The Last Half-Century

The Last Half-Century

Societal Change and Politics in America

Morris Janowitz

The University of Chicago Press
Chicago & London

The University of Chicago Press, Chicago 60637
The University of Chicago Press, Ltd., London
Published 1978
Printed in the United States of America
82 81 80 79 78 54321

MORRIS JANOWITZ is the Lawrence A. Kimpton Distinguished Service Professor in the Department of Sociology at the University of Chicago.

Library of Congress Cataloging in Publication Data

Janowitz, Morris.
The last half-century.

Includes indexes.
1. United States—Social conditions—20th century.
2. United States—Politics and government—20th century.
3. Social change. 4. Social institutions. I. Title.
HN57.J2479 309.1'73'09 78-17715
ISBN 0-226-39306-2

To Gayle
and
to our daughters of the Middle Border

Contents

Tables

Preface

I have written this book for my students—past, present, and future. It would be more accurate to say that I think of my students, undergraduate and graduate, as the persons I hope will read it.

It is impossible to pursue the kind of sociology which interests me without the active involvement of students. They are infectious carriers of enthusiasm. The very fact that they take nothing for granted is the central source of their academic importance. Universities are progressively more required to deal with difficult and endless issues of administration. The price of academic administration is high, almost excessive in the procedures which must be adhered to. Therefore one must rely on all possible sources of fervor and initiative; each new cohort of students makes its contribution to energizing the university in its pursuit of intellectual goals.

I hope that this book will demonstrate to new students that an enduring intellectual core of sociology exists and that this core of the discipline cannot be separated from its substantive achievements. I hope that this book will be of relevance to social scientists who have a continuing interest in the synthesis of sociological research. This is a difficult and at points tedious task. Therefore "sophisticated" scholars and "hard-nosed" critics must proceed through this volume at their own risk.

We are in a period in which various intellectual cults have become fashionable and serve to fragment academic thought. There is little likelihood that a drastic reformulation of sociological thought will take place, or that there will be rapid progress toward a unification of the strands of sociological thought, especially in its linkages to the other social sciences. Therefore the task of maintaining a national intellectual culture for sociology and the social sciences remains important. At present the conservation of the effective heritage of sociology is as important as the generation of new knowledge.

I have felt the need to make explicit my intellectual and empirical sources in approaching the topic of societal change in the United States from the point of view of social control. In a sense this exercise—and the complexity and scope of the topic mean that it is no more than an exercise—is a form of intellectual autobiography. It reflects a fusion of my continuing exposure to the various strands of the Chicago school of sociology, with its multiple research traditions, and my interest in political sociology. In the end to make explicit the basis of my argument does not free one from one's intellectual background, but one hopes that it serves to underscore the limitations of that background.

This study of macrosociology and social control grows out of the generous support accorded to the Center of Social Organization studies of the Department of Sociology, University of Chicago, by the Russell Sage Foundation. For over a decade, the center has supplied a focal point for graduate students and faculty concerned with the institutional links between the metropolis and the national society.

I was able to develop the outline of this study during the academic year 1972–1973 while I served as Pitt Professor at Cambridge University and Fellow of Peterhouse. An all too brief Guggenheim Fellowship in the summer and fall of 1975 supplied the leave during which I started the initial draft. The routines of the University of Chicago and the Near Southside of Chicago made it possible for me to spend the early mornings in preparing the final draft. I first separated out the manuscript which was published under the title *Social Control of the Welfare State*, an effort which helped fashion the scope and direction of this study.

I had the opportunity to push ahead with these efforts because my academic colleagues devoted their energies to the ever increasing administrative burden of the University of Chicago. I am deeply appreciative of my debt to Evelyn Kitagawa, Chairman of the Department of Sociology, and John T. Wilson, President of the University of Chicago.

The intellectual origins of this undertaking go back to my undergraduate experience at Washington Square College, 1936–1941, and especially to two of my teachers: Bruce Lannes Smith, who introduced me to political sociology; and Sidney Hook, whose course on the philosophy of history presented a critical approach to the grand theories of societal change. In addition, his teaching of pragmatism saved me from the burdens of both materialism and idealism.

The book came to completion because of the supportive and collegial academic life of the quadrangles of the University of Chicago. I had the benefit of a most intense and detailed reading and criticism of the manuscript by Edward Shils and Jerry Suttles; their extensive comments were indispensable. In addition, numerous associates read and commented on specific chapters: Odin Anderson, Bernard Barber, Bruno Bettelheim, Margaret Fallers, Kirsten Grønbjerg, Paul Hirsch, James Jacobs, Jack Ladinsky, Dwaine Marvick, Michael Schudson, David Street, and Mayer Zald. I wish to also thank Robert Bogart and Ray Hutchinson for their comments and suggestions.

I

Frame of Reference

One

Sociological Objectives

The State of Sociology

This study deals with social control in advanced industrial society, especially the United States, and particularly the half-century after World War I. The United States is representative of those "Western" advanced industrial nations which have been faced with marked strain in their political institutions. These nation-states have been experiencing a decline in popular confidence and a distrust of the political process, an absence of decisive legislative majorities, and an increased inability to govern effectively, that is, to balance and to contain competing interest-group demands and resolve political conflicts.

The present study uses the sociological idea of social control as one perspective applicable to the macrosociology of the nation-state in order to explore the sources of these political dilemmas. In its classical definition and continuing basic meaning, "social control" does not imply coercion or the repression of the individual by societal institutions. Social control is, rather, the obverse of coercive control. Social control refers to the capacity of a social group, including a whole society, to regulate itself. Self-regulation must imply a set of "higher moral principles" beyond those of self-interest.

Since the end of World War II, the expanded scope of empirical research has profoundly transformed the sociological discipline. The repeated efforts at "theoretical reformulation" have left a positive residue, but there have been no new conceptual "breakthroughs" which are compelling. An important intellectual task in contemporary sociology is the concerted and detailed effort to organize and to make more "sense" out of the vastly increased body of empirical research.

This intellectual task can be described as "codification" of sociological knowledge. In pursuing such codification, sociologists will have to make do with the existing alternative main lines of sociological thought plus their own elaborations. The notion of "systemic analysis," to be discussed below, denotes a strategy for synthesis which avoids both excessive closure and diffuse eclecticism. This study of social control is conceived of as an example in this genre. Sociology is seen as a monographic discipline informed and enriched by its theoretical formulations. The empirical core includes the ever increasing body of quantitative trend indicators of social change. To speak of sociology in these terms is not to downgrade theory. General formulations do more than make possible the element of continuity and accumulation that has been achieved. Theoretical considerations inhibit analysis based on mechanical extrapolation of existing patterns and trends.

Any effort at codification is guided by a conception of the history and development of the sociological discipline. The dominant view is to write the history of sociology as a discipline which was first rooted in philosophical and speculative reasoning and which steadily developed an empirical base. In this view, it is convenient to trace the origins of sociological thinking to writers of antiquity and to emphasize that it was August Comte and then a number of mid-nineteenth-century figures who structured the scope of sociology by their theoretical and speculative writings. Thereafter, the history of the discipline has been the step-by-step incorporation of various systematic empirical procedures into the evolving analytic schemes. However, there is another historiography of sociology which may be more helpful for codification and for exploring sociological theory and social control. In this alternative, the initial emergence of the discipline in the nineteenth century included more than the generalized and philosophic sociological thought. Sociology had a two-track origin, since the impulse to "do sociology" led men to engage directly in empirical research. In the United States, Great Britain, and France, as early as the 1830s, there were extensive empirical accomplishments which were in effect independent of the "theoretical" writings of the classical masters of sociology.[1] These research efforts grew; many were penetrating, imaginative,

1. Philip Abrams, ed., *The Origins of British Sociology, 1834–1914* (Chicago: University of Chicago Press, 1968). The history of social research in the United States is covered by Robert C. Davis, "The Growth of Social Research in America: The Nineteenth Century" (unpublished manuscript). See also Charles E. Rosenberg, *No Other Gods: On Science and American Social Thought* (Baltimore, Md.: Johns Hopkins Press, 1969), and Anthony Oberschall, *Empirical Social Research in Germany, 1848–1914* (The Hague: Mouton, 1965). Roger L. Beiger, "The Development of French Sociology, 1871–1905," Ph.D. dissertation, University of Michigan, 1972.

and painstaking, and they contributed to the recording of the social history of the nineteenth century. However, because this research lacked a theoretical framework and a stable institutional base, much of it was not cumulative and did not realize its full intellectual potential.

In this two-track history, sociology as a fusion of an analytic and empirical discipline emerged both in the United States and in Europe immediately after 1890 when it developed its university base.[2] At that time, there was a sustained effort to join the concerns of the grand figures of sociological writing with the increasing scale of empirical research. This fusion was essentially institutionalized by the appointment of professors of sociology, and on occasion by the organization of departments of sociology at universities. The institutionalization of sociology was far greater in the United States than in Western Europe and remained so until the end of World War II.

The development of sociology and the momentum of sociology as an academic discipline—and its continuing energy—rest as much with its empirical interests as with its theoretical debates. My study proceeds from such a view of the history of sociology.

The organization of sociology as an academic discipline gave rise to three new developments which have left their enduring mark. First, relating sociological theory and empirical research became an explicit, enduring task for teachers of sociology.[3] Moreover, in the initial institutionalization of sociology, research and teaching were seen as compatible and mutually reinforcing. Second, the university base made it possible to engage in cumulative empirical research, as opposed to the earlier situation, in which individual investigators worked with little knowledge of previous efforts. Third, the university organization of sociology offered a mechanism for training new students and researchers. Since 1890 sociology has grown continuously in numbers of workers, financial support, and university recognition. The expansion of sociology rested on the growth of the universities in industrial societies. The discipline, like others in the social sciences, gained impetus from its claim that the application of the scientific method would contribute to progress and to social and political justice.[4] This is not to

2. Edward Shils, "Tradition, Ecology, and Institution in the History of Sociology," *Daedalus* 99 (1970): 760–825.

3. Albion Small was one of the most energetic spokesmen for this point of view during the early development of sociology. See Vernon K. Dibble, *The Legacy of Albion Small* (Chicago: University of Chicago Press, 1975).

4. Although the conviction that the development of sociology would benefit society was inherent in the very origins of the discipline, it was during the 1930s that this outlook was more explicitly articulated. See, for example, Karl Mannheim,

deny the powerful academic and intellectual concerns which invigorated sociological inquiry, but rather to recognize that the ideas of the eighteenth-century Enlightenment, which pervaded the discipline and encompassed scholars of divergent theoretical viewpoints, assisted in its institutionalization and growth.[5]

Three-quarters of a century of growth in the scope and size of the sociological enterprise, however, resulted in a decisive and rather suddenly perceived strain on the Enlightenment assumptions of the discipline. At the end of the 1960s, the outlook, intellectual aspirations, and optimism of sociologists were badly shaken. Then the phrase "crisis in sociology" gained extensive currency because it indicated the troubled mood of those sociologists who were no longer certain of the outcome of their endeavors.[6]

No doubt some sociologists have been disappointed by the capacity of their discipline to alter the sociopolitical process; others have become personally discontented with the life-style of a teacher in the university setting, and as a result they have less zeal for their intellectual endeavors. If the crisis in sociology is an intellectual rather than a personal or political issue, it must mean that sociology is progressively less able to contribute to the clarification of social change in contemporary society. There is no need to exaggerate the maturity of sociology and the cumulative character of its research efforts. Nor is there any need to overlook the vast amount of marginal, even trivial, research. The rapid expansion of personnel and research resources has resulted in extensive internal fragmentation and a massive production of research of limited scholarly relevance. Most of these efforts will leave little intellectual residue. To the outside observer, the intrusion of political and bureaucratic considerations into the sociological enterprise is conspicuous. In particular, scholars from related disciplines find it difficult to keep informed and to identify and use the important, lasting contributions of sociology.

But the present state of sociology is not to be assessed in terms of the wide range of its undertakings but rather by the vitality of its relevant

Man and Society in an Age of Reconstruction (New York: Harcourt, Brace, 1940); Robert S. Lynd, *Knowledge for What* (Princeton: Princeton University Press, 1939); Harold D. Lasswell, *Democracy through Public Opinion* (Menasha, Wisc.: Banta, 1941).

5. Keith Baker, *Condorcet* (Chicago: University of Chicago Press, 1975), analyzes the linkages between the Enlightenment and the emergence of the social sciences including sociology.

6. Alvin W. Gouldner, *The Coming Crisis of Western Sociology* (New York: Basic, 1970).

streams, even if they are minority efforts.[7] Therefore, while some sociologists may experience a personal "crisis" in their work, there is no basis for asserting that a crisis exists in the intellectual aspects of the discipline. The crisis resides in the real world. The advanced industrial nations with parliamentary institutions are experiencing crises in their ability to regulate themselves, particularly in their political institutions. The intellectual *Fragestellung* (posing of the question) linked to the idea of social control is a relevant standpoint for assessing this crisis in political legitimacy.

Since this study involves the synthesis of available research, the present state of empirical sociology is crucial. I do not believe that sociology, as I use its results, has during the twenty-five years since 1945 offered only a distorted view of social conflict and social control in the United States. Of course, there is much in sociology which has no bearing on the topics at hand, a great deal with which I disagree, and even more which is of little relevance. However, much of what I discard has been and will continue to be useful to other sociologists concerned with the continuing tasks of codification—of "making sense" of particular research. Essentially, there is enough—in fact, more than I can handle—in the research accomplishments of the discipline of the past three decades so that I can proceed with the task at hand. For each error, distortion, and omission of sociologists in the period since 1945, one can find relevant literature and penetrating contributions. Contemporary sociology has a momentum and a logic which derive from its classic writers, but this momentum is strongly reenforced by contemporary research efforts.

There are naturally many limitations and weaknesses in sociology as an intellectual discipline. Given the scope and goals of my study, the most troublesome is the persistent difficulty of linking the concepts and methods of the working sociologist to an effective historical perspective. This is not to focus exclusively or predominantly on epistemological issues or on questions of the philosophy of the social sciences.[8] It is, rather, to draw attention to the challenge to separate significant changes

7. Neil J. Smelser and James A. David, eds., *Sociology* (Englewood Cliffs, N.J.: Prentice Hall, 1969). This effort to structure and overview the field of sociology is the result of a special report prepared by the Survey of the Behavioral and Social Sciences between 1967 and 1969 under the auspices of the Committee on Science and Public Policy of the National Academy of Science and the Problems and Policy Committee of the Social Science Research Council.

8. Robert Nisbett, *Social Change and History: Aspects of the Western Theory of Development* (New York: Oxford University Press, 1969).

in the patterns and forms of social control over time from refinement in the categories and details of social research during the period under investigation. This issue will be encountered repeatedly.

The "Crisis" of Political Legitimacy

These observations about the tasks and state of sociology help assess the idea of "the crisis of political legitimacy" in advanced industrial society. I have no quarrel with this terminology if it is thought to be a point of entrance to the analysis of the complex dimensions in the stalemate of parliamentary institutions in advanced industrialized nations. It is a formulation compatible with the long-standing concern of political sociologists with the vulnerabilities of democratic institutions in mass society.[9] In particular, political sociologists have focused on the problems which the extension of the popular franchise generates for multiparty political systems.

However, the crisis of political legitimacy also is an ideological slogan which distorts and oversimplifies sociological investigation of modern political institutions. It is an expression of the "crisis in sociology" perspective which also justifies a lack of personal political responsibility, on the one hand, and utopianism, on the other.

In any case, an adequate analytic perspective does not result from substituting one concept for another. The increased concern of sociology with power concepts has been a contribution, but only a partial one. The extensive literature and debate of "conflict" versus "consensus" theories have proved relatively sterile. This controversy failed to recognize the essential and persistent interplay of both these dimensions in social change.

A social-control perspective aspires to a holistic analysis of the United States in seeking to explain its profound political tensions.[10] As will be discussed below, the original formulations of social control by pioneer sociologists at the turn of the century deemphasized political institutions for an examination of what they believed to be the underlying, fundamental social processes of society. The strategy of my analysis, however, is to incorporate into the social-control perspective the main

9. Otto Kirchheimer, *Politics, Law and Social Change* (New York: Columbia University Press, 1969); Maurice Duverger, *Political Parties: Their Organization and Activity in the Modern State* (New York: Wiley, 1959); Robert Dahl, *A Preface to Democratic Theory* (Chicago: University of Chicago Press, 1956).

10. Morris Janowitz, "Anthropology and the Social Sciences," *Current Anthropology* 4 (April 1963): 149–54.

outlines of the social stratification and institutional dimensions of the sociology of politics.[11] This perspective is offered as an alternative to contemporary approaches to macrosociology which have become rooted either in notions of economic determinism or in the social psychology of political participation and political norms.

The social-control perspective brings into focus the regulatory arrangements of a society with a complex division of labor. Such an approach implies particular attention to norms, but hardly at the expense of excluding underlying ecological, technological, and economic variables. The pioneer figures who used the social-control concept paid attention to a broad range of normative mechanisms, including custom, tradition, public opinion, patterns of public and private morality, and the institutional base of the family, school, and religion. The intellectual strategy of this research is to attempt to ensure the explicit infusion of the relevant dimensions of the "substructure" of society—ecological, technological, and economic—into a holistic approach.

The core issue is to account for the gradual emergence in the post–World War II period of weak political regimes in Western political democracies, including the United States. They may be reasonably described as weak or stalemated regimes because they are unable to produce effective and authoritative policies to manage economic and social tensions and political conflict. The electoral process is less likely to result in a decisive political majority or a unified political coalition—or, in the United States, an executive-legislative balance which represents a clear political mandate. The executive is either faced with a limited majority or unable to mobilize its nominal majority; the opposition does not clarify or sharpen alternatives or improve legislative decisions.

Despite an underlying political consensus in the population, the legistive institutions are unable to generate consistent decision making on day-to-day issues. A multitude of interest groups make for piecemeal and unstable compromises which do not add up to an integrated sociopolitical approach. One resulting paradox is the fact that, despite the decline of public confidence and trust in the political process, there is strong, pervasive popular demand for continued, expanded governmental intervention. Only a minority of the electorate are committed to "withdrawal," while most of the electorate, in one fashion or another,

11. Morris Janowitz, "The Logic of Political Sociology," in *Political Conflict* (Beverly Hills, Calif.: Sage Publications, 1974), pp. 5–35.

see their self-interest as requiring active legislative decisions and administrative decrees.

The apparatus of government has grown immense during the period between the end of World War I and the end of the Vietnam conflict. It has become more powerful in its ability to collect revenue, to engage in civilian and military enterprise, and to regulate and intervene in human affairs. To speak of a weak political regime is not to deny this obvious, pervasive expansion of government. It is, rather, to emphasize the limited capacity of elected officials to direct coherently the activities of government and to resolve the divergences in government policies and practices.

The difficulties of parliamentary control can be seen in the patterns of mass political participation common to these advanced industrial nation-states. The voting patterns which produce governments with weak majorities, unstable coalitions, or even minority governments are persistent. In general, there has been an increase in the proportion of the population who declare themselves unaffiliated with the major parties and/or who shift in their electoral choices more and more from one election to the next. This detached political perspective, as would be expected, had been accompanied by a decline in belief in the effectiveness of the legislative processes and the administrative apparatus of government. Students of social control must do more than explain patterns of personal deviant behavior, such as suicide, criminality, and personal unhappiness, important though these may be.[12] They must also analyze the patterns and subjective definition of citizens' participation in the political process.[13]

Trends in patterns of social stratification remain the appropriate beginning point for such an analysis. The underlying changes in social stratification resulting from technology, occupational structure, patterns of urbanization, and economic resource allocation do not appear to have increased or produced a highly "alienated" or "anomic" electorate. On the contrary, the social stratification patterns result in a highly "fragmented" electorate with a considerable solidarity within its component social segments. During a continuing period of deficit na-

12. This perspective derives from the classic study of Emile Durkheim, *Suicide: Étude de sociologie* (Paris: Alcan, 1897).

13. See Charles E. Merriam and Harold F. Gosnell, *Non-Voting: Causes and Methods of Control* (Chicago: University of Chicago Press, 1924) for one of the early studies which initiated the stream of systematic research concerned with the subjective aspects of political participation.

tional economy, these groupings increase their demands for collective economic aid and governmental benefits. Under the conditions of an advanced industrial society, however, the competing self-interests of individuals and groups are not easily resolved or aggregated into effective, stable political preferences.

But the social-control perspective requires an institutional level of analysis. The outcome of the changes in social structure and the manifestations of the "crisis" of political legitimacy are in part the result of the response of political institutions and political parties. The great strain on social control is not only the result of the influence of the social structure on political institutions but also the ensuing constricted response of the political institutions. Modern society is one in which the political party and the administrative agencies of government affect all sectors. To speak of the decisive consequences of the political parties on "social structure" and to recognize the supremacy of political institutions does not imply either effectiveness or legitimacy. Their level of effectiveness and their contribution to social control are precisely what is at stake, both as a historical reality and as the key issue in the macrosociology of a nation such as the United States.

Since the end of World War II, the structure of political parties in the advanced nations has remained relatively unchanged.[14] Nevertheless, especially in the United States, the parties have come to require far greater resources to perform their political tasks.[15] Paradoxically, the mobilization of these resources appears to make them less responsive. Nor has the influx of new cadres of personnel acting for underrepresented groups improved the internal functioning of the major parties.

As a result, trends in political behavior, especially measures of electoral behavior, become important indicators of the effectiveness of social control in advanced industrial societies with multiparty systems. The "crisis" in political legitimacy emerges not as a sudden manifestation, the outcome of a particular historical event or political personality, but rather as the result of continuing sociopolitical change. Wars and military conflicts supply the historian with appropriate points of historical demarcation, and these can be used in sociological analysis. They link historical perspective to social control because they encom-

14. Herman Finer, *Theory and Practice of Modern Government* (London: Methuen, 1932); Maurice Duverger, *Political Parties* (New York: John Wiley, 1954; Sigmund Neumann, *Modern Political Parties* (Chicago: University of Chicago Press, 1956).

15. See chapter 13 below for a discussion of this topic.

pass both the dynamics of internal social structure and the effect of changes in the world arena. To the extent that a distinction can be made between industrialism and advanced industrialism, the cumulative influence of the technological and bureaucratic developments associated with World War II can be taken as the historical threshold, although the essential forms had been manifested by the end of World War I. They involved the emergence of the welfare state and the extension of political participation associated with wartime pressure, developments which became institutionalized after World War II.[16] In the early 1920s, the United States and other industrialized nations were adapting their institutions to the consequences of World War I. Likewise, the early 1970s, with the cease-fire in Vietnam and the decline of conscription in the United States and Western Europe, marked the end of an era both domestically and in the relations between the industrialized nations and the so-called developing nations.

These historical events supply a rationale for delimiting the time relevant for macrosociological change. I have asserted that the period from 1920 to 1970 represents the transformation of the United States from an industrialized nation to an advanced industrialized nation. But a broad study such as this depends not so much on an appropriate time span as on the availability of valid research, on macrosociological dimensions, but also on examinations in depth of patterns and trends in microsociology, of informal relations, and of face-to-face interactions. In the 1920s sociologists launched a variety of field studies which now serve as benchmarks for historical comparisons. These were studies of considerable depth and sophistication and involved a wide range of bureaucratic institutions and community structure. Long-term social indicators of macrosociological dimensions in the United States are obviously more abundant, but they supply only partial, imprecise indicators of the microsystems involved in social control. It is the availability of selected sociological monographs which can be utilized for ap-

16. For a discussion of the extension of social welfare in industrial society, see R. M. Titmuss, *Essays on "The Welfare State"* (London: Allen and Unwin, 1958); Arthur Marwick, *Britain in the Century of Total War: War, Peace, and Social Change, 1900–1967* (London: Bodley Head, 1968); Otto Kirchheimer, "Confining Conditions and Revolutionary Breakthroughs," *American Political Science Review* 59 (December 1965): 964–74. See also Derek Fraser, *The Evolution of the British Welfare State: A History of Social Policy since the Industrial Revolution* (London: Macmillan, 1973); Harold Wilensky and Charles N. Lebeaux, *Industrial Society and Social Welfare* (New York: Russell Sage Foundation, 1965).

proximate historical comparisons with contemporary research findings that makes the comparison over time minimumly feasible.

During the second half of the 1960s, the "crisis" of political legitimacy, the strain of social change and political constriction, produced a variety of parapolitical movements outside the institutionalized parties that engaged in outbursts of violent symbolism and in violence. In that period there was an increase in efforts to extend civic participation into the management of administrative agencies of government and of voluntary associations. These efforts, in part a response to parapolitical movements, implicitly recognized the limitations of periodic national elections as mechanisms of social and political control.

Sociological literature failed to anticipate the full scope and intensity of these social movements, although one can find analyses of the marked levels of societal strain. To some degree this reflected the defects of sociological analysis, but one cannot expect such predictive power. More important is the intellectual reaction of sociologists to these events. Of course, many sociologists were naïve and exaggerated the "revolutionary" implications of such manifestations. However, many of the sociological writings about the agitation followed the classic model of the natural history of social movements.[17] Their authors perceptively focused on the impending transformation of the protest movements into "interest groups" and highlighted their built-in limitations in altering patterns of social control. It was no profound sociological discovery that the protest movements of this period would lead to increased diffuse political violence but hardly to a "revolution" or a "revolutionary situation." Nevertheless, their explosive character requires students of social control to reexamine violence and coercion in social change.

When there is a crisis in political legitimacy, what is the relation between reliance on violence and coercion and the search for effective social control in an advanced industrial society? This question manifests itself at every point in sociological analysis where patterns of social control are ineffective.

Historians have made it clear that, regardless of the vast and immeasurable amount of human misery which coercion and violence have

17. Lyford P. Edwards, *The Natural History of Revolution* (Chicago: University of Chicago Press, 1970); Crane Brinton, *The Anatomy of Revolution* (Cambridge: Harvard University Press, 1938). See also Robert E. Park, *The Crowd and the Public*, trans. Henry Elsner, Jr., and Charlotte Elsner (Chicago: University of Chicago Press, 1972). For an overview approach, see Ralph Turner and Lewis Killian, *Collective Behavior* (Englewood Cliffs, N.J.: Prentice Hall, 1957).

produced, the threat and use of force in the past have been essential for achieving social and political "progress." But to explicate the "principles of force" is another matter; that is to identify the conditions under which force produces positive contributions to social control. Sociologists have speculated repeatedly on this issue; but how much further has the analysis been pressed beyond the aspirations of Georges Sorel?[18] Repeatedly in this study we will confront these baffling intellectual issues.

However, the perspective of social control is grounded in assumptions about human interaction and mutual influence. Thus it raises the difficult issue of the consequences of force and coercion on those who initiate or manage their use—whether the goal be the maintenance or the change of a social structure. Perhaps the assertion which needs to be remembered is that the use of force and coercion in the search for social control operates within narrow limits in relations within advanced industrialized societies. This does not neglect the unanticipated, extensive, and diffuse patterns of violence under advanced industrialism. Nor does it deny the decisive importance of the restrained use of force as an "ultimate sanction"; the foundation of the state rests on its legitimate monopoly of force. But this observation points out the self-defeating implications for those who must rely extensively on force and coercion to achieve social control in its traditional meaning. Such as calculus of force and coercion reflects at least two trends. First, there has been an increase in the professed moral sensibilities of the citizenry (compatible with political indifference under conditions of ineffective political institutions); second, the complexity of societal organization has made anticipating the consequences of force—especially given the expanded power of force—much more unpredictable.

Moreover, in evaluating the actual and potential consequences of using force and coercion to direct social change, we must consider whether the existing categories of political ideology are adequate for the analysis of social control. The social-control perspective has had, in the past, the task of penetrating political rhetoric in order to examine actual practices and operative norms; the same perspective should be able to serve the same analytic purpose now.

The alternative consequences of the search for effective social control cannot be analyzed adequately in terms of existing conventional

18. Georges Sorel, *Reflections on Violence* (New York: Huebsch, 1914).

ideological categories—radicalism, conservatism, or incremental liberalism. A body of theoretical writings affirm this assertion and a mass of empirical data highlight that these categories are limited in describing mass opinion as well as patterns of institutional practice. These categories of political analysis imply a final result, a resolution, and an "end" state, when we are dealing with a continuous and continuing social process. But the study of macrosociology and, as a result, the analysis of social control are too often dominated by a narrow format fashioned by "conventional" political discourse. The "resolution" or "outcome" of ineffective social control does not necessarily conform to the categories of political ideology, which tend to underestimate the actual extent of popular consensus. In the course of this analysis it is necessary at least to assume that, for an advanced industrial society, the political alternatives include results such as chronic tension, repeated minicrises, and a variety of patterns of stalemate and indecision.[19]

Systemic Disarticulation: Illustrative Propositions

In 1920, the United States had a population of 105.7 million; by 1970, 203.2 million. The growth in population was accompanied by an increase in the "economy of scale" of bureaucratic organizations and by an elaboration of the division of labor. The enlargment of these magnitudes ensured continued concern with an evolutionary perspective in sociological analysis. However, simplified conceptions of societal evolution had been pointedly and continually criticized.[20] The reformulations were more subtle and differentiated. During the half-century under discussion, the new conceptual approaches have ranged, for example, from "cultural lag" to "multilinear change."[21]

19. Barrington Moore, Jr., *Reflections on the Causes of Human Misery and upon Certain Proposals to Eliminate Them* (Boston: Beacon Press, 1972); Barrington Moore, Jr., "Revolution in America?" *New York Review of Books* (January 30, 1969), pp. 6–12.

20. R. C. Lewontin, "The Concept of Evolution," *International Encyclopedia of the Social Sciences* (New York: Crowell Collier and Macmillan, 1968) 5: 202–9.

21. William F. Ogburn, *Social Change with Respect to Culture and Original Nature* (New York: Huebsch, 1922); Julian Stewart, *Theory of Culture Change: The Methodology of Multilinear Evolution* (Urbana: University of Illinois Press, 1955). A penetrating empirical analysis of societal "evolution" and family patterns has been offered, by Winch and Blumberg, which rejects a linear model. Instead, the relations between societal complexity and familial complexity is seen as "curvilinear, with minimal at the extremes of societal complexity (hunting-gathering and urban-industrial) and the maximium at some intermediate level." See Robert F. Winch and Rae Lesser Blumberg, "Societal Complexity and Family Organization," in *Selected Studies in Marriage and the Family*, ed. Robert F. Winch and Louis

In varying degrees, the new orientations have been freed from traditional rigidities and from "overdeterminism." The implicit and explicit directionality, be it that of "progress" or of a negative utopia, was no longer binding in social evolutionary thinking. Second, no doubt more significant, the assumption of one uniform set of phases or stages had been abandoned; unilinear evolution gave way to concepts of multilinear development. Third, the evolutionary process was no longer seen as "automatically" implying the elaboration of coordinating mechanisms. If one argued that increases in magnitude and complexity produced a more elaborate allocation of "social roles," there was no reason to assert that there was an inherent emergence of integrative institutions. And most important, from the point of view of the analysis of societal change and social control, there was no reason to assert that the evolutionary process meant that larger, more complex social forms would displace and render extinct smaller, simpler social institutions. On the contrary—the research evidence collected over a half-century underlined, for example, that primary groups were not displaced by the growth of bureaucratic structures. Nor were neighborhoods eliminated by the expansion of the scale of metropolitan community, nor were nations displaced by supranational units. The smaller units became more specialized and internally differentiated, and survived.

The intellectual residue of the evolutionary perspective is that of a grand metaphor. In the setting of the United States as an advanced industrial society, it is an image which emphasizes as a dominant feature, the discontinuities, disjointness, or more pointedly the disarticulations, of the component institutions and organizations. The internal elaboration of social forms is not matched by effective connections among constituent elements.

The dictionary definition of "disarticulation" is, a condition of a lack of unity or integration. Conversely, "articulation" means the state of forming or fitting into a systematically related whole. These meanings make sociological sense and are appropriate for an analysis of social change and social control. One does not have to predicate a "higher level" of articulation in the United States at the end of World War I to assert that the population increase and the elaboration of the division

Wolf Goodman (New York: Holt, Rinehart and Winston, 1968); Rae Lesser Blumberg and Robert F. Winch, "Societal Complexity and Familial Complexity: Evidence for the Curvilinear Hypothesis," *American Journal of Sociology* 77 (March 1972): 898–920.

of labor in the ensuing half-century have not been accompanied by the emergence of effective institutions of coordination and self-regulation appropriate for a democratic polity. The clear implication is that extensive institutional disarticulation increases the probability of conflict and in turn of violence.

If the grand metaphor of social evolution is limited for purposes of historical comparison, there is little to be gained by a cyclical imagery of organization, disorganization, and reorganization, although a case can be made for it. The cyclical theories of change—or, rather, "spiral" analogs—have the advantage of being free of pathos and overdeterminism. From either perspective, the important point is that one avoids an approach which stimulates and emphasizes the extrapolation of existing trends. And there are plausible reasons to believe that selected trends in the United States, especially normative ones, reached self-limiting levels as of the middle 1970s.

In essence, the time encompassed in this study is that of the emergence of the United States as an advanced industrial society, that is, in the evolution from an industrial society to an advanced industrial society. It has been argued that a nation becomes effectively industrialized when less than 50% of the labor force is engaged in primary production (agriculture, mining, and forestry). If we use this criterion, England was "industrialized" before 1841, France before 1866, and the United States by 1880. Such a criterion places a large burden on census types of definitions of occupations. However, it is one of those judgments which is useful in eliminating pointless debate about historical periods. In any case, scholars are less likely to offer arbitrary criteria about the advent of an advanced industrial society, especially in relation to the labor force. Would it make sense to assert that the mark of an advanced industrial society is a labor force of which 10% or less are engaged in primary production?

Throughout this study, societal change is seen as much in the transformations wrought by total war as by "peacetime" industrial developments per se. Diverse writers have emphasized the influence of war and war-making on the social institutions of advanced industrialism.[22] The emergence of advanced industrialism is perceived as at least a two-stage process, arising first as a consequence of World War I and then as a

22. For example, Harold D. Lasswell, "The Garrison State," *American Journal of Sociology* 46 (January 1941): 455–68; Richard Titmuss, "War and Social Policy," *Essays on the Welfare State* (London: Allen and Unwin, 1958).

consequence of World War II. And in a real sense World War II was an extension of the societal processes of World War I. But for the United States, both the Korean conflict and the Second Indochina War led to the termination of the trends initiated by the two world wars. This line of argument has fashioned the historical scope of this study of social change and social control.

Is there a parallel between the "evolutionary" developments of society and the refinement of theories of macrosociology? The history of sociological theory—or rather the intellectual history of sociology—can be described as a shift in emphasis from single variable philosophies of history (unidimensional formulations) to a stronger concern with multiple causation, or "multivariate" analysis.[23] It may be more accurate and revealing to speak of the cyclical emphasis in this regard. Comprehensive models based on unified and simplified forms of determinism continue to have great intellectual attraction and influence. At the same time, the fierce substantive interests of competing sociologists recurrently challenge the grand formulations but hardly replace them.

The logic of "systemic analysis," as used in this study and explicated in chapter 3, requires a "multivariate" notion of causality, that is, an ordered and reasoned conception of the flow of influence.[24] While this approach avoids simplified closed systems of determinism, it does not force one into "mere" eclecticism. A number of hypotheses and propositions are offered about the sources and consequences of the disarticulation of advanced industrialism. In the United States, they are designed to account for the emergence of weak political regimes. The goal is to

23. Despite the enormous outpouring of literature on the "methodology" of the social sciences, two modern classic contributions still dominate the intellectual scene, namely, Morris R. Cohen, *Reason and Nature: An Essay of the Meaning of Scientific Method* (Glencoe, Ill.: Free Press, 1931); Morris R. Cohen and Ernest Nagel, *Introduction to Logic and Scientific Method* (New York: Harcourt, Brace, 1934).

24. It is unfortunate but of limited consequence that the term "systemic analysis" can easily be confused with "general system theory" or "system analysis." See Ludwig Von Bertalanffy, "General System Theory," *Yearbook* (February 1956): 1. These in fact have very different meanings. Systems analysis is the effort to import, into the social sciences, physical and biological science models. It is an intellectual orientation which has been strongly reinforced by cybernetic thinking. Systems analysis emphasizes closure and self-contained analytic formulations built on imputed logico-deductive procedures and on formal categories which are designed to be logically exclusive. Systemic analysis, by contrast, as described in chapter 3, seeks to take into account the limitations of closed systems. It is more concerned with generating a body of hypotheses with some degree of concreteness which reflect historical developments. Systemic analysis tries to "put together" or to organize plausible, reasoned, and meaningful hypotheses about societal change.

account for the normative order which has emerged; but this hardly dictates a "normative" explanation or a normative "theory of macrosociology." On the contrary, in the classical formulation of macrosociology: (*a*) the point of entrance is to investigate the ecological-technological-economic structure of social organization and the resulting social stratification of the nation-state; (*b*) the intermediate step is to explore the interactive processes which create societal institutions and institutionalize norms and values; and (*c*) the final step is the analysis of elites, power, and decision-making processes which are based on conscious efforts to intervene in and fashion patterns of political participation. I hope that the analysis is enriched by utilizing both a "contemplative" approach—a reflective examination of historical trends in societal change—and a "manipulative" approach—an analysis of social change from the point of view of the potentials for explicitly and with intent directing the processes of societal change.[25] The word "manipulative" is used not in a negative or pejorative sense but to reflect conscious, deliberate collective problem solving. The term "policy analysis" has come to substitute for the manipulative approach, but this relabeling should not obscure the essential intellectual goal.

Thus the first part of this study focuses on charting three basic societal trends: political participation, social stratification, and military participation. The second part deals with the structures of social organization: bureaucratic organization, residential community, and with societal socialization, particularly those institutions of mass persuasion and the regulation of legitimate coercion. The final part emphasizes the manipulative standpoint and includes strategic contributions—positive and negative—of the social sciences to rational institution building for more effective social control: the management of interpersonal relations, experiments in community participation, and organization of political leadership.

The rationale of this study is that, in an advanced industrial society, the patterns of electoral behavior—including the quality of electoral participation—supply central indicators of social control. The electoral process is the central mechanism of self-regulation. A "liberal" democracy must rely extensively on the economic marketplace as a mechanism for allocating resources; but in an advanced industrial society, national legislation and administrative regulation create the framework within

25. Harold D. Lasswell, *World Politics and Personal Insecurity* (New York: McGraw Hill, 1935).

which the marketplace functions. Under advanced industrialism, periodic elections are limited in effectively adjudicating institutional disarticulation. As a result, the basic issue of public policy is to develop extralegislative agencies, local and national, which *are* capable of resolving conflict and of strengthening the system of periodic competitive elections.

The following hypotheses about the master trends in societal change in the United States need to be examined for 1920 to 1976. They have parallels in the multiparty nation-states of Western Europe.

1. *Political Participation*

There has been a long-term trend of attenuation of the relatively stable citizen attachment to one or another of the two major parties. The indicators of this trend, especially since 1952, have been the decline in "identification" with a political party by the electorate and the growth of "independent" political self-conceptions, the increase in party switching from one national election to the next, and the growth of ticket splitting. This trend of electoral participation has resulted in the development of weakened or stalemated national political regimes, that is, an inability to produce decisive and clear-cut combined presidential and legislative majorities. Periodic national elections have not, since 1932, produced a "critical election" that resulted in a significant realignment of political support or new stable national coalitions.

2. *Social Stratification*

There has been long-term growth in the proportion of the gross national product distributed by the agencies of government. A person's position in the system of social stratification is thus not only a function of his occupational position but is also increasingly related to the claims and expectations generated by the welfare state. Likewise, social stratification reflects the persistence or growing importance of cleavages based on age, sex, region, and primordial attachment of race, ethnicity, religion, and the like. The long-term trends have been toward a more differentiated and segmented configuration of social stratification. Society-wide categories of social class give way to more differentiated social groupings which can be appropriately called "ordered social segments" in order to describe the pattern of social stratification.[26]

26. Meyer Fortes and E. E. Evans Pritchard, eds., *African Political Systems* (Milford: Oxford University Press, 1940), pp. 1–23, for a related discussion of "ordered segmentation."

3. *Political Participation, Social Stratification, and Social Control*
From the social-control point of view, the changes in social stratification and the growth of the welfare state make it more difficult for the individual and his household to calculate enlightened self-interest and group interest. The result is that the citizen and his household have chronic difficulty in aggregating and expressing political preferences by the alternatives posed in periodic national elections. The segmentation of the social structure also contributes to the fragmented, unstable electoral patterns. In other words, trends in social stratification strategically influence electoral behavior which reflect the attenuation of stable political party preferences.

4. *Military Participation*
The concepts of the citizen-soldier and of wars of limited duration which operated until and through World War II supplied a system of military participation compatible with a parliamentary regime. There is even reason to believe that civil-military relations based on conscription strengthen democratic electoral institutions. The decline of the citizen-soldier, the rise of the all-professional military, and the continuous military tensions in international relations have, since 1945, strained the multiparty electoral system. I suggest that, during the mobilization of World War I and World War II, military service, despite its unequal burdens, operated both as an index and as an agency of social equality, and integrated the military participant into the larger society. However, participation in the limited wars of Korea and especially Vietnam has increased social inequality and differentiated the participant and the veteran from the larger society. The outcome of the shift from conscription to an all-volunteer military is problematic, but there is no reason to anticipate that it will simplify civilian management and control of the armed forces. Likewise, the change in the function of the military toward deterrence, because it involves continuous and enlarged "peacetime" operations about which there is political controversy, also increases the strain on civil-military relations.

The second part of this study focuses on the social organization of an advanced industrial society and especially on the sources and consequences of institutional disarticulation. We are interested in two levels of exploration: initially, in the influence of ecological, technological, and economic factors on the development of societal institutions; and then in the institutionalization of norms and values in bureaucratic institutions, the residential communities, and in two different groups of agencies of societal socialization, namely, those of mass persuasion, and those of legitimate coercion. In this context, the role of family and educational institutions and of religious and ethnic attachments are explored. The following hypotheses are guides for this phase of the study.

5. Bureaucratic Institutions
The industrial sector represents the prototype of hierarchical bureaucratic organization, although the labor force in "service" types of organizations, including "human services institutions," has grown rapidly. Since the end of World War I, the resort to violence in labor-management relations has declined and the processes of collective bargaining have increased. Nevertheless, high levels of institutional disarticulation continue, as indicated by worker resistance to increased productivity, worker discontent, and a pattern of labor-management relation basically characterized by opposition and adversary perspectives. Institution building for increased and effective patterns of social control has been limited, and the chronic problems of "stagflation" and of the effective management of the welfare state have been avoided. Equivalents can be found in service bureaucracies and "socializing" institutions, such as schools, mental hospitals, and prisons, where the disarticulation reflects cleavages between management and staff and between the management-staff sectors and clients or the "public."

6. Residential Communities
The emergence of advanced industrial society has not been accompanied by the disappearance of the "local community" in the metropolis but by specialization of function and of social networks. Although use of local facilities has declined, the strength of community networks and sentiments derives from the specialized household patterns and the processes of socialization which remain in the residential community. The level of household income, the territorial distribution of socioeconomic groups, and the increasing length of the journey to work have produced increased disarticulation between the central city and the suburban area and between residence and work.

Because the political system emphasizes territorial representation and because government functions, including welfare state functions (some of which are geographically based) have expanded, the importance of local residential citizen participation has grown since the end of World

War II. Local citizen organizations and local political participation articulate and balance competing self-interests, and relate local citizens to the larger political process. However, the pattern of local citizen political participation has been fragmented and very partially linked to the larger political process and therefore has made only limited contributions to social control.

Because of the magnitude and the complexity of the division of labor of an advanced industrial society, social control requires societal socialization processes which strengthen personal control. For the purposes at hand, the mass media, mass persuasion, and the institutions of legitimate coercion are central.

7. *Societal Socialization: Mass Media and Mass Persuasion*

An advanced industrial society supplies the technological and economic resources with which a system of mass media is built. The disarticulation of the institutional sectors of an advanced industrial society would be impossible without corresponding positive contribution by the mass media. On balance, a wide variety of research and systemic analysis highlights this fundamental contribution by the mass media to both the development of personal controls and societal integration. However, the long-term positive contribution of the mass media to effective social control has declined, and there are significant disruptive or self-defeating consequences of the role of the mass media as agencies of societal socialization. The popular culture content stresses material consumption and has shifted to a strong emphasis on the expression and gratification of interpersonal impulses—a form of psychological symbolism which weakens both personal and social control. Popular culture content also stresses an enormous amount of violence, which operates in the same direction. In the area of public affairs, the television style of personalized reporting and advocacy journalism does not necessarily contribute to clarifying self-interest; it is more likely to strengthen suspicion. Finally, there is reason to believe that, since 1952, the impact of the mass media on elections has increased in part because of the weakening of party affiliation, and this increased impact does not always strengthen consent and acceptance of the electoral process.

8. *Law and Legitimate Coercion*

Law is not just another "set of norms"; because it seeks to express legitimate coercion, it has special relevance in the analysis of social control. Moreover, the law is designed not only to influence the behavior of the alleged criminal but also to define and socialize citizens into the larger society. The long-term trend has been seen as a proliferation of the scope and details of legal regulation, both by legislative and administrative action and by judicial decisions. The declining ability of the law, or at least its limitations, as an agency of socialization can be seen as manifest in the steady diminishment of trust and confidence in legal institutions, including the Supreme Court.

The limits on the legitimacy of the legal system can be explained in part by two hypotheses. First, the response of the court system to the increase in criminality has undermined popular acceptance of judicial procedures. The short-term increase in criminality is a function of the increase in the youth population and in increased unemployment and underemployment. The response of the courts, as seen by the citizenry, has been mainly to extend and reenforce their citizenship rights—that is, "to be too lenient." Second, while there is popular support for equality of opportunity for excluded social segments, the attainment of such equality by judicial decision fails to provide self-generating acceptance, so that the decisions are viewed as arbitrary.

Any analysis of legitimate coercion requires examination of the popular reaction to the forms of political protest, including those using coercive symbolism and tactics. The eruption of violent protest in the 1960s was short-lived despite the longer-term decline in trust in both political and legal institutions. The residues have been increased diffused violence and very limited conspiratorial or "terrorist" types of outbursts.

The final part of the analysis shifts to the "manipulative" or policy standpoint. It is designed to assess the consequences of premeditated efforts at institution building in the search for more effective social control. It focuses on the specific contributions of social science and social-science analysis. Three points of social and public policy illustrate the intellectual concerns of the last half-century. The first is the arena of the management of interpersonal relations, deviant behavior, and associated tensions, that is, the personal behavior syndrome. Here, the concern is with personality theory and the broad elements of psychological analysis. The second is the arena of community, that is, the syndrome of citizen local participation. Here, the concern is with the sociological analysis of the metropolis. The third arena is the structure of political elites, that is, the fashioning of their self-conceptions and strategies; here the concern of analysis is on "political economy."

Sociological Objectives

Two criteria are used to assess the influence of these on public policy. One is the clarity, consistency, and relevance of the intellectual formulation and the associated strategy of intervention. The other is the exploration of their actual effect on institutional building for social control. The underlying hypothesis is one that almost defies exploration because of the complexity of the issues involved.

9. *Consequences of Social-Science Analysis*

On balance, the contribution of social analysis, as reflected in the arenas of social and public policy, has been positive, although hardly with a marked consequence. The argument is not unidimensional. There is a sharp distinction between the nature of the influence—positive versus negative—and its scope and intensity. Paradoxically, the influence of personality analysis, it will be argued, has been on the whole positive, but the scope and intensity—the operative—have been limited. In the analysis and the strategies of community organization and citizen participation, the scope and effect have been noticeable. However, the direction and outcome have been mixed, and at times even disruptive, although the long-term effect and potentials have been positive or at least weighted toward the positive. The analysis of political behavior and "political economy" which focuses on the electoral system and elite formation, it will be argued, has had extensive consequences of both scope and intensity; however, the direction and contribution to effective social control have been consistently positive and at important points disruptive or negative. From an overall point of view, the line of reasoning to be developed runs counter to much evaluation of the social sciences and their social and political consequences. I do not believe that, in general, the results of social sciences are devices by which the elite maintain themselves in power or distort reality. Nor do I believe that the development of social sciences has contributed to a decline or eclipse of reason and common sense. The performance of social scientists is not without defects and limitations. No uniform and oversimplified assessment can be offered; it is essential not to exaggerate their influence.

All these hypotheses are offered with full recognition of the unending debate in sociological analysis about the connection between sociological knowledge and human values. Despite the intensity of the debate, I must assert that I am still committed to be belief in a "value-free" sociology—as Max Weber intended and not as vulgarized by some contemporary debate.[27] I believe that there is a meaningful difference between a fact and a statement of preference, and that the search for objective description and analysis of social reality is a legitimate, if most difficult, enterprise.

To Max Weber, "value-free" social science was linked to academic freedom, since he believed that social research should be free of the values of the Prussian state, the bureaucracy that controlled the university system in which he taught. Of course, group interest impinges on and threatens to distort observation of social reality. But even more important, every statement of fact threatens the interest of some social group, so vested interests erect strong barriers to social research. But we cannot get caught in an infinite regression. Social research is a collective and professional enterprise, and it can and does make progress by means of its own norms of consensual validity, although the issues of self-regulation and social responsibility of the social scientists require constant clarification and reformualation. The very notion of social control, elaborated in the next chapter as an approach to social analysis, also encompasses the contributions or lack thereof which result from the efforts of social scientists themselves.

27. Max Weber, "Der Sinn der 'Wertfreiheit' der soziologischen und "okonomischen Wissenschaften," *Logos* 2 (1917); See also Max Weber, *On the Methodology of the Social Sciences*, trans. Edward A. Shils and Henry A. Finch (Glencoe, Ill.: Free Press, 1949); Max Weber, "On Universities," trans. Edward A. Shils (Chicago: University of Chicago Press, 1974).

Two

The Idea of Social Control

Social Control and Conformity

When sociology emerged as an intellectual discipline, the idea of social control was a central concept for analyzing social organization and the development of industrial society. I realize that "social control" has taken on pejorative connotations in some sociological quarters. It is also used as a vehicle for social criticism of contemporary institutions, especially for their imputed excessive constraint and surreptitious manipulations.

In the development of sociology, however, the term referred to a generic aspect of society and served as a comprehensive basis for sociological examination of the social order. It was one intellectual device for linking sociological analysis to the human values and philosophical orientations of some pioneer sociologists interested in "social progress" and the reduction of irrationality in social behavior. In 1925, George Herbert Mead wrote that "social control depends, then, upon the degree to which the individuals in society are able to assume the attitudes of others who are involved with them in common endeavors."[1] He was articulating, in his own conceptual terms, a widespread orientation in American sociology that had already been reflected in the first volume of the *American Journal of Sociology* in 1896.[2] There George Vincent, a sociologist who still felt at ease with the language of social philosophy, offered the formulation: "social control is the art of combining social

1. George Herbert Mead, "The Genesis of Self and Social Control," *International Journal of Ethics* 35 (1925): 251–77.

2. For an intellectual history of the philosophic issues during the period in which sociology was developing in the U.S., see R. Jackson Wilson, *In Quest of Community: Social Philosophy in the United States, 1860–1920* (London: Oxford University Press, 1968).

forces so as to give society at least a trend toward an ideal."[3] Fundamentally, social control referred to the capacity of a society to regulate itself according to desired principles and values. Sociological analysis must explore the conditions and variables likely to make this goal possible.

The immediate task is to trace the intellectual history of the concept of social control and to assess its contemporary utility. Because some sociologists have come to define social control as meaning the social psychology of conformity, sociological theory and analysis have suffered. This type of thinking contributes to the difficulty of relating the sociological enterprise to other social-science disciplines, to social philosophy, and to professional practice and social policy. A new term had to be invented or the earlier meaning had to be reconstituted. I have chosen to retrace the intellectual history—of "social control" since I believe that the concept in its original meaning can help to integrate bodies of empirical data with sociological theory, to codify research findings, and to handle questions of social value in sociological analysis. Moreover, one of my central arguments is that a close examination of the intellectual history of the idea of social control reveals that, despite the constriction of its original meaning in some quarters, its broad generic meaning has had persistent vitality for the study of the social order.

"Social control" has served and continues to serve as a shorthand notation for a complex set of views and viewpoints. It has been a "sensitizing concept," in the terminology of Herbert Blumer, or a "theoretical orientation," in that of Robert K. Merton. Moreover, social control has been directly linked to the study of total societies. It has stood for a comprehensive focus on the nation-state which has come to be called "macrosociology."

The opposite of social control can be thought of as coercive control, that is, the social organization of a society which rests predominantly and essentially on the threat and the use of force. Of course, even in the most repressive totalitarian nation-state, the agents of repression are limited in scope by some primitive, if unstable, set of norms. However, and more pertinent, any social order, including a society which has a relatively effective system of social control, will require an element of

3. George Vincent, "The Province of Sociology," *American Journal of Sociology* 1 (January 1896): 488.

coercion—but presumably a limited one, circumscribed by a system of legitimate norms.[4]

The intellectual investment in the idea of social control derives from a rejection of economic self-interest theories. The concept of social control has been characterized as that outlook which holds that the individualistic pursuit of economic self-interest can account for neither collective social behavior nor the existence of a social order and does not supply an adequate basis for the achievement of "higher ethical goals." Much writing about social control must be understood as the effort of sociologists to accept the relevance but at the same time to identify the limitations of marginal-utility analysis.

Formally, one can think of social organization, the subject matter of sociology, as the patterns of influence in a population of social groups. Social control is therefore not to be conceived as being the same as social organization; rather, it is a perspective which focuses on the capacity of a social organization to regulate itself. This generally implies a set of goals rather than a single goal. Social control is a perspective which, while committed to rigorous testing, requires the positing of a set of values.

Social control was not originally the expression of a conservative political outlook—nor has it necessarily been so subsequently. Many early American sociologists who used the term were religious socialists; others had a "progressive" outlook. It is more to the point to emphasize that these early formulations parallel sociologists' contemporary interests in "value maximization." While social control involves the capacity of constituent groups in a society to behave in accordance with their acknowledged moral and collective goals, it does not imply cultural relativism. The term has continuity because social control can be conceived as resting on a value commitment at least to *(a)* the reduction of coercion, although it recognizes the irreducible elements of coercion in a legitimate system of authority, and *(b)* the elimination of human misery, although again, it recognizes the persistence of some

4. Personal control is the psychological and personality counterpart of social control. Personal control focuses on the capacity of the person to channel his energies and to satisfy his needs while minimizing disruption and damage to himself or others. Personal control implies mastery over one's psychological environment and encompasses psychological conditions that enhance rationality. See Bruno Bettelheim and Morris Janowitz, *Social Change and Prejudice* (New York: Free Press, 1964).

degree of inequality. One should add a third element, namely, *(c)* a commitment to procedures of redefining societal goals in order to enhance the role of rationality; this, however, may be considered inherent in the first two.

Early sociologists in the United States were vague about their social goals and their notions of the "ideal." Frequently, the ideal that was offered was no better defined than the spontaneously emerging consensus. At times, these writers did no more than assert that the ideal referred to norms which were rationally accepted and internalized in contrast to the conditions of coercive controls. Sociologists have become much more specific about the goals they wish to see maximized and therefore much more precise about the analysis of different patterns and mechanisms of social control.

To assert that social control is a generic aspect of society is to indicate a concern with the consequences of social organization on the pursuit of social values within a society. From this standpoint, there are a variety of types and mechanisms of social control. Each is the result of particular antecedent variables and each has a different effect on social behavior. The task of empirical social research is to investigate these forms and consequences of social control. This means determining which forms of social control are most effective—that is, which forms enable a social group to regulate itself in accord with a set of "higher norms" with a corresponding reduction of coercive control.[5]

This perspective explicitly negates the assertion that social organization per se represses personality, social creativity, and collective problem solving. Social control is not the achievement of collective stability. The vital residue of the classical standpoint is that social control organizes the cleavages, strains, and tensions of any society—peasant, industrial, or advanced industrial. The problem is whether the processes of social control can maintain the social order while transformation and social change occur. From this point of view, there is a parallel between social control and stability or repression. The argument is just the opposite: social control, to the extent that it is effective, "motivates" social groups. All this seems obvious; but, in part, the purpose of a theoretical orientation is to make the obvious inescapable.

5. In the contemporary period Amitai Etzioni defines control in a fashion similar to the classic orientation found in social control. "Control—the process of specifying preferred states of affairs and revising ongoing processes to reduce the distance from these preferred states." His theoretical model is derived from cybernetics. Amitai Etzioni, *The Active Society* (New York: Free Press, 1968), p. 668.

The Idea of Social Control

Exploration of the social-control idea requires one to recognize that its emergence was part of a continuing critique of and response to the "Gemeinschaft-Gesellschaft" model. Under the influence of philosophical pragmatism and empirical research, the dichotomous categories of Gemeinschaft-Gesellschaft were found to be both oversimplified and inadequate.[6] I speak not only of the original exposition of Ferdinand Toennies but also of the work of parallel or related writers. These include Henry Maine (status and contract), Emile Durkheim (mechanical and organic solidarity), Charles Horton Cooley (primary and secondary groups), Robert Redfield (folk culture and urban culture), Louis Wirth (urbanism as a way of life), Ralph Linton (ascription and achievement), and Talcott Parsons (pattern variables).[7]

The converging elements of these formulations have had a strong influence on sociological theory and analysis. At the same time, there is a tradition of criticism of the writings of Toennies and his followers that is almost as long-standing and enduring as the Gemeinschaft-Gesellschaft model itself. Among the European sociologists who have dissented from Toennies's orientation are Georg Simmel, Herman Schmalenbach, Theodor Geiger, and Rene König.[8] The accumulated empirical evidence from anthropological and sociological sources with a historical perspective indicates that peasant societies are not really wholly Gemeinschaft entities, as the term was used by Toènnies. The model's inability to account for the variety of solidary collectivities that emerge in advanced industrial societies is equally noteworthy.

6. Ferdinand Toennies, *Gemeinschaft und Gesellschaft* (Leipzig: Reisland, 1887).

7. Henry Maine, *Ancient Law* (London: Murray, 1861); Emile Durkheim, *De la division du travail social* (Paris: Alcan, 1893); Charles Horton Cooley, *Social Organization: A Study of the Larger Mind* (New York: Scribner, 1909); Robert Redfield, "The Folk Society," *American Journal of Sociology* 52 (January 1947): 293–308; Louis Wirth, "Urbanism as a Way of Life," *American Journal of Sociology* 44 (July 1938): 3–24; Ralph Linton, *The Study of Man* (New York: Appleton-Century, 1936); Talcott Parsons, *The Social System* (Glencoe, Ill.: Free Press, 1952).

8. Georg Simmel, "Die Kreuzung Sozialer Kreise," *Soziologie* (Munich: Duncker & Humboldt, 1922), pp. 305–344; Theodor Geiger, *Demokratie ohne Dogma: Die Gesellschaft Zwischen Pathos und Nuchternheit* (Munich: Szczesny, 1963); Theodor Geiger, *Die Masse und ihre Aktion: Ein Beitrag zur Soziologie der Revolutionen* (Stuttgart: Enke, 1926); Renate Mayntz, *Theodor Geiger: On Social Order and Mass Society* (Chicago: University of Chicago Press, 1969); Herman Schmalenbach, "The Sociological Category of Communion," in *Theories of Society*, ed. Talcott Parsons and Edward Shils (New York: Free Press, 1961), pp. 331–47; Rene Kőnig, "Die Begriffe Gemeinschaft und Gesellschaft bein Ferdinand Toennies," *Kolner Zeitschrift für Soziologie und Sozialpsychologie* 7 (1955): 348–420.

Much of the criticism of the Gemeinschaft-Gesellschaft approach is not an effort to reject its central concern with societal transformation,[9] but an attempt to recast the approach to make it effectively applicable to the analysis of the various historical paths by which societies have become urbanized and industrialized. It is difficult, if not impossible, to think of the emergence of modern society in terms of an "evolutionary" transformation from "community into society" that is the result of a limited number of basic variables and a linear model of social change and societal transformation. Thus, this criticism has freed the model from its historical mythography and refashioned its conceptual dimensions and variables into testable hypotheses.

Consequently, the notion of social control has been formulated and elaborated to present a more adequate approach to social change and social order. Sociological theories of the social order thereby have come to reject the assertion that the Gemeinschaft aspects of societal structure are only residues of some previous stage of social organization, and the Gesellschaft dimensions, the reality of industrial and urban society. Instead, social organization encompasses, at any given moment, essential and elaborated elements of both Gemeinschaft and Gesellschaft in varying scope, intensity, and consequence. The analysis of social control is an analysis of the interplay of those variables which can be related to both Gemeinschaft and Gesellschaft attributes. Moreover, the social-control concept is directly linked to the idea of voluntaristic action, to articulated human purpose and actions—that is, to various schemes of means and ends. Therefore it is designed to prevent the overdeterministic sociology which is inherent in the Gemeinschaft-Gesellschaft model. Social control presents a format of influence based on the notion of interaction and mutual relations among social groups. To speak of mutual influence is hardly to deny the elements of inequality and imbalance in social relations.

9. Robert A. Nisbet is representative of those sociological theorists who are aware of the centrality of the concepts of Gemeinschaft-Gesellschaft in contemporary research and who emphasize the necessity of departing from the original mechanistic and linear model of change. In *The Social Bond*, he writes, "a relationship that begins as a Gesellschaft type . . . may in time become increasingly characterized by Gemeinschaft relationships among members" (Nisbet, *The Social Bond: An Introduction to the Study of Society* [New York: Knopf, 1970], p. 109). For an empirical based critique see Oscar Lewis, "Tepoztlan Restudied: A Critique of the Folk-Urban Conceptualization of Social Change," *Rural Sociology* 18 (June 1953): 121–34.

The Idea of Social Control

Sociologists who have used the concept of social control have in effect been following the intellectual lead of Auguste Comte, for whom the central problem of sociological analysis was the effect of industrialization on the social order and the consequences of the resulting individualism on the moral order. The classic writers, including Karl Marx, Emile Durkheim, and Max Weber, addressed themselves to the issues Comte raised. One can translate much of the corpus of sociological writing on macrosociology into the language of the framework of social control, but that would obscure rather than clarify the issues involved. Instead, it is possible to focus directly on that distinct sociological stream which in varying degrees makes explicit use of the social-control idea. It has been mainly an American stream, but it was influenced by and influenced European thought and research. It presents both unity and continuing elaboration. In part, the unity is grounded in a number of central theoretical issues which reflect a skepticism about the evolutionary overtones in sociological theory, including the Gemeinschaft-Gesellschaft framework.

First, the original writers and, in time, the subsequent ones, have manifested a philosophical outlook concerned with the limits of rationality in pursuing social and moral aims. Their outlook has reflected pragmatism, as was the case for most of the writers who used social control, but for some it has also included aspects of phenomenology. An essential component of this orientation has been the rejection or, rather, the avoidance of either idealism or materialism.

Second, the adherents of social control have been writers concerned with informal, face-to-face relations as aspects of social structure. In contemporary language, they have been preoccupied with the interface between micro- and macroanalysis.

Third, these sociologists have been persistently concerned with empirical exploration of their ideas. They have been self-critical about appropriate empirical techniques, continually searching for various types of documentation and data, and fully aware of the complex, elusive character of proof in sociology.

There is thus a direct intellectual continuity from the earliest efforts to formulate the components of social control to its usage by contemporary research sociologists aware of its intellectual background and theoretical purpose. Social control hardly implies that the task or subject matter of sociology is the "adjustment" of men to existing social reality; on the contrary, since its early usage, this stream of sociological discourse has focused on efforts of men to realize their collective goals. Thus there is a direct connection between the early writers on social control and particular efforts in contemporary research, such as that on juvenile delinquency by Albert J. Reiss, Jr., who conceptualizes his operational measures in terms of social control and refers to social control as "the ability of social groups or institutions to make norms or rules effective."[10]

There is also a continuity between the early analysis of social control which included the study of social and political movements—the processes of revolution, of protest, and of institution building, as described in the seminal study by Lyford Edwards—and contemporary interests in collective behavior.[11] Thus the theoretical and empirical tasks of sociology which uses the social-control orientation have been and are to identify and wherever possible to quantify the magnitude of the variables which facilitate or hinder the group pursuit of "higher" collective and moral goals.

The pioneer sociologists who thought in terms of social control worked on specific empirical topics and in time applied their efforts to a very broad range of topics in social research. Initially, they did tend to focus on macrosociological issues, such as law and the formation of legal codes, the emergence of public opinion and collective behavior, informal and mass media communications, and "traditional" elements, such as customs, "mores," and religion. Louis Wirth, an articulate spokesman for this intellectual tradition, asserted the centrality of the processes of "persuasion, discussion, debate, education, negotiation, parliamentary procedure, diplomacy, bargaining, adjudication, contractual relations, and compromise." For him, these had to serve as the means for arriving at a sufficient degree of agreement to make the ongoing life of society possible, despite differences in interests.[12]

At this point an important caveat must be emphasized. Much of the empirical and substantive writing about social control deals with norms and normative behavior. Norms are often used as the indicators of social control—the dependent variables, so to speak. But social control

10. Albert Reiss, Jr., "Delinquency as the Failure of Personal and Social Control," *American Sociological Review* 16 (April 1951): 196–207.

11. This study was prepared in collaboration with Robert E. Park. It demonstrates the manner in which the empirical study of revolution was related to the elaboration of the social-control concept. Lyford Edwards, *The Natural History of Revolution* (Chicago: University of Chicago Press, 1927).

12. Louis Wirth, "Consensus and Mass Communications," *American Sociological Review* 13 (February 1948): 1–15.

does not rest on an exclusively normative conception of social organization and society. As will be demonstrated, it certainly did not in its origins and cannot if it is to serve as a guide to empirical research and to the codification of research findings. On the contrary, the continuing relevance of social-control theory reflects the fact that its assumptions and variables incorporate the ecological, technological, economic, and institutional dimensions of social organization.

Early Usage of "Social Control"

In tracing the intellectual history of social control as it emerged into a sociological outlook, one must avoid imposing more of a conceptual framework on the early writers than they actually offered. However, these men did have intellectual ambitions to explore, through a holistic approach, the classical problem of accounting for the existence of a social order. The phrase "social control" figures for the first time prominently in the writings of E. A. Ross, who was strongly influenced by Gabriel Tarde, a sociologist with great insights into French society who was deeply involved in empirical social research. Tarde did not emphasize the term, but he did present a broad analysis of the complex processes needed to produce social agreement through mass persuasion. He was concerned with the mechanisms required to generate effective leadership and legislation which would regulate social change.

While working at Stanford University in 1894, Ross decided that the social-control idea was a "key that unlocks many doors."[13] Again and again, Ross used the concept to explain how men "live closely together and associate their efforts with that degree of harmony we see about us." Basically, Ross was concerned with the social conditions that created harmony. Much of his writings consisted of detailed descriptions of the social-control mechanisms that attracted considerable attention.[14] Aware of the coercive elements in industrial society, he

13. E. A. Ross noted that Herbert Spencer had employed the word "control" in 1892 in his *Principles of Sociology*, vol. 2, part 4. See E. A. Ross, *Seventy Years of It—An Autobiography* (New York: Appleton-Century, 1936), p. 56. While Spencer did not give it central importance in his analysis, his usage undoubtedly influenced E. A. Ross. Also see Edgar F. Borgatta and Henry J. Meyer, *Social Control and the Foundation of Sociology* (Boston: Beacon, 1959).

14. The intellectual orientation encompassed in social control was more generally present in the works of many sociologists who wrote in the last decade of the nineteenth century but did not explicitly use the term. For example, Lester Ward wrote, "teleology is essentially the utilization of natural forces, causing them to do what the agent perceives to be useful and wills to be done." Lester Ward, *Outline of Sociology* (New York: Macmillan, 1899), p. 245.

focused on the devices of persuasion—interpersonal and institutional. He was impressed with the extent to which persuasion—as well as manipulation—was operative. His analysis encompassed processes from face-to-face interaction and sociability to public opinion and legal control. However, he was interested not merely in devices of persuasion but also in a generic conception of society which would explain those devices which operate to "find a means of guiding the will or conscience of the individual members of society."[15] His usage of "social control" brought the term into the center of sociological inquiry, but other sociologists would use the idea more rigorously and enrich its intellectual relevance.

During the founding of sociology in the United States, two major figures—Charles Horton Cooley and W. I. Thomas—gave centrality to social control and its relation to rational control in their writings. Their interests converged, but the differences were important.[16] Cooley was a more systematic and coherent thinker than Ross and his approach to social control was based on a thoughtful, normative orientation. His main preoccupation reflected the pervasive influence of pragmatism among the sociologists of that period.[17]

His approach rests on an interactional social psychology which he helped develop. Social control was essential for the growth of the self through the process of interaction. Likewise, social control rested to an important degree on self-control. Cooley used the notion of the primary group—face-to-face relations—but he had few constructions to deal with the internalization of norms, although he asserted that "individuality" was crucial for effective and meaningful social control.

However, Cooley struggled to relate his interactional approach to the larger society. Cooley's link with the classic question of social order and his outlook on social control under conditions of industrialization are summarized in his chapter, "Social Control in International Relations." In his words, "A ripe nationality is favorable to international

15. E. A. Ross, *Social Control: A Survey of the Foundations of Order* (New York: Macmillan, 1901), p. 59.

16. William G. Sumner never explicitly used "social control," yet, because of the issues raised in the volume *Folkways*, his name is linked to this concept. Sumner defined "folkways" as habits and customs which serve as the basis for the "regulation and imperative" for succeeding generations. William G. Sumner, *Folkways* (Boston: Ginn, 1906).

17. In 1911, L. L. Bernard published his treatise on social control, which contained a sociological critique of utilitarian philosophy. These themes were later emphasized in sociological analysis as part of the "theory of action." L. L. Bernard, *The Transition to an Objective Standard of Social Control* (Ph.D. dissertation, University of Chicago, 1911).

order for the same reason that a ripe individuality is favorable to order in a small group. It means that we have coherent, self-conscious and more or less self-controlled elements out of which to build our system [of nations]."[18]

Thomas approached social control from different but related principles of pragmatic philosophy. In his view, the essential issue for both sociologists and persons of public and social affairs was to increase the importance and effectiveness of "rational control in social life." Open-mindedly—and in a sense paradoxically—like many European sociologists, Thomas raised the question of the influence of rational thought in weakening the social fabric of society. "We are less and less ready to let any social process go on without our active interference and we feel more and more dissatisfied with any active interference based upon a mere whim of an individual or a social body, or upon preconceived philosophical, religious or moral generalization."[19]

Unlike Cooley, Thomas was trained in classical literature and history, and he developed an interest in the comparative sociological study of specific cultures and societies. He knew the writings of Toennies, whose formulation he rejected because of its simple evolutionary bias, its failure to describe adequately either peasant society or modern social organization, and particularly its implied hostility to individual freedom and creativity. Thomas offered no single set of determinant causes of social change, although he was the most systematic of the founding sociologists concerned with social control. Thomas had a comprehensive outlook on the dimensions of social organization and social control. He offered a differentiated orientation which sought to incorporate variables reflecting ecology, economy, and technology into his analysis of social control and which, of necessity, suffered because of its eclecticism. He saw society in institutional terms as consisting of a set of irreducible social groups, from primary groups to complex bureaucratic structures. Social control depended on effective linkage or articulation among these; social disorganization resulted from their disarticulation.

While Ross was stimulated by Tarde to propose the term "social control," the writings of Georg Simmel were important ingredients in fashioning the outlook of W. I. Thomas and, later, Robert E. Park,

18. Charles H. Cooley, *Social Process* (New York: Scribner, 1920).

19. W. I. Thomas and Florian Znaniecki, *The Polish Peasant in Europe and America* (New York: Knopf, 1927); Morris Janowitz, *W. I. Thomas: On Social Organization and Personality* (Chicago: University of Chicago Press, 1966), p. 37.

both of whom tried to develop an empirical base for analysis of social control in the metropolis. In his classic "The Mental Life of the Metropolis," Simmel manifested his resistance to the categories derived from the Gemeinschaft-Gesellschaft model.[20] He was concerned with the changing and alternative bases of group life. He did not conceptualize individuality as inherently self-destructive or destructive of social control. The analysis of individuality had to include the possibilities of forms of autonomy and personal freedom.[21]

Simmel's writings did not express any existing philosophy of history. However, they articulated with the orientation of those American sociologists who were of the pragmatic persuasion. In particular, Simmel did not conclude that the complexity of modern society and its range of group affiliations automatically implied the loss of individuality, or that it was necessarily disintegrative. His "Die Kreuzung socialer Kreise," translated by Reinhard Bendix as "The Web of Group Affiliations," argues the opposite. Each new group to which a person becomes affiliated "circumscribes" him more exactly and more unambiguously.[22] In other words, as a person becomes affiliated with a social group, he surrenders himself to it. However, the larger the number of groups to which the individual belongs, the more unlikely or improbable it will be that other persons will exhibit the same combination of group affiliations. Therefore, "the person also regains his individuality because his pattern of participation is unique." In essence, Simmel rejected the assertion that participation engendered only social constraint and conformity, or alternatively, that individuality resulted only from withdrawal. He held that individuality was the result of a pattern of social participation and the outcome of specific types of social control.

The central themes of Durkheim's writings converge with the early formulation of social control and are thus a related aspect of the intellectual history of the concept. He did not use the term or an equivalent. But his persistent search for the "determination of moral facts" is his version of the problematic issue involved in social control; this is perhaps most clearly seen in *Sociologie et Philosophie*.[23] However, his

20. Georg Simmel, "Die Grosstadt und das Geistesleben," *Die Grosstadt, Jahrbuch der Gehe-Stiftung*, vol. 9 (1903).

21. Donald Levine, *Georg Simmel: On Individuality and Social Forms* (Chicago: University of Chicago Press, 1971), passim.

22. Georg Simmel, *Conflict and the Web of Group Affiliations* (Glencoe, Ill.: Free Press, 1955), pp. 140–41.

23. Emile Durkheim, *Sociologie et Philosophie* (Paris: Alcan, 1924).

empirical study of *Le Suicide* has come to supply the link between his work and the subsequent generation of writers concerned with social control.[24]

One cannot overlook the existence of a body of literature criticizing Durkheim for failing to effectively analyze the internalization of the norms on which he rests his analysis. Durkheim's framework has also not served as a contribution to critical evaluation of the Gemeinschaft-Gesellschaft themes in sociology but has, in effect, been incorporated into this dominant perspective. While his work has been an important stimulus to empirical research, in contrast to the main body of writing on social control, his orientation has presented a relatively "overdeterministic" frame of reference without adequate exploration of the voluntaristic components in the "moral order."

Diffusion of the Concept

By 1920, "social control" had emerged in the United States as representing a central theoretical thrust by which sociologists sought to integrate their substantive and empirical interests. For the next twenty years, while sociology was becoming institutionalized as an academic discipline, the writings of Robert E. Park and Robert M. MacIver—although they were very different—maintained the notion that social control is a device for integrating diverse elements of sociological analysis.[25]

Social control was used as the organizing theme of the national convention of the American Sociological Association in 1917. There a wide range of empirical topics were explored, such as child welfare, immigration, labor relations, and economic organization. The papers presented tried to be explicit in evaluating the effectiveness of elements in the process of social control.[26] In 1921, Robert E. Park and Ernest W. Burgess asserted in *Introduction to the Science of Sociology*, that "All social problems turn out to be problems of social control."[27] In contemporary language, social control is the outcome, in various forms and content, of social organization. It is a construct which helps to re-

24. Emile Durkheim, *Suicide* (Paris: Alcan, 1897).

25. Ralph H. Turner, *On Social Control and Collective Behavior* (Chicago: University of Chicago Press, 1967); Leon Bramson, *Robert MacIver on Community, Society, and Power* (Chicago: University of Chicago Press, 1970).

26. Scott E. W. Bedford, ed., "Social Control," *Publications of the American Sociological Society* 12 (Chicago: University of Chicago Press, 1918).

27. Robert E. Park and Ernest W. Burgess, *Introduction to the Science of Sociology* (Chicago: University of Chicago Press, 1921), p. 785.

late and interrelate the "dependent variables" of empirical research. Moreover, sociologists of the early period saw social control as a vehicle for joining sociological analysis to "social problems" and social policy.

To understand the full connotations of social control in that intellectual setting, one has only to turn to its references and cross-references. Social control encompassed law and leadership, key elements for understanding how society regulated itself. In the Park and Burgess volume, the list of cross-references even included "participation," and the explication of this cross-reference was based on an analysis of the "immigrant problem" viewed as a problem in lack of participation.[28]

Sociologists then did not perceive social control as a mechanism of conformity. Society did not and could not exist on the basis of conformity but required active collective problem solving. Nor did the explicit philosophical preferences of these sociologists permit them to equate social control with conformity. Social control raised the question of how society regulated itself and changed. Park and Burgess postulated a sequence or "natural history" of collective behavior that was rooted in conflict and from which new forms of social control could emerge. "Social control and the mutual subordination of individual members to the community have their origin in conflict, assume definite organized forms in the process of accommodation, and are consolidated and fixed in assimilation."

Park's explication of social control drew on analogies from the competitive processes of ecology, to which he added those forms of social communication which constrained the ecological processes.[29] Park formulated the underlying processes of social control in a way that fused ecological, institutional, and normative variables. "Competition and communication, although they perform divergent and uncoordinated social functions, nevertheless in the actual life of society supplement and complete each other. Competition seems to be the principle of individuation in the life of the person and of society—communication, on the other hand, operates primarily as an integrating and socializing principle."[30] He went on to argue that the initial consequence of new forms of communications is to intensify competition. However, "in the long

28. Ibid., p. 766.

29. Turner, *Social Control*, passim.

30. Robert E. Park, *Race and Culture* (Glencoe, Ill.: Free Press, 1950), p. 431; Robert E. Park, *Human Communications* (Glencoe, Ill.: Free Press, 1952), pp. 240–62.

run," improved communication can contribute "to humanize social relations and to substitute a moral order for one that is fundamentally symbiotic rather than social."

In contrast, Robert MacIver's interest in political theory and the role of the state led to his bringing into social control the dimension of coercion, and especially of legitimate force, in a fashion which paralleled Max Weber's orientation. For MacIver, some coercion was involved in social control; the issue was the amount and the minimization of coercion.

MacIver accepted that social control was the modern equivalent of the classic issue of social order. Social control meant both elements: the institutional mechanisms by which society regulated individual behavior; and the "way in which patterned and standardized behavior in turn serves to maintain the social organization."[31] He investigated social control in nineteenth-century utopian communities in the United States, searching for hypothetical equivalents of existing patterns of social control and particularly interested in the capacity of purposefully constructed utopian communities to adapt to social change and to engage in collective problem solving. Reflecting his frame of reference, he concluded that, because the social organization of these communities permitted very limited, or insufficient, individualization, they were incomplete societies and therefore suffered a very high rate of "mortality."[32]

During the 1920s and early 1930s, "social control" supplied an essential bridge to the influential work of institutional economists. In the United States, these included Thorstein Veblen, John Maurice Clark, Wesley C. Mitchell, and Walton H. Hamilton.[33] They believed that the mechanisms of the marketplace and competition supplied an essential but partial basis for understanding economic behavior. Clark presented the core of the institutional economists' effort to make use of the so-

31. Robert M. MacIver and Charles Page, *Society* (New York: Rinehart, 1949), p. 137.

32. Other sociologists who before 1940 pursued the analytic aspects of social control included Kimball Young, L. L. Bernard, and Paul Landis. Kimball Young, *Introductory Sociology* (New York: American Book Co., 1934); L. L. Bernard, *Social Control* (New York: Century Co., 1937); Paul Landis, *Social Control: Social Organization in Process* (New York: Lippincott, 1939).

33. These institutional economists supplied a body of scholars with sociological interest, who for more than two decades produced important research on industrial and economic organization. With the decline of the institutional school of economists, sociologists, unfortunately, have failed to incorporate fully the topics of the social control of economic and industrial life into their domain.

ciological notion of social control.[34] He was committed to the centrality of utilization of market mechanisms for allocating resources. However, it was clear to him that the basic structure of modern society does not rest in the competitive economic process. Society requires a set of informal and formal norms which highlight "cooperative" arrangements. He rejected the notion of the society-wide organization as derived from the competition of large-scale or different types of economic organizations. He asserted that the governmental system—legislative and legal—supplies the framework for the cooperative elements of the modern economic system. He examined economic exchanges and controls—from antitrust legislation to price control—in terms both of immediate economic consequences and of the normative and institutional implications for the larger system of social control.

The connection between sociology and economics during that period is reflected in the article on social control prepared by an institutional economist, Helen Everett, which appeared in the original *Encyclopaedia of the Social Sciences* (published 1930–35). She argued that, given the inability of economic institutions to organize society effectively, the concept of social control had become central. Social control was applicable to more than economic management. "During the past few decades, the interest in social control has been steadily gaining ground. The forces at work in this development are discernible at many different levels of complicated corporate life. Largely as a result of the technological and economic changes of the past decades there has been a breakdown of individualistic assumptions in almost every field of thought, particularly in ethics, psychology, law, education and religion."[35] She was impatient because sociologists had not accomplished more in the area of the analysis of social control, as she focused on the requirements of institution building and of developing new modes of participation in economic affairs.

Comparable to this linkage of social control with economics was the work of "realist" scholars in law, politics, and psychology. One of the most outstanding writers in the sociology of law was Roscoe Pound, whose study of *Social Control through Law* anticipated contemporary approaches.[36] In political science, Charles E. Merriam made use of the

34. John Maurice Clark, *Social Control of Business* (Chicago: University of Chicago Press, 1926).

35. Helen Everett, "Social Control," *Encyclopaedia of the Social Sciences*, 4 (London: Macmillan, 1931): 344–49.

36. Roscoe Pound, *Social Control through Law* (New Haven: Yale University Press, 1942).

process of social control to launch empirical research into political and governmental institutions.[37] During this period, another vigorous intellectual current which fed the concern with social control derived from the writings of Mary Parker Follett, the psychologist of administration. With profound insight, she was moving toward a sociological formulation of administrative control that would encompass the essentials of the social process, and she broke with the view of administration as a system of constraints. "We get control through effective integration. Authority should arise within the unifying process. As every living process is subject to its own authority, that is, the authority evolved by or involved in the process itself, so social control is generated by the process itself. Or rather, the activity of self-creating coherence is the controlling activity."[38]

By the 1930s, the theoretical and empirical concerns of American sociologists with social control had begun to have a discernible effect on European thought. Two European sociologists, Karl Mannheim and Georges Gurvitch, followed the American literature closely and served as focal points of reinterpretation.

In *Man and Society in an Age of Reconstruction*, Mannheim made social control a central point of departure for his analysis.[39] Interested in political sociology, he introduced and focused attention on the role of parliamentary institutions in the processes of social control in an advanced industrial society. For him, freedom was a particular type and quality of social control; it was required under advanced industrialism if social planning were not to degenerate into authoritarian rule. He also believed that the processes of social control, to be effective, had to rest on strong parliamentary institutions. Influenced by Max Weber, he sought to analyze, in broadest terms, the transformation of social structure and authority relations, and he highlighted the shift which he saw toward indirect authority with the concomitant profound strains on social control. His work was striking in the extent to which he incorporated the detailed findings of empirical sociological research on American social structure. In essence, Mannheim prepared the intellec-

37. Charles E. Merriam, *The Role of Politics in Social Change* (New York: New York University Press, 1936).

38. Mary Parker Follett, *Dynamic Administration*, ed. Henry C. Metcalf and L. Urwick (London: Management Publication Trust, 1941); Paul Pigors, *Leadership or Domination* (Boston: Houghton Mifflin, 1935).

39. Karl Mannheim, *Man and Society in an Age of Reconstruction* (London: Kegan Paul, 1940).

tual groundwork for incorporating political sociology and the analysis of mass society into the study of social control.

Gurvitch, in a mixture of flamboyance and careful scholarship, used social control as a concept for emphasizing the "humanistic" and creative aspects of social relations. He speaks of social control as coinciding with the "sociology of the human spirit"—and delimits its content as the common name for the sociology of religion, morality, law, knowledge, art, and education.[40]

Conceptual Continuity

Although social control persisted as a coordinating term of reference in American sociology through 1940, its constricted focus was already coming into being. The alternate formulation of social control as a process of socialization leading to conformity was being postulated by sociologists who called themselves social psychologists. This trend becomes evident when one examines, not the theoretical treatises of the period, but the titles of doctoral dissertations and journal articles concerned with socialization and the processes of persuasion, interpersonal and mass.

How does one account for this shift? First, in part, there is a natural history of sociological ideas. Under the influence of empirical research, broad conceptions which have been sources of stimulation eventually become changed into more specific topics of research. However, this is a convincing but hardly adequate explanation. Review of the literature and interviews with figures active during this period do not permit the conclusion that the diffuseness and inherent shortcomings of the social-control idea—and there are many—account for the apparent transformation. It is necessary to point to additional considerations.

Second, power analysis and the modified versions of economic determinism derived from the writings of Karl Marx had the unanticipated consequence of weakening a concern with the "voluntaristic" and purposeful process which seeks to modify the social order. This occurred during the Great Depression and the New Deal—which created ideological and political currents that impinged on sociology, in a fashion comparable to the events of the 1960s, which made the idea of social control or any equivalent "unpopular." The result was an oversimplified

40. Georges Gurvitch, "Social Control," in *Twentieth Century Sociology*, ed. Georges Gurvitch and Wilbert E. Moore (New York: Philosophical Library, 1945), p. 292.

focus on power and power relations without sufficient reference to the institutional and normative elements of the social order. Moreover, to speak of social control was perceived as impeding those social and economic changes which members of the sociological profession considered essential.

As a result, after the interruption of academic life during World War II, social control more and more came to reflect the specialized interests of sociologists concerned with institutions dealing with socialization and resocialization, such as the mental hospital or the school. One of the notable exceptions was the 1954 treatise by Richard T. La Piere, *A Theory of Social Control*, which sought to incorporate the growing body of empirical social psychology into a traditional conception of social control.[41] The research topics covered under "social control" at the national and regional meetings, and in journal and monograph publications, show that the processes of social control in these terms were investigated in an ever widening range of institutional settings. Paradoxically, the relevance of these empirical researches rested in their findings about the limitations of dominant leaders and organizational administrators in enforcing norms and the capacity of informal groups to modify norms or participate in redirecting goals. Even in investigating the enforcement of norms, such sociologists and social psychologists were forced to recognize the requirements of institutional life and the societal order. On occasion they sought to deal with basic issues by relabeling "social control" as "social regulation."[42]

The delimitation of social control as the process of social conformity, although widely utilized in sociological research, did not and could not

41. Richard T. LaPiere, *A Theory of Social Control* (New York: McGraw-Hill, 1954).

42. See Elaine Cummings, *Systems of Social Regulation* (New York: Atherton, 1968). Of course, it would be an error to conclude that the narrow social psychological definition of social control as conformity was accepted by all social psychologists of either the psychological or sociological persuasion. Many social psychologists concerned with social values resisted. Without effective reference to the previous literature they came eventually almost to reinvent the older conception of social control. A thoughtful example of this countertrend is in Scott and Scott. They boldly introduce their work with the assertion, "even a purely objective attitude toward the phenomenon of social control provides some safeguard against the concept of control by a superman, for either good or evil purposes. This is the fact that control is always a mutual affair." Paul Scott and Sarah F. Scott, eds., *Social Control and Social Change* (Chicago: University of Chicago Press, 1971). See also Eugene Litwak, "Three Ways in Which Law Acts as a Means of Social Control: Punishment, Therapy and Education," *Social Forces* 34 (October 1955): 217–23.

displace the continuity in the classical usage of the concept. The new reliance on biological and electronic analogies has not completely displaced or rendered obsolete this traditional line of sociological thinking. In fact, after 1945, a period of marked expansion in sociological efforts, the idea of social control was not completely submerged under the results of delimited empirical work but continued to appear and reappear with persistence and vitality in general writings of a range of sociologists.

Any review of the continuity and vitality of the idea of social control must accord an important place to the writings and research of Everett Hughes and his students. As the post–World War II expansion of academic sociology began, Hughes published his influential essay on "Institutions."[43] For him, one central issue of social control was the socialization and the organization of occupational, and especially professional, groups. Hughes's theoretical and empirical writings stimulated an important body of literature analyzing and assessing processes of regulation and self-regulation of skilled groups in modern society.[44]

Hughes drew on social anthropology. In particular, the research of British and American social anthropologists reinforced the interest of students of social control in intensive field work during a period when the emerging trend in sociology was toward survey research methodology. Anthropologists who sought to use the social-control concept to integrate their ethnographic materials and maintain linkages with intellectual traditions of sociology by this approach included Raymond Firth, Max Gluckman, S. F. Nadel, J. S. Slotkin, and Jack Goody.[45]

The post–World War II "functionalist" continued to be concerned with an orientation toward social control. Talcott Parsons's interest in the concept derived from his explication of Emile Durkheim. In *The Structure of Social Action*, he asserted that "he [Durkheim] not only gained great insight into the nature of social control, but also into the

43. Everett C. Hughes, "Institutions," *New Outline of the Principles of Sociology*, ed. Alfred McClung Lee (New York: Barnes & Noble, 1946), pp. 225–81.

44. Everett C. Hughes, *Men and Their Work* (Glencoe, Ill.: Free Press, 1958).

45. Raymond Firth, *Elements of Social Organization* (London: Watts, 1951); Max Gluckman, *The Judicial Process among the Barotse of Northern Rhodesia* (Manchester: Manchester University Press, 1955); S. F. Nadel, "Social Control and Self Regulation," *Social Forces* 31 (March 1953): 265–73; S. F. Nadel, *The Theory of Social Structure* (Glencoe, Ill.: Free Press, 1957); J. S. Slotkin, *Social Anthropology* (New York: Macmillan, 1950); Jack Goody, "Fields of Social Control among the Lodagoba," *Journal of the Royal Anthropology Institute* 81 (1957):75–104.

role and importance of moral conformity."[46] In *The Social System* (1951), the analysis of social control figures more prominently in his exploration of the patterning of deviant behavior. Parsons's writings have had a strong influence on the study of deviance by a variety of empirical research sociologists.[47]

A number of Parsons's immediate students continue to explicate the issues of social control. In *Human Society*, Kingsley Davis has joined his conception of functionalism to the idea of social control. "It is through them [social controls] that human society regulates the behavior of its members in such ways that they perform activities fulfilling societal needs—even, sometimes, at the expense of organic needs."[48] He focuses on institutional arrangements for regulation and control by comparing the mechanisms of social control in totalitarian societies with those in the multiparty states of the West. Likewise, the "social control" of science has been used to focus attention on both the conditions under which science develops and in the social and political consequences of scientific knowledge. Bernard Barber, in *Science and the Social Order*, has probed the direct involvement of scientists in wartime research and the new orientations toward their social responsibility that have emerged.[49]

The continuing influence of the issues of social order were to be manifested, after 1945, by a group of sociologists concerned with macrosociology. Reinhard Bendix and Bennett Berger, students of the

46. Talcott Parsons's analysis seeks to assess the contributions and the degree of convergence of a number of classical sociologists to the extension and reformulation of basic questions of the social order. Thus this volume is a key resource in the intellectual history of sociology and the issues involved in social control. Parsons, *The Structure of Social Action* (New York: McGraw-Hill, 1937). Compactly, Percy Cohen has reviewed these linkages; his effort makes possible the conclusion that "modern sociology" has, in effect, abandoned the older question of how society emerged and concentrates on how the social order persists. Cohen, *Modern Social Theory* (London: Heineman, 1968), especially chap. 2.

47. While a great deal of this writing and research on deviance came to reflect the narrower view of social control, the expositions listed here deal with broad societal issues and thereby reflect earlier formulations: Alexander Clark and Jack P. Gibbs, "Social Control: A Reformulation," *Social Problems* 12, no. 4 (Spring 1965): 498–514; Jack Gibbs, "Conceptions of Social Control," in *Social Control*, ed. Peter K. Manning (New York: Free Press, forthcoming); Richard M. Stephenson, "Involvement in Deviance: An Example and Some Theoretical Implications," *Social Problems* 21 (Fall 1973): 173–89.

48. Kingsley Davis, *Human Society* (New York: Macmillan, 1948).

49. Bernard Barber, *Science and the Social Order* (Glencoe, Ill.: Free Press, 1952); Bernard Barber et al., *Research on Human Subjects: Problems of Social Control in Medical Experimentation* (New York: Russell Sage Foundation, 1973).

history of sociology, displayed a strong concern with issues of social order and the conditions under which it is maintained. Following directly on Simmel's formulations, they postulate alternative consequences of group participation in a fashion which converges with traditional notions of social control. They emphasize that social participation in its generic form produces more than "socializing" effects, the central concern of empirical sociologists.[50] They also stress the potentiality of an alternative set of outcomes, "individualizing" effects, which require a careful, richer language of analysis. The individualizing effects are not equated with personal anomie but are at the root of autonomy, creativity, and problem solving, elements consistent with and to some degree essential for a social order and effective social control.

In another way, Edward A. Shils has sought to explicate the dimension of social order and social control of a mass society.[51] The essential transformation of modern society rests not only in its industrial and technological base but also in the effort to incorporate the "mass of the population" into central institutional and value systems of society as a result of the social and political process of fundamental democratization, to use Mannheim's terminology. Shils has tried to give a normative dimension to the ecological structure of the nation-state with his emphasis on the "center" and the "periphery."[52] The particular relevance of Shils's writings lies in his use of "civility" to characterize the patterns of interaction and social relations required for the reduction of coercion and manipulation in the social order of mass society.

It is interesting that George Homans, before his acceptance of the "behavioral" mold of conditioning psychology, used "social control" in its "traditional" meaning. In this he was stimulated by Mary Parker Follett's writings. "Social control is not a separate department of group life—instead control, to a greater or lesser degree, is inherent in everyday relationships between members of the group."[53] For Homans, interaction supplies the basis for empirical investigation of social control in "at least two somewhat different languages."[54] Social control can be

50. Reinhard Bendix and Bennett Berger, "Images and Concept Formation," in *Symposium on Sociological Theory*, ed. L. Gross (Evanston, Ill.: Row, Peterson, 1959), pp. 92–118.

51. Edward A. Shils, "The Theory of Mass Society," *Diogenes*, no. 39 (1962), pp. 45–66.

52. Edward A. Shils, "Centre and Periphery," *The Logic of Personal Knowledge* (London: Routledge & Kegan Paul, 1961).

53. George Homans, *The Human Group* (New York: Harcourt Brace, 1950), p. 365.

54. Ibid., p. 94.

described in terms of "distribution of goods, such as money, and intangible goods, such as the enjoyment of high social rank."

Concerned with the historical transformation of societies, Barrington Moore, Jr., in a different style, poses the question traditionally associated with social control.[55] He considers himself, not a student of the abstract principles of the human group, but a sociologist of comparative sociopolitical systems. For Moore, social control involves an element of repression, conscious or unconscious. He feels that "in the mature man, we simply call it self-control." Moore has thus approached social control from the reverse side, namely, how much conformity does an advanced industrial society require? First, he is attracted to the idea that, in such a society, more of "this ancient virtue" is required than less. The societal context for self-control derives from the fact that the practical problem is compounded by a paradox. "There may be less of the self-control now imposed by scarcity," while "a wider range of material opportunities and temptations may require a stronger exercise of this capacity."

Second, Moore, strangely enough, finds the primary need for conformity in the arena of culture, whether broadly defined (as anthropologists define culture), or narrowly defined to include certain appreciated cultural, artistic, and intellectual attainments. It is not the arena of technology that generates the need for conformity but "the simple fact that the achievements of human culture require effort and discipline, not only to create them but merely to appreciate them."[56] This line of reasoning is not an expression of a sense of sociological perversity; it represents Moore's search for the requirements of an advanced society able to regulate and control itself.[57]

Thus the social-control idea has been a central formulation in the origin and development of sociology as an intellectual discipline. Moreover, particular sociologists have not abandoned the intellectual heritage and problematic issues associated with social control, for there can be no sociology without a concern for the elements of a social order.

55. Barrington Moore, Jr., "Reflections on Conformity in Industrial Society," *Political Power and Social Theory* (Cambridge: Harvard University Press, 1958), pp. 179–96.

56. Ibid., p. 186.

57. Andrew Hacker has restated the issues of contemporary political elite theory in terms of social control in "Liberal Democracy and Social Control," *American Political Science Review* 51 (December 1957): 1009–26; see also S. Cook, "Comment on Hacker's 'Liberal Democracy,'" *American Political Science Review* 51 (December 1957): 1009–39.

An inventory of contemporary usage indicates that efforts to substitute the language of social systems or biological and cybernetic models do not supplant older conceptualizations. In fact, Wilbert E. Moore has concluded, in his assessment of "social structure and behavior," that the "old-fashioned sociological term, social control, seems appropriate to revive," to handle the combination of external controls and individual internalization of the moral order.[58] The particular term is not the issue, of course. The issue is the analytic formulation which highlights the preconditions and variables that maximize the self-regulation of society and take into consideration the realities of social constraints, whether they have their origins in ecological, economic, or normative factors.

It would be an error to assess the relevance of the idea of social control mainly in terms of the continuity it supplies to sociological analysis. The advantages of such continuity cannot be overlooked. However, the case for the centrality of social control rests more decisively on its relevance for bringing integrated meaning—codification—to diverse bodies of empirical research. Especially during expansion of empirical research, the tasks of codification relate not only or even primarily to the integration of findings on a specific and delimited area of research but more to the linkages between diverse subject matter areas and problematic concerns. This was precisely the objective the original users of the concept had in mind and it remains an essential part of the concept's continuing relevance. In time, given the persistent sociological debate about values and the utility of sociological knowledge, the relevance of the idea of social control rests equally on its approach to value.

The core element in the idea of social control is that of self-regulation; therefore social control implies effective self-regulation. In order to have meaning in this sense, social control must be grounded in value analysis. One cannot make use of the idea of social control without specifying at appropriate points the meaning of self-regulation in terms of value alternatives. Social control requires the investigator to confront the related question of the methodology of sociology and the values which he holds in his citizen role and the values which are being maximized in his hypothetical constructs. These observations do not imply that the term dictates a particular resolution to these problems. Thus it is appropriate to return to the discussion of the intellectual origins of the moral orientations of those who first used the concept.

58. Wilbert E. Moore, *Order and Change* (New York: Wiley, 1967), pp. 171–219.

It would be both efficient and effective if the sociologist could solve or, at least for the moment, settle the issue of "relevance" by being able to orient himself to a single or overriding value. This was the outlook of the early American sociologists who made use of the idea of "progress" as their central value. They thought of the specific content of progress as being filled in by the relatively spontaneous interaction among persons and social groups guided by a generalized commitment to rational enlightenment and particularly to the containment of coercion.

To the extent that there is sophistication and realism among sociologists, it has come to be manifested in their commitment to a format of multiple goals and multivalues. To think in terms of a single central value would be naïve or unsociological. It would be most general and difficult to operationalize. Moreover, sociologists have come to accept that the pursuit of any single value is likely to generate distortions in personal and social control, and even sometimes to increase reliance on coercive control. For the members of an advanced industrial society, to be committed to a system of social and political democracy implies a balancing not only of interest but also of values and goals.

The literature on social organization and social control contains many efforts to classify the goals of social behavior into categories which meet both the requirements of "value categories" and the problematic concerns of sociological analysis. None of this effort has had great influence on the development of the sociological discipline, although it is impossible to proceed without recognition of its content. The desire to link sociology to issues of social policy and the policy sciences has only stimulated the alternative formulations of value-grounded constructs.

Harold D. Lasswell's writings demonstrate the advantages and limitations of such an intellectual endeavor. He seeks to use the same rubrics for both the categories of means and of ends in his analysis of the process of social change. He gave wide currency to value analysis by his formulation of the "value pyramid" in terms of the three categories of income, safety, and deference, applicable to both the means and ends of social behavior.[58] He defined a democratic society as a society which minimizes the use of coercion, but which also permits and encourages multiplicity of goals, in terms of both broadening access and limiting inequalities. His very concern with the range of goals in a democratic society led him progressively to refine and elaborate the categories of his goal analysis. Finally, he presented eight values both as means and ends in social organization; power, respect, rectitude, affection, well-being, wealth, skill, and enlightenment.[59]

Each step in the elaboration of a categories system of value analysis makes the tasks of empirical research more complicated and the procedures of use more difficult and arbitrary. The need for avoiding diffuse eclecticism emerges and remains crucial. In the context of social control, this study makes the value assumption that the role of coercion and its reduction are still the central issue. This formulation is compatible with those of the early sociologists of social control. This is hardly to assert that the reduction of coercion is universally overriding. The sociologist is concerned not only with the role of legitimate force in state power but also with the conditions under which force is related to the attainment of particular social and political objectives in the absence of effective systems of social control. The issues of coercion versus persuasion which constitute pervasive dimensions of value analysis are ones that continue the original orientations of sociologists concerned with social control.

59. Harold Lasswell and Abraham Kaplan, *Power and Society* (New Haven: Yale University Press, 1950), p. 86.

Three

The Logic of Systemic Analysis

Revolutionary versus Incremental Paradigms

The development of sociological theory in general, and more specifically of those aspects which deal with social control, has not been characterized by "scientific revolutions." Thomas S. Kuhn has offered the idea of a scientific revolution which produces a new paradigm and becomes binding on the empirical research of investigators.[1] This orientation does not consider that science proceeds by a continuous process of accumulation and by testing particular hypotheses. Rather, at specific moments, noteworthy issues which are unresolved force a fundamental and "radical" reorientation and hence a scientific revolution in which basically new premises and models are suddenly introduced. Kuhn calls such moments revolutions because they provide no opportunity for a compromise between the old and the new format.

Such a historiography of science may be applicable to the physical and biological sciences. It may even be relevant for aspects of the social sciences, such as the introduction of marginal utility analysis in economics.[2] However, it describes neither the emergence and growth of sociology as a discipline nor, especially, the conduct of research in 1945–1975 which is more explicitly concerned with propositional analy-

1. Thomas S. Kuhn, *The Structure of Scientific Revolutions* (Chicago: University of Chicago Press, 1962). A critical appraisal is presented in Dudley Shapere, "The Structure of Scientific Revolutions," *Philosophical Review* 73 (July 1964): 383–93. Reservations about the application of Kuhn's approach for economics are expressed by Dudley Shapere, "The Paradigm Concept," *Science* 172 (May 14, 1971): 706–9.

2. A. W. Coats, "Is there a 'Structure of Scientific Revolutions' in Economics?" *Kyklos* 22 (1969): 289–95; Martin Bronfenbrenner, "The 'Structure' of Revolutions in Economic Thought," *History of Political Economy* 3 (1971): 136–51; Leonard Kunin and F. Stirton Weaver, *History of Political Economy* 3 (1971): 391–97; George J. Stigler, "Has Economics a Useful Past?" *History of Political Economy* 1 (1969): 217–30.

sis and quantification. Of course, sociology has had its commanding figures with a decisive influence. Over three-quarters of a century, sociology has gradually developed a loose but productive framework; but in Kuhn's view, the history of a discipline is the result of a series of scientific revolutions.

Different analyses of the practice of scientists have been presented. For example, Joseph J. Schwab, biologist and philosopher of science, examined some "4,000 scientific papers written by European and American scientists over the past five centuries in the biological sciences, the physical sciences and three 'behavioral sciences.'" The investigator is guided, according to Schwab, by a set of important decisions which he must make at specific points in his work and which guide the nature and result of his inquiry. Available alternatives in this decision-making process are limited and have important common elements within and between disciplines. Moreover, in his view, these alternatives have not changed significantly over time. He identifies a pattern of five issues for decision; each has a set of standard alternatives and subalternatives. Scientific progress depends on the outcome of these decisions for the problem under investigation. Whatever the applicability of this approach to physical and biological science, it bears a strong resemblance to the intellectual history of sociological inquiry.[3]

The development of sociology as a discipline, particularly in terms of the influence of theoretical formulations on empirical research, can better be characterized as incrementalist rather than revolutionary. This is a crucial aspect of systemic analysis. Thus, the intellectual history of social control, like that of sociology more generally, does not manifest any scientific revolutions as those who have employed the term interpret it; it has been characterized by a number of overlapping orientations. Continuity rather than revolutionary displacement, and elaboration instead of contradiction, have been its scientific history.

It can be argued that sociology is not a mature discipline and therefore that Kuhn's format is irrelevant. Such a contention makes little sense if one thinks in terms of the number of years encompassed in the history of sociology or the amount of effort expended. However, a more pointed assessment might be that the notion of a paradigmatic discipline is not applicable. By the criterion of Thomas Kuhn, which

3. Joseph J. Schwab, "What Do Scientists Do?" *Behavioral Science* 30 (January 1960): 1–27. The decision points he gives are: the forms of principle for enquiry; criteria for the judgement of principle; reliability-validity; stable vs. fluid enquiries; guiding, collecting, interpreting.

emphasizes the importance of textbooks, this is clearly the case. He refers to the reliance in mature disciplines on the use of textbooks as a method of training future scientists. In such disciplines, the graduate and the undergraduate student is almost wholly dependent on textbooks throughout his training and is not required to expose himself beyond textbooks until he begins his own or collaborative research efforts. However, in sociology, monographic literature supplies an important pedagogical tool not only for transmitting theoretical knowledge and research approaches, but also for stimulating the collegial solidarities which are part of the scientific effort.[4]

It is legitimate to ask why the sociological enterprise has not produced binding paradigms capable of displacing competing ones. The history of the discipline has been characterized by persistent efforts to explicate alternative theoretical approaches in order to assess their convergence. Sociologists have worked intelligently and critically for varying degrees of theoretical synthesis. These efforts cannot be dismissed, but their contributions to the achievement of a paradigmatic discipline are at best very partial. In fact, the reverse can be argued. The preoccupation with theoretical reformulations has diverted attention and energy from the basic task of codification of empirical results which might have fashioned a more unified discipline. Sociologists have not made the sustained efforts at codification of available research findings in the

4. The history and influence of textbooks of sociology in the United States have yet to be written. In sociology, there was a long tradition of a few textbooks of respected intellectual worth. In the past, outstanding textbooks were both introductions to the discipline for undergraduates concerned with general education and also tools for graduate training and standard references for research workers. However, preparation of such textbooks has declined. W. I. Thomas's *Source Book of Social Origins* (Chicago: University of Chicago Press, 1909) served for a decade or more to affect the main themes of sociology. It was replaced by Robert E. Park and Ernest W. Burgess, *Introduction to the Science of Sociology* (Chicago: University of Chicago Press, 1921), which had a life of more than two decades. The increasing diversity of sociology in the United States was reflected by the appearance of two textbooks which served as alternatives and in time replaced the Park and Burgess "green Bible," as it was called. William F. Ogburn wrote *Sociology* (Boston: Houghton Mifflin, 1940). Robert McIver's *Society*, (New York: Farrar and Rinehart), written with the assistance of Charles H. Page, lived from its first appearance in 1937 past its final revision in 1947. After World War II, *Human Society* (New York: Macmillan, 1949) by Kingsley Davis and George Homans, *The Human Group* (New York: Harcourt, Brace, 1950) occupied a comparable intellectual position. There are additional examples. But, after 1950, the role of introductory treatises changed. The need to appeal to ever larger audiences of students with limited intellectual background resulted in textbooks' having less interest for apprentice sociologists in graduate school. One interesting exception was Gerhardt Lenski's *Power and Privilege* (New York: McGraw-Hill, 1965).

fashion advocated by Robert K. Merton and others.[5] Codification in this sense implies the goal of reformulating hypotheses and theoretical orientations not by logical or formal analysis in the first instance but by careful assessment of the convergence and divergence of specific empirical findings.

Moreover, one cannot attribute the "present state" of sociological theory to the social factors encompassed by the "sociology of knowledge." Men of very different ideological and political persuasions have tried to construct sociological theories and they have worked under extremely varied institutional arrangements. No doubt sociology bears the imprint of its charismatic personalities, and its empirical efforts have been fashioned by the manner in which research is organized in university departments and in research centers. Moreover, the writings on the "sociology of sociology" seem to comment on specific currents rather than to illuminate underlying and generic characteristics of the discipline.

The structure of sociological knowledge is an intellectual issue, a question of epistemology if one wishes to use this term. Sociological abstractions and the manner in which they have been combined have not produced competing models or paradigms which are subject to decisive empirical rejection. This is but another acknowledgement of the absence of revolutions in sociology. It is doubtful that a logical or formal argument can be deduced to explain or buttress this assertion; it is an assessment of the intellectual history and accomplishments of sociology for over three-quarters of a century and an inference thereby of its enduring characteristics.

Such a line of reasoning should not obscure the elements of convergence that have emerged. Paradoxically, there is much greater convergence in actual sociological reasoning than is reflected by scientific debates.[6] The very notion of systemic analysis reflects the absence of paradigmatic forms but highlights the degree of meaningful and realistic convergence. However, mutual toleration of differing perspectives, especially toleration based on indifference, cannot be considered con-

5. Robert K. Merton, *Social Theory and Social Structure* (Glencoe, Ill.: Free Press, 1957), pp. 99–101. See also Frank R. Westie, "Toward Closer Relations between Theory and Research: A Procedure and an Example," *American Sociological Review* 22 (April 1957): 149–54.

6. John C. McKinney, "Methodological Convergence of Mead, Lundberg, and Parsons," *American Journal of Sociology* 59 (May 1954): 565–74.

vergence; convergence involves the search for common elements, theoretical and empirical, and the common recognition of sociological knowledge and data.

The main basis for the convergence that exists in sociological thought as it relates to social control derives from the central idea held by sociology's founders, because of intellectual and moral convictions, that any frame of reference—be it economic or psychological—which stressed individualistic self-interest would not supply an adequate basis for analyzing the social order and processes of social control. Early sociologists were certain that such a framework would not only distort social reality but also would not supply a basis for contributing to purposeful social intervention and social policy. It is not farfetched to point out that the articulation of the sociological framework was in good part a reaction to other intellectual orientations. The intellectual history of sociology as a discipline underlines its effort to distinguish itself not only from history and social philosophy but also particularly from economics and psychology. An important theme in the theoretical writings of sociologists was directed precisely at this task; Talcott Parsons's monumental *Structure of Social Action* was in this genre.[7]

Since much of sociology was built on an intellectual reaction to and criticism of other systems of analysis, sociological reasoning has had elements of a negative or residual paradigm. In emphasizing the limitations of individualistic psychology and economics which stressed self-interest, sociologists became committed to undifferentiated terms such as society and "group." More specifically, "social organization," while it is far from a universal notion in the intellectual history of sociology, is probably the most common single term of interest. It serves almost as a nodal point of collegial commitment, as much as a basis of theoretical derivations.

The concept of "social organization" signaled the emergence of formal sociological writing in the nineteenth century; after more than a century of formulation, reformulation, and diffusion, it remains the acknowledged focal point of divergent interest, if only because of its generality. Auguste Comte in *Positive Philosophy* can be thought of as the originator, or at least explicit formulator, of the term. Herbert Spencer, who first used the term in his *Social Statistics* in 1851, does not

7. Talcott Parsons, *The Structure of Social Action* (New York: McGraw-Hill, 1937).

dispute the priority of "invention" but accords to Comte the priority of usage.[8] From then on it became a kind of intellectual reference to a common interest among a group of scholars. Beginning with his earliest writings, W. I. Thomas consistently took social organization as his main point of reference.[9] For him, social organization was an approach to the total society, in that it encompassed social stratification, social institutions, and cultural patterns. When Durkheim wrote *The Division of Labor in Society*, he incorporated the term "social organization" as a general statement of the subject matter of sociology.[10] It is difficult to locate the German equivalent of "social organization" in the writings of Max Weber. The more cumbersome formulation, "types of solidary social relations," was his equivalent. However, in translation, Talcott Parsons preferred, probably correctly, to use the terminology of theory of social and economic organization.[11] The notion of social organization thereby gained additional currency including subsequent German sociology.

The growth in sociological research after 1945, which produced considerable specialization, only resulted in the increased intellectual attractiveness of the concept of social organization. For example, in the debate in the *American Journal of Sociology* in 1959, generated by Otis Dudley Duncan and Leo Schnore, on "cultural, behavioral, and ecological" perspectives, all parties agreed that the study of social organization was the core of the discipline.[12] This centrality comes not from any precise theoretical logic but from the tradition of a common core of research and subject matter interests.

Even the sociologically oriented social psychologists—those who do not search for an independent discipline of social psychology—have begun to assert their attachment to this rubric, but of course, from their

8. Herbert Spencer, *Autobiography* (New York: D. Appleton, 1904), vol. 2, appendix B, p. 487, in correspondence to G. H. Lewes.

9. The essentials of his formulation are presented in "The Relation of Sex to Primitive Social Control," *American Journal of Sociology* 3 (May 1898): 754–76. The articulation of the concept of social organization with empirical research is developed in his study of *The Polish Peasant in Europe and America*, 5 vols. (Boston: Badger, 1918–20).

10. Emile Durkheim, *De la division du travail social: Etude sur l'organization des sociétés supérieures* (Paris: Alcan, 1893).

11. A. M. Henderson and Talcott Parsons, trans., *Max Weber: The Theory of Social Control and Economic Organization* (New York: Oxford University Press, 1947).

12. Otis Dudley Duncan and Leo F. Schnore, "Cultural, Behavioral, and Ecological Perspectives in the Study of Social Organization," *American Journal of Sociology* 65 (September 1959): 132–53.

own vantage point. Moreover, it would be obvious and redundant to point out that the usage of social organization is compatible with the full range of "causal" theories, from technological and economic determinism to normative interpretation of social interaction. Any effort to subsume these diverse elements in a highly general and systematic formulation is no doubt legitimate, but it produces a formulation which is intriguing, of circumscribed utility, and with tautological overtones. Such a generalized formulation might read approximately: "Social organization represents the pattern of influence in a population of social units. For any population under analysis, one social unit has influence over another to the extent that the first conditions the second's behavior. This conditioning may be direct or indirect, but social influence situations are interactive in that they are two-way, that is, reciprocal."[13]

The concept of social organization has not moved sociology toward an axiomatic discipline. Instead, it has led sociologists to concentrate their empirical investigation on underlying structures and more common social processes.[14] This is precisely what is involved in systemic analysis. The study of drug addiction and alcoholism has become part of the broader analysis of deviant behavior. Investigations of work teams, delinquent gangs, and neighborhood cliques have developed some integration by being transformed into the study of small groups, while empirical investigations of doctors, schoolteachers, and certified public accountants add up to comparative research on professions and professional influence. All this is another expression of the incremental dimensions of the sociological discipline. For better, or for worse, sociology has not shed its reliance on the classic concept of social organization, on which the idea of social control depends, although it has been able to use it for intellectual integration and clarification.

Another suggestive indicator of incremental convergence is the changing and more simplified categories that have come to be used in the classification of sociological theories. Any such system of classification is arbitrary, and classification can be a self-contained undertaking of limited import. But over time there has been a trend toward using more coherent, simpler systems of categorization which reflect in part elements of convergence in sociological analysis.

13. I am indebted to my colleague Guy E. Swanson for the assistance he has given me over the years in dealing with these issues in the analysis of social organization.

14. Edward Shils, "The Calling of Sociology," in *Theories of Society*, ed. Talcott Parsons et al. (New York: Free Press, 1961), pp. 1405–48.

There is also arbitrary element in selecting a number of sociologists concerned with the classification of sociological theories. But three over a period of thirty years indicate an interesting trend. In 1928 Pitirim Sorokin declared that there were nine types of theories.[15] They were: mechanistic, synthetic, geographic, biological, bio-social, bio-psychological, sociologistic, psychological, psycho-sociologistic. These had nineteen subcategories. Donald Martindale in 1960 reduced the list to five major categories.[16] They were: positivistic organicism, conflict theory, sociological formalism, social behaviorism, and sociological functionalism. Otis Dudley Duncan and Leo Schnore were satisfied with three major categories: cultural, behavioral, and ecological.[17] In essence this trend reflects a sharper focus on a more limited number of alternative formulations of causal relations.

Styles of Theory Construction

If an observer required additional evidence of the nonparadigmatic outlines of sociology, he could find it in the unending discussion of the philosophy of science as its issues apply to sociological research. Sociologists entertain differing notions about the nature of sociological explanations. As sociology became an academic discipline, it became philosophically concerned with the applicability and limits of positivism, and in time, the potentials of logical positivism as a basis of sociological inquiry. This involvement with positivism has not resulted in the partition of sociology. While there are extreme phenomenologists in sociology who reject the relevance of positivism, most "working" sociologists are concerned with the appropriate balance of emphasis in the discipline. It is as if the participants required the close proximity of their opponents for stimulation.

The basic issues become clear if one considers the inquiries that sociologists actually undertake rather than the formulae they claim to adhere to. However, because sociology is incremental, each sociologist does not start afresh. The investigator must make a number of decisions about the logic of his approach which are influenced by past accomplishments. He has a set of alternative ways of constructing his cate-

15. Pitirim Sorokin, *Contemporary Sociological Theories* (New York: Harper, 1928), p. xxi.

16. Donald Martindale, *The Nature and Types of Sociological Theory* (Boston: Houghton Mifflin, 1960), passim.

17. Otis Dudley Duncan and Leo Schnore, "Cultural Perspectives," passim.

gories and defining the properties of social organization which can be thought of as his style of theory construction. (The possibility of a revolutionary breakthrough is never denied, but there is no basis for anticipating its immediate or even remote eventuality.) Systemic analysis as one style of theory construction supplies a set of decisions about five categories of analysis: general versus middle-range theory; equilibrium versus developmental analysis; interdependent versus autonomous structures; generalized versus differentiated units of analysis; and social versus socioenvironmental boundaries.

General Theory versus Middle-Range Theory

Immediately after 1945, sociologists debated the alternative merits of general theory versus theory of the middle range. Like many such sociological issues, it has subsided without clear-cut resolution. However, on this issue, systemic analysis is explicit: it rejects the relevance of these alternative formulations because they are both part of a common approach. The terms of reference in the distinction were offered with specific intellectual objectives in mind by Robert K. Merton. He was concerned that sociological theory not be limited to the history of ideas, but that theory construction have an influence on empirical research and that empirical research, in turn, on the reformulation of sociological theory.[18] He was writing in the context of his own work as a member of a university-affiliated center during a period of expansion of survey research methodology. He wanted to relate the findings of this methodology to the broader, more enduring interests of academic sociologists. It may well be that the language of his argument created a debate which he did not intend. His formulations gave rise to an antithesis between his approach and that of the comprehensive-system builders, particularly Talcott Parsons and his colleagues. The difference between these approaches is one in preferred degree of abstraction and generality of concepts and propositions.

Merton argues "from all of this it would seem reasonable to suppose that sociology will advance in the degree that its major concern is with developing theories of the middle range and will be frustrated if attention centers on theory in the large. I believe that our major task today is to develop special theories applicable to limited ranges of data, theories, for example, of class dynamics, of conflicting group pressures,

18. Robert K. Merton, *Social Theory and Social Structure* (Glencoe, Ill.: Free Press, 1957), pp. 85–117.

of the flow of power and the exercise of interpersonal influence, rather than to seek at once the 'integrated' conceptual structure adequate to derive all of these and others."[19] There is a close affinity between this style of theory construction and that of systemic analysis. The emphasis is on a range of testable hypotheses for which no single postulated schema will suffice. The language is consonant with the requirements for the study of social control.

But any set of hypotheses requires a group of givens on which they can rest. Systemic analysis refers to testable and delimited hypotheses to be found in theories of the middle range. But there can be no testable hypotheses without some elements—explicit, at that—of a general theory.[20] The argument appears overdrawn at best, except to the extent that particular general theories do not generate testable hypotheses. Naturally, there is considerable latitude in the logical structure, specificity, and their substantive content of the givens. The result of the enormous discussion of this so-called controversy is to point out that some theories, because of their global character or their internal definitions and categories, do not produce testable hypotheses.[21] In the language of systemic analysis, such testable hypotheses do not have a life of their own but are derived in part from, or at least dependent on, elements which are to be found in what Robert K. Merton calls grand theory.

An essential aspect in the debate between the advocates of grand theory and advocates of middle-range analysis centers on the appropriate theoretical terms of reference in a sociological analysis. Again, at this point, the observer might be struck by the lack of agreement in the theoretical terms of reference which sociologists employ in their empirical research efforts. Every abstraction is not a theory, nor can the term "concept" be applied to every abstraction. Much of the discussion in sociology about appropriate theoretical terms of reference is both commonplace and arbitrary. But to dismiss these problems as being a form of oversophistication and to engage in excessive elaboration is self-defeating. It is more important to note the degree of operative convergence in sociological analysis, since systemic analysis does require terms which will expedite the translation of findings from one investigation to another and from one subject to another.

19. Ibid., p. 9.

20. See Ralf Dahrendorf, "Out of Utopia: Toward a Reorientation of Sociological Analysis," *American Journal of Sociology* 64 (September 1958): 115–27.

21. For an explanation of this, see Maurice Mandelbaum, "Societal Laws," *British Journal for the Philosophy of Science* 8 (1957): 211–23.

The Logic of Systemic Analysis

The implicit and explicit issues in the debate between grand theory and middle-range theory resolve themselves when there is a degree of logical clarity which makes it possible to separate the hypotheses that are being tested in a given research from the assertions (assumptions) on which they rest and which are therefore taken for granted in the course of the investigation.[22] This distinction is essential if any real progress is to be made in codification of research findings.

It is important to distinguish between types of givens. There are those givens which are no more than assumptions. They are taken for granted during the course of a particular investigation, and can be weakened by specific empirical findings. Such assumptions are different from the "overarching" givens, those *postulates* found in grand theory, which represent basic outlooks and are not likely to be rejected by particular empirical research but can be abandoned or modified only by the long-term superiority of alternative sets of hypotheses drawn from an alternative theoretical perspective. In the absence of revolutionary science, this is indeed slow, difficult, and painful. Thus, while systemic analysis is not grounded in the distinction between grand theory and middle-range theory, it does explicitly recognize the centrality of those formulations in the analysis of social control which are not immediately subject to empirical investigation.

Equilibrium versus Development Analysis

Sociology reacts strongly to developments in other research disciplines. In particular, it continues to reflect the imprint of biological and physiological constructs. The analogy between society (or the social order) has been too tempting to avoid. The intellectual record spans attempts to incorporate Charles Darwin's evolution and natural selection to the contemporary development of cybernetics and the biology of the brain.[23] The most persistent influence has been by the use of the analogy of equilibrium. Distinct from such analogous reasoning has been the efforts to explore the linkages of biological factors and social organization or social behavior as a research task.

22. I am indebted to my colleague Amos Hawley for the assistance he has given me on these issues of analytic terminology.

23. Of the extensive literature on cybernetics, the following references are illustrative of those which have been widely read and cited by sociologists: Norbert Wiener, *Cybernetics* (New York: Wiley, 1948); William R. Ashby, *Design for a Brain* (New York: Wiley, 1952); and W. Sluckin, *Minds and Machines* (Baltimore: Penguin, 1960).

Equilibrium, as a property of social organization heavily emphasized by L. J. Henderson and his disciples, has to be juxtaposed to the alternative which might best be called developmental analysis.[24] Systemic analysis acknowledges the priority of the developmental posture, at least as a point of entry; at this decisive point it finds equilibrium analysis too confining.

In the extensive literature on equilibrium analysis, the underlying postulate is the inherent tendency of the component subsystems and the overall system of social organization to remain in a steady state. Modifications and deviations tend to be eliminated, reduced, or narrowly restricted. The equilibrium approach, in effect, perpetuates the older distinction between static and dynamic analysis. It asserts the necessity of stipulating in advance all the variables required. In this view, understanding social structure is a prerequisite for explicating social change.[25]

Theoretical orientations which make use of the property of equilibrium handle the question of change by the "principle of emergence," a philosophical construct of long tradition. However, as pointed out by various philosophers, including Abraham Edel, this "principle" is not without problems and limitations for empirical investigators.[26] As applied to social organization analysis, the "principle of emergence" has been described: ". . . at various levels of organizational complexity systems emerge which have properties which cannot be inferred from or explained in terms of the operation of their component parts or elements and that these emergent properties must be treated as causally relevant variables in the theory. By implication, at each emergent level, certain new degrees of freedom are created."[27] This formulation asserts that the new properties cannot be inferred from the prior state, but it

24. Bernard Barber, ed., *L. J. Henderson: On the Social System* (Chicago: University of Chicago Press, 1970). For a discussion of the alternative developmental approach see Harold D. Lasswell, *World Politics and Personal Insecurity* (New York: McGraw-Hill, 1935), pp. 3–26; see also G. Poggi, "A Main Theme of Contemporary Sociological Analysis: Its Achievements and Limitations," *British Journal of Sociology* 16 (1965): 283–94. For a penetrating analysis of history and the analysis of social change which converges with "systemic analysis" in its concern with the appropriate level of analysis and abstraction see Ernest Gellner, *Thought and Change* (London: Weidenfeld and Nicholson, 1964).

25. See particularly Talcott Parsons, *The Social System* (Glencoe, Ill.: Free Press, 1951), chap. 11, "The Process of Change in Social Systems," pp. 480–535. Parsons argues that "a general theory of the processes of change in social systems is not possible in the present state of knowledge" (p. 486).

26. Abraham Edel, "The Concept of Levels in Social Theory," in F. Gross, ed., *Symposium of Sociological Theory*, (Evanston, Ill.: Row Peterson, 1959), pp. 167–95.

27. Ibid., p. 171.

is still causally relevant. The property of emergence violates the development toward theoretical closure which the equilibrium format is designed to facilitate. Thus equilibrium analysis is as much an aspiration as a reality.

Developmental analysis is both more time-bound and more interested in making explicit so-called emergent properties. It does not make the sharp distinction between static and dynamic analysis or between structural analysis and the analysis of social change. There are many unsolved and unsolvable problems of such a format, but it supplies a more realistic and comprehensive orientation, beginning with the aspiration that the postulates of change be explicit and substantive, rather than implicit and purely formal—as is often the case in the equilibrium format. To use such an orientation may well "mess up" the analysis. For example, secondary, intervening variables are stated in advance; but the possibility that additional elements will be introduced to the analysis cannot be ruled out in advance.

If equilibrium analysts, or some of them, postulate that social change occurs gradually, developmental analysis postulates that the rates of social change vary and are a subject for empirical investigation.[28] Likewise, if equilibrium analysis implies that change has its locus outside the system under analysis, in developmental analysis change can originate within and outside the social organization under investigation.

It is a primary responsibility of the sociologist to collect and chart empirical indicators of social change. At this point, sociology and "history" converge. All empirical sociology is history, but history is not all empirical sociology. The collection of social indicator data cannot be limited to particular hypotheses but must reflect the collective judgment of social scientists about the range of descriptive data required to write contemporary social history. In the 1920s such a research notion was presented in the writings of William F. Ogburn. Almost a half-century later, the institutionalized collection of such indicators in sociology has begun to occur."[29]

Developmental analysis at times postulates some hypothetical end state, for example, Harold D. Lasswell's "garrison state."[30] The goal is

28. President's Research Committee, *Recent Social Trends* (New York: McGraw-Hill, 1933).

29. Eleanor B. Sheldon and Wilbert E. Moore, *Indicators of Social Change* (New York: Russell Sage Foundation, 1968).

30. Harold D. Lasswell, "The Garrison State," *American Journal of Sociology* 46 (January 1941): 455–68. See also Guenther Roth, "Socio-historical Model and Developmental Theory," *American Sociological Review* 40 (April 1975): 148–57.

to examine social change in terms of movement toward or away from this construct. This emphasis in developmental analysis includes the charting of "master trends," to use C. W. Mills's term, which supply the societal context for the investigation of particular institutions.[31] Within such a historical and analytic framework, it becomes feasible to explore the limits of equilibrium analysis.

To argue that developmental models are more appropriate for the study of society hardly implies that systemic analysis of social control has no aspirations for general formulations. It does mean that sociologists must pay attention to "historical" issues in research. To aspire to narrow the distinction between history and sociology is commendable only if the sociologists remain aware of the looseness of notions such as the "principle of emergence" and other escape hatches that historians have allowed themselves.[32]

Likewise, there is the question of the appropriate time span involved in developmental analysis, a subject on which sociologists have not displayed great expertise. There is no general answer; but sociologists have erred in limiting the periods in their developmental analysis, whether the object of study is a particular institutional innovation or a pattern of societal change. Explanations of the limits vary; the dramatic character of particular contemporary events, inherent limitations of sociological inquiry and available data, or even the desire to participate in policy making. However, intellectual criticism of sociological research has had an increasing influence on broadening and extending sociological time perspectives.[33] In summary, systemic analysis encompasses a

31. Hans Gerth and C. Wright Mills, *Character and Social Structure: The Social Psychology of Social Institutions* (New York: Harcourt, Brace and World, 1953).

32. There is no reason to suppose that modern research efforts, with their better resources and elaborate methodology, are always superior to earlier efforts. Studies of racial tension and violence make interesting comparisons possible of the period immediately after World War I and the 1960s. One of the most comprehensive analyses deals with Chicago during 1919, Chicago Commission on Race Relations, *The Negro in Chicago* (Chicago: University of Chicago Press, 1922). The detailed documentation for this volume was collected by the sociologist Charles S. Johnson under the guidance of Robert E. Park, and the published report is based on an integrated effort. For 1965–1970, immense amounts of data were collected by the Congress, federal commissions, and university and social research groups. Some of these materials permitted refined measures of statistical analysis, including the use of Guttman-type scaling procedures. But not for a single community did these efforts produce the penetrating analysis presented in *The Negro in Chicago*.

33. For a brilliant example of comprehensive historical treatment of the persistence and change of a complex social entity which encompasses the full and

concern with the equilibrium model and an emphasis on developmental analysis; the actual admixture is related to both the specific research issue and the style of the investigator.

Interdependent versus Autonomous Structures

One aspect of sociological theory which has fairly general acceptance is that embodied in the holistic approach. The elements of social organization have meaning in terms of all other elements. Most of the founding figures of sociology made some equivalent reference to the idea of holistic analysis. The incremental development in sociology has reaffirmed this notion; the influence of social anthropology has reinforced it.[34] However, sociologists require frequent reminders of this aspect of sociological theory, because it is very difficult to implement in research.

The emphasis of holistic analysis makes the meaning and relevance of any factor or dimension of analysis rest on an understanding of all the other factors and dimensions; this is an essential part of the pursuit of macrosociology. For better or worse, sociology is the discipline concerned with "the context." However, sociological theories based on a holistic framework, as Pierre L. van den Berghe points out, can use fundamentally different conceptions of explanation and causality.[35]

In fact, to speak of a holistic orientation is to refer to no more than the view that, in social organization, causation is to some degree reciprocal among the component elements.[36] It does not answer the question of the degree of interdependence of the components in any particular social organization. On this essential issue—the degree of postulated interdependence among component structural elements—sociological writers differ consistently and to a considerable degree; the direction of systemic analysis is to take for granted at least a considerable degree of actual and potential autonomy between elements, or to assert that there are conditions under which such autonomy is operative.

necessary temporal sequences, see Donald Levine, *Greater Ethopia: The Evolution of a Multi-ethnic Society* (Chicago: University of Chicago Press, 1974).

34. Lloyd A. Fallers, *Social Anthropology of the Nation State* (Chicago: Aldine, 1974).

35. Pierre L. van den Berghe, "Dialectic and Functionalism: Toward a Theoretical Synthesis," *American Sociological Review* 28 (October 1963): 695–705.

36. See Alvin Gouldner for a related analysis of reciprocal and autonomous relations in social organizations, "The Means of Reciprocity: A Preliminary Statement," *American Sociological Review* 25 (April 1960): 161–78.

The distinction of equilibrium versus developmental analysis is relevant at this point. Equilibrium versus developmental analysis postulates different degrees of interdependence. Equilibrium orientations assert a great degree of effective interdependence of component elements of any given social organization. In this type of theory construction, the structure of a society is characterized by a continuous network of persons and groups, so that a change in one component has a direct and discernible effect throughout the entire social organization.

However, if one proceeds by means of systemic analysis, the degree of interdependence is problematic; more specifically, developmental analysis asserts that some autonomous groups are required to achieve effective integration in a given social organization.[36] Thereby systemic analysis, which uses developmental constructs, rejects the idea of complete and comprehensive interdependence.

In particular, the very notion of social control in an advanced industrial society underlines the crucial role of autonomous or relatively autonomous groups. This asserts no less than that some groups in an advanced industrial society will be autonomous or relatively so if the process of social control is to be effective. There is no reason to deny the possibility that in a primary group, a community, a large bureaucracy, or nation, effective social control is compatible with and requires some autonomy in particular constituent groups. In fact, examination of social control in an advanced industrial society indicates that, because of the increased complexity of the division of labor, the importance of such autonomous structures is enhanced if social rather than coercive control is to be achieved.

Generalized versus Differentiated Units of Analysis

Directly related to the degree of interdependence is the decision which sociologists must make about the units of analysis (and the objects of analysis). In this decision, systemic analysis differs from the dominant motif, since there is a strong tendency in sociological theory to develop and utilize a single basic, highly generalized unit for sociological analysis. For example, sociologists use various notions of a basic "social atom" from which the component elements of social organization are derived and in terms of which social structure can be analyzed. Social role is one formulation of the basic social molecule and the social act is in effect the atomic element.[37]

37. For an early contribution, see Florian Znaniecki, *The Social Role of the Man of Knowledge* (New York: Columbia University Press, 1940).

Talcott Parsons advanced this type of analysis. He spoke of the institutionalization of the social role, the mechanism by which more complex systems are created.[38] The intellectual goal is to produce an orientation of the widest generality, applicable to all institutional arrangements. It is interesting to note that theories of social organization which stress the close interconnection of the component elements are the ones which tend to postulate a single basic unit of analysis. These theories also tend to proceed by means of an equilibrium approach.

Likewise, an orientation which rests on a single, generalized unit of analysis tends to use a single object of analysis. The analogy with the biological notion of organism is again at work. Talcott Parsons offers the social system as his object of analysis, and he holds that society—the nation-state in the modern context—is the most complete social system.[39] While the notion of social system can be applied to other objects of analysis, they are all derivative from the nation-state as a social system. In this regard, George Homans's theoretical orientation has many common features with Talcott Parsons's conception of social systems. He presents the human group as the appropriate object of analysis. The human group is best characterized as the obverse of total society, namely, the primary group defined in classic terms of the small, face-to-face collectivity.[40] Homans builds his case on the argument that "perhaps we cannot manage a sociological synthesis that will apply to whole communities and nations, but it is just possible we can manage one that will apply to the small group.[41] In other words, the small group, the human group, for George Homans, like the social system (the total society) for Talcott Parsons, is not only the appropriate object of analysis; it is also a conception of sociological inquiry and a strategy of analysis.[42]

Systemic analysis, drawing on empirical practices as much as on theoretical forms, takes a very different stance with respect to the units and objects of analysis. The notion of a single molecular unit of analysis

38. Talcott Parsons, *The Social System* (Glencoe, Ill.: Free Press, 1951), passim.
39. Ibid., p. 19.
40. George Homans, *The Human Group* (New York: Harcourt, Brace, 1950).
41. Ibid., p. 31.
42. Both approaches have intellectual attractions. Talcott Parsons's focus on the total society not only supplies continuity with long standing concerns about the social order but also carries a face validity, namely, that total society is obviously most complex and therefore the core of sociological inquiry. George Homans's posture appears to carry with it an important seed of intellectual restraint and modesty. In his view, how can sociologists attack the total society when they do not understand the small group? Actually, sociologists have not been constrained to accept either formulation of a single object of analysis, nor need they do so.

does not generate a guide to the variables to be employed in research. Likewise, to postulate a single unit or object of analysis—particularly if it is couched in a highly abstract format, such as the social system or the human group—is incomplete. It remains necessary to construct additional taxonomies of group structure to generate testable hypotheses.

There is, of course, a strong element of taste or preference in this theory construction. The unitary approach excessively detaches theory construction from social reality. On the other hand, an elongated collection of units and objects, reflecting the wide research interests of sociologists and having no internal logic, is self-defeating.[43] In short, an appropriate set of units and objects of analysis seeks a balance between concreteness to guide empirical research and a degree of analytical generality.

In the elaboration of sociological theory, the simple distinction between "community" and "society" served to identify units and objects of analysis. These terms are not simply empirical entities; they are also analytical categories. The independent variables are linked to the "community" (the unit of analysis) and were designed to explain its transformation into "society" (the object of analysis); these distinctions also imply the reverse flow of influence from "society" to "community." The schema presents a balance between abstract categories and concrete realities which continues to have a strong appeal to empirical sociologists.

But the distinction between "community" and "society" was hardly sufficient to incorporate the empirical observations of the founding figures in sociology. Sociologists like Charles Horton Cooley identified the primary group as an essential component in accounting for the social order. Likewise, since the earliest writings of Herbert Spencer, sociologists have sought analytically to distinguish "institutions" from "society."

By the turn of the century, a relatively standardized set of units and objects of analysis had come into the terminology of primary groups, communities, institutions, and societies.[44] For students of social control, these early distinctions have remained crucial, although the definitions

43. At this point, systemic analysis converges with the idea of grounded theory. Grounded theory, however, does not sufficiently emphasize the positive assistance that the intellectual heritage of sociology affords the empirical investigator, nor does it specify the formal issues that must be resolved by the investigator. See Barney Glaser and Anselm Strauss, *The Discovery of Grounded Theory: Strategies for Qualitative Research* (Chicago: Aldine, 1967).

44. In *The Polish Peasant in Europe and America*, 5 volumes (Boston: Richard G. Badger, 1918–20) by W. I. Thomas and Florian Znaniecki, published in 1918,

have been refined and modified. These structures were offered as elements of "holistic" analysis and not the result of ad hoc observation. Each rested on analytic definition and delimitation. For systemic analysis these analytic categories continue to serve as rubrics for research and for codification of existing empirical research.

Systemic analysis seeks to avoid the investigation of primary groups, communities, and institutions that are detached from their social context and their interrelations.[45] A great deal of empirical research into social organization has emerged as the study of samples of such structures, as if they were detached and self-contained objects of analysis. In essence, systemic analysis focuses on a set of differentiated analytic entities. This focus is designed to supply a framework sufficiently comprehensive to pursue the investigation of macrosociology. Macrosociology is the study of the most complex and most comprehensive social group, namely, the nation-state. The nation-state must be seen in its relations to the world-wide system of nation-states. For other historical periods, macrosociology encompasses other sociopolitical objects, for example, the city-state. But in the modern period, the nation-state has emerged as the "universal" format, although there are some nation-states which are no more than urban centers without hinterlands.

In the origins of sociology, macrosociology was the central intellectual concern, and explicitly concerned with cross-national or cross-societal comparisons. The idea of social control articulated with the centrality accorded to macrosociological analysis. However, under the influence of more and more delimited empirical investigation, this orientation receded; it has gradually reemerged since 1945. In the present state of sociology, sociologists must recognize, tolerate, and accept the inherent limitations of sociological orientations which deal with total societies and are thus global in perspective. It was the very global character of social control that supplied its original intellectual attractiveness but which, in time, limited its usefulness because of its diffuse formulations.

During the last quarter-century, an effort to revitalize macrosociology has been made in two directions. There has been a great expendi-

one of the earliest systemic studies of comparative social organization and social structure, these categories were defined as the irreducible minimum and none were thought of as merely residual.

45. Charles P. Loomis and Zona K. Loomis's observations on systemic linkages are relevant here. "This is the process whereby the elements of at least two social systems come to be articulated so that in some ways and on some occasions they may be viewed as a single system." Charles P. Loomis and Zona K. Loomis, *Modern Social Theories* (Princeton, N.J.: Van Nostrand, 1961).

ture of energy to analyze, by means of various statistical models of causality, quantitative indicators collected in cross-national data banks. The limitations of the quality of these data have been counterbalanced by the wide measures that have been investigated, many of which reflect central issues of social control. These data are essential aspects of comparative macrosociology, but when they are statistically and mathematically analyzed as a self-contained "data base" the results are self-defeating. One overriding conclusion, negative though it may be, has been that the variety of nation-states cannot be analyzed as if they constitute a single universe.

On the other hand, macrosociology has been characterized by persistent efforts to construct comprehensive, ideal, and logico-deductive models of the nation-state of the "social system," efforts which have been influenced by Weber's writings. These models, more often than not, have been definitional rather than deductive. Their intellectual worth has rested, not on the testable hypotheses that have been generated, but in their insistence on a holistic orientation which converges with the goals of a social-control perspective. But comparative macrosociological analysis is not limited to the analysis of national statistical indicators or the elaboration of ideal types. It involves, at a minimum, for the issues at hand, an examination of the articulation (or disarticulation) of the set of essential social units (e.g., primary-group structure, community, bureaucratic organization) which constitute a society and their comparative juxtaposition with one another or another society.

Social versus Socioenvironmental Boundaries

Systemic analysis must address itself to the boundaries of social organization. This is a crucial decision in social theory, since it involves imputing causal processes. The interplay of the "material" conditions of society and the "normative" elements of social control has been at the center of sociological inquiry. One solution—implicit or explicit in many normative perspectives—has been to narrow the boundaries of social organization, to exclude the material environment, and to focus on social interaction. Normative theories take cognizance of the external environment in terms of the manner in which it is defined by social institutions and by the "strains" that develop over the allocation of resources. Theoretical orientations of this variety often emphasize the equilibrium mode of analysis. The advantage of such an approach is that the sociologist can claim that he is operating at one level of analysis—and the appropriate one, at that. From Emile Durkheim onward, such a direction has been explored in the interest of logical rigor, analytic simplicity, and theoretical closure. Such theories are very attractive, precisely because they challenge sociological thinking and popular thinking which emphasize the importance of the material environment.

But systemic analysis seeks to incorporate the environment into the boundaries of social organization more directly and explicitly, whether the environment is considered in ecological, technological, or economic terms, or a combination of these. Systemic analysis of this kind presents a "socioenvironmental" framework. Sociological writers have tried in different ways to deal with these environmental boundaries. First, the ecological orientation postulates the external environment as an essential (even *the* essential) dimension of social organization which operates directly and without mediating mechanisms, by means of competitive and associational processes.[46] Second, and more often, technological and economic dimensions are incorporated as the prime variables in generating the forms of social structure and social organization. This is, of course, the logic of classic "economic determinist" theories of social class conflict. Alternatively, technological and economic sectors of society have been explicitly juxtaposed to the normative and cultural sector by sociologists like William F. Ogburn. The resulting "imbalance" between these spheres determines patterns of social change and social control.[47] Third, there are those sociologists who proceed on a much delimited basis and identify particular aspects of the external environment, for example, geographic distance, for exploring specific "vulnerabilities" of social organization.[48] All these strategies are relevant for systemic analysis, although they do not postulate invariant causal priority for any particular environmental or economic-technological element. (If one had to select a single "prime cause," technology might be the most effective and satisfactory—or rather, a technological-economic determinism—but at least sociology has kept itself from that self-defeating requirement.) Instead, some reciprocal influence is thought to be operative. To define the boundaries of social organization as being socioenvironmental in this sense implies that one's orientation has a

46. Amos Hawley, *Human Ecology; a Theory of Community Structure* (New York: Ronald, 1950).

47. William F. Ogburn, *Social Change: With Respect to Culture and Original Nature* (New York: Huebsch, 1922).

48. Arthur L. Stinchcombe, *Constructing Social Theories* (New York: Harcourt, Brace and World, 1968), pp. 216–30, "Geopolitical Concepts and Military Vulnerability."

degree of openness to reflect historical specifics. It weakens the effort to create a highly deductive system. But such is the problem of a systemic analysis approach to social control in an advanced industrial society.

Thus, to summarize partially, systemic analysis rejects the distinction between grand theory and theory of the middle range. It rests on a series of givens in order to put forward a body of testable hypotheses. Systemic analysis attributes the greater relevance to developmental over equilibrium analysis and, correspondingly, takes into account those component elements of social control which are not completely interdependent. The degree of interdependence is problematic, but effective social control in an advanced industrial society requires at least some relatively autonomous social groupings. In turn, rather than to postulate a basic and universal social unit of analysis, such as social role, and a highly abstract object of analysis, for example the social act, it requires a set of analytically differentiated units and objects of analysis. These should be linked to the imputed causal processes. Finally, systemic analysis is not limited to a set of social interactional boundaries but makes use of a socioenvironmental conception of boundaries.

From the beginnings of sociology as an organized discipline, total societies have been taken as the central objects of analysis, with analytic entities, such as the primary groups, communities, and institutions, as the irreducible components.[49] It is interesting that the term "macrosociology" has become prominent to describe the comparative analysis of total societies in terms of complex linkages of these constituent elements. The goal of systemic analysis is not to arrive at a single body of propositions which conform to a unified theoretical perspective. The objective is to establish overlapping hypotheses which are given a degree of coherence by related assumptions and by master societal trends which describe the historical context. This is the essential character of systemic analysis. Likewise, sociological knowledge is thought of not only as more generalized formulations but also as substantive findings—the contents of its monographs and its charting of social trends.

Such a stance does not mean the slightest retreat from the "principles" of scientific inquiry. It does not mean that theory construction in sociology seeks to make a virtue out of imputed weaknesses. On the

49. Regional and worldwide patterns of "international" relations among total societies are hardly excluded thereby. On the contrary, social control in advanced industrial societies is directly influenced by the supranational systems which modern technology and organization have helped to fashion.

contrary, it means that the investigator seeks to make a series of appropriate decisions about both the formal and empirical aspects of his undertaking, which reflect the heritage of the discipline as well as his own immediate experiences.

Personality, Politics, and Social Control

The systemic approach to social control uses the separation of the concept of personality from that of social organization, on the one hand, and of political institutions (politics) from social organization, on the other. Concern with the subjective aspects of social organization or "the definition of the situation" is a central aspect of sociological tradition. Normative theories of social organization and those formulated in terms of symbolic interaction postulate a notion of social personality or the equivalent as an essential aspect of sociological analysis. However, sociologists are less and less prepared to attribute importance to personality as a distinct and separate level of analysis. In fact, a negative orientation toward personality has grown more pronounced and articulate since the end of the 1950s. Efforts to create a specialization entitled "personality and social organization" have not been very successful.

But it is highly arbitrary to explore changes in patterns of social control without assessing the importance of the personality factor and variables in psychodynamic terms, or to put aside the body of empirical knowledge developed by students of personality which bears directly on the processes of social control. From a substantive point of view, the very fact that personality constructs have come to be so extensively utilized in the management of interpersonal and institutional relations requires a wider intellectual aperture than sociologists are prepared to use. At this juncture, three points can be made.

First, at the level of analogous reasoning, social control is the outcome of social organization and personal control the outcome of personality. When personality theorists use the idea of personal control, they can proceed with a relative degree of theoretical clarity and a measure of objectivity. Personal control has come to refer to the ability of a person to organize his impulses and energies and to satisfy his needs and impulses while minimizing disruption or even damage to himself or others.[50] Personal control implies mastery over one's self and en-

50. Erik H. Erickson, *Childhood and Society* (New York: Norton, 1950). See also Dennis Wrong, "The Oversocialized Conception of Man in Modern Sociology," *American Sociological Review* 26 (April 1961): 183–93.

compasses those psychological conditions that enhance self-restraint and rationality. Personal theorists do not reduce these processes to conformity (or adjustment) or to rationality. The systemic analysis of personality is concerned with the mechanisms that result from the interplay of internal resources and the psychosocial environment. The analogy might serve to indicate to sociologists the advantage of proceeding in comparably comprehensive and objective terms of reference.

Second, if one seeks to go beyond reasoning by analogy, the distinction between personal and social control assists one in guarding against excessive sociological reductionism. It can be postulated that the consequences of social organization cannot completely and persistently override the influence of personality. In essence, this postulate seeks to give concrete substance to the process of internalization of norms and values associated with social control. In any given social group, the degree and extent of internalization of group norms and values vary. Effective internalization results in a pattern of attitudes and perspectives which is relatively "quasi-normal" in distribution. Personality variables help to account for these patterns of internalization. The extensive research on ethnic and racial prejudice, as well as on more generalized political attitudes, supplies documentation for such an assertion. The repeated effort to "wash out" differences within particular social groups by adding "social" variables fails to undermine this observation. In fact, empirically, it is among populations that are markedly homogeneous in social terms that the effect of personality variables in producing differences in attitude and value patterns emerges most clearly.[51] Variations in values within relatively homogeneous social groups are a striking characteristic of an advanced industrial society; the result is to complicate the tasks of social control.

In addition, one can offer a more direct formulation of the effect of personality on social organization; namely, that the personality of a given individual—strategically located—can on certain occasions override the variables of social organization and alter patterns of social control. The great man in history, local or national, is not an artificial problem. Sidney Hook's *The Hero in History* is relevant for those who are concerned with this issue.[52] At this point systemic analysis converges

51. For a theoretical analysis, see Herbert Goldhamer, "Opinion and Personality," *American Journal of Sociology* 55 (January 1950): 346–54.

52. Sidney Hook, *The Hero in History: A Study in Limitation and Possibility* (New York: John Day, 1943).

with the interests of historians and political scientists concerned with personality and social change.

Sociologists can and have justified their indifference to personality variables in this context on the grounds of the immense problems of data collection, especially where large populations are involved. However, at a minimum, personality variables can be thought of as reflecting differing levels of effective or ineffective personal control which cannot be inferred directly from the person's position in the social structure; differences in family socialization are obviously the root dimension. These personality variables, therefore, may serve as intervening variables in conditioning patterns of group participation in response to interpersonal and mass communications.

By way of illustration: In an advanced industrial society, self-selection operates with significant consequences in allocating professional careers. Again and again in the analysis of the process of professional socialization in educational and institutional settings, research findings of the last quarter-century emphasize the importance of self-selection.[53] The norms of professional groups, a key element in social control, are not only the result of bureaucratic structures but also involve the effect of selection and self-selection in processes which in turn are conditioned by personality variables. Therefore, in the study of social control of professional groups, sociologists cannot dismiss the personality dimensions.

Third, the explication of systemic linkages between personality and social organization has the advantage of reducing the saliency of the misleading metaphor that social control deals with the relations of the "individual to society." Personality constructs are relevant in this regard because there is a body of theory which rejects the distinction between the "individual" and "society." Instead, we are dealing with different aspects of group processes. Personality can be conceived in terms of group characteristics—that is, predispositions—emotional, cognitive, and normative. One starting point is the classic argument presented by Sigmund Freud in *Group Psychology and the Analysis of the Ego*: "The contrast between individual psychology and social or group psychology, which at first glance may seem to be full of signifi-

53. An extensive body of research has been collected for the military profession. See John P. Lovell, "The Professional Socialization of the West Point Cadet," in *The New Military: Changing Patterns of Organization*, ed. Morris Janowitz (New York: Russell Sage Foundation, 1964), pp. 119–58.

cance, loses a great deal of its sharpness when it is examined more closely. . . . In the individual's mental life someone else is invariably involved, as a model, as an object, as a helper, as an opponent; and so from the very first individual psychology in this extended but entirely justifiable sense of the words, is at the same time social psychology as well."[54] This type of reasoning runs through the psychology of pragmatism as developed by John Dewey and incorporated into symbolic interactionalism by W. I. Thomas and George Herbert Mead.[55] Thus the incorporation of personality variables into the study of social control, even in the ad hoc amplification of specific mechanisms of social control by means of personality variables, does not require "shifting" the focus of analysis to the "individual" but, rather, persistent concern with alternative conceptualization of group processes.

The delimitation between social organization and political organizations (or politics) presents another, but related, set of issues inherent in avoiding unreflective sociological reductionism. Sociologists are generally prepared to analyze political institutions with the same concepts and strategy that they would any other institutional arrangement. A reasonable but incomplete case can be made for this orientation. In fact, some sociologists have been inclined to think of politics as epiphenomenal, since they believe that the essential issue is to probe beyond manifest political arrangements (e.g., leadership) into realities of underlying social structure (e.g., population groups).

Influenced by the writings of Karl Marx and Max Weber plus the methods of empirical social research, sociological modes of analysis in turn came to influence political science and political analysis. The emergence of the so-called "behavioral persuasion" among political scientists represented the infusion of sociology into the study of political parties and the organs of government. However, the systemic analysis of social control does not permit such an easy solution to the linkages among social organizations, political institutions, and the "political order." This is particularly the case of an advanced industrial society where it is essential to assert the "supremacy of politics" by means of a differenti-

54. Sigmund Freud, *Group Psychology and the Analysis of the Ego*, trans. James Strachey (London: International Psychoanalytic Press, 1922).

55. See especially Neil Coughlan, *The Young John Dewey: An Essay in American Intellectual History* (Chicago: University of Chicago Press, 1973). The writings of Harry Stack Sullivan are particularly relevant for highlighting common elements in dynamics of personality theory and interactional social psychology. See *Conceptions of Modern Psychiatry* (Washington: William Alanson White Psychiatric Foundation, 1945).

ated party system in the regulation of the social order. Instead, the systemic analysis of social control finds it reasonably appropriate and necessary to emphasize again and again the distinction between social organization and political institutions.

The view that political institutions derive from the pattern of stratification emerged and persisted as a dominant theme in the empirical sociology of political behavior. This orientation was, of course, stimulated by the formulation of Karl Marx and his disciples that political conflict is produced by the social stratification of classes which reflects the economic factors and the social relations generated by the mode of production. But sociologists with different conceptions of social stratification—including skill, education, and cultural characteristics—also made use of such an orientation. In this mode, sociologists have written contemporary social history with great richness of detail.

Their interests have ranged from describing local community stratification, as in the case of W. Lloyd Warner's study of Yankee City and Robert and Helen Lynd's *Middletown in Transition*, to national stratification patterns by large-scale sample surveys. The purpose has been to trace the consequences of social hierarchies on political control.[56] The focus in this kind of analysis of politics is mass political participation. The causal direction has been from underlying ecological, economic, and occupational structure to social strata to a set of group interests which fashion mass political participation.

The social-stratification perspective focuses on inequality. Social-stratification investigations of industrial society with multiparty parlimentary systems are designed to measure inequality; and measures of inequality are used to reveal the quality of the social order and to assess its political institutions. The crisis of political legitimacy is rooted in and fashioned by inequality. Inequality is postulated as the barrier to an effective moral and political order. Political institutions essentially reflect underlying social conflict and serve as the arena in which such conflict is acted out.

The social-control perspective has come to use an augmented conceptualization which includes an "institutional" dimension to probe the "crisis of political legitimacy" in advanced industrial society. The so-

56. W. Lloyd Warner and Paul S. Lunt, *The Status System of a Modern Community* (New Haven: Yale University Press, 1942); Robert and Helen Lynd, *Middletown in Transition: A Study in Cultural Conflict* (New York: Harcourt, Brace, 1937).

cial-stratification conception focuses on the core hierarchies of economic and socioeconomic position, while social organization encompasses the institutional patterns, informal and formal, communal and bureaucratic. It is because of the writings of Max Weber and of a variety of political scientists that sociologists have become more explicitly concerned with an institutional orientation toward politics and political behavior.[57]

Political institutions—political parties, political elites, and the host of parapolitical agencies—must be considered as active in the process of social change and political conflict. Sociologists have had to confront the implications of the assumption that the emergence of modern society implies a historical process of a degree of separation of political institutions from economic and social structures. As this differentiation evolves, political institutions become more involved in managing economic and social affairs of the advanced industrial society. Political institutions thereby become objects of direct sociological inquiry because of the necessity of establishing the conditions under which they operate as independent sources of societal change.

The empirical materials of much of political sociology and an important component of political science are rooted in the analysis of the effect of socioeconomic and social-stratification factors on political attitudes and collective political behavior; the direction of the flow of influence (the causal model) is from the social structure to the organs of government. But the process is interactive. The informal and formal institutions of party and political leadership need to be seen as supplying independent elements to the processes of social control and social change. Political parties are mechanisms for accommodating the strains and conflicts of social structure, and political parties and elites are more than reactive elements. The policies they generate have an influence on social structure, since they fashion the definitions, content, and boundaries of political conflict.[58]

The specialized character of political institutions and the central organs of government is the central issue. The "political order" is an expression of those institutions which deal with the legitimate monopo-

57. Morris Janowitz, "The Logic of Political Sociology," in *Political Conflict* (Beverly Hills, Calif.: Sage Publications, 1970), pp. 5–35.

58. Maurice Duverger, *Political Parties: Their Organization and Activity in the Modern State* (New York: Wiley, 1954); Avery Leiserson, *Parties and Politics* (New York: Knopf, 1958).

lization of coercion.[59] This dimension gives them their special character. Political power is not merely the summation or the aggregation of power relations in other spheres of social and economic behavior. While political power rests on all forms of social and economic relations, it has its own structure and its own logic. Therefore the sociological intrusion into political analysis has served—much to the amazement of many sociologists—to maintain and even strengthen the intellectual specialization of political science as a discipline; that is, in reality, to reinforce by definition and empirical reality the distinction between social organization and political institutions. Again this degree of intellectual differentiation is an essential element of systemic analysis.

Sociology has its boundaries defined in part by intellectual contact with related disciplines. The growth in the scope of effort involved in sociology has lead to a stronger emphasis on an intradisciplinary focus among sociologists. But systemic analysis proceeds by continuous concern with an interdisciplinary focus.[60] There is no reason to suppose that an interdisciplinary focus will result in new and closed paradigms. Rather, it serves as an explication of the incremental strategy and specific research decisions that sociologists must continually make and remake in their study of macrosociology, which sees political institutions as active and voluntaristic elements in societal change and social control.

59. The explanation of the basic formulation of Max Weber has led to a stream of scholarly writing. Of particular relevance for this study is Harold D. Lasswell, *Politics: Who Gets What When and How* (New York: McGraw-Hill, 1936).

60. A distinction should be made between cross-disciplinary and interdisciplinary efforts. Cross-disciplinary procedures involve the wholesale and intact transfer of the concepts and methods of one discipline to the subject matter of another discipline. A case in point is the use of the mode of economic analysis to study the economic returns of marriage or of crime. Interdisciplinary research involves selective infusing of concepts and procedures and includes a two-way intellectual process.

II

Master Trends, 1920-1976

Four

Political Participation: Emergence of Weak Regimes

Elections as Indicators of Social Control

Is it possible to identify a series of closely related measures which may serve as macrosociological indicators of the level and effectiveness of social control in an advanced industrial society such as the United States? Such measures would have to be available for the period under investigation with some degree of specificity, stability, and accuracy. Social control is a unifying concept, and it is hardly to be anticipated that it would lead directly to a single or a specific number of operational measures. However, systemic analysis requires that the essential dimensions and consequences of social control be explored in approximate operational terms, especially by means of trend data.

The tour de force of Emile Durkheim's empirical research rested on his selection of suicide as his central operational measure of societal integration and social solidarity.[1] The enduring relevance of his research strategy derived from the fact that his "operational measure"—suicide—could be linked to his conceptual orientation, in which the division of labor was seen as the basic element in social organization. While most of his analysis involved comparing social groups within France, his strategy produced a version of macrosociology which made use of cross-national comparisons. The various forms of social integra-

1. Emile Durkheim, *Suicide: Etude de sociologie* (Paris: Alcan, 1897). See also Thomas Masaryk, *Der Sebstmord als sociale Massenerscheinung der moderner Civilisation* (Vienna, 1881); Henry Morselli, *Suicide: An Essay on Comparative Moral Statistics* (New York, 1882); Louis I. Dublin, *Suicide—A Sociological and Statistical Study* (New York: Ronald, 1963); Jack D. Douglas, *The Social Meanings of Suicide* (Princeton: Princeton University Press, 1967). Baruch Kimmerling has sought to use suicide rates in Israel as a measure of societal integration which could be linked to the political tensions associated with changes in the levels of the Arab-Israeli conflict; Baruch Kimmerling, "Anomie and Integration in Israeli Society and the Salience of the Arab-Israeli Conflict," *Studies in Comparative International Development* 9 (1974): 64–89.

tion and their obverse produced three types of suicide—anomic, egoistic, altruistic. These social indicators rest on the subjective definition of the act of suicide. Therefore, the data available to Durkheim, and to later sociologists did not permit a direct and independent basis for categorizing his statistical data on suicide into these different types. As a result, his analysis has a certain circularity which has yet to be overcome.

Despite this defect, the boldness with which he used his trend and comparative data created a model for investigating patterns of social control. In particular, the idea that deviant behavior can be used as a measure in understanding the complex processes of social control has stimulated sociologists concerned with long-term patterns of social change and macrosociology. Thus Herbert Goldhamer has presented long-term documentation from the nineteenth to the mid-twentieth century on the rate of mental illness which challenges the hypothesis that there has been a secular growth in the incidence of mental breakdowns during this period of industrialization.[2]

It is not necessary to reject deviant behavior as an indicator of social control in order to offer an approach more directly linked to macrosociological concerns. Could one use the measures generated by the electoral system in the United States to examine social control? The results of elections would be seen as indicators of the institutional arrangements produced by party organization and legislative representation. Such a systemic analysis could proceed through time and through comparison with other industrial nations.

The advantage in utilizing these indicators of social control is that it helps one to keep in mind that the United States is both an advanced industrial nation and a nation with Western political institutions. The distinction is crucial. To speak of Western industrialized societies is to focus on the centrality of parliamentary institutions—political regimes based on multiparty systems and elected legislatures ("parliamentary political systems" or "parliamentary regime" is used to encompass the presidential form of the United States and the cabinet form of Great Britain, the Federal Republic of Germany, etc.). To speak of

2. Herbert Goldhamer and Andrew Marshall, *Psychosis and Civilization: Two Studies in the Frequency of Mental Disease* (Glencoe, Ill.: Free Press, 1953). Andrew Henry and James Short, in *Suicide and Homicide* (Glencoe, Ill.: Free Press, 1954), probed the long-term linkages of these two forms of social behavior with changes in the business cycle. The analysis makes use of these measures in order to trace the effect of economic institutions on societal patterns of social control.

Western industrial societies is to point to the particular historical pattern of secularization which distinguished Western Europe, and the United States, from other parts of the world.

The world society comprises nation-states of such variation in level of industrialization, in size, and in resources that to speak of a common subject matter for comparative macrosociology requires considerable caution and much self-restraint.[3] Yet the double distinction between industrialized and nonindustrialized and parliamentary and nonparliamentary systems is the overriding rationale in the use of election as an indicator of social control.[4] Raymond Aron's point of departure is productive for comparative analysis. Europe, including the United States, as seen from Asia (or Africa or Latin America), does not consist of two fundamentally different worlds, the Soviet world and the Western world. "It is one single reality: industrial civilization."[5] This is an essentially external viewpoint which focuses on the economic-technological base of these nation-states. However, viewed from the inside, that is, by juxtaposing one industrial nation and another, it is necessary to incorporate Aron's additional explication. From an internal point of view, "the characteristic of each type of industrial society is dependent on politics." Each industrial nation can choose its political forms, "liberal or tyrannical democracy," with "deep and profound consequences."[6] In this sense, the Soviet Union is not a Western industrial society.

Electoral systems and institutions of representation are almost "universals" among industrialized nations, although in some these institutions may be only pro forma. It is the image if not the reality of electoral systems and parliamentary institutions which is the universal element. However, the effective characters of these institutions are revealing indicators of internal social organization. There are no industrialized nations without a formalized electoral institution. The "mechanics" of political elections have penetrated deeply in the so-called developing nations. In the search to maintain political legitimacy, political elites

3. For a comparative analysis of total societies which focuses on size, see Norton Ginsburg, *Atlas of Economic Development* (Chicago: University of Chicago Press, 1961).

4. See E. A. Wrigley, "The Process of Modernization and the Industrial Revolution in England," *Journal of Interdisciplinary History* 3 (1972): 225–59.

5. Raymond Aron, *18 Lectures on Industrial Society* (London: Weidenfeld and Nicholson, 1967), p. 42. Japan is encompassed in this comparison.

6. Raymond Aron, *Democracy and Totalitarianism*, trans. Valence Ionescu (New York: Praeger, 1969), p. 11.

of industrialized states seek to validate their rule by claiming that sovereignty resides in the "people." Much scholarship has been devoted to examining the extensive definitions of who constitutes a citizen or at least who are members of the polity.[7] The "mass society" is one in which there are no formally excluded social elements.[8] Whether the system is multiparty or single-party, it appears impossible to govern without at least the symbolism of organized representation. However, the distinction between a parliamentary regime and a one-party state is critical—not a matter of degree but a crucial threshold.

In addition, it is necessary to focus on the transformation of religious symbolism. This was the strategy of Max Weber in his efforts to account for the temporal priority of economic development in Western Europe.[9] Such an approach focuses particularly on the separation of religious beliefs and religious structures from the secular state and from science—relevant elements in economic development. However, if one focuses on normative content, the sociopolitical definition of "citizenship" as it has evolved in the West seems a more adequate and more comprehensive basis for exploring the differences between the West and other sociopolitical regimes of the world community. The idea of citizenship has gradually evolved in the West, derived from earlier Greek and Roman formulations and elaborated by the ideological dimensions of the French and American Revolutions.[10] "Citizenship" gives meaning to the concept of Westernization in that it asserts the political centrality of legislative institutions, that is, legislative institutions based on widening spheres of competitive elections. As T. H. Marshall has underlined, national revolutions which gave impetus to modern definitions of citizenship concentrated first on political rights.[11] These political rights established the legitimacy of the national state and in turn created the definition of economic and social rights of citizens,

7. R. R. Palmer, *The Age of Democratic Revolution: A Political History of Europe and America, 1760–1800* (Princeton: Princeton University Press, 1964).

8. Edward A. Shils, "The Theory of Mass Society," *Diogenes* 39 (1962):45–66.

9. Max Weber, *The Theory of Social and Economic Organization*, trans. A. M. Henderson and Talcott Parsons, ed. Talcott Parsons (New York: Oxford University Press, 1964), pp. 329–41.

10. Morris Janowitz, "Military Institutions and Citizenship in Western Societies," *Armed Forces and Society: An Interdisciplinary Journal* 2 (Winter 1977): 185–204. Samuel E. Finer, "State and Nation Building: The Role of the Military," in *The Formation of National States in Western Europe*, ed. Charles Tilly (Princeton: Princeton University Press, 1975), pp. 84–163.

11. The historical background of the extension and enlargement of the conception of citizenship is presented by T. H. Marshall, *Citizenship and Social Class* (Cambridge: Cambridge University Press, 1950).

as embodied in the goals of social welfare. Even the broad notion of "citizenship" is not comprehensive enough for analyzing electoral behavior as an indicator of social control. The act and consequences of voting have meaning in the light of the trends in mass opinion about mutual respect and deference, in particular, respect accorded to minority groups in industrial society. Our analysis of trends in electoral behavior needs to be and will be supplemented by an examination of trends in mass public opinion which reveals the operative social integration of the nation-state.

The emergence of an electoral system with multiparty institutions occurred over the centuries, if England is used as the prototype.[12] But, of course, the experiences of Britain provided only a partial model for Western Europe; no single nation embodies the complete historical sequence. However, it is important to stress that each of the leading nation-states of Western Europe, and the United States, experienced at least one armed political revolution in the course of the development of its political institutions. The electoral institutions which have emerged have often appeared fragile but have endured with considerable resilience.

The diffusion of Western institutions has involved both industrial technology and organization and the ideal of democratic political institutions. But the limited, declining viability of these political arrangements outside Western Europe and certain associated nations has been a major trend since the middle of the nineteenth century, especially since the end of World War II.

The diffusion of Western political norms has been limited by the counterdevelopment of colonial forms. The origins of European colonial expansion in the sixteenth century reflect political, religious, military, and economic initiatives. The political symbolism of the American and French Revolutions has contributed to the decline of the European colonialism throughout the world community. The attraction of the Russian and Chinese revolutions helped complete the process of decolonialization and intensified the political and ideological debate about the appropriate format for institutions of representation.

There is no regime, whatever the degree of coercion it employs on its subjects, that can totally avoid public discussion or token acknowledgment of a "desirable" system of representation and participation.

12. Walter Bagehot, *The English Constitution* (New York: D. Appleton, 1900); see also Samuel Beer, *British Politics in the Collectivist Age* (New York: Knopf, 1965).

In general, personal dictatorship of the old-fashioned variety has been abandoned or is being pushed aside by the pressure of technological necessity. Few political leaders are prepared to justify their political power and legitimacy without asserting the appropriateness—if only in the future—of some consultative procedure. The fact that most of the institutions of the world community designated for representation are at best plebiscitarian does not deny the increasing universalism of the "symbolism" of rule in the name of the mass of the population and of "political participation."

Every nation-state—including the developing nations—has political opposition. Ruling groups not only privately calculate the costs and effectiveness of repressive rule, but incorporate into their official rhetoric pronouncements about ideal representative arrangements.[13] In this sense, one can identify elements of consensus in one-party states and forms of "public opinion" in totalitarian nations.[14] But these observations serve only to underline that the use of elections as measures of social control can be applied only to a limited number of countries with truly competitive national elections. In terms of basic realities, as of 1964, Robert A. Dahl concluded that, by his definition, of the 113 nation-states of the world community, only "about thirty had political systems during the previous decade in which legal party opposition had existed."[15] Since that year the number of nation-states with legal party opposition has continuously declined.

The subject of this study is the United States. Meaningful comparisons can be made only with the Western nation-states that have fairly equivalent competitive electoral procedures. A body of comparative analysis prepared by scholars such as Maurice Duverger, Herman Finer, and Sigmund Neumann sets the institutional context.[16] The relevance of their perspective for the analysis of social control rests in the recognition by political scientists in this intellectual tradition that an effective competitive electoral system does more than the specific task of selecting leaders and creating political conditions for making legitimate deci-

13. See, for example, Alex Inkeles, *Public Opinion in the Soviet Union* (Cambridge: Harvard University Press, 1962).

14. See, for example, Paul Hollander, *Soviet and American Society: A Comparison* (New York: Oxford University Press, 1973).

15. Robert A. Dahl, *Political Oppositions in Western Democracies* (New Haven: Yale University Press, 1966).

16. Maurice Duverger, *Political Parties: Their Organization and Activity in the Modern State* (New York: Wiley, 1951); Herman Finer, *The Theory and Practice of Modern Government* (London: Methuen, 1932); Sigmund Neumann, *Modern Political Parties: Approaches to Comparative Politics* (Chicago: University of Chicago Press, 1956).

sions. If effective, it serves to reinforce the norms of rule by consent. This goal is achieved if the political procedures accord a positive role to the opposition, both in the election and in the subsequent elected parliament.

Therefore the question arises: Are the quantitative results and measures of electoral behavior adequate and useful for describing the self-regulating dimensions of social and political control? The empirical problems are formidable but the solutions are rewarding.[17] It is necessary to encompass not only the hard data of electoral outcomes but also popular definitions of electoral systems and the processes of interpersonal contact and communication generated by the electoral process. The term "political participation" in the democratic context refers not only to the formalism of parliamentary bodies but also to a system of primary-group, face-to-face, political intercourse between the electorate and their representatives.

For my purpose, the comparable element in the Western electoral systems (including the United States) has come into being in the emergence of a profound strain on political legitimacy which these nations have been experiencing since the mid-1960s. While this trend is operative regardless of the size of the nation, there is a particular similarity for the United States, Great Britain, and, to a lesser extent, West Germany, and in a related form for France and Italy with their large Communist constituencies. There are noteworthy differences in the social organizations of these nations, but, given the range in the world community, we are dealing with "similar" social structures. Likewise, differences in political organization in these nation-states loom large and pointed. However, the similarity in the format of the political "crisis" in their electoral systems highlights the commonality.

As mentioned in chapter 1, the phrase "crisis in political legitimacy" may be more obscuring than clarifying. The crux of the political problem is the prolonged inability of the electoral system to produce clear-cut, effective parliamentary majorities. In addition, there is the increased inability of a parliamentary opposition to make positive political contributions and, thereby, to contribute to the self-regulation of an advanced industrial society.[18] Opposition elements serve as powerful veto groups, as legislative barriers rather than as political resources

17. Stein Rokkan, *Citizens, Elections, Parties* (Oslo: Universitetsforlaget, 1970). For a review of relevant empirical research, see Lester W. Milbarth, *Political Participation* (Chicago: Rand McNally, 1965).

18. Otto Kirchheimer, "The Waning of Opposition in Parliamentary Regimes," *Social Research* 24 (1957): 127–56.

for collective problem solving. As a result, there has been an increase in the concentration of political power in the "chief executive." But it would be an error to overlook the difficulties and instabilities in the position of the chief executive and, in turn, his particular inabilities to utilize his office consistently and meaningfully because of the absence of an effective legislative base of support.

The changing pattern of electoral behavior in the United States over the last half-century, although it conforms to this Western industrialized nation-state format and especially parallels Great Britain's, reflects the social and political structure of the American nation-state.[19]

The period 1920–1976 is the setting for exploring the master trends and the transformation of electoral behavior. A combination of the analysis of election statistics and survey research overcomes the defect of a limited time perspective so frequent in "political behavior" research.[20]

A key notion in assessing election trends as indicators of social control is that of the critical or realignment election.[21] In the research literature, the elections of 1896 and of 1932 are cited as critical elections because these served to restructure political alternatives and produce decisive political decisions. Three elements are operative. First, the critical election produces a new majority; that is, there is a marked realignment in the social and economic support of the majority and minority blocs. Second, the shift is pronounced and relatively durable. Third, these two elements imply that the restructuring of the patterns of voting creates a decisive political majority which has important, persistent political consequences. The realignment election thus represents a decisive accomplishment in self-regulation. Political developments precede such critical elections. There was the emergence of a

19. David Butler and Donald Stokes, *Political Change in Britain: Forces Shaping Electoral Choice* (London: St. Martin's, 1969).

20. Philip Converse, "Change in the American Electorate," in *The Human Meaning of Social Change*, ed. Angus Campbell and Philip E. Converse (New York: Russell Sage Foundation, 1972), pp. 263–337. See also W. D. Burnham, "The Changing Shape of the American Political Universe," *American Political Science Review* 54 (March 1965): 7–28; W. D. Burnham, "The End of Party Politics," *Trans-Action* 7 (December 1969): 12–22. The alternative emphasis on patterns of continuity is to be found in Paul T. David, *Party Strength in the United States 1872–1970* (Charlottesville: University Press of Virginia, 1972).

21. V. O. Key, Jr., "A Theory of Critical Elections," *Journal of Politics* 17 (February 1955): 1–18; Duncan McRae and J. Meldrum, "Critical Elections in Illinois, 1888–1958," *American Political Science Review* 54 (September 1960): 669–83; W. D. Burnham, *Critical Elections and the Mainsprings of American Politics* (New York: Norton, 1970).

"populist" vote in 1894 before the election of 1896. The campaign of Alfred Smith represented the preliminary step in reorienting the Democratic party in 1928 and the precondition for the Franklin D. Roosevelt political coalition of 1932 and thereafter.

It may well be that the passage of time and the limitations of empirical data help create in retrospect the image of a realignment election. Therefore, more time may be required to identify the critical election since 1932; however, this argument does not seem persuasive. Instead, a trend hypothesis is an element in the explanation of the "crisis" of political legitimacy. It is that, since 1945, there has not been a critical election in the United States in response to the emerging sociopolitical issues of the post–World War II period. Instead there has been a pattern of continuous, marginal, and volatile political aggregation. In other words, the election of 1932 was the last critical election thus far, despite the extensive change in the social demography of the electorate. Of course, there is no reason to assume that another critical election will not take place. In chapter 5 I will argue that, in large part, the parliamentary stalemate reflects changes in the social structure–changes accentuated by the emergence of the welfare state. In part the explanation involves the organization of the U.S. party structure. It will be argued in chapter 13 that the political parties have not developed effective internal discipline and management.

A competitive election, to work effectively, must create a stable majority able to rule. The balance between the majority and the minority must be such that the minority–by itself or in coalition with the other political elements–maintains a reasonable chance of success in future elections; if the majority becomes excessively preponderant, the viability of the electoral system as a mechanism of self-regulation is weakened. But the opposite has come to characterize the pattern of electoral behavior in the United States and generally in Western Europe. The outcome of national elections has been to produce a growth of "weak" or minority governments. The forms and patterns are diverse. The margin of victory for the leading party can be slim; or the victorious party may obtain only a minority of the vote; or its legislative majority may be too narrow to justify speaking of it as a governing party. In the presidential system the chief executive may find himself with the opposition party in the legislative majority. The result is hardly an effective system of checks and balances, but rather political fragmentation or disarticulation and a variety of forms of stalemate.

Even when important legislation is passed, it can represent a complex and unwieldy compromise of administrative practices.

For the United States, the indicators of electoral outcome do not present a series of discrete political outcomes, but rather an overall pattern of transformation in the results of political participation which distinguishes the period 1920–1948 from that of 1948–1972 (Table 4.1).

TABLE 4.1 Trends in U.S. National Elections, 1920–1972: Political Participation and Political Mandate

	Turnout		Presidential Mandate	Legislative Mandate	
Year	Presidential Election (Percent)	President	Popular Vote Plurality (Percent)	House of Representatives Plurality (No. of Seats)	Senate Plurality (No. of Seats)
1920	44.0	Harding	Rep. 26.3	169	23
1924	44.0	Coolidge	Rep. 25.2	14	10
1928	52.0	Hoover	Rep. 17.3	38	5
1932	52.4	Roosevelt	Dem. 17.7	193	25
1936	56.9	Roosevelt	Dem. 24.3	242	50
1940	58.9	Roosevelt	Dem. 9.9	106	38
1944	56.0	Roosevelt	Dem. 7.5	52	18
1948	51.1	Truman	Dem. 4.5	92	2
1952	61.6	Eisenhower	Rep. 10.7	0	1
1956	59.3	Eisenhower	Rep. 15.4	−33	−2
1960	62.8	Kennedy	Dem. 0.2	89	30
1964	61.8	Johnson	Dem. 22.7	145	36
1968	60.9	Nixon	Rep. 0.7	−51	−14
1972	55.7	Nixon	Rep. 23.2	−47	−14
1976	53.3	Carter	Dem. 0.9	149	11

In the first period, the electoral system created a relatively stable majority political regime which was Republican and lasted for three presidential terms. It was replaced in 1932 by a stable Democratic majority political regime which persisted for an even longer period of time, namely, five presidential terms. However, during 1952–1972, the outcome has been neither that of a relatively stable political regime nor, with one exception, even a single term of control of both the presidency and both legislative houses by the same party.

While political historians do not identify the election of 1920 as critical, it did replace the Wilson administration and create a Republican majority which persisted until 1932. The electoral competition gave the Republican presidents decisive popular mandates (ranging from 26.3% in 1920 to 17.3% in 1928); moreover, these presidents had working majorities in both houses of Congress throughout the period.

In 1928 the first movement toward a critical election can be seen—at least in retrospect. The drop in the popular vote for the president was noteworthy but limited; it was the decline in senatorial seats for the Republicans that signaled the emergence of the new Democratic party with its new strength and base in the North.

The 1932 election was a critical election because it created the new Democratic party majority, a majority which persisted both in the popular vote for the president and in the composition of both houses of Congress. The trend in the popular presidential majority was consistently downward after 1936 but still reached 7.5% in 1944. The popular Democratic presidential position was paralleled by a consistent majority in both houses, which was tempered at critical points because of the importance of the North-South political split. Thus, from 1920 through the election of 1944, the electoral system created relatively clear-cut political regimes.

In retrospect, the election of 1948 had the elements of an election antecedent to a critical election. The popular advantage of the Democratic president continued to decline; it reached 4.5%. While the House of Representatives returned a decisive majority of Democratic legislators, the Democratic majority in the Senate was reduced to two members. The pattern of political disarticulation began to appear.

The outcome of the 1952 election, however, was not that of a critical realignment election. In contrast to the majority political regimes of 1920–1944, the elements of the "weak" political system had their origins not in the particular political events of 1968–1972 but had been foreshadowed in the election of 1952. The long-term trend from 1952 to 1972 can be described in part as a period of decline in the national legislative strength of the Republican party. However, we are dealing with more than the relative electorate strength of the major parties. We are dealing with basic changes in political attitudes and electoral decisions.

In 1952 Dwight D. Eisenhower was elected by a decisive majority (10.7% advantage), but not by a margin of the magnitude accorded post–World War I Republican presidents or Roosevelt in the first two elections of the New Deal. Moreover, he did not have a majority in the legislature as a whole. The distribution was balanced in the House of Representatives, and the number of Republican senators exceeded the number of Democrats only by one. For the first time since 1920, the United States government was not based on a relatively unified political regime. In 1956, Eisenhower increased his popular vote so that the advantage reached 15.4%; but the pattern of political disarticulation had come into being. In both houses of Congress, the Democratic party was in the formal majority. They had only two seats more than the Republicans in the Senate, but 33 seats more in the House of Representatives.

National elections continued essentially in this format through 1972. In 1960, the Democratic president was elected without an effective popular mandate, although he had a working majority in both houses of Congress (30 in the Senate, 89 in the House). Only in the 1964 election did Lyndon B. Johnson re-create the conventional pre–World War II majority political regime with a landslide popular mandate and a marked increase in the Democratic majority in both houses of Congress. However, the result of the 1964 election could not be taken as a critical election of realignment; it had signs of a minicritical election of limited scope and duration. In 1968, Richard Nixon was elected as the head of a minority political regime. He collected only a plurality of the popular presidential vote (43.4%) and his advantage over the Democratic candidate was limited to a miniscule 0.7%. The strength of the George Wallace vote, which totaled 13.6%, rendered Nixon, in effect, a minority president. Moreover, the Democratic party held a working majority in both houses of Congress (14 in the Senate and 51 in the House). The pattern of a disarticulated political regime was even more pronounced in the 1972 election. Nixon achieved a landslide popular majority—a 23.2% advantage over his Democratic contender—but the dominance of the Democratic legislators in both houses of Congress remained.

In 1976, the Democratic party obtained clear-cut majorities in both houses of Congress, especially in the House of Representatives. However, James Carter's popular mandate was in effect nominal; 50.1% of the total vote cast for the office of the president and 0.9% advantage of the two party Democratic-Republican vote. Thus, one can note that the "weak" or stalemate format of political regimes in the United States was not the result of the Vietnam War but has been in existence in one form or another throughout the post–World War II period.

The implications for the social-control perspective are clear. If one assumes that the election outcome is a measure of the ability of the society to regulate itself, then the absence of critical elections or stable majority political regimes indicates significant limitations in the pattern of social control. Thus these data highlight the strains on the central institutional mechanisms for developing effective social control. Next, by examining crucial measures of citizen participation in national elections, we can explore the long-term trend.

Trends in Electoral Participation

Vast effort has been expended in analyzing electoral behavior with data derived from official statistics and a variety of sample surveys.[22] The pragmatic self-interest of political leaders and their professional staffs, plus the popular concern with elections, have coincided with the goals of social scientists.[23] Despite the inadequacies of the available research we have an impressive body of basic information.[24] For 1920–1940, measures of trends are limited to voting results, and, even when augmented by refined ecological and statistical analysis, must remain incomplete. The use of sample surveys started in the 1930s and was markedly expanded in the 1950s.

Despite the well-grounded reservations of the research specialists, the available documentation bears directly on the issues of social control, because a group of survey election studies with varying degrees of theoretical explicitness help clarify underlying statistical trends. The questions which have been asked about election data have changed in focus, so that the gap between the collection of aggregate data and sample statistics and the systemic analysis of the electoral process has narrowed. Sample survey studies of voting behavior started with an effort to describe who voted for whom, and were expanded to articulate with the classical issues of representation, consent, and the effectiveness of collective problem solving.

The earliest opinion polls sought not only to estimate the preference of the citizenry for particular parties and candidates but also to describe the social correlates of political preference and choice. One of the first academic studies on the 1940 election, conducted by Paul F. Lazarsfeld and his associates, cast these issues into a social-stratification approach of political participation.[25] Voting patterns were assumed to be the

22. S. M. Lipset, P. F. Lazarsfeld, A. H. Barton, and J. Linz, "The Psychology of Voting: An Analysis of Political Behavior," in *Handbook of Social Psychology*, ed. Lindzey (Reading, Mass.: Addison Wesley, 1954), 2: 1124–75.

23. Mark Abrams, "Political Parties and the Polls," in *The Uses of Sociology*, ed. Paul F. Lazarsfeld et al. (New York: Basic Books, 1967), pp. 427–34.

24. For an effort to summarize this literature which emphasizes the difficulties of interpretation, see Philip E. Converse, "Change in the American Electorate," in *The Human Meaning of Social Change*, ed. Angus Campbell and Philip E. Converse (New York: Russell Sage Foundation, 1972), pp. 263–337.

25. Paul F. Lazarsfeld, Bernard Berelson, and Helen Gaudet, *The People's Choice* (New York: Columbia University Press, 1948).

expression of the social position of the participating citizen; social-economic level, place of residence, and religion formed the basis for an "index of political predisposition" which was offered as a basis for explaining the patterns of political participation in the election. It was a voting model of social stratification: low income, urban, and Catholic, independently (and more so in combination), produced a Democratic decision. Lazarsfeld and his associates sought to investigate the effect, limited but important, of the campaign and the significance of face-to-face and personal pressure and influences. For the 1952 national election, the University of Michigan group, Angus Campbell and his associates, sought partially to refute and partially to elaborate the Lazarsfeld social-stratification model by offering an alternative set of social and psychological variables, dealing with motivation. Their index encompassed party identification, issue orientation, and candidate orientation to explain the 1952 election.[26] Because of its tautological overtones, the motivation model did not have the intellectual relevance and durability of the Lazarsfeld approach.[27] In refined fashion, voting studies have continued to identify the explanatory power of the social stratification variables in accounting for mass electoral participation; attitudinal variables have come to be used as secondary explanatory elements.

When the specific variables employed by Lazarsfeld in 1940 were applied to a national sample in 1948, their explanatory power was indeed limited.[28] Obviously, it could be argued that by 1948 the campaign issues had altered. A comprehensive explanation of voting behavior requires an analysis of social profiles of the citizenry, and the changes in political alternatives offered by the political leaders and their party organization. However, there is a consistent inference to be drawn from the Lazarsfeld research and from those studies which have been pursued in the same framework since 1940. The results indicate that the linkage between standard social-stratification variables and the patterns of political preference has declined since 1948. Here, sociological research and the reading of contemporary history converge; the applica-

26. Angus Campbell, Gerald Gurin, and Warren E. Miller, *The Voter Decides* (Evanston, Ill.: Row, Peterson, 1954).

27. See Heinz Eulau for a critical assessment of the Angus Campbell study, *American Political Science Review* 54 (December 1960): 993–94.

28. Morris Janowitz and Warren E. Miller, "The Index of Political Predisposition in the 1948 Election, *Journal of Politics* 14 (November 1952): 710–27.

tion of standard measures over time reveals that we are dealing with "real" changes. The model of the "lower" social strata on the Democratic side and the upper social strata on the Republican, the model of the 1932 political realignment, became progressively less pertinent.[29]

To assert that the relevance of social-stratification explanations is declining is not to discard this stratification approach as the point of entrance. More refined measures of social differentiation, which include community setting, age, race, and ethnicity, help increase the explanatory power of the social-stratification model.[30] Moreover, under advanced industrialism, social-stratification patterns which influence political behavior come to include age and sex as a more explicit basis of social differentiation in the political arena. National surveys with limited samples tend to underemphasize the subtleties and complexities of social-stratification variables. But fundamentally, we are dealing with basic changes in the system of social stratification to be discussed in chapter 5 and changes in the political alternatives offered by the political parties.

Moreover, from the perspective of social control, the relevance of election studies based on sample surveys does not hinge on explaining the social and the psychological correlates of the vote. The more central questions are those raised by political sociologists and political theorists about the election as a process of consent; to what extent did the election conform to the desired goals of a legitimate process of political decision making and collective problem solving? Thus, the fundamental issue is the effectiveness of voting participation as a system of representation.[31] Under the acknowledged stimulation of Edward Shils, Bernard Berelson in his 1948 replication of the original Lazarsfeld election study was explicitly concerned with the extent to which the

29. James Davis, "Subjective Social Class, Party Identification and Presidential Vote, 1952–1972," unpublished paper, National Opinion Research Center, 1975.

30. David Segal and David Knoke, "Political Partisanship: Its Social and Economic Bases in the United States," *American Journal of Economics and Sociology* 29 (July 1970): 253–62; Norval D. Glenn, "Massification versus Differentiation: Some Trend Data from National Surveys," *Social Forces* 46 (December 1967): 172–80; for an analysis of age as a political variable see Ronald Inglehart, *The Silent Revolution: Changing Values and Political Styles among Western Publics* (Princeton: Princeton University Press, 1977).

31. For an exposition of the issues raised by classical democratic theory as they relate to voting survey studies, see Dennis F. Thompson, *The Democratic Citizen: Social Science Theory in the 20th Century* (Cambridge: Cambridge University Press, 1970).

political participation of the citizenry conformed to the ideal standards presumed to be required of a democratic election based on consent.[32]

The presidential election of 1952 produced a reorientation in election studies; they sought to close the gap between empirical indicators and political theory, and converged with the perspective of social control. This shift reflected both the political realities of that election and intellectual trends. The effect of Eisenhower's personal "charisma" and the growing influence of television raised the question of the quality of the debate and the extent to which the 1952 campaign reflected political consent versus mass persuasion. At the same time, the intellectual perspectives of political macro-sociology were being applied to the analysis of the electoral system; in particular, the writings of Joseph Schumpeter had become central.[33] He assigned central importance to the competitive nature of the electoral process as the hallmark of a political democracy. His approach led to analyses of the electoral process which sought to assess, by means of empirical survey data, the quality of the electoral process as a mechanism of self-regulation and collective problem solving.[34]

The research literature covering the 1950s and the early 1960s did not uniformly emphasize the arrival of an era of comprehensive consent.[35] While the analysis of the 1952 election indicated the broad base of consensus which was generated, the strain on and defects in the electoral system could be explicitly identified.[36] Exclusion from the electoral process of large segments of the citizenry, especially minority groups, bespoke ineffective patterns of social control which would sub-

32. Bernard Berelson, Paul F. Lazarsfeld, and William N. McPhee, *Voting* (Chicago: University of Chicago Press, 1954). Berelson acknowledged the influence of Edward Shils in stimulating his research group to explore the linkages between democratic theory and survey findings.

33. Joseph Schumpeter, *Capitalism, Socialism and Democracy*, 3d ed. (New York: Harper, 1950).

34. Morris Janowitz and Dwaine Marvick, *Campaign Pressure and Political Consent* (Chicago: Quadrangle, 1964); Anthony Downs, *An Economic Theory of Democracy* (New York: Harper, 1957); V. O. Key, Jr., *The Responsible Electorate: Rationality in Presidential Voting, 1936–1960* (Cambridge: Harvard University Press, 1966.). The University of Michigan's research group's adaptation to this intellectual trend came with publication of Angus Campbell et al., *Elections and the Political Order* (New York: Wiley, 1966).

35. An explicit formulation of the rise of a "permanent consensus" is to be found in the writings of Robert E. Lane, "The Politics of Consensus in an Age of Affluence," *American Political Science Review* 59 (December 1965): 874–95. See also S. M. Lipset, "The Changing Class Structure and Contemporary European Politics," *Daedalus* (Winter 1964), pp. 271–303.

36. Janowitz and Marvick, *Campaign Pressure*, passim.

sequently have their conflict-ridden political impact. Likewise, the research data from 1952 onward identified those segments of the voting population whose political decisions did not have a sufficient or stable definition of self-interest to contribute to a meaningful process of consent. These electoral analyses were concurrently being augmented by sociological writings which pointed out deep strains in the political parties and related institutions for generating consent. These themes were found in the research strategies of sociologists such as Edward Shils, William Kornhauser, Harold Wilensky, Robert Hamilton, and Melvin Seeman.[37] The idea that sociologists without exception accepted, for the period after 1952, the idea of the "permanent" decline of sociopolitical conflict is hardly accurate.

These research currents need to be interpreted in the context of the earlier observation that the 1952 election did not produce a critical political realignment—as might have been expected in light of the issues of the post–World War II period. It is possible to examine four specific trends in electoral participation which extend over the half-century from 1920 to 1975 and highlight the transformation in the electoral process. These trends help explain the increasing inability of the electoral process since 1948 to generate cohesive majority political regimes. We are dealing with relatively long-term trends and not the particular manifestations of the elections of 1968–1972. To emphasize the increased ineffectiveness of social control is not to offer and accept projections of existing trends into the future. We are dealing with (*a*) the level of voting participation; (*b*) shifts in voting patterns from one election to the next; (*c*) changes in patterns of party affiliation; and (*d*) the level of beliefs about the legitimacy and effectiveness of the electoral process and elected officials. The election of 1952 is used as the dividing point for the period, 1920 to 1976. Each of the trends is formulated to highlight the balance of change versus persistence.

37. Edward Shils, *The Torment of Secrecy: The Background and Consequences of American Security Policies* (Glencoe, Ill.: Free Press, 1956); William Kornhauser, *The Politics of Mass Society* (Glencoe, Ill.: Free Press, 1959); Harold Wilensky, "Life Cycle, Work Situation and Participation in Formal Associations," in *Aging and Leisure*, ed. by R. W. Kleemeier (New York: Oxford University Press, 1961), pp. 213–43; Harold Wilensky, "Orderly Careers and Social Participation," *American Sociological Review* 26 (August 1961); 521–39; Richard Hamilton, *Class and Politics in the United States* (New York: Wiley, 1972); Melvin Seeman, "On the Personal Consequences of Alienation in Work," *American Sociological Review* 32 (April 1967): 273–85; Melvin Seeman, "On the Meaning of Alienation," *American Sociological Review* 24 (December 1959): 783–91.

First, since 1952 the long-term secular increase in voting participation has not been effectively maintained. Given the increasing levels of education, wide exposure to the mass media, and politicalization of minority groups, the persistence of a high level of nonvoting and even specific increases in nonvoting is particularly noteworthy. This trend can be perceived as a direct measure of the electoral process's ineffectiveness as a mechanism of social control without asserting that everyone "must" vote in a democratic polity. However, there is no basis for offering the hypothesis that there has been a decline in popular interest in politics; the limitations in voting participation are not directly related to a decline in the level of political interest.

Second, since 1952 there has been an increase in the magnitude of shifts in voting patterns from one national election to the next. The post–World War II period has not been essentially characterized by a two-party system composed of two large and relatively stable voting blocs, with the outcome from one election to the next resulting from rather small shifts in voter preference. On the contrary, increasingly important segments of the electorate are prepared to change their preference for president and also to engage in ticket splitting.

Third, the number of citizens who are prepared to describe themselves as independents or as having no party affiliation has increased since 1952, and especially among young voters. Specifically, it is hypothesized that there has been a change in the character of those citizens who call themselves independent; as of 1952, the bulk of the independents had weak involvements in politics and marginal partisan preferences. The subsequent trend has been one in which independents are increasingly persons with strong interests in politics and articulated political demands. The greater extent of "informed" ticket splitting is another manifestation of this. When considered together with the persistent levels of nonvoting plus changes in preference for political candidates, this increase in independent political orientation underlines the growth of attenuation of stable affiliation with the two majority parties.

Fourth, in the period 1964–1976, there has been a marked reduction in the trust and confidence placed in the electoral system and in the outcome of elections. This trend is linked to the specific influence of the military intervention in Vietnam and has been strengthened by the political events surrounding the Watergate investigation. However, it antedates the first years of the 1970s.

None of these trends can be taken as measures per se of political apathy or depoliticalization of the citizens of the United States.[38] They are, more, manifestations of the tension and pronounced disarticulation between political goals and available political means.[39]

First, voting participation from 1920 on must be seen in the context of the historical trend from 1896. Political historians have documented the decline in voting during 1896 to 1912.[40] While electoral reform had an influence whose magnitude cannot be effectively estimated, it is difficult to accept the view that improved election procedures which reduced fraud were the decisive element in the downward trend in voting of that period. Instead, it took a number of years to assimilate each new annual increment of immigrants into the national voting system. But the task of assimilating these new immigrants who came in large numbers during this period was also only a partial element. One cannot rule out the political setting and the limited range of political issues offered to the citizenry as important factors. During these years the pattern of party competition served to dampen participation to an important degree. In fact, the reversal in the downward trend in presidential voting occurred during the election of 1916, when the issues of World War I intensified the competition between the parties.

After 1920, the increasing levels of turnout probably reflected the participation of politically assimilated immigrants and the expanding concentration of newly enfranchised women voters as well as the higher levels of education in the population. But none of the available sources permit the conclusion that changes in the demographic and social-stratification dimensions of the citizenry could account for the increased voting. During the period after 1920, and especially after 1930, more

38. James Spence found the same master trends in Britain as for the United States. James Spence, "Trends in Political Participation in Britain Since 1945," in *Sociological Theory and Survey Research*, ed. Timothy Leggatt (London: Sage Publication, 1974), pp. 313–34. He concluded that political apathy could hardly effectively characterize the strains and dissatisfaction with the results of political participation.

39. Walter E. Burnham presents an analysis in which he speaks both of "party decomposition" and "depoliticalization." Walter E. Burnham, *Critical Elections and the Mainsprings of American Politics* (New York: Norton, 1960), pp. 91–134. See also Walter E. Burnham, "American Politics in the 1970's: Beyond Party?" in *The Future of Political Parties*, ed. Louis Maisel and Paul M. Sacks (Beverly Hills, Calif.: Sage Publications, 1975), pp. 238–75.

40. Robert E. Lane, *Political Life: Why People Get Involved in Politics* (Glencoe, Ill.: Free Press, 1959), pp. 16–22.

competitive politics influenced turnout and increased voting participation. From 44% turnout in the presidential election of 1920, the level of voting increased steadily until it reached 58.9% in 1940 (Table 4.1). But the trend has not been consistently upward since then. In 1944 and 1948 the turnout failed to reach the level of 1940; in fact, there was a downward phase, with 56.0% in 1944 and 51.1% in 1948, with the vote, to some undetermined extent, dampened by the wartime mobilization and demobilization. In terms of secular trends, the election of 1952 produced a new high point in presidential voting. Research gives the impression that the electoral competition—which was more between political personalities than about political issues—was a crucial factor.[41]

From 1952 to 1968, the overall turnout remained fairly stable (from 59% to 62%). In the strongly contested election of 1972 between Richard Nixon and George McGovern, voter participation dropped markedly to 55.7%, while the Carter-Ford campaign resulted in a lower figure of 53.3%. Thus, for 1960 to 1976, and especially for 1972, in the United States the level of competitive politics, which remained intense, did not produce increased levels of national electoral participation. We are speaking of actual participation, not interest in politics. No doubt, there is a point at which, hypothetically, the level of turnout becomes so high as to weaken elections as a system of self-regulation. This would be at the point at which the ability to mobilize new elements has been effectively curtailed and this element of uncertainty in the outcome eliminated. That level of participation has hardly been reached in the United States.

These observations about voting in national elections hardly imply that the changes in the level of participation have been the same in various social groups. Although the available data are not definitive, the configuration is much to the contrary, and, interestingly enough, reveals an increased incorporation of underrepresented groups. There is sufficient evidence to assert that the level of participation of women has increased more rapidly than that of men since 1948.[42] From being underrepresented, by 1968 women had a higher level of voting than men in national presidential elections. Likewise, the political involvement of blacks, especially Southern blacks, in 1960–1970 increased at a

41. Janowitz and Marvick, *Campaign Pressure*, pp. 40–54.

42. Marjorie Lansing, "Women: The New Political Class," in *A Sampler of Women's Studies*, ed. Dorothy Gris McGuigan (Ann Arbor: Center for Continuing Education of Women, 1973), pp. 59–76.

faster rate than that of the white population.[43] The assimilation of these two groups, as well as other minority elements, in two national elections, has increased the representativeness of the electorate and at the same time increased its heterogeneity. These trends imply that for some traditionally involved groups a short-term ceiling and some actual decline have been reached in political involvement.

The import of trends in electoral turnout in the United States does not rest in direct comparison of the differences with other industrialized nations of Western Europe and of Canada and Australia. In these nations, the level of turnout is generally higher than in the United States. The lower rate of participation in the United States is a function in part of higher residential mobility and the absence of electoral reform to deal with it. Again, more centrally, the explanation seems to involve a paradox which reflects political values. In Western Europe, the residues of traditional central authority and individuals' obligation to governmental procedures seem to propel the responsibility to vote. In the United States, to some degree, the highly individualist notions of civic responsibility apparently weakened pressures to conform to the obligation to participate in elections. Lower levels of electoral participation reflect the oft-mentioned stronger negative attitudes toward organized politics, particularly in concept content. But the essential issue is not these differences between the United States and Western Europe per se, but rather new points of similarity. For example, Great Britain has experienced a similar leveling off and actual decline in the latter half of the 1960s and the first half of the 1970s.

Trends in voter turnout must be assessed for the industrialized nations in the context of the continuing higher educational background of the citizens. Education has been the key variable which social scientists utilizing survey results have emphasized, education as a positive correlate of electoral participation. The failure of turnout in the United States to continue to increase and its short-term decline in 1952–1972 is not a result of educational limitations. The most important expansion came in the second half of the 1960s as Southern blacks with limited educational background registered and voted in increasing numbers.

Data on voting patterns need to be augmented by data on expressed interest in politics and on other types of political activity. National survey research data from 1952 to 1976 indicate no clear-cut trend, es-

43. Converse, "Change," pp. 303 ff.

pecially no sustained decline in interest. One trend series reported by Converse pointed out that, in 1952, 37% of the electorate reported that they were "very much interested" in the presidential campaign; by 1968 the figure was 39%.[44] Nie et al. reported national samples for 1956–1972; the trend was that of increased interest from 30% with "strong interest" up to 42% in 1968, and down to 39% in 1972, but still at a higher level than encountered in 1956.[45] The American Institute of Public Opinion data, which extend over a long period, are more revealing. During the period 1952 to 1976, no secular trend was encountered, and the level of expressed interest ranged by their measure from a low of 56% in 1956 to a high of 65% in 1960. The relevant observation is that fluctuation of interest depended on whether the presidential race was one-sided or not. During elections in which the contenders were more closely balanced, interest was higher, that is in 1952, 1960, and 1968; the level of interest was lower in 1956, 1964, and 1972.[46]

During this period, there were slight increases in self-reported membership in "political clubs or organizations," attendance at "political meetings, rallys, dinners, etc." and in the percentage of the population who had engaged in party work or made campaign contributions. The measured increase varies between different national samples, but the increase in the trend is clear. Thus, for example, attendance at "political meetings, rallys, dinners, etc." rose from 7% in 1952 to 16.5% in 1972. As far as mass political participation is concerned, the pattern is not one of apathy or depoliticalization, even when the measure of voting turnout is used; rather, new responses to the disarticulation of the electoral process were at work.

The increased magnitude of shifts in voting patterns from one election to the next is a sharp indicator of the transformation of the electoral system as a process of social control and self-regulation. One way to measure this trend is to compare directly the net shifts from election to election in the advantage given to the Republican or Democratic presidential candidate. The gross shifts, including those which cancel themselves out, would be more accurate. A measure of such shifts is

44. Ibid., pp. 332–33. The text of the question asked was "Some people don't pay much attention to the political campaigns. How about you? Would you say that you have been very much interested, somewhat interested, or not much interested in following the political campaigns so far this year?"

45. Norman H. Nie et al., *The Changing American Voter* (Cambridge: Harvard University Press, 1976), p. 281.

46. American Institute of Public Opinion, Oct. 25, 1976.

available only for years during which sample surveys were completed. But it is assumed that both the gross and the net measures are closely associated.

TABLE 4.2 Net Two-Party Shift in Presidential Election: Index of "Volatility," 1920–1972

Election Period	Percent Shift in Two-Party Vote	
1920 to 1924	1.1	
1924 to 1928	7.9	
1928 to 1932		(realignment election)
1932 to 1936	6.6	
1936 to 1940	14.4	
1940 to 1944	2.4	
1944 to 1948	3.0	
Average 1920 to 1948		5.9 (without realignment election)
1948 to 1952	15.2	
1952 to 1956	4.7	
1956 to 1960	15.6	
1960 to 1964	22.9	
1964 to 1968	22.0	
1968 to 1972	22.5	
Average 1948 to 1972		17.1

If one examines the period from 1920 to 1948, leaving out the realignment election of 1932, the shift in voting from one election to the next is moderate. The average two-party shift for these six presidential elections was 5.9 percent points. (See Table 4.2.) However, for 1948 to 1972, the volatility of electoral behavior was much greater.[47] In fact, the average two-party shift was three times as great; for the seven presidential elections, the average shift was 17.1 percentage points. (If one included the third-party voting in 1968, the magnitude of the switching would be even greater.)

Another reflection of the detachment from two-party attachments is reflected in the long-term increase in "ticket splitting." Electoral reform, plus higher levels of education, have been at work in developing a self-definition of more "sophisticated" political behavior. But, as will be argued below in the analysis of patterns of social stratification, this trend reflects the complexity and ambiguity of translating self-interest into a clear-cut political decision. The documentation on the long-term growth of ticket splitting is indeed impressive. It shows that, if social researchers have a historical perspective, they collect revealing data re-

47. See also Norman H. Nie et al., *Changing American Voter*, pp. 345–56.

lated to the long-term patterns of political and social control. In Table 4.3, Paul T. David demonstrates the continuous growth in ticket splitting from 1872 to 1970.[48] His analysis is based on the differences in six pairs of voting decisions involving the president, governor, senator, and

TABLE 4.3 Index of Ticket Splitting: Average Differences between Party Office Percentages, 1872–1970

Time Period	P-G*	P S	P-R	G-S	G-R	S-R	Pair averages
Democratic							
1872–1894	6.5	0.0	6.3	0.0	5.3	0.0	6.0
1896–1930	8.5	—	7.9	—	6.0	—	7.5
1914–1930	—	10.6	—	7.0	—	6.4	8.0
1932–1970	11.1	10.9	10.4	7.4	6.3	6.6	8.8
Republican							
1872–1894	6.0	0.0	4.9	0.0	5.1	0.0	5.3
1896–1930	7.5	—	6.8	—	5.6	—	6.6
1914–1930	—	9.0	—	6.1	—	6.3	7.1
1932–1970	9.5	9.3	8.6	7.5	6.4	6.4	8.0

*The symbols used as column heads indicate the various pairing combinations for president, governor, senator, and representative in Congress: P-G, president and governor; P-S, president and senator; P-R, president and representatives (statewide); G-S, governor and senator; G-R, governor and representatives (statewide); S-R, senator and representatives (statewide). The computations are based on the biennial series for each office in each state.

SOURCES: Paul T. David, *Party Strength in the United States, 1872–1970* (Charlottesville: University Press of Virginia), p. 16.

representatives. There has been no reversal in the century-long trend in increased ticket splitting. The available sources indicate that this trend increased after 1948.[49] Cox has calculated a "minimal" measure which produced the following results: 1932: 3.19; 1936: 3.82; 1940: 3.16; 1944: 2.96; 1948: 5.35; 1952: 6.37; 1956: 6.80; 1960: 5.22; 1964: 7.24.[50] Survey research shows the same trend; findings from the Survey Research Center, at the University of Michigan, indicate the respondents in their national sample who voted "a straight ticket, state and local" declined

48. Paul T. David, *Party Strength in the United States, 1872–1970* (Charlottesville: University Press of Virginia, 1972), p. 16.

49. Milton Cummings, "Split Ticket Voting and the Presidency and Congress," in *Congressmen and the Electorate: Elections for the U. S. House and the President, 1920–1964*, ed. Milton Cummings, Jr. (New York: Free Press, 1967); Edward Cox, *Voting in Post-War Federal Elections* (Dayton, Ohio: Wright State University, 1968); see also, for an overall summary, Walter DeVries and Lance Torrance, Jr., *The Ticket Splitter* (Grand Rapids, Mich.: Erdmans, 1972).

50. Cox, *Voting*.

from 72% in 1948 to 50% in 1966. Ticket splitting is to be found roughly equally among citizens who consider themselves to be Republicans and those who consider themselves to be Democrats.

The third trend which highlights the transformation of political participation is the gradual but persistent increase in the proportion of the electorate who consider themselves to be independents. The Gallup surveys since 1938 have charted the long-term decline in Republican affiliation, the relative stability of Democratic attachments, and the gradual increase in that proportion of the citizenry who consider themselves to be "independents" (Table 4.4). In 1940, 38% of the Gallup

TABLE 4.4 Trends in Political Party Identification, 1940–1974

"In politics, as of today, do you consider yourself a Republican, a Democrat, or an independent voter?"*

18 and older	Rep.	Dem.	Independent
1971	26%	45%	29%
1972	28	43	29
1973	26	43	31
1974	24	42	34
21 and older			
1940	38	42	20
1950	33	45	22
1960	30	47	23
1964	25	53	22
1965	27	50	23
1966	27	48	25
1967	27	46	27
1968	27	46	27
1969	28	42	30
1970	29	45	26

*The proportion who do not classify themselves in one of the three categories—ranging from 2-3%—has been excluded in each set of figures.

national sample classified themselves as Republicans, and the figure declined steadily to 24% by 1974. The concentration of Democrats increased from 42% in 1940 to a high point of 53% in 1964 and subsequently declined until in 1974 it stood at 42%. The trend for independents ranged from a low of 20% in 1940 to 34% in 1974. The result was that the relative balance between Republican and Democratic affiliation of the pre–World War II period gave way to an increasing preponderance of Democratic affiliation. For the period from October

1952 to November 1970, the findings of the Survey Research Center confirm these trends.[51] The trend toward "independent" affiliation is even more pronounced among young people.[52] In fact, among college students, by 1974 almost one-half called themselves independents.

There is no reason to believe that the growth in the proportion of the electorate who call themselves "independent" represents a decline in political interest and involvement. In fact, there is evidence to the contrary—an increasing concentration of the political independents think of themselves as politically responsible and "sophisticated." It is appropriate to compare the characteristics of the political independents as recorded by surveys in 1952 and with those of 1968 to 1972. In this case, the results are not the outcome of applying a more refined set of categories to the more contemporary period as contrasted with cruder categories for the earlier period. In the 1952 election, survey data underlined that the majority of those citizens who called themselves "independent" had weak political interests and limited political involvements. Their political participation in the electoral process was marginal, and they were the individuals most likely to be influenced by the mass media. There is good reason to believe that this had been the case at least since the realignment election of 1932. By 1972, the independents had changed to an important extent. They had come to include a marked concentration of persons with strong interests in the political process. They tended to be younger and better educated persons who thought of themselves as engaged in a continuing calculation of their self-interest and political responsibility. In fact, among the younger, better educated members of the electorate, these independents began to reach a majority.

Students of voting behavior have sought to use the social-psychological conception of political competence to measure political involvement. Because of the difficulty of conceptualization and operational measures, the results are difficult to assess. However, the available materials for 1948 to 1972 do not support any inference of fundamental or extensive political withdrawal. In fact, one analyst of this type of data has argued that the "indicators of political attentiveness and activism appear to have edged forward over the past two decades [1950–1970] in something like the measure that advances in education, with which all are

51. Reported in Burnham, *Critical Elections*, p. 121.

52. Philip Converse, "Of Time and Partisan Stability," *Comparative Political Studies* 2 (July 1969): 139–71.

clearly correlated, would lead one to expect."[53] This basic trend, or at least persistent level of involvement, is of course compatible with increasing levels of distrust and frustration.

The fourth trend, an increased distrust of the electoral process, rests on data which cover mainly the post–World War II period and especially the period since 1968. While there is strong evidence to support the long-term increase since 1952, and especially since 1968, there is no available empirical basis for extending this trend back to the decade of the Great Depression.

One sensitive indicator of the magnitude of the declining public confidence in the electoral process as constituted can be seen in the responses to the question, "Do you think it will make any important difference in how you and your family get along financially whether the Democrats or the Republicans win?" This formulation is not without ambiguities, since some of those who report no "difference" may be expressing basic satisfaction. Nevertheless, the national sample responses to this question are striking both for the high percentage who report "no difference" and the gradual upward trend; in 1952, 53%, and by 1964, 66%.[54]

A more direct measure, which yields a much more marked shift in mass attitudes, is the level of confidence placed in the Congress. From surveys by the Survey Research Center, the trend was reported as dropping from 62% of a national sample in 1958 reporting "high" level of trust in government to 35% in 1970.[55] Gallup used a three-point scale for rating the "present Congress in Washington": good (including excellent), fair, or poor. In 1963, by this approach, 39.6% said good, 49.7% fair, and 10.7% poor. By 1974, a comparable three-point rating revealed a distribution of 17.6%, 60.9%, and 15.3%, respectively.[56]

This downward trend in confidence about governmental and political authority became more pronounced in the final years of the 1960s. The Harris survey, which appropriately compared the years 1966 with 1975, highlights the short-term decline in mass confidence in the appointed and elected officials of government.[57] The text of the question

53. Converse, "Change," p. 334.

54. Inter-University Consortium for Political Research, *Codebooks of Election Studies*, n. d.

55. Institute of Social Research, *Newsletter* (Winter 1972), p. 5.

56. D. Garth Taylor, "Confidence in the Legislative Branch," NORC, unpublished report, April 1975.

57. *Current Opinion* 1 (November 1972): 3.

was "As far as people running (insert name of institution) are concerned, would you say you have a great deal of confidence, only some confidence, or hardly any confidence at all in them?" The relative positions of the military, federal, and executive branches and Congress can be judged by comparison with that of medicine. Medicine ranked highest in 1966 with 72% expressing "a great deal of confidence"; but in 1975 the level of confidence had dropped to 43%. The Supreme Court, Congress, and the executive branch of government all experienced sharp declines in the levels of confidence which they were able to generate: U.S. Supreme Court, 51% in 1966 versus 28% in 1975; Congress, 42% in 1966 versus 13% in 1975; Executive Branch of Federal Government, 41% in 1966 versus 13% in 1975. A similar attitude was revealed in the summary measure used by the Gallup survey, on the level of satisfaction "with the way this nation is being governed." In 1971, 37% responded "satisfied"; by 1973 the level of satisfaction had declined to 26%, which must be judged a profound low.[58] For the period 1958 to 1973, the Survey Research Center constructed an index of trust in government which moved from positive 50 to negative 30 during those years.[59]

The imagery of the president and satisfaction with the performance of the president are, of course, important indicators of this trend. The long-term trend for the president of the United States since the Truman regime has been that of rapid decline in popularity after each election of a new president, with the exception of J. F. Kennedy. In each case, one central factor of dissatisfaction has been involvement in military operations abroad. In the case of Nixon, approval shifted from nearly 70% in January 1973 to 20% in January 1974, probably the widest recorded shift in mass opinion on any particular topic in the history of national survey research.

The declining level of trust and confidence in "government" is, of course, reflected in the prestige of elected officials. The question used

58. Attitudes toward governmental agencies and governmental officials are hardly expressive of particularistic opinions; they reflect a person's underlying orientation toward public authority. In a sample survey of adults in the Detroit area, collected in 1954, it was found that attitudes toward government agencies conformed to a Guttman scale revealing a general orientation toward governmental authority. The relative position of particular agencies reflected their effectiveness, but a person's general orientation was linked to his basic orientation toward authority. Morris Janowitz et al., "Public Administration and the Public—Perspectives toward Government in a Metropolitan Community" (Ann Arbor, Mich.: Institute of Public Administration, 1958), passim.

59. Institute for Social Research, *Newsletter* (Winter 1974), p. 5.

to measure trends has been "If you had a son, would you like to see him go into politics as a life's work?" The finding that the majority of the citizenry would be reluctant serves as a measure of the low prestige and trust of the elected official. However, this measure is reflective of the more general attitude trends toward governmental legitimacy.

TABLE 4.5 Trends in Prestige of Elected Officials, 1943–1973

"If you had a son, would you like to see him go into politics as a life's work?"

Year	Yes	No	No Opinion
1943	18%	69%	13%
1945	21	68	11
1953	20	70	10
1955	27	60	13
1965	36	54	10
1973	23	64	13

SOURCE: The Gallup Opinion Index, July 1973, report no. 97.

From Table 4.5 it can be seen that since 1943 the percentage of the population who approved of "their" sons' entering politics rose from 18% to 36% in 1965. Thereafter the trend declined to 23% in 1973. The better educated, younger persons were more positive about the career of an elected official. Distrust is not a sudden development of the Nixon regime; it has been an aspect of the emergence of "weak" political regimes. However, comparison of national samples in 1972–1974 indicates that the Watergate affair had a specific and discernible consequence. Interesting enough, the contribution it made to declining trust in government was not primarily in the event itself or in Nixon's role, but in the action of President Ford in pardoning Nixon.[60]

THE MORAL CONTEXT OF POLITICS

These four trends in electoral behavior have occurred in the context of extensive changes in mass opinion, especially in attitude patterns which reflect the "moral context" of politics.[61] Attitudes toward minor-

60. "Watergate Crisis," *Institute for Social Research Newsletter* (Summer 1975), pp. 4–5.

61. A limited number of content analysis studies on the moral context supply longer time series for the period 1920–1970. While these studies are informative, they do not articulate directly with the issues of the moral context of politics. One of the most widely known is that of Leo Lowenthal, who studied the long-term changes in the heroes of popular fiction and highlighted the shift from "idols of production" to "idols of consumption." Leo Lowenthal, "Biographies in Popular Magazines," in *Radio Research, 1942–43*, ed. Paul F. Lazarsfeld and Frank Stanton (New York: Duell, Sloan and Pearce, 1944), pp. 507–48. See also P. Johns-

ity groups, especially concerning their human dignity and political rights, constitute key indicators of social change and social control. Hostile prejudice toward minority groups based on their ascriptive characteristics constitutes a painful central barrier to the process of fundamental democratization and the achievement of effective social control in an advanced industrial society. Indicators of sociopolitical change must do more than measure income, education, and well-being; they must be used to assess the trends in mutual respect, which is an essential element of effective social control. Fortunately, there is a considerable body of national data concerning attitudes toward minority groups in the United States which serves this goal. Syndromes of extreme racial and religious prejudice are closely linked to opposition to the two-party parliamentary system. In the simplest terms, joint outspoken hostility toward blacks and Jews—not "polite" prejudice—is linked to antidemocratic political extremism.

For the period that data exist, namely, from approximately the middle of the 1930s, the long-term trend has been continued decline in expressed prejudice toward Jews and blacks. Since the 1930s, when systematic national sample surveys became institutionalized, attitudes toward minority groups have been one topic which has been continuously researched. The weight of the evidence is most persuasive.

Despite the sociopolitical tensions of the 1960s and the impact of inflation and unemployment in the first half of the 1970s, there has been a decline in expressed levels of ethnic and racial hostility.[62] The research data which we needed to take into account are mainly in the form of repeated national public opinion surveys. After the 1960s militant socio-

Heine and Hans H. Gerth, "Values in Mass Periodical Fiction, 1921–1940," *Public Opinion Quarterly* 13 (1949): 105–17. It would be important to carry the Lowenthal study forward in time to see if there has been a shift in this trend. There is reason to believe that after 1960 the emphasis has been on the management of interpersonal relations and on minority group figures. See chapter 9. Trend analysis of Protestant sermons has been effectively utilized in pointing up a secular shift from optimism to persistent pessimism. T. Hamilton, "Social Optimism and Pessimism in American Protestantism," *Public Opinion Quarterly* 6 (1942): 280–83. One of the earlier long-term context values studies which focused on social values was prepared by Hornell Hart, "Changing Social Attitudes and Interests," President's Research Committee, *Recent Social Trends in the United States: Report* (New York: McGraw Hill, 1933). See also James A. Davis, "Communism, Conformity, Cohorts, and Categories: American Tolerance in 1954 and 1972–73," *American Journal of Sociology* 81 (November 1975): 491–513.

62. For an analysis of the sociological and psychological issues involved, see Bruno Bettelheim and Morris Janowitz, *Social Change and Prejudice* (New York: Free Press, 1975).

political movements, despite the diffusion of criminal and political violence and the weakening of political legitimacy, there continued to be a long-term decline in expressed prejudice that has persisted up to 1976. The outburst of racial violence in 1964–1969 did not interrupt this trend.

The documentation on the long-term decline in expressed anti-Semitic attitudes has been assembled by Charles Herbert Stember in *Jews in the Mind of America*, which draws on a large number of national and specialized surveys.[63] Thus Stember identified twelve different measures of anti-Semitic attitudes covering the period 1938 to 1962, dealing with a range of items from the "Jews are a race" to "Jews have too much power." For each of these, there is a clear-cut decline.[64] The greatest decline deals with opposition to working with Jews, namely, "it would make a difference if employees were Jewish," which declined from 43% to 6%.

The only source relying on survey research data which tends to resist acknowledging the long-term decline in anti-Jewish attitudes is the Anti-Defamation League–sponsored study analyzed by Gertrude J. Selznick and Stephen Steinberg.[65] Their argument is based on inferences from a single sample and cannot be considered as refuting the mass of materials presented by Stember and other investigators. The exposition by Selznick and Steinberg indicates that they hold that anti-Semitism has not declined sharply since 1952. Clearly, an important part of the decline of anti-Jewish feeling took place during the years from 1945 to 1952, as knowledge of the Holocaust in Europe spread and as the post–World War II full employment economy emerged, but the continued decline since 1952 remains noteworthy.

In fact, in addition to the findings assembled by Stember, the results presented by Otis Dudley Duncan and colleagues on the basis of very careful comparisons of the findings of the Detroit Area Study highlight the continued downward trend.[66] Because of the precise sampling procedures, this source is invaluable for assessing change in prejudice attitudes, although obviously the Detroit metropolis cannot be assumed to

63. Charles Herbert Stember, *Jews in the Mind of America* (New York: Basic Books, 1966).

64. Ibid., p. 94.

65. Gertrude J. Selznick and Stephen Steinberg, *The Tenacity of Prejudice: Anti-Semitism in Contemporary America* (New York: Harper and Row, 1969).

66. Otis Dudley Duncan, Howard Schuman, and Beverly Duncan, "Social Change in Metropolitan Detroit: The 1950s and 1971" (University of Michigan, unpublished report), p. 92.

represent the United States. A comparison of the sample of adults in metropolitan Detroit in 1958 and 1971 revealed that the attitude that "the Jewish people have been trying to get too much power in the country" dropped—among Protestants, from 27% to 22%; among Catholics, from 26% to 20%. There was a comparable drop in the belief that Jews were "less fair in their business dealings" than Protestants and Catholics.

The long-term decline in prejudiced attitudes toward blacks has been documented by various national survey agencies. The Gallup survey has made use of a projective type of question, namely, willingness to support a "Negro" for president. In 1958, the percentage prepared to vote for a qualified black was 38; by 1971 it had reached 69%.[67] The findings of the National Opinion Research Center focused on changing attitudes toward racial integration.[68] For example, in 1942, approximately 44% of the white population was willing to endorse integrated transportation; by 1970, the figure had risen to 88%. Similarly, Angus Campbell has reported that attitudinal support for "strict segregation" found in the University of Michigan national samples fell from 24% in 1964 to 19% in 1970, to approximately 10% in 1974.[69]

These data indicate that, even during controversy and outbursts concerning school busing, the overall pattern of decline in racial hostility continued. (Negative attitudes toward busing are discussed in chapter 12.)

The response to the question whether "relations between white and black were getting better, getting worse or staying pretty much the same," is revealing. In 1972, 48% had said "getting better," compared with 58% in 1974. In both years, this proportion was much larger than those who said "getting worse."[70] Likewise, during 1964–1974, the "proportion who felt that the government should protect the rights of black people to equal accommodations in public places rose from 56 to 75 percent," while the proportion who felt that "civil rights leaders are

67. *The Gallup Opinion Index*, November 1971, report no. 77.

68. Paul B. Sheatsley, "White Attitudes toward the Negro," *Daedalus* (Winter 1966), pp. 217–38; Andrew M. Greeley and Paul B. Sheatsley, "Attitudes toward Racial Integration," *Scientific American* (December 1971), pp. 13–19. See also Mildred A. Schwartz, *Trends in White Attitudes toward Negroes* (Chicago: National Opinion Research Center, 1967); and Angus Campbell, *White Attitudes toward Black People* (Ann Arbor, Mich.: Institute for Social Research, 1971).

69. Angus Campbell, *Newsletter*, Institute of Social Research (Autumn 1975), pp. 4–7.

70. Ibid., p. 7.

trying to push too fast" dropped from 68% to 40%. These changes were taking place in the context of a self-reported increase in interracial contacts by whites with blacks in their neighborhoods, with friends, and at work. The proportion of whites who described their social space as all white dropped between 1964 and 1974 as follows: neighborhood, 80% to 61%; friends, 81% to 53%; work, 53% to 39%. While the gap between social behavior and verbal behavior on these issues remains immense, these data underline the continued and noteworthy transformation of attitude patterns.

These trend data, of course, describe verbal behavior—attitudes expressed in the setting of a semipublic interview. It can be argued that, during the last decade, respondents—to use the terminology of the survey research specialist—have learned to conceal their prejudice. Therefore the findings are superficial. There can be no doubt that there is a great need to augment these standardized interviews with research that probes more deeply and explores the extent of latent hostilities and the role of prejudice as a mechanism of defense, especially as an aspect of projective reactions. But we interpret these data as reflecting the emergence of a gradually shifting set of social and moral norms. Within the framework of an interactional social psychology and buttressed by the assumptions of a phenomenologist orientation, verbal expressions of this type are a form of social reality with their own validity. The very fact that the United States has been gradually and continuously altering its expressed attitudes toward minority groups reflects the political and moral context in which institutional changes have operated. Obviously, it would be an error to continue to extrapolate these trends mechanically into the future.

Even Gertrude J. Selznick, who has emphasized the persistence of anti-Semitism in the United States, came to the same conclusion in 1966, when she asserted that "the possibility of anti-Semitism becoming a major issue is more a question of a prejudiced elite gaining control over an apathetic majority than in the overturn of a sympathetic government by a prejudiced and involved public."[71]

71. Charles Y. Glock, Gertrude J. Selznick, and Joseph L. Spaeth, *The Apathetic Majority: A Study of Public Responses to the Eichmann Trial* (New York: Harper and Row, 1966). Such an analysis of public opinion is, however, much too mechanistic to deal with the American electorate. First, it underestimates the capacity of political leaders to mobilize irrational elements in public opinion during a crisis situation; and second, it fails to recognize the important contribution that marginal voters play in the final outcome of narrow contested elections.

Moreover, it is essential to examine the extent to which the black community was, in its own perspective, becoming polarized from the outlook of the white community in the 1960s. From the point of view of a democratic society, a decline in prejudice among the majority group is significant to the extent that the minority group also comes to believe that the society at large is concerned with the injustices it suffers.

There is only a limited number of trend data on black attitudes toward the white community.[72] The all-too-limited evidence indicates some increase—but hardly a profound trend—in the distrust the black community feels for the white community. Within the black community, interest in integration, especially in school integration, increased and reached a plateau. Comparison of national samples of black respondents reveals that in 1964, 68% believed that the government in Washington should see to it that "white and Negro children are allowed to go to the same school."[73] By 1970, it had risen to 84%, but by 1974 it had fallen somewhat.[74] Similar increases were encountered in demands for public accommodations, housing, and especially general questions of desegregation. Further, dissatisfaction among blacks with the pace of change increased. In 1964, 23% believed that civil rights leaders were moving too slowly; by 1970, 39% believed so. Nevertheless, there is little evidence of a sharp growth in black hostility toward the white population. More than half of the black respondents felt, in 1974, "relations between white and black people have been getting better," and fewer than 10% felt that relations were getting worse.[75]

While the central trend of U.S. attitudes has been toward a decline in ethnic and racial intolerance, there may have been a hardening in outlook among the hard-core extremists. "Hard-core" refers not only to ethnic and racial attitudes but also to opposition to democratic political forms. There can be no doubt that the events of the 1960s saw an extensive mobilization of such sentiments, but whether and how much this hard-core has grown is problematic. In particular, it is im-

72. William Brink and Louis Harris, *The Negro Revolution in America* (New York: Simon and Schuster, 1964).

73. Angus Campbell, *White Attitudes toward Black People*, p. 130.

74. Campbell, *Newsletter*, p. 7.

75. For evidence of short-term, selective increases in antiwhite and negative attitudes among a national sample of blacks during 1968 to 1971, see Howard Schuman and Shirley Hatchett, *Black Racial Attitudes: Trends and Complexities* (Ann Arbor, Mich.: Institute for Social Research, 1974).

portant to compare the public support of the "radical right" in the 1960s with the support for "native fascist" movements of the 1930s. During the 1930s, the extent of the "native fascist" appeal has been estimated as ranging from 8% to 10% at most.[76] It is doubtful whether a larger percentage could be assigned to popular support for the "radical right" in the 1960s.

George Wallace's entrance in the national political arena represents the focal point of the radical right during the post–World War II period. While Wallace populism has appealed to the economically submerged groups in American society, his strategy has involved various degrees of explicitness on prejudiced themes. The Wallace movement has been analyzed mainly in terms of the social basis of those who have supported him.[77] From the point of view of trend analysis, the levels of support he could mobilize reflect the capacity of the two-party system to contain and limit his appeals.

In 1967, national Gallup surveys revealed that Wallace had a positive image among 43.2% of the adult population; in October 1968, approximately 21% indicated their intention to vote for him. However, the election results in November 1968 gave him only 13.5% of the total voting electorate. The decline reflects his inability to translate a preference into a concrete voting decision. Nixon's campaign, with its Southern strategy, had its effect in appealing to Wallace supporters. There is, in the United States, strong resistance to third-party voting, which is often defined as "wasting your vote." Nevertheless, ten million voters represented a noteworthy success for Wallace. Of course, all of the total popular vote for George Wallace cannot be thought to represent a "radical right" sentiment.

If popular support for the radical right is defined as involving both "extremist" racist attitudes and a strong commitment to authoritarian government, only a limited majority of Wallace voters fall into that category. The rest were responding to broad populist appeals to the underdog on specific issues. Nevertheless, if one assesses the overall and long-term influence of the national political parties as contributing to the decline in ethnic and racial prejudice, Wallace's ability to mobilize

76. Samuel Flowerman and Marie Jahoda, "Polls on Anti-Semitism," *Commentary* (April 1946): 82–86.

77. Seymour M. Lipset and Earl Raab, *The Politics of Unreason: Right-Wing Extremism in America, 1790–1970* (New York: Harper and Row, 1970), pp. 338–427.

a significant minority of the electorate has constituted a temporary but deep break in this process of social control and one with basic long-term consequences.

If one accepts the reality and relevance of the decline in expressed hostility toward blacks and Jews, it is possible to offer the hypothesis that certain sociological correlates linked to intolerance, such as education, age, income, and the like, which individually and in combination have strong explanatory power, do not supply a penetrating explanation of the trend data. It is unfortunate that the published reports on the sample surveys do not contain sufficient statistical analysis to permit assessing the magnitude of the variance explained by each of these variables. No doubt education is one of the pivotal variables, but it would be an error to reify it and emphasize the popular conclusion that lack of education is *the* key factor in prejudice. It would be especially distorting to assert that increased levels of education will continue to result in a decline in ethnic intolerance.

Instead, a more comprehensive explanation can be linked to the process of social control. Since the early 1940s, social control in the United States has had a positive effect on reducing ethnic intolerance. In particular, the influence of the mass media and the legal system, and the performance of the national political parties, have redefined and restrained the scope of expressed ethnic and racial intolerance. However, the influence of the agencies of social control has not necessarily been accompanied by stronger personal control in this regard. In the absence of strong personal control, the durability of this decline—especially in times of tension and crisis—is problematic. Likewise, a portion of decline in prejudice may not have resulted from effective tolerance, but rather from indifference. Such indifference, it can be argued, is an expression of the fragmentation of social relations and the disarticulation of institutional linkages, including political linkages, and thus it cannot be viewed as effectively strengthening the values of mutual respect required for a democratic society. In other words, the long-term decline in intergroup prejudice is not a clear-cut contribution to social control because it has been accompanied by growth of distrust of government and a weakening of the electoral process.

The moral context of political participation encompasses not only the shift toward more tolerant intergroup attitudes; there is also a more "liberal" trend, in social attitudes in areas such as pornography, abortion, and sexual practices. However, the growth of these liberal sentiments has not been accompanied by a comparable shift toward liberal political symbolism. National surveys have collected the conservative-liberal preferences for the period 1936 to 1974. Of those who expressed a choice, the long-term trend is one of striking stability. In fact, the concentration of conservative attachment rose from 53% in 1936 to 59% in 1974, while the preference for liberal symbolism correspondingly declined. From the 1962 sampling, there appears to have been a

TABLE 4.6 Political Preferences: Conservative versus Liberal, 1936–1974

Year	Conservative	Liberal
1936	53%	47%
1962	51	49
1974*	59	41

*For 1974, the text of the question was "If an arrangement of this kind (two new political parties) were carried out and you had to make a choice, which party would you personally prefer—the conservative party or the liberal party?" Percentages are of those respondents who expressed a preference.

SOURCE: *The Gallup Opinion Index*, report no. 107, May 1974.

slight liberal shift which developed during the Kennedy regime and which was clearly reversed after his assassination. The elements of stability and change are most sharply highlighted when the conservative-liberal preferences are classified by party preference. In 1936, Republicans divided 80% conservative and 20% liberal; in 1974, the division remained essentially the same, 83% conservative and 17% liberal. If there was a shift, it was in the conservative direction. However, for the Democrats, the division was 37% conservative and 63% liberal in 1936. By 1974, those who called themselves Democrats had shifted toward the conservative, with 50% in each category. Moreover, of those who called themselves independents in the 1974 sampling and expressed preferences, the majority described themselves as conservative (54%). No doubt the content and meaning of conservative and liberal have shifted, but the shifts of electoral behavior have occurred in the context of strong stability of "ideological" attitudes.

In partial summary, patterns of political participation as revealed by electoral behavior, and especially when augmented by indicators of mass opinion, serve as measures of the long-term strain and decline in effective social control in the United States at the national or macrosociological level. There is little reason to be satisfied with formulations that focus on concepts such as withdrawal, privatization, or even alienation, for they do not supply a meaningful orientation for the analysis of sociopolitical change. On the contrary, systemic analysis requires a focus on the extent of disarticulation in the social patterns of political participation—on the relations between available means and desired ends.

It will be recalled that the strategy of our analysis is to use social stratification and social participation as the point of entrance for explaining these patterns of political participation and thereby in turn for the analysis of changing patterns of social control. The next step is to examine the master trends in social stratification in the United States.

Five

Social Stratification: Occupation and Welfare

Impact of Advanced Industrialism

In the dominant sociological perspective, the social stratification of an advanced industrial society, as well as its transformation, is best understood in terms of the division of labor; that is, by occupational categories. The intellectual heritage of sociological theory dictates such a research stragegy. Social stratification obviously encompasses the economic, bureaucratic, and cultural forms which regulate relations within and between occupational and professional groups, as well as ownership of and access to property.

From this point of view, the first step in the macrosociology of industrial society is to construct indicators of social strata and social classes based on occupational analysis. These indicators are supplemented by measures of human settlement and urbanization. The obvious, persistent realities of inequality—economic, social, and political—reinforce the vast energy expended in the measurement of occupational structure. The complexity of the subject and its potential for statistical and mathematical analysis also make it one of continued academic fascination.

Disputes among advocates of different "theories of society" and social change often proceed on a level concerned with the appropriate definition of social stratum and social class. In these debates, the concept of occupational groups is the key issue. From these efforts has come the conviction that a central task of contemporary sociology is to construct societal-wide morphologies of social structure—that is, of social classes and strata. To use the critical terminology of Lloyd Fallers, the dominant sociological perspective is that of a "stratigraphic" image of society.[1] The result is the view of social stratification as an analog to geological strata—massive layers in hierarchical array which pervade uniformly throughout the entire society or nation-state.

The limits of this perspective are marked, especially from the point of view of the systemic analysis of social control. Therefore this chapter probes alternative formulations of social stratification—which, of course, must be rooted in the sociological tradition of the division of labor and occupational indicators.[2] To assert that a person's social position is a function of his relations to the mode of production makes sense, but requires a realistic notion of the complexity of this relation. The goal is to "break with" the "stratigraphic" image of social stratification for the more differentiated, multifaceted conception epitomized in the notion of the "ordered social segmentation" of an advanced industrial society.[3] To move in this direction, it is necessary to remember that the division of labor and the resulting occupational structure are more than a manifestation of the productive processes of industrialism. They continue to be grounded in the effect of the collective enterprise of the state, in particular, the effect of military institutions and warmaking, and, in the twentieth century, the consequences of the rise of the welfare state.

For the moment it is necessary to recall the proposition which constitutes the core of our argument. The emergence of "stalemated" parliamentary government under advanced industrial society is in part a result of the changes in the system of socioeconomic stratification generated by the rise of the welfare state. Because of the growth in the proportion of the gross national product distributed by the agencies of government—federal, state, and local—a person's social position is not only a function of his occupational position but also of the claims and expectations he holds for welfare. From the point of view of social control, these changes make it more difficult for the individual citizen to calculate and articulate his enlightened self- and group interest and to formulate his political preference in periodic elections.

1. Lloyd A. Fallers, *Inequality: Social Stratification Reconsidered* (Chicago: University of Chicago Press, 1973), pp. 3–29; see also Talcott Parsons, "An Analytical Approach to the Theory of Social Stratification," *American Journal of Sociology* 45 (May 1940): 841–62.

2. Emile Durkheim, *De la division du travail social* (Paris: Alcan, 1893).

3. The notion of ordered segmentation forcuses on the spatial or social ecological dimensions of social stratification. It is in part derived from the writings of British and American social anthropologists, although equivalent formulations are to be found in the sociological traditions of urban community research.

To probe the relevance of the propositions, it is necessary and makes sense to turn back to the sociological writings of Auguste Comte, Karl Marx, Herbert Spencer, Max Weber, and other nineteenth-century sociologists.[4] Despite their differences in style of analysis and personal goals, they converged in what they believed to be the tension between industrial society and militarism. The forms of militarism have undergone profound change, as have those of industrialism. One cannot speak of the occupational structure and social stratification of an advanced industrial society without confronting the consequences of military institutions and war on the various strata of society. Therefore, in the next chapter, the social stratification of advanced industrial society is seen within this perspective.

The sociological perspective which stressed the interplay and juxtaposition of industrial and military society was first elaborated by Saint-Simon.[5] He was influenced by Condorcet, who had sought to fuse the aspiration of Francis Bacon for a science of society with his own interest in the social and political values of Rousseau and Locke.[6] Saint-Simon emphasized the antithetical character of military society to industrial society and his premature conclusion that, with the growth of industrialism, "military society" would decline and become useless. Subsequently, both Comte and Spencer maintained the distinction between industrial and military society and anticipated a decline in militarism with the growth of industrial organization.[7] This juxtaposition of military institutions and industrialism led Marx also to observe that in the long run industrial forms would make military institutions obsolete. However, for this stage of development, war and proletarian revolution were essential preconditions.[8] While these exercises in "futurology" appear naive in retrospect, they remain pertinent in their focus on the tensions between industrial and military institutions.

However, our task is to examine the results of the preoccupation of sociologists with the long-term development and changes in the division

4. Auguste Comte, *Cours de philosophie positive*, vol. 6 (Paris: Baillière et fils, 1877). Karl Marx, *The German Ideology*, part 1 (for updated translation, see Robert C. Tucker, ed., *The Marx-Engels Reader* (New York: Norton, 1922), pp. 110–64); Herbert Spencer, *Principles of Sociology* (London: Williams and Norgate, 1872).

5. C. Saint-Simon, *L'Industrie, Oeuvres de Saint-Simon*, ed. Barthélemy d'Enfantin (Paris: E. Dentu, 1868), vol. 18.

6. Keith Baker, *Condorcet: From Natural Philosophy to Social Mathematics* (Chicago: University of Chicago Press, 1975.)

7. Spencer, *Principles*, vol. 1, part 2, pp. 576–96.

8. Karl Marx, *The Communist Manifesto*.

of labor produced by advanced industrialism. The continuing analysis of the influence of industrialism on internal social structure has produced descriptive and analytic materials which in effect have undermined the "stratigraphic" image of social stratification. Sociologists have so extensively elaborated and modified their view of the occupational structure that they have begun to undermine the "classic" formulations of societal-wide social strata based on occupational categories.

Social scientists, mainly by means of the data assembled by the U.S. Bureau of the Census for the Bureau of Labor Statistics, have classified occupational categories into social strata and charted the shifts from 1900 to 1970. The results give empirical meaning to the notion of an advanced industrial society.[9] As summarized in Table 5.1, we are dealing with a dramatic decline of the agricultural sector (41.7% of the male working force in 1900 to 8.4% in 1960) and the emergence of a "middle" white-collar stratum (from 17.6% of the male working force in 1900 to 41.2% in 1975). While the "lower" blue-collar stratum expanded (from 40.8% of the male working force in 1900 to 53.9% in 1975), the rate was slower than those of the white-collar stratum and more specifically the "lowest" grouping, laborers, except farm and mine, actually declined (14.7% to 7.4%). These trends contribute to the image and reality of the proliferation of the "middle majority."

This type of occupational categorization gives the impression of the persistence of sharp boundaries between the social strata and the continuing relevance of a "stratigraphic" format. The categories remain the same; the changes which have taken place are in the relative concentration in specific groupings. In reality, the occupational structure during 1900 to 1970 has undergone a process of increased differentiation. The number of readily discernible skill groupings within each of the two major stratum (white-collar–blue-collar) has greatly increased and the boundaries between the strata are less clear-cut.[10]

9. Otis Dudley Duncan, "Occupation Trends and Patterns of Net Mobility in the United States," *Demography* 3, no. 1 (1966): 1–18; Alba M. Edwards, "Comparative Occupation Statistics for the United States, 1870 to 1940," (Washington, D.C.: Bureau of the Census, Government Printing Office, 1943) presents an early analysis of trends in occupational distribution.

10. Gerhard Lenski, "American Social Classes: Statistical Strata or Social Groups?" *American Journal of Sociology* 58 (September 1952): 139–44; Edward O. Laumann, *Prestige and Association in an Urban Community* (Indianapolis: Bobbs-Merrill, 1966); Richard Hamilton, *Class and Politics in the United States* (New York: Wiley, 1972); William Form, *Blue Collar Stratification: Autoworkers in Four Countries* (Princeton: Princeton University Press, 1976); Reeve Vanneman,

TABLE 5.1 Distribution of Male Working Force by Major Occupational Groups, 1900–1975

Major Occupation Group	1900	1910	1920	1930	1940	1950	1960	1970*	1975*
White Collar	*17.6%*	*20.2%*	*21.4%*	*25.2%*	*26.6%*	*30.5%*	*35.4%*	*41.0%*	*41.2%*
Professional, technical, and kindred	3.4	3.5	3.8	4.8	5.8	7.2	10.4	14.0	14.6
Managers, officials, and proprietors, except farm	6.8	7.7	7.8	8.8	8.6	10.5	10.8	14.2	14.0
Sales workers	4.6	4.6	4.5	6.1	6.4	6.4	7.0	5.6	6.1
Clerical and kindred	2.8	4.4	5.3	5.5	5.8	6.4	7.2	7.1	6.5
Blue Collar	*40.8*	*45.0*	*48.1*	*49.9*	*51.7*	*54.5*	*56.2*	*53.7*	*53.9*
Craftsmen, foremen, and kindred	12.6	14.1	16.0	16.2	15.5	19.0	20.6	20.1	20.4
Operatives and kindred	10.4	12.5	14.4	15.3	18.0	20.5	21.3	19.6	17.5
Service workers, including private household	3.1	3.8	3.7	4.8	6.1	6.2	6.5	6.7	8.6
Laborers, except farm and mine	14.7	14.6	14.0	13.6	12.1	8.8	7.8	7.3	7.4
Farm	*41.7*	*34.7*	*30.5*	*24.8*	*21.7*	*14.9*	*8.4*	*5.3*	*4.8*
Farmers and farm managers	23.0	19.7	18.4	15.2	13.3	10.0	5.5	5.3	4.8
Farm laborers and foremen	18.7	15.0	12.1	9.6	8.4	4.9	2.9		
Total	*100.1*	*99.9*	*100.0*	*99.9*	*100.0*	*99.9*	*100.0*	*100.0*	*99.9*

*Data not strictly comparable with earlier years due to reclassification of census occupations.

SOURCE: Otis Dudley Duncan, "Occupation Trends and Patterns of Net Mobility in the United States," *Demography* 3 (1966): 1–18, tables 1–5, for years 1900 to 1960; for 1970 and 1975 *Statistical Abstracts*, and U.S. Bureau of Labor Statistics, *Employment and Earnings*.

Of course, the ordering from the top to the bottom is systematically related to income and education, but two changes can be noted. The disparity between income and education is considerable and has probably increased; the number of occupations which do not fit directly into a continuous hierarchy is noteworthy and has probably increased.[11] The consequence is that the boundaries between the white-collar and blue-collar strata are not sharply discernible and represent a high degree of arbitrary designation. The same holds true for the more specific occupation groupings within the two strata. The notion of ordered social segmentation becomes more applicable and relevant to describe the realities of social stratification.

In addition, a "stratigraphic" format has been associated with a pyramidal structure, but the movement from industrialism to advanced industrialism transforms this pattern to more of a "flask"-shaped labor force. This transformation implies a greater degree of complexity than that encompassed by the "stratigraphic" model. The full scope of the transformation becomes clear when Table 5.1 is examined. By 1900 the pyramidal occupational structure had a relatively narrow base; by 1960 the flasklike bulge was pronounced.

The increased magnitude in the labor force of white-collar occupations with a more complex division of labor and higher skill level, has led to the concept "postindustrial society" to describe the profound alteration in the social stratification. However, "postindustrial society" has not been particularly useful in breaking away from stratigraphic imagery.[12] At the root of this concept is a technological determinism which has altered the occupational structure. If one had to select a brand of "traditional" determinism, this technological perspective has advantages over its competitors, but the present maturity of sociology has rendered such a choice unnecessary.

From the point of view of postindustrial society, the occupational structure is the key to social structure—and changes in the occupational

"The Occupational Composition of American Classes: Results from Cluster Analysis," *American Journal of Sociology* 82 (January 1977): 783–807.

11. The notion of status crystallization has been coined to handle such inconsistencies; see especially Gerhard Lenski, "Status Crystallization: A Non-Vertical Dimension of Social Status," *American Sociological Review* 19 (August 1954): 405–13; Gerhard Lenski, "Social Participation and Status Crystallization," *American Sociological Review* 21 (August 1956): 458:64.

12. Daniel Bell, *The Coming of Post-Industrial Society: A Venture in Social Forecasting* (New York: Basic, 1973). For a more precise and succinct statement of his argument, see Daniel Bell, "Post-Industrial Society: Technocracy and Politics," *Survey* 17, no. 78 (1971): 1–24.

structure are decisive in social and political change. Technology transforms the elite structure; businessmen as entrepreneurs give way to new men of power. Following James Burnham's *Managerial Revolution* and C. W. Mills's *Power Elite*, Daniel Bell has argued that, in a postindustrial society, the men of power are the scientists, engineers, information specialists, and the like.[13]

This line of reasoning rests on the analysis of shifts in the occupational structure as formulated by Colin Clark, namely, shifts from primary and secondary sectors to secondary and tertiary ones.[14] Bell seeks to extend Clark's treatment by identifying tertiary (transport, recreation), quaternary (trade, finance, insurance, and real estate), and quinary (health, education, research, and government) sectors. This classification is rather arbitrary and not likely to provide an effective approach to the classification of census data. The change in the occupational slope is epitomized by the shift from that of the semiskilled worker and engineer in industrial society to that of the professional and technical scientist in postindustrial society. The master trend is toward more capital-intensive technology.

Such a view of social stratification has two chief difficulties. First, in many sectors the economic limits of capital-intensive technology have been or are being reached, particularly in specific service areas, such as education, health, and welfare enterprises. Here change and adaptation require new forms of labor-intensive inputs (rather than science-based technology) for greater "human" returns. Second, the postindustrial society arguments rest on the belief that the shift from primary to secondary to "tertiary," "quaternary," and "quinary" sectors—that is, from the production of goods to that of services—progressively eliminates "labor." It has underemphasized the extent to which the service sector merely restructures work, with all its corresponding discontents. For example, the sorting rooms of the parcel post depots of the United States Post Office are industrial types of establishments. Men and women work with less fatigue, but the form of technology and task elaboration is essentially assembly-line production. This format is found in the growing areas of food service, health facilities, maintenance work,

13. James Burnham, *Managerial Revolution* (Bloomington: Indiana University Press, 1960); C. W. Mills, *The Power Elite* (New York: Oxford University Press, 1956).

14. Colin Clark, *The Conditions of Economic Progress*, 3d ed., largely rewritten (London: Macmillan; New York: St. Martin's Press, 1957). See also Victor R. Fuchs, *The Service Economy* (New York: Columbia University Press, 1968).

and even record keeping and data processing, especially in banking and commerce. The knowledge basis of the control systems in these institutions hardly eliminates work. While the size of the industrial labor force does not increase, the characteristics of industrial assembly work spill over into the tertiary sector. One noteworthy change in the conditions of work under advanced industrialism is that employees engaged in service tasks are not employed as individuals or in small establishments; they are organized into massive hierarchical organizations.

In the industrial sector, and more and more in the service sectors, although physical strain and fatigue in the classic sense have been reduced, the realities of work dissatisfaction remain immense.[15] "Industrial sabotage" refers to the expression of opposition to the existing organization and the control of work procedure; and there are in the white-collar sector equivalent forms of organizational resistance, if not sabotage. Trade union organization represents a demand for higher wages and a response to the discontent with the conditions of work, including the conditions of work in service and the tertiary sector. Absenteeism is widespread; corruption is especially extensive in the middle and upper levels, regardless of the emergence of new information-control systems. Continuity rather than fundamental transformation in patterns and organization of work is operative. There is little basis for speaking of postindustrial society; more accurately, in the period under consideration, U.S. society has shifted from an industrialized to an advanced industrial society.

In an advanced industrial society, men and women think of themselves as members of skill and professional groups rather than as affiliates of broad social strata or social classes. Of course, occupation—skill and professional status or the lack of them—serves as one shorthand notation of social position in society. But the details of occupation, even the refined details, supply only a partial basis for the analysis of effective authority, because the refinement of the division of labor has been accompanied by an elaboration of bureaucratic structures within and between occupational and skill groups. This is the sociological message from Max Weber to Karl Mannheim to Ralf Dahrendorf.[16] Occupa-

15. Department of Health, Education, and Welfare, *Work in America* (Cambridge: MIT Press, 1972).

16. Max Weber, "Wirtschaft und Gesellschaft," in *Grundriss der Sozialoekonomik*, 2: 650–78; Karl Mannheim, *Man and Society in an Age of Reconstruction* (New York: Harcourt, Brace, 1940); Ralf Dahrendorf, *Class and Class Conflict in Industrial Society* (Stanford: Stanford University Press, 1959).

tional analysis is not limited to static elements in the division of labor, but includes institutionalized processes for acquiring, exercising, and regulating various levels of skill.

The empirical tasks of research into social stratification have been summarized by Harold Wilensky: "With advancing industrialism and urbanism traditional indices of class, present income and occupational category no longer serve to distinguish life styles and mass political attitudes and behavior."[17] An increasing focus on social mobility—upward, downward, and in all its variant forms—is required to amplify the stratigraphic model of social hierarchies.[18] Simple, crude measures of movement from "blue collar" to "white collar" or vice versa do not reflect the complexity of social mobility, especially career mobility. Career involves variation in education—the prestige of the institution, the content of the educational experience, and the details of job assignment and the potentials for ascent. In describing careers and shifts in job, it is possible to speak of orderly versus disorganized careers, and of dead-end jobs versus assignments with modest or with high career potentials. These are essential aspects of social stratification.[19]

Closely related is another major limitation in the stratigraphic model, namely, its inability to capture the multiple bases of social differentiation. An industrial society separates work from family and community; this observation may well be the enduring relevance of Karl Marx's sociological analysis. The social hierarchies of work and of family and community are intertwined, but with important elements of disarticulation. In effect, to separate work from residential community attenuates but does not extinguish the network of localistic social relations and the

17. Harold Wilensky, "Work Careers and Social Integration," *International Social Science Journal* 2 (1960): 543–74; Harold Wilensky, "Class, Class Consciousness and American Voters," in William Haber, ed., *Labor in a Changing America* (New York: Basic, 1966), pp. 12–28; James Alden Barber, Jr., *Social Mobility and Voting Behavior* (Chicago: Rand McNally, 1970); Kenneth Thompson, "Upward Social Mobility and Political Orientations," *American Sociological Review* 36 (April 1971): 223–35. For an alternative approach to these issues see Norbert Wiley, "America's Unique Class Politics: The Interplay of the Labor, Credit and Commodity Markets," *American Sociological Review* 32 (August 1967): 531–41.

18. Pitirim Sorokin, *Social Mobility* (New York: Harper, 1927).

19. Everett C. Hughes, "Institutional Office and the Person," *American Journal of Sociology* 43 (November 1937): 404–13. Students of occupational and professional stratification must confront such findings as those reported by the U.S. Department of Labor, Bureau of Labor Statistics, that almost one-third of members of the labor force have transferred to a different detailed occupation from 1965 to 1970; Dixie Sommers and Alan Eck, "Occupational Mobility in the American Labor Force," *Monthly Labor Review* 100 (January 1977): 3–19.

primordial attachments which are nourished, fashioned, and developed in urban settlements, and reinforced by voluntary associations and the mass media.[20] While the functions of local residential communities become more specialized, the consequences of these territorial attachments are not merely derivations of "social class." (The linkages between community structure and social control will be explored in chap. 8.)

Of course, there were pioneers in sociology—Frederic LePlay, Charles Booth, or W. I. Thomas—who tried to connect their analysis of industrial society with the empirical realities and who were aware that occupational and "social class" interests were fundamentally mediated by communal and primordial attachments, racial, religious, ethnic, national, or primarily local.[21] In effect, they and their disciples never accepted the stratigraphic definition of social structure.

The stratigraphic image of social structure, with its common-sense focus on occupation, does not adequately integrate the manifold and separate bases of social differentiation. With the advent of advanced industrialism, age paradoxically became more and more a societal-wide dimension of self-identification and collective attachment which penetrates the basic mechanisms of social control.[22] Likewise, under advanced industrialism the ascriptive characteristics of race and sex emerge as profound sociopolitical issues, in good measure because they produce inequality in social stratification and economic reward among minority-group members and women who have the required educational and skill levels. William Wilson, in *The Declining Significance of Race*, has summarized the research data and documentation on the occupational stratification of blacks.[23]

20. Talcott Parsons, "Age and Sex in the Social Structure of the United States," *American Sociological Review* 7 (October 1942): 604–16.

21. Frederic Le Play, *Les ouvriers européens*, 2d ed., 6 vols. (Tours: Mane, 1877–1879); Charles Booth, *Life and Labour of the People in London*, 2d ed., 9 vols. (London: Macmillan, 1882–1897); W. I. Thomas with Florian Znaniecki, *The Polish Peasant in Europe and America*, 5 vols. (Boston: Richard G. Badger, 1918–1920) (Vols. 1 and 2 originally published by the University of Chicago Press, 1918).

22. Edward A. Shils, "Primordial, Personal, Sacred and Civil Ties," *British Journal of Sociology* 8 (June 1957); Gerald Suttles, *The Social Construction of Communities* (Chicago: University of Chicago Press, 1972).

23. William Wilson, *The Declining Significance of Race: Blacks and Changing American Institutions* (Chicago: University of Chicago Press, 1978); see also Stanley H. Masters, *Black-White Income Differentials: Empirical Studies and Policy Implications* (New York: Academic Press, 1975); David L. Featherman and Robert M. Hauser, "Changes in the Socio-economic Stratification of the Races,

The income gap for better educated—in particular college graduates—blacks declined in 1960–1975. But for those blacks with limited education, the differential persisted and in certain categories has increased. The narrowing of income differentials for better educated women has been gradual, but these economic differentials for the female group as a whole have resisted change and have been at points enlarged.[24] The socioeconomic position of women is related to their rapid increase in the labor market after 1970 as older women have sought employment; there has also been a sharp increase in female heads of household. The number of women in the labor force has doubled between 1950 and 1974. However, the median weekly earnings of women in full-time jobs in 1974 were about 60% of those of men. For "year-round full-time" workers, women's median annual earnings were 57% of men's—a ratio that ranged from 38% for sales workers to 64% for professional-technical workers.

Older, better educated women compete successfully in the service sector with younger black men of modest education. Again, the stratigraphic hierarchy is less descriptive of the more differentiated occupational competition between ordered social segments.

In fact, the student of social stratification must recognize the full range of criteria by which groups are differentiated in an advanced industrial society. In the United States in 1976, 9.6% of the population had a handicap which resulted in a major limitation of their activities.[25] Medical progress has meant an increase in the number of handicapped persons, since effective treatment can be given to larger numbers of industrial and traffic accident victims and in general the lives of handicapped persons can be prolonged. Their handicaps affect their earning capacity, contribute to a sense of group identity, and serve as the basis of collective political action.

While inequality remains a dominant characteristic of an advanced industrial society, broad socioeconomic strata are less adequate as corre-

1962–1973," *American Journal of Sociology* 82 (November 1976): 621–51; Reynolds Farley, "Trends in Racial Inequalities: Have the Gains of the 1960s Disappeared in the 1970s?" *American Sociological Review* 42 (April 1977): 189–208.

24. James A. Sweet, *Women in the Labor Force* (New York: Academic Press, 1973); David L. Featherman and Robert M. Hauser, "Sexual Inequality and Socioeconomic Achievement in the United States, 1962–1973," *American Sociological Review* 41 (June 1976): pp. 462–83; Donald J. Treiman and Kermit Terrell, "Women, Work and Wages—Trends in the Female Occupational Structure," in Kenneth Land and Seymour Spilerman, eds., *Social Indicator Models* (New York: Russell Sage Foundation, 1975), pp. 157–200.

25. U.S. Center for Health Statistics, Vital and Health Statistics, sec. 10, no. 96.

lates of sociopolitical behavior than a combination of social origin, education, and career, plus elements of social differentiation such as sex, age, and community attachments (including ethnic-religious identification). There is every reason to substitute for the stratigraphic image or to supplement it with a perspective of the ordered social segments if one seeks to explore political perspective and the resulting patterns of social control. When the idea of ordered social segments is applied, the distinction needs to be made between the bureaucratic occupation setting and the primordial communal affiliations of the individual and his household.

However, the most critical assessment of the conventional analysis of stratigraphic perspective does not derive from empirical critiques, but from an assessment of the intellectual history and political usage of the inherent terms of reference. As is often the case in social-science analysis, the vitality of a frame of reference has its own momentum—or inertia, if you will—which resists scrutiny because it imposes a sense of order on the human environment. Only a direct attack on the origins—both intellectual and political—can overcome such rigidities. Thus the "stratigraphic" approach to social structure in language and political consequences is a modern invention. Its limitations result in part from the fact that it has served both as a device for sociological analysis and as a rhetorical basis for political activity. And it is very difficult to separate the two.

This argument, which reflects the analysis presented by Lloyd Fallers, focuses on the historical relevance and political utility of appeals in the name of social class as a strategy in the struggle and pursuit of political democracy and subsequently in its subversion. We are speaking of the experiences of Western parliamentary systems and their emergence before advanced industrialism. For this historical context, the claim is made that the "stratigraphic" mode was the appropriate language of political appeals during the "age of democratic revolutions."

No doubt the experiences of the Greek city-states and of the early Roman Republic are relevant to this intellectual and political heritage. The particular accomplishments of city-states of Italy, the Hanseatic League, and the record of the Netherlands are germane for such analysis.[26] But the focus at this point is on the emergence of the nation-state, as epitomized by the English, American, and French revolutions, during

26. Henry Kamen, *The Iron Century: Social Change in Europe, 1550–1660* (London: Weidenfeld and Nicolson, 1971).

the period in which national revolutions emerged as the precondition for the development of parliamentary political regimes—a historical sequence of most limited frequency. My reading of the range of comparative historical and macrosociological treatises (in particular R. R. Palmer, *The Age of Democratic Revolution* and Barrington Moore, Jr., *Social Origins of Dictatorship and Democracy*) leads to the necessity of confronting this basic issue.[27] The emergence of these parliamentary regimes, while they are linked to the expansion of the middle class, cannot be accounted for in the conventional terms of social-stratification patterns, either by comparisons with those industrializing nation-states which did not develop parliamentary institutions or by comparisons of the timing and format of those which did develop such political agencies. To speak of the emergence of Western representative institutions in the eighteenth and nineteenth centuries involves reference to the content and form of ideological movements and political leadership. Of the elements involved, two are crucial. First is the political definition offered by the "revolutionaries" to justify the use of force and the political meaning they imposed on citizen participation in military institutions. (These elements are examined in chap. 6.) Second, the use of social class appeals creates a political system for containing communal and primordial differences, for expanding political participation, and for creating political formulas for handling competing economic interests by balancing them or at least modulating them by means of limited parliamentary intervention.[28]

Terms such as "class" and "stratum" are modern constructs even in the West. It is extremely important that the *Shorter Oxford English Dictionary* (third edition) gives 1772 as the date of first occurrence for "class" as in the social layer sense. The more technocratic term "social stratum" apparently did not appear until as late as 1902. How were the various forms of inequality described before these terms were used?

Available scholarship underlines that forms of inequality were referred to and debated in a medieval context. This meant that the debate about the nature of the church in relation to the evolving secular state

27. R. R. Palmer, *The Age of Democratic Revolution: A Political History of Europe and America*, 1760–1800, 2 vols. (Princeton: Princeton University Press, 1970); Barrington Moore, Jr., *Social Origins of Dictatorship and Democracy* (Boston: Beacon, 1966).

28. For a description of the expansion of mass political participation, see Reinhard Bendix, *Nation-Building and Citizenship: Studies of Our Changing Social Order* (New York: Wiley, 1964); Stein Rokkan, *Citizens, Elections, Parties* (Oslo: Universitets forlaget, 1970), especially chap. 1.

and associated institutions was overriding; equality had to do with the religious and the secular. At the same time, the language of feudalism created an organic conception of society—a collection of orders and estates; and the system of subinfeudation and localism before the emergence of a centralized monarchy and the nation-state rejected the notion of societal-wide strata.[29]

The emergence of parliamentary political regimes rested on the exclusion of particular groups, and on the partial inclusion and participation of others. The exclusion and containment of specific groups assisted in maintaining the political and economic advantages of traditional feudal elements. These exclusionary practices in retrospect highlight the gradualism in the process of political institution building; but the gradualism cannot obscure the transformation in political authority and power which the "age of democratic revolution" produced. Legitimate sovereignty came to be lodged in a set of secular institutions which permitted competitive national elections; elections were the basic instrument both for generating consent and for exercising political power.

From the point of view of strengthening social control, both nationalism and parliamentary regimes required extensive and expanding reliance of universalist principles. The political achievement of nation building in Western industrializing societies was the formula that was used to extend and to "universalize" political participation. It was to draw and develop a political construct—the citizen; symbolized and sloganized by the notion of "one man, one vote." The notion of the citizen avoided formalizing political power in terms of primordial and communal groups, an approach which would have been and has been fatal. Nor was political participation formalized in terms of corporate economic groups, but in terms of individual persons. Of course, the citizen's effective power was a function of his position in the social structure; and explicit property requirements set the standard for the extension of the franchise. But the idea of citizen serves to contain, limit, and make manageable the political issues generated by economic differences.

The citizen was essentially a person who had an occupation; this tended to exclude the economically marginal and women. But it meant that citizens came to think of themselves and to be appealed to in terms of the occupational social strata with which they were affiliated. Politi-

29. Marc Bloch, *Feudal Society* (Chicago: University of Chicago Press, 1961).

cal activists who sought to aggregate power came more and more to emphasize the universality of social status.

The language of the students of society both reflected and influenced this political process. The designation of the citizenry as members of occupationally based social classes served ideological and political functions which were initially compatible and conducive to parliamentary regimes. It was an effective basis for enlarging the citizenry and the electorate. It was, in fact, the most universal criterion and one that could be effectively used. But it could also be manipulated so that "paupers" and persons with very small incomes could be excluded. Also, it created a balance of political elements which expanded and diffused political power. In the main, it initially assisted those who came to think of themselves as members of the middle stratum in their conflicts with the older upper status groups. Subsequently, it supplied the basis for alliances between the middle-income skill groups and the lower-income labor groupings. In addition, the political appeals that were generated and the self-conceptions of social class that were implanted in the citizenry could, in varying degrees, operate without producing political divisions that were irreconcilable by parliamentary procedures. Throughout the nineteenth century, Great Britain escaped such divisions by expanding the franchise; in the United States the issue of slavery presented such a cleavage. In France, social class based demands interrupted the stability and legitimacy of parliamentary institutions, but never undermined them. Prussia and modern Germany as nation-states represent one of the variants of paths toward industrialism, in which parliamentary institutions failed to take hold until the onset of advanced industrialism and then in good measure because they were externally imposed.

In part, this argument rests on the observation that the "stratigraphic" model has greater plausibility in the nineteenth century than in the twentieth century, although even for the earlier period it failed to capture the realities of the interplay of the division of labor and the other bases of social differentiation. The language of social class was most effective as a political strategy in developing industrialism in the Western mode. While the apparatus of the central region and local government operated to the advantage of particular elite groups, the legislative organs of government adapted to the changing demands of emerging groups. The rise in the standard of living was a result of developments in the "private sector." Thus the economic tasks assigned to parliamentary institutions were manageable by the available political mechanisms of debate and bargaining. These economic tasks were more regulative than distributive of the results of economic enterprise. But with the extension of the welfare state, especially after World War I and the Great Depression, the tasks of the legislative arena changed. The very notion of a person and his household's position in the social structure and their relation to the means of production altered fundamentally and, as shall be argued, the relevance of stratigraphic notion of social structure became attenuated.

Distribution of Welfare Claims

"Welfare state" here refers to governmental practices of allocating at least 8% to 10% of the gross national product to welfare, i.e., public expenditures for health, education, income maintenance (including deferred income), and community development (including housing). These allocations can take the form of monetary transfers, expenditures for services, and in-kind benefits (for example, food stamps, public housing). By 1935, the United States had almost reached this level; by 1975, the percentage was approximately 20%.

The "welfare state" and welfare expenditures are not synonymous. The welfare state rests on the political assumption that the well-being of its citizens is enhanced not only by allocations generated from their occupations and the marketplace but also from grants regulated by the central government. The welfare state involves at least two additional elements. Under the welfare state, the extent and nature of welfare expenditures are conditioned decisively by parliamentary regimes; that is, they reflect political demands and consent, and not authoritarian decisions. Second, it is accepted as legitimate for the political system to intervene through governmental institutions in order to assist its citizens in the pursuit of their personal and "household" goals.

The welfare state rests on the availability of some form of economic surplus, or economic profit—individual or collective—that can be reallocated in terms of a set of moral principles. The welfare state requires that industrial and commercial enterprise create a profit—an economic surplus—that supplies the material basis of welfare.

Economists speak of a system of national accounts to describe the total national economy. National accounts are the total sum of the economic transactions in both private and public sectors. The new terminology does not obscure the fact that the system of national accounts requires some conception of profit compatible with the various traditions of economic thinking. In fact, it makes little difference whether one draws on classic economic formulations or on those specifically offered by Karl Marx. One can speak in terms of either the labor theory of value or of the exchange theory of value. Industrial and commercial enterprises generate profit and an economic surplus, which can be used for social welfare purposes. The allocation of economic surplus is central to Marx's perspective, since it reflects the social relations of society and influences the patterns of social conflict. In simple terms, "capitalist" societies produce surplus profit that cannot be utilized effectively for the workers' welfare. Instead, surplus profit produces disruption because of the pressure for imperialist expansion and imperialist war—both of which create the conditions for political conflict and the transformation of capitalism to socialism and socialism into communism.

The inability of a "capitalist" society to make meaningful use of its economic profits leads to social misery, depressions, and imperialist wars, it is argued from this point of view. The contrary assumption seems more pertinent. Societal trends and the processes of politics have produced a "permanent" system of deficit government spending. Whether one uses a fiscalist or a monetarist point of view, or both, chronic inflation and persistent high levels of unemployment have come to be called by economists "stagflation." The increase in the demand for social welfare with effective allocation of economic resources makes political management of the welfare state very difficult and in effect distorts its fundamental goals.

The national economy and the pattern of national accounts for advanced industrial societies under parliamentary regimes have been modified by the welfare state.[30] Expenditures for social welfare have increased at a rate greater than that of the gross national product, and they have overtaken military expenditures in the United States. Our first step is to examine the growth in welfare expenditures from 1929 to 1974 in Table 5.2. Total expenditures in constant 1974 prices rose from over $10.9 billion to $241.7 billion from 1929 to 1974. In per capita terms, the growth was from $88 in 1929 to $1,125 in 1974; the level of expenditures more than doubled in the decade since 1965. When

30. For the historical background of public expenditures before the expansion of welfare allocations, see Richard Musgrave and J. M. Culberston, "The Growth of Public Expenditures in the United States, 1890–1948" *National Tax Journal* (June 1953): 97–115.

the effect of social welfare expenditures on social stratification and on social control is analyzed, the assumption is warranted that progressively the relative availability of economic resources to support the development and maintenance of welfare services has declined. In fact, the trend has been toward creating a "negative" surplus in Western industrialized societies.

TABLE 5.2 Trends in Welfare Expenditures, 1929–1974
Total and per capita social welfare expenditures under public programs in the United States in 1974 prices

	Constant Fiscal Year 1974 Prices		
	Total Social Welfare Expenditures		Implicit Price Deflators (1974–100)
Fiscal Year	Amount (in millions)	Per Capita	
1929	$ 10,882.4	$ 88.83	36.0
1950	44,107.0	287.31	53.1
1955	53,916.7	322.82	60.3
1960	78,237.6	428.56	66.6
1965	109,118.6	554.82	70.5
1970	176,472.6	850.64	82.5
1971	199,453.2	951.87	86.0
1972	216,044.3	1,021.08	88.8
1973	232,410.9	1,089.93	91.9
1974	241,736.9	1,125.59	100.0

Source: *Social Security Bulletin* (Washington: GPO, Jan. 1975) p. 10.

To what extent do social welfare expenditures account for a rising fraction of the gross national product and total government expenditures (Table 5.3)? Welfare expenditures as a fraction of the GNP have risen steadily with the exception of the years during World War II. In 1935, they constituted 9.5% of the GNP; by 1973, the figure was 17.6%. Welfare expenditures also can be measured as a fraction of total governmental expenditures. On the basis of this measure, there has also been an increase, but in a more varied pattern. By 1935, welfare expenditures in the Great Depression rose to 48.6% of total government expenditures. In the post–World War II (1955) economic prosperity, the figure dropped to 32.7%, but it rose steadily, so that in 1973, for federal, state, and local levels, it reached 53%. The growth of welfare expenditures varies by type of program. On a per capita basis, income maintenance and social security programs expanded approximately 40 times during the period 1935 to 1973; health programs, 23 times; educa-

TABLE 5.3 Social Welfare Expenditures under Public Programs, 1935–1974 (In millions of dollars, except for percentage figures)

Year	Total Social Welfare*	Social Insurance*	Public Aid	Health and Medical Programs	Veterans Programs	Education	Housing	Other Social Welfare Programs	All Health and Medical Care†	Total Social Welfare as Percent of: GNP	Total Social Welfare as Percent of: Government Expenditures For All Purposes*
1935	6,548	406	2,998	427	597	2,008	13	99	543	9.5	48.6
1940	8,795	1,272	3,597	616	629	2,561	4	116	782	9.2	49.0
1945	9,205	1,409	1,031	2,354	1,126	3,076	11	198	2,579	4.4	8.4
1950	23,508	4,947	2,496	2,064	6,866	6,674	15	448	3,065	8.9	37.6
1955	32,640	9,835	3,003	3,103	4,834	11,157	89	619	4,421	8.6	32.7
1960	52,293	19,307	4,101	4,464	5,479	17,626	177	1,139	6,395	10.6	38.0
1965	77,175	28,123	6,283	6,246	6,031	28,108	318	2,066	9,535	11.8	42.4
1967	99,710	37,339	8,811	7,628	6,898	35,808	378	2,848	15,823	12.9	42.4
1968	113,840	42,740	11,092	8,459	7,247	40,590	428	3,285	20,039	13.8	43.2
1969	127,741	48,772	13,439	9,004	7,934	44,283	518	3,792	22,934	14.2	44.9
1970	145,894	54,676	16,488	9,753	9,018	50,848	701	4,408	25,232	15.3	47.8
1971	171,901	66,304	21,304	10,800	10,396	56,885	1,047	5,075	28,583	17.0	51.8
1972	192,749	74,715	26,092	12,771	11,465	60,741	1,396	5,569	33,392	17.5	53.4
1973	214,179	86,118	28,697	12,640	12,952	65,258	2,180	6,335	35,819	17.5	55.2
1974 (prel.)	242,386	98,502	33,628	14,054	13,923	72,763	2,582	6,934	41,311	18.0	55.8

*Although total social welfare and social insurance expenditures include that part of workmen's compensation and temporary disability insurance payments made through private insurance carriers and self-insurers, such private payments have been omitted in computing percentages relating to all government expenditures.

†Combines health and medical programs with medical services provided in connection with social insurance, public aid, veterans and other social welfare programs.

SOURCE: *Statistical Abstracts of the United States* (Washington: GPO, 1974), p. 273.

tion, 20 times; and veterans' benefits, 12 times. As of 1976, income maintenance and social security payments have come to constitute the largest segment of social welfare expenditures, having reached over $155 billion annually. These data indicate that since 1955, expenditures for social welfare have been less and less the result of a "Keynesian" policy designed for economic expansion. Instead, the logic of social welfare expenditures has become more and more a system of self-sustaining expansion in response to the social and political definitions of welfare requirements. The careful comparison of the growth of selected welfare expenditures from 1960 to 1970 prepared by Kirsten Grønbjerg emphasizes that political factors were as important as economic need.[31]

The growth of welfare expenditures in the United States has been accompanied by the following economic trends. One, after 1955, the United States federal government entered a period of long-term budget deficit spending. From the Korean War until 1975, during four years there was a budget surplus ($10.8 billion), while in 18 years there was a total budget deficit ($182 billion). Moreover, for the single fiscal year 1976, a deficit of $68 billion was constructed, which increased the total negative balance for 1955 to 1976 by 27%. The growth of state government indebtedness has also been marked during 1955 to 1975. The total outstanding state debt, not including local units, stood at $18.5 billion in 1960 and reached $47.9 billion in 1970.

Two, the United States has not been able to sustain a long-term growth rate of 3%, which is considered standard for a welfare state concerned with minimum standards of living, greater social equality, and the increase in the older, dependent segment of the population. For 1945–1975, in the United States, the overall rate of economic growth has been somewhat higher than that of Great Britain, but below that of Germany, France, and Italy.

Three, "stagflation" has produced chronic inflation, especially if one applies the criterion of more than 5% annual increase in the consumer price index. For the United States, increases in the consumer price index of more than 5% were recorded in 1969 (5.3%) and 1970 (5.9%). The impact was decisively registered in 1973, since the percent increase was 6.2% in 1974, when it reached 11.0% and remained at 8.5% for 1975. There are differences in the extent to which the new economics is operative in the major industrialized nations. For example,

31. Kirsten A. Grønbjerg, *Mass Society and the Extension of Welfare, 1960–1970*, (Chicago: University of Chicago Press, 1976).

in 1973 the rate of inflation in Germany was 6.5%; in France and Italy it was markedly higher, over 10%; and in Great Britain it exceeded 20%.

Four, the growth in welfare expenditures has been accompanied for the United States by a constriction in the pattern of capital accumulation. From 1960 to 1973, in the United States national output devoted to fixed investment averaged 17.5%. This was lower than in Japan, West Germany, and France, which had high percentages (24% or more), and below even that in Canada, Italy, and Great Britain, which had low investment percentages.

The effects of increased welfare expenditures and the associated economic trends are pervasive on the pattern of social stratification, although the precise details and consequences are very difficult to identify. The social incidence of the welfare system varies widely. The welfare state is based on the assumption that the lowest social stratum requires additional resources. The emergence of the welfare state has produced a system whose official goal is "assisting" those at the bottom of the social structure. But the long-term trend has been one in which there has been a diffusion of social welfare upward and throughout the social structure. The upward direction of welfare expenditures has been increased by the regressive character of social security taxes. A person who earned $16,500 in 1976 paid 5.85% of his income in social security taxes, while a person who earned $100,000 contributed less than 1%. For millions of workers, social security taxes exceeded income taxes.

The classic question, "What are the consequences of the mode of production on the social structure?" is valid to the extent that it encompasses the consequences of the social welfare system. The normative rationale of social welfare is based on aspirations for universal treatment and standards. Thus, as such, welfare operates in direct opposition to the particular rewards of occupation and work systems of exchange. As a result, efforts are constantly being made to link welfare payments for income maintenance to work and work incentives; but this linkage is most difficult to achieve. Welfare payments are designed not only for the lowest social stratum but also to deal with the life problems of the population of an advanced industrial society in which inequality is linked to race, sex, age, family composition, and medical and mental health.

The fundamental question is the extent to which social welfare programs and the transfer payments which they generate have redistributed income. The available research answers are not clean-cut or conclusive. (Of course, the redistribution of wealth depends as well on the system of taxation.) There is research by Herman Miller that focuses on the conclusion that, during the expansion of the welfare state under the New Deal and throughout World War II, income became more equally distributed and there was also a gradual reduction of the population below the imputed poverty line.[32] Since 1950 substantial and continued redistributions of income have not occurred. However, other studies, especially those by Robert J. Lampman and Gabriel Kolko, are critical of these conclusions and emphasize the persistence of inequality.[33] A conference of economic experts sponsored by the Institute for Research on Poverty, University of Wisconsin in 1976 highlighted the extent of disagreement.[34]

Moreover, the question of the extent to which the pattern of income distribution reflected the expansion of employment and increased level of economic productivity versus the effect of social welfare legislation remains unanswered, and the experts are divided. Some economists emphasize that the growing welfare transfer payments have not resulted in a greater degree of income equality, especially for the period 1960–1970.[35] Others point to some contributions to income equality by welfare expenditures.[36] (The stream of transfer income payments rose from $28.5 billion in 1950 to $158.8 billion in 1975.) Finally, the pattern of

32. Herman Miller, *Income Distribution in the United States* (Washington: Department of Commerce, Bureau of the Census, 1966); Lee Soltow, ed., *Six Papers on the Size Distribution of Wealth and Income* (New York: Columbia University Press, 1969); Daniel B. Radner and John C. Hinrichs, "Size Distribution of Income in 1964, 1970, and 1971," *Survey of Current Business* 54 (October 1974): 19–31; Congressional Budget Office, "Poverty Status of Families Under Alternative Definition of Income," Background Paper no. 17, January 13, 1977. The context for assessing these trends is by cross-national comparisons. Kuznets has shown that there is greater income inequality in underdeveloped than in developed nations; Simon Kuznets "Quantitative Aspects of the Economic Growth of Nations, VIII, Distribution of Income by Size," *Supplement to Economic Development and Cultural Change*, vol. 11 (January 1963).

33. Robert J. Lampman, *The Share of Top Wealth Holders in National Wealth 1922–1956* (Princeton: Princeton University Press, 1962); Robert J. Lampman, *Ends and Means of Reducing Income Poverty* (Chicago: Markham, 1971); Gabriel Kolko, *Wealth and Power in America: An Analysis of Social Class and Income Distribution* (New York: Praeger, 1962); See also James N. Morgan et al. *Income and Welfare in the U.S.: A Study* (New York: McGraw Hill, 1962).

34. Sheldon Danizer, "Trends in Economic Inequality in the U.S. since World War II: A Conference," *Focus* 1 (1976–1977): 9–12.

35. Morgan Reynolds and Eugene Smolensky, "The Post-FISC Distribution: 1961 and 1970 Compared," *National Tax Journal* 27 (December 1974): 515–30.

36. Robert D. Plotnick and Felicity Skidmore, *Progress against Poverty: Review of 1964–1974* (New York: Academic Press, 1975).

income distribution could and would have been more unequal without such increased transfers.[37]

But the influence of the welfare state on social structure requires a broader approach than the assessment of the degree of equality of disposable income for households. In addition to money transfers, the welfare state renders direct services or extends benefits at reduced costs. We are particularly interested in those which extend beyond the lower income groups, particularly in the areas of housing, higher education, and medical services.

One of the most important mechanisms for creating new economic equities has been the widespread diffusion of homeownership under extensive mortgage assistance that started after World War I and expanded after World War II.[38] Homeownership penetrates deeply into modest and low income families (except for the very lowest, it is not strongly related to family income). Homeownership by modest and middle income families has been facilitated by government-subsidized insurance of mortgages, and low-interest federal- and state-insured veterans' mortgages, which are a form of social welfare that has extended upwardly throughout the social structure.

The dispersion of welfare allocations received impetus from the extension of higher education. Expenditures for education have produced high rates of economic return and have influenced the pattern of social mobility. Since 1945, there has been massive extension of public support for education. The federal contribution went disproportionately to support higher education until the middle of the 1960s. Access to higher education is directly related to occupational position; as a result, these educational benefits serve to link the middle class—old and new—to the structure of the welfare state.[39]

37. For a comprehensive description of the socioeconomic position of low-income households see James N. Morgan, Katherine Dickinson, Jonathan Dickinson, Jacob Benus, and Greg Duncan, eds., *Five Thousand American Families: Patterns of Economic Progress*. Vol. 1: *An Analysis of the First Five Years of the Panel Study of Income Dynamics*. Vol. 2: *Special Studies of the First Five Years of the Panel Study of Income Dynamics*, Ann Arbor: Institute for Social Research, University of Michigan, 1974–1975. Vol. 3: Greg J. Duncan and James N. Morgan, eds., *Five Thousand American Families: Patterns of Economic Progress*.

38. Glen H. Beyer, *Housing and Society* (New York: Macmillan, 1965), pp. 117–249; Raymond J. Struyk and Sue A. Marshall, *Income and Urban Home Ownership* (Washington, D.C.: Urban Institute, 1974); Congressional Budget Office, *Homeownership: The Changing Relationship of Costs and Income, and Possible Federal Roles* (Washington, D.C., Government Printing Office, 1977).

39. Joseph A. Rechman, "The Distributional Effects of Public Higher Education in California," *Journal of Human Resources* 5 (Summer 1971): 361–70; Richard Freeman, *The Overeducated American* (New York: Academic Press, 1976).

At the core of the welfare state benefits are the income-maintenance programs, from old age payments to rent supplements to food stamps. These programs extend well beyond the lowest social stratum. Thus, for example, over 100,000 members of the armed forces in the early 1970s were eligible to receive food stamps; for a period students were eligible for food stamps. Old age insurance has become important for members of the middle strata to relieve themselves of or shift the burden of caring for aging parents. Veterans' benefits are social welfare, since they are as much designed to overcome liabilities as they are to be rewards. The emerging medical insurance programs are more and more broadly based. It is significant that aspects of these programs are closely linked to the cost of living index rather than to levels of productivity.

Efforts to diffuse stock ownership as an approach to altering wage earner–employer relations have been studied. Ownership of stock, like that of insurance policies, serves as a vehicle for underwriting welfare payments. However, the ownership of stock has not been a major device for weakening the distinction between wage earner and owner of equity capital. The direct ownership of stock has not diffused deeply and extensively into middle income groups in the United States. Nor have the schemes by which industrial establishments distribute stock been noteworthy in their impact.[40] The 1974 legislation on employee stock ownership was designed to facilitate such schemes by adding a tax deferment advantage.

But it is the vast growth of health and pension plans in industrial and commercial firms, often in conjunction with trade union groups, which creates new linkages between wage earners and the "mode of production." These schemes depend on the economic returns of investments. As of 1975, by means of pension funds, employees of U.S. firms owned at least 25% of the existing equity capital and the figure was projected to rise to 50% by 1985. There are inadequate data on the social incidence of this type of welfare equity claim, but it can be estimated that between one-third and one-half of the blue-collar families by 1970 had such "stakes," of real importance to their standard of living. Such private welfare schemes are closely linked with and supported by the welfare state. The federal government seeks to facilitate them by research

40. According to the New York Stock Exchange data, the 1975 profile of stockowners indicated that there were 25.2 million Americans who held stock, a drop of 18.3% from the 30.8 billion in 1970. The average owner was 53 years of age and had an annual household income of $19,000, compared with an $11,000 average for the total population.

and information. In 1974 legislation was passed establishing governmental standards and regulations; these programs are in effect subsidized, as they are closely monitored by the government.

Interest-group politics is at the heart of the expansion of welfare expenditures. The claims and demands of occupational groups are expressed by voluntary association networks. Ideological and humanitarian goals—and the realities of inequality and disability of an advanced industrial society—supply the political and rhetorical context. Each occupational group has a short-term, relatively clear-cut interest that competes and conflicts with those of other groups. The political process is unable to impose a national scheme or an integrated economic policy and instead reacts by a series of compromises without "grand design" and without effective contribution to social control and self-regulation of the welfare state. (Some innovations have been inconsistent.) Each claim for social welfare has its inherent relevance, legitimacy, and high priority; the ranking of one claim against another is theoretically very difficult and in the political arena even more difficult to adjudicate. How do elected officials balance the demand for increased old age benefits against youth employment training programs without resort to the strength of pressure groups?

But this analysis needs to be extended in order to explain the emergence of weak and "stalemated" political regimes; it is necessary to assess the effect of the welfare benefits on popular political perspectives and participation. The influence of the welfare state on the social structure modifies and transcends conventional interest-group politics. Political conflict becomes more than the struggle between competing occupational and interest groups. Each person and each member of the household must confront an elaborate set of contradictory or competing and often ambiguous issues in the pursuit of self-interest—immediate or long term. The new social and economic structure produces a fusion of claims and expectations about wages, property, income, and welfare. A person's relations to the means of production is by no means characterized by a simple set of alternatives. One's linkage to the mode of production under these conditions is based both on one's occupation and on the institutions of social welfare.

The claims and expectations of one's occupation remain central. Yet, the spread and increased weight of welfare equity claims mean that the admixture of property rights, private welfare returns, and benefits of social welfare are also important components of one's socioeconomic self-conception and realities. The task of assessing one's self-interest becomes continuous and more complex, and the pursuit of one's personal or group goals almost defies direct political and programmatic articulation. There is no reason to assume that a decline in political interest and participation under such circumstances is the result. The outcome is a transformation of the patterns and consequences of political participation. In 1920–1950, "conventional" occupational interest-group politics tended to produce relatively stable political attachments, which permitted integrated preferences that shifted slowly. It created a political setting that generated a form of bargaining politics by political leaders who could make fairly accurate assessments of popular demands and preferences. The election arena rested on large and relatively stable blocs; political competition was directed to segments of the electorate that shifted gradually, except for those special occasions which produced sharp and lasting changes in political alignment in critical elections.

Political competition had for 1920 to 1950 built-in self-generating limits. This was the political process of a social structure which could operate as if the "stratigraphic" model had some reality. The political process could use a modulated language of social strata to build the political base for the welfare state. But the social base of the welfare state has meant that electoral politics since 1950 have been less and less able to produce effective political solutions and have instead contributed to the emergence of weak political regimes. Closer examination of the social stratification correlates of electoral behavior helps clarify this process.

Group Consciousness and Political Self-Interest

Our argument is that, under advanced industrialism, patterns of participation in national elections serve as an index of social control and its effectiveness. More specifically, the logic of the social-stratification perspective toward political participation implies that the division of labor and changes in it generate elements of group consciousness and conceptions of political self-interest. These conceptions of self-interest fundamentally condition actual patterns of mass political participation under a parliamentary system. Of course, the systemic analysis of social control, as already emphasized, requires a further examination of the institutional structure of the political parties and the related agencies of mass persuasion.

At this point, it is necessary to assess the empirical research about the connections between occupation and social stratum, and the trends in mass political behavior that have been associated with weak political regimes. To what extent have the trends in occupational structure and welfare altered conceptions of group consciousness and levels of satisfaction, the raw materials of political competition and political conflict? In what way have social position and changes in social position had consequences for popular political perspective and political participation? Examination of findings of this research indicates a striking stability in popular consciousness about one's sound position for the years 1945 to 1975 for which survey data are available.[42] In particular, for the period 1952 to 1972, change in political participation hardly reflected sharp changes in this dimension of social self-conceptions. Moreover, many of the relevant shifts in popular political perspectives—for example, a distrust of political processes—are distributed throughout the social structure and not concentrated in particular strata. Again, these findings emphasize the limited value of a rigid stratigraphic conception of social structure. Even when one thinks of more delimited ordered segments of the social structure, it is clear that personality and social psychological differences within groups are operative, in part by means of communication and interpersonal influence.

The ideal body of survey research data for the analysis of the effect of group consciousness on political participation would require at least three sample points in time: one in the 1930s, one in 1952, and one in 1972. For the members of each sample, we would need data on social position and other aspects of social differentiation and measures of self-definition in group terms, plus conceptions of political self-interest and actual political behavior. In the absence of such data, it is necessary to examine a range of trends, so that the conclusions rest on a measure of plausibility and convergence of different sources.

41. Peter Drucker, *The Unseen Revolution: How Pension Fund Socialism Came to America* (New York: Harper and Row, 1976).

42. Reported in D. Garth Taylor, "Subjective Social Class," unpublished paper, National Opinion Research Center, April 1975. For earlier studies of trends in subjective social class in the United States, see Robert E. Lane, "The Politics of Consensus in an Age of Affluence," *American Political Science Review* 59 (December 1965): 874–89; Charles W. Tucker, "A Comparative Analysis of Subjective Social Class: 1945–1963," *Social Forces* 46 (June 1968): 508–14; Richard F. Hamilton, "Reply to Tucker," *American Sociological Review* 31 (April 1966): 192–199; E. M. Schreiber and G. T. Nygreen, "Subjective Social Class in America: 1945–1968," *Social Forces* 48 (March 1970): 348–56.

The stratigraphic model implies that group self-conceptions reflect the realities of the division of labor and of relations to the mode of production. Of course, economic determinists speak of false social group consciousness, especially with the rise of the mass media, which are able to manipulate the representation of socioeconomic reality. They argue that, under the continuous influence of societal contradictions, especially of depressions and wars, societal conditions engender "correct," or at least realistic, self-conceptions. In actuality, the social self-conceptions that men and women hold of themselves are not only a function of their work and communal settings but also of the social definition that they have internalized from their educational experiences and from the mass media.

This admixture of personal consciousness and the influence of educational institutions and the mass media creates problems in the mass observation of the subjective aspects of social stratum and social class.[43] Sample surveys highlight these difficulties, since the form of the question influences the encountered social forms. To use the findings on subjective definition of social strata and social class, it is necessary to remember the "artificial" nature of the social interaction of the survey interview: two persons who are strangers are engaged in a structured and potentially manipulative conversation detached from the context of social realities. But it is the standardized elements in survey research which give it its social-science relevance. The more categories for classifying social position the interviewer presents to the citizen, the larger the percentage of the sampled population who place themselves in the upper and middle groupings. Thus, on the basis of data reflecting the years 1972–1974, if the choice was twofold—middle or working class—45% thought of themselves in the higher stratum; if the choice is fourfold—lower class, working class, middle class, or upper class—those designating themselves in the upper two strata rises to 49%; if the choice is fivefold—lower class, working class, middle class, upper middle class, or upper class—then those including themselves in the upper three strata rises to 54%.

Nevertheless, during the post–World War II period, the long-term trend in social class identifications has been upward to a limited degree. Three different versions of the question produce the same minor upward trend: the number of "upper or middle" based on the two category question rose from 37.8% in 1952 to 45.0% in 1972; the four-

43. Taylor, "Social Class," passim.

category question from 43.6% in 1948 to 48.9% in 1974; and the five-category series from 46.2% in 1955 to 54.3% in 1973.

A crude "time series" analysis indicates that the important variable in accounting for this limited upward shift is level of education. Increases in amount of education produce a stronger concentration of upper status self-conceptions. In a real sense, educational experience—or the lack of it—implants conceptions of social position, and the stratigraphic self-image is as much a reflection of educational level as any single variable.

In the light of these findings about social class identifications and the previously discussed trends in occupational structure, it is appropriate to reassess the well-known but limited linkage in the United States between social status and political behavior. Our interest is more pointed and more complicated: what are the direct connections, if any, between the long-term changes in social stratification in the United States and the observed trends in electoral behavior which have contributed to the emergence of weak parliamentary regimes?

Vigorous scholars have sought to apply quantitative research methods to the study of political sociology in the United States.[44] Unfortunately, most of their efforts are not directly applicable to the systemic analysis of social change and social control. In part, the available measures of social position which have been utilized are very crude, even in terms of the stratigraphic image. This stream of research has relied on cross-sectional analysis without having adequate longitudinal data. Moreover, the modes of statistical analysis have not been adequate to isolate and identify the measures of social position in contrast with other types of variables. Few studies are directly relevant and highlight two converging conclusions. If one assumes a social stratification basis of political participation, then the "conventional" measures of economic strata, or social class for 1950 to 1975, are of limited and declining pertinence in explaining patterns of party and preference and the growth of a volatile electorate.

But there should be no misunderstanding about the scope of these observations. Electoral participation and the resulting patterns of social control do reflect the struggle for "well-being" between the "haves" and the "have-nots." The increased complexity of political issues and

44. For an early summary, see S. M. Lipset, *Political Man* (Garden City, N.Y.: Doubleday, 1960); Richard F. Hamilton, *Class and Politics in the United States* (New York: Wiley, 1972).

the emergence of "stagflation" economics weakened but did not eliminate the political definition of the Democrats as the party of the "have-nots" and the Republicans as that of the "haves." The definition of relative deprivation and the location of those who believe themselves to be either absolutely or relatively deprived have been transformed. The proportion of the electorate who think of themselves as Republicans has declined, those who accept the symbol of Democrat have remained constant, while the independents have grown.

Of course, a hierarchical approach to partisan affiliation is tempered and distorted by the strong tendency of those with professional education, especially those employed in bureaucratic settings, to defect from their social "position" and affiliate with the Democratic party. The social hierarchy of political affiliation is further distorted by the under-representation of the lowest stratum in the Democratic category as well as by a persistent defection of skilled workers to the Republican party. Moreover, foreign policy preferences are even less related to social position in the stratigraphic sense and therefore also attenuate the connection between social stratification and electoral behavior.

From the point of view of social control, the central issue is the differences in the social correlates of mass political behavior in parliamentary nations. We are dealing not with a uniform historical process but rather with the different but closely related political patterns of advanced industrial societies because of varied patterns of ordered social segmentation. For the early 1960s, massive reanalysis of sample surveys places the socioeconomic stratification of political orientation in the United States in a meaningful cross-national comparison with West Germany and England.[45] If one wishes to use the stratigraphic model, these national samples have particular relevance, since the social-stratification categories involved—income, occupation, and prestige—were not arbitrary but were formulated to reflect the historical and contemporary setting of the three nation-states.

It is no startling finding that for the United States, the linkage between social strata (socioeconomic status groups in this case) and party affiliation (liberal versus conservative) was the lowest; it was highest for Great Britain, and intermediate for West Germany. (Cramer's V, for the United States, is .162; .284 for West Germany; and .394 for Great Britain.) For this period, in all three countries, socioeconomic status

45. Morris Janowitz, *Political Conflict: Essays in Political Sociology* (Beverly Hills, Calif.: Sage Publications, 1970), pp. 88–115.

emerged as the strongest variable in explaining "liberal" or "conservative" attitude. However, it is striking that this method of analysis identified a different dimension of social cleavage as the next most important variable for each of the three countries. For the United States it was race; for Germany, religion; and for Great Britain, sex. For each nation, additional variables could be identified which to some extent help explain the pattern of party affiliation. Nevertheless, the first two variables explain the basis of party affiliation at that time. In other words, mass political affiliation in these societies can be seen as rooted in the occupational division of labor if at the same time these categories are related to overriding dimensions of social cleavage which reflect the specific pattern of ordered segmentation. To account for the change in political attitudes in 1965–1975, there is every reason to believe that age has emerged with increased salience for all three nations.[46] However, all these variables must be seen in the context of the new economics and the welfare state.

An examination through time of various sets of national samples for the United States from 1952 to 1974 reveals a decline in connections between social stratum or social class position and Democratic and Republican affiliation, or in actual voting in presidential campaigns. While the economics of "stagflation" increased the salience of economic and standard of living issues, there was no evidence that social position defined in societal-wide categories as of 1975 had become decisively more important; in fact, given the diffuse and variegated influence of inflation and the welfare state, this was not to be expected.

Using occupationally based data, Philip Converse argued that, for 1944 to 1965, the importance of social class as a correlate of presidential voting declined.[47] Robert Axelrod came to the same conclusion for 1952 to 1968 on the basis of the decline of low-income groups in the Democratic vote.[48] The most comprehensive analysis, James Davis's for 1952 to 1974, makes use of social class identification (subjective social

46. Paul R. Abramson, *Generational Change in American Politics* (Lexington, Mass.: Lexington Books, 1975).

47. Philip E. Converse, "The Shifting Role of Class in Political Attitudes and Behavior," in Eleanor E. Maccoby, *Readings in Social Psychology*, 3d ed. (New York: Henry Holt and Co., 1958), pp. 388–99.

48. Robert Axelrod, "Where the Votes Come From: An Analysis of Electoral Coalitions, 1952–1968," *American Political Science Review* 66 (March 1972): 11–20. For an analysis of the association between income and partisanship in the United States, see David Segal, "Political Partisanship: Its Social and Economic Bases in the United States," *American Journal of Economy and Sociology* 29 (July 1970): 253–62.

class, in his terminology) to account for both party identification and presidential vote.[49] In summarizing his findings about social class and voting patterns ("middle class" voting disproportionately for Republicans, "lower class" for Democrats), he concludes that "The system as a whole tended to deteriorate during the period." His analysis also highlights the growth of the "independents" in the middle and upper middle groupings.

In contrast, three basic attitude trends and their social correlates illuminate the patterns of group consciousness which help fashion political self-interest and the volatility of electoral participation. The three are economic and consumer satisfaction, political alienation (that is, generalized political distrust), and attitudes toward the welfare state and welfare expenditures. In essence, from the end of the Great Depression to the national election of 1976, there has been stability in popular levels of economic satisfaction. It is impossible to argue that the decomposition of party affiliation has been an expression of feelings of a profound economic crisis or even marked and widespread decrease in satisfaction with one's standard of living. At the same time, there has been a long-term, consistent, and finally noteworthy increase in generalized distrust of the political process. The data presented below indicate that this distruct is not highly concentrated but dispersed widely throughout the social structure.

In contrast to the relative overall stability in economic satisfaction, popular perspectives on welfare expenditures have fluctuated widely. As will be documented below, first there has been a growth in support, followed by a discernible decline with the advent of "stagflation," and a second, but much more limited, increase in support as the recession of the 1970s deepened. Again there is only a limited association between position in the social structure as measured by occupation and social class and attitude about welfare. Moreover, there are only narrow differences between those with Democratic and those with Republican affiliation. If one thinks in terms of economic self-interest calculations, the electorate is engaged in making very short-term, narrow, unstable, and even highly personalistic judgments about the costs and benefits

49. James Davis, "Subjective Social Class, Party Identification and Presidential Vote 1952–1972," unpublished paper, NORC, 1975; See also Norval Glenn "Class and Party Support in the United States: Recent and Emergent Trends," *The Public Opinion Quarterly* 27 (1973): 1–20; David Knoke, *Change and Continuity in American Politics: The Social Bases of Political Parties* (Baltimore: Johns Hopkins University Press, 1976).

of the welfare state. An examination of the details of these trends is therefore in order.

A revealing long-term indicator of political self-interest can be derived from measures of consumer and economic satisfaction; the "standard of living" is at the heart of political demands. Since 1938 public opinion surveys have continuously measured consumer satisfaction and relative deprivation.[50] The operational procedure has been to ask the citizenry whether they "are better or worse off financially than one year ago."

The remarkable aspect of these data is the essential stability and gradual improvement that have been recorded over four decades (see Table 5.4). The trends encountered are consistent with the realities of economic conditions. The fact that, even during affluent prosperity, there has been little change reflects the reality and perception of each citizen's continuing relative position in the income hierarchy. From the years of the Great Depression to 1956, the long-term trend has been one of gradual, persistent increase in the level of satisfaction with one's standard of living, and a decrease in relative deprivation (decline in percentage reporting that they were worse off).

From 1959 to 1974, there was no further increase in level of economic satisfaction. A rough plateau had been reached; in fact, a certain decline can be noticed. After 1969 the impact of stagflation is noticeable. The number of the population who report that they are better off drop from a high point of 40% in 1956 to 31.2% in 1974, while the no-change category rises from 35% to 45.4%. However, the striking datum is that the worse-off category remains in effect constant, at about 23%.

While, from the crude available data, those at the top suffered less, the effect did not increase directly as one moved down the social structure. No doubt more refined data would indicate the relative advantage of those groups which have been able through governmental or trade union intervention to link their income to increase in the cost of living. When one examines the occupation correlates of these responses, the well-known pattern of the "superior" position of the skilled workers can be seen clearly. Thus, for 1970 the clerical and sales group and the unskilled workers reported an increase in "worse off" (approximately

50. For the background of this type of research see George Katona, *The Mass Consumption Society* (New York: McGraw Hill, 1964).

TABLE 5.4 Trends in Financial Satisfaction and Relative Deprivation, 1938–1974

Evaluation of financial situation	1938[a]	1942[b]	1948[c]	1952[c]	1956[c]	1959[c]	1964[d]	1969[d]	1973[e]	1974[e]
Better off	26.0	30.9	29.0	33.0	40.0	38.0	35.0	34.0	32.5	31.2
No change	43.0	46.9	28.0	29.0	35.0	34.0	43.0	41.0	45.4	45.4
Worse off	31.0	21.3	39.0	35.0	23.0	27.0	22.0	25.0	23.7	23.1
Don't know/no answer	—	—	4	3	2	1	—	—	—	—

a. "Are you better off or worse off than you were a year ago?" (AIPO)
b. "Financially, are you better off or worse off than last year?" (AIPO)
c. "Would you say that you people are better or worse off financially than one year ago?" (Survey of Consumer Finances)
d. "We are interested in how people are getting along financially these days. Would you say that you and your family are better off financially than you were a year ago?" (Survey of Consumer Finances)
e. "So far as you and your family are concerned, would you say that you are pretty well satisfied with your present financial situation, more or less satisfied, or not satisfied at all?" (NORC)

25% each), while the professional and technical, the managers and self-employed, and the skilled workers reported the same level of dissatisfaction (15% approximately) and self-employed with a slightly higher level of 18%. The most fundamental division came, of course, from those who were not in the labor force (chronically unemployed, ill, broken families, and youth and old age). Those in this category reporting "worse off" reached 40%. One cannot make direct inferences that the welfare system modulated the response of these persons. There is a body of research for the period before World War II which highlights that an important element of the chronic unemployed became apathetic and resigned to their situation.[51] But with the growth of the welfare state, the disposed and deprived segments of society are more likely at last to have negative and resentful attitudes about their economic position.

Political alienation, with all its vagueness and conceptual limitations, has been charted by national samples from 1952 to 1968. Sociologists have been deeply concerned with the meaning of alienation.[52] The weakness of the notion of political alienation is that this terminology tends to overlook the problem of specifying the particular social groupings and agencies from which the citizen believes he is alienated. In effect, the measures of alienation cannot be taken as indicators of actual political behavior; as indicated in chapter 4, there has been no effective enlargement of "depoliticalization"—to use that awkward but trenchant term. The measures of alienation reflect citizen affect toward the institutions of political decision making; not one in effect dealing with a measure of distrust. In fact, in the national elections of 1964 to 1972, voting was not related to trust in government. Likewise, those with low trust in government were slightly more interested in these political campaigns.

The various measures of political alienation—that is, generalized distrust—have independently and in combination revealed the following

51. E. Wight Bakke, *The Unemployed Man* (London: Nisbet, 1933); Ewan Clague, Walter J. Couper, and E. Wight Bakke, *After the Shutdown* (New Haven, Conn.: Yale University Press, 1934); E. Wight Bakke, *Citizens Without Work: A Study of the Effects of Unemployment Upon the Worker's Social Relations and Practices* (New Haven: Yale University Press, 1940); Marie Jahoda, Paul F. Lazarsfeld, and Hans Zeisel, *Marienthal: The Sociology of an Unemployed Community* (Chicago: Aldine, Atherton, 1971).

52. For a critical assessment of the analytic problems involved in the concept of alienation, see Melvin Seeman, "Alienation Studies," *Annual Review of Sociology* 1 (1975): 91–123.

attitude trends.[53] For 1952 to 1974, there has been a long-term increase in reported alienation which corresponds with previous reported trends of distrust of government. This trend went from a decrease from 1952 which ended with the 1960 election and was followed by a more continuous increase in reported political alienation from the 1964 to the 1972 elections.

James S. House and William M. Mason have, on the basis of a time series analysis, sought to identify the social-stratification correlates of this trend in political alienation and distrust.[54] In effect, their interpretation centered on the narrower and more usable definition of political alienation, namely, mistrust of government. In terms of the stratigraphic image, they found that occupation was unrelated to increased alienation. It is important that they found that increased levels of alienation occurred "remarkedly uniformly [sic] across demographic groups." Actually, the traditional variables of survey analysis used for measure of political attitudes, such as region, sex, age, education, income, and occupation were not very pertinent for accounting for these changes in verbalized political alienation. If one sought to highlight a single variable, from their analysis, it would be that increased feelings of alienation were to be found among better educated persons, and to a limited extended age was operative in that both young and old persons revealed higher levels of alienated attitudes. Clearly, social personality dimensions and interpersonal process within specific social groupings is at work. Moreover, in the context of the growth of the welfare state, it is central that those who were more alienated were also those who preferred an expansion of the welfare state, while those desiring less governmental intervention were less alienated. The high concentration of antagonism toward and distrust of government institutions among those segments of the population who wish to see more government intervention was identified by samples drawn in 1953–1954; and the

53. Philip E. Converse, "Changes in the American Electorate," in *The Human Meaning of Social Change*, ed. Angus Campbell and Philip E. Converse (New York: Russell Sage Foundation, 1972), pp. 326–31; James S. House and William M. Mason, "Political Alienation in America, 1952–1968," *American Sociological Review* 40 (April 1975): 123–47; Otis Dudley Duncan, Howard Schuman, and Beverly Duncan, *Social Change in a Metropolitan Community* (New York: Russell Sage Foundation, 1973).

54. James S. House and William M. Mason, "Political Alienation," passim. Converging results were obtained by Luther B. Otto and David Featherman, "Social Structural and Psychological Antecedents of Self-Estrangement and Powerlessness," *American Sociological Review* 40 (December 1975): 701–19.

analysis of these data foreshadowed increased instability and volatility of political preference.[55]

The influence of the changes in social stratification and the expansion of the welfare state on political self-interest can be clarified by assessing the long-term shifts in attitudes toward "welfare spending" (Table 5.5). If one examines the full sweep of the three decades from 1935 to 1975, attitudes toward the welfare state—as measured by support for "welfare spending"—fluctuated widely. This pattern of attitudes contrasts with the relative stability in feelings of consumer satisfaction. Moreover, the fluctuations cut across various social groupings. There is a general tendency for those at the bottom of the social structure to support increased welfare spending to a greater degree than those at the top. However, the changes over time are not easily explained by reference to a simple split between "haves" and the "have-nots."[56]

The available data support attenuation of linkages between conventional categories of social stratification and political orientation (including party orientations). These data in a deeper sense support the hypothesis of the increased complexity in defining economic self-interest and in articulating self-interest with available political alternatives. In short, we are dealing with a long-term trend in which the original increase in support for social welfare expenditures has given way to a more reserved and critical attitude in which welfare orientations in particular are not highly correlated with political party orientations.

From 1935 to after World War II there was a sharp, steady increase in support for welfare programs and welfare expenditures. By 1950, 43.9% of the population reported in a Gallup survey that they were in favor of increased welfare spending. Initially this trend reflected the influence of the first New Deal programs and the increased public awareness of these efforts. The massive expansion of governmental enterprise during World War II and the attendant economic prosperity increased support for welfare spending. Two elements were at work; the confidence of the political leaders and the popular feeling that if the public sector could spend massive amounts to fight a worldwide war, it could help those Americans in need.

55. Morris Janowitz et al., *Public Administration and the Public Perspectives Toward Government in a Metropolitan Community* (Ann Arbor, Mich.: Institute of Public Administration, 1958).

56. Michel E. Schlitz, *Public Attitudes toward Social Security, 1935–1965.* (Washington: GPO, 1970).

TABLE 5.5 Trends in Attitudes toward Welfare Spending, 1950–1975

Year	1950[a]	1961[b]	1973[c]	1975[c]
Total % for increased spending. Number of respondents sampled in parenthesis.	43.9 (1379)	40.2 (3747)	20.7 (1432)	24.7 (1405)
Region				
East	47.2 (509)	36.1 (954)	18.7 (342)	18.5 (325)
Midwest	38.2 (521)	37.0 (1123)	20.7 (425)	22.5 (427)
South	34.3 (216)	32.1 (1048)	19.5 (478)	26.1 (498)
West	45.8 (203)	35.5 (594)	20.6 (252)	26.1 (234)
Race				
White	41.5 (1355)	32.5 (3325)	14.7 (1302)	19.5 (1317)
Black	58.2 (55)	57.4 (394)	53.8 (195)	53.9 (167)
Occupation				
Prof, Tech	39.6 (159)	32.6 (365)	22.5 (360)	21.2 (179)
Mgr, Adm	30.4 (191)	29.7 (491)	8.4 (203)	12.0 (209)
Clerical	41.3 (259)	33.3 (291)	16.0 (268)	23.1 (273)
Blue, skilled	51.4 (142)	36.7 (531)	12.9 (155)	26.9 (175)
Blue, Unsk	51.7 (420)	39.6 (1110)	27.2 (475)	27.5 (480)
Income Quartile				
Top		30.8 (915)	12.4 (370)	15.6 (437)
Second		36.0 (848)	11.5 (347)	19.3 (342)
Third		34.6 (1123)	20.5 (366)	27.3 (264)
Bottom		40.5 (763)	36.5 (307)	34.5 (359)
Education				
0-11 yrs.	47.4 (700)	37.3 (1971)	25.5 (548)	26.8 (533)
High School	39.0 (403)	35.9 (1129)	13.1 (482)	21.1 (498)
College	33.6 (342)	26.6 (606)	20.3 (462)	22.0 (450)
Age Cohort				
New (Vnam)		26.4 (72)	23.0 (483)	28.4 (574)
Young (WW2)	51.2 (211)	41.9 (1157)	18.2 (440)	20.0 (390)
Middle (Dep)	43.3 (584)	34.1 (1333)	17.4 (397)	20.2 (346)
Old (WW1)	37.5 (638)	29.8 (1140)	20.9 (177)	20.7 (174)
Religion				
Protestant	36.1 (985)	34.6 (2633)	18.3 (418)	23.2 (384)
Catholic	52.2 (341)	32.5 (850)	17.9 (386)	19.4 (360)
Trade Union Membership				
Either R or Spouse belongs	57.2 (258)		17.0 (418)	23.2 (384)
Neither	38.4 (1131)		20.8 (1070)	23.5 (1094)
Party Affiliation				
Independent	42.2 (289)	36.5 (743)	19.1 (519)	21.6 (555)
Republican	29.1 (485)	30.6 (1036)	8.8 (339)	18.0 (328)
Democrat	51.2 (646)	37.1 (1892)	26.4 (611)	28.0 (597)

Table 5.5 (Cont.)

Year	1950[a]	1961[b]	1973[c]	1975[c]
Political Orientation				
Liberal	49.5 (432)			34.8 (420)
Middle	44.4 (522)			18.7 (557)
Conservative	28.4 (377)			17.3 (416)
Subjective Social Class				
Lower, Working			23.6 (721)	26.0 (784)
Middle, Upper			16.3 (765)	20.5 (692)

Questions

a. AIPO 454—"Do you think U.S. government spending should be increased, decreased, or remain the same on the following . . . social welfare, health, and social security?"

b. AIPO 651—"Do you think that the government in Washington is spending too much tax money for welfare programs to help people in the United States, or do you think it isn't spending enough?"

c. General Social Survey—"We are faced with many problems in this country, none of which can be solved easily or inexpensively. I'm going to name some of these problems and for each one I'd like you to tell me whether you think we're spending too much money on it, too little money, or about the right amount . . . welfare."

However, by 1961, a plateau had been reached in support of public welfare expenditures (the percentage in support had dropped slightly to 40.2%). Attitudes toward welfare spending were influenced by the massive expansion of expenditures for aid to dependent children. This program encountered racial hostility; in addition, it was clear to much of the citizenry that the political leaders were reluctant or unable to formulate more effective welfare programs for this particular welfare category. The basic support for welfare expenditure rested on the expansion of old age benefits, which enabled much of the population to be relieved of some of the burden of parental support. However, from 1960 to 1973, support for social welfare expenditures dropped markedly, so that by 1973 the fraction of the population in favor of increased welfare spending stood at 20.7%. Opposition to social welfare focused on the continued growth of the aid to dependent children and the failure of the political leadership to modernize the system and introduce a more acceptable family allowance system. More broadly, the onset of "stagflation" undermined the confidence of much of the population in continued economic growth and led them to press for economic retrenchment. The theme of "welfare cheating" also had its negative impact. During this period the population emphasized the greater importance of controlling inflation than of handling employment or dealing with unemployment. However, as unemployment rates continued to rise after 1973, there was for the first time since 1960 a limited growth in public opinion in support of increased welfare expenditures. This support was based on popular acceptance of the need to help the chronically unemployed and also to raise payment to old age insurance recipients who were suffering under stagflation.

What were the social correlates of these trends? For 1950 to 1975, there was a decline in regional differences and correspondingly the emergence of a national norm, so to speak; in particular, the South was no longer the most antiwelfare. (In part this convergence was an artifact of the decline in overall level of support.) Income differences were clear-cut but, as of 1975, they were less than anticipated. In 1975, 15.6% of the top quartile supported more welfare spending, while for the bottom quartile the figure only reached 34.5%. The differences by occupational groupings were less marked and very unsystematic. The gap in prowelfare attitudes between the professional technical at the top of the structure and the unskilled blue-collar at the bottom was very limited; 21.2% compared with 27.5%. In fact, there was considerable uniformity among all occupational groupings, except that the managerial administrative category was the most strongly opposed (12% in favor). Educational level has become even less related to welfare expenditures. The survey data indicate that higher levels of education work to reduce the opposition to welfare encountered among those in the more privileged positions in the social structure. The trend toward convergence is highlighted by the decline in differences among Catholic and Protestant, young and old, and even union members and nonmembers, although each of these changes reflects decreasing overall support. The only persistent element of cleavage is the difference between whites and blacks, which has grown dramatically; in 1950, those in support of welfare spending were 41.5% white and 58.2% black; by 1975 for whites it had dropped to 19.5% and for blacks it persisted at 53.9%. Thus, the data on social characteristics income, occupation, education, age, and even religion, indicate that a simple stratigraphic approach to welfare attitudes is not very revealing; we are dealing with complex interrelations between ordered segments of the populations and their life chances, their broad ideological outlook, and personalized judgments.

It is not particularly striking that the difference between Republicans and Democrats has declined over time. This is most sharply revealed in the pattern of attitudes which emerged in the short-term changes from 1973 to 1975; the increase in support for welfare is greater among Republicans than among Democrats. In good measure this reflects the influence of increased unemployment among white-collar and middle-class groupings (since World War II, unemployment compensation has increased in the middle-class groups as compared with working-class ones).

If one wishes, one can think of the political process as a constant struggle between the haves and the have-nots. But the political definitions which have emerged are not those of a simple and direct confrontation between a stratum at the bottom and another at the top. On many crucial issues and interests, the differences between haves and have-nots is no greater than those within various social segments. The resulting diffuse and unstructured definitions of political self-interest help explain the trends in political participation which have resulted in the decomposition of party affiliation and increased fluidity of electoral choice. But the master trends in industrialism and social welfare are accompanied by those of military participation and military operations, which must be explored next.

Six

Military Participation and Total War

Rise and Decline of the Mass Armed Force

Along with expanded political participation and industrial development, modern war and the transformation of military institutions constitute a third series of master trends which have contributed to the problems of social control. The social stratification and the institutional structure of the United States reflect its involvement in four major international wars fought with conventional weapons: World War I, World War II, Korea, and the Second Indochina War. Despite their profound differences, these conflicts can be thought of as an interrelated sequence of military engagements.[1] In addition, the United States has responded to the development and deployment of nuclear weapons, which have decisively altered the role of organized violence in international relations.[2] Nuclear weapons produce a new threshold in the role of force in the international arena.

Any exploration of the influence of modern warfare and military institutions on advanced industrialism must assess the historical literature on the connections between military institutions and sociopolitical change. John U. Nef, in *War and Human Progress*, sought to summarize the documentation; he concluded that industrialism and economic progress would have come into being and advanced without the "stimulus" of war; the tempo might have been slowed, but overall, in his view, war was a barrier to the development of "civilization."[3]

1. Russell F. Weigley, *The American Way of War: A History of United States Military Strategy and Policy* (New York: Macmillan, 1973); Raymond Aron, *The Century of Total War* (Boston: Beacon Press, 1955).

2. Bernard Brodie, *The Absolute Weapon* (New York: Harcourt, Brace, 1946); *War and Politics* (New York: Macmillan, 1973).

3. John U. Nef, *War and Human Progress* (Cambridge: Harvard University Press, 1950). See also Arnold Toynbee, *War and Civilization* (New York: Oxford University Press, 1950), which presents the essence of his multivolume *Study of History*.

Quincy Wright, the empirically oriented political scientist, interpreted the detailed findings of his monumental *Study of War* in the following terms: "The preceding survey suggests that in the most recent state of world civilization war has made for instability, for disintegration, for despotism and for unadaptability, rendering the course of civilization less predictable and continued progress towards achievement of its values less probable."[4] If war and military institutions have been barriers to the development of civilization, they have fashioned the modern nation-state which is our concern. These formulations are so global as to limit their explanatory utility and to permit an abdication of responsible moral judgments. Thus, Harold D. Lasswell used the concept the "garrison state" to chart the destructive and disruptive consequences, including the unanticipated strain of prolonged international warfare, on liberal democracy.[5]

These historical overviews do not substitute for systemic analysis of the linkages among war, military institutions, and specific elements of sociopolitical change. There is no theoretical or empirical basis for formulating the issue in the extreme, universalistic form of Stanislaw Andreski: that the stratification in a society varies inversely with the extent of military participation, namely, that the greater the military participation, the more equalitarian the society.[6] It is more to the point that social historians and sociologists have underlined that the realities of total war as practiced in the West during World War II produced fundamental societal changes by expanding the active electorate and intensifying its political demands, thereby resulting in elements of "fundamental democratization," to use Karl Mannheim's phrase.[7] Richard Titmuss and others have pointed out that the economic and social mobilization for World War II fashioned the governmental institutions required for the welfare state and created the political demands which resulted in the necessary fiscal allocations.[8] However, the underlying question which must be confronted is much broader and

4. Quincy Wright, *A Study of War* (Chicago: University of Chicago Press, 1942) 1: 272. See also Pitirim A. Sorokin, *Man and Society in Calamity* (New York: Dutton, 1942).

5. Harold D. Lasswell, "The Garrison State," *American Journal of Sociology* 46 (January 1941): 455–568.

6. Stanislav Andreski, *Military Organization and Society* (London: Routledge and Kegan Paul, 1968), pp. 73, passim.

7. Karl Mannheim, *Man and Society in an Age of Reconstruction: Studies in Modern Social Structure* (New York: Harcourt, Brace, 1940), pp. 44ff.

8. Richard M. Titmuss, "War and Social Policy," in *Essays on "The Welfare State"* (London: Allen and Unwin, 1958).

encompasses fundamental issues of "nation building" in the West. Given the destructive and disruptive aspects of warfare, how does one account for the character of nationalism and the nation-state in the West since the sixteenth century?

The nation-state in the West, with its parliamentary institutions, cannot be explained—as most macrosociologists explain it—as the result of a particular sequence of circumstances and conditions which produced capitalism and the resulting forms of industrialism. The West has also been the locus of the emergence of modern military institutions with their peculiar admixture of bureaucratic structure and professional relations.[9] To examine "modernization" and nation building in the West and the United States, it is necessary to account for the historical reality that capitalism and industrialism first emerged in this region of the world, as did the "modern" military institutions—which displaced all other forms of military organization throughout the world. Moreover, and this is crucial, these military institutions and their leaders, supported by the organizational weight and firepower at their disposal—were made subject to civilian parliamentary control to varying degrees.[10] One cannot ask too frequently why the military officers of the Western nation-states and the United States in the nineteenth century did not decisively dominate their societies, as has been typical of many "societies" throughout the world seeking to become modern nation-states. The history of the West is the history not only of the early emergence of the industrial forms of production and modern military institutions but also of the specialized civilian control of military institutions.

My analysis of the emergence of the Western nation-state diverges from standard analysis.[11] To assert that it diverges is an overstatement, since in effect the line of analysis reflects at best the need to come to terms with the central issues posed in the writing of August Comte, Herbert Spencer, and Max Weber, as well as Karl Marx and Friedrich Engels. These writers saw feudal military institutions as barriers to the

9. Jacques van Doorn, "The Officer Corps: A Fusion of Profession and Organization," *Archives Européennes de Sociologie* 6 (1965): 262–82.

10. Alfred Vagts, *A History of Militarism: Romance and Realities of a Profession* (New York: Norton, 1937).

11. Reinhard Bendix, *Nation-Building and Citizenship* (New York: Wiley, 1964). For another emphasis, see S. F. Finer, "State and Nation-Building in Europe: The Role of the Military," in *The Formation of Nation-States in Western Europe*, ed. Charles Tilly (Princeton: Princeton University Press, 1975).

development of capitalism, industrialism, and the modern nation-state. Their analyses differed about the variables which accounted for the transformation of feudal military institutions, but they were all concerned with the consequences of military organization and revolutionary outbreaks for sociopolitical change and on the total society.

In Great Britain, Herbert Spencer, with his typology of the "militant" society, focused on the negative effects military institutions had on industrial society and its evolution.[12] In Germany, Max Weber was concerned with the legitimate institutionalization of coercion as the essential element in the emergence of the nation-state. Max Weber was fully aware of the centrality of the armed forces in fashioning nationalism. He understood that military organization was the prototype of modern organizations: "The discipline of the army gives birth to all discipline."[13] He recognized the linkages between military service and citizenship. But, in the thousands of pages in his collected works, at most twenty are devoted to military themes.[14] It is understandable that Weber's disciples did not continue his approach and avoided such matters.[15]

Max Weber implies that the Protestant ethic, which he held so firmly in the center of his analysis of the transformation of feudalism into capitalism, contributed to the required organization and discipline of military institutions. Strong, independent urban centers and the essential long-term differentiation of the secular state from religious institutions required a containment of feudal power based on landed estates. Max Weber argued that those conditions which brought about the rise of strong urban economic centers were the same as those which transformed feudal military institutions.

12. *Herbert Spencer on Social Evolution*, ed. J. D. Y. Peel (Chicago: University of Chicago Press, 1972). Heritage of Sociology Series.

13. Max Weber, *Economy and Society*, ed. Guenther Roth and Claus Wittich (New York: Bedminister, 1968), 3: 1155.

14. Weber's essay, "The Origins of Discipline in War," is one of the most profound of his writings. He probes the emergence of modern forms of military discipline, and considers the effect of technology on modern military organization. His analysis rejects a technological determinism. Modern technology is an essential prerequisite for the bureaucratic military discipline absent in the feudal armies. However, charismatic leadership and ideological content established the basis of effective organized military discipline associated with the professional armies of the Western nation-state. See Max Weber, "The Origins of Discipline in War," *Economy and Society* 3: 1150–55.

15. Emile Durkheim, in contrast to Max Weber, was completely uninterested in analyzing armed forces as part of the "social division of labor" and the processes of societal change.

Karl Marx's theory of armed conflict and revolutionary change required him to describe the military institutions of the nineteenth century, although this topic was actually of greater concern to Friedrich Engels.[16] The economic determinist view asserted that the accumulation of resources by the expanding bourgeoisie undermined feudally based military formations. This occurred at varying rates in Western Europe; but fundamentally, the transformation of military organization was a response to changes in the mode of production. Military organization was at best reactive, so to speak. However, Frederick Engels departed from—or, more accurately, amplified—this line of reasoning. He believed that the forms of military organization that arose under bourgeois influence had an independent influence on sociopolitical change. In particular, he believed that conscription incorporated wide segments of society into the political process and thereby spread democratic practices:[17] "Contrary to appearance, compulsory military service surpasses general franchise as a democratic agency." This is one, albeit incomplete, form of the argument that military service in Western Europe contributed to the notion of citizenship. Engels judged this contribution to be of continuing, central importance. It is in the writings of Gaetano Mosca, particularly in *The Ruling Class*, that the initial comprehensive analysis of the connection between conscription and political forms is presented.[18]

Because of the accumulation of historical scholarship, we are in a position to offer a more systemic analysis, which includes an examination of the ideological and political conceptions of citizenship.[19] This approach throws light on the rise and decline of the modern mass armed force. We are concerned with 1920–1975, which saw the "perfection" of the mass military institution, and, in turn, its transformation by means of the elimination or constriction of conscription. But it is necessary to examine, even briefly, the trends of the last two centuries, since military institutions have a profound ability both to change and to maintain their traditional logic. In particular, we must be concerned

16. Karl Marx, *The 18th Brumaire of Louis Bonaparte* (New York: International, 1969); Friedrich Engels, *Anti-Duhring: Herr Eugen Duhring's Revolution in Science* (Moscow: Foreign Language Publishing House, 1954), pp. 219–56.

17. Friedrich Engels, *Anti-Duhring.*

18. Gaetano Mosca, *The Ruling Class* (New York: McGraw-Hill, 1939).

19. Morris Janowitz, "Military Institutions and Citizenship in Western Societies," *Armed Forces and Society* 2 (1976): 185–204.

with the normative and ideological context of civil-military relations and the notions of the "citizen"-soldier, which were grounded in the impact of the nationalist revolutions—the American, the French, and the earlier Cromwellian. With the decline of the mass armed force after 1945, the character of modern military institutions undergoes basic change, especially as they influence social stratification and the processes of social control.[20]

Social stratification and inequality in the United States has been fundamentally conditioned by the structure of its military institutions and by the patterns of popular military participation. Our underlying assumption is that the rise of the mass armed force in the West and in the United States had elements which were compatible with, and, in fact, reinforced parliamentary democracy. The more specific hypothesis is linked to the system of conscription which came into force during the twentieth century. It was based on the tradition of the citizen-soldier of the United States. During the mobilization of World War I and World War II, the military personnel system, although it had obvious inequalities, operated to strengthen social equality and to integrate participants into the larger society. However, participation in the limited wars of Korea and especially of Vietnam had increased social inequality and differentiated the participant and the veteran from the larger society.

Two organizational and normative features of the Western military institutions are relevant. A component of personalized feudal authority persisted in the officer corps which could relatively easily be transferred to civilian political leadership. Parliamentary processes were strengthened by the broadening base of recruitment of officers and rank and file, especially by the normative content of conscription by which mass political participation was legitimatized by military service.[21] In turn, the decline of the mass armed forces after 1945 and the transformation of the military into an all-volunteer force in the 1970s have the potential of increasing the strain in civil-military relations and of attenuating the citizen-soldier concept.

20. Morris Janowitz, "The Decline of the Mass Army," *Military Review* (February 1972), pp. 10–17; Jacques van Doorn, "The Decline of the Mass Army in the West: General Reflections," *Armed Forces and Society* 1 (1975): 147–58.

21. For another perspective, see V. G. Kiernan, "Conscription and Society in Europe before the War of 1914–1918," in *War and Society: Historical Essays in Honor and Memory of J. R. Western*, ed. M. R. D. Foot (London: Paul Elek, 1973), pp. 141–58.

We are dealing with the organization of military forces and with the changing pattern of military strategy. The conception of military service under the citizen-soldier format and wars of specific and delimited duration were more manageable by parliamentary regimes. It is therefore necessary to examine the hypothesis that the shift in military function toward a strategy of deterrence, because it involves continuous and enlarged "peacetime" military operations about which there is political debate, also increases the strain in civil-military relations.

The end of military conscription in the United States on June 30, 1973 can be taken as the symbolic date of the decline—or rather, transformation—of the mass armed force. For the first time the United States undertook to maintain an expanded military establishment without conscription. The professional cadre of officers and enlisted personnel to be expanded by citizen-soldiers in times of emergency gave way to a more regularized "force in being." With the doctrine of deterrence, military forces had to narrow the distinction between "wartime" and "peacetime" operations. After the advent of nuclear weapons in 1945, the military establishments of the Western parliamentary democracies after 1945 were transformed more and more into a "force in being" with a heavier reliance on volunteer personnel. Great Britain eliminated conscription in 1962. By 1975, Denmark, the Netherlands, and Belgium had contracted the length of conscript service and projected plans for an all-volunteer armed force. In France, the end of conscription was more remote because of political traditions, but public debate on the subject was intense and the military forces had in effect started a transition toward a mixed system. The Federal Republic of Germany has a special politico-military position because of the division of Germany, but in West Germany, alternative civilian service to military service was well developed and extensive; moreover, the military authorities had even explored the possibility of a professional cadre augmented by a citizen militia. The image and reality of the conscript military—a dominant historical theme of nineteenth-century Europe—had, in effect, been extensively undermined.

Conventional scholarship places the origin of the mass armed force immediately after the American and French Revolutions: the modern professional mass armies of Western Europe emerged from the post-feudal institutions created in the eighteenth century by the absolute monarchies.[22] This view of military history emphasizes the influence

22. Theodore Ropp, *War in the Modern World* (New York: Collier-Macmillan, 1962); see also O. L. Spaulding, Hoffman Nickerson, and J. W. Wright, *Warfare:*

of modern technology and modern forms of military organization, and focuses on the transformation of the military in France and Germany—in the center of Europe—from its feudal antecedents into its professional and bureaucratic character.

But there is a good reason to alter this historical overview, especially for the tasks of analyzing civil-military relations in the framework of social control. It is more accurate to locate the initial development of the modern military system in the Netherlands (at the periphery of Europe—innovations often take place at the periphery) at the end of the sixteenth century. On the other hand, greater emphasis must be given to the effects of the American, French, and Cromwellian Revolutions, focusing on the normative and political context of the emergence of the Western military institutions.

In the Dutch struggle against the Spanish at the end of the sixteenth century, a basic ingredient of the modern military was the mercenary forces which they developed. These forces were the first to use modern organizational discipline. As Maury Feld has demonstrated, they were a forerunner of Max Weber's rational bureaucratic organization.[23] Modern military organization had its roots, not in the gradual transformation of feudal and postfeudal institutions, but in mercenary units. The social structure of the Netherlands supported this development. The Netherlands had strong middle-class elements located in relatively independent urban centers; the outlook of the feudal gentry did not dominate the organization of military forces. But it can hardly be asserted that the economic interests of the bourgeois created these new military institutions, although they supplied the preconditions. We are dealing with conscious efforts at institution building; we are dealing with relatively autonomous steps toward professionalization based on the study of past military enterprises and on a conscious effort at trial and error in the persistent application of scientific and engineering principles which could be pursued more successfully in the relative absence of the norms of landed aristocratic groups.[24] (The city-states of Italy used mercenaries, but this did not contribute to the development of modern professional armies.)[25]

A Study of Military Methods from the Earliest Times (London: Harrap, 1924); Michael Howard, *War in European History* (London: Oxford University Press, 1976).

23. Maury Feld, "Middle-Class Society and the Rise of Military Professionalism: The Dutch Army 1589–1609," *Armed Forces and Society* 1 (1975): 419–42.

24. Ibid.

25. Michael Mallett, *Mercenaries and Their Masters: Warfare in the Renaissance* (Totowa, N.J.: Rowman and Littlefield, 1974), p. 207.

However, the political definitions of the American and French Revolutions contributed decisively to the institutionalization of military service in a format which contributed to civilian control. The core was that military service was an aspect of citizenship. This took place only in the West. Two ideas are central in this regard. First, because of the political definition of the American and French Revolutions, citizenship was linked to and validated by military service; this form of conscription has been an essential component in the emergence of Western parliamentary institutions. (Conscription in the nineteenth century was also compatible with monarchial regimes in Prussia and Austria, Hungary and with serflike sociopolitical relations with Czarist Russia.)[26] The second idea involves the transformation of the postfeudal military to the bureaucratic and professional armies of the nineteenth century. The "heroic" model of the Western officer corps, rooted in European feudalism, has been important in facilitating the acceptance of parliamentary and civilian control. The military elite, or at least a significant portion traditionally conservative because of their conception of personal fealty, could readily transfer their allegiance from the monarchy to the leaders of the new regimes.[27] The failure or the reluctance of the professional military to intervene directly in the political process in the nineteenth-century West more extensively than they did requires explanation. Throughout the nineteenth century, the military's behavior was contained compared with military groups of the developing nations since 1945.[28] The military leaders at various times in the development of Western political institutions monopolized coercive power to at least as great a degree as the military in developing societies after World War II. Moreover, they often operated in a setting in which political parties were as weak as or even weaker than those in the new nations. Therefore, the rise of the mass armed force and its implication of civil-military relations require systemic analysis in terms of *(a)* technology and organizational format, *(b)* social stratification and professionalization, and *(c)* the normative content of citizenship and mili-

26. Richard Hellie, *Enserfment and Military Change in Muscovy* (Chicago: University of Chicago Press, 1971).

27. This theme has not been extensively researched but is revealing in biographical and literary sources.

28. Morris Janowitz, *The Military in the Political Development of New Nations* (Chicago: University of Chicago Press, 1964); Morris Janowitz, *Military Institutions and Coercion in the Developing Nations* (Chicago: University of Chicago Press, 1977).

tary service. These variables operate to explain the subsequent decline of the mass armed force.

Technology and organizational format.—Most historical writing about emergence of the mass armed force emphasizes the technological dimension. The sociological approach is to regard technology as a set of factors fashioning organizational format. The technological base of the mass armed force has rested on the increase in firepower effected by the introduction of the rifle and modern artillery, and on the development of transportation and communication systems permitting the concentration of large numbers of men and machines. These technological innovations could utilize the manpower produced by conscription and thereby contribute to the strengthening of large-scale "nationalized" bureaucratic military organization and to the weakening of feudal conceptions of military life.

However, citizen participation in the military antedated the new technology. Modern technology was only incipient during the French and American Revolutions. Likewise, modern technology has been incorporated into military systems where the notion of citizenship and its political implications have been completely absent. At best, technology can be considered a facilitating variable in determining the military's role in the emergence of the modern state.

Modern technology also contributed to the development of the strategic conception of total war.[29] Progressively larger proportions of the civilian population have been mobilized into the military or into war-related production. The slaughter of human beings has increased, especially with the introduction of airpower, with less and less regard to the distinction between the military and the civilian. The deployment of nuclear weapons represents the "perfection" of the modern military by vastly increasing its destructiveness. At the same time, advanced technology carries the "seeds of its own destruction," since the outbreak of total nuclear war can no longer be perceived as in the national interest. After 1946, the military function shifted from making war to deterrence, to the extent that rational considerations could be applied.[30] Peripheral war prolonged conscription in the United States,

29. Raymond Aron, *The Century of Total War.*

30. Morris Janowitz, "Toward a Redefinition of Military Strategy in International Relations," *World Politics* 26 (Summer 1974): 473–508.

but in time the altered strategy eliminated or reduced conscription among Western industrialized nations. All-volunteer professional forces augmented by various types of part-time soldiers, or short-term militias, have been emphasized.

Social stratification and professionalization.—The emergence of the mass armed force has changed the social stratification of the military and transformed the military into a bureaucratic institution with its own format of professionalism. Despite important structural differences from nation-state to nation-state, a generalized pattern of stratification of the military in Western nations—including the United States—has been identified. It contrasts with the development of the military in other regions of the world. The officer corps of Western Europe before the French Revolution was an elite whose social recruitment was rooted in the landed aristocracy, especially in the minor gentry. Its social recruitment not only gave it its conservative political outlook but was also an integral aspect of its code of honor, despite the fact that the armed forces became more and more technical and professionalized. The system of land tenure enabled a social enclave to persist where traditional values could be maintained and from which "reliable" officers were recruited.

A body of scholarship traces the broadening of the social origins of members of the military profession as new technology and mass armies developed. In all the militaries of Western Europe for which studies of historical trends are available, the professionalization of the military in the nineteenth century meant the introduction of middle-class elements into a structure dominated by the upper class with its close connections to the landed gentry. Karl Demeter in his study of *The German Officer Corps* presents the prototype of this type of officer corps. Comparable trends have been documented in Great Britain, France, Italy, Belgium, Sweden, and Norway, and earlier in the Netherlands.[31]

Even before the French Revolution, technological necessity and the growth in size of the military establishments in Western Europe required that middle-class officers be introduced to fill the cadres of artillery, engineering, and logistical specialists. The French Revolution,

31. Karl Demeter, *The German Officer-Corps in Society and State 1650–1945* (New York: Praeger, 1965); Morris Janowitz, *The Professional Soldier: A Social and Political Portrait* (Glencoe, Ill.: Free Press, 1960, revised 1971), pp. 79–103; Bengt Abrahamsson, *Military Professionalization and Political Power* (Beverly Hills, Calif.: Sage Publications, 1972), pp. 20–58.

of course, speeded up the social transformation of the French military establishment (the absence of a comparative process in England permitted the feudal type of domination to persist through much of the nineteenth century).[32] In France, the transformation represented a balance between the infusion of new nonnoble personnel and the persistence of noble personnel. S. F. Scott has traced the extent to which traditional components persisted in the "revolutionary" armies.[33] At the lower ranks of the officer corps the influx of new personnel was most extensive, including men promoted from noncommissioned status; at the higher ranks, a carryover in personnel predominated. As of 1793, nobles still constituted 70% of the generals.

By the end of the nineteenth century, however, throughout Western Europe, middle-class personnel were extensive in the military and frequently dominated it in number, except in selected elite infantry and calvary units with high personalistic attachments to surviving monarchies. But the concentration of numbers was less important than the fact that political conservative traditions and the heroic model persisted until World War II. In the United States, although there was no feudal tradition, a comparable social selectivity in recruitment served to develop a similar set of values. Recruitment was concentrated among native-born white Protestant families from rural and hinterland backgrounds, especially in the South.

Social origin and recruitment does not determine political behavior. As professionalization grows, there are more and more links between political behavior and professional socialization. Jacques van Doorn has traced the development of military professionalism, with its heroic component which developed within a bureaucratic structure.[34] In the nineteenth century, the social role and professional format of the officer corps of Western industrialized nations were compatible with the variety of political forms, but this compatibility included acceptance of and alliance with struggling democratic institutions. In England,

32. Katharine Chorley has sought to investigate the conditions under which "armed forces" either support or do not oppose revolutionary movements, using the historical materials of Western Europe, Russia, and the United States. Katharine Chorley, *Armies and the Art of Revolution* (London: Faber, 1943).

33. S. F. Scott, "The French Revolution and the Professionalization of the French Officer Corps, 1789–1793," in *On Military Ideology*, ed. Morris Janowitz and Jacques van Doorn (Rotterdam: University of Rotterdam Press, 1971), pp. 5–56.

34. Jacques van Doorn, "Political Change and the Control of the Military: Some General Remarks," in *Military Profession and Military Regimes: Commitments and Conflicts*, ed. Jacques van Doorn (The Hague: Mouton, 1969), pp. 11–35.

France, and the United States, revolutionary movements influenced the officer corps, although there was continuity and only gradual transformation from feudal forms. The heroic model inhibited the officers' direct intervention in politics. In England, the professional officers felt that the civilian political leaders were men with whom they had strong social, political, and often familial affiliations.

Thus the residue of the heroic model, with its emphasis on traditional values and personal allegiance to the ruler, permitted acceptance of the emerging parliamentary forms. This is not to assert that, in the nineteenth century, the military profession was without political influence or that its political power was only the result of struggles between competing civilian elite groups. Rather, social origins, and the social mold of the military with its upper-class sense of guardianship of the state, worked in the United States and Great Britain, on balance, to serve the processes of internal parliamentary government. In France, the balance was more unstable and disruptive, but the military did not fundamentally undermine the parliamentary system, although at times challenging its existence; one outcome of the Napoleonic period was a constitutional monarchy and a legislative arena. On the other hand, the officer corps that emerged in Germany was compatible with and served to support the monarchial-civil service regime, moreover, the officer corps had its own direct representative at court and in the central organs of the government.

In sharp contrast, for example, the Ottoman military did not rest on a feudal social structure in Western European terms. The system of land tenure and the sultan's position ruled out an independent nobility either as a source of officer recruitment or as a political check on the sultan's power. Instead, for centuries the armed forces were recruited by the Ottoman Empire from a diverse base, including a slave type of component, in order to strengthen the sultan. Military service was a form of government service under the sultan's authority.[35] It had no specific conservative orientation reflecting attachment to a landed upper class. In the absence of a feudal and heroic tradition, the Turkish military leaders, as they have developed modern armed forces, have been committed to their own notions of revolutionary political change and accessible to and involved in direct domestic political action.

35. Morris Janowitz, "Some Observations on the Comparative Analysis of Middle Eastern Military Institutions," in *War, Technology and Society in the Middle East*, ed. V. J. Parry and M. E. Yapp (London: Oxford University Press, 1975), pp. 412–40.

Military Participation and Total War

During the first half of the twentieth century in Western industrialized nations, the growth of the military establishment, more than the social origins or professionalization of its officers, contributed to its increased political weight. With the decline of the mass armed force and the movement to an all-volunteer system, social recruitment reemerges as a more important variable, since participation becomes less representative. In the post–World War II period, the trend in much of the West has been toward a heavier self-recruitment in the officer corps, especially among sons of noncommissioned officers. There is evidence of disproportionate reliance on sources such as special preparatory schools catering to old service families with regional affiliations. The existence of an unrepresentative officer corps during the emergence of the all-volunteer force does not necessarily present a "putschist" threat to parliamentary institutions, but it does weaken the legitimacy of military institutions and its ability to extend citizenship. Moreover, selective factors in recruitment tend to increase the conservative political bias of the officer corps and to produce more rigid attitudes toward international affairs, and thereby to aggravate the problems of effective social control.[36]

Military Institutions and Citizenship

Trends in civil-military relations do not merely reflect technological developments and patterns of social recruitment; they are rooted in ideological and normative content, in particular, in a sense of nationality. Military institutions have been central in fashioning the type of nation-states that emerged in Western Europe and the United States. In fact, the armed forces of the nineteenth and twentieth centuries epitomize modern nationalism. But modern nationalism hardly ensures the emergence of political democracy.[37] The analytic terrain that requires investigation is complex and the theoretical formulations involved are easily misunderstood. Political democracy is linked to the normative notion of "citizenship." To the extent that mass armies in the West defined their recruits in terms of political and normative ideas of citizenship, military service functioned as an essential contribution to politi-

36. Jerald G. Bachman and John D. Blair, " 'Citizen Force' or 'Career Force': Implications for Ideology in the All-Volunteer Force," in *The Social Psychology of Military Service*, ed. Nancy L. Goldman and David R. Segal (Beverly Hills, Calif.: Sage Publications, 1976), pp. 237–54.

37. Alfred Vagts, *A History of Militarism.*

cal institutions. Of course, the political meaning of military service is generated and imposed by political elites external to the military. There is another factor in the mass conscript army which contributes to the democratic political institution: revolutionary nationalism, in the United States and especially in France, broke the monopoly of the higher social groups over the officer corps. In theory, and to some extent in reality, members of all social groups could become officers.

However, military conflict also created social and political tensions which weakened democratic political institutions. Moreover, throughout the nineteenth and early twentieth centuries, civil-military relations were influenced by the "military-industrial complex" of that time. Industrial groups aligned themselves with the military (e.g., Krupp under Kaiser Wilhelm, and Schneider during the Third French Republic) in such a manner as to strain parliamentary control over the officer corps.

Reinhard Bendix, in *Citizenship and Nation Building*, argues that the extension of the franchise is the key indicator of nation building in Western Europe in the nineteenth century.[38] Stein Rokkan has also developed this theme in considerable detail.[39] Such analyses are too circumscribed. Alternatively or in amplification, I argue that, starting with the French and American Revolutions, participation in the national army has been an integral aspect of the normative definition of citizenship. In those conflicts, political leaders armed extensive groups in the civil population breaking with tradition. That the rank and file could and should be armed and would be loyal was "revolutionary." The establishment of the principle that the officer corps was open to recruits from all groups was similarly revolutionary. Under feudal and post-feudal arrangements from the Renaissance to the neo-Classical age, 1417–1789, military formations were officered by groups dominated by the nobility and were manned by mercenaries, men impressed into service, and small groups of volunteers.[40] In the Italian city-states, particularly those with republican forms, some degree of military service was required of citizens.

38. Reinhard Bendix, *Nation-Building and Citizenship*. "Similar questions were raised with regard to universal conscription, since arms in the hands of the common people were considered a revolutionary threat."

39. Stein Rokkan, "Mass Suffrage, Secret Voting and Political Participation," *European Journal of Sociology* 2 (1961): 132–52. See also "The Comparative Study of Political Participation," in *Essays on the Behavioral Study of Politics*, ed. A. Ranney (Urbana: University of Illinois Press, 1962).

40. T. Ropp, *War in the Modern World*.

Military Participation and Total War

The citizen-soldier concept originated in the Greek city-state and in the early Roman military system, where the connections among military service, control of the armed forces, and political democracy were explicitly formulated and institutionalized. Some of the leaders of the French Revolution referred explicitly to these classic ideas and practices. Moreover, the citizen-soldier format had its institutional antecedents, before the American and French Revolutions, in the militia and national guard units. Variations of these types of units were widespread both in Western Europe and in the North American British and French colonies. The part-time service of their officers and the more representative character of their members anticipated the social format of the mass citizen-conscript armies. Particularly in France, the national guard units played an important role in armed conflicts of the Revolution.

The legitimacy of these revolutionary movements and the political democracies they sought to establish rested on the fact that citizens had been armed and had demonstrated their loyalty through military service.[41] Military service became a hallmark of citizenship and citizenship the hallmark of a political democracy. The citizen army which used civilian reservists was not only an instrument of nationalism but also a device for the political control of the military professionals. To stress the political and normative consequences of mass military service is not to overlook the requirement that the military leaders of the mass armed forces which emerged during the nineteenth century had to be depoliticized or politically contained if any variant of political democracy were to be achieved and institutionalized.

While it is possible to speak of the emergence of modern armed forces in Western Europe in the nineteenth century, such a general observation cannot obscure the variations in the organizational and normative bases of mass participation in the military in different nations. The connection between citizen-soldier and the effective extension of the franchise, with its influence on political institutions, reflects different historical patterns in Germany, France, Great Britain, and the United States. In France the conception of the citizen-conscript was most clearly enunciated as a principle designed to assist civilian political control of the military. Conscription was institutionalized early and widely

41. It is interesting that social anthropologists concerned with political institutions have turned their attention to the analogies of the presence or absence of the idea of "citizenship" as a central approach of the politico-jural structure of tribal and peasant societies. See, for example, Meyer Fortes, *Kinship and the Social Order: The Legacy of Lewis Henry Morgan* (Chicago: Aldine, 1969).

accepted; it has been gradually reformed and expanded, with the result that it has served as an accepted institution in French social structure. In contemporary France, the political commitment to conscription remains the strongest among Western nations, although, with the development of nuclear weapons and the end of the French empire, it has come under increasing attack, especially by extreme radical movements. In the United States the ideological and political bases for the citizen-soldier have been strong and extensive from the American Revolution. The forms of local militia were rooted in obligatory citizen service. However, national and military requirements made it possible to avoid introducing conscription except in wartime, until the end of World War II. From World War I onward, citizen military service has been seen as a device by which minorities could achieve political legitimacy and rights. Until Vietnam, for example, blacks pressed to be armed and integrated into the fighting military as a sign that they had effectively attained citizenship and the concomitant privileges. Americans of Japanese descent, who were subject to indignities and arbitrary internment after the attack on Pearl Harbor, volunteered for all-Japanese combat units in order to demonstrate their loyalty and reaffirm their citizenship. While professional officers have informally been excluded from elected office, with the exception of a number of wartime heroes who became president, service as a citizen-soldier has been a powerful asset for candidates seeking election to the Senate and House of Representatives.

Germany's parliamentary institutions until after World War II were weak in comparison with those in France, Great Britain, and the United States. Nevertheless, the connection between military service and the extension of the franchise was explicit in "nation building" in Germany. For example, in 1871 Bismarck expanded male suffrage to a limited extent immediately after the unification of Germany in response to the political realities created by new forms of military service. In contrast, throughout most of the nineteenth century, British military institutions were an admixture of feudal forms and slowly emerging professional officers.[42] The extension of the franchise was also very gradual and limited. World War I transformed the structure of the British military. Conscription was not instituted in Great Britain until after World War I had caused enormous manpower losses. The political consequences of

42. Gwyn Harries-Jenkins, *The Army in Victorian Society* (London: Routledge and Kegan Paul, 1977).

extensive military mobilization produced legislation in 1918 which completed the extension of the franchise and was explicitly linked to the necessity of giving political rights to those who had been conscripted.[43]

It is essential to keep in mind the distinction between the process of "modernization" in the West—Westernization, if you will—and the equivalent processes of sociopolitical change leading to the emergence of the nation-state in other regions that occurred later. The traditional Ottoman Empire before the nineteenth century had military formations which rivaled those of the West. However, the "modernization" of the Ottoman military depended on important Western technology and Western organizational procedures. Modern military elements were, so to speak, grafted onto the Ottoman social structure, and the associated industrial development lagged until well into the middle of the twentieth century. Japan in the second half of the nineteenth century introduced both Western technology and military forms and experienced a simultaneous and continuous development of its industrial and military institutions. But neither the Ottomans nor the Japanese developed or assimilated the notion of citizenship as an aspect of military service; instead, the growth of parliamentary institutions of control over the military was inhibited, slow, and fragmented.

The American and French Revolutions were social and political movements whose ideological and normative content and leadership styles had independent effects on "nation" building. The ideological content of these movements fashioned the social cohesion of the central leaders and contributed to the mobilization of activist cadres, both military and civilian. They involved extensive armed conflict against existing standing armies, in which the revolutionary forces were victorious because they could mobilize new rank-and-file cadres and use professional officers. Moreover, the effective consequences of these revolutionary movements were not military dictatorships or oligarchies, but parliamentary institutions of varying stability and effectiveness.

Three elements in the ideological content of the American and French Revolutions (and, on an equivalent basis, of the Cromwellian Revolution) were significant in influencing their character and consequences. First, their ideology and political propaganda were explicitly nationalist.

43. Arthur Marwick, *Britain in the Century of Total War: War, Peace and Social Change 1900–1967* (London: Bodley Head, 1968), p. 110; Philip Abrams, "The Failure of Social Reform: 1918–1920, *Past and Present* 24 (April 1963): 43–64; B. A. Warles, "The Effect of the First World War on Class and Status in England, 1910–1920," *Journal of Contemporary History* 11 (January 1976): 27–48.

That is, they created a national symbolism of identification within which to press for sociopolitical change and to demand social and political justice, more in France than in the United States. National symbols were offered in contrast to existing localistic and traditional boundaries. The idea and appeal of nationalism as a basis for collective action were powerful and enduring. Nationalist symbolism supplied a basis for the political legitimacy of revolutionary leadership and a particularly effective basis for organizing the armed forces. Nationalist ideology was a convenient vehicle by which feudal elements could find their social, professional, and political positions in the emerging polity and in the postrevolutionary mass armed forces.

Second, the ideological and normative definition of citizenship and the notion of civic participation in the revolutionary armed forces were equally pervasive and powerful. The legitimacy of these forces was based on an appeal to defend individual freedom and achieve social and political justice. To arm the ordinary person and to declare his right to bear arms was revolutionary, serving the immediate requirements of raising military cadres and drawing participants from different social strata. But this was not only a military formula. It was a political definition which enlarged the concept of who were effective members of the polity. Like nationalism, it supplied a key ingredient in the expansion of the electorate. The duties and obligations of the armed citizen set the framework for the concept of the electorate in civil society, although actual enfranchisement came later.

From the Cromwellian Revolution onward, the actual competence of military leaders to rule in Western nation-states has, indeed, been limited. Philip Abrams's study of the Cromwell military government by generals and colonels has shown it had problems comparable to the difficulties of the contemporary military oligarchies of new nations.[44] The generals and colonels could not convert their ability to seize power into a legitimate base for a stable government. In the United States, historians emphasize George Washington's political commitment to civilian rule, but this represented the pervasive ideological and normative definitions of the American Revolution.[45]

44. Philip Abrams, "Restoring Order: Some Early European Cases," in *On Military Intervention*, ed. Morris Janowitz and Jacques van Doorn (Rotterdam: Rotterdam University Press, 1971).

45. Richard H. Kohn, *Eagle and Sword: The Federalists and the Creation of the Military Establishment in America, 1783–1802* (New York: Free Press, 1975).

Military Participation and Total War

For 150 years, the notions of nationalism and citizenship participation supplied a basis for transforming the military from a status group into more and more of a civil service organization of the state. In Germany, where the concept of citizenship was weak, the military continued to operate as a detached status group, as a state within a state, even after World War I. The National Socialist regime, with its ruthless and distorted forms of "democratization," ended the Prussian military assumptions. The reconstructed armed forces, after the Allied victory, have a conventional modern Western format.[46] In most Western European nations with modern industrial systems, the standing armies could exist alongside parliamentary systems—a special historical development of limited frequency. This has been so not only because of the patterns of civilian social structure but also because the military had come to accept the legitimacy of the political system.

The decline of the "political ideal" of mass armed force and the citizen-soldier started with the destructive impact of World War I and was deepened by the military consequences of World War II. The potentials of nuclear destruction made it difficult for the individual to perceive his military relevance. Likewise, the sense of nationality among West Europeans but also among Americans was attenuated. While this trend is clearly discernible, it should not be overstated. Feelings of national identity remain deep-seated and are readily mobilized in periods of tension and crisis. The weakening of a sense of nationality and the contraction of mass armed forces do not automatically strengthen parliamentary institutions. The attenuation of nationalist sentiments and ideology is not caused only by the increased destructiveness—actual and nuclear potential—of war. It is also a popular expression of an advanced industrial society with a high level of income and education that produces strong antiauthoritarianism and pronounced hedonistic concerns. Negative attitudes toward military service become widespread as the logic of nationalism is questioned and as the rationale for the military is obscured by the reality of nuclear weapons. Social and political movements become intensified. Only a tiny minority of college-educated youth were prepared to engage in confrontation politics de-

46. Eric Waldman, *The Goose Step is Verboten: The German Army Today* (New York: Free Press, 1964); Dietrich Genschel, *Wehrreform und Reaktion: Die Vorbeitung der Innere Fuhrung 1951–1956* (Hamburg: R. V. Decker's Verlag G. Schenck, 1972).

signed to "undermine" contemporary military institutions, while a much larger group are hostile to the forms of military authority.

A convergence of consequences derives from the new dimensions of technology, social stratification, and the normative content of social and political movements in Western advanced industrial nations. All these dimensions imply a continuing and even increased potential for the separation of the military from the larger society to render it a more isolated body with selective relations with that society. The consequence is a greater ideological differentiation between those who offer themselves for a military career and the greater part of the population who accept the necessity of a military but accord it limited moral legitimacy. Our analysis of the social stratification of the United States as an advanced industrial society highlights that the new forms of occupational stratification, as well as the age, sex, ethnic-religious, and racial differences do not supply the basis for "revolutionary" social conflict but do create social divisions which are persistent and disruptive. Issues of civil-military relations, such as the internal position of the military and the military's role in foreign affairs, to be discussed below, also burden the parliamentary system of an advanced industrial society. The allocation of military costs and inequalities of military participation as well as the purposes of military operations all contribute to weakening the patterns of social control with the decline of the mass armed force.

War and Inequality

The major wars which the United States has fought in the twentieth century have consumed immense economic and human resources. Various indicators are available to chart the different impacts of these wars and of military institutions on the social structure of the United States. At stake is the hypothesis that over time military participation and its influence have become more unequal. Trends which encompass the half-century from World War I to the advent of the expanded all-volunteer military make it possible to assess the consequences of the decline of the mass armed force. Of course, such trend analysis is limited by the fact that more adequate data exist for the Korean and Second Indochina Wars.

Without losing sight of the human misery and misfortune, let us mention three topics of special relevance for the analysis of the changing patterns of social control: (*a*) trends in expenditures for the military compared with spending for welfare; (*b*) the differential patterns of military service and of combat casualties by social groupings; and (*c*) the consequences of military service on veteran status, including the transition back to civilian life.

Trends in Military Budgets

Examination of the trends in military expenditures reveals the competition between the programs of national defense and those of welfare. These trends also help assess the argument that persistent and high-level military expenditures are required in the United States in order to maintain economic "prosperity"; in this view, the economy would collapse without this form of reinvestment of the economic surplus. However, military expenditures have their consequences in a transformed system of national accounts; it is difficult to speak of an economic surplus which presents problems of reinvestment. In the simplest terms, persistent deficit spending by governmental units during 1965 to 1975, plus a decline in the proportion of the gross national product allocated for industrial capital reinvestment, coupled with high levels of consumption, have produced a decline and, in fact, an absence of an effective economic surplus.

The transformation of the national accounts in the United States is reflected in the trends in total government spending as a percentage of the national income during the period from the Great Depression to the depression of 1973 (see Table 6.1). The increase in the proportion of the national income allocated by government spending has been steady and pronounced. From these data it can be seen that government spending as a fraction of the national income rose from 11.9% in 1929 to 38.6% in 1973. Since World War II, the pattern of governmental expenditure has been one of an essential decline in the proportion allocated to the military. As indicated in Tables 5.2 and 5.3, the long-term increase in the welfare budget has been more rapid than that of the military. The total mobilization of World War II produced a dramatic fluctuation in military expenditures. However, Korea, and subsequently Vietnam, resulted in less fluctuation in the long-term downward trend in such expenditures. The height of the Korea War produced a military budget of 16.0% of the national income; in 1967 the Vietnam military budget reached 11.1% of the national income, which was only a limited increase over the previous years. This was in part due to the fact that each successive military engagement involved a more limited

TABLE 6.1 Government Spending as a Percentage of National Income, 1929–1975

Year	Total Spending[1]	Defense Spending[2]	Domestic Spending[3]
1929	11.9%	0.8%	11.1%
1933	26.6	1.5	25.1
1939	24.2	1.6	22.6
1944	56.4	47.9	8.5
1949	27.2	6.1	21.1
1953	33.2	16.0	17.2
1959	32.8	11.5	21.2
1960	32.8	10.8	22.0
1961	34.9	11.2	23.7
1962	34.9	11.3	23.7
1963	34.6	10.5	24.1
1964	33.9	9.7	24.2
1965	33.1	8.9	24.2
1966	34.2	9.8	24.4
1967	37.2	11.1	26.1
1968	38.0	11.0	27.0
1969	37.6	10.2	27.3
1970	37.8	9.3	28.5
1971	37.5	8.3	29.1
1972	39.1	7.9	31.2
1973	38.6	7.0	31.6
1974	40.1	6.8	33.3
1975	43.4	6.9	36.5

1. Expenditures of federal, state, and local government as defined in national income accounts.
2. Purchases of goods and services for national defense as defined in national income accounts.
3. Total spending minus defense spending.

SOURCE: *Economic Report of the President* (Washington, GPO, 1974), pp. 249, 265, 328.

war mobilization and a continued expansion of the civilian national economy. Thus, the long-term trends in the decline in military expenditures can be described by the observation that in the 1960s, the military expenditures ran about 10% of the gross national income, while in the early 1970s, the figure dropped to below 7.0%. In 1975, the first increase in the proportion of the national income for military expenditures was projected.

With the advent of the all-volunteer force, the military establishment contracted from a high point of 3.5 million personnel in the height of Vietnam intervention in 1968 to almost 2 million persons in 1975 (see Table 6.2). As the military shifted more to a force in being, personnel costs rose to well over half the military expenditures. One significant aspect of military budget expenditures is the continuous rise in the cost of military pensions as delayed military manpower expenditures. By 1975 these costs had reached $6 billion and were projected to rise to over $20 billion by 1985. As noted previously, the basic increase in government expenditures in the post–World War II period has been in welfare expenditures. If we define welfare as governmental expenditures for health, education, and income maintenance (plus classes of housing and community development programs), welfare expenditures rose from 9.5% of the gross national product in 1935 to 17.6% in 1973. A significant increase was recorded in interest payments for the national debt, but increases in welfare expenditures are at the heart of the transformation of the national accounts.

TABLE 6.2 Trends in U.S. Military Participation, 1900–1975

Year	Total Uniformed Personnel	Military Participation Ratio*
1900	125,923	0.32
1905	108,301	0.25
1910	139,344	0.29
1915	174,112	0.34
1920	343,302	0.63
1925	251,756	0.43
1930	255,648	0.41
1935	251,799	0.39
1940	458,365	0.69
1945	12,123,455	16.93
1950	1,460,261	1.90
1955	22,935,107	3.54
1960	2,476,435	2.77
1965	2,653,142	2.76
1970	3,066,000	3.06
1975	2,129,000	

*For purposes of trend reporting, the military participation ratio is computed as the ratio of male personnel in the armed forces to the total male population for the particular year.

On the central economic issue of the importance of military expenditures in the United States as a stimulus or as an essential element in maintaining economic "prosperity," the available bodies of sophisticated research by Murray Weidenbaum, Stanley Lieberson, and Clark Nardinelli and Gary B. Ackerman all come to negative conclusions.[47] A

47. Murray Weidenbaum, *The Modern Public Sector* (New York: Basic Books, 1969); Stanley Lieberson, "An Empirical Study of Military-Industrial Linkages," *American Journal of Sociology* 76 (January 1971): 562–84. Clark Nardinelli and

very few large firms are almost entirely or crucially dependent on military contracts. However, for the late 1960s, among the 50 largest industrial companies, only 12 were among the 100 biggest military contractors, and these firms had a ratio of military contracts to sales of 4% or less. Such economic dependency is hardly pronounced. Even more relevant, at the macrolevel, either of the industrial sector or of the total economy, military contracts were revealed to be of limited economic consequence. Lieberson, using a Leontie F input-output model, demonstrated that a reduction in military expenditures in the 1960s of 20% could result in an output and employment reduction from about 16% in aircraft production to 5% in electronics equipment, with generally compensating results in other economic sectors but on a highly dispersed, diversified basis. This type of analysis does not deal with day-to-day political pressures. No doubt the concentration of the impact of a reduction would generate considerable political pressures against reduction as compared with mobilizing support among the diversified corporations that would benefit. Moreover, it can be argued that this type of economic analysis does not take into account the indirect effects of military expenditures in stimulating consumer demand, but the substitutability of such effects is obviously very great if welfare expenditures or tax reductions are taken into consideration.

In any case, Nardinelli and Ackerman's analysis for 1905–1973 sought to analyze the direct effect of the magnitude of military expenditures on the growth of the gross national product.[48] Their results, based on careful regression analysis, indicated that military expenditures "crowd out" private expenditure, or, in short, that military expenditures had a negative effect on the real growth of the gross national product. This was especially the case for 1946–1973. There is no adequate body of data about the income distributions and redistributions resulting from military expenditures. But it is known that the rate of profit in investments in military-related industries is lower than in non–military-related industries, in part because of the volatility of demand and because of public regulation.[49] However, there is no reason to expect that the economic

Gary B. Ackerman, "Defense Expenditures and the Survival of American Capitalism: A Note," *Armed Forces and Society* 3 (1976), 13–16. Stephen Cobb, "Defense Spending and Defense Voting in the House: An Empirical Study of an Aspect of the Military-Industrial Complex Thesis," *American Journal of Sociology* 82 (July 1976): 163–82.

48. Nardinelli and Ackerman, "Defense Expenditures."

49. Weidenbaum, *Modern Sector*, passim.

distributions from military-related industries are markedly different from those of other industrial sectors.

Thus a partial summary can be offered about the consequences of the military budget of an advanced industrial society such as the United States. There is no reason to assert that the military budget is required for the maintenance of economic development or high levels of employment. On the contrary, military expenditures in the context of the welfare state have various negative economic consequences. This is not to deny the obvious implication that a reduction in the military budget would release funds for the expanding goals of the welfare state, although not sufficiently to meet expanding demands. Nor does this conclusion overlook the fact that the economic goals of particular industrial groupings and their political spokesmen have specific influence on the political economy.

Social Incidence of Military Service

In addition to trends in military expenditures, the impact of war and military institutions on the social structure obviously requires examination of trends of manpower mobilization and the resulting patterns of military participation, including especially the distribution of casualties. As background analysis of U.S. social structure, there is available the ambitious, almost grandiose, effort of Pitirim Sorokin to chart the pattern of manpower mobilization and the incidence of military casualties from the twelfth century to the twentieth century, that is, to 1925.[50] He focused on France, England, Austria-Hungary, and Russia. He concluded that "the curse or privilege to be the most devastating or most bloody war century belongs to the twentieth; in one quarter century it imposed on the population a 'blood tribute' far greater than that imposed by any of the whole centuries compared. The next place belongs to the 17th and then comes the 18th century; the nineteenth appears to be the least bloody of all these centuries concerned."[51]

Sorokin therefore rejects the notion of an evolutionary development of more destructive military institutions. In his words, "the curve fluctuates and that is all." Moreover, he concluded that the size of the military does not indicate the relative magnitude of the casualties incurred.

50. Pitirim A. Sorokin, *Social and Cultural Dynamics*, vol. 3, *Fluctuation of Social Relationships, War, and Revolution* (New York: American Book Co., 1937), chap. 11, pp. 335–80.

51. Ibid., p. 342.

The analysis of the social distribution of military service starts with an exposition of long-term trends in mobilization. The basic trend data on the magnitude of military mobilization for the United States for 1900 to 1975 are presented in Table 6.2. Of course, military operations have involved the mobilization of civilian employees into the military establishment and in war-based industries. But for the purposes at hand, the numbers of military personnel supply the appropriate indicators.[52]

The underlying change has been from a professional cadre designed for rapid expansion in time of conflict to a more stable force in being. In particular, the ground forces have rested on the mobilization format of rapid expansion during conflict and equally rapid contraction after hostilities. The naval forces have had more of the character of a force in being because of the long lead time required to construct naval vessels. Likewise, after 1945, the air force has also been more of a force in being. The task of deterrence has meant that the ground forces have become more of a force in being as well. As a result, the data presented in Table 6.2 show a decline in intermittent fluctuations in the absolute size of the armed forces. Instead of rapid expansion followed by rapid contraction, shifts are more gradual. This table also presents the military participation ratio, that is, the ratio of males mobilized to the total male population. This measure, which takes into account the total size of the civilian population, also reveals since the end of World War II the same emerging pattern of greater manpower stability.

From the point of view of social control, there is a paradoxical or unanticipated dimension in this long transformation. One might well have anticipated that the sharp fluctuation in the size (and correspondingly in the level of activity) of the military establishment would place a powerful strain on civil-military relations and the mechanisms of social control. This has been the case; however, until the outbreak of World War II, the sharp decline in the size of the military establishment after military operations meant that the institutional arrangements in the United States did not have to deal with the complex tensions of a permanent large armed force. Civilian control was based on the ability

52. By means of the cooperative efforts of the Advisory Panel on Comparative Military Institutions, basic statistical data on military manpower have been collected for the United States and the major nation-states of Western Europe for 1900 to 1975. See David Curry, "A Comparative Analysis of Military Institutions in Developed Nations," Ph.D. thesis, University of Chicago, 1976. For an analysis of the U.S. data see David Curry, "The Case of the United States," unpublished report, University of Chicago, April 1976.

of the political authorities to collapse the armed forces after hostilities. However, the system of social control since 1945 has had to face a military establishment without precedence in the American experience: that of a "permanently" expanded armed force—based first on conscription and, after 1973, on an all-volunteer force; each of these developments was unprecedented for the United States. It is particularly incorrect to assert that the United States has traditionally operated with an all-volunteer system. The colonial and postcolonial militias were based on obligatory service, and the theme of the citizen-soldier was operative in the national guard formations. Throughout most of its history, the United States was able to rely on a small volunteer force for tiny wars and border security, while active involvement in intense military operations has rested on conscript forces. Since Vietnam, the United States has had its first experience with long-term commitment to an expanded all-volunteer manpower system during a period in which the military have been assigned extensive operational goals and missions.

In Table 6.3, the relative fluctuations in the size of the U.S. armed forces for five-year intervals are presented. This measure of relative fluctuations (as presented in the second column) is the sum of the absolute values of percentage change in size during each period. This measure of relative fluctuations (as presented in the second column) is the sum of the absolute values of percentage change in size during each period. This measure indicates both change in magnitude and frequency

TABLE 6.3 Relative Fluctuation in the Size of U.S. Armed Forces, 1901–1970*

Years	Relative Fluctuation
1901–1905	22.0
1906–1910	38.3
1911–1915	22.9
1916–1920 (WW I)	742.2
1921–1925	60.6
1926–1930	5.0
1931–1935	7.9
1936–1940	66.9
1941–1945 (WW II)	574.1
1946–1950	152.7
1951–1955 (Korea)	154.9
1956–1960	16.6
1961–1965	18.9
1966–1970 (Vietnam)	44.7

*Sum of the absolute values of percentage change in size during each five-year period.

of change. The long-term decline in fluctuation is most dramatic when linked to the four major conflicts. Thus, for World War I, the measure of change 1916–1920 was 742.2, while for World War II, the measure declined to 574.1, even though the number of personnel mobilized was greater. The Korean War produced a measure of 154.9, and in the Vietnam conflict the change measure dropped to only 44.7. In the post-Vietnam period, with an all-volunteer structure, the fluctuations have become gradual and modest; in fact, they appear to be less than in the period from 1900 to 1915.

In exploring the degree of social inquality associated with the expanded military service since 1940, we must confront two issues. First, what is the social stratification of military service, that is, how has military service, regardless of military assignment, been distributed among the various social groupings? Second, what has been the incidence of combat assignments and casualties among those who were mobilized? There are two dimensions to the second question: What has been the actual distribution of casualties? To what extent have popular concern and agitation emerged about the inequality of sacrifice among different social groups?

For 1940 to 1975, military service was distributed throughout the social structure, although not without some selectivity. The almost total mobilization of World War II set the framework for "democratization" of military participation in the United States. In fact, the effect of World War II was to overrepresent the higher-status groups because health, psychiatric, and educational screening deemphasized the very lowest socioeconomic groups. Moreover, during World War II, there was an effective absence of extensive educational deferments, so that there was little or no underrepresentation of the highest socioeconomic groupings. Educational deferments were introduced after World War II and had a cumulative effect on recruitment until they were eliminated and replaced by a lottery system in December 1970.

It can be argued that the Selective Service System after 1948 tended to draw more heavily from the upper (the "solid") working-class strata and the broad lower-middle-class strata. One systematic source of data reenforced this view of the social stratification of military service, namely, the national survey on the distribution of military service conducted in 1964 by the National Opinion Research Center.[53] It reported the underrepresentation of the lowest-income groups on the basis of

53. National Opinion Research Center, report no. 117 (Chicago: National Opinion Research Center, 1966).

educational and health criteria, and a parallel underrepresentation of the upper-status groups because of educational deferments; also, sons of farmers tended to be underrepresented.

However, the reanalysis of a more elaborate national survey of social stratification and social mobility conducted on a large sample of 33,164 men in 1973 and analyzed by more rigorous methods presented a more detailed and more precise overview of the social incidence of military service which highlighted the degree of representativeness of conscription rather than the amount of selectivity.[54] Neil Fligstein, who completed this reanalysis, concluded that "all in all the draft must be viewed as relatively equitable."[55] Where there were over- and underrepresentation, the magnitudes were not marked. Of central importance, social position as measured by father's occupation, throughout the entire period of Selective Service (including the Vietnam conflict), was unrelated to military service. However, when socioeconomic position is distinguished from race, race is negatively related to military service, namely, blacks were consistently underrepresented. Sons of farmers were also underrepresented. Moreover, during World War II and Korea, older age cohorts tended to be underrepresented in military service; but by the Vietnam conflict, age emerged as unrelated to military service.

On the important issue of education, it is necessary to make a distinction between father's education and the individual's. Higher levels of father's educational attainment were positively related to military service throughout the entire period. In World War II and Korea, higher educational level of the individual was positively related to military service. Only in the Vietnam period was higher educational attainment of the individual's negatively related to military service but not markedly so. In part this reflects education deferments and the efforts of college students to avoid military service. Thus, as was expected, the public definition of inequalities of service had greater influence than the actual incidence of service.[56]

The issue of inequality in incidence of military service rests more on the distribution of combat casualties than on the patterns of military service per se. In this regard, the experiences and reactions of the

54. Neil Fligstein, "Military Service, the Draft and the G.I. Bill: Their Effects on the Lives of American Males, 1940–1973," report, University of Wisconsin–Madison, 1976. The data were collected in 1973 by the "Occupational Changes in a Generation Survey."

55. Ibid., p. 42.

56. Ibid., passim.

United States differ from those of Western Europe. In Western Europe the magnitude of military casualties in World War I was the dominant sociopolitical influence. France had 1,300,000 battle deaths; Germany, 1,700,000; and Great Britain, 900,000. In Great Britain, these losses extended throughout the social structure, from the top to the lowest stratum. During World War I and in the postwar period there was little discussion of the social incidence of these casualties; what was discussed were the actual losses and their enervating effect on critical social institutions. Humanistic writings of the post–World War I period have emphasized this theme. In addition, the indifference of the military leaders to these casualties and the limited military results which they achieved had a pervasive consequence on public attitudes.

World War II produced a "democratization" of danger, as air warfare exposed the civilian population to military operations. However, in both France and Great Britain, the battle casualties (plus civilian deaths as a result of air warfare) were much fewer than during World War I. France suffered 210,000 battle deaths; Great Britain was 240,000, plus 60,000 civilian deaths. But the physical destruction from aerial bombardment was widespread. Germany had more military casualties in World War II than in World War I; 3,500,000, compared with 1,700,000, aside from the prisoners of war who were not returned and the civilian deaths from air warfare. But it is impossible to discover any uniform and direct linkage between the extent and impact of military casualties and post–World War II adaptation and recovery.

All the major military conflicts of the United States during the twentieth century were fought on foreign soil; there was no physical destruction. The scope of military participation and of military casualties is presented in Table 6.4 for these military conflicts.

For the United States, the greater intensity and scope of World War II compared with the other conflicts is striking, although it will be argued that the Vietnam conflict has the greater disruptive consequences on the patterns of social control. In World War I, 4.7 million persons were mobilized, with a military participation ratio of 5.57, compared with 16.3 million in World War II, or a military participation ratio of 16.93. The military participation ratio has been calculated on a one-year basis, that is, the ratio of persons on active duty in a particular year out of the total population. For World War I, the year was 1918; for World War II, 1945; for the Korean conflict, 1952; and for Vietnam, 1968. These years were the years of the highest level of manpower mobilization for each war. In the Korean conflict, the total who served in the military was 5.7 million with a military participation ratio of 4.60; the number reached 8.8 million for Vietnam, with a military participation ratio of 3.60. Another revealing measure of the effect on manpower and on the social structure is the average duration of military service; in World War II it reached 33 months, compared with 12 months in World War I, 19 months in Korea, and 23 months in Vietnam.

TABLE 6.4 Trends in U.S. Military Mobilization and Military Casualties, World War I-Vietnam Conflict

	World War I	World War II	Korean Conflict	Vietnam Conflict
Personnel mobilized (per 1,000)	4,744	16,354	5,764	8,811
Military participation ratio	5.57	16.93	4.60	3.60
Average duration of service (months)	12	33	19	23
Battle deaths (per 1,000)	53	292	24	46
Percent killed	1.1	1.7	0.4	0.5
Wounded, not mortal (per 1,000)	204	671	103	304
Percent wounded	4.3	4.1	1.8	3.4

SOURCE: U.S. Department of Defense, Office of the Secretary, *Selected Manpower Statistics*, annual; and unpublished data.

While the measurement of battle casualties is complex, the documentation shows not only the greater degree of mobilization and longer length of service but also the higher incidence of battle deaths in World War II. In World War I, 1.1% were killed, and the incidence of wounded (not mortal) was 4.3%. While firepower and destructive capacity of the military technology greatly increased by World War II, the incidence of battle deaths rose to 1.7%, despite the increased proportion of military personnel in noncombat posts. No doubt improved medical technology reduced the incidence of battle deaths, but the percent wounded also declined compared with World War I. Both the Korean conflict and the Vietnam conflict resulted in lower incidence of battle deaths and wounded than World War II (Korea, 0.4% deaths, 1.8% wounded; Vietnam, 0.5% deaths, 3.4% wounded). These trends underscore the observations of Pitirim Sorokin that there are no evolutionary trends toward increased deaths in military conflict through time.[57] Moreover, while battle casualties were traumatic at every level

57. Sorokin, *Fluctuation*, passim.

of societal organization and had enduring consequences, compared with the major powers and especially with Germany in World War II, U.S. casualties were more limited.

In fact, during the brief period of World War I and in the longer and more extensive mobilization of World War II, both the magnitude of the casualties and their social representativeness did not become an issue of political debate. The existence of terminal geographical goals and the steady progress toward these goals were at work. However, during the Korean War, the level of casualties became defined as a political issue and there was extensive concern about the magnitude of the casualties incurred. (The public support and opposition to the Korean and Vietnam interventions are explored below.) The lack of clear military objectives and the continued prolongation of hostilities were causes of the increasing popular disaffection with that military effort. After the Korean War, there was some debate in academic circles concerning the social unrepresentativeness of the combat casualties, but it was hardly a matter of heated controversy or agitation. However, as the military intervention in Vietnam developed, university-based charges of the unrepresentativeness of casualties became a central note of political dissensus and popular agitation. The claim, supported by reports, that black Americans were a disproportionate share of the battlefield casualties in the ground combat operations was covered by the mass media.

The controversy about the incidence of combat casualties was broadening to a generalized criticism of inequalities of the Selective Service system, especially the procedures of student deferments. These agitations led to the establishment of a President's Commission on Selective Service and to certain reforms, including the ending of education deferments.[59] These reforms did not eliminate the popular criticism of Selective Service, which was a target for opposition to the war in Vietnam.

In the aftermath of Vietnam, analysis of the incidence of combat casualties was a topic worthy of detached, rigorous research. The central issue, from the point of view of effective social control, was the

58. John E. Mueller, *War, Presidents and Public Opinion* (New York: Wiley, 1973), presents a comprehensive analysis of the existing survey data.

59. The National Advisory Commission on Selective Service, *In Pursuit of Equity: Who Serves When Not All Serve?* (Washington: GPO, 1967); see also the *President's Commission on an All-Volunteer Armed Force* (Washington: GPO, 1970).

extent to which the inequalities which resulted were racial versus the extent to which they were based on socioeconomic position. Moreover, there was no reason to assume that the social incidence of casualties in the officer ranks would be the same in the enlisted groups.

Despite the importance of the topic, research on the social composition of U.S. military casualties has been limited. There is no adequate research for World War II, although there is extensive analysis of the distribution of casualties by military rank.[60] The one study of Korean casualties, based on data collected in Detroit, indicated an overrepresentation of blacks, although from a methodological point of view the findings are not definitive.[61] An analysis of casualty data for a sample of 380 Wisconsin men killed in Vietnam prior to December 31, 1967, found that, in contrast to a control sample of male Wisconsin high school seniors, almost twice as many of the group of casualties came from poor families (27.2% versus 14.9%).[62] Sons of workers, regardless of income, tended to be substantially overrepresented. But neither of the studies addresses the social incidence of casualties in the enlisted ranks in comparison with the casualties among officers, and the degree to which inequality was a function of socioeconomic status versus racial characteristics.

Gilbert Badillo and David Curry investigated the topic on a large sample—namely, all army personnel killed in action between 1964 and mid-1968 in Cook County, Illinois; they augmented their analysis by including all casualties, regardless of service between mid-1968 and 1972.[63] They found a significant negative relationship between socioeconomic level (as measured by community characteristics) and the incidence of casualties. In short, they confirmed the overrepresentation of casualties in the Vietnam War among those of lower socioeconomic origins. However, when other relevant variables were controlled, there was no significant relation between racial composition and the inci-

60. Gilbert W. Beebe and Michael DeBakey, *Battle Casualties* (Springfield, Ill.: Charles C Thomas, 1952).

61. Albert J. Mayer and Thomas F. Hoult, "Social Stratification and Combat Survival," *Social Forces* 34 (December 1955): 155–59. Criticisms of the methodology of this research are contained in Gilbert Badillo, "Socio-Economic Status, Military Participation and Casualties," Master's thesis, Brown University, June 1975.

62. Maurice Zeitlin, Kenneth Lutterman, and James Russell, "Death in Vietnam: Class, Poverty and the Risks of War," *Politics and Society* 3 (Spring 1973): 313–28.

63. Gilbert Badillo and David Curry, "The Social Incidence of Vietnam Casualties: Social Class or Race?" *Armed Forces and Society* 2 (1976): 397–406.

dence of casualties. Inequality of sacrifice was a matter of socioeconomic position and not of racial characteristics of the enlisted force.

The military system assigned persons with low or limited educational background (and thereby low social status) to combat positions where, regardless of race, they could function effectively, and assigned those with higher educational background to technical and support positions. This system of personnel allocation accounted for the differential incidence of combat casualties by social status. The concentration of black Americans in the lowest socioeconomic strata is a result of the structure and practices of civilian society, not in the first instance of military institutions. Military institutions, in effect, were perpetuating the pattern of civilian socioeconomic stratification, but not its pattern of racial stratification. The higher incidence in the enlisted ranks of combat casualties among low status groups may have been operative in World War I and World War II, but the mobilization of blacks into combat units was very limited. Thus, it was the addition of the visible racial dimension that exacerbated in the public definition the disruptive sociopolitical impact of this form of inequality.

On the other hand, this study revealed that among officers, the higher socioeconomic status (as measured by the community from which the officer came), the greater the incidence of casualties. The process of personnel allocation was reversed among officers and reflected the same mechanisms of assignment. Either because of technical requirements or because of organizational definition, officers of higher educational background (and thereby of higher social status) were assigned to more dangerous tasks. This operated both in the utilization of ROTC officers and academy graduates as combat troop leaders in the ground forces and in the involvement of college graduates in the air formations. In a limited war—limited in mobilization and in objectives—social inequality of casualties resulted. These inequalities were to some extent operative in previous wars, but in the Vietnam intervention, the political emphasis and importance of this pattern grew and supplied an important element of protest and dissensus.

Socioeconomic Position of Veterans

Another social indicator of the influence of military institutions on the social structure is the socioeconomic status of the citizen-soldiers after they return to civilian employment. Four major wars and a prolonged period of conscription have made veteran status a pervasive dimension of social differentiation. As of 1974, 42.3% of the male population 18 years and over were military veterans (Table 6.5). The massive demobilization after World War II made the decisive contribution to this trend. As of 1945, before the demobilization started, 13.2% of the male population 18 years and over were veterans. By 1955, it was 35.2%. By 1965, the figure rose to 42.1% and remained at the same level in 1973 (42.7%).

If the all-volunteer force remains approximately at the 2 million level, and if women are approximately 10% to 15% of the military force, over 30% of the eligible male 18-year-old age cohort will have to serve on the average for four to five years. Under these conditions, the concentrations of male veterans in the population will decline only gradually. Furthermore, in Table 6.5, the age grading of the veteran population is demonstrated.

We are not dealing with a homogeneous veteran population, but with a series of service generations which have had very different military experiences and have different experiences in transition to civilian society. As of 1975, the surviving veterans of World War II were 53.5 years in average age and already converging in their interests with those of World War I. In contrast, the veterans of Vietnam had an average age of 27.0 and were oriented to educational opportunities, career decisions, and employment.

Research on the effects of short-term military service and the consequences of veteran status presents a complex set of issues because of the difficulty of obtaining adequate longitudinal data. Such research must deal with the difficulties involved in drawing inferences about the relative importance of family and social background characteristics in contrast to the effect of military experience and the particular set of circumstances which confronted demobilized citizen-soldiers. The analysis of veteran status is also complicated by ideological overtones. It is necessary to remember that military service which involves combat produces overwhelming sacrifices and trauma for a limited fraction of the population; these are impossible to calculate in terms of the criteria of social stratification research, such as occupational mobility and income and social economic status. On the other hand, military service does give access to education—both military and civilian after service—for persons who have failed at or have been inadequately served by civilian educational institutions. Thus the research strategies which have been employed only rarely provide detailed and precise data to ex-

TABLE 6.5 Trends in Veteran Population, World War I to 1974
Living Veterans, by Age and Period of Service, 1974
(In thousands, except as indicated. As of June 30, 1974. Estimated.)

Age in 1974	Total: Number	Total: Percent	World War I	World War II	Korea, including World War II	Korea only	Vietnam, including Korea	Vietnam only	Service between Korea and Vietnam only
All ages	29,265	42.3	1,075	13,759	5,958	4,703	7,088	6,628	3,099
18–19 years	48	1.2	—	—	—	—	48	48	—
20–24 years	1,139	12.1	—	—	—	—	1,139	1,139	—
25–29 years	3,620	44.8	—	—	—	—	3,570	3,570	50
30–34 years	2,703	40.4	—	—	—	—	1,637	1,637	1,066
35–39 years	2,356	42.1	—	(Z)	560	560	231	204	1,592
40–44 years	3,361	60.4	—	83	2,932	2,894	169	20	364
45–49 years	4,204	73.2	—	3,016	1,592	1,160	145	6	22
50–59 years	8,166	76.5	1	8,074	726	83	133	4	5
60 years and over	3,668	27.7	1,075	2,586	148	6	16	(Z)	—
Average age years	45.5	(X)	79.4	54.4	44.9	42.9	28.9	27.7	35.7

TABLE 6.5 Continued

Period of Service	1945	1950	1955	1960	1965	1970	1972	1973	1974
All veterans	6,455	19,023	21,802	23,811	25,259	27,647	28,804	29,073	29,265
Percent of males age 18 and over	13.2	37.0	35.2	42.1	42.1	42.7	43.1	42.7	42.3
War veterans	6,455	19,023	21,798	22,431	22,107	24,522	25,691	25,967	26,166
Spanish-American War	164	118	72	36	15	5	3	2	1
World War I	3,821	3,518	3,150	2,673	2,121	1,536	1,291	1,184	1,075
World War II	2,469	15,386	15,405	15,202	14,969	14,458	14,122	13,955	13,759
Korean conflict	(X)	(X)	3,999	5,482	5,718	5,867	5,908	5,936	5,958
And service in World War II	(X)	(X)	828	962	1,150	1,262	1,259	1,261	1,255
No service in World War II	(X)	(X)	3,171	4,520	4,568	4,605	4,649	4,675	4,703
Vietnam	(X)	(X)	(X)	(X)	456	4,173	5,976	6,557	7,088
And service in Korean conflict	(X)	(X)	(X)	(X)	22	255	350	406	460
No service in Korean conflict	(X)	(X)	(X)	(X)	434	3,918	5,626	6,151	6,628
Service between Korean conflict and Vietnam only	(X)	(X)	4	1,380	3,152	3,125	3,113	3,106	3,099

– Represents zero. X Not applicable. Z Less than 500.

SOURCE: U.S. Bureau of the Census, *The Statistical Abstract of the United States, 1975*, 96th edition (Washington, D.C., 1975), pp. 331, 332.

amine the social processes involved in the transition from military to civilian life. One early exception is the study of felons paroled to the U.S. Army during World War II completed by Hans Mattick.[65] The research issue was whether being paroled to the U.S. Army serves as a better transition to civilian society than being paroled directly to the then existing civilian agencies. The results document the superiority of the military environment over civilian parole agencies in preparing paroled criminals for successful adjustment to civilian life.

Despite the difficulties involved, a number of specific studies have been accumulated which permit a reasonable assessment of the trends in the effect of short-term military service and veteran status on the patterns of social stratification. The benefits for veterans and the effectiveness of these benefits progressively decreased from World War II to Korea and Vietnam. In part this is due to the more limited societal and administrative support for veterans after World War II. In addition, in civilian society there has been an increased access to civilian education, and veteran status is less significant in facilitating such access. This has largely been the result of the expansion of community and junior colleges. The amount of compensatory advantage from educational opportunity that resulted from being a veteran has declined since World War II.

Most available research studies have tended to demonstrate the higher socioeconomic position of veterans than of nonveterans, although occasional studies question these findings.[66] One central theme which points

64. Ibid., p. 401.

65. Hans W. Mattick, "Parole to the Army: A Research Report on Felons Paroled to the Army During World War II," presented at the Eighty-seventh Annual Congress of Corrections, Chicago, August 1957.

66. Otis D. Duncan and Robert W. Hodge, "Education and Occupational Mobility: A Regressive Analysis," *American Journal of Sociology* 68 (May 1963): 629–44; Charles B. Nam, "Impact of the G.I. Bill on the Educational Level of the Male Population," *Social Forces* 43 (October 1964): 26–32; Elton F. Jackson and Harry J. Crockett, Jr., "Occupational Mobility in the United States: A Point of Estimate and Trend Comparison," *American Sociological Review* 29 (August 1964): 5–15; I. G. Katenbrink, Jr., "Military Service and Occupational Mobility," in *Selective Service and American Society*, ed. Roger W. Little (New York: Russell Sage Foundation, 1969); Gary R. Nelson and Catherine Armington, *Military and Civilian Earnings Alternatives for Enlisted Men in the Army* (Arlington, Va.: Institute for Defense Analysis, 1970); Otis Dudley Duncan, D. L. Featherman, and Beverly Duncan, *Socio-economic Background and Achievement* (New York: Seminar Press, 1972); Harley L. Browning, Sally C. Lopreato, and Dudley L. Poston, Jr., "Income and Veterans Status: Variations Among Mexican Americans, Blacks, and Anglos," *American Sociological Review* 28 (February 1973): 74–85. See also Bernard Udis and Murray Weidenbaum, "The Many Dimensions of the Military Effort," in *The Economic Consequences of Reduced Military Spending*, ed. Bernard Udis (Lexington, Mass.: Heath, 1973), pp. 38–39.

to the advantages of veterans is that the studies stress that such advantages are most strongly concentrated among men from low-status and minority groups. This conclusion was to be expected because the military offers such persons involvement in an orderly environment compared with the disorganized settings from which they came; it also serves to engender goals and aspirations previously not fashioned or mobilized.

With the completion of the analysis of the 1970 census data on veterans by Wayne J. Villemez and John D. Kasarda, a comprehensive body of data was available which placed these issues in a sequence required for the systemic analysis of social change and social control.[67] These data make it possible to examine the differential effect of the experiences of World War II, Korea, and Vietnam. They underline the declining "positive" influence of short-term military participation on civilian socioeconomic status. These data support the hypothesis of the growing disarticulation of military institutions from civilian social structure and the declining relevance of military service to the process of national integration.

Villemez and Kasarda found that both for whites and nonwhites the civilian earnings of veterans were greater than those of nonveterans. However, as of 1970 we are dealing with a declining trend; the largest advantage was for the World War II veterans, with smaller differences for Korean veterans and an opposite trend for Vietnam veterans. These differences cannot be attributed primarily to a time lag, since with the passage of time the influence of Korea and Vietnam would approximate that of World War II; however, basically, the linkages which operated in World War II were lesser for Korea and Vietnam. This can be seen in the results of the regression analysis of the key variables collected by the U.S. 1970 Census. A direct effect of veteran status on income for whites and nonwhites is present, but not large. Instead, veteran status had a more important influence on income through the indirect effect of education. Thus, the educational attainment generated by military service—both in and after service—is central in accounting for the consequences of short-term military service. In this regard, the total mobilization of World War II resulted in a program of educational benefits for veterans which exceeded in coverage, amount, and flexibility those resulting from Korea and especially from Vietnam. Likewise, the expansion of civilian educational opportunity, during 1950 to 1975,

67. Wayne J. Villemez and John D. Kasarda, "Veteran Status and Socioeconomic Attainment," *Armed Forces and Society* 2 (1976): 407–20.

meant that the importance of educational opportunities in the military and those available through the G.I. Bill were of declining importance, except for the persons in the most submerged groups in society. Thus, the findings of Villemez and Kasarda stress the importance of the educational benefits for minority-group members. The high levels of unemployment after Vietnam contributed to the declining relevance of military experience; the Vietnam veteran faced higher rates of unemployment, which depressed their overall income level.

Jack Ladinsky has integrated the available documentary and statistical evidence about the level of social disruption among veterans in the aftermath of World War II, Korea, and Vietnam.[68] He focuses not only on the level of unemployment encountered by veterans but also on the adequacy and flexibility of government programs after each of the conflicts. The almost total mobilization of World War II was followed by a period of employment expansion, augmented by massive government programs, especially educational and vocational training programs, which were relevant to skill acquisition and for the morale and self-esteem of the veterans involved. One striking outcome was the narrow gap encountered in the post–World War II surveys between the attitudes and outlook of veterans and the larger society.[69] Military experience, including combat, did not produce a set of attitudes, identifications, and expectations sharply at variance with the "home front" population. The definition of the war converged, and even more important, the home front opinion basically supported the massive military operations and the returned military personnel.

U.S. intervention in Korea and especially in Vietnam was based on a very different relation between the home front and the overseas military forces. The Vietnam military operations, with their frustration and the widespread popular indifference and even outright hostility among civilians, had the effect of heightening sensitivity among the veterans. It was a military campaign which developed political opposition groups within the armed forces. The efforts of the military commanders to cope with the pressure and tensions of military service, especially of combat service in Vietnam, by means of extensive rotation, supplied a temporary control mechanism, but one which weakened military effectiveness. Paradoxically, the system of rotation undermined small unit

68. Jack Ladinsky, "Vietnam, the Veterans and the Veterans Administration," *Armed Forces and Society* 2 (Spring 1976): 435–67.

69. Leo Crespi and G. Schofield Shapleigh, "The Veteran–A Myth," *Public Opinion Quarterly* 20 (1948): 361–72.

cohesion and military leadership effectiveness and thereby further contributed to the discontent and frustration of military service.[70]

Ladinsky has also carefully examined the evidence of the influence of Vietnam on the sense of "alienation" and on the antisocial behavior of Vietnam veterans. The expectation that the Vietnam experience would produce "hordes" of men with heightened "killer" tendencies was hardly grounded in reality. The small percentage who were engaged in combat limited this possibility. Moreover, available research data on the impact of combat do not overlook the extensive personal and psychological costs and misery, but emphasized that the bulk of those exposed to combat adapted rapidly to peacetime environments.[71] Drug use was widespread, more so than in previous military engagements. But the personality characteristics and the specific patterns of deviant behavior cannot be judged as the basic issue in the transition of Vietnam veterans to civilian society. The incidence of enduring psychiatric casualties is difficult to estimate, although it is a persistent tragedy. The essential issue was the adequacy of governmental and institutional response to the returning veterans.

In the context of a military failure and the persistent and growing economic dilemmas of stagflation, the government and private response was circumscribed. As Ladinsky has documented, the level and scope of veterans' programs and benefits were more limited than after World War II.[72] It was not until 1974 that benefits were increased sufficiently to render the G.I. Bill more effective. The Veterans Administration had become a complex, rigid bureaucracy. Its operating procedures were more oriented to the needs of and requirements of older veterans, especially to health and pension problems. The veterans' lobby represented these older veterans rather than the new groups. The transition from military service was thus more difficult, more prolonged, and more disruptive for the veterans of Vietnam than for the veterans of World War II or even Korea.

Military Goals and Political Consent

The analysis thus far has emphasized the consequences for social structure of the accumulated military sequences of the last half-century. However, both elite and popular expectations concerning "future" mili-

70. Paul L. Savage and Richard A. Gabriel, "Cohesion and Disintegration in the American Army: An Alternative Perspective," *Armed Forces and Society* 2 (1976): 340–76.
71. Ladinsky, "Vietnam," pp. 437–54.
72. Ibid., passim.

tary operations have a crucial influence as well. The growth in military potentials has paradoxically been accompanied by increased limitations on military intervention by the United States.[73] For the United States, an advanced industrial society, its military goals have been transformed, although the process has been slow, painful, and incomplete. In order for military institutions to have basic legitimacy, the strategy of conventional "offensive" military operations has been replaced by the conceptions of military deterrence.[74] The very idea of deterrence has come to be continually scrutinized in the light of changing technology and political realities. It is being replaced by politico-military conventions such as stabilizing versus destabilizing military systems, and the positive pursuit of arms control and disarmament.[75] Despite support for extensive military budgets, the goals and purposes of military operations and the position of military institutions and the military profession in the domestic social order have become since 1945 a continuous source of political controversy which deeply strains effective social control. Just as the development of the welfare state creates new society-wide cleavages, military policy and civil-military relations are persistent sources of tension, straining social control.

The advent of nuclear weapons presented a new threshold in international relations and transformed the logic of warfare. However, the tremendous destructive capacity of conventional weapons and the havoc they had wrought in World War II had already seriously undermined "classical" military strategy in the Western parliamentary democracies. In the Eastern European nations and the USSR the military has undergone less change because it has the additional functions of internal police operations and youth socialization and ideological indoctrination.[76]

For industrialized nations with open systems of mass media, civilian political leadership and mass public opinion have reacted with horror, plus apathetic withdrawal, to the prospect of a "broken back" nuclear war. Public opinion polls, with all their crude limitations, emphasize the

73. Morris Janowitz, "Toward A Redefinition of Military Strategy in International Relations."

74. See note 2.

75. Morris Janowitz, "Beyond Deterrence: Alternative Conceptual Dimensions," in Ellen Stern, ed., *The Limits of Military Intervention* (Beverly Hills, Calif.: Sage Publications, 1977).

76. See especially Dale R. Herspring and Ivan Volgyes, "The Military as an Agent of Political Socialization in Eastern Europe: A Comparative Framework," *Armed Forces and Society* 3 (1977): 249–70.

almost total rejection of the use of nuclear weapons in military intervention to defend allied nations, although nuclear weapons are tacitly accepted as an element of deterrence. In fact, in the United States, the leaders of both political parties have been consistent in agreeing that there are no conditions under which the outbreak of a general nuclear war between the major industrialized nations would produce results in the national interest of the United States.

The symbolic and psychological aspects of nuclear weapons and the threats of nuclear blackmail have become new components of international competition. Domestic political debate about the size structure of nuclear forces which are required for deterrence and the role of conventional forces in deterrence has emerged as central in each presidential election since 1960. Likewise, the strategy of deterrence requires positive steps toward arms control; as a result, the issues of arms control and the extent to which the Soviet Union can be "trusted" become part of the political debate concerning military objectives. If one thinks of the social structure of the United States in broad stratigraphic terms, there is no simple direct linkage between a person's position in the social structure and his or her popular demands about "defense policy," and national military objectives.[77]

The USSR's procurement of nuclear weapons in the first half of the 1950s resulted in a considerable popular concern about the danger and prospect of the outbreak of a nuclear war.[78] With the passage of time, the expectation of the outbreak of a nuclear war has receded in popular thinking. By 1975, public opinion surveys were no longer measuring the extent of this concern—a certain measure of the atrophy of this preoccupation. (We are speaking only of public opinion and not of the actual trends in the likelihood of general war.)

Of particular importance for social control in the United States has been the absence of mass support for civilian defense. The USSR has supported a significant and continuing program of investment in civil defense as an aspect of its nuclear stragegy and a device of domestic coercive control. In the United States, the efforts to develop civil defense in the 1950s failed and in fact produced a strong popular reaction. Opposition arose not only because of the belief that such a measure would be futile and also because the public did not wish to "bother"

77. John E. Mueller, *War, Presidents*, pp. 116–54.
78. John E. Mueller, "Changes in American Public Attitudes Toward International Involvement," in Ellen Stern, ed., *Limits*, pp. 323–44.

with the details of civilian defense which were considered an interference with personal prerogatives. Intensification of the nuclear arms race and the proliferation of nuclear weapons into developing countries could well stimulate interest in civil defense, but such a development in the United States would again produce a new source of political controversy.

Along with nuclear weapons, conventional military strategy and military operations have contracted as a result of the decline of overseas colonialism. Since World War II, it has been demonstrated that conscript forces are not able to maintain political hegemony in overseas colonial possessions, leaving aside the problematic case of Algeria. Nor have U. S. specialized forces in "counterinsurgency" performed with much effectiveness or "distinction" from a political point of view. U.S. politico-military goals in the post–World War II period have, on balance, been committed to the process of decolonization. The initiatives pursued by the United States have contributed to British decolonization, especially in India, and were crucial in the decolonization of the Dutch empire in Indonesia. Although it had no colonial aspirations, it is ironic that the United States found itself as the inheritor of the French effort at recolonization of Indochina, with both unsuccessful and tragic political results.[79]

In anticipation of the future, deterrence strategy has assigned a role in maintaining nuclear deterrence in Western Europe to conventional forces. Likewise, deterrence strategy asserts that conventional forces are relevant in countering the direct deployment of ground troops by the Soviet Union outside the boundaries of the Warsaw Pact nations. However, extensive ambiguity exists about the future logic and legitimacy of limited war. Thus, in assessing the effect of military institutions—past, present, and future—on the social structure, the reality and imagery of limited war have particular significance which is as central as the calculations about nuclear weapons. In fact, it can be argued that the management and disposition of conventional forces, particularly ground forces, become the political indicators of U.S. military intent and goals in the world community. At this point it is thus necessary to review the trends in popular support of and opposition to limited war, that is, the extent of delegitimation of military preparations and operations.

79. David Halberstam, *The Best and the Brightest* (New York: Random House, 1972).

Popular opposition to involvement in limited war is hardly a new phenomenon. In the nineteenth century the United States fought three "little wars," and about each there was considerable internal dissent and organized political opposition.[80] In each of these wars—War of 1812, Mexican War, Spanish-American War—limited military forces achieved specific and negotiable goals, namely, new territory.

While direct comparisons are difficult, there is good reason to believe that the War of 1812 was the most unpopular of the three and probably the most unpopular in U.S. history. The declaration of war passed by a small margin; and when it became clear that the conquest of Canada would be difficult, if not impossible, the war was disliked throughout the nation. Opposition was so strong that a secessionist movement was launched, but the Peace of Ghent and Jackson's victory in New Orleans ended the war and dissipated the political opposition. Political opposition to the Mexican War was extensive and grew as the war progressed. President James K. Polk pressed for the war in 1846, following a border incident. Although the military aspects of the war were successful, antiwar Whigs gained control of Congress and an acceptable peace treaty was negotiated on February 2, 1848.

During the first phase of the Spanish-American War, the defeat of the Spanish forces in Cuba and in the Philippines produced little dissent, since the goals were thought to be humanitarian. However, the second phase, the Philippines Insurrection, dragged on for three years. The successful efforts by the U.S. Army which suppressed the indigenous revolt led to the annexation of the Philippines, but produced considerable dissent in the United States. The Filipinos lost over 200,000, since the war involved burning villages and produced extensive civilian casualties. While the popular hostility to intervention in the Philippines served to inhibit similar undertakings in the immediately following years, the intervention did not have a profound or lasting political influence.

For the period since 1945, an impressive body of trend data exist on mass attitudes about United States military involvements. When the trend findings of these sample surveys of public opinion are assessed, the available data have come to be treated with considerable sophistication. Superficially, the vast amount of data collected, often by poorly

80. Samuel Eliot Morrison, Frederick Merk, and Frank Friedel, *Dissent in Three American Wars* (Cambridge: Harvard University Press, 1970).

constructed questions which tend to impose a public attitude where one does not exist, make it possible for the advocate to construct ingenuous interpretations in support of widely divergent conclusions. However, when one approaches with skepticism and a sense of reality, the regularities in long-term trends emerge clearly. The mass mobilization and the pursuit of total war with definable and attainable geographical goals produced a continuing decline in popular dissent during World War II. On the other hand, the partial mobilization supporting the interventions in Korea and Vietnam, and the more limited and diffuse war, produced a persistent increase in popular dissent.

For each military engagement, it has been possible to construct an index of popular dissent based on a series of standardized public opinion questions which were asked throughout the period involved.[81] The scores are not equivalent for the three periods, but each index charts trends. For the year prior to Pearl Harbor, the dissent index was 34%, while from 1942 on through 1944, the figure dropped markedly to an average of 8% or a decrease of 26 percent points. In 1950, at the beginning of the Korean War, the dissent index was only 20%, compared with 50% at the end of active hostilities in 1953. In the case of the Vietnam intervention, by 1965, the dissent index was 24% and it continued to rise steadily up to 57% in 1970. While the Korean War produced a sharp increase in the first year and a leveling of dissent thereafter, popular opposition to involvement in Vietnam grew continually and gradually.

The growth in opposition to the military intervention in Korea and Vietnam has been linked by John E. Mueller to the incidence and especially the increase in combat casualties.[82] In essence, this measure is an indicator of the passage of "combat" time and the continuation of a struggle without discernible geographical goals. In addition, it is necessary to emphasize the moral definition of the intervention, especially as dramatized by the mass media and by visible protest movements. The greater opposition to the military intervention in Vietnam than in Korea reflects not only the higher casualties and the length of the conflict but also the level of popular legitimacy of the intervention.

Mueller's research is particularly important in that he failed to uncover unidimensional "hawk-dove" attitudes as a basis for distinguishing

81. Robert B. Smith, "Disaffection, Delegitimation and Consequences: Aggregate Trends for World War II, Korea and Vietnam," in *Public Opinion and the Military Establishment*, ed. Charles C. Moskos, Jr., (Beverly Hills, Calif.: Sage Publications, 1971), pp. 221–51.

82. Mueller, *War, Presidents*, pp. 35ff.

supporters and opponents of the war. Popular attitudes toward foreign and military policy are dominated by the imagery of the president and conspicuous party leaders. Shifts in attitudes reflect the initiative of such leaders. Moreover, while there is a tendency for upper educated groups to be less hawkish and lower educated groups to be more hawkish, again, the stratigraphic approach hardly accounts for the pattern of attitudes toward this military intervention. The explanation of attitudes toward the Korean and Vietnam Wars rests in an interplay between position in the social structure, the network of interpersonal contacts, and the person's reaction to organizational pressures and political leadership.

Korea and Vietnam, plus the acceptance of the realities of nuclear weapons in Soviet hands, have had a long-term effect on U.S. popular attitudes in support of military intervention in general and in support of specific allies. As of 1975, expressed willingness of Americans to support the use of U.S. military forces for the defense of foreign nations was lower than during the height of the "cold war." The same level of support was operating as of the time immediately before the United States entered World War II.[83] Since the end of 1969, the level of support for military intervention has declined, but only to a limited degree, indicating that a plateau has been reached. Willingness to send troops abroad is highly selective and variable, and the following pattern can be taken to indicate no more than relative rankings: Mexico, 42%; England, 37%; West Germany, 27%; Japan, 16%; Brazil, 15%; and Nationalist China, 8%. Expressed willingness to support military intervention tends to be higher for countries the closer they are geographically to the United States. Economic linkages to the United States, existence of a formal military alliance with the United States, and rule by a non-communist government—regardless of the type of rule—also make a positive contribution. There is stronger popular support for intervention by American troops for defense against an external attack than against indigenous insurgency. Likewise, support for the use of nuclear weapons is extremely limited and much lower than during the early 1950s.

These opinions and normative trends are reinforced by the long-term shift from 1950 to 1975 in declining support for defense spend-

83. Bruce Russett and Miroslav Nincic, "American Opinion on the Use of Military Force Abroad," unpublished paper, undated, pp. 3–6. See also John Rielly, ed., *American Public Opinion and U.S. Foreign Policy 1975* (Chicago: Chicago Council on Foreign Relations, 1975).

ing, an attitude pattern which articulates with increased resistance to U.S. military intervention.[84] In the spring of 1976, the U.S. Congress increased the percentage of the gross national product to be spent for defense for the first time since 1967. This increase was effected at a time when approximately 40% of the population expressed a preference to reduce the military budget while 50% were opposed to reducing the military. The growth of resistence to military expenditures was compatible, by U.S. standards, with high levels of budgetary spending for defense, namely, 6%–8% of the gross national product. In essence, the normative pattern which had been emerging after Vietnam was support for extensive military expenditures, but increasing strong popular resistance to limited interventions.

Thus, we are drawing on a long tradition of unpopularity of limited war. The limited wars of the nineteenth century were unpopular and became more so through time. But unpopularity was limited to attitudes and opinion, not to overt resistance. No doubt, in the nineteenth century, the United States had a stronger popular anti-imperialist sentiment than was found in Western Europe. Moreover, the expansionist tendencies could be absorbed by enlarging the frontier. However, popular opposition to limited war, it is argued, in the post-Vietnam period operates in a very different domestic and international setting. We are no longer dealing with episodic military interventions with discrete, contained sociopolitical consequences. Instead, each military intervention takes place in the context of a more politicized domestic electorate sensitive to the cumulative outcome of previous military interventions. Presidential and congressional initiatives leading to military intervention are likely to produce considerable, but not universal, mass support. But the stability and endurance of such mass support are likely to be of relatively short duration and subject to fragmentation. In addition, because specific military interventions are not likely to produce clearly discernible and decisive results, they will serve only to exacerbate the domestic cleavages concerning military policy.

For the United States, as for advanced industrialized nations of Western Europe, the transformation of the logic and legitimacy of military operations has been accompanied by a shift in organizational format, that is, by the decline of the mass armed force.[85] From the

84. Russett and Nincic, "Opinion," pp. 6–18.

85. Morris Janowitz, "The All-Volunteer Military as a 'Sociopolitical' Problem," *Social Problems* 22 (February 1975): 432–49.

point of view of effective social control, the emergence of an expanded all-volunteer force strains and calls into question the traditional basis of the legitimacy of military service and the military profession. As a result, there are sustained efforts to reinforce the legitimacy of military service by balancing "military tradition" with new managerial practices and financial incentives. In theory and in practice, under the older mobilization system, the armed forces required small cadres of professionals. By means of conscription, the citizen-soldier who was mobilized—officer and enlisted personnel—supplied the required manpower, skills, and motivation. The conscript system also served as a political device for civilian control and for defining citizenship and thereby, as argued above, was compatible with the mechanisms of parliamentary systems.

The legitimacy of the citizen-soldier was enhanced by the fact that, roughly speaking, the military was a cross section of the larger society. The society was, in effect, defended by all of its ordered social segments. This ideology was institutionalized, in particular by the provisions which required congressional selection of cadets for the service academies; a selective and self-perpetuating cadre was thereby ruled out. Of course, in peacetime, the enlisted ranks of the military were drawn from predisposed and marginal civilian groups.[86] The officer corps, as it was fashioned into a nationwide system from the turn of the century, has been described as disproportionately native-born, Southern rural, and Protestant, reflecting the values of the American hinterland.[87] Over the three-quarters of the twentieth century, the trend in recruitment has been toward broader social representation. But the legitimacy of the armed forces was reinforced by the vast World War II mobilization, through which the ranks of the military became much more representative.

The Selective Service System produced at the enlisted level a relatively representative cross section after World War II. Recruitment into the officer corps was also fairly representative. But the graduates of the military service academies dominated at the general officer level. The pattern of relative social representativeness not only enhanced the

86. For a historical account, see Jack D. Foner, *The United States Soldier between Two Wars: Army Life and Reforms, 1865–1898* (New York: Humanities Press, 1970).

87. Morris Janowitz, *The Professional Soldier*, pp. 79–103.

basis of legitimacy but also facilitated the system of indoctrination in nonpartisan outlook and the acceptance of the rules of the game of democratic political control.

The expanded all-volunteer force has rapidly altered the social basis of recruitment of both officer and enlisted ranks. It has raised the potential of a military, at the officer level, with stronger self-selection, with distinct implicit political outlook, and with increased social distance from the larger society, or at least with specialized and selective linkages with the larger civilian society. Within the enlisted ranks, the trend in recruitment was to almost exclude persons with college backgrounds. The all-volunteer military is less socially representative of the larger society. In the army in 1961, 18% of the enlisted ranks had had some college education. During the first six months of calendar year 1973, of new enlistments, fewer than 3% had had some college education. In broader terms, recruitment decreased the concentration of persons from middle-class background and increased those from lower socioeconomic positions. The basis of this trend was the growing concentration of minority groups, blacks, Spanish-speaking, etc. In 1962 the overall concentration of blacks in the armed services stood at 9.2%. By 1974, with the introduction of the all-volunteer force, the figure for enlisted blacks in the ground forces was 19.9%. Since blacks reenlist in the ground forces at a higher rate, their overrepresentation becomes more persistent, while the percent for first enlistment was higher.

The patterns of increased unrepresentativeness in the officer corps were more complex and had started before the introduction of the all-volunteer force. Conscription had a strong influence on social recruitment into the officer corps. A significant number of men entered the officer corps as an alternative to service as enlisted personnel, and some of them elected to become career soldiers. Alternatively, enlisted personnel decided after entering military service to become officers. In the ground forces, it has been estimated that one-third of the active-duty officers as of 1970 had served as enlisted personnel. The suspension of conscription ended such channels of recruitment to a considerable extent. Instead of a broadening of the basis of recruitment, since the 1960s one of the main trends in officer recruitment has been increased self-recruitment by sons of officers and of noncommissioned officers. The percentage of cadets entering the service academies from military families was approximately 30% in 1975.

There has also been a trend toward geographical imbalance in the recruitment of ROTC officers. The concentration of ROTC candidates in New England and the Midwestern states has declined, while there has been a corresponding increase in the South and Southwest, especially from schools outside the metropolitan areas in those regions. These trends in officer recruitment indicate a drift toward a more conservative, even right-wing orientation in the officer corps. This drift is strengthened by the system of socialization, which operates to a limited extent to select out those officers who do not conform to the somewhat conservative mold.[88]

In the United States, the all-volunteer format emphasized the importance of economic incentives. This, plus the rise of cost-benefit analysis procedures in military management, has contributed to new norms, at both the officer and the enlisted level. Military service outwardly is seen more and more as "another occupation." But the military profession, because of its involvement in the management of the instruments of violence, is disposed to reject a predominantly economic model and seeks to retain "special" elements in its organizational and professional setting. The overall trends toward civilianization of the conditions of employment have their limits and countertrends focus on heroic imagery, ideological symbolism, interpersonal relations, and on style of life, as, for example, the insistence on short hair.

While the internal format of the all-volunteer military emerges gradually, the end of conscription and the decline of the citizen-soldier concept attenuate the connection between military service and the societal definition of citizenship. With the end of hostilities in Vietnam, the armed forces required only fewer than half of eligible males who became 18 each year. Under conditions of "peacetime" conscription, if only a fraction of those eligible are required for military service, it becomes very difficult, if not impossible, to devise popularly acceptable procedures to determine who will serve and who will not. A system of conscription which does not rest on widespread and almost universal service of the eligibles loses its validity and legitimacy. Moreover, the alternative of a system of national service encompassing both

88. John P. Lovell, "The Professional Socialization of the West Point Cadet," in *The New Military*, ed. Morris Janowitz (New York: Russell Sage Foundation, 1964), pp. 119–57; David Edwin Lebby, "Professional Socialization of the Naval Officer: The Effect of the Plebe Year at the U.S. Naval Academy," Ph.D. thesis, University of Pennsylvania, 1970.

military and civilian service, even on a voluntary basis, was rejected.[89] As a result, the significance of military service as a mechanism for defining citizenship has been fundamentally undermined.

The change in the logic of military preparations and the introduction of the all-volunteer force have produced a complex set of popular perceptions of the military profession. Survey data indicate that the armed forces continue to rank as the most trusted institution in the United States.[90] The trust and confidence have not declined in the decade from 1965 to 1975, while other government and private institutions have suffered dramatically. The basic values of nationalism and the centrality of persistent support of the defense function are operating. But there is considerable public distrust of the civilian leadership who direct the military establishment; and the professional officer is not held in very high esteem and does not rank high in prestige.

Clearly, the military profession has a form of legitimacy because of the importance assigned to it in a world community based on nuclear deterrence and without international mechanisms of social control. At the same time, the high costs of defense and the lack of clarity about the military goals, especially conventional military intervention, create political controversy and dissensus, since there is no ready calculus for translating enlightened self-interest into definitions of national well-being and the public interest.

The analysis of the influence of military institutions, especially the format of conscription, has indicated that, despite the destructive aspect of modern warfare, military service and wartime mobilization have been compatible with the institutional basis of political consent and with vitality of democratic parliamentary procedures. In fact, the evidence indicates that the conception of citizenship which included military service in the United States was a positive asset. Moreover, the growth of the welfare state has been related to the mobilization of World War I and World War II, in the institutional framework it created, the confidence it gave the political elites, and the popular political demands for social justice and equality it generated. However, patterns of military participation after 1945 have been more

89. Morris Janowitz, "The Logic of National Service Systems," in *The Draft*, ed. Sol Tax (Chicago: University of Chicago Press, 1967), pp. 73–90; see also Morris Janowitz, "Volunteer National Service," *Record*, special issue (Teachers College, Columbia University, September 1971).

90. David R. Segal and John D. Blair, "Public Confidence in the Military," *Armed Forces and Society* 3 (1976): 3–11.

unequal and present elements of increased disarticulation in civil-military relations. There is considerable support for the new hypothesis that the military logic of deterrence, accompanied by the decline of the mass armed force and the advent of the all-volunteer force, creates new political cleavages and controversy which strain the search for effective social control. There is a direct analogy with the growth of the welfare state, but the strains of military defense and civil-military relations appear more intractable, since they extend beyond the domestic political arena, and the enlargement of domestic political participation does not readily produce effective and viable resolutions of political-military affairs.

III

The System of Social Organization

Seven

Bureaucratic Institutions: The Hierarchical Dimension

The Centrality of the Industrial Sector

Superficially, one of the most visible dimensions of an industrial society —and especially of an advanced industrial nation—is its pervasive presence of bureaucratic institution based on the hierarchical principle of social organization. Under the hierarchical principle, the basic components of a bureaucracy operate in specialization of task, allocation of position along a vertical scale, and explicit rules for recruiting and promoting personnel. However, industrialization generates a widespread ecological and institutional separation of bureaucratized work from household and residence.[1] Each person, so to speak, finds himself or herself enmeshed in two different but overlapping social worlds. Only rarely are occupation and work fused with residence; for example, in particular religious orders, in specialized intellectual and artistic enclaves. Even in the military, a progressively larger proportion of the personnel reside in the civilian community. There are, of course, special populations who live in particular "human services" institutions, such as mental hospitals and correctional institutions.

Limited separation of work and household, of course, helps characterize primitive and peasant society.[2] And the emergence of a significant separation was the primary interest of nineteenth-century writers investigating the societal consequences of industrialization and urbanization. The master trends in political behavior, social stratification, and military participation have influence on social control in the context of this separation.

1. Amos H. Hawley, *Urban Society: An Ecological Approach* (New York: Ronald Press, 1971), especially pp. 176–99.
2. Lloyd A. Fallers, *Inequality: Social Stratification Reconsidered* (Chicago: University of Chicago Press, 1973), pp. 28–34.

The assumption of the social-control perspective is that the pursuit of economic self-interest alone cannot create an effective self-regulating society. For an effective system of social control, it is assumed necessary to have an appropriate articulation between the social organization of work and the social organization of household and residence. Hypothetically, the social aspirations and practices generated in the "social world" of work must interact and aggregate with those generated by the "social world" of residence and household to facilitate the pursuit of a set of principles of "higher moral worth." In reality, the division of labor in an industrial society creates varying articulation-disarticulation patterns between the hierarchical bureaucracies of production and service and the communal social fabric. Each increment of disarticulation contributes to attenuating the patterns of social control. The effects of industrialization and urbanization, and the consequences of the major trends of social change, are not the linear emergence of isolated, individualized persons who are to be described as atomized. Our systemic analysis explicitly rejects the model of socialization implicit in the classical distinction between *Gemeinschaft* and *Gesellschaft*. The interaction between informal face-to-face relations and the goals and formal structure of the institutions of work, of community, and of residence continuously creates new social solidarities. Effective social control is a reflection of the interplay of the primary-group relations–the microsystems–and the larger collectivities, bureaucratic organization, and community structures.[3] Each individual participates in his occupational grouping and related bureaucratic structures through a network of primary groups; and an equivalent network of primary groups operate in his household-community. Primary-group relations and their connections with the large institutional structures are hardly a residual phenomenon, but the essential and ongoing ingredient of processes of socialization and social control.

The manner in which the face-to-face relations articulate or disarticulate with the bureaucratic institutions and communal organizations supplies essential indicators of the patterns of social control and their effectiveness. The content of norms, as has been repeatedly emphasized by sociologists, does not emerge from informal interactions. Primary groups reinforce or attenuate norms and social goals which derive from the moral culture of society.

3. Michel Crozier, "The Relationship between Micro- and Macrosociology," *Human Relations* 25 (July 1972): 239–51.

Much social reform has sought alternative strategies for new linkages between work and household-residence (see chapter 12). Utopian thinkers have tried to create new miniature societies which would join work and residence in a rural setting, while after World War II similar utopian institutions have been advocated for the metropolis.[4] Some vocal supporters of business enterprise have urged that the industrial corporation become the all-encompassing institution for managers and workers, with the implication that executives would supply the essential leadership. After the ambitious plans and then failure of the Pullman experiment, business leaders have gradually retreated from advocating the construction of business-sponsored communal utopias.[5] Likewise, advocates of revolutionary transformation claim that only a single mass party ruling in the name of the dictatorship of the proletariat can overcome the disarticulation resulting from the separation of work and family and eliminate poverty and the discontent of industrialism. The theory of self-regulation falls back on a vision of pluralistic attachments and linkages between work and residence. This is what is meant by democratic pluralism.

Without accepting any single-minded notion of evolutionary trends, our analysis hypothesizes that, from 1920 to 1976, the level of articulation between the industrial sector and the social organization of household-community has declined. Given the greater required interdependence of these societal sectors and the growth in complexity and scale of social organization, it can be argued that the disarticulation and the resulting strains on social control have increased. Moreover, we are dealing with changed social definitions which demand higher levels of institutional effectiveness.

4. Harry W. Laidler, *Social-Economic Movements: an Historical and Comparative Survey of Socialism, Communism, Co-operation, Utopianism, and Other Systems of Reform and Reconstruction* (New York: Crowell, 1947); Alice Felt Tyler, *Freedom's Ferment: Phases of American Social History from the Colonial Period to the Outbreak of the Civil War* (New York: Harper and Row, 1962); Paul Goodman, *Utopian Essays and Practical Proposals* (New York: Village Books, 1964); William Hedgepeth and Dennis Stock, *The Alternative: Communal Life in New America* (New York: Macmillan, 1970); Dick Fairfield, *Communes, U.S.A.* (San Francisco: Alternatives Foundation, 1971); Rosabeth Moss Kanter, *Commitment and Community: Communes and Utopias in Sociological Perspective* (Cambridge: Harvard University Press, 1972); Rosabeth Moss Kanter, *Communes: Creating and Managing the Collective Life* (New York: Harper and Row, 1973).

5. Stanley Buder, *Pullman: An Experiment in Industrial Order and Community Planning, 1880–1930* (New York: Oxford University Press, 1967).

Therefore the immediate task is to assess the available research on the connection between bureaucratic work and household-community. It is thus initially necessary to examine basic trends in the internal organization of work (in this chapter) and of residential community (in the next chapter). The underlying hypothesis about industrial organization can be stated with more concrete reference to the patterns of social change. Since the end of World War I, there has been a decline in the resort to violence in labor-management relations and an expansion of collective bargaining. These trends have been accompanied by a continued and even heightened pursuit of narrow self-interest without any corresponding development of mechanisms for linking occupational interests with communal or with broader collective societal interests.

The following hypotheses are offered to explore this overall trend:

First, managerial authority in the industrial sector has shifted from reliance on domination to manipulation (this trend is to be found in all types of bureaucratic organizations, including "human services" institutions). This in part accounts for the decline of industrial violence; nevertheless, managerial attitudes toward trade unions remain essentially those of an adversary. Industrial management has shifted toward professional executives who are cautious and narrow in defining their responsibilities. Even where owners control the enterprise financially, management authority has undergone the same transformation.

Second, the decline in violence in industrial relations has not significantly eliminated worker resistance to increased productivity or improved quality control. While work satisfaction in the industrial sector varies greatly, depending on industrial and communal conditions, in the 1960s and 1970s employee concern with the conditions of work generally and job dissatisfaction among young workers have increased. Even in the absence of strong social class consciousness, at the informal primary-group level and in the behavior of organized trade unions, a strong oppositionist or adversary orientation persists among industrial workers. They thus support narrow business unionism and are indifferent to or resist broader schemes of worker participation.

Third, as a result of the adversary outlooks of economic entrepreneurs, industrial managers, and most trade union leaders, the collective bargaining system which has evolved in the United States has not shown initiative about the economic issues of the welfare state and of stagflation, including the low rates on capital formation and the limited increase in economic productivity of the U.S. economy.

Industrial organization is the prototype of the bureaucratic organization.[6] Of course, industrial production was probably not the earliest historical locus of "modern" large-scale enterprise. In terms of the aggregation of men and material resources and especially of the development of the logic of the bureaucratic discipline, the military in the fifteenth and sixteenth centuries is the innovative case.[7] Military institutions in the United States continue to be the largest single aggregation of personnel and resources under single managerial control. Moreover, the service sector—professional, skilled, and semiskilled—represents the growth of an advanced industrial society. Nevertheless, the industrial sector, with its efficiency and adaptiveness, remains the central component of the vitality of an advanced industrial society. It still represents the economic core of the society because of its crucial contribution to the gross national product. The industrial sector—supplemented by the agricultural and extractive sectors—supplies the essential resources for the well-being of the nation-state; in particular, it supplies the economic surplus on which the service economy and the welfare state are based.[8]

There was a time when the simple terms "factory" and "manufacturing plant" were used instead of the more global "industrial establishment." The factory remains the site of the organization of human labor by means of machinery which is propelled by more and more efficient energy. With the introduction of new forms of energy and new forms of technology, the essential characteristics of the factory

6. Arnold S. Feldman and Wilbert E. Moore, "Industrialization and Industrialism: Convergence and Differentation," in *Comparative Perspectives on Industrial Society*, ed. W. A. Faunce and W. H. Form (New York: Little Brown, 1969).

7. See, for example, Maury D. Feld, "Middle-Class Society and the Rise of Military Professionalism: The Dutch Army 1589–1609," *Armed Forces and Society* 1 (1975): 419–42.

8. Andrew Schoenfield, *Modern Capitalism: The Changing Balance of Public and Private Capitalism* (London: Oxford University Press, 1965). For another point of view, see P. A. Baran and Paul M. Sweezy, *Monopoly Capital: An Essay on the American Economic and Social Order* (New York: Monthly Review Press, 1966), and Paul M. Sweezy and Harry Magdoff, *The Dynamics of U.S. Capitalism, Corporate Structure, Inflation, Credit, Gold and the Dollar* (New York: Monthly Review Press, 1972).

were defined; division of labor and routinization of task, resulting in factory work and its discontents as well as in new forms of economic exploitation.[9]

The increase in industrial productivity has produced the decline in the proportion of the labor force required for factory work and for employment in industry. These trends supplied the basis of Colin Clark's analysis of economic progress and industrial development, with its emphasis on the decline of the primary (agriculture and fishing) and secondary (manufacturing sector) and the growth of the service sector of society.[10] Of course, since 1900, the proportion of the labor force engaged in industry has declined. Even if one adds the mining and construction sectors, the same trend is clearly observable.

These trends can be seen for 1950 to 1975 for the nonagricultural establishments. If one combines mining, construction, and manufacturing—the goods-related sectors—the proportion of the labor force has declined from 40.9% to 28.9%, while the services-related establishments rose from 59.1% to 71.1%. The concentration of government employees increased from 13.3% to 19.8%.

However, it is essential to examine the extent to which industrial work can be found in the service sector, both public and private. Aggregate statistics on the location of the labor force do not reveal actual conditions of work and employment. It has become appropriate to speak of industrial type of work in the service sector, that is, those tasks in which workers are engaged in very routine operations, in some form of assembly line or in segmented operations in which they have little control over the work flow and limited opportunity for variation of task. Such conditions obtain in important areas of clerical work, food handling, communications enterprises, transportation and maintenance organization, and the "human services" institutions. The "industrial" component of service employment has grown and been intensified, as jobs have become more specialized and more routine. Likewise, an important number of the industrial type of tasks in the service sector are in small establishments, especially in food service and retailing, where workers receive few of the benefits available in larger establishments—which are also more likely to be unionized.

9. Harry Braverman, *Labor and Monopoly Capital* (New York: Monthly Review Press, 1974); Daniel Bell, *Work and Its Discontents: The Cult of Efficiency in America* (Boston: Beacon Press, 1956).

10. Colin Clark, *The Conditions of Economic Progress*, 3d ed. (London: Macmillan, 1957).

Therefore, estimates of the fraction of the labor force engaged in "industrial type" employment vary greatly. Some analysts believe that if one combines those persons engaged in industrial, extractive enterprise, and construction, plus the "industrial type" jobs in the service sector, the group has grown as a percentage of the labor force.[11] One such estimate concluded that in 1900, 50.7% of the labor force were "workers"; by 1970, the figure was 69.1%. While this estimate is high, the notion of the industrial type of employment prevents one from accepting idealized notions about the decline of tedious and boring work associated with the idea of postindustrial society.

From the perspective of social control, the starting point in the analysis of the social organization of U.S. economic enterprise—and industrial enterprise in particular—is the focus developed by those economists who have sought to investigate the degree of concentration on industrial production and the extent of separation of ownership of the "means of production" from the actual control. This tradition of research, launched by Adolf A. Berle, Jr., and Gardiner Means, has dealt with the largest corporate enterprises and has continued to be pursued energetically.[12] The results of this research served as indirect measures of the processes of bureaucratization.[13]

11. Braverman, *Labor*, p. 379.

12. Gardiner C. Means, "The Growth in the Relative Importance of the Large Corporation in American Economic Life," *American Economic Review* 21 (March 1931): 10–42; Adolf A. Berle, Jr., and Gardiner C. Means, *The Modern Corporation and Private Property* (New York: Macmillan, 1933). For an overview of the intellectual history and concepts in the economic analysis of industrial organization, see George J. Stigler, *The Organization of Industry* (Homewood, Ill.: Richard D. Irwin, 1968). A comprehensive analysis of industrial organization in a comparative and cross-national frame of reference is presented by Frederic Pryor, *Property and Industrial Organization in Communist and Capitalist Nations* (Bloomington: University of Indiana Press, 1973); Frederick Pryor, *Public Expenditures in Communist and Capitalist Nations* (Homewood, Ill.: Richard D. Irwin, 1968).

13. National Resources Committee, *The Structure of the American Economy* (Washington: GPO, 1939); Raymond W. Goldsmith and Rexford C. Parmelee, *The Distribution of Ownership in the 200 Largest Nonfinancial Corporations (Temporary National Economic Committee Monograph)* no. 29 (Washington: GPO, 1940); R. A. Gordon, *Business Leadership in the Large Corporation* (Washington: Brookings Institution, 1945); R. Sargant Florence, *Ownership, Control and Success of Large Companies: An Analysis of English Industrial Structure and Policy, 1936–1951* (London: Sweet and Maxwell, 1961); Henry Manne, "Buyers and the Market for Corporate Control," *Journal of Political Economy* 72 (April 1965): 110–20; W. G. Shepherd, "Trends of Concentration in American Manufacturing Industries, 1947–1958," Review of Economics and Statistics 46 (May 1964): 200–212; R. J. Larner, "Ownership and Control in the 200 Largest Nonfinancial Corporations, 1929 and 1963," *American Economic Review* 56 (September 1966): 777–87; C. S. Breed, "The Separation of Ownership from Control," *Journal*

If one assumes that the industrial order operates in terms of the reality and the legitimacy of competitive capitalism, then the greater the concentration of control, the greater the degree of departure from classical theory and the more likely both restrictive and exploitative economic performance. Likewise, the greater the separation of ownership from control, the greater the potentiality for managerial control of industrial enterprises for considerations other than those of profit. Unfortunately, measures of ownership and control, important though they be, supply only indirect and at best partial indicators of the performance of industrial enterprise. They are even more indirect as in reflecting actual patterns of managerial authority and business norms. It is essential to go beyond the morphological structure and formal legal arrangement of economic enterprises in order to describe the transformation of "capitalism" in an advanced industrial society. I agree with those sociologists who point out that we have more critical inquiry into the behavior of the lower middle class than we have about the upper levels of industrial and economic enterprises.[14] It is appropriate to examine the scope and trends in concentration of industrial enterprise and the imputed consequences.[15] In terms of classical theory, the nonfinancial sector in the United States is characterized by concentration. The definition of oligopoly employed by economists is that of four firms with a sales concentration of 50% or more. As of 1966, the proportion of manufacturing firms of this type was 28.6%.[16] The variation in concentration was marked; in 1950 for automobiles it was 90%, cigarette and cigars 70%, petroleum refining 39%, woolen yarn 15%, and sawmills, 4%. Economists have therefore sought to

of Economic Studies 2 (1966): 29–46; R. Joseph Monsen, Jr., J. S. Chin, and D. E. Cooley, "The Effect of Separation of Ownership and Control on the Performance of the Large Firm," *Quarterly Journal of Economics* 82 (August 1968): 435–51; Jean-Marie Chevalier, "The Problem of Control in Large American Corporation," *Anti-Trust Bulletin* 14 (1969): 163–80; Brian V. Hindley, "Separation of Ownership and Control in the Modern Corporation," *Journal of Law and Economics* 13 (April 1970): 185–221; Robert J. Larner, *Management Control and the Large Corporation* (New York: Dunellen, 1970); Philip H. Bunch, Jr., *The Managerial Revolution Reassessed* (Lexington, Mass.: Heath, 1972).

14. Maurice Zeitlin, "Corporate Ownership and Control," *American Journal of Sociology* 79 (March 1974): 1073–1119.

15. For early efforts to deal with these issues, see Edward S. Mason, "Price and Production Policies of Large-Scale Enterprise," *American Economic Review, Supplement* (March 1939), pp. 61–74; Edward S. Mason, "The Current Status of the Monopoly Problem in the United States," *Harvard Law Review* (June 1949), pp. 1265–85.

16. F. M. Scherer, *Industrial Market Structure and Economic Performance* (Chicago: Rand McNally, 1973), p. 60.

formulate a theory of workable competition, and economic debate centers on the extent and consequences of workable competition, resulting from the existing degree of concentration.[17]

Therefore, the central question is whether, over the long run—and in our case since 1920—there has been a trend toward increased concentration. M. A. Adelman has set forth the complexities and difficulties involved.[18] G. Warren Nutter, among others, has collected the required detailed data.[19] As of 1951, the results, based on a variety of measures, could be summarized by the conclusion, "any tendency either way if it does exist, must be at the pace of a glacial drift."[20] Research covering the years up to 1966, using other measures, indicates a modest drift toward increased concentration.[21]

The merger movement has been used as an index to the process of concentration. It appears that there have been three waves of mergers in the U.S. economy, in general.[22] The first occurred roughly between 1887 and 1904; the second, between 1916 and 1929; and the third, after World War II. The magnitude of these merger movements has declined; the effect of the post–World War II mergers has been modest with that of 1887–1904. According to Scherer, "it would be equally incorrect to say that the movement had no effects on concentration. But the effect was generally modest."[23] Thus, as one measure, between 1950 and 1962, the 200 largest manufacturing corporations increased their share of all manufacturing corporation assets from 48.9% to 55.0%.

In the 1960 decade, the merger movement assumed a new direction, namely, an emphasis on conglomerates. Mergers were more and more designed to acquire diversified industrial establishments rather than to consolidate ownership within a type of industry. In part the conse-

17. S. Peterson, "Anti-Trust and the Classic Model," *American Economic Review* 47 (March 1957): 60–78; Steven H. Sosnick, "A Critique of Concepts of Workable Competition," *Quarterly Journal of Economics* 72 (August 1958): 380–423.

18. M. A. Adelman, "The Measurement of Industrial Concentration," *Review of Economics and Statistics* 33 (November 1951): 269–96.

19. G. Warren Nutter, *The Extent of Enterprise Monopoly in the United States: 1899–1939* (Chicago: University of Chicago Press, 1951); see also H. A. Einhorn, "Competition in American Industry, 1939–58," *Journal of Political Economy* 74 (October 1966): 506–11.

20. Adelman, "Measurement," p. 295.

21. Similar results have been obtained by Nutter, *Extent*.

22. Scherer, *Industrial Market*, p. 103.

23. Ibid., p. 111.

quences of anti-trust regulation were at work; acquisition across industrial sectors was less likely to encounter anti-trust regulation. In addition, business executives sought diversified industrial holdings in order to assist their economic success during a period of rapid technological and market change. The extent of acquisition for conglomerate goals was noteworthy. In the eight-year period of 1960 to 1968, the 25 largest conglomerate acquiring firms purchased 695 firms costing over $20 billion. These firms often included highly successful ones, in contrast to the earlier merger movement which emphasized weak companies. The thrust of these conglomerates was mergers lead by financial leaders rather than by industrial managers. The economic issues were those of financial control rather than industrial management, and therefore fundamental questions of socio-political consequences and responsibilities were raised. By the end of the 1960s the rate of these mergers slowed.

There appear to be limits to the trend toward concentration and the formation of conglomerates, although they have by no means been reached. In part, they are linked to the declining economies of scale. Or to state the issue otherwise, for nonfinancial corporations to achieve economy of scale, there is no need for very high economic concentration. "It is evident from the studies of scale economies in particular industries and the observation of broad survival patterns that in many and perhaps most American industries high concentration is not a technological, marketing, or financial imperative."[24] The degree of competition is augmented by governmental intervention, since antitrust programs—administrative and judicial—have had a discernible effect. Even more important are the constant developments of technology and new consumer tastes which permit new bases of competition to arise. But the essential question, which is more difficult to answer, is the consequence of different degrees of concentration on economic performance, especially profits and profiitability. The accumulation of results underlines that the degree of concentration is not notably related to the persistence of high levels of profit. The same is true of conglomerates. These findings indicate that a form of workable competition operates in the United States. Such a conclusion is not a statement about the direct and indirect political consequences of economic concentration, or an assessment of the social implications of the operating managerial strategies.

24. Ibid., p. 103.

A group of research studies by Joe Bain, H. Michael Mann, and George J. Stigler report that, for particular groups of industries, high concentration produces higher profits.[25] However, these studies were based on limited samples. As Yale Brozen has indicated, they were limited to short intervals.[26] When, for the corporations covered by these studies, he examined the persistence of profits over time, he found no relations between higher profits and the degree of concentration.[27]

After thirty years of research and debate, the findings on the scope of separation and ownership and control are not definitive, although a reasoned argument does emerge which highlights the significant extent of this separation. If one focuses on the largest nonfinancial corporate enterprises in the United States—and this highlights the conformation of the industrial enterprise to the hierarchical industrial model—it is clear that separation of ownership from operating control has taken place.[28] The extent has probably been overstated and has been questioned by Philip H. Burch, Jr., and Maurice Zeitlin.[29] For example, the ability of financial leaders and family groupings to maintain control of particular industrial or groups of corporate enterprises is pronounced and reflects their energy and ingenuity as well as the existing legal and banking arrangements. Any assessment of the structure of corporate enterprise must also consider the pattern of control in the financial sector and the mechanism for controlling the flow of credit. Moreover, in the process of capital accumulation, industrial managers at times transform themselves into ownership groups. The distinction between owner (or entrepreneur) and manager is not fixed and unchanging.

25. Joe Bain, "Relation of Profit Rate to Industry Concentration: American Manufacturing, 1936–1940," *Quarterly Journal of Economics* 65 (August 1951): 293–324; H. Michael Mann, "Seller Concentration, Barriers to Entry, and Rates of Return in Thirty Industries, 1950–1960," *Review of Economics and Statistics* 48 (August 1966): 203–307; George J. Stigler, "A Theory of Oligopoly," *Journal of Political Economy* 44 (February 1964): 44–61; see also Norman R. Collins and Lee Preston, *Concentration and Price-Cost Margins in Manufacturing Industries* (Berkeley: University of California Press, 1968).

26. Yale Brozen, "Concentration and Profits: Does Concentration Matter?" *The Anti-Trust Bulletin* 19 (1974): 381–97.

27. Yale Brozen, "The Antitrust Task Force Deconcentration Recommendation," *Journal of Law and Economics* 13 (October 1970): 279–92; Yale Brozen, "The Persistence of 'High Rates of Return' in High Stable Concentration Industries," *Journal of Law and Economics* 14 (October 1971): 501–12.

28. See note 13.

29. Philip H. Burch, Jr., *The Managerial Revolution Reassessed: Family Control in America's Large Corporations* (Lexington, Mass.: Lexington Books, 1972);

However, the crucial findings deal with the economic performance of owner-dominated enterprises compared with manager-administered ones. Research indicates that there is very little difference between manager-dominated industrial enterprises and those which can be described as owner-controlled, as manifested by rates of return on invested capital, growth rates, and other key economic indicators.[30] This does not deny the possibility of important differences in the political behavior and conceptions of social responsibility among the leaders of these two groupings. While the topic of sociopolitical orientations of economic dominants will be discussed in chapter 13, at this point, it is relevant to point out that a body of data emphasize that absentee owners of industrial enterprises are much less responsive to and effectively involved in local community affairs.[31] While the categories of absentee ownership are usually not operationalized exactly like the distinction between ownership and control, the overlap is very high.

The consequences of both economic concentration and the separation of ownership from control need to be examined in the context of the trends in profits in the United States over time. On the basis of careful research, William D. Nordhaus has reported a long-term decline in the level of corporate profits in the United States.[32] His analysis of the share of profits in the GNP, from 1948 to 1973 reveals, for the period 1971–1973, that profits were 57% of the 1948–1950 average. Other measures indicate a comparable decline. The findings made corrections for changes (*a*) in accounting conventions and depreciations provisions, (*b*) the financial structure of corporations, (*c*) the burden of corporate taxation, and (*d*) the price level.

Maurice Zeitlin, "Corporate Ownership and Control: The Large Corporation and the Capitalist Class," *American Journal of Sociology* 79 (March 1974): 1073–1119.

30. A. D. H. Kaplan, *Big Enterprise in a Competitive System* (Washington: Brookings Institution, 1964); David R. Kamerschen, "The Influence of Ownership and Control on Profit Rates," *American Economic Review* 58 (June 1968): 432–47.

31. C. Wright Mills and Melville J. Ulmer, *Small Business and Civic Welfare; Report of the Small War Plants Corporation to the Special Committee to Study Problems of American Small Business* (U.S. Senate, 79th Congress, 2d Session, Document Number 135, Serial No. 11036, Washington: GPO, 1946); Robert O. Schulze, "The Bifurcation of Power in a Satellite City," in *Community Political System*, ed. Morris Janowitz (New York: Free Press, 1961); Michael Aiken, "The Distribution of Community Power: Structural Bases and Social Consequences," in *The Structure of Community Power*, ed. Michael Aiken and Paul E. Mott (New York: Random House, 1970), pp. 487–525.

32. William D. Nordhaus, "The Falling Share of Profits," *Cowles Foundation Paper*, No. 408 (New Haven: Cowles Foundation for Research in Economics at Yale University, 1974).

All in all, the economic performance of corporations in the United States has led economists to speak of an alternative pattern of corporate behavior.[33] Rather than maintain the fiction of competitive behavior and the drive to maximize profit, economists offer a more institutional notion, namely, the "managerial theory of the firm," in which various goals leads not to maximization of profit but to a form of "satisfice."[34]

After 1950 the structure of U.S. industrial establishments has been strongly influenced by the rapid growth of multi-national corporations, particularly those in which U.S. financial holdings play a major role. In effect, the export of U.S. industrial products has come to be rivaled by the export of U.S. capital used to create multi-national firms located abroad. Such investments by U.S. businesses increased from $3.8 billion in 1950 to $11.2 billion in 1960, to $32.2 billion in 1970. This represents a rate of growth of approximately 10% per year. By comparison, U.S. exports of manufactured goods have expanded about 5% per year in the 1960s. The growth of multi-national corporations reflect the obvious advantages in lower labor costs and immediate access to foreign markets.

The immediate consequences of this overseas investment is the exporting of "jobs," many millions of jobs; it is, of course, difficult to estimate the total number in the period 1945 to 1976. Moreover, the internationalization of industrial corporations, and associated financial institutions in the first instance of U.S. firms, but likewise of Japanese and Western European firms represents an enormous concentration of economic power with attendant implications for social control. There emerge persistent and complex tensions and conflict between the international operations of multi-national corporations and the nation

33. Fritz Machlup, "Marginal Analysis and Empirical Research," *American Economic Review* 36 (September 1946): 519–54; Fritz Machlup, "Theories of the Firm, Marginalist, Behavioral, Managerial," *American Economic Review* 57 (March 1967): 1–33; Edward S. Mason, ed., *The Corporation in Modern Society* (Cambridge: Harvard University Press, 1960); R. M. Cyert and J. G. March, *A Behavioral Theory of the Firm* (Englewood Cliffs: Prentice-Hall, 1963); Robin Morris, *The Economic Theory* of *"Managerial" Capitalism* (London: Macmillan, 1964); John Kenneth Galbraith, *The New Industrial State* (Boston: Houghton Mifflin, 1967; W. J. Baumol, *Business Behavior, Value and Growth* (New York: Harcourt, Brace and World, 1967); Oliver E. Williamson, *Corporate Control and Business Behavior* (Englewood Cliffs, N.J.: Prentice-Hall, 1970); William J. Baumol and Mark Stewart, "On the Behavioral Theory of the Firm," in *The Corporate Economy: Growth, Competition and Innovative Potential*, ed. Robin Morris and Adrian Wood (Cambridge: Harvard University Press, 1971), pp. 118–42.

34. Scherer, *Industrial Market*, pp. 27–38.

states in which the multi-national factories are located; and, in particular, the national regulatory agencies have limited effect.

From the point of view of social control, the existing statistical data on concentration and on separation of ownership from control within the United States do not adequately reflect the normative patterns which influence the industrial executive in the pursuit of profit and in the management of labor relations. First, the revelations of various antitrust suits highlight the extent to which cooperative and collusive practices develop informally in opposition to the regulations enforcing competition. It is very difficult to assess the extent and influence of these informal—and even the formalized—practices. Second, since the New Deal, the basic conception of private property has undergone extensive change by legislation and by judicial intervention. The normative changes, which are replete with difficulties and inconsistencies, have had the long-run consequence of limiting property rights, as shown by sociologists such as Wilbert Moore and Philip Selznick.[35] As a result, owners and managers of industrial enterprises must respond not only to the degree and forms of competition but also to the web of new normative standards about limitation on property and labor rights. None of these normative definitions eliminate the primacy of profit, but do change the institutional context under which profit can be pursued.

It is still relevant to remember the distinction between managers and corporate owners, but only as it supplies a basis for probing the normative patterns which condition their actual behavior—economic and otherwise. Measures of the separation of ownership and control and the degree of concentration of these indicators are not adequate. In particular, we are interested in the changing patterns of corporate and managerial authority as the context of these norms.

Such a perspective was held by early writers on the social control of business, e.g., John Maurice Clark.[36] This perspective was also opera-

35. Philip Selznick, *Law, Society and Industrial Justice* (New York: Russell Sage Foundation, 1969), see especially chap. 4, "Collective Bargaining and Legal Evolution." Analysis of industrial organization as a form of social organization has been deeply influenced by Thorstein Veblen. See especially his *Theory of Business Enterprise* (New York: Scribner, 1932); *The Engineers and the Price System* (New York: B. W. Huebsch, 1921); Neil J. Smelser, *The Sociology of Economic Life* (Englewood Cliffs, N.J.: Prentice-Hall, 1963).

36. Wilbert E. Moore, *Industrial Relations and the Social Order* (New York: Macmillan, 1947), especially chap. 22; John Maurice Clark, *Social Control of Business* (Chicago: University of Chicago Press, 1926).

tive in the seminal work of the laissez faire economist Frank H. Knight in *Risk, Profit and Uncertainty*, which was grounded in classical economic theory and incorporated a normative approach of social control.[37] In this study, Knight stressed that the successful men in business were those who were concerned with seeing that their enterprises worked. Although fixed salary was less of a motivation to them than the prospect of profit, the nature of the competitive enterprise system carried with it self-restraints and limitations on competition which emerged pragmatically. In short, Frank H. Knight was already describing the limited forms of professionalism in industrial management which had come into being and was anticipating their further growth. This growth, which had to take place in a profit-oriented context, needs to be explored.

Managerial Strategies and Authority

Although the industrial sector of the United States has been extensively described by economists in the categories of patterns of concentration, ownership, and control, from the point of view of social control, the factory system must be viewed in terms of authority patterns and the influence of the formal goals of profit making on the informal realities in the conflicts between "management" and "labor." In this view, the industrial sector is rooted in the realities of market relations based on the level of technology, and conditioned by the particular parliamentary regimes. The historical context of industrialization in the United States was one of limited governmental intervention.[38] Technological determinism is unable to deal with the different patterns of economic growth and the wide variation in the societal consequences of parallel technological growth.[39] To speak of technology in a systemic analysis is to assert that it serves as a point of entrance for the analysis of social change.[40]

Technological innovation to a large extent is derivative from the growth of science. The institutional logic of science, which creates for

37. Frank Knight, *Risk, Profit and Uncertainty* (Boston: Houghton Mifflin, 1921).

38. Reinhard Bendix, *Work and Authority in Industry: Ideologies of Management in the Course of Industrialization* (New York: Wiley, 1956), p. 5.

39. See David S. Landis, *The Unbound Prometheus: Technological Change and Industrial Development in Western Europe from 1750 to the Present* (Cambridge: Cambridge University Press, 1969).

40. Charles Perrow, "A Framework for the Comparative Analysis of Organizations," *American Sociological Review* 32 (April 1967): 495.

itself a strong element of autonomy, requires such autonomy for its continued but fragile development.[41] The observations by students of the history and sociology of science about the institutional and societal conditions which facilitate or retard the growth of science are secondary to this central but difficult to comprehend conclusion. Moreover, the fact that there has arisen a new term, "national science policy," indicates that, under advanced industrialism, the growth of science can no longer be taken for granted; if only because of budgetary limitations, national governments deliberately formulate policies to fashion the growth of science, but seldom with the anticipated consequences.

However, there is no simple connection between scientific development and technological innovation, and between technological innovation and economic growth.[42] Much debate has focused on the organizational resistance to both scientific and technological developments.[43] In an advanced industrial society, such resistance crumbles; and the central task of the industrial entrepreneurs and managers becomes that of selecting between a large number of competing avenues of technological development, since the process of technological development itself has become institutionalized and routinized. In terms of changing patterns of social control, it is even more important that the mental attitudes of the scientist and the technologist become an organizing principle which influences those executives responsible for the day-to-day management of industrial enterprises. A critical outlook toward existing procedures and a concern with the application of the scientific method to the "problems" of industrial production and organization become pervasive. Of course, the managerial perspective is subject to the control of the calculus of profit making. But the effort to apply the scientific perspective is a basic component of the growth of professions generally and the managerial perspective in industrial organizations.

Industrial management, it is necessary to keep in mind, reflects the societal context, in particular, the character of the political regime.[44]

41. Joseph Ben-David, *The Scientist's Role in Society: A Comparative Study* (Englewood Cliffs, N.J.: Prentice-Hall, 1971).

42. Joseph Schmookler, *Invention and Economic Growth* (Cambridge: Harvard University Press, 1966); John Jewkes, David Sawers, and Richard Stillerman, *The Sources of Invention* (New York: Norton, 1958).

43. Robert K. Merton, *The Sociology of Science: Theoretical and Empirical Investigation* (Chicago: University of Chicago Press, 1973).

44. Alfred D. Chandler, Jr., *Strategy and Structure: Chapters in the History of the American Industrial Enterprise* (Cambridge: MIT Press, 1962).

The legislative system in the United States helps explain the strong adversary outlook which industrial management developed to their labor force. In contrast to Great Britain and Western Europe, the United States represents the extreme case in the adversary perspective. Industrial relations were characterized by widespread violence until the end of the 1930s and by the low proportion of the labor force enrolled in trade unions.

The initial phases of industrialization in the United States took place without extensive intervention by the central government; and even that was based on weak political authority and limited legitimacy. As a result, employers in the United States have been able to set their own standards of behavior. In contrast, developments in Great Britain and Germany had continuity with feudal patterns of responsibility, so that the central government inhibited the use of force against industrial labor. In Germany, the authoritarian state was deeply involved in the process of industrialization and was active in the nineteenth century in regulating the social position of the workers. In Great Britain the central government's role was more circumscribed, but it was based on far-reaching traditional authority. In Great Britain particularly, and inherent in the growing liberal and utilitarian movements which undermined traditional and feudal restraint against "free trade and commerce," was the concept of the state as a regulating mechanism.[45] Government sought to contain the hostility of the industrial employers toward efforts to organize the labor force. In the United States the state gradually emerged as a regulating mechanism, but it faced persistent opposition from both entrepreneurs and managers. Until the New Deal, business groups thought of themselves as private government and were prepared to press their opposition to trade unions and left-wing political movements. Industrial executives learned the economic limits of their laissez-faire ideology; but they used the ideological implications of competitive economics to develop, maintain, and justify their stand against trade unions.

Our hypothesis is that there has been a long-term shift in forms of industrial authority from discipline based on domination to that involving manipulation. While this trend can be seen in industrial organization, it is a general trend that has also operated in the military estab-

45. A. V. Dicey, *Lectures on the Relation between Law and Public Opinion in England during the Nineteenth Century* (London: Macmillan, 1930). See especially "The Debt of Collectivism to Benthamism," pp. 303–10.

lishment and in large-scale organizations more generally.[46] By domination we mean influencing an individual's behavior by giving commands and explicit instructions about desired behavior without reference to the goals. Domination involves threats and negative sanctions rather than positive incentives. It tends to produce mechanical compliance. By manipulation we mean influencing an individual's behavior by indirect techniques of group persuasion and by an expansion of group goals. Manipulation involves positive incentives rather than physical threats, though it does retain the threat of exclusion from the group as a form of control. The techniques of manipulation take into account the individual's predisposition.

This hypothesis rests on no simple-minded value orientation. In fact, it seeks to penetrate the external manifestations of authority patterns before applying value judgments. Douglas McGregor tried to deal with this issue by speaking of theory *x* and theory *y* models of organization.[47] If, for some, "manipulation" has negative overtones, another phrase may be used. However, "manipulation" is used as in scientific experimentation; it refers to the conscious rearrangement of factors for the achievement of specific goals. It draws on Max Weber's formulations of rationality and the rationalizing of the institutional process of modern society.[48] It draws on the fundamental distinction between functional and substantive rationality of Karl Mannheim and the writings of Edward Shils on types of power and status.[49]

A variety of social scientists have discussed this transformation of authority and its built-in limits and concomitant instabilities. Georges Friedman in 1946 refers to the shift from discipline to morale.[50] Other

46. Morris Janowitz, "Changing Patterns of Organizational Authority: The Military Establishment," in *Military Conflict: Essays in the Institutional Analysis of War and Peace* (Beverly Hills, Calif.: Sage Publications, 1975), pp. 221–38.

47. Douglas McGregor, *The Human Side of Enterprise* (New York: McGraw-Hill, 1960); see also D. S. Pugh, "Modern Organization Theory," *Psychological Bulletin* 66 (October 1966): 235–51; T. Burns, "On the Plurality of Social Systems" in *Operational Research and the Social Sciences*, ed. J. R. Lawrence (London: Tavistock, 1966), pp. 165–78.

48. Max Weber, "Charisma and Its Transformation," in *Economy and Society: An Outline of Interpretive Sociology*, ed. Guenther Roth and Claus Wittich (New York: Bedminster Press, 1968).

49. Karl Mannheim, *Man and Society in an Age of Reconstruction* (New York: Harcourt, Brace, 1940); Herbert Goldhamer and Edward Shils, "Type of Power and Status," *American Journal of Sociology* 45 (1939): 171–82. These trends in authority relations were taken into account by C. Wright Mills in his early works; see Hans Gerth and C. Wright Mills, *Character and Social Structure: The Psychology of Social Institutions* (New York: Harcourt, Brace, 1953).

50. Georges Friedmann, *Problèmes humaines du machinisme industriel* (Paris: Gallimard, 1946); for an analysis of the influence of informal organization on

writers, drawing on Emile Durkheim, have spoken of mechanistic versus organic patterns of management.[51] National culture and national value systems deeply influence the content, scope, and consequences of this basic transformation. A number of detailed participant-observation studies on the organizational climate of "modal" industrial establishments highlight the cross-national differences. For example, we have Ronald Dore's comparison of the British and the Japanese factory, and Michel Crozier's analysis of the French industrial setting.[52] These profound cultural differences modify but do not reverse or undo the basic long-term hypothesis for nation-states governed by parliamentary regimes.

Finally, this transformation is not a simple evolution. Indeed, the growth of manipulative authority, while it represents a decline in "revolutionary" confrontation, is accompanied by strains and tensions in the industrial sector. Moreover, if the shift toward manipulative authority involves a reduction in coercion and force in industrial relations, this hardly implies a concomitant reduction in personal aggression or in various forms of criminality.

The complexity of the technology base and the division of labor requires this transformation of authority, especially if parliamentary institutions are to operate. As organizational forms become more intricate and as the scale of organization increases, bureaucratic authority has altered. To maintain effectiveness, authority systems have had to become less arbitrary, less direct, even less "authoritarian." The importance of persuasion has grown. An authority system based on rigid discipline operates when there is a simple division of labor where coordination involves no more than compliance or adherence to rules. The "morale" system of manipulative authority implies that coordination is too complex to rely on mechanical compliance and requires positive initiative. Even on the routinized assembly line, workers accumulate a measure of individual power which can be expressed by failure to

working procedures, see E. L. Trust and K. W. Bamforth, "Some Social and Psychological Consequences of the Longwall Method of Coal-Getting," *Human Relations* 4 (1951): 3–38.

51. T. Burns and G. Stalker, *The Management of Innovation* (London: Tavistock, 1961), pp. 96–125; M. W. Flinn, "Social Theory and the Industrial Revolution," in *Social Theory and Economic Change*, ed. Tom Burns and S. B. Saul (London: Tavistock, 1967), pp. 9–34.

52. Ronald Dore, *British Factory—Japanese Factory: The Origins of National Diversity in Industrial Relations* (Berkeley: University of California Press, 1973); Michel Crozier, *The Bureaucratic Phenomenon* (Chicago: University of Chicago Press, 1963).

perform or by outright noncompliance with work standards, without immediate sanctions being applied.

The shift from authority based on domination to that based on manipulation occurs within a wage system and profit-oriented context. It is hardly sufficient to assert that men work for wages; and it is insufficient, although correct, to assert, that with the growth of manipulative authority, the importance of nonwage issues grows with the process of collective bargaining. With the transformation of authority the mechanism and the assumptions involved in setting wages change. The collective bargaining process, as defined in the U.S. pattern of industrial relations, has meant a decline in the resort to coercion and greater reliance on negotiations which are supposed to be based on the realities of the economic relations. Because of the adversary orientation of managers and trade union leaders, minimum governmental intervention is desired, and this has been generally accepted by labor leaders. In reality, as explored below, collective bargaining operates in the United States in terms of a limited range of important immediate issues without much concern for the totality of the economic system—that is, without an implicit or explicit attention to the interplay of policies of wages, profit, productivity, and social welfare.

While technological development supplies the initial explanation for the transformation of managerial authority, it is not enough. Social control in the industrial sector, or rather its limitation, involves the normative definition of work and industrial relations and the cultural content of societal values about work and industrial relations.

In the advanced industrial nations with parliamentary regimes, there is a strong emphasis on equality of opportunity and of reward, plus pressure for security of tenure. It is by no means easy to explain how an advanced industrial society such as the United States, with its concern with professionalization, at the same time places an equal or even higher value on social equality. Individuals and social groups are not consistent in their values; as a result there is a profound difference between professed goals and actual practices. But such a well-worn observation is not sufficient.

The emphasis on social equality has independent ideological origins in religious and political movements. Second, as Joseph Schumpeter emphasizes, the infusion of the scientific outlook into the managerial perspective contributes to the acceptance of the idea of social equality.[53] The critical spirit generated with the scientific spirit has a negative influence on traditional "business" values. The industrial manager does not give up his basic economic commitments; he modifies important elements to accept new values. Especially, he develops a surface acceptance of various notions of equality particularly equality of opportunity. Managers become involved in efforts to create a new sociopolitical balance encompassing minority groups and women. In other words, the instabilities of managerial authority are a reflection of the tensions between an industrial system which rests on strong components of professionalization and expertise and at the same time generates its own commitment to various and expanding forms of equality as goals and as institutional practices.

The publication by Frederick Taylor during 1903 to 1912 of his three major writings, later republished under the title *Scientific Management*, serves as an effective historical point to anchor the long-term transformation of managerial authority in industry.[54] (In the military, the 1905 publication of an article by Captain M. B. Stewart helps identify the initial stages in the shift toward managerial authority.)[55] These writings reflect the organizational difficulties industrial leaders and military commanders had to face. Support for the hypothesis on the shift in managerial authority rests not only on the contents of published materials but also on a few participant-observation studies, documentary sources, and primary reports.

Actually Taylor had started his research, lecturing, and writing on rationalizing industrial production in the 1880s. Parallel writings had begun to appear in Germany through the efforts of Hugo Munsterberg, who had studied at the University of Leipzig under the direction of Wilhelm Wundt. Munsterberg took up residence at Harvard University, where he sought to infuse the German experimental psychology tradition into efforts to develop a system of scientific management. Interest in scientific management has persisted as in the managerial perspective in the United States. From the point of view of social control,

53. Joseph Schumpeter, *Capitalism, Socialism and Democracy*, 3d ed. (New York: Harper, 1950).

54. Frederick W. Taylor, *The Principle of Scientific Management* (New York: Harper and Bros, 1911), p. 191; see also Charles S. Maier, "Between Taylorism and Technocracy: European Ideologies and the Vision of Industrial Productivity in the 1920's," *Journal of Contemporary History* 5 (April 1970): 27–66.

55. Captain M. B. Stewart, "The Army as a Factor in the Upbuilding of Society," *Journal of the Military Service Institute* 36 (1905): 391–404.

scientific management represented a recognition—incomplete or even distorted—that the wage incentive system would not suffice as an effective basis of industrial organization. At the turn of the century, managerial ideology, in varying degree, was based on a piece rate wage incentive system, violent opposition to the various forms of trade unionism, and an admixture of religious rationalization of the responsibility of industrial leaders for the welfare of the worker. Taylorism recognized that a profound and extensive source of informal and organized opposition existed in the social life of the plant, even in the absence of trade unions. It focused mainly on the restructuring of the task of work but had broader implications for the structure of industrial relations, since it assigned no role to the trade unions or to worker participation in management decisions.

Until the entrance of the United States into World War I, there is little basis to conclude that scientific management was of more than marginal consequence in industrial relations. It supplied a rationalization to speed up technological innovation. It served to facilitate the work of efficiency engineers and in turn to increase worker opposition and hostility as well as productivity. "Scientific management," although it was a response to the increasing complexity of industrial work, did not relate to the realities of industrial life—either the immediate informal life of the plant or the larger, more encompassing realities of organized labor-management relations. Industrial executives moved slowly to new forms of authority under the influence of technology.

During World War I, the federal government pressured management to sponsor labor-management committees which foreshadowed the long-term trends toward manipulative authority. But with the end of World War I, the opposition to trade unions reasserted itself and violence and coercion continued. Groups of radical unionists engaged in bitter strikes. The effective trade union movement involved only a small fraction of the working-class occupations. It depended mainly on skilled workers and followed business unionism and adversary tactics. Recognition by industrial executives that the traditional system has strong limitations as well as moral defects led to various stock-distribution system schemes, of little or no lasting consequence.

Opposition to the expansion of trade unions meant that more and more steps were taken at the plant level to introduce management-dominated innovations. It was in the 1920s that the famous Hawthorne studies were undertaken.[56] The lasting debate about their intellectual contribution should not obscure the fact that they represented a managerial effort—even though a paternalistic one—to deal with industrial inefficiency and discontent. They were also destined to have limited immediate influence, since they failed to deal with the fundamental issues of group representation and participation. From a research point of view, they documented that any system of effective management which did not rely on extensive violence would have to take into account the intimate solidarities among members of the labor force. In retrospect, they underline that a concern with "human relations," without effective institutions for relevant participation at the plant level, would be an incomplete system of social control.

The Great Depression meant that entrepreneurs and industrial managers had to face comprehensive political initiatives which called into question the existing pattern of industrial relations. By means of a series of enactments, the federal government intervened to increase the legitimacy, scope, and power of the trade union movement; Norris LaGuardia (Anti-Injunction) Act of 1933; Section 7A National Industrial Recovery Act of 1933; National Labor Relations Act of 1935 (the Wagner Act). As a result, the trade union movement made extensive gains in the mass production industries. Management had to face the extension of collective bargaining about wages and the intrusion of trade unionism at the shop floor. The trade union movement was an essential ingredient in a national political coalition which enacted Keynesian fiscal measures to increase consumer demand and which instituted legislation to develop the welfare state.

The New Deal produced a dramatic, persistent decline in industrial violence; in these years there were major transformations of managerial authority and strategy.[57] The sit-in produced a short-term and rela-

56. Elton Mayo, *The Human Problem of an Industrial Civilization* (New York: Macmillan, 1933); *The Social Problem of an Industrial Civilization* (Boston: Division of Research, Graduate School of Business Administration, Harvard University, 1945); F. J. Roethlisberger and William J. Dickson, *Management and the Worker: An Account of a Research Program Conducted by the Western Electric Company, Hawthorne Works, Chicago* (Cambridge: Harvard University Press, 1939); T. N. Whitehead, *Leadership in a Free Society* (Cambridge: Harvard University Press, 1936); a retrospective assessment of these research efforts is presented by Henry Landsberger, *Hawthorne Revisited* (Ithaca: Cornell University Press, 1958); see also Alex Carey, "The Hawthorne Studies: A Radical Criticism," *American Sociological Review* 32 (June 1967): 403–16.

57. Philip Taft and Philip Ross, "American Labor Violence: Its Causes, Character, and Outcome," in *Violence in America: Historical and Comparative Per-*

tively inhibited series of confrontations, more symbolic than destructive. The political coalition on which the New Deal was based plus the new labor legislation and the fiscal and welfare measures provided the context for sharp societal change. One of those almost unanswerable questions is whether, in the absence of political intervention, managerial strategies would have undergone such extensive transformation. In any case, we are dealing not only with New Deal legislation but also with the effect of World War II experiences on managerial perspectives and strategies. The wartime programs of governmental management of fiscal policy and the governmental intervention in labor relations laid the basis for the expansion of the welfare state, as described above, and strengthened the legitimacy of collective bargaining. In the name of wartime goals, managerial and labor resort to violence was strongly deemphasized and the mechanisms of bargaining and negotiation were strengthened. Entrepreneurs and industrial managers faced a more sophisticated trade union movement, equipped with its own economic experts, the growth of a group of independent labor negotiators who were available for the resolution of the industrial disputes, and an expansion of federal and state arbitration services.

After World War II no antilabor movement reemerged comparable to that after World War I. The adversary model, and the existing collective bargaining system, became more institutionalized. In terms of wage and incomes policy, various economists have argued that the fact that only a minority of the labor force was organized was of secondary importance, since the unionized segment of the industrial labor force set the wage scale and the nonunionized segment followed shortly thereafter.

This thesis is by no means generally accepted; in fact, the counterarguments warrant careful consideration. In the United States, the limited percentage of the labor force which is unionized has had a great influence on labor-management negotiations. It has, with other factors to be discussed below, contributed both to a defensive stance on the part of trade union leaders and to reinforcing the circumscribed "business" trade unionism at the expense of societal-wide responsibilities.

It was inevitable that the industrial leaders would launch political initiatives to counter aspects of the Wagner Act and the expansion of

spectives, ed. Hugh D. Graham and Ted R. Gurr (New York: Bantam Books, 1969), pp. 281–395.

the trade union movement during World War II. At the state level there has been a trend to pass "right to work" laws. At the federal level, the Taft-Hartley Act and the Griffin-Landrum Act were designed to limit trade union power. The strategy of the Taft-Hartley Act was to constrain the labor movement's ability to conduct strikes, while at the same time limiting the role of the government. The Griffin-Landrum Act required greater disclosure of trade union activities and more effective election procedures and internal management of the trade unions. The outcome of this latter legislation was, of course, that the federal government's involvement in the regulation of the trade unions increased, since the government was assigned surveillance and the enforcement of due process.

In contrast, in Western Europe, in the post–World War II period, many consultative innovations designed to increase mutual responsibility in industrial management had been launched, especially in West Germany and Sweden, in the form of codetermination. With the advent of stagflation the adversary orientation of managerial authority in the United States remained essentially intact. Limited experiments in modifying the U.S. formula of labor-management negotiations were advocated, for example, Secretary of Labor John Dunlop's efforts to invigorate the President's Committee on Labor-Management. By 1976, these attempts had a record of no accomplishment.[58]

It has mattered little whether in effect the particular factory or corporate organization was directed by a financial entrepreneur; that is, whether it was owner-managed or administered by a group of industrialists without effective financial ownership. Whatever the type of financial control, the trend toward "managerial authority" continued. If the corporate establishment was large and based on extensive, elaborate technology, a limited group were responsible for its day-to-day administration. These administrators display a strong professionalization. Their explicit laissez-faire ideology, which is reinforced by their

58. The opposition of the existing top leadership of the trade unions to such an approach is indicated by the statement of George Meany, chief spokesman for the AFL-CIO. It was his opinion that the "group (President Ford's Labor-Management Committee) should function independently of government and as a forum for confidential discussion and, on occasion, release recommendations to the public" (*New York Times*, May 7, 1976, p. 5); see also Bernard Barber, "Is American Business Becoming Professionalized? Analysis of a Social Ideology," in *Sociocultural Theory, Values and Sociocultural Change: Essays in Honor of Pitirim A. Sorokin*, ed. E. A. Tiryakian (New York: Free Press, 1963), pp. 121–45.

membership in voluntary associations and participation in informal community-based networks, is constantly being circumvented in their actual practices. This tempering is a result of their technical expertise, which has engendered a self-critical approach, and of their intimate day-to-day primary-group encounters with other managerial experts who appreciate "effective" administration.[59] Industrial managers are motivated to perform their tasks of administration and short-term innovation with considerable energy and competence, although they are uncertain about their broader strategic role as managers of the larger industrial order. They are strongly committed, nevertheless, to the idea that their adversary relation to unions—a reasoned, consistent, and legalistic opposition—serves the national economy. Their contact with lawyers and legal personnel reinforces such commitments.

Professionalization among industrial administrators is not without strong ambiguity. The behavior of industrial executives—with or without significant ownership claims—reveals that they are not men with extensive and "overpowering" risk-taking proclivities. "He is not the restless dynamic individual of an earlier generation who, owning his company, pioneered new lines and 'risked his shirt' building up a new business organization."[60] Economists have noted that even the entrepreneur who has extensive holdings—through family control systems or legal entities—is more frequently not the plunger but the careful and cautious investor. Only a small number of self-made and highly individualist entrepreneurs, operating often at the periphery of the industrial and economic mainstream, fill the classic entrepreneurial model.

As in any other skill group, professionalization of the industrial executives is conditioned by their social recruitment and education, and the organization of their work. Sociologists have expended much effort in describing the recruitment of business entrepreneurs and industrial executives. F. W. Taussig and C. S. Joslyn documented, on the basis of a large sample of industrialists of the 1920s, that there was considerable mobility into the higher ranks.[61] After World War II, there is little reason to believe that there has been a marked decline in opportunities for social mobility.[62] (The important issue of the social and

59. Melville Dalton, *Men Who Manage: Fusions of Feeling and Theory in Administration* (New York: Wiley, 1959).

60. Gordon, *Business Leadership*, p. 71.

61. Frank William Taussig and C. S. Joslyn, *American Business Leaders: A Study in Social Origins and Social Stratification* (New York: Macmillan, 1932).

62. W. Lloyd Warner and James Abegglen, *Occupational Mobility in America Business and Industry, 1928–1952* (Minneapolis: University of Minnesota Press, 1955).

political attitudes of those business leaders who come from upper status versus those of leaders from a more modest background has not been investigated, however.) Their essential findings were that those in managerial positions had a great deal of opportunity for upward mobility and in this respect conformed to the model of professionalization. Inherited connections no doubt supply a person with considerable advantages in the struggle for advancement. However, the career development of industrial executives is based on a strong element of meritocracy. Education has come to have a more important influence in career development. The modern corporate executive is better educated and better trained technically than the owner-entrepreneur of the turn of the century or even of the 1920s.[63] Recruitment has been "democritized" as a broader range of colleges and universities are found in the backgrounds of the higher ranks of industrial leaders.

What about the influence of professional training on the self-conceptions of the industrial executive and on his world view and on his sense of sociopolitical responsibility? The influence of technical and business education, including legal education, appears to be narrowing the focus of attention of the industrial executive and generating, as in other professional groups, a circumscribed conception of the task to be performed and a strong emphasis on career advancement. Close relations with peers on the job tend to reinforce this type of specialization and task performance, while the broader range of personal and friendship contacts with other sectors of the economic system serve mainly to reinforce a conservative ideology.[64] The businessman of the 1970s was clearly better informed than his counterpart of the 1920s. Higher education and increased exposure to the mass media meant that the elite businessmen are more interested in national social and political affairs.

However, the commitment to a laissez-faire ideology, and particularly the opposition to the growth of welfare benefits, cannot obscure doubts and uncertainties. The comprehensive survey of 1200 businessmen published in 1977 highlighted their rejection of an ideology that business is concerned only with making profit.[65] "Only 28 percent endorsed the traditional dictum that the social responsibility of business is to 'stick to business.' " Moreover, 69% agreed with the statement,

63. Gordon, *Business Leadership*, p. 324.

64. For a comprehensive study of business ideology, see Francis X. Sutton et al. *The American Business Creed* (Cambridge: Harvard University Press, 1956).

65. Steven N. Brenner and Earl A. Molander, "Is the Ethics of Business Changing," *Harvard Business Review* 55 (January-February, 1977): 57–71.

"profit is really a somewhat ineffective measure of business's social effectiveness."

The outcome is a perspective among both financial entrepreneurs and industrial managers rooted in desirability of a workable if not classic economic competition. In fact, industrial relations in the United States are in part the result of the operating procedures of executives who seek to balance the search for profits with a circumscribed professionalism. As a result, by the mid 1970s, the outcome was a level of performance of the industrial sector of the United States in which comparison with the pattern of industrial relations in Western Europe—especially West Germany— *(a)* has a lower rate of increases in economic productivity, *(b)* has a lower rate of reinvestment of capital in industrial plant, and *(c)* has profound defects in quality control. The decision-making of the industrial executive (*a*) emphasizes the centrality of the control of inflation, (*b*) resists responsibility for "full employment" and instead is concerned with the reduction of costs, including labor costs, and *(c)* accepts collective bargaining and seeks to define collective bargaining as negotiations about short-term wages.

Labor relations are thought of as a form of battle institutionalized by a set of legal decisions designed to contain the conflicts of interests of an advanced industrial society. The managerial approach is to resist governmental regulation and any form of trade union participation in the management of industrial affairs—and to resist even those forms of participation which would not alter the legal structure of property rights but operate on the basis of consultative procedures. The exception is the limited effort at distribution of property rights by means of stock options and bonuses as work incentives.

The resulting pattern of industrial relations, especially when the union and worker responses are examined below, creates a weak and disarticulated institutional basis for the effective social control of competing economic interests. Industrial managers are aware of the defects and difficulties in industrial relations. The ambiguity in which they, especially the operating executive, find themselves, leads at points to toleration of criminality in labor-management's bargaining process, collusion with competing establishments, informal or formal, to circumvent the antitrust legislation and norms of a competitive market, and corruption in the form of bribes to influence competitors or governmental officials and potential purchasers of products.

The analysis thus far has focused on managerial patterns in the industrial sector. In the following section, the responses and initiatives of the industrial workers and industrial unions are examined from the point of view of social control.

WORKER INITIATIVES: INFORMAL AND COLLECTIVE

The responses and the initiatives of workers and their leaders in the United States as the industrial sector and industrial type of work in the service sector expanded have produced a very low percentage of unionization of the labor force (Table 7.1), particularly compared

TABLE 7.1 Union Membership as a Proportion of the U.S. Labor Force, 1930–1974

Year	Total U.S. Union Membership (thousands)	Percent of Total Labor Force	Percent of Non-agriculture Employment
1930	3,401	6.8	11.6
1940	8,717	15.6	26.9
1950	14,267	22.3	31.5
1960	17,049	23.6	31.4
1965	17,299	22.4	28.4
1970	19,381	22.6	27.6
1972	19,436	21.8	26.7
1974	21,643	21.7	25.8

SOURCE: *Handbook of Labor Statistics, 1971*, p. 307; *Statistical Abstract of the United States, 1976.*

with Western Europe. In 1930, 11.6% of the employees in nonagricultural establishments were unionized, and in the total labor force, only 6.8%. New Deal legislation and the "sit-in" strikes produced immediate results: from 13.7% of the nonagricultural labor force in 1936, the figure rose to 22.6% in 1937, and grew steadily until it reached 35.5% in 1945. From the end of World War II on, the proportion of the nonagricultural labor force in unions declined gradually until 1974, when the figure stood at 25.8%. Only the increase in white-collar unionization, especially in public services, offsets this decline in trade union membership in industry.

One approach to the limited success of trade unionism has been to explore the classic question of the failure of socialism in the United States. Subsequent to the writings of Werner Sombat, historical and sociological literature has sought to trace the ideologies, strategies, and political behavior of organized labor groups in the United States with regard to socialism. The core of socialism deals not with the central government's fiscal management of the economy or the growth of welfare expenditures, but rather with the demand for government ownership of the means of production.

These writings manifest a great convergence. One focus has been on societal elements such as the absence of a feudal tradition, the social and geographical mobility, the higher standard of living, the extreme cultural, ethnic, and racial heterogeneity of the industrial labor force, and the extensive system of secondary and higher education which has produced a more "middle-class" social structure. While researchers have pointed out that the differences in the rate of social mobility in the United States and Western Europe may not have been as great as popular discourse asserted, there is no reason to believe that from 1920 to 1960 they were equal.[66] The larger cadre of university graduates and the proliferation of professional specialists which could be supported by the higher standard of living have produced more extensive social mobility in the United States than in Western Europe.[67]

Socialist-oriented scholars have debated whether the Socialist movement in the United States has been too doctrinaire; the rigidity, it is argued, prevented the Socialist leaders in the United States during 1910 to 1920 from developing an effective strategy and an organized political base which would be comparable to those of the Socialist movements of Western Europe and Great Britain. The Socialist party had grown to 120,000 by 1912, it had elected 1,200 public officials throughout the United States, and was publishing over 300 periodicals.[68] Convinced party cadres existed; but there can be no doubt that the Socialist leaders of the United States did not effectively organize their potential rank and file, just as the right-wing groups of the 1930s failed to organize their constituency.[69] But it is very difficult to judge the consequences of the lack of organizational skill and the imputed rigidities of the social leaders. Perhaps as important, the Socialist movement in the United States between World War I and World War II had to face and was weakened by the Communist party with its fanatical opposition to competitive working-class organizations.[70]

66. Reinhard Bendix and S. M. Lipset, *Social Mobility in Industrial Society* (Berkeley: University of California Press, 1959).

67. Thomas G. Fox and S. M. Miller, "Economic, Political and Social Determinants of Mobility," *Acta Sociologica* 9 (1965): 76–93; Morris Janowitz, "Social Stratification and Mobility in West Germany," *American Journal of Sociology* 64 (July 1958): 6–24.

68. James Weinstein, "The Problems of the Socialist Party: Before World War One," in *Failure of a Dream?* ed. John H. M. Laslett and Seymour Martin Lipset (New York: Anchor, 1974), pp. 300–341.

69. David Shannon, *The Socialist Party of America* (New York: Macmillan, 1955); Morris Janowitz, "Native Fascism in the 1930's" in *Political Conflict* (Beverly Hills, Calif.: Sage Publications, 1970), 149–70.

70. Nathan Glazer, *The Social Basis of American Communism* (New York: Harcourt, Brace, 1961).

Efforts to organize industrial workers into "left-wing" associations had to confront the same kind of opposition which the trade union movement encountered. While comparisons with Western Europe are difficult if not impossible to make, the opposition appears to have been highly effective. With the decline in industrial violence, and both the expansion of collective bargaining and the incorporation of onetime Socialists into the New Deal, worker response overwhelmingly continued to support "business" trade unionism. In this long-term process, employers and managerial groups have had great influence in "defining the situation," in setting the terms of reference, and in conditioning the response of trade unions, as would be expected in any setting of imbalance of power. (This is not to assert that the workers were merely reacting; as in the case of majority-minority group relations, the behavior of the minority group is not merely the response to the strategies and practices of the majority or the powerful.)[71] After the decline of violence against trade unions, labor leaders came to accept a "definition of the situation" paralleling employers' groups. They believed collective bargaining should focus on immediate wage issues and resisted a positive role by the federal government. As mentioned above, they believed that collective bargaining should be negotiations between economic groups without interference or guidelines from the federal government or even from mutually generated national guidelines.

One of the rare efforts to formulate a broader conception of labor-management collective bargaining was offered by Clinton S. Golden and Harold J. Ruttenberg, two officials of the United Steel Workers Union.[72] Their formulation explicitly sought to avoid traditional socialistic goals of "nationalization" of basic industry and emphasized broader responsibility for the trade union movement. They anticipated the European movement toward codetermination. The book had practically no influence on public opinion.

Workers' initiatives in response to industrialization involve and are conditioned by the informal, intimate social relations of the factory. The separation of place of work and place of residence in an advanced industrial society has its direct implications. The literature on the history of trade union and left-wing movements acknowledges the centrality of these dimensions. From the limited available materials, it is

71. Ralph Ellison, *Shadow and Act* (New York: Random House, 1964).
72. Clinton S. Golden and Harold J. Ruttenberg, *The Dynamics of Industrial Democracy* (New York: Harper and Bros., 1942).

clear that localistic and particularistic social solidarities, not atomized persons, were the basis for constructing workers' organizations. From the early history of Socialist trade union movements to the contemporary studies of working-class politics such as that of the steel workers in South Chicago by William Kornblum, the strength of industrial worker movements depends on the articulation between in plant social solidarities and communal institutions outside the factory—more often than not the local tavern or the church is crucial.[73]

For the period under investigation we have a few realistic observations of actual social life of the factory. Before World War II, sociologists concentrated more on community-based social solidarities. One of the first adequate descriptions and analysis, based on prolonged participant observation of the informal organization of industrial workers in the United States, was the research work of Donald Roy prepared in the late 1940s.[74] He was particularly concerned with the effect of technological processes on the informal organization of work groups, a theme which has become more and more central in the analysis of industrial relations. His research encountered not isolated "anomic" workers but a complex admixture of particularistic solidarities, with strong oppositionist orientations. There were elements of class consciousness, but a stratigraphic model would hardly encompass the complex social life of the factory, which involved skill, length of time, ethnic background, age, type of work, and sex. His research underlines that much of the oppositionist outlook was a manifestation of antagonism between informal groups and supervisory personnel. Moreover, the cleavages aggregrated into strong resistance to production quotas and continuous interpersonal tensions and hostility which undermined morale and influenced performance.

The observations and interpretation by Donald Roy help give meaning to the findings of the Elton Mayo experiments. The populism of the U.S. setting and the pervasive opposition to authority and absence of a deferential perspective to established authority have not been confined to the political arena, but as of the end of 1940 were widespread in the industrial sectors of the United States. If in the United States

73. Morris Janowitz, *The Community Press in an Urban Setting* (Glencoe, Ill.: Free Press, 1952); William Kornblum, *Blue Collar Community* (Chicago: University of Chicago Press, 1974).

74. Donald Roy, "Restriction of Output by Machine Operators in a Piecework Machine Shop," Ph.D. dissertation, University of Chicago, 1952; Donald Roy, "Quota Restriction and Goldbricking in a Machine Shop," *American Journal of Sociology* 57 (March 1952): 427–42.

the trade union movement has not been based on or engendered a strong ideological commitment to Socialist symbols, it could use a diffuse but personal antagonism to the direct presence of supervisory and managerial authority. (Roy's research is revealing in its focus on the interpersonal difficulties and exploitation of women in the industrial setting and their extensive sexual molestation by coworkers and by supervisory workers, which has only gradually declined.)

It is, of course, a reality that men and women learn to live with their immediate circumstances. Social scientists are again and again "amazed" to observe that industrial workers accept their life chances. Donald Roy found that, along with the manifestations of discontent, workers in industrial establishments developed considerable job satisfaction; this conclusion has been confirmed by subsequent investigators.[75] This is not simply resignation but satisfaction with their tasks, as they find personal gratifications. As a result, there is a wide variation in the level of job satisfaction and in the extent of oppositional solidarities. Gradually over the years social scientists have undertaken studies of the factors within the industrial work setting which influence the degree of work discontent.

At the core is the sheer monotony, and the unpleasant, unsanitary, and unsafe conditions which reflect technology and also the lack of concern with making the workplace tolerable. Investigators such as Joan Woodward present a detailed picture of the different patterns of industrial organization in, for example, factories which operate by making batches of a product versus those that operate on a continuous assembly production.[76] Blauner has used public opinion surveys to highlight the technological base which contributed to workers' satisfaction, by comparing the automobile assembly line, the textile factory, the printing plant, and the highly automated chemical establishment.[77] The more complex the machinery and the more individual responsibility and variation the technology produces and permits, the greater the satisfaction. In short, the greater the invested capital per work, the higher the level of workers' satisfaction.

75. See especially William H. Form, *Blue Collar Stratification: Autoworkers in Four Countries* (Princeton: Princeton University Press, 1976).

76. Joan Woodward, *Industrial Organization: Theory and Practice* (Oxford: Oxford University Press, 1965).

77. Robert Blauner, *Alienation and Freedom: The Factory Worker and His Industry* (Chicago: University of Chicago Press, 1964); see also Martin Meissine, *Technology and the Worker* (San Francisco: Chandler, 1969).

It is not enough to observe that, in general, job satisfaction increases with increases in pay or with greater investment in capital–technological or human investments or more pleasant conditions of work.[78] There are occupational enclaves where workers have high self-esteem and a sense of competence based on family tradition, skill components, or even a sense of danger. Worker satisfaction can derive from ethnic solidarity both inside and outside the plant and from participation in community institutions.[79] Participation in trade unions—especially as a leader—is another important source of gratification. The emergence of a union can contribute to a sense of social solidarity and worker satisfaction, even though the union may be engaged in adversary strategies. It is not a simple matter to summarize the constellation of relations within the factory, or among the factory and the community and the larger society, which operate to overcome the discontents of industrial and industrial type of work, but there is no need to portray a pattern of universality of oppositionist attitudes and behavior.

It is rare that social research produces penetrating research which highlights the consequences of the separation of work, community, and residence, and the tensions between industrial work and the social organization of the larger society. One such study uses the "propensity to strike" as a crucial indicator of industrial relations and as a measure of the consequences of the disarticulation of the organization of work from the organization of the larger society.[80] Clark Kerr and Abraham Siegel for the interwar period carried out extensive international comparisons of the propensity to strike in different industries. A range of economic measures were found to be inadequate in explaining it: sensitivity of the industry to the business cycle, structure of the product market, the elasticity of demand for the product, labor as a percent of total cost, the profitability of the industry, the average size of the

78. Richard Renck, "Industrial Organization and Employee Morale," Ph.D. dissertation, University of Chicago, 1965; R. W. Revans, "Industrial Morale and Size of Unit," *Political Quarterly* 27 (July-September 1956): 303–11.

79. William H. Form, "Auto Worker and Their Machines: A Study of Work, Factory, and Job Satisfaction in Four Countries," *Social Forces* 52 (September 1973): 1–15; Melvin Seeman, "The Urban Alienation: Some Dubious Theses from Marx to Marcuse," *Journal of Personality and Social Psychology* 19 (August 1971): 135–43.

80. Clark Kerr and Abraham Siegel, "The Interindustry Propensity to Strike—An International Comparison," in *Industrial Conflict*, ed. Arthur Kornhauser et al. (New York: McGraw Hill, 1954), pp. 189–212; see also David Britt and Omer R. Galle, "Industrial Conflict and Unionization," *American Sociological Review* 37 (February 1972): 46–57.

plant, the state of technological change, the rate of expansion or contraction of the industry. Instead, the social location of the worker in the community and the society was more critical; those described as "the isolated mass"—sharply differentiated and separated from the larger society—the miners, sailors, longshoremen, loggers, etc., had the greater propensity to strike. Those described as "the integrated individual and the integrated group" were less likely to strike. Clearly, this distinction involves both formal and informal connections with the larger society.

No adequate body of trend data describes long-term shifts in job satisfaction in the United States. Job satisfaction has increased but probably not as much as one might have hoped for. However, one is struck by the observation, drawn from at least two relevant studies, that there has been an embitterment, a deepening of dissatisfaction in the 1960s among young workers who have entered the heavy industry mass-production factories. Both the research by Harold Sheppard and Neal Herrick and the large-scale study sponsored by the Department of Health, Education, and Welfare on assembly work underline the split between the older and younger worker, with the young worker as the carrier of job dissatisfaction.[81]

The dissatisfaction among young workers is in part a continuation of traditional attitudes toward factory work. But the social definition of factory work has undergone a change for the new generations who have been exposed to the formal requirements of high school education. The older generation of industrial workers were immigrants either from Europe or from rural areas who had had very little formal education and for whom the entrance into the industrial employment was anticipated and desired. The younger worker who enters the factory—and especially the assembly-line factory—believes that he is settling for less than the desired occupation stressed by the school system. The definition of desirable work, as conditioned by the mass media, is not that of the factory setting.

Moreover, the educational experience fails to be an institutional bridge from school to the work situation. Often, the old workers,

81. Harold L. Sheppard and Neal Herrick, *Where Have all the Robots Gone? Work Dissatisfaction in the 1970's* (New York: Free Press, 1972). Special Task Force to the Secretary of Health, Education and Welfare, *Work in America* (Cambridge, Mass.: MIT Press, 1973); Raymond A. Katzell and Daniel Yankelovich, *Work, Productivity and Job Satisfaction: An Evaluation of Policy-Related Research* (New York: Psychological Corporation, 1975).

especially those who entered the factory before 1945, were concentrated in enclaves close to the work site so that their socialization into the local communal institutions supported the informal organization of the factory.[82] Local residents were available in the factory to assist in the socialization of the new worker into the factory. After 1945, especially with the recruitment of black workers, the disarticulation between work and community life grew as workers were recruited from greater distances and more variegated residential settings. Adjustment to the work setting became more difficult and the integration of new people into trade union organization slowed. As a result, the concentration of discontent is particularly high among young workers, high enough to reduce their participation in existing trade unions. For the young workers, collective bargaining about immediate economic issues is taken for granted; often they are more interested in issues of style of management, grievance procedures, and authority relations.

The tensions and pressure of "stagflation" have been accompanied by a sharp increase in contested elections among industrial types of unions. The picture presented by sociologists of the structural inability of trade unions to generate internal political democracy has been starkly overdrawn. To a considerable extent these contested elections relate to economic issues, and to some extent they relate to personalities and to ethnic and racial divisions in the labor force. But perhaps the most pervasive cleavage which these conflicts manifest is age, the older versus the younger workers. It is not incompatible to have high disaffection among young workers and at the same time to have leaders arise to challenge the older entrenched leadership. The insurgent leaders are of the middle generation, but with a strong admixture of younger workers in their thirties—which is very young by trade union standards. A limited amount of opposition in the industrial trade unions in the early 1970s has been inspired by radical ideology, but more important is this age split.

The internal cleavage in trade unions hardly obscures their basic rationale, namely, to achieve short-term economic benefits for the membership. On the basis of their exemption from antitrust legislation and with the advantages derived from legislation in support of collective bargaining, trade unions have succeeded in limiting the entry of workers in a variety of sectors as well as restricting work quotas, particularly in construction. Trade union efforts have resulted in set-

82. Kornblum, *Blue Collar.*

ting wages in particular industries which are clearly above equivalent skill level, for example, in transportation—in both the railroads and trucking. The influence of trade unions can be inferred by comparing the wages of clerical workers with various categories of blue-collar workers, since this comparison reflects marked differences in degree of unionization. As of May 1971, the data collected by the Bureau of Labor Statistics indicate that the earning for full-time clerical workers was less than that of blue-collar workers; for example, the weekly wage of clerical workers was $115 while craftsmen and foremen earned $167, operative and kindred workers $120, and nonfarm workers $117.[83] In addition to the more extensive fringe benefits which union workers enjoy, with the advent of stagflation, some trade unions have been important to their members by obtaining automatic cost of living increases, a wage pattern almost wholly absent among unorganized workers.

Thus it is necessary to keep in mind that a person's relations to the economic order (and the mode of production) under advanced industrialism cannot be adequately inferred from the categories of occupation, education, and prestige, although such variables are essential components. This is the case not only because of the previously mentioned limitations in the stratigraphic conceptions of social structure. It is also the result of the social organization of the industrial order in the United States, which, while it conforms to the general pattern of a shift toward managerial authority and the decline of discipline based on domination, has fashioned a particular type of trade unionism. The trade union movement has a narrow definition of labor-management relations and therefore is reluctant to include the central issues of stagflation—declining productivity, low national investment in capital development—and the allocation for social welfare. The result is a strong tendency to export these issues into the political arena with little or limited effort to adjust differences within the industrial sector. Thus another crucial dimension is added to the strain on the political regime. While there has been a reduction in overt coercion in the industrial arena, violent confrontations have given way to chronic conflict which strain and weaken patterns of social control. At this point it is appropriate to examine the changing basis of authority in noneconomic institutions.

83. Paul O. Flaim and Nicholas I. Peters, "Usual Weekly Earnings of American Workers," *Monthly Labor Review* (March 1972), pp. 28–38.

"Human Services" Bureaucracies

The term "organizational behavior" involves an attempt to construct models of bureaucratic organizations without reference to the distinction between industrial and service organization or any other such substantive distinction.[84] The transformation in institutional authority for the industrial executive is paralleled in service institutions and especially in "human services" institutions—educational, health, mental health, correctional, and related types of organization. These institutions have the goal of directly influencing social personality. From the point of view of social control, the distinction between industrial (including service organizations) and these "human services" organizations remains relevant. The continuous efforts to reform these institutions in order to improve their internal milieu highlight their special character. The criteria for judging the performance of these organizations are more difficult to formulate; they cannot be effectively evaluated in terms of financial considerations, although cost measures are of importance.

We have relevant case studies in depth over time which make it possible to trace the transformation of different classes of these institutions, especially the trends in prison organization and authority. It is not an accident that the prison has served as a continuing site for the empirical study of the dilemmas of social control. The prison is a complex social system which could be studied intensively by a single investigator. In the study of the prison one could observe the persistent, irreconcilable conflicts between the desires and needs of the prisoners and the demands of the larger society. The handling of these conflicts serves as a measure of the moral order of the larger society.

The original classic study was completed by Donald Clemmer in 1940.[85] From Donald Clemmer onward investigators have sought to

84. Tom Burns, "On the Plurality of Social Systems," in *Operational Research and the Social Sciences*, ed. J. R. Lawrence (London: Tavistock, 1966), pp. 165–78; James L. Price, *Organizational Effectiveness: An Inventory of Propositions* (Homewood, Ill.: Richard D. Irwin, Inc., 1968); Charles Perrow, *Organizational Analysis: A Sociological View* (London: Tavistock, 1970); Stanford M. Dornbush and W. Richard Scott, *Evaluation and the Exercise of Authority* (San Francisco: Jossey-Bass, 1975); D. J. Hickson, "A Convergence in Organization Theory," *Administrative Science Quarterly* 16 (September 1966): 224–37.

85. Donald Clemmer, *The Prison Community* (Boston: Christopher Publishing House, 1940). Important subsequent studies include Gresham Sykes, *The Society of Captives; A Study of a Maximum Security Prison* (Princeton: Princeton University Press, 1958); David Street, Robert Vinter, and Charles Perrow, *Organization for Treatment* (New York: Free Press, 1969); James Jacobs, *Stateville: The*

trace the influence of prison goals and policies on the informal intimate organization and, in turn, the consequences of primary group on the social climate of the institution. The authority system of the prison generates by its very nature oppositional solidarities among its inmates. However, the major thrust of prison research over time has been to trace the changes in authority and its consequences on the social life of the inmates.[86]

The transformation of authority in the prison, like the transformation of authority in industrial society, has been a gradual process and has produced extensive conflict and strain. The movement toward more "managerial" authority in "human services" institutions, including prisons and correctional institutions, has been an expression of humanitarian goals in the larger society. Pressure for change has also resulted from the belief that custodial types of institutions are inefficient; the same resources could be used with greater results. In addition, a social technology based on advances in dynamic psychology and organizational research has been elaborated for managing "human services" agencies, and it is a technology which has become more complicated and more complex.[87] The phrase from "custody to treatment" epitomizes these trends. Moreover, during the 1960s the courts intervened with considerable effect in correctional institutions to strengthen the requirements for due process in the management of inmates.

Despite these efforts, there is no reason to assess the transformation of prison authority as resulting in an increased capacity to rehabilitate

Penitentiary in Mass Society (Chicago: University of Chicago Press, 1976); See also Douglas Lipton, Robert Martinson, and Judith Wilks, *The Effectiveness of Correctional Treatment: A Survey of Treatment Evaluation Studies* (New York: Praeger, 1975).

86. Erving Goffman acknowledges his debt to the work of Donald Clemmer and the tradition of participation observation studies correctional and "people processing" institutions. He offers the notion of total institution. See Erving Goffman; *Asylums: Essays on the Social Situation of Mental Patients and Other Inmates* (Garden City, N.Y.: Anchor, 1961). However, this "ideal type" model oversimplifies his analysis. The concept suffers because it produces stereotypical notions rather than a series of testable hypotheses. First, it exaggerates the boundaries between the internal organization of the institution and the larger society. Second, it overstates the barriers between staff and clients, especially in medical and mental health settings. Third, it fails to recognize the range of responses among inmates which are produced by different staff strategies and by the availability of increased resources—human and material. Thus he underemphasizes those settings in which there is cooperation and mutual support between management and elements of the staff. And as a result, it fails to account for the difference in organizational climate in various types of institutions.

87. For an overview of these issues see Lloyd Ohlin, *Theoretical Studies in Social Organization of the Prison* (New York: Social Science Council, 1960).

the inmates. In the prison, rehabilitation does not succeed or fail wholly as a result of the influence of institutional experience; it also requires satisfactory socioeconomic conditions and effective transitional agencies in the external community. The traditional correctional agency has been a repressive institution. Organizational change has moved it toward the benign category, with more orderly and more due process routines. This is not an advance to be dismissed. But to speak of an institutional capacity for rehabilitation is to refer to an aspiration yet to be achieved. Therefore, the quality of the treatment of the inmates while they are in prison is an appropriate criterion for judging the consequences of changes in authority patterns. And this criterion is a clear measure of the moral values of the larger society. Benign institutions are desired in functional terms as well, since with the passage of time the incidence of criminal behavior in each age cohort declines.

The process of innovation means that new specialists in "human relations" are introduced into the prison with professional perspectives which are at variance with the traditional custodial hierarchy. These new personnel render not only particular services but, in fact, serve as a "public presence." The result is to alter the hierarchical structure by shifting from one single unified table of organization to a more diffuse formal structure and to open the boundaries of the organization to persons and agencies from the external community.

The pressure for change first produces limited modification toward manipulation, then because of increased pressures more change is generated, innovations increase internal tensions and can contain unrealistic components. Then because of the resulting internal conflict between the old and the new perspectives and personnel, a shift back takes place—but not necessarily to the original format. This natural history has continued to repeat itself with gradual long-term changes. One of the most striking sources of conflict and instability as the institution becomes more open to external groups is that the criminal groups from which inmates come can at times become powerful forces in the internal conduct of the prison.

Institutions which have undergone these changes reveal the gradual and realistic movement toward a new internal milieu. It remains the milieu of a prison but one organized on principles more compatible with the goals of social control in the larger society. James Jacobs's study of the social history of a large midwestern prison—Stateville—over a half-century supplied an analysis of this long-term process of organizational adaptation. Quantitative survey data on the behavior and attitudes of inmates in different types of youth correctional institutions collected at the same time offer additional supporting evidence.

In these comparisons, the informal social organization of the inmates is the basic indicator of institutional change. With the decline of repressive custodial authority based on domination, the inmates' informal organization moves away from solitary opposition to a more differentiated pattern of response including varying forms of interaction and support between inmates and staff. In the adult institution, whose inmates include repeated offenders, the interaction with staff heightens a portion of the inmates' realistic appraisal of their self-interest, and leads them to more effective use of their energies. (Without overstating the consequences, it should be stressed that Daniel Glaser's assessment of the federal prison system—with its highly selected inmate population—in the 1960s, when the process of transformation was in process, revealed that in the first two to five years after their release, the period of greatest vulnerability, only about one-third of the men released are returned to prison.)[88]

For youth institutions, a body of research on the informal social organization of the inmates highlights the extent to which the traditional opposition culture can be altered by increased resources and by effective managerial strategies. By comparing treatment in benign and custodial institutions, one is able to connect the influence of managerial strategies with the resulting inmate culture.[89] The inmates of the benign institutions were less hostile to the goals of the institution, and in particular developed inmate patterns of interaction with the staff which were less oppositional. They had more extensive sociometric patterns of friendship and chose less oppositional persons as their in-

88. Daniel Glaser, *The Effectiveness of a Prison and Parole System* (New York: Bobbs-Merrill, 1964).

89. Clarence Schrag, "Leadership Among Prison Inmates," *American Sociological Review* 19 (February 1954): 37–42; Stanton Wheeler, "Socialization in Correctional Communities," *American Sociological Review* 26 (October 1961): 697–712; Charles R. Tittle, *Society of Subordinates* (Bloomington: Indiana University Press, 1972). See especially Street, Vinter, and Perrow, *Organization*. Other relevant research includes Oscar Grusky, "Organizational Goals and the Behavior of Informal Leaders," *American Journal of Sociology* 65 (July 1959): 59–67; Bernard B. Berk, "Organizational Goals and Inmate Organization," *American Journal of Sociology* 71 (March 1966): 522–534.

formal leaders. The sharp difference in the normative climate was between the custodial and the benign institutions; intensive effort at treatment produces few differences from the benign institutions.

The movement to transform correctional institutions constantly faces crucial limitations in fiscal resources, especially in a period of increasing crime rates. However, in contrast to the transformation of the industrial plant, the crucial threshold was reached by the intervention of courts. From 1964, the courts of the United States, including the Supreme Court, asserted their authority to review the internal procedures and standards of prison and correctional institutions. The result was a new basis for institutionalizing the trend toward managerial authority. This intervention hardly eliminated the fundamental difficulties facing correctional institutions, but it did stabilize the efforts to institutionalize managerial authority oriented toward a benign social order. Not only have steps been taken to develop a set of rights for prisoners, but also components of due process were strengthened and their durability greatly increased in contrast to the previous unstable reform movements.

Prisons and correctional institutions have since the 1960s become more accessible to external religious, education, welfare, and community groups. The new legal procedures and codes also legitimize this public presence and put the formal and informal structure of the prison under stronger external scrutiny. The first steps have been taken to build institutions that will assist inmates in their transition to the community to which they return. Other "human services" institutions, such as the mental hospital, have undergone analogous changes, but the degree varies depending on the type of client and the scope of judicial review, for judicial review has become crucial in institutionalizing the movement toward manipulative authority.[90] In mental hospitals, the widespread use of drugs obscures the consequences of these organizational changes.

If one returns to the concept of hierarchical bureaucracy as the prototype, or rather the embodiment, of the institutional arrangements of

90. Alfred H. Stanton and Morris S. Schwartz, *The Mental Hospital: A Study of Institutional Participation in Psychiatric Illness and Treatment* (New York: Basic Books, 1954); M. Greenblatt, R. H. York, and E. Brown, *From Custodial to Therapeutic Patient Care in Mental Hospitals: Explorations in Social Treatment* (New York: Russell Sage Foundation, 1955); Clagett G. Smith and James A. King, *Mental Hospitals: A Study in Organizational Effectiveness* (Lexington, Mass.: Lexington Books, 1975).

an advanced industrial society, all institutional sectors of society have moved away from authority based on domination. The rate is varying, and often unexpected. As a result, the efforts to accommodate to the new format and to create new and relatively durable structures emerge as the underlying subject of the analysis of social control.

In the "human services" institutions, the new forms of managerial authority contribute to, or are at least compatible with, more humane practices and with a more benign milieu, even if there is little evidence of increased rehabilitation. Thus, in a real sense, the consequences are a moral contribution to the search for social control. In contrast, the implications of the new forms of authority in the industrial and related institutional sectors involved the basic articulation of the social structure.

It is premature to assess the consequences of the underlying trends in industrial and nonindustrial organization until there has been greater explication of the consequences of the separation of work and household community and an examination of the structure of community organization—both formal and informal. However, the development of a bureaucratic system of industrial relations in the United States which emphasizes short-term issues and which conforms to a mold of adversary relations has not been accompanied by an effective set of norms and institution arrangements on which to base social control of the "ordered segments" of an advanced industrial society. This is especially the case for dealing with economic conflicts in the context of stagflation. Because of the centrality of the separation of work and residence, an effective system of social control could not be generated within the confines of the industrial sector. This is the assumption of the social-control perspective. The formal and informal trends in community institutions, as set forth in the next chapter, highlight additional sources of disarticulation in the social organization of an advanced industrial society which must be dealt with in the search for more effective social control.

Eight

Residential Community: The Geographical Dimension

The Basis of Community

The hierarchical structure of bureaucratic organizations is paralleled by a geographical dimension based on the territorial distribution of human settlements.[1] If the social organization resulting from the division of labor cannot be reduced to a simplified stratigraphic image, neither can the residential patterns of the social bloc, the neighborhood, and the local community—the constituent elements of the metropolis—be summarized by a neat and simplified cartographic map with easily discernible, precise, and comprehensive boundaries. Industrial society, as has been stressed, separates work and residence; advanced industrial society increases this separation.

The separation of work and residence, in effect, creates residential communities which vary in their stability, diffuseness of boundaries, and internal cohesion. Likewise, in any residential settlement the members' involvement and sense of attachment vary greatly. But in terms of the social-control perspective, the moral order of a society, with its defects, strain, and difficulties, cannot be reduced to the consequences of its division of labor. The content and effectiveness of its moral values are crucially conditioned by the social organization of its familial-residential communities. In a parliamentary system which does not rely on a single mass political party, under advanced industrialism the importance of family-residential communities as one basis of political participation is even selectively intensified.

1. Kingsley Davis, "The Origins and Growth of Urbanization in the World," *American Journal of Sociology* 60 (March 1955): 429–37. For the United States see Brian J. L. Berry, *Growth Centers in the American Urban System*. Vol. 1: *Community Development and Regional Growth in the Sixties and Seventies*. Vol. 2: *Working Materials on the U.S. Urban Hierarchy Organized by Economic Regions* (Cambridge, Mass.: Ballinger, 1973).

Residential Community

In one form or another, various sociologists have repeatedly described the societal trend as essentially that of increasing atomization of interpersonal relations. Their anticipated result was that the durable units with effective solidarity would be those linked to occupation and the attendant social classes. The persistently forecasted "disappearance" of the local community with the development of advanced industrialism in Western Europe and the United States has not come into being.

Human settlement under advanced industrialism responds to technology and economic trends—to population growth, deconcentration of population density, enlarged economic interdependence, increased magnitude of organization, and the emergence of powerful and more flexible modes of transportation—although each of these trends of course has its limitations.[2] As in the case of the transformation of bureaucratic structures in the industrial sector, the processes of societal change are not adequately described by a linear model from Gemeinschaft to Gesellschaft. From the beginnings of sociology as an academic discipline, there has been a stream of sociologists who asserted that the spatial organization of household-residence was not a residue or an artifact of "earlier" societies. To the contrary, the residential community in the urban metropolis has been described as an adaption to social change; it is a social construction and a political one as well.[3] None of these sociologists implied that the local community structures were strong, viable, and effectively articulated into the larger society. Rather, the tradition of community research simultaneously emphasized both the strong solidarities that could develop in communal

2. Amos Hawley, *Urban Society: An Ecological Approach* (New York: Ronald Press, 1971); D. W. G. Timms, *The Urban Mosaic: Towards a Theory of Residential Differentiation* (Cambridge: Cambridge University Press, 1971); for an extensive bibliographic overview of relevant statistical research, see Jack P. Gibbs and Kingsley Davis, "Conventional Versus Metropolitan Data in the International Study of Urbanization," in *Urban Research Methods*, ed. Jack P. Gibbs (Princeton: Van Nostrand, 1961), pp. 419–35.

3. Robert E. Park and Ernest W. Burgess, *Introduction to the Science of Sociology* (Chicago: University of Chicago Press, 1921), p. 163; Robert E. Park, "The City: Suggestions for the Investigation of Human Behavior in the Urban Environment," in *The City*, ed. Robert E. Park, Ernest W. Burgess, and Roderick D. Mc Kenzie (Chicago: University of Chicago Press, 1925), pp. 1–46. George Hillery, Jr., *Communal Organizations: A Study of Local Societies* (Chicago: University of Chicago, 1968), p. 65; Suzanne Keller, *The Urban Neighborhood: A Sociological Perspective* (New York: Random House, 1968); Rene König, *The Community* (New York: Schocken, 1968); Roland L. Warren, *The Community in America*, 2d ed. (Chicago: Rand McNally, 1972). See also Anselm Strauss, *Images of the American City* (Glencoe, Ill.: Free Press, 1961), for an analysis based on literary and humanistic sources.

settlements and their institutional weaknesses, especially in their connections with the larger society. These sociologists were sensitive to the vulnerabilities of communal institutions to external sources of social change and their limitations as bridging mechanisms to the political process. They recognized that localistic sentiments could be barriers to participation in the large metropolis.

"Community" is not to be thought of as the convergence or likeness of social interests and moral values. This is the usage emphasized by Robert MacIver and his disciples, a usage which has some validity but obscures the systemic analysis of the separation of work and residence.[4] As a point of departure, community can be conceived as a geographically based form of social organization which directly supplies its members with the major portion of their sustenance needs. The daily transactions of goods and services offers a basis for delimiting boundaries and identifying the structure of the community. Of course, sustenance is broadly defined, and in fact has its full meaning when associated with socialization and transition through the stages of the life cycle. A person's sustenance needs are met by institutions which diffuse throughout the nation-state and involve the world economy, to the extent that such an economic system exists. But the household-residential community operationally is delimited by the scope of daily transactions. In the metropolis, local territorially based social systems emerge out of these transactions, and these patterns are what is meant by the local urban community. (The neighborhood is often used as an equivalent term to local urban community, but it more often refers to smaller social blocs which reflect local social solidarities and patterns of self-help.) The social reality of the residential community is a reflection of a series of service and socialization institutions and the symbolic definition imposed on the locality in order to create a social order in which households seek to survive. The local urban community is represented by a set of symbols which in varying degrees are internalized by the residents, for without symbolic identifications there is no local community. However, sociologists also stress the "institution building"

4. Robert MacIver, *Community: A Sociological Study*, 3d ed. (London: Macmillan, 1936); see also William J. Goode, "Community Within a Community: The Professions," *American Sociological Review* 22 (February 1957): 194–204. For an intellectual and literary overview of the use of the term "community," see Wilson Carey McWilliams, *The Idea of Fraternity in America* (Berkeley: University of California Press, 1973).

by governmental agencies, political groups, and voluntary association which are required if a local urban community is to exist and survive.[5]

Obviously a local urban community in an advanced industrial society is not the same as the local communities associated with peasant, feudal, or even rural society.[6] We are not dealing with those social conditions under which a person and his household find themselves submerged in a local social entity in which there is little opportunity for individuation or for partial or total withdrawal. Community in the metropolitan setting is not the coercive format of the "ideal type" of small town as portrayed by the novelists of the 1920s such as Sherwood Anderson. Nor does the notion of community refer to some futuristic form in which local relations are completely bureaucratized and depersonalized. Residential community in the social structure of Western Europe and the United States in the latter half of the twentieth century involves important components of voluntarism, self-interest, and contractual relations designed to benefit the well-being of the person and his household.

Many different formulations have been utilized to highlight the realities of a residential community in a society with an industrial order based on rational considerations of self-interest, for example, the notion of a community of "limited liability."[7] A person's relation to his community—his social investment in his community is such that, when the community fails to serve his needs, he will withdraw. Withdrawal implies either actual departure from the local community or merely a decline or lack of involvement. Some degree of withdrawal is inherent in social change. Withdrawal takes place with aging of the householders. We are dealing both with the life cycle of the person and the cycle of the community; but older communities can renew their population and their institutional networks.

Withdrawal accompanies changes in the ethnic, racial, and occupational composition of a community. Numerous persons develop a "psychic" commitment to an area which persists after the community

5. Gerald D. Suttles, *The Social Construction of Communities* (Chicago, University of Chicago Press, 1972), passim.

6. Edward Shils, "Primordial, Personal, Sacred and Civil Ties," *British Journal of Sociology* 8 (June 1957): 130–45.

7. Morris Janowitz, *The Community Press in Urban Setting*, 2d ed. (Chicago: University of Chicago Press, 1967).

fails to serve their needs; and the extent of withdrawal varies from community to community, from group to group. But for most persons there is a point at which he cuts his losses, and therefore the term community of "limited liability."

The service functions—shopping, banking, health, and leisure—which take place in the local community have undergone drastic change since the end of World War I. The reliance on locally based service institutions has sharply declined. But the local community has specific functions which are not easily or in actuality transferred to other groups. The residential social organization is the locus within which the life cycle is given its moral and symbolic meaning to the extent that such meanings develop. Each generation seeks—although it does not necessarily succeed—to invest in the next generation, with the result that school and the related agencies of socialization persist as central institutions of the locality. Even the consumption-oriented locality with few children—the area of single people and older couples without children, adjoining the central business district—is replete with a variety of "schools," formal and informal, to indoctrinate each new generation of adult newcomers in the values and practices of the locality. These community "schools" teach the new consumer skills such as baking natural bread, basket weaving, karate, muscle control, and transcendental meditation.

But the socialization process is not merely the outcome of nurturing and sustaining of each person through his life cycle. The local residential organization is the social area for developing links to political institutions, especially in a society in which political responsibility is widely diffused and readily avoided. Within the social space of family residence, persons have the opportunity, and in varying degrees the necessity, of aggregating or balancing the competing self-interests which they pursue.

The systemic analysis of community therefore rests on the assertion that the emergence of more complex and more differentiated institutions does not mean the essential elimination of older arrangements, although it does imply their adaptation and their specialization. In particular, the growth in size, scale of organization, and complexity of human settlement does not mean that personalized relations are being replaced by impersonalized ones. On the contrary, our underlying assumption is that the separation of work and residence multiplies the number. range, and content of personal attachments. These attachments contribute to the culture of the metropolis.[8] The emergent patterns of interaction can be pervasive and powerful for the individual who is a member of a "literary set," a religious cult, a political sect, or the like. No one has argued and demonstrated this assertion as effectively as Herman Schmalenbach in his analysis of modern youth movements and his concern with "communion."[9]

On the other hand, ordered segmentation can lead to a paucity of interpersonal interaction and support which fails to serve the psychic economy of the person. The rooming house stands as the symbol of the threshold of social isolation and sheer loneliness which urban society is capable of engendering. An extraordinary range of interaction and attachments emerge within a given metropolis. From the point of view of the analysis of social control, we are concerned to underline that the increased range of informal and organized contacts can contribute to a measure of autonomy, personal freedom, and creativity required for the community of "limited liability."

During the half-century since the end of World War I, local communities in the United States have been the locus of intense group conflict along communal dimensions as well as along racial and ethnic lines. The accumulated research on the metropolis underlines the continuing sequence of competition, conflict, and partial accommodation. Despite the predictions of large-scale organized armed conflict, during this half-century the residential community has not been the locus of "revolutionary" confrontation. Community tensions and conflicts exist and they reflect socioeconomic position. In fact, as there has been a long-term decline of purposive violence in the industrial sector, the observation can also be offered that from 1920 to 1976, there has been a parallel transformation of community-based and communally organized violence. The racial riots of the 1960s constituted a short-term deviation in this long-term trend. (The historical transformation of urban riots is explored in chapter 10.) This observation hardly denies that the intensity, persistence, and scope of diffuse violence and criminality in the inner city have seriously weakened and distorted local political institutions. Nevertheless it is basic to our orientation that

8. Georg Simmel, "Die Grossstadt und das Geistesleben," in *Die Grossstadt: Jahrbuch der Gehe-Stiftung*, vol. 9 (1903).

9. Herman Schmalenbach, "Die soziologische Kategorie des Bundes," *Die Dioskuren: Jahrbuch für Geisteswissenschaften* 1 (1922): 35–105.

residential areas throughout metropolitan centers, regardless of their socioeconomic status, have become more important as loci for political decisions and political participation.

The bulk of the expenditures of the welfare state are occupation-based and work-related; for example, social security, unemployment compensation, and some aspects of health insurance. However, there is an increasingly important welfare expenditure associated with the broadened definition of citizenship which funnels through community-based institutions.[10] This has particularly been the case for public education, housing, and community development. But struggles over allocations, especially those for public education, have become more and more intensified as community conflicts. Innovative programs such as WIN (Work Incentive Now) and CETA (Comprehensive Employment and Training Act) designed to reform welfare payments are typically community-based; important health services are more and more explicitly related to community organization.

We are dealing with the citizenry's awareness of the increased relevance of the local community as a source of chances. Demands for local control or participation reflect the desire for a larger share of public expenditures; but they also reflect the increased pressure to ensure some supervision over and accountability in the performance of the agencies of the welfare state, particularly those which penetrate the residential community.[11]

Previously we have argued that appeals in the name of "social class" have been the vehicle for the extension of political participation during the emergence of industrialism in Western Europe and the United States. With the advent of the welfare state, the dimension of territoriality—the residential community—moves into the forefront of political rhetoric and conflict. In other words, under advanced industrialism, political leaders find it necessary to augment the appeals of social class with those advocating community participation and community "equity." Our underlying assumption is that since 1920 the importance of local family-residential social organization has been maintained and

10. T. H. Marshall, *Citizenship and Social Class* (Cambridge: University of Cambridge Press, 1950); Harold Wilensky, *The Welfare State and Equality: Structural and Ideological Roots of Public Expenditures* (Berkeley: University of California Press, 1975); Morris Janowitz, *Social Control of the Welfare State* (New York: Elsevier, 1976).

11. Gerald D. Suttles, "Community Design: The Search for Participation in a Metropolitan Society," in *Metropolitan America in Contemporary Perspective*, ed. Amos H. Hawley and Vincent R. Rock (New York: Wiley, 1975), pp. 235–98.

even selectively increased as a basis for integrating the person and his household into the political process and for balancing self-interest with larger societal responsibilities. The services performed by the welfare state dictate these sociopolitical trends, but we cast the problem as well in terms of the consequences of the increased separation of work and residence. Two hypotheses can guide systemic analysis of the residential community in the metropolitan setting.

First, although increased separation of work and residence has been accompanied by a declining use of local facilities, the strength of community networks and sentiments continues to derive from the specialized household relations and the processes of socialization which remain in the residential locality. (Because of the disruptive factors which impinge on the residential locality, Gerald Suttles's term "the defended community" is a very appropriate one.)[12]

Second, because the political system emphasizes territorial representation and because of the expansion of governmental functions, including those of the welfare state, local voluntary associations become more important as mechanisms for articulating and linking the citizenry to the larger political process. However, these patterns of civic and political participation have been fragmented and are very partially connected to the larger metropolitan structures. Therefore they have made only limited contributions to social control. In fact, a great deal of local voluntary association participation serves only to intensify pressure group representation and enlarge sociopolitical conflict, and thereby complicate the tasks of the local, state, and national legislative bodies.

These trends must be seen in the context of the historical changes in urban settlement, local and metropolitan, in the United States since the end of the Civil War. The emergence of a national industrial system and the associated financial and service enterprises has been accompanied by a decline in the ability of the business elites to directly dominate local politics and local political decision making. In chapter 13, the resulting growth of a loosely differentiated political elite, without the benefit of strong party organization, will be examined. The ability of the trade unions directly to influence local politics and to use local political institutions as a basis for national political goals has grown correspondingly. But the effectiveness of "organized labor" is greatly limited because only a fraction of the wage earners are in

12. Gerald D. Suttles, *The Social Construction of Communities* (Chicago: University of Chicago Press, 1972), pp. 21–44.

trade unions. Thus the residential community has become the locus of a network of competing and cooperating voluntary associations which link the local residents to the fragmented, decentralized political parties. The explorations of the social organization of the residential community and these networks of association start with an examination of the trends in metropolitan growth and residential settlement.

Residential Settlement and Resource Distribution

The dynamics of metropolitan growth in the United States since the turn of the century reveals a continuous suburbanization of human settlement and an unanticipated rapid growth of population after World War II. However, the structure of U.S. urban centers is based on the aftermath of long conflicts in Western Europe between the cities and the hinterland. In Western Europe for over a millennium, urban centers had to struggle fiercely for economic, cultural, and political "freedom," and for a relative autonomy from the feudal agricultural hinterland. Massive scholarship, including the writings of Max Weber, identifies the conditions which made possible the emergence of strong and relatively independent cities.[13] The development of these cities were the precondition for the "modernity" of the nation-state. The cities which emerged early in Western Europe have been linked to the emergence of parliamentary systems.

The U.S. colonies were a fragment of Western Europe; and the American cities developed from this Western European historical threshold. The capacity of these urban centers from their very beginnings to enhance their population, economic, technological, and cultural resources has been truly extensive, even in the South, where a strong plantation system took hold.[14] The urban centers have been dominant despite the system of geographic representation which gave

13. Max Weber, "The City (Non-Legitimate Domination)," in *Economy and Society: An Outline of Interpretive Sociology*, ed. Guenther Roth and Claus W. Wittick (New York: Bedminster, 1968), pp. 1212–1372. Henri Pirenne, *Les villes du moyen âge: Essai d'histoire économique and sociale* (Brussels: M. Lamertin, 1927); N. S. B. Gras, *An Introduction to Economic History* (New York: Harper and Row, 1922); Adna F. Weber, *The Growth of Cities in the Nineteenth Century* (New York: Macmillan, 1899); Lewis Mumford, *The Culture of Cities* (New York: Harcourt, Brace, 1938).

14. Carl Bridenbaugh, *Cities in the Wilderness: The First Century of Urban Life in America, 1625–1792* (New York: Ronald, 1938); Charles N. Glaab and A. Theodore Brown, *A History of Urban America* (New York: Macmillan, 1967); Sigmund Diamond, "From Organization to Society: Virginia in the Seventeenth Century," *American Journal of Sociology* 63 (March 1958): 457–75.

strong political advantages to the hinterland, advantages which have persisted through advanced industrialization.

However, the high degree of structural differentiation from the hinterland and the relative institutional autonomy of U.S. cities contributed to the outward spread and deconcentration of population. The history of urbanization in the United States has been that of a system of self-propelling urban centers without noteworthy intervention by the central government until after World War II. In the absence of a grand design, these population centers have had boundaries which have been particularly subject to great urban sprawl. The resulting decay of the central city became politically visible in the 1960s, although ecologists have plotted the pattern of deconcentration of population extending back before 1900.

The long-term trend in human settlement in the United States as a whole has been threefold; growth in population, the increased concentration of the population in metropolitan centers, and the suburbanization of the population resident within the metropolitan centers.[15] Since the end of the nineteenth century, the percentage of the nation's population living within the metropolitan area has shifted from 31.7% to 68.7% as of 1970, while the proportion residing in the suburban ring during this period has grown from 30.3% to 54.0%.[16] In fact, faster rates of growth in the suburban ring have occurred in every decade since 1900 for every region in the nation. After 1930, the process of deconcentration became intensified when the absolute population growth in the suburbs exceeded that in the central cities. By 1950, the process of deconcentration had reached the point where, in the central cities of the Northeast and North Central region, the population had started to decline.

Population density per square mile provides a revealing indicator of long-term deconcentration. However, this density is influenced by the extensive territorial annexations which have changed the political boundaries of the central city and the suburbs. The long-term trend underlines "gross" decline in density; but refined analysis which takes into account those boundary changes resulting from annexation complicates

15. Brian J. L. Berry, *Metropolitan Area Definition: A Re-Evaluation of Concept and Statistical Practice*, working paper no. 28 (Washington: Bureau of the Census, Department of Commerce, 1968).

16. John D. Kasarda and George V. Redfearn, "Differential Patterns of Urban and Suburban Growth in the United States," *Journal of Urban History* 2 (November 1975): 43–66.

the configuration. For the purposes at hand, the results calculated by John Kasarda and George Redfearn on the trend in the population density per square mile of U.S. central cities and suburban rings for 1900–1970 are relevant. They analyze the data in terms of the date when each city attained metropolitan status, adjusting for annexation. Despite continuous population growth in the United States and especially the rapid post–World War II population increase, the density of human settlement declined in the central cities. Moreover, the later the area attained metropolitan status the lower the population density of both its central cities and suburban rings. However, Kasarda offers a more refined analysis based on decade by decade changes while more stringently holding constant the changes in boundaries. These results show that the decline in concentration is more extensive in the older cities—those in the Northeast and the North Central area—and deconcentration did not have its full effect until after 1950. In fact, newer cities in the West, where population grew after extensive annexation, have experienced some increase in density in terms of constant area. After 1970, this process of deconcentration of residential settlement and of population redistribution continued and even accelerated. According to urban demographers, since 1970 the metropolitan areas of the United States have grown more slowly than the nation as a whole and much less rapidly than nonmetropolitan United States.[17] This development contrasts with preceding decades as far back as the early nineteenth century and represents an intensification of population dispersion.

Population deconcentration and reduced density illustrate the consequences of modern transportation. Cities which grew before 1880 were organized without effective mechanical transportation and thus were dense. By 1890 electric mass-transit systems increased the separation of work and residence; and after 1920 the automobile had the same effect.[18] The streetcar, the electric train, and the automobile each contributed to the "lower initial density levels in cities which developed during their technological eras."[19]

17. Brian J. L. Berry and Donald C. Dahmann, *Population Redistribution in the United States in the 1970s* (Washington: National Academy of Sciences, 1977), p. 36.

18. Sam Bass Warner, Jr., *Streetcar Suburbs* (Cambridge: Harvard University Press, 1962); Joel A. Tarr, *Transportation Innovation and Changing Spatial Patterns: Pittsburgh, 1850–1910* (Pittsburgh: University of Pittsburgh Press, 1972); Kenneth T. Jackson, "Urban Deconcentration in the Nineteenth Century: A Statistical Inquiry," in *The New Urban History: Quantitative Explorations of American Historians*, ed. Leo F. Schnore (Princeton: Princeton University Press, 1975).

19. Kasarda and Redfearn, "Differential Patterns," p. 61.

It is appropriate to inquire whether classical theories of population growth have contributed to the systemic analysis of community and metropolitan organization. The classical theories of population transition linked to industrialism and urbanism explain effectively the growth of population in the nineteenth century mainly as being a result of the spread of public health measures.[20] The subsequent lower birthrates fit into theories of population which involve the continued development of public health measures, namely, the spread of contraceptive devices and the changing norms of an industrialized society in which the economic value of children declines.[21] However, theories of population designed to explain the rising birthrates for the period after World War II are less satisfactory.[22] They tend to involve ad hoc "psychological factors" and seek to account for variations in birthrates among stratigraphically defined social groupings. The results, however, do indicate that voluntaristic elements have come to account for population dynamics more than before 1945.

Nevertheless, the details of population trends since 1920 contribute to an understanding of the increased disarticulation between the locus of occupation and residential community, especially if one compares the pattern of population growth during 1920 to 1945 with that between 1945 and 1976, since for the second period the population dynamics tended to strain local and metropolitan social organization to a much greater extent.

Three observations are in order. First, the birthrate and total population growth during 1920–1940 was low to medium and relatively constant compared with the period after 1940, when it was high and variable. (Table 8.1). Second, the pattern of population growth in the

20. Philip M. Hauser and Otis D. Duncan, eds., *The Study of Population* (Chicago: University of Chicago Press, 1959).

21. In the 1950s various social scientists including David Riesman, asserted that the United States had in effect entered a post-Malthusian period; there was no problem of the ratio of population to resources; the institutional problem was to cultivate the ability of the population to consume. Two decades later, with remarkable candor and intellectual honesty, Riesman modified this thesis as presented in his *The Lonely Crowd*; see David Riesman, "The Lonely Crowd: Twenty Years After," *Encounter* 33 (October 1969); 36–41. For our purposes there is no need to substitute optimistic assessment for equally pessimistic ones, but rather to recognize the continuing fluctuating influence of resource limitations on population and metropolitan growth.

22. Charles F. Westoff, Robert G. Potter, Jr., Philip C. Sagi, and Elliot G. Mishler, *Family Growth in Metropolitan America* (Princeton: Princeton University Press, 1961); Charles F. Westoff, Robert G. Potter, Jr., and Philip C. Sagi, *The Third Child: A Study in the Prediction of Fertility* (Princeton: Princeton University Press, 1963).

second period changed or "distorted" the structure of the population pyramid to a much greater extent. In particular, the ratio of young and old persons to the middle group increased. In other words, the ratio of dependent persons to active wage earners grew. Both these trends strained communal institutions, especially those of education and welfare, which had to adapt to a rapidly increased population—particularly

TABLE 8.1 Components of Population Growth, 1930–1974

	Total					Population Increase Ratio:
		Net Increase		Net Civilian	Net Civilian	Immigration
Year	Population (1,000)*	Total (1,000)	Percent	Immigration (1,000)	Immigration Rate†	to Natural Increase
1930	122,487	1,128	0.9	113	0.9	10.0
1935	126,874	853	0.7	—2	—	—0.2
1940	132,054	1,221	0.9	77	0.6	6.3
1945	139,767	1,462	1.1	162	1.2	11.1
1950	151,135	2,486	1.7	299	2.0	12.0
1955	164,588	2,925	1.8	337	2.0	11.5
1960	179,386	2,901	1.6	327	1.8	11.3
1965	193,223	2,315	1.2	373	1.9	16.1
1970	203,849	2,227	1.1	438	2.1	19.7
1974	211,205	1,591	0.8	360	1.7	22.6

SOURCE: Adapted from U.S. Bureau of the Census, *Current Population Reports*, series P-25, no. 545.
* x Population as of Jan. 1,
† y Rate per 1,000 of the mid-year population

the mass educational system, which by 1970 was facing further disruption because of drastic reduction in the size of the entering age cohorts. Finally, the social composition of the population increase was also very different during these two periods. In the first, the contribution to population growth by foreign-born persons was low and relatively stable; in the second, the ratio of new foreign born immigrants to native births was much higher. To speak of the social demography of the United States as an advanced industrial society is to make special references to the high inflow of permanent foreign immigrants (Table 8.1). This trend is similar to the period immediately before World War I in that immigration also strained the community institutions of socialization and welfare. After 1945 a proportion of the immigrants were trained professionals who integrated rapidly, but most were unskilled. There is, of course, no reason to assume that all of these trends will continue; in fact, the birthrate had begun to decline by 1958.

The metropolitan pattern of residential settlement which results from population growth and deconcentration reflects the location of economic enterprise and of employment opportunities. Basically, underlying resource distribution has produced greater overall socioeconomic differentiation and resulting disarticulation between central city and suburban ring. In the centrifugal direction, the long-term trend has been a loss of blue-collar jobs in the central city. Between 1947 and 1967, the central cities of the 23 largest and oldest Standard Metropolitan Statistical Areas (SMSA's) lost annually on an average nearly 85,000 positions.[23] For 1960 to 1970, John Kasarda found for 101 comparable SMSA's that there were a loss of 828,257 blue-collar jobs. (This loss was most heavily concentrated in the older cities of the Northeast and the North Central region.) On the other hand, during the same period there has been an increase of 1,119,134 blue-collar jobs in the suburban ring. In the centripetal direction, white-collar employment has increased in the central cities, although the increase has been greater in the suburban ring. In other words, the growth of white-collar jobs has prevented greater decline of employment in the central city. To a considerable degree this is the result of the concentration of particular professional, financial, and governmental services in the core of the metropolis.

As a result, the profiles of occupations of the labor force, by place of work, in 101 SMSA's during 1960 to 1970 central city and suburban ring presented in Table 8.2, appear to have converged. However, in fact, the social organization of the central city and the suburban ring, in terms of human settlement—that is, the residential location of different occupational groups and the distribution of household resources—has increased in divergence and contributed to increased disarticulation.

The apparent convergence of occupational profile classified by place of work is the result of increased frequency and extended length of the journey to work.[24] What is crucial, as has been repeatedly and

23. John D. Kasarda, "The Changing Occupational Structure of Metropolitan America: Apropos to the Urban Problem," in *The Changing Face of the Suburbs*, ed. Barry Schwartz (Chicago: University of Chicago Press, 1976), pp. 113–35.

24. James N. Morgan, "A Note on the Time Spent on the Journey to Work," *Demography* 4 (1967): 360–62; John Kain, "Post War Metropolitan Development: Housing Preferences and Auto Ownership," *American Economic Association Papers and Proceedings* 57 (May 1967): 223–34; Amos Hawley, *Urban Society: An Ecological Approach* (New York: Ronald Press, 1971), p. 191; John Kain, "The Distribution and Movement of Jobs and Industry," in *The Metropolitan Enigma*,

TABLE 8.2 Changes in Occupational Structure, Central City and Suburban Ring, 1960–1970

(Mean Number of Employees by Occupation in 101 Longitudinally Comparable SMSA Central Cities and Suburban Rings, 1960–1970.).

	Mean Number of Central City Employees		
Occupational Category	1960	1970*	Change 1960–70
Professional and Technical	16,015	20,138	4,123
Managers and Proprietors	12,458	11,354	–1,104
Clerical Workers	26,915	30,002	3,087
Sales Workers	11,113	9,813	–1,300
Craftsmen	18,041	16,043	–1,998
Operatives	25,078	19,838	–5,240
Laborers	5,676	4,668	–1,010
Service Workers	15,669	15,713	44
Farm Workers	232	203	–29
	Mean Number of Suburban Ring Employees		
Occupational Category	1960	1970*	Change 1960–70
Professional and Technical	9,392	16,203	6,811
Managers and Proprietors	5,787	8,288	2,501
Clerical Workers	10,066	18,411	8,345
Sales Workers	5,209	7,921	2,712
Craftsmen	11,684	14,575	2,891
Operatives	14,263	17,501	3,238
Laborers	3,649	4,363	714
Service Workers	8,393	12,630	4,237
Farm Workers	2,691	1,506	–1,185

*Central city and suburban employment figures adjusted for annexation between 1960 and 1970.

SOURCE: John D. Kasarda, "The Changing Occupational Structure of Metropolitan America: Apropos to the Urban Problem," in Schwartz, *The Changing Face of the Suburbs.*

extensively documented, is that the socioeconomic gap in the residential population of the central city and the suburban ring has increased for the second period of our analysis. By the second decade of this century the average distance from home to work was 1.5 miles, on the basis of data from the Chicago area, which in this regard does not appear atypical.[25] By 1960 the trip averaged 4.7 miles. On the basis of

ed. James Q. Wilson (Cambridge: Harvard University Press, 1970), p. 1–40. For a general analysis, see Kate K. Leipman, *The Journey to Work* (New York: Oxford University Press, 1944); the burden for women is discussed in Julia A. Ericksen, "An Analysis of the Journey to Work for Women," *Social Problems* 24 (April 1977): 428–35.

25. Beverly Duncan, "Factors in Work-Residence Separation: Wage and Salary Workers, Chicago 1951," *American Sociological Review* 21 (February 1956): 48–56.

the sample of 101 SMSA's adjusted for annexation, the increase in the journey to work across the boundaries of the central city has been documented for 1960 to 1970, for both blue-collar and white-collar workers.[26] This is augmented by the increase in the number of metropolitan residents who travel beyond suburban ring boundaries to work outside of the SMSA.

These data hardly reflect the full scope of the long-term process of deconcentration of employment locations; we are dealing not only with the increased length of time in the journey to work but also with an enlargement in the diversity of direction. The centrifugal and centripetal flows result in an increased diversity in the direction of the flow of traffic to work. This is accompanied by a similar diverse pattern of traffic flow in the utilization of urban services and leisure activities, basically reflecting the decline in dominance of the central business district and the rise of service centers throughout the metropolitan area.

Beneath the web of daily transportation, the distribution of the population reveals a continued increase in the difference in the social composition between the central city and the suburban, with the concentration in the core of the metropolis of the low-income, minority-group persons and households with limited educational backgrounds. This population includes the highest incidence of social disabilities—poverty-stricken pensioners, broken and incomplete families, and ill and handicapped persons. Within the central city there is an important but very small number of high-income households who reside in the high-rise apartment houses constructed since 1960 to hold and attract persons seeking the life-style of the central city. However, from an overall point of view, while the idea of a middle majority has relevance for the suburban ring, the central city has become more and more the locus of the socially deprived.

The economic consequences of human settlement, employment location and family resources have been to exacerbate the economic strain confronting the welfare state. As examined previously, the United States as an advanced industrial society has had to face a chronic public deficit in the economic resources available for welfare.[27] The management of this deficit is complicated by the unequal distribution of house-

26. Kasarda, "Changing Structure."

27. Morris Janowitz, *Social Control of the Welfare State* (New York: Elsevier, 1976), passim.

hold incomes between the suburb rings and the central city and the requirements for social welfare expenditures.

The existing mechanisms of taxation and revenue allocation are persistent barriers to the creation of metropolitan-wide fiscal systems. But the pattern of disarticulation also involves the services and burdens the central city maintains for the suburbs, without adequate economic support by the suburbs. The suburbs have been able to resist undesirable land usage and the incorporation of low-income social groups. One of the most dramatic examples is the enforced territorial segregation of commercialized vice into the central city for the benefits of suburban clients. The irony of the ecology of prostitution is that, while the deconcentration of population was in process, particular declining neighborhoods near the central business district serve as the centers of vice without high public visibility. However, the efforts to preserve and renew selected local communities in the central city bring the local residents into direct confrontation with organized vice seeking to use these neighborhoods for its purposes.

The rapid emergence of a municipal fiscal crisis after 1970, especially in New York City, has served to manifest dramatically the consequences of the economic differentiation of the suburbs from the central city.[28] As a result, the ecology of employment opportunities and the distribution of economic resources in each metropolitan center establish the social segregation of the population which takes place in each local urban community and/or neighborhood. The pattern of population distribution is more than the result of economic competition and available income per se. Three basic variables are operative: income, family status, and ethnic and/or racial composition for 1920 to 1970.[29] There is good reason to believe that they have been operative over a longer period of time, but data for small areas have been collected by the U.S. census only since 1920. Economic status since 1930 remains the dominant factor by which persons locate themselves, the significance of family status has declined. On the other hand, the importance of ethnic-racial status has increased.

28. Congressional Budget Office, *New York City's Fiscal Problem*, background paper no. 1 (Washington, D. C.: Government Printing Office, 1975).

29. For an overview of this research literature and an analysis of the census data for the city of Chicago see Albert Hunter, *Symbolic Communities: The Persistence and Change of Chicago's Local Communities* (Chicago: University of Chicago Press, 1974).

Residential Community

What overall patterns emerge from these data on the population composition of the local community areas? No single set of categories will suffice, but in varying degrees, the idea of zones, sectors, and multinucleation are applicable. In fact, it is striking that the classic pattern of Burgess's zones linked to distance from the center of the metropolis with increasing income and "familialism" persists to a considerable degree.[30] One line of modification is that some zones have been altered into elongated and enlarged sectors, as conceptualized by Homer Hoyt.[31] This shift is the result of the corridors of transportation that have been created, which have attenuated and elongated the concentric character of urban growth. In addition, there has been a trend toward multinucleation reflecting the rise of service centers outside the downtown central business district.[32]

In addition to population trends the influence of the residential community on social control is complicated and weakened because, since 1920, metropolitan deconcentration and increased flexibility of transportation have caused a decline in the use of local service facilities.[33] At the macrolevel this decline can be measured by the increase in centralized shopping centers and complexes for rendering professional service. From 1954 to 1974, over 14,000 shopping centers have been constructed, most of which serve suburban populations. The increases in selected service functions in the central business district also served to contribute to this centralization. At the microlevel, we have available Albert Hunter's restudy of a local urban community in Rochester, which in 1940 had 13,030 residents and which had declined to 11,890 by 1970.[34] From 1949 to 1974, the percent who made use of local facilities—as measured by five blocks from home, declined for grocery shopping, small purchases, church, movies, and doctor visits, and only bank-

30. Hunter, *Symbolic Communities*, pp. 19–66; Avery M. Guest, "Retesting 'The Burgess Zonal Hypothesis': The Location of White Collar Workers," *American Journal of Sociology* 76 (May 1971): 1094–1108; Lee J. Haggerty, "Another Look at the Burgess Hypothesis: Time as an Important Variable," *American Journal of Sociology* 76 (May 1971): 1084–93.

31. Homer Hoyt, *The Structure and Growth of Residential Neighborhoods in American Cities* (Washington: Federal Housing Administration, 1939).

32. Chauncy D. Harris and Edward L. Ullman, "The Nature of Cities," *Annals* 242 (November 1945): 7–11.

33. Stuart Chapin, *Human Activity Patterns in the City: Things People Do in Time and in Space* (New York: Wiley, 1974).

34. Albert Hunter, "Loss of Community: An Empirical Test Through Replication," *American Sociological Review* 40 (October 1975): 537–53.

ing—increased. (See Table 8.3.) In general the decline in the use of local facilities was faster and was most extensive among higher groups than among lower groups, but the trend penetrates deeply into all the ordered segments of the metropolis. The decline was present in the suburban developments more than in the central city. And it is also to be found among the black and Spanish-speaking enclaves.

TABLE 8.3 Trends in Neighborhood Behavior and Attitudes, 1949 and 1974 (Local Area in Rochester)

Informal Neighboring Percent saying "often" or "sometimes" versus "rarely" or "never" . . .	Foley – 1949 N = (446)	Hunter – 1974 N = (154)
chat with neighbors	73.9%	79.7% n.s.
exchange favors	58.5	56.5 n.s.
exchange things (tools, recipes, etc.)	41.2	51.3 *
visit informally in home	38.7	47.4 n.s.
ask neighbors advice	26.1	30.8 n.s.
have picnics, parties	17.2	26.0 *
Number of neighbors chat with on block	64.1% at least half	47.3% all or most, vs. some, a few or none
Location of friends	24.4 at least half live within five blocks	34.9 2 or 3 of 3 best friends live in area
Sense of Community Index Percent who think district . . .	Foley – 1949 N = (448)	Hunter – 1974 N = (154)
is a small community in city	51.1%	59.9% n.s.
claims greater loyalty than city as whole	41.3	43.7 n.s.
has a special name	53.5	64.5 *
has particular boundaries	44.8	61.2 *
has particular activities solely for local residents	35.6	60.4 *

*Significant difference T_1 vs. T_2 at .05 level

SOURCE: Albert Hunter, "Loss of Community" *American Sociological Review* (October 1975)

The trends in population settlement and the ecology of the social composition of the urban locality set the stage for the hypothesis that the deconcentration of population and the decline in the use of facilities do not necessarily weaken community identification and community participation. There is no reason to assume that social changes which produce new forms eliminate all the older structures. The transformation in the journey to work and the decline in the use of local facilities mean that the local urban community and the neighborhood have specialized and narrowed their function. Our argument is that, in particular, the atrophy of local sustenance institutions has been accompanied by an intensification of the importance of the socialization function throughout the life cycle and the new ingredients of the socialization cycle. Instead of the classical Gemeinschaft-Gesellschaft format with its inherent empirical limitations, we speak of a socialization perspective, which applies to the entire household as it locates and relocates from one human settlement to another and demonstrates over time its varying capacity to internalize the norms of the new locality.

Local Socialization and Territorial Boundaries

Community studies such as the two monographs on Middletown by Robert and Helen Lynd and the multivolume investigation of Newburyport by W. Lloyd Warner and his associates have been based on the premise that community research supplies the locus of the study of total society.[35] In this view, the "community study" affords the opportunity for the investigator or the small research team to undertake an intensive and comprehensive investigation on the basis of a holistic approach. (There is an analogy between the tradition of communities studies and the holistic study of the prison and custodial institutions.) However, one does not confront the total society when one investigates a community, especially the relatively small and "separate" town or city which is the object of much community research. On the contrary, the power of the community study tradition lies precisely in its use of a specialized perspective. It highlights the distinctive consequences of territoriality on social structure and societal organization, and especially on the socialization of successive generations. Community research requires the sociologist to identify the boundaries—real and symbolic—and the social space in which the person and his household exist and proceed through the life cycle.[36]

35. Robert S. Lynd and Helen M. Lynd, *Middletown* (New York: Harcourt, Brace, 1929); Robert S. Lynd and Helen M. Lynd, *Middletown in Transition* (New York: Harcourt, Brace, 1937). In the "Yankee City Series," see particularly W. Lloyd Warner and Leo Srole, *The Social Systems of American Ethnic Groups* (New Haven: Yale University Press, 1945).

36. For a discussion of the distribution of socioeconomic population groups in metropolitan areas, see James Beshers, *Urban Social Structure* (New York: Free Press, 1962), pp. 87–108.

The transitory character of social relations in the metropolis is not a barrier to the proliferation of intricate and elaborate social patterns rooted in community organization.[37] Men and women and their offspring exert themselves energetically to create a variety of residential life-styles in an advanced industrial society. Higher standards of living make this feasible. For an effective system of social control, territorial attachments must be articulated into the larger political structure of each metropolitan center—a state of affairs which is yet to be achieved and which remains problematic. However, there is no possible answer to the Hobbesian issues of the existence of a social order without reference to the powerful, persistent contribution of the local community to the search for a moral order.

It can be argued that there are few succinct and conclusive hypotheses or precise statistical models which derive from the accumulated efforts to study the social format of the residential community. It appears that the weight of scholarship has produced detailed portrayals of social reality and a concern with style, language, and expression. The sociology of the urban locality in this view presents the essential ethnography. Urban sociology is one of the all too few bridges between sociology and humanistic analysis; in particular, the community study is the vehicle for approaching the existential problems of daily life. And in turn, despite the continuing criticism of sociology by humanists, the "modern" novel in the United States demonstrates the deep influence of the sociological enterprise on creative writers, such as Richard Wright, Ralph Ellison, and Saul Bellow have demonstrated.

37. Community research has been enriched by investigators schooled in the traditions and methods of social anthropology who have worked in small population centers; both Robert and Helen Lynd and W. Lloyd Warner reflect this perspective. But from the very origins of urban sociology, sociologists have sought to explore the local communities—the social worlds—that exist in the expanding massive centers of population. This tradition, as practiced by Charles Booth in England, George Simmel in Germany, and W. I. Thomas, W. E. B. DuBois, Robert E. Park, and Ernest W. Burgess in the United States, has stimulated a continuous stream of research which focuses on the consequences of territoriality in the metropolis. This intellectual tradition encompasses rich institutional and interpersonal analysis based on participant observation and includes the efforts to develop statistical social indicators of local community life. Selected examples of early efforts include Roderick D. McKenzie, *The Neighborhood: A Study of Local Life in the City of Columbia, Ohio, 1923* (Chicago: University of Chicago Press, 1923); Bessie Clenahan, *The Changing Neighborhood* (Los Angeles: University of Southern California Studies, 1929); Frank Sweetser, Jr., *Neighborhood Acquaintance and Association: A Study of Personal Neighborhoods* (New York: Columbia University Library, 1941).

However, the richness of detail should not divert attention from our observations on long-term trends in the format and symbolic character of residential localities. The community studies of the 1920s can be compared with those of the 1960s and 1970s, and their similarities and contrasts supply revealing if not necessarily completely representative findings. Since 1945 we are not limited to Chicago studies, but can look to efforts ranging from Boston to Los Angeles; in addition, the growth and effect of the community press have been increasingly used as revealing statistical measures.[39]

The point of departure is the observation that, in the United States, geographical, territorial, and institutional place names—precise or vague—and not ethnic designations serve as the basis for the social construction of community images and boundaries. The social organization of the metropolis is fundamentally molded by the pattern of racial and ethnic segregation. However, by 1976 ethnicity did not operate as an explicit or primary basis of the cognitive maps and designation held by the citizenry of their residential localities. Even the racial segregation and segregation of Spanish-speaking populations operate in a complex fashion. These characteristics contribute to the larger boundaries of the black and Spanish enclaves; but these ghettos have become differentiated into smaller localities described by place names which reflect geography, institutions, and social status, the constituents of ordered social segmentation.

In a setting of continuous residential mobility, community sentiment can be based on a short history which is passed on by word of mouth.[40]

38. Ralph Ellison, *Shadow and Act* (New York: Random, 1964).

39. Morris Janowitz, *The Community Press in an Urban Setting: The Social Elements of Urbanism* (Chicago: The University of Chicago Press, 1967); Alex S. Edelstein and Otto N. Larsen, "The Weekly Press' Contribution to a Sense of Urban Community," *Journalism Quarterly* 37 (October 1960): 489–98; Otto N. Larsen and Alex S. Edelstein, "Communication, Consensus and the Community Involvement of Urban Husbands and Wives," *Acta Sociologica* (1960), pp. 15–30; Scott Greer, *The Emerging City: Myth and Reality* (New York: Free Press, 1962); Scott Greer and Ella Kube, "Urbanism and Social Structure: A Los Angeles Study," in *Community Structure and Analysis*, ed. Marvin B. Sussman (New York: Crowell Company, 1959), pp. 93–114; Scott Greer, "The Mass Society and the Parapolitical Structure," *American Sociological Review* 27 (October 1962): 634–46; Scott Greer, *Metropolitics: A Study of Political Culture* (New York: Wiley, 1963), see especially chap. 5, "Who Was Listening?"

40. The construction of community boundaries can become the explicit task of governmental agencies. In New York City, the City Planning Commission consciously sought to develop community planning areas which articulated with the natural settings of localities. Local planning boards were established in 1949 by

But the group memory of a locality can quickly be extinguished or just forgotten. However, it must be emphasized again and again that a cartographic representation with fixed boundaries is an oversimplified picture of the territorial images in the minds of men and women.[41] The social space of a resident is not only diffuse but multiple, as it reflects various household needs and practices and indicates his sentiments, attachments, and actual local participation. Moreover, an important minority of residents hold more than one tenet and identification; they see themselves as members of a particular locality and, at the same time, as residents of a larger sector of the city. These images are not part of zero sum game. The real distinction between community and society can best be noted in the hierarchy of images the resident holds of his daily social space, in contrast to the multidimensional strength and weakness of his feelings of national identification as a citizen.

Albert Hunter in 1967–68 undertook a massive effort to chart the perceptions of social space—the symbolic communities of the central city—building on the work by Ernest W. Burgess.[42] His findings are not fundamentally different from those about other major metropolitan

Mayor Robert F. Wagner, then Borough President of Manhattan, and were mandated in all boroughs by the City Charter. In June 1966, the Commission announced 24 criteria for marking the boundaries and sought community comment on these criteria. In addition to connections with health, school, welfare policy, and urban renewal districts, these criteria included physical factors, lines of the original villages of the city, and historical areas, such as Yorkville in Manhattan or Riverdale in the Bronx.

41. For a discussion of the statistical and perceptual measures of community boundaries, see William Form, Joel Smith, Gregory P. Stone, and James C. Conley, "The Compatibility of Alternative Approaches to the Delimitation of Urban Sub-Areas," *American Sociological Review* 19 (June 1954): 434–40; Eshref Shevky and Wendell Bell, *Social Area Analysis: Theory, Illustrative Application and Computational Procedures* (Stanford: Stanford University Series in Sociology, no. 1, Stanford University Press, 1955); Eshref Shevky and Marilyn Williams, *The Social Areas of Los Angeles and Berkeley: Analysis and Typology* (Los Angeles: University of California Press, 1949); Kevin Lynch, *The Image of the City* (Cambridge: MIT Press, 1960); O. D. Duncan et al., *Statistical Geography: Problems in Analyzing Areal Data* (Glencoe, Ill.: Free Press, 1961); George A. Theodorson, (ed.), *Studies in Human Ecology* (Evanston, Ill.: Row, Peterson, 1961); Roger M. Downs and David Stea, *Image and Environment: Cognitive Mapping and Spatial Behavior* (Chicago: Aldine, 1973). See also series of working papers prepared by Harold F. Goldsmith and Elizabeth L. Unger dealing with the analysis of 1970 Census materials; Harold F. Goldsmith and Elizabeth L. Unger, "Differentiation of Urban Subareas: A Re-examination of Social Area Dimensions," Laboratory Paper no. 35, November 1970; "Social Areas: Identification Procedures Using 1970 Census Data," Laboratory Paper no. 37, May 1972; "Social Rank and Family Life Cycle: An Ecological Analysis," Laboratory Paper no. 43, May 1972; distributed by National Institute of Mental Health, Mental Health Study Center.

42. Hunter, *Symbolic Communities*, passim.

centers, except that Chicago has been more extensively researched. In the 1920s Ernest Burgess defined 75 "exhaustive and mutually exclusive" community areas. He was aware of many smaller neighborhoods and of the complexity of the symbolic boundaries of local areas, but he tried to construct a simplified map both for statistical research and for the administrative use of the municipality. Albert Hunter's map of localities offers a much more complex and varigated pattern. While Burgess focuses on 75 community areas, Hunter charted both neighborhood and community areas and emerged with a much larger number of operative localities–over 200 in effect.[43] This growing nucleation is a national trend, particularly in the older central cities of the Northeast and Midwest. But it is also to be found in the newer cities of the West and Southwest with their extensive suburbanization and deconcentration of population. However, as sociologists face historical change, it is difficult to know whether the number of subjectively defined communities have increased or whether our more refined methods of research lead to more elaborated categories and more detailed findings.

A powerful continuity is manifested by the fact that 43% of those surveyed by Hunter used the same place names encountered by Burgess one-half century earlier. In essence, territorial community in the metropolis rests on some sense of descent even if it is encompassed only by geographical continuity. Moreover, the Hunter survey found that an overwhelming 86% of the residents were able to offer specific place names for the locality in which they resided.

The extent to which residents' images of the locality contained both a center and a periphery is striking.[44] The periphery followed the boundaries of parks, vacant land, railroads and elevated lines, expressways, and city limits, in descending order. The center was generally a shopping area, a major intersection, or a group of community facilities. But the symbolic elements, not the physical artifact, defined the periphery, since there were infrequently alternative physical or geographical possibilities.

Historical reconstruction of the images of the local community is difficult. However, by 1920, despite the massive ethnic enclaves, cognitive definitions of the local community seldom emphasized ethnic

43. Ibid., pp. 67–94.

44. Edward Shils, "Centre and Periphery," in *The Logic of Personal Knowledge: Essays Presented to Michael Polanyi on his Seventieth Birthday, 11th March 1961* (London: Routledge and Kegan Paul, 1961).

designation. Historical accounts of local communities based on the reports of old settlers which go back as far as the Civil War period reveal that the ethnic concentrations seldom produced ethnic names for communities. The occasional designation of Greektown, Little Italy, or Polonia referred to the persistence of ethnic service centers for local residents, suburbanized ethnics, and clientele from the metropolis. It was as if the cognitive labels of residential localities indicated the aspiration to link the ethnic residents to the larger metropolis. In fact, most ethnic enclaves were composed of various nationalities—this mixture produced the essential preconditions for both acculturation and assimilation.

It was in the black ghetto that ascriptive designation persisted the longest. For example, in Chicago up to the outbreak of World War II, the residents of the black ghetto thought of themselves as residents of Bronzeville.[45] As the ghetto expanded, however, they took over the older names.

We are interested in the correlates which explain different degrees of community cohesion and account for the strength of a person's identification with his locality. Even the crude measure, whether a person does or does not make use of a place name to identify his residence, is revealing of community social organization. Persons from upper-status backgrounds hold clearer cognitions and more elaborated conceptions of the social space in which they reside than do lower-status persons. They are also persons with extensive voluntary association membership. However, these variables cannot be considered to be very explanatory. The single variable which has the most influence is a measure of community socialization, namely, length of residence. Thus, of those who lived in the local community less than one year, 27.5% did not know the name, while of those who lived in the community 20 years or more, the figure dropped to 9.7%. Controlling length of residence weakened and attenuated the difference between whites and blacks on this measure of community identification.

Cognitive definitions and images of one's residential community need to be related to the strength of positive and negative attitudes. The data collected by Albert Hunter confirm other studies which underline the relatively high degree of community satisfaction throughout the various social segments, in both the central city and the suburb. These

45. St. Clair Drake and Horace R. Cayton, *Black Metropolis: A Study of Negro Life in a Northern City* (New York: Harcourt, Brace 1945).

attitudes are an aspect of the syndrome of the "community of limited liability," a high degree of satisfaction is frequently compatible with a willingness and even proclivity to move to a "better" community. Even more striking, the long-term trend in satisfaction with one's local community is a consistent positive sentiment, in contrast to more rapidly fluctuating patterns of satisfaction with one's financial position and in particular in contrast to the increased negativism toward the central institutions of society. It is as if the local community had served as a "defended" refuge from the tensions of the larger society, as a social space for partial retreat.[46]

Thus, of a sample of 600 respondents interviewed in 1950, only 12.5% were dissatisfied with their community.[47] This is comparable to the percent (12.4) encountered by Hunter in his survey almost two decades later on an equivalent population.[48] The findings of Scott Greer for metropolitan St. Louis for the mid-1950s, which included suburban areas, produced similar results.[49] The Hunter sample revealed that about 50% were clearly positive; this percent is comparable for national samples collected in 1973 and 1974.[50]

Relevant national trend data are available on attitudes toward "your housing situation."[51] From 1963 to 1971, those who responded that they were satisfied varied in a narrow range from 74.6% (1963) to 79.2% (1969) to 77.4% (1971). This is particularly striking given the variation in feeling of relative deprivation concerning one's financial condition.[52] As was to be expected, there was a limited positive association between satisfaction with one's residential locality and membership in

46. Gerald D. Suttles, *The Social Order of the Slum: Ethnicity and Territory in the Inner City* (Chicago: University of Chicago Press, 1968).
47. Janowitz, *Community Press*, p. 128.
48. Hunter, *Symbolic Communities*, p. 118.
49. See John C. Bollens, *Exploring the Metropolitan Community* (Berkeley: University of California Press, 1962).
50. Tom W. Smith, "Satisfaction With Community," unpublished report, National Opinion Research Center, April 1975.
51. Tom W. Smith, "Satisfaction With Housing," unpublished report, National Opinion Research Center, April 1975.
52. Satisfaction with community and the quality of life in one's local community has come to be characterized in the mass media as centering on crime and the fear of crime. Survey data do show the salience of the problem, but the trend has not been markedly higher since 1965. This is a topic on which responses are very sensitive to the wording of the question. The question which has been used reflects the difficulty of operationalizing the boundaries of the local community when one uses national surveys. "Is there any area around here that is within a mile, where you would be afraid to walk alone at night?" In 1967 this indicator stood at 36% and by 1974 it had reached 45%.

the more privileged social segments of the metropolis. But again, this association was not very strong; very high levels of satisfaction could be found in low-income neighborhoods, while certain categories of middle-class suburban residents express only average levels of satisfaction.

However, these data show that since 1920 the decline in the use of local facilities has had limited influence on the cognitive definitions and images that the residents hold of their locality. Even more important, the increasing diversity of patterns of journey to work and to service and leisure facilities is unrelated to and has not weakened positive community sentiment and attitudes as well as actual informal and formal participation in the local environment.[53]

In essence, the idea of loss of community fails to capture the realities of the network of interpersonal relations and primary group ties that are constantly being fashioned and refashioned. Yet, as in the case of the interpersonal ties that emerge in the industrial and work settings, there is no reason to assert that they effectively support the linkage between the locality and the institutions and political organs of the larger metropolis; in fact, they are far from adequate in this regard, although they are vital in accounting for the operative level of social control.

Support for the perspective of the neighborhood and local community as a viable system of local socialization comes from both cross-sectional national survey data and longitudinal comparisons of particular

53. Patterns of land usage, traffic, and architectural design strongly influence the patterns of social interaction and the network of primary-group relations in the localities of the metropolis. The sociological tradition has encompassed a concern with the consequences of these factors for the microorganization of neighborhood and local communities. Generalizations about the influence of these physical and environmental dimensions are difficult to formulate. One can emphasize that proximity and openness stimulate social contact as does heterogeneity of the usage of space. But such observations seem tepid, except that one can point to the extensive failure of large-scale housing developments to contribute to a sense of neighborliness. Summarizing the results of the wide range of research and development work conducted by the faculty and graduate students at the University of Chicago in 1945 to 1975 on urban development, and drawing on my own experience in social planning (Hyde Park–Kenwood Redevelopment, South Commons, and South Loop Community), I emphasize that the ability of the local residents to participate in the management of the physical resources and to help maintain them or refashion them is as powerful a factor in developing effective social interaction as the physical and environment factors themselves. See John Zeisel, *Sociology and Architectural Design* (New York: Russell Sage Foundation, 1975); Clare C. Cooper, *Easter Hill Village: Social Implications of Design* (New York: Free Press, 1975).

community studies over the last half-century. It is perhaps understandable that the most impressive body of national sectional data derives from a British study. The British have had a long intellectual tradition in the application of survey procedures to the study of the local communities, and an even longer governmental tradition of concern to preserve viable localities. A detailed large-scale survey conducted on behalf of the Royal Commission on Local Government was undertaken in 1967 which collected an extensive data on patterns of local social bonds and participation. In addition, the sample was so designed that pertinent ecological and social organization variables could be analyzed.[54] There are no comparable data for the United States.

There is little reason to believe that the overall findings and relations for Great Britain are significantly different from those for the United States. The relevance of these data rests on their coverage of the internal social organization of the locality. Linkages between the locality and the larger society by means of voluntary associations, administrative agencies, and political institutions are likely to show some differences between the two countries. It is also necessary to take into account the higher rate of residential mobility in the United States than in Great Britain (and elsewhere in Western Europe), since length of residence is an important variable in accounting for the strength of local social bonds.[55] But the comparability between the United States and Great Britain in the internal organization and patterns of social behavior of neighborhoods is reinforced by the findings of a comparative survey of localities in Bristol, England, in 1957 and Columbus, Ohio, 1958 and 1959.[56] One of the central differences was the stronger emphasis on and salience of personal and familial privacy in Great Britain.

The central findings of the British Royal Commission study on social bonds—friendship and kinship—on community sentiment and at-

54. The survey interviewed 2199 adults and was designed to assist the Royal Commission on Local Government in England in making recommendations to restructure the size and format of local government units. A random sample was drawn from 100 local authority areas throughout England (excluding London) in numbers "correctly proportionate to the population which is contained within three main types of local authority of different population sizes. . . . " The original findings were published as *Community Attitude Survey: England* (London: HMSO, 1969). A detailed reanalysis is presented by John D. Kasarda and Morris Janowitz, "Community Attachment in Mass Society," *American Sociological Review* 39 (June 1974): 328–39.

55. Larry H. Long, "On Measuring Geographical Mobility," *Journal of the American Statistical Association* 65 (September 1970): 1195–1202.

56. H. F. Bracey, *Neighbors: Subdivision Life in England and the United States* (Baton Rouge: Louisiana State University Press, 1964).

tachment are relatively clear-cut by the standards of social research. They converge with and explicate the findings of earlier and more limited analyses completed in the United States. Community size and density have limited consequences for a person's social bonds in his locality and limited effect on his community participation as well as his community sentiments. Persons who live in large, dense urban settlements have no weaker or more limited informal and kinship ties than the residents of smaller and less densely populated areas. Instead, the single most important variable leading to stronger social bonds is length of residence. Higher social class had a positive effect on stronger social bonds but again much less than length of residence. Likewise, family cycle and presence of children were also a secondary variable in strengthening local social bonds, as has been emphasized by various other communities surveys; this process operates by means of the social relations generated by the school and associated institutions.

In addition to length of residence, the findings of the Royal Commission underline the importance of voluntaristic effort in the social construction of local communities. Persons with more education, as has been frequently emphasized, have stronger interest in their local community and are more likely to be directly involved in its voluntary associations. Moreover, membership in local voluntary associations strengthen particular local social bonds, community sentiments, and attachment regardless of the social position of residents. Thus it is useful to point out that integration of a person in a local area reflects less "societal-wide social status," such as occupation and race, and more local "social position"—in particular, length of residence, number of children, and patterns of daily behavior.[57]

These findings highlight the consequences of size and density—the key variables on the Gemeinschaft-Gesellschaft perspective. Residence in communities of increased size and density does not result in a substitution of secondary organizational for primary and informal contacts. The data suggest that organizational ties foster more extensive primary contacts in the local community. None of these conclusions deny the relevance of the metaphor "loss of community" as a basis for social criticism and for creating new social goals. However, available cross-sectional data hardly support the linear conception of the growth of atomization or "alienation" of the person and his household as a basis for probing the defects in social control.

57. Hunter, *Symbolic Communities*, p. xiii.

The central importance of residential mobility moves the analysis into the longitudinal mode. The development of urbanization and advanced industrialism in the United States has not been accompanied by an increase in the amount of residential mobility. Amos Hawley reports, for example, that in every census since 1850 the proportion of the population (adjusted for age differences) reported living in the state of birth has varied between 66% and 70%; he concludes that very little change has occurred.[58] Moreover, most household moves take place during the ages of 25 to 35, and after that there is a marked increase in residential stability. U.S. Census data indicate that there are also secular trends toward a decreasing overall rate of residential mobility. Between March 1975 and March 1976, 17.7% of the population changed addresses; five years earlier the migration rate was 19.1%, and it was 20.1% 15 years earlier. We are not faced with a "social doomsday machine" by which the increase in scale and complexity produces ever quickening paces of geographical mobility.

The most explicit longitudinal study of the social organization of a residential community is the restudy of one locality in Rochester first carried out in 1949 by Donald L. Foley and repeated by Albert Hunter in 1974.[59] The study has the drawback that it deals with a local area close to a university in which the residents have displayed a strong commitment to central city values and to racial integration. It is therefore a rather special case, but this type of community can be found in increasing numbers in one form or another in each major metropolitan area. The data collected at the two points in time over one-quarter of a century on "informal neighboring" and on the residents' "sense of community" reveal clearly the strengthening during this particular period of the community of limited liability. (See Table 8.3). Although there was a decline in the use of local service facilities, the level of informal neighboring remained the same or increased, while the expressed sense of community increased significantly.

Community studies, when placed in a historical context, broaden longitudinal comparison. Every metropolitan center has its "Gold Coast" and urban renewal has throughout the United States included widespread efforts to maintain and expand the "Gold Coast" of the

58. Amos Hawley, *Urban Society: A Ecological Approach* (New York: Ronald Press, 1971), p. 177.
59. Albert Hunter, "Loss of Community: An Empirical Test through Replication," *American Sociological Review* 40 (October 1975): 537–53.

central cities. The "Gold Coast" of Chicago is "special" only in that, for purposes of historical comparison, we have available *The Gold Coast and the Slum*, by Harvey W. Zorbaugh, a monograph published in 1929 which deals with a locality characterized by high residential mobility, a wide range of social components—as wide as could be encountered—and the presence of strong resistance to collective community organization.[60]

One-half century after the publication of *The Gold Coast and the Slum*, the boundaries of the area have not changed; it is still delimited by North Avenue on the north, Lake Michigan on the east, and the Chicago River on the south and west. However, the name has changed from the "Lower Northside" to the "Near Northside." The area has been transformed more by the pouring of concrete than by changes in social forms. Rooming houses have been replaced by four-story apartments, while near Lake Michigan the older brownstone mansions have given way to luxury high-rise apartments. Adjoining the Chicago River, Little Italy, once the site of blighted single-family units, has been recast into a massive high-rise public housing project for blacks.

The social extremes in the populations remain and population density is high.[61] The blacks have replaced the ethnics; and while the socialites have declined in numbers they have not vanished. They have been augmented by hardworking business and banking executives plus "big time" professionals. The former flow of native-born immigrants with a rural background and a high school education seeking to penetrate the cultural and social life of the area have been replaced by college graduates from suburban enclaves with similar aspirations.

Despite the social heterogeneity, high residential mobility, and institutional fragmentation, Zorbaugh found a strong sense of local identity. A striking portion of the residents worked in or near the area. But the

60. Harvey W. Zorbaugh, *The Gold Coast and the Slum* (Chicago: University of Chicago Press, 1929).

61. The consequences of crowding and high density in neighborhoods are intriguing. Many city planners emphasize the importance of relatively high density to support essential facilities and to stimulate interpersonal interaction and informal "socializing." But at what point does high density become crowding and "injure" interpersonal and family relations, especially among low-income households? The limited research data are not conclusive but tend to "discount" or deemphasize the consequences. Alan Booth and John N. Edwards, "Crowding and Family Relations," *American Sociological Review* 41 (April 1976): 308–21; for a review of the literature and careful empirical study which produced negative findings. Most of the research deals with varying degrees of crowding, but the real issue may be the very limited but important fraction of households living under very crowded conditions.

atmosphere of the area reflected not its work habits but its relatively self-contained informal social contacts and its local institutions which catered to the tastes of the residents. It was and remains an area in which adults "socialize" and develop differentiated tastes. Zorbaugh emphasized the weakness of the central voluntary association—The Lower North Community Council, which started out as an all-purpose organization during World War I and survived as a defensive community maintenance group. One of the sharpest changes over the decades has been the growth in number and vitality of local community organizations still strongly oriented toward a defensive posture. These voluntary associations, although they had specific purposes and goals, express a generalized concern for the fate of the area. The local party organization and especially the alderman have become closely connected to these voluntary associations; the alderman is a link between these voluntary associations and the municipal government.

In sharp contrast to the "Gold Coast" study are community studies of older industrial concentrations and their surrounding neighborhoods. These are the enclaves of industry and community—mainly of the older settlements of the East and the Middle West—which are being replaced by the newer working-class suburbs throughout the United States, as studied by Bennett M. Berger, which are removed from the industrial plant sites.[62] But the old-fashioned "working class" localities, for example, the steel mill areas of South Chicago, present the pre–World War II pattern of more limited separation of work and residence. As portrayed in *Blue-Collar Community* by William Kornblum, residential cohesion played a significant role in supporting the emergence of active trade unionism.[63] While new technology and plant relocation have been gradually eliminating these mixed locales of industry and residence, they continue to serve as ecological centers for blacks and Spanish-speaking groups entering the industrial order. The incorporation of these minorities into the mills and trade unions is more complicated, since often they enter the factories before they move into the immediate neighborhoods.

One basic contrast with the "Gold Coast" is that the socialization process in South Chicago focuses on the young people and the next generation; the "care and feeding" of the adults is taken for granted

62. Bennett M. Berger, *Working Class Suburb: A Study of Auto Workers in Suburbia* (Berkeley: University of California Press, 1960).

63. Kornblum, *Blue-Collar*, passim.

and is not the issue. Especially since the Vietnam War, the stable local educational system and associated youth-serving institutions have had to face social change and strained patterns of social control. The educational system operated with some effectiveness because it was taken for granted that preparation for a career in the mills was the effective goal. This goal supplied an operating logic even though more and more young men sought other types of employment. Since 1965 the desired goal for young men has been not to enter the mills and there has been increasing pressure to educate the young women for active employment rather than only household duties. The influx of Mexican and black minorities has only served to compound the education dilemma. The voluntary associations and political organizations are active and closely linked to the ethnic structure of the locality. However, over time there is a strain on the sense of community, as these organs have limited influence on the tensions created by ethnic succession and by the problems and limitations that family and educational institutions encounter in seeking to socialize the next generation.

There is a rich tradition of sociological writings which focus on the strain—and imputed increasing strain—resulting from the gap between family socialization and the realities of the industrial and occupational setting.[64] Each community study highlights the wide variation in patterns of transition by which young people move from residential community to the world of work, but the central patterns of convergence are striking.

Although the post–World War II period has witnessed a short-term increase in "familism," the long-term trends have been toward smaller families, more employed wives, an increase in the number of divorces, and a larger proportion of the population living in incomplete or reconstituted families.[65] According to Census Bureau data in 1976, 65% of U.S. households had both a husband and wife living together, and

64. See the studies of family networks in industrial society prepared by social anthropologists; for example, Raymond Firth, Jane Hubert, and Anthony Forge, *Families and Their Relatives: Kinship in a Middle Class Sector of London* (New York: Humanities Press, 1970); Elizabeth Bott, *Family and Social Network* (New York: Barnes and Noble, 1971); Ernest W. Burgess and Harvey J. Locke, *The Family: From Institute to Companionship* (New York: American Book Co., 1953).

65. Paul C. Glick, *American Families* (New York: Wiley, 1957); Kingsley Davis, "The American Family in Relation to Demography Change," in *U. S. Commission on Population Growth and the American Future: Demographic and Social Aspects of Population Growth*, ed. Charles F. Westoff and Robert Parke, Jr. (Washington: GPO, 1972), pp. 237–65; Clarence Glick, "Some Recent Changes in American Families," *Current Population Reports*, series P-23, no. 52 (Washing-

this was a decline from 71% in 1970. In that six-year period, the number of families headed by women rose 33% and the number of men living as "primary individuals"—either alone or with nonrelatives—jumped by 61%. Likewise the increase in illegitimate children has been marked both for whites and blacks, for example, it has been estimated that over 50% of the first children born to black mothers were illegitimate in 1969.

Each of these trends complicates the task of local socialization; while the research findings are hardly conclusive, the argument has strong plausibility. In addition to family composition, the increased separation of the locus of work from residence places additional burdens on family structure to effect the necessary transition of its offspring; the task therefore rests increasingly on the public school system—a task which it is unable to accomplish.[66] Thus it has become a commonplace for social critics and sociologists to point to the limited capacity of the educational institutions to supply an appropriate transition from family to adult occupation.

For the United States, the comprehensive high school has been the regulating and bridging institutional mechanism from childhood to gainful employment. It was an educational system which sought a balance between preparation for an increasingly complex division of labor and the development of a sense of collective identity loosely linked to residential locality. During 1920 to 1940 the comprehensive high school operated to some extent as a device to overcome barriers to higher education based on geographical and community segregation. It was not the goal of the comprehensive high school to increase social and economic equality; its goal was to extend potential access to higher education.[67] Moreover, until the outbreak of World War II, the comprehensive high school was at least compatible with

ton: Department of Commerce, 1975); For an overview of alternative types of family arrangements, see Ira L. Reiss, *The Family System in America* (New York: Holt, Rinehart and Winston, 1976).

66. For an interesting formulation of these issues, see Theodore Caplow, *The Sociology of Work* (Minneapolis: University of Minnesota Press, 1954).

67. Gordon C. Wayne, *The Social System of the High School* (New York: Free Press, 1957); David Gottlieb and Tom Reeves, *Adolescent Behavior in Urban Areas* (New York: Free Press, 1963); James S. Coleman, *The Adolescent Society* (New York: Free Press, 1966); Jerald G. Bachman et al., *Youth in Transition*, vol. 3: *Dropping Out—Problem or Symptom?* (Ann Arbor: Institute for Social Research, 1971); see also, for the historical background, Lawrence Cremin, *The American Common School: An Historic Conception* (New York: Teachers College, Columbia University, 1961).

the needs of youngsters who were to enter blue-collar occupations. There was a steady exodus from the comprehensive high school into the world of work without undue emphasis on rigid and artificial attendance requirements. More important, the size, location, and values of the comprehensive high school were not antithetical to the realities of occupational life in industry.

Extensive research literature on the post–World War II transformation of the comprehensive high school underlines the strain on its capacity to serve as a local institution of socialization. The comprehensive high school has found itself operating in a changed labor market in which the age of entrance into the industrial and service sectors has been raised by legislative and administrative decrees, by the increase in minimum wages, and by employer–trade union negotiations. The removal of youngsters from the labor market has been a humanitarian, welfare, and economic goal. However, the long-term changes in the comprehensive high school have exacerbated the task of youth socialization and effective transition from community to occupation, especially in a period of raising the age of entrance into the labor market.

Since 1945 the size of the high school has been increased, under educational policy which has claimed that larger high schools are required to effect an adequate comprehensive education.[68] The results have been a weakening of local community ties and greater difficulty of maintaining internal order in many high schools. Paradoxically, the larger size of the comprehensive high school has not meant that individual schools are able to maintain a relatively representative student body. In fact, there has been a growth in the homogeneity of the student body in individual units, which reduces the school's ability to serve as a bridging institution to the larger society. This increased homogeneity is the result of the growth in the scale of social segregation in local areas, particularly in the central city with its black ghetto. Moreover, the loss of industry in the central city has meant that the geographical proximity of the factory to the comprehensive high school has declined; likewise, the relocation of service-oriented establishments either in the central business district or in suburban cities has also removed these "work institutions" from the local community. As a result, the "social world" of the high school is more disarticulated and more removed from the reality and symbolic presence of work and employment.

68. James Conant, *The American High School Today: A First Report to Interested Citizens* (New York: McGraw-Hill, 1959).

The increased requirement of school attendance has been accompanied by a growth in the dominance of the value of the college preparatory curriculum. This trend has been reinforced by the values emphasized in the mass media. These long-term changes have increased the difficulties much of the youth population has in making the transition to an adult occupation. In particular, the impact has been most painful for youngsters from low-income households without a tradition of family involvement in the industrial setting and for certain youngsters from middle strata who have found prolonged participation in an educational setting particularly difficult.

The expansion of the mass education system has increased the emphasis on age grading and limited as well as specialized the range of contacts youngsters have with adults. (Since is it both impossible and undesirable to revert to earlier educational forms, there have been many recommendations and a few experiments to modify secondary education toward goals of a new mixture between work experience and classroom experience.[69] With the termination of conscription even the armed forces have contracted in their capacity to serve as a bridge between school and adult occupational life.[70] These trends help account for the increase in deviant and criminal behavior among youth groups, as well as the strength of the counterculture, fundamentalist youth religion, and parapolitical youth movements which operate in the post-Vietnam "youth scene," with less attention from the mass media. The process of transition from community to occupation is more and more regulated by nonlocal institutions of socialization, particularly the mass media, the legal and criminal justice system, and the bureaucratized social welfare services.

The pressure and pace of the life cycle are overriding, for it generates the basis of communal attachments of each new and successive generation. The disruption and tension associated with the transition into an occupation outside of one's residential community hardly stand as permanent barriers to the subsequent development of local residential attachments that come with marriage and the passage of time. We are not dealing with a "middle-class" phenomenon but with one that penetrates into the lower segments of the social structure. Thus a most

69. Morris Janowitz, *Institutional Building in Urban Education* (New York: Russell Sage Foundation, 1969); James S. Coleman et al., *Youth Transition to Adulthood* (Chicago: University of Chicago Press, 1974).

70. Wayne J. Villemez and John D. Kasarda, "Veteran Status and Socioeconomic Attainment," *Armed Forces and Society* 2 (1976): 407–20.

powerful indicator of the intersection of the industrial order and the geography of the locality is that deviant and criminal behavior declines markedly after the age of twenty-five regardless of social and legal policy. At this age, the aspirations to have a stable household of one's own imply that most of the next generation seek to enter the labor market and at the same time develop their own communal network in a fashion at least compatible with the norms of the larger metropolis. However, the social costs of transition are high. The incidence of temporary disruption grows as the rate of persistent youth unemployment under "stagflation" has increased, while there are those who are permanently affected. The tensions and strain of incorporating new cohorts into a relatively stable communal life fall not only on the younger generation but also increase the discontent of the older generation and generate the tensions between age groups. The obverse of the strain on the comprehensive high school as a local institution is the disarticulation of the institutions designed to handle the socialization and support of those entering later maturity; for constructing one's own household does not include care of one's aging parents under the social definition of the welfare state.

We are not merely dealing with interpersonal processes by which a person and his household struggle to make the transition through the stages of the life cycle. We are also dealing with institutional processes and the issues of "institution building." Local socialization throughout the life cycle not only relates the person and his household to the industrial and occupational order but also fashions political orientations and behavior. It is a classic theme that the political process in the United States traditionally rested on a network of voluntary associations, including local voluntary associations. But the increased separation of work and residence has changed this structure and the network of community-based voluntary association in the half-century since the end of World War I.

Communal Attachments and Voluntary Associations

We have reached the point in our analysis of the separation of work and residence where we need to examine the consequences of local voluntary associations on the processes of social control. Two sets of considerations are involved. First, to what extent do occupational, professional, and economic groupings dominate local voluntary associations, and how important are specifically territorial and communal variables, especially ethnic and religious ones? Second, and even more important for the social-control process, is an assessment of the strength and weakness of the linkages between local voluntary associations and the various levels of partisan political parties.[71] Full assessment of these dimensions of social organization of the United States will await an examination of the research findings on the conscious and contrived efforts to expand citizen participation which have taken place since the 1960s with the "War on Poverty" and the local community control movement, although the origins date back to 1920 and earlier. One basic question is whether these intensified local community activities have influenced the conduct and outcome of the regular elections. (These topics are explored in chapters 12 and 13 to the extent that there are relevant research studies.)

Our analysis of the strains in the national electoral system is rooted in the argument that it is progressively more difficult for the citizenry to calculate their political self-interest on the basis of occupational and work place affiliations. To what extent, if any, does participation in community-based voluntary associations adjudicate conflicts of group interest and to mold stable and effective political orientations? It is not possible to accept a simpleminded notion that local community participation necessarily assists the resolution of group conflicts among the ordered social segments of an advanced industrial society. Increased community participation can represent intensified tension between local groups and contribute to the disarticulation of administration and politics. It can, in effect, as in the case of particular work place groupings, serve mainly to push the resolution of differences upward to the national level rather than to operate as a means of conflict resolution. The hypothesis that we are developing is that, on balance, given the increased differentiation of the occupational structure and the extension of welfare benefits, local community associations serve to a limited extent to resolve conflicts of interest. In other words, without this mechanism of social control, the tasks of the national political process, especially the national election, would be significantly more difficult. However, the limitations and ineffectiveness of these local networks remain immense. This is especially the case since local voluntary associations have shifted their relative emphasis from self-help to a stronger concern with interest-group representation. Our hypothesis implies that

71. Constance Smith and Anne Freedman, *Voluntary Associations: Perspectives on the Literature* (Cambridge: Harvard University Press, 1972).

all too frequently the consequence of local participation is to reinforce the stalemate of the political process on which this analysis of social control is based.

The separation of work and residence obviously creates a dual system of voluntary association which the political parties must seek to coordinate. Manifestly, the influence of the work-based associations exceed those which are embedded in the familial residential setting; but the full power balance is complex and subtle. The contrast between economic-based voluntary associations and community organizations is rooted in vast differences in their power base; economic interest groups represent vastly greater concentrations of influence. The plethora of voluntary associations spawned by the industrial order are explicit in asserting that their rationale and primary goals are economic self-interest; their activities are rationalized by an ideology of economic self-interest serving the goals of larger collectivities. In the absence of an operative democratic socialist ideology in the United States, there have come to exist voluntary associations of economic entrepreneurs, industrial managers, professionals, and trade unionists. All, except a handful, are prepared to bargain but without aspiring to rule. These voluntary associations operate on the principle that the elected political representatives will define the collective or public interest if each presses narrowly for its presumed economic self-interest. In reality, these organizing principles cannot be applied without important components of collective social responsibility, but these are derivative, implicit, and secondary.

From the point of view of social control, community voluntary groups operate from a different set of organizing principles—from a different set of goals which influence and rationalize their activities. They speak explicitly in the name of moral standards and of collective responsibility. At times, the territorial boundaries of community interests can be very narrow or ill defined, and the definition of their collective responsibility can clash—even violently—with the imputed goals of the larger metropolis. However, the fact that local groupings compete and struggle for public resources should not obscure their underlying ideology, which seeks to give content to the idea of collective responsibility. The moral standard that neighbors—the local residents—have collective responsibilities permeates their organizing principles.

72. Morris Janowitz and Gerald D. Suttles, "The Social Ecology of Citizenship," forthcoming.

The collective defense of the community flows from the task of socializing the new residents and the next generations.

In the local community, the person and his household have the opportunity—by no means generally realized—to both internalize and aggregate the cost and benefits of alternative public policies.[72] At least the aspiration of the public interest is not lost as a goal. Each citizen is forced to consider his definition of the "good community" and to confront the costs he will have to endure for such a social order. For example if he wishes to call the police to complain about a rowdy party, he will have to bear the hostility of his neighbors; and there is no shifting the burden to a third party.

At an endless number of interaction points, the neighborhood and community are the locus where the motives and desires of economic self-interest encounter direct face-to-face reality testing. The family across the hall that will water the plants and take in the mail is participating in mutual self-help and not an economic exchange. Such patterns of interpersonal assistance, if they have any vitality, influence both the goals and tactics of the local voluntary associations. And in turn, the accomplishments—and, more often, the lack of accomplishment—of local community initiatives serve as realistic "civic education" about the larger political process. It is painfully obvious that the geographical scope of community organizations do not articulate with the jurisdictions of the political and administrative units of metropolitan government. Yet it is crucial to keep in mind that an essential characteristic of the political parties in a multi-party political system is that they are organized on a geographical basis. Therefore, contests for political power are waged in the smallest territorial units. The political parties must seek to penetrate the locality and present themselves as legitimate to the citizenry of the residential community.

Political competition is thereby strongly influenced by the relative ability of different economic groupings to penetrate and to use local voluntary associations or to create voluntary associations which represent their political interests. This topic is central if one is to explore the influence of community associations on the resolution or intensification of sociopolitical conflict. In particular, to what extent does associational membership contribute to strengthening the political participation of lower-income and lower-status social groups? Do the communal associations of the "lower class" serve as a political counterweight to the work place "pressure" groups of the middle and upper strata?

A considerable amount of social history underlines that the rise to political power of the reconstructed Democratic party in 1932 was facilitated and maintained through the New Deal by local religious, communal, and ethnic associations which "mobilized" low-income social groupings. Community-based associations have remained vital for these groupings, but there is no body of data to "measure" the extent to which there has been an attenuation of such organizational support.

The economic interest associations of the middle strata, and especially of the elite, in the main grow directly out of work-place contracts and arrangements. This is hardly to deny that for the middle strata—entrepreneurial and managerial, as well as for the wide range of professional, semiprofessional, and white-collar personnel—their informal social contacts are generated as a result of their work contacts. Nevertheless, their membership in community organizations is "in addition to" and separate from their affiliation in economic interest and professional associations. In turn, these economic "pressure" groups have not found it necessary or appropriate to strive to penetrate residential localities. In part residence patterns are at work; although white-collar and upper-status households are residentially segregated, there is little territorial concentration of these households by particular industrial sectors or employers or even by particular managerial or skill groups. But more important, higher levels of education and greater skill differentiation have led to economic interest groups which are specific to particular occupational settings.

In contrast, the trade union movement in the United States has energetically tried to strengthen its institutional base and expand its political influence by using local community and religious organizations. Until the end of World War II, those mass production industrial complexes which drew labor force from the immediate or particular environs facilitated trade union efforts to mobilize strength from local communities; and in turn the trade unions came to dominate the communal and political organizations of the locality. C. W. M. Hart's analysis of the auto workers union in Windsor, Canada, highlighted the complexities and inherent limitations in extending trade union influence into residential communities even in a municipality where the automobile industry thoroughly dominated the local economy.[73] As William Form has shown, it is the skilled worker who supplied trade union leadership in

73. C. W. M. Hart, "Industrial Relations: Research and Social Theory," *Canadian Journal of Economic and Political Science* 15 (February 1949): 52–73.

local community affairs.[74] However, the long-term trends toward dispersion of industrial plant and the increased length and diversity in the journey to work have weakened the links between trade unions and local community after 1960. The trade union became more and more an occupationally based interest group with less support from the community-based leadership. In localities dominated by an unskilled and unorganized labor force, church groups make a contribution to the sociopolitical balance. The task of community leadership falls more upon indigenous personnel with limited external support or to a limited number of political party agents; and thereby such "working-class" localities have few direct linkages with the industrial sector.[75] Thus when trade unions seek to mobilize their membership in elections, they must more and more rely on specially constructed organizations, in effect on ad hoc bureaucratic organizations which try to penetrate local communities in a fashion similar to political parties (See chapter 13).

Connections between work and community of residence are related to trends in ethnic composition and the strength of ethnic identifications, including, of course, racial identifications. The contrast and comparison between the post–World War I period and the period at the end of the Vietnam conflict are strong and well documented, even though there are no adequate national surveys which measure attitudes and self-concepts. At the end of World War I, public interest in the "nationality" question (as it was labeled then) was intense, since the war had mobilized national patriotic and ethnic sentiments. The sociologists who wrote in the 1920s emphasized the strength of nationality and ethnic solidarities; they did not hold the superficial view that a comprehensive "melting pot" was rapidly developing.[76] In fact, from a policy point of view, they opposed mechanical efforts at "Americanization"; as pluralists they believed that ethnic solidarities and associated forms of self-help were essential for national integration. Robert E. Park and Ernest W. Burgess wrote, "the condition of his (the Immi-

74. William H. Form, "Occupation and Social Integration of Automobile Workers in Farm Countries: A Comparative Study," *International Journal of Comparative Sociology* 10 (March–June 1969): 95–116; William H. Form, "The Internal Stratification of the Working Class: System Involvements of Auto Workers in Four Countries," *American Sociological Review* 38 (December 1973): 697–711.

75. For a series of Western European case studies, see Jerome F. Scott and R. P. Lynton, *The Community Factor in Modern Technology*, UNESCO Tensions and Technology Series, no. 1, 1952.

76. W. I. Thomas, with assistance of Robert E. Park and Herbert A. Miller, *Old World Traits Transplanted* (New York: Harper and Bros., 1921).

grant's) Americanization is that he shall have the widest and freest opportunity to contribute in his own way to the common fund of knowledge ideas and ideals which make up the culture of our common country."[77] In fact, the main contribution of these sociologists was that they underscored the institutional process which reinforced and maintained certain components of ethnic identity in the United States; in particular, they were aware of voluntary association and political groups as conditioners of ethnicity. While they stressed the durability of ethnic sentiments, they were not romantics, and they saw the strong pressures toward both acculturation and assimilation. The passage of time since World War I has influenced ethnic relations in a fashion continuous with these original analysis. The long-term trend has been a weakening of ethnic solidarity and the specialization of its scope.

At any given moment it is necessary to separate the new immigrants who enlarge the ethnic social base from the older elements and their descendents, for whom the persistence of ethnic identity is problematic. Restrictions in 1920 brought a long interruption in the flow of immigrants. However, after World War II, a strong unanticipated surge developed. While the magnitude never reached the pre–World War I concentrations, the post–World War II figure that about 20% of the population growth resulted from the foreign-born immigrant, is very high for an advanced industrial society. (See Table 8.1.) Moreover, the new arrivals included trained professionals, university professors, journalists, and political leaders, which resulted in highly visible groups of new immigrants.

Both patterns of residence and language supply important indicators of ethnic cohesion and solidarity and serve to correct the image of a "rapid" melting pot. Ecological research highlights the relative persistence of residential segregation (or concentration) of ethnic groupings.[78] These studies measure ethnicity by descent, namely, foreign-born

77. Robert E. Park and Ernest W. Burgess, *Introduction to the Science of Sociology* (Chicago: University of Chicago Press, 1921), p. 769.

78. Nathan Kantrowitz, "Ethnic and Racial Segregation in the New York Metropolis, 1960," *American Journal of Sociology* 74 (May 1969): 685–95; Nathan Kantrowitz, *Ethnic and Racial Segregation in the New York Metropolis; Residential Patterns Among White Ethnic Groups, Blacks and Puerto Ricans* (New York: Praeger, 1973); Avery M. Guest and James A. Weed, "Ethnic Residential Segregation: Pattern of Change," *American Journal of Sociology* 81 (March 1976): 1088–1112; Thomas L. Van Valey, Wade Clark and Jerome E. Wilcox, "Trends in Residential Segregation: 1960–1970," *American Journal of Sociology* 82 (January 1977): 826–44; for the intellectual background of this type of research, see Stanley Lieberson, *Ethnic Patterns in American Cities* (New York: Free Press, 1963).

versus native-born, and by the means of the "nationality" heritage of the offspring of the foreign-born. In particular, these studies emphasize that residential segregation persists with suburbanization. In essence, higher socioeconomic status reduces the amount of residential segregation of ethnic groups, but from an overall point of view ethnicity has an independent effect. The quantitative measures of ethnic segregation do not reveal an "overwhelming" concentration which produce ideal "enclaves" but rather still a significant tendency to aggregate.

But the crux of "ethnic" segregation is the continuous expansion of the black ghetto since 1920, and of the Spanish-speaking ghetto since 1950. In the black ghetto, ecological segregation envelops almost all of the black social structure. But even the self-containedness of the black ghetto has weakened. First, a larger and larger proportion of black wage earners work outside the ghetto. Second, there has been a fundamental shift in the housing market for black residents in the central city. Since 1965 the "dual housing market," enforced by prejudice and informal sanctions, has weakened. The differential pricing in housing—both in rental property and in owner-occupied residence—has declined and in some areas by 1976 the cost of comparable housing for blacks was lower than for whites.[79] The increased supply of housing for blacks has been in part the result of the suburbanization of whites following the long-term relocation of job opportunities. Third, the emergence of a limited but noteworthy number racially integrated residential communities has altered the social definition of the territorial distribution of black population. The definition of racial integration is not a numerical balance, since at any given percentage level the reality might well be a transitional phase from an all-white to an all-black community. The definition of residential integration is economic-based;

79. The decline of the dual housing market may well have had a strong effect on the racial succession in residential neighborhoods. For 1920 to 1960, the research literature placed a strong emphasis on the "tipping point." In the process of competition, invasion, and succession, population change was described as following a definite pattern. First, the rate of change was low as the initial blacks entered a white community and remained relatively low until the blacks constituted between 20% and 40% of the population. Then the character of the neighborhood or community underwent rapid change: and this point was called the tipping point. There is reason to believe that the increase in housing available to blacks and the greater difficulty of low-income white families to suburbanize has changed this into a more continuous and gradual process. Data collected and analyzed for 1963 to 1967 point in this direction. See George S. Piccagli, "Racial Transition in Chicago Public School: An Examination of the Tipping Point Hypothesis," Ph.D. dissertation, University of Chicago, 1975.

whites sell or rent to blacks and blacks in turn rent or sell to whites. Likewise, the opening up of suburbs for blacks has had an effect even though the number involved has been limited. The supply of housing for blacks in the suburbs has come to exceed the economic demand, since the reluctance of blacks to suburbanize is in part a personal and group preference for central city location. Nevertheless, the central black ghetto found in each U.S. metropolis is a contiguous enclave in which the full range of income and occupational groupings—each ordered segment of the black community—are to be found.

Geographic concentration is only an indirect indicator of ethnic solidarity and self-conceptions, especially of the changes in the social basis of ethnic identification. Therefore, language has become the more crucial quantitative measure. On the basis of the extensive documentation collected by Joshua A. Fishman, the decline in "language loyality" can be taken as a strong indicator of the overall weakening of ethnic attachments. By 1960, the non-English language resources of the United States were "undoubtedly smaller than they had been a decade or two previously."[80] As of 1960 it was estimated that 19 million persons or 11% of the entire U.S. population possessed a non-English mother tongue. The flow of new immigrants from Spanish-speaking countries injected important new foreign-language speakers. But given the long-term history of U.S. immigration, to point to one-tenth of the population as foreign-language speakers does not warrant describing this percentage as "high." Moreover, the key measure would be the ability of households of foreign-language speakers to transmit the command of the mother tongue to their children, and there are very few data on this. The continuing decline of the foreign-language press despite the new immigrants is another measure of the long-term decline in language loyalty.

Beyond residential concentration and language loyalty, more direct measures of ethnic solidarity and self-conceptions are required, particular measures which highlight the difference between assimiliation and acculturation.[81] Acculturation refers to incorporation into the occupational structure and the acceptance of key values of the larger society; assimilation implies loss of a sense of consciousness of descent and par-

80. Joshua A. Fishman, *Language Loyalty in the United States* (The Hague: Mouton, 1966), p. 392.

81. Eric Rosenthal, "Acculturation without Assimilation? The Jewish Community of Chicago, Illinois," *American Journal of Sociology* 65 (November 1960): 275–88.

ticular group identity. In the absence of adequate national survey data on long-term trends in ethnic identification, my estimate is that more than half the adult population of the United States as of 1976 did not have a meaningful or relatively clear or discernible ethnic sentiment (including racial identifications). Some indication of the construction of ethnic identifications can be drawn from community studies—past and present—which reveal the changing meaning and scope of ethnic identification in the United States. (The implied comparison is with other industrialized national settings, such as Scottish ethnicity or Flemish ethnicity, which supply the basis of nationalistic party politics.) From the community studies of 1920 and 1930, one is struck by the pervasive and almost coercive character of ethnicity and ethnic solidarity. Ethnicity and associated religious sentiments were central themes in the sense of personal consciousness. For example, Elin Anderson's study of Burlington, Vermont, published in 1938, shows the comprehensive character of ethnicity, based on the close overlap between ethnicity and occupation.[82] But the trends have been toward a decline in the linkage between ethnicity and occupation and a decline in the centrality of ethnicity as occupation has gained in salience.

The comparison with the stream of literature generated after 1950 is clear. The documentation that has been collected brings into focus the importance of voluntary associations and conscious efforts—particularly of political groups—to maintain and strengthen ethnic symbolism. This conclusion emerges in the wider range of literature on particular ethnic groups and in *Beyond the Melting Pot*, by Nathan Glazer and Daniel P. Moynihan, with its special focus on New York City. Regional variations reflect differences in recency of immigration and ethnic composition, but do not alter the observation.[83] Ethnicity is a characteristic which is paramountly linked to politics and political institutions. Ethnicity erupts from its subdued format in political pressure and political conflict, and in this regard it operates as another very important element of cleavage among ordered social segments. Many ethnic coalitions are a manifestation of similar economic positions or similar relation to the welfare state; concern with foreign relations is variable but obviously more intense among the more recent immigrants and the Jewish-American community.

82. Elin Anderson, *We Americans: A Study of Cleavage in an American City* (Cambridge: Harvard University Press, 1938).

83. Nathan Glazer and Daniel P. Moynihan, *Beyond the Melting Pot* (Cambridge: MIT Press, 1963).

Cross-sectional surveys of ethnic groupings support these observations, since these studies can classify their respondents into generations, and reveal the persistent political salience of ethnicity indentifications. Neil C. Sandberg's study of Polish-Americans in metropolitan Los Angeles, with its careful research design, documents the decline in the cultural basis of Polish-American identity from the first to the fourth generation.[84] In turn, political participation, especially metropolitan politics, supplies a purpose for ethnic solidarity, since it is a basis on which political coalitions are created.

The Jewish-American community is an interesting case, since the "reversal" of the assimilation trends has been described as most marked. Community studies which incorporate survey research by Sidney Goldstein and Calvin Goldscheider and by Marshall Sklare underline the transformation in the symbolism of Jewish group solidarity.[85] The immigrants from Eastern Europe thought of themselves primarily as members of a "people," an ethnic group with a distinct culture, a language —Yiddish—and an enduring religious heritage. The third generation instead view themselves essentially as a religious group rooted in biblical symbolism and emphasizing the importance of Hebrew and the heritage of Israel. The pronounced trends toward assimilation which reached a high point in the 1930s have been slowed. However, Jewish demographic trends have included very low birthrates and persistently high intermarriage. Therefore, "survival" in the United States implies less sheer numbers and more vitality of the committed elements, augmented by new immigrants from both the USSR and Israel.

In fact, intermarriage, reflecting acculturation through education and employment, is the basic manifestation of the attenuation of ethnic attachments. In the 1930s, the argument was first presented that, with acculturation and assimilation, the United States was experiencing and would continue to experience a triple melting pot; that is, there would be intermarriage across ethnic lines but within the three religious group-

84. Neil C. Sandberg, *Ethnic Identity and Assimilation: The Polish-American Community; Case Study of Metropolitan Los Angeles* (New York: Praeger, 1974). For a social history of particular Italian and Slavic immigrants, see Josef Banton, *Peasants and Strangers* (Cambridge: Harvard University Press, 1975).

85. Marshall Sklare and Joseph Greenblum, *Jewish Identity on the Suburban Frontier: A Study of Group Survival in the Open Society* (New York: Basic Books, 1967); Sidney Goldstein and Calvin Goldscheider, *Jewish Americans: Three Generations in a Jewish Community* (Englewood Cliffs, N.J.: Prentice-Hall, 1968). For an interpretative analysis, see Jacob Neusner, *American Judaism: Adventure in Modernity* (Englewood Cliffs, N.J.: Prentice-Hall, 1972).

ings: Protestants, Catholics, and Jews. In fact, there has been a long-term increase in both interreligious marriage and interethnic marriage. Data on the extent of religious intermarriage in the United States is limited. The findings of the Current Population Survey of 1957 indicate that at least 25% of the married couples were interreligious marriages and the amount has probably increased since that date.

Likewise, the documentation on interethnic marriage even among Catholics is striking; for example, in a sample of 1575 Catholics surveyed in 1964, the limits and range of ethnic endogamy were marked. On the low end—and the term "low" is hardly appropriate—27% of the Chicano group married outside their ethnic groups; on the high end, 47% of the Catholics of English descent did likewise.[86]

The "revival" of ethnicity and ethnic identity in the 1960s needs to be placed in an historical framework. One aspect of visibility of ethnic sentiments is that portion concentrated in the central city. In part this reflects the settlement pattern of the new immigrants and the persistence of older lower-income people. However, the increased political involvement and participation of blacks and Spanish-speaking groups contribute to the imagery of an ethnic revival while in effect we are dealing with the entrance into the political arena of formerly excluded groups. Second, there is an increase in "intellectual" ethnicity linked to higher education and to the interest of third and subsequent generations in their personal and group heritage. In this regard, ethnic concern in the "middle class" is the equivalent of upper-class preoccupation with genealogy. Accordingly, the general English-language mass media and not foreign-language press have reinforced this attenuated aspect of ethnic consciousness.

It seems reasonable to conclude that, while acculturation continues, the rate of assimiliation has slowed, but hardly stopped. In any case, the crucial issue is the connection between ethnic solidarities and local and wider political institutions. The analysis presented by W. I. Thomas in his classic study of Poles in Chicago before World War I revealed that the Poles—like other ethnic groups—had direct access to local political leaders.[87] At the same time, most ethnic groups of the

86. Harold J. Abramson, *Ethnic Diversity in Catholic America* (New York: John Wiley, 1973). The early formulation of the "triple melting pot" was presented by Ruby Jo Reeves Kennedy, "Single or Triple Melting Pot? Intermarriage Trends in New Haven, 1870-1940," *American Journal of Sociology* 49 (January 1944): 331–39.

87. W. I. Thomas and Florian Znaniecki, *The Polish Peasant in Europe and America*, 5 vols. (Boston: Richard G. Badger, 1918–1920).

period were organized on a national basis, and religious institutions served to support the national scope of ethnic voluntary associations. In short, ethnic associations were both local and national. (This was not the case for black associations until after World War II.) Thus, ethnic associations had community attachments, and dealt with local conflicts and issues while at the same time they functioned to integrate ethnic groups into the wider political structure, including the national structures. During World War I, and to a lesser extent during World War II, national government agencies stimulated ethnic voluntary associations and reached out to incorporate them as part of the war effort and as aspects of international political warfare.

There is fragmentary evidence that ethnic and ethnic-religious sentiments dampen the disruptive consequences of geographical mobility.[88] Members of ethnic groups transport their communal institutions and voluntary associations as they change residential location. Nonetheless, the deconcentration of human settlement and the increased range of daily and residential mobility have served to weaken the territorial basis of ethnic solidarities. And the ethnic basis of local community organization has declined while geographical and territorial affiliations per se become more pertinent. Ethnic groupings emerge more and more as a specialized type of "interest group" which involves an important emphasis on self-respect. Ethnic leaders remain aware of and sensitive to their geographical basis, but ethnic political participation is managed increasingly by metropolitan and national mass media and organizational specialists. The last step in the transformation is that presidential candidates cannot operate without special staff advisers on ethnic affairs, whose task is to mobilize the ethnic constituency as much as to transmit the respective demands of the groups involved.

By examining five national sample surveys, David Knoke and Richard B. Felson have been able to assign a realistic quantitative "weight" to the ethnic factor in political behavior.[89] For 1952 to 1968 they note a small and declining "covariation" between ethnic stratification (as measured by ethnic prestige in the stratigraphic image) and political

88. Charles Jaret, "Residential Mobility and Local Jewish Community Organization in Chicago," Ph.D. dissertation, University of Chicago, 1976.

89. David Knoke and Richard B. Felson, "Ethnic Stratification and Political Cleavage in the United States, 1952–68," *American Journal of Sociology* 80 (November 1974): 630–42; for another emphasis, see M. Parenti, "Ethnic Politics and the Persistence of Ethnic Identification," *American Political Science Review* 61 (September 1967): 717–26.

party identification. We are dealing with an "ethnic factor," since controls for socioeconomic stratification do not eliminate the linkage. Such data prevent one from overemphasizing the ethnic "factor" even in local politics and help one keep in mind the importance of voluntary associations in maintaining these identifications.

In essence, we return to the original definition of the residential community as the community of limited liability. This means that the vitality of the residential community and its contribution to the sociopolitical balance and effective social control, in the U.S. context, rest on and are conditioned by the voluntary associations which link the citizen to the administrative and political agencies of the welfare state. It is not a simple matter to identify these social realities, and the efforts of sociologists to map the massive details of these interpersonal and interorganizational networks are truly heroic.[90]

The conflicts of interest which concern locally based voluntary associations are frequently pushed upward in the political structure, as in the case with occupationally based conflict. In fact, particular local issues, such as racial integration by means of school busing, have produced explosive conflict. But in the context of the community of limited liability even these racial conflicts tend to be resolved or transformed by the redistribution of population. "Communal" conflict has rarely in the United States resulted in the development of paramilitary voluntary associations with persistent destructive consequences, as has characterized communal and ethnic politics in other national settings.

But on a day-to-day basis, the system of local community-voluntary associations is a manifestation of the elaborate network of associational membership in the United States. The level of participation in the United States in voluntary associations has been shown to be higher than that in most Western European parliamentary nations.[91] Moreover, the network is heavily embedded in localities, in part reflecting the greater separation of local and national government, a characteristic which distinguishes the United States from most Western European nations.

But it would be an error to accept the conclusions of those writers who emphasize that even this extensive network of voluntary associ-

90. Edward O. Laumann and Franz U. Pappi, *Networks of Collective Action: A Perspective on Community Influence Systems* (New York: Academic Press, 1976).

91. Gabriel Almond and Sidney Verba, *The Civic Culture* (Boston: Little, Brown, 1965), chap. 11.

ations encompasses only a minority of the citizenry. First, the long-term trend appears to be one of increasing levels of such participation.[92] Thus, one national survey in 1955 revealed that 64% of the adult population were not members of a single voluntary association; but by 1962 the figure dropped to 57%. The increase was particularly strong in black communities.[93] The data collected by Gabriel Almond and Sidney Verba found in 1959 that 57% of the adult population were members of voluntary associations.[94] The differences between these studies in part reflect whether or not labor unions are enumerated as voluntary associations. Moreover, since the early 1960s the amount of participation has increased, especially at the local level. In any case, we are not dealing with a fixed pattern; a person becomes involved in a voluntary association at specific times when needs and controversies arise; so membership during one's lifetime is higher than cross-sectional data indicate. Likewise, the network of voluntary associations is extended by a person's access through his relatives and friends. Thus the survey by Hyman and Wright mentioned above which reported 64% were not members of voluntary associations also indicated that when the respondents were classified by households the number of nonparticipants dropped sharply to 47%.[95] The network of participation has been described in detail by Edward O. Laumann, based on a 1965–1966 sample from the Detroit Area study, showing that among native-born males, excluding those over the age of 65, 83% were members of one

92. Herbert H. Hyman and Charles R. Wright, "Trends in Voluntary Association Membership of American Adults," *American Sociological Review* 36 (April 1971): 191–206; James Curtis, "Voluntary Association Joining: A Cross-National Comparative Note," *American Sociological Review* 36 (October 1971): 872–80.

93. J. Allen Williams, Jr., Nicholas Babchuk, and David R. Johnson, "Voluntary Associations and Minority Status: A Comparative Analysis of Anglo, Black and Mexican Americans," *American Sociological Review* 38 (October 1973): 637–45; for other relevant studies see Basil G. Zimmer and Amos H. Hawley, "The Significance of Membership in Associations," *American Journal of Sociology* 65 (September 1959): 196–201; Nicholas Babchuk and Alan Booth, "Voluntary Association Membership: A Longitudinal Analysis," *American Sociological Review* 34 (February 1969): 31–45; Andrew M. Greeley, "Political Participation among Ethnic Groups in the United States," *American Journal of Sociology* 80 (July 1974): 170–204; Frank Clemente and William Sauer, "Voluntary Associations and Minority Group Status: Comment and Extension," *American Sociological Review* 40 (February 1975): 115–17; Susan Welch, John Comer, and Michael Steinman, "Ethnic Differences in Social and Political Participation: A Comparison of Some Anglo and Mexican Americans," *Pacific Sociological Review* 18 (July 1975): 361–82.

94. Almond and Verba, *Civic Culture*.

95. Hyman and Wright, "Trends."

voluntary association; the incidence of two, three, and four memberships was noteworthy.[96]

The available data on voluntary associations have been reported in a fashion which conforms to the stratigraphic image of society; therefore the persons at the top of the social structure are seen as more involved in voluntary association than those at the bottom. While this pattern makes "sense," in reality the network of participation reflects the complexity of the ordered social segments of an advanced industrial society.[97] A linear association between position in the social structure and strength of voluntary association membership is an oversimplification; for example, some blue-collar workers, with strong trade union and church affiliation, have more effective voluntary associational anchors than do large numbers of the "white-collar" population.

Neither the limitations on the available documentation nor the complexity of the patterns of participation obscures the conclusion that more extensive involvement in voluntary associations is linked positively to both stronger local social bonds and stronger communal identifications as well as to higher levels of political participation in elections, both local and national.[98] As stressed above, we are dealing with a local socialization process in which length of residence is a key variable associated with increased voluntary association membership. It is essential to avoid simple causal chains of explanation. Instead, two systemic observations can be made which throw some light on the influence of voluntary associations in aggregating and balancing local community interests and in influencing local political institutions. Both these observations deal with the interplay of social stratification variables and community political participation.

First, if one "decomposes" the available quantitative survey data on political behavior, one encounters a local political context, or, if you will, a local political culture which has a strong and independent effect on civic participation. In this regard, "local" has a multiple or tiered meaning; it refers to metropolitan as opposed to national, and commu-

96. Edward O. Laumann, *Bonds of Pluralism: The Form and Substance of Urban Social Networks* (New York: Wiley, 1973), p. 140.

97. For an overview of this literature, see William Glazer and David Sills, *The Governments of Association* (Totowa: Bedminster, 1966); Murray Hausknecht, *The Joiners* (Totowa: Bedminster, 1962).

98. Marvin E. Olson, "Social Participation and Voting Turnout: A Multivariate Analysis," *American Sociological Review* 37 (June 1972): 317–33; Almond and Verba, *Civic Culture*.

nity as opposed to metropolitan.[99] The sociological truism that applies is that indicators of political behavior which we use as measures of effective social control cannot be adequately inferred from the social background or stratification characteristics of the citizenry. (In essence, this is an elaboration of the analysis presented in chapter 5.) The same background characteristics produce different community and political perspectives, depending on the concentration of these characteristics in a given community. Thus, for example, those persons who have social background characteristics likely to produce Republican perspectives are less likely to behave politically as Republicans if they find themselves in mainly Democratic communities.[100] The concentration of political partisans can be taken as a crude indicator of the political culture of the locality.

The second systemic observation is that, along with the existing political context, "civic leadership" comprises an important set of variables accounting for the character of community perspectives and participation. Only a very limited amount of social research has been designed to clarify the strength and dynamics of local leadership as opposed to the concern with social-stratification variables. It is indeed a rare piece of research that permits Howard Schuman to point out that the difference in "social demography" of 15 cities in the United States does not account effectively for the difference in patterns of racial attitudes. It is necessary to take into account the institutional and cultural setting.[101]

Robert C. Angell's classic study of the moral integration of cities (his terminology for effective social control) emphasized the key im-

99. The regional tier should not be overlooked. In essence, the same occupational and social position produced different electoral perspectives depending on the regional context. "The South" is the most conspicious in this regard. While there is evidence that the South is converging with national norms, the persistence of regionalism is striking. See Norvall D. Glenn and J. L. Simmons, "Are Regional and Cultural Differences Diminishing?" *Public Opinon Quarterly* 31 (1967): 176–93.

100. David R. Segal and Marshall W. Meyer, "The Social Context of Political Partisanship," in *Quantitative Ecological Analysis in the Social Sciences*, ed. Stein Rokkan (Cambridge: MIT Press, 1969), pp. 217–32; David R. Segal and Stephen H. Wildstrom, "Community Effects on Political Attitudes," *Sociological Quarterly* 11 (1970): 67–86.

101. Howard Schuman and Barry Gruenberg, "The Impact of City on Racial Attitudes," *American Journal of Sociology* 76 (September 1970): 211–61. Richard F. Curtis and Elton F. Jackson, *Inequality in American Communities* (New York: Academic Press, 1977). Differences in trust in government and satisfaction with local institutions in 15 cities is presented in Peter Rossi et al., *The Roots of Urban Discontent: Public Policy, Municipal Institutions and the Ghetto* (New York: Wiley, 1974).

portance of three social-stratification variables—residential mobility, cultural heterogeneity, and socioeconomic differentiation—in accounting for different levels of moral integration in the major cities of the United States in his sample.[102] However, he found that the character of community leadership and of local civic participation in voluntary associations, although difficult to operationalize, had to be taken into account to explain those cities which displayed higher than anticipated levels of moral integration. Moreover, when the moral integration of these cities in 1940 is compared with their situation in 1970, social-stratification variables declined in importance, and by inference, the variables of civic leadership increased in importance.[103] This is essentially the conclusion which most local community power studies have generated.

In addition, local community organizations have undergone changes in the post–World War II period which have contributed to their influence. First, in response to the increased nucleation and fragmentation of the urban environment, the number of local community organizations throughout the United States, and in particular in metropolitan centers, have increased as they have come to reflect smaller localities. For example, the number of neighborhood and local community organizations in the city of Chicago had grown to over 250 by 1967–1968.[104]

At the same time, by conscious effort, local community organizations have sought to adapt themselves to the shifting boundaries of political units and to the enlarged territory of agencies which are much more inclusive than the natural area of neighborhoods and local communities. The proliferation of separate voluntary associations has been accompanied by a strong movement toward hierarchical federation of voluntary associations. In fact, one-half of the neighborhood and local community organizations were affiliated with a "roof organization" representing wide sectors of the central city. These roof organizations varied from loose federations to multitiered organizations with complex constitutions and staffs and extensive financial resources. Even the highly individuated Gold Coast of Chicago has witnessed the same development. The increased number of local organizations in the "Near

102. Robert C. Angell, "The Moral Integration of American Cities," *American Journal of Sociology* 57, pt. 2 (July 1951), pp. 1–140.

103. Robert C. Angell, "The Moral Integration of American Cities, 2," *American Journal of Sociology* 80 (November 1974): 607–29.

104. Hunter, *Symbolic Communities*, p. 163.

Northside" community area has produced a Committee on Community Organization to coordinate the various groups. The effectiveness and durability of these roof associations vary widely. These coordinating agencies become successful when the competing local leaders develop a measure of internal accommodation and compromise. The trend toward hierarchical federation has increased the actual and potential capacity of the community organizations to operate as more than veto groups. However, as of 1976 the persistent divide between central city and suburban organizations remains to be bridged, although basic issues of mass transportation and the management of the environment supply the initial basis for broader political coalitions.

But the sign that the network of voluntary associations are effective is their emergence into a national grouping with direct representation in the nation's capitol. The connections within metropolitan centers have even more strikingly been accompanied by the formation of national federations. Many functional "grass-roots" organizations, such as religious and education groups, have national hierarchies, for example, the networks of parent-teacher associations. Likewise, professional associations concerned with community organization, in part or in whole, for example, social workers and, more recently, urban social and physical planners, are national entities. The National Association of Inter-Group Officials represents the extent to which professional specialization has developed. But the clearest demonstration of the articulation of local grass-roots groups into national federations is in the citizens' lead associations, National Association of Neighborhoods, National Neighborhoods, and National People's Action, groups which came into prominence in the 1970s.

Our analysis of community organization has been based on the assertion that the local residential community has come more and more explicitly to be an area of political competition. The evidence presented thus far supports or at least is compatible with the hypothesis that, on balance, and regardless of their weakness, these networks of organizations have made a political contribution to resolving, or at least balancing, competing group interests. However, the full exploration of this conclusion requires an examination of the linkages between community organization and the changing character of party organization. (See chap. 13.)

However, at this point, it must be remembered that our analysis of social organization in the urban metropolis has, in the last two chapters, been based on the juxtaposing of the hierarchical dimension of bureaucratic institutions against the territorial dimension of residential communities. The increase in the scale of bureaucratic organization and the enlargement of the means of transportation are the proximate causes, but there is no reason to accept the notion of a simple evolutionary model in the division of labor and a loss of community in the residential sector.

The increase in scale does not result in increased uniformity and homogeneity in the community organization of an advanced industrial society. On the contrary, the outcome is greater differentiation and greater interdependence. Fortunately, these trends do not confirm those classic theories which anticipated impersonality and atomization of social relations. Yet, unfortunately, interdependence does not produce and ensure integration and coordination within the metropolis or between the metropolitan concentrations and the total society. The result is the repeated observation that partisan politics, and especially the electoral system has emerged as the central coordinating element; but the inherent and operative limitations of election decisions contribute fundamentally to the defects in social control.

The system of social organization cannot be reduced to the intersection of the dimensions of bureaucratic hierarchy and communal territoriality. The systemic analysis of bureaucracy and community must be augmented by a focus on the societal-wide system of persuasion and coercion—in particular, on the institutions of the mass media and of law enforcement, which are the next stage in our analysis of the processes of social control.

Nine

Societal Socialization: Mass Persuasion

Social Personality and Personal Control

The logic of systemic analysis includes a safeguard against excessive, rigid sociological reductionism. Instead, in the systemic analysis of social change and social control, it is both desirable and essential at points to interject conceptions of personality or, more to the point, conceptions of social personality. This is appropriate because the social-control perspective focuses on the mechanisms of socialization and on the processes of internalization of norms or, in the older language, on the degree to which the person accepts values guided by "higher moral principles" rather than merely by the pursuit of self-interest.

Despite the modest research accomplishment, the formulations of personality and culture offer one point of departure.[1] This type of social psychology has enduring relevance because it focuses on authority and the subjective dimensions of authority. The students of personality and culture have sought to incorporate into their analysis the realistic constraints on institutional authority. They have also been sensitive to the historical setting; one cannot speak of culture without appropriate time referents. But one remains uneasy about the problems of empirical investigation, for all too often the results still appear too oversimplified.

It is no fatal flaw; but the "outside" observer rather than the "inside" participant appears best prepared to undertake such investigations, for in fact they may require considerable personal and social distance. As a result social-psychological reactions to authority are reported by Ruth Benedict for the Japanese; by Margaret Mead for the Russians;

1. Alex Inkeles and Daniel Levinson, "National Character: The Study of Modal Personality and Sociocultural Systems" in *The Handbook of Social Psychology*, vol. 4, ed. Gardner Lindzey and Elliot Aronson (Reading, Mass.: Addison-Wesley Publishing Co.), pp. 418–506; Clifford Geertz, "A Study of National Character," *Economic Development and Cultural Change* 12 (January 1964): 205–9.

by Henry V. Dicks for the Germans; by Lucien Pye for the Chinese.[2] The insider appears reluctant or inhibited. At best Michel Crozier, the French sociologist, has presented specific themes in his analysis of authority relations in French bureaucratic settings; and the same approach is pursued in the analysis by Geofrey Gorer, the English anthropologist, of English character structure.[3] Most telling, from the point of view of the tasks at hand, the intellectual apparatus and methodology of the study of personality and social structure have not been energetically and extensively applied to the citizenry of the United States. No doubt the very heterogeneity of the United States resists such an intellectual enterprise. The massive study of *The Authoritarian Personality*, stimulated by the "Frankfurt school" while residing in the United States, is highly selective because of ideological considerations.[4] It deals only with authoritarianism of the "right" and omits that of the "left." The fundamental finding that tolerant attitudes toward minority groups are concentrated among those who are "antiauthoritarian"—in opposition to the existing authority structure—is a serious oversimplification. Nevertheless, one can "measure" authoritarian attitudes and they do relate to political attitudes and political behavior.

But the exploration of social control does not rest on the search for a general theory of action which fuses sociological and personality theories. Instead I believe that sociological analysis of social change and social control in a specific historical period both requires and is enriched by the incorporation of particular conceptions and variables of social personality. This is merely a continuation of the intellectual heritage of sociology, which includes a persistent emphasis on the distinction between personal and social disorganization.[5] The important consideration is that we are dealing not with exclusively infantile so-

2. Ruth F. Benedict, *The Chrysanthemum and the Sword* (Boston: Houghton Mifflin, 1946); Margaret Mead, *Soviet Attitudes toward Authority* (New York: McGraw Hill, 1951); Henry V. Dicks, "Personality Traits and National Socialist Ideology," *Human Relations* 3 (1950): 111–54; Lucien Pye, *The Spirit of Chinese Politics: a Psychocultural Study of the Authority Crisis in Political Development* (Cambridge: MIT Press, 1968).

3. Michel Crozier, *The Bureaucratic Phenomenon* (Chicago: University of Chicago Press, 1964); Geoffrey Gorer, *Exploring English Character* (London: Cresset Press, 1955).

4. Theodor Adorno et al., *The Authoritarian Personality* (New York: Harper, 1950); Edward Shils, "Authoritarianism: 'Right' and 'Left,'" in *Studies in the Scope and Method of the Authoritarian Personality*, ed. Richard Christie and Marie Jahoda (Glencoe, Ill.: Free Press, 1954), pp. 24–49.

5. Morris Janowitz, ed., *W. I. Thomas: On Social Organization and Social Personality* (Chicago: University of Chicago Press, 1966), pp. 11–36.

cialization but with the formation of personality throughout the entire life cycle.

Nor does the inclusion of personality dimensions imply that the sociologist must constantly shift or enlarge his frame of reference. It does imply that the analysis of the changing patterns of social control in an advanced industrial society is assisted by such incorporations even though the result is to undermine, or at least retard the search for paradigmatic models. Moreover, if one holds a perspective which requires the enlargement of both voluntarism and rationality in the management of societal institutions, an interface with the elements of social personality and motivation becomes inescapable.

Theories of personality abound and are constantly being explicated. But there is a basic meaning—a primitive meaning—which has emerged and which impinges directly on the study of social control. When one talks about personality, one refers to relatively enduring predispositions—emotive and attitudinal—to behave; they are the externalization of internal "psychic states" which carry over from one interpersonal and social setting to the next. This line of reasoning can be found in diverse sources, such as W. I. Thomas, who spoke of the "organization of attitudes" and the resulting "definition of the situation" as he made use of an interactional psychology.[6] It is equally present in Erik H. Erikson's emphasis on the "stages of man" and the resulting modalities of social life.[7] To ground one's perspective toward personality in psychoanalytical theories produces a very different set of intellectual priorities.[8] But these and related formulations work against belabored sociological reductionism, on the one hand, and general systems theories, on the other hand. I use the term "social personality" to encompass the convergence in these orientations toward personality which sees the organization of attitudes as (1) rooted in intrapsychic states, (2) strongly impacted during childhood, and (3) nevertheless capable of being refashioned throughout the life cycle.

There is another simple but overriding element in the incorporation of social personality into the analysis of social control. A person's at-

6. W. I. Thomas, *The Child in America: Behavior Problems and Programs* (New York: Knopf, 1928).

7. Erik H. Erikson, *Childhood and Society* (New York: Norton, 1950), chap. 7.

8. Harold Lasswell, *Psychopathology and Politics* (Chicago: University of Chicago Press, 1930), pp. 261–63; Alexander Goldenweiser, "Some Contributions of Psychoanalysis to the Interpretation of Social Facts," in *Contemporary Social Theory*, ed. Harry Elmer Barnes, Howard Becker, and Francis Becker (New York: Appleton-Century, 1940), pp. 391–430.

tachment to and participation in the more remote societal institutions are not only mediated by intimate and primary groupings and local social organizations. The connections between the person and the society (and the state) have more direct dimensions of great symbolic content.[9] These more direct linkages among the mass of the citizenry and elite groups cannot be explored without references to social-psychological and personality content. Thus, it is necessary to distinguish the processes of microsocialization and local socialization from those of societal socialization. Of the various possibilities, our strategy is to focus on the interplay between those instrumentalities of mass persuasion and those of legitimate coercion and lawful sanction, for the outcome is at the heart of the long-term trends in social control.

The substantive meaning of social control is grounded in persuasion, although, as argued in chapter 2, the mechanisms of social control assume a minimum—an irreducible minimum—of legitimate coercion and physical sanctions. However, the terms "persuasion" and "coercion" have their common-sense and their "primitive" social-science meanings by reference to the personality concept. Persuasion is "to induce by arguments," and to "affect beliefs." It is not possible to think about social control without assuming that the person is engaged in periodic modification of his beliefs on the basis of persuasion, both interpersonal and mass.

On the other hand, coercion is the "use of physical force to control a person or a group." The brute efforts to negate a person's "will" imply that there is a core of attitudes and predispositions to behave which characterized the person and his social groupings. The goal of coercion—even of legitimate coercive sanction—is not only to modify behavior but to condition underlying personality as well.

Systemic analysis seeks to emphasize and clarify the distinction between persuasion and coercion. The value orientation of the social-control perspective works to this end. However, in reality, aspects of persuasion, especially mass persuasion, and coercive sanctions become fused and difficult to separate. The term "coercive persuasion" is a lin-

9. The direct relation between the person and the nation-state is epitomized by the not infrequent response of well-educated and highly politically involved voters in the 1976 presidential election who resolved their indecisions only when actually in the voting booth. As reported by one respondent, "I entered the voting booth committed to the idea that I would not vote for President. But when I saw the label, 'President,' I knew I had no option but to vote for the highest office in the land, and then I finally gave in and voted for Carter."

guistic barbarism but it is not a sociological contradiction. It refers to direct use of symbols to achieve coercive controls. Coercive persuasion is to be found in social mechanisms, from the intensive small group "encounters" which have been called brainwashing to particular forms of behavior modification.[10] In effect, the elements of meaningful persuasion have been removed, and from the perspective of social control we are dealing with an essential reliance on coercive control.

On the other hand, we also have the idea of and actuality of symbolic force or symbolic coercion. From the writings of Georges Sorel until those of Frantz Fanon, these notions have attracted attention, especially among university-based intellectuals.[11] Violence and the various forms of coercion are characterized, not in terms of the physical element and physical consequences, but rather in terms of their symbolic content and manifestation. The resort to violence sets in motion, for the person and the group, social-psychological processes of personal emancipation and social development. In this view, the application of coercion is to be seen as an educative process. From the perspective of social control, such a formulation is at best a play on words. The definition and the application of symbolic violence are to be seen as a specialized form of violence and coercion.

By contrast, as argued in chapter 2, the goal of social control is the reduction of violence and coercion, by strengthening group self-regulation. Such self-regulation is enhanced by the strength of personal control. It should be recalled that personal control means a person's capacity to channel his energies and to satisfy his needs and impulses while minimizing damage to himself and to others.[12] Personal control—to the extent that it operates—cannot be only the result of intimate or local or metropolitan socialization. Personal control and the resulting contributions to social control involve macrosociological or societal-wide mechanisms of socialization. In this sense the social organization of an advanced industrial society rests on a national system of persuasion and legitimate coercion, and the resultant internalization of the operative norms. Thus it is not metaphysical to assert that the person has direct connections with the nation-state. For our purposes the mass media and the coercive aspects of the legal system are central in fashioning these linkages.

10. H. Schein, *Coercive Persuasion: A Socio-Psychological Analysis of American Civilian Prisoners of the Chinese Communists* (New York: Norton, 1961).

11. Georges Sorel, *Réflexions sur la violence* (Paris: Rivière, 1946).

12. See Bruno Bettelheim and Morris Janowitz, *Social Change and Prejudice* (New York: Free Press, 1964), pp. 198–244.

Societal Socialization: Mass Persuasion

Mass persuasion and law enforcement have a symbolic content which bears directly on personal control. They have a symbolic imagery and a psychological content which give meaning to the statement that the individual in modern society, despite its elaborate complexity, has direct relations to the state. The systemic analysis of social control which emphasizes social institutions cannot neglect these direct linkages, although they do not lend themselves to simple operational measures.

In chapter 3 it was argued that the distinction between individual and group psychology was not effective for the analysis of social control; and this observation is pertinent to assessing the trends in the effect of the institutions of mass persuasion and legitimate coercion. Our task is not limited to making use of "psychological" variables to explain differences in attitudes and values within particular social groups or social segments. Instead, personal control emerges as an equivalent conception to social control, which has particular relevance in exploring a person's attachment or lack of it to the larger societal collectivity.

There are value judgments involved in relating social control to personal control; but we are not dealing with a set of personal preferences. We are dealing with the subjective dimension of changing patterns of institutional authority. In a competitive political democracy, the mass electorate—even those members of limited education—must be able, in theory and practice, to choose deliberately between political candidates. This deliberate choice can be heavily influenced by communal traditions and concern for the personalities of the contenders, but there must be, over the long run, a component of autonomy in the decision.

The idea of personal control is not based on an "oversocialized" human being for whom the exercise of autonomy creates "destructive" strain and personal conflict.[13] In the most fundamental terms, personal control implies that there is acceptance of external authority, not mere submission to authority. In turn, the person's social personality has been molded to permit some degree of autonomy with respect to external authority, or at least to have some element of psychological distance or realistic awareness about authority processes.

An elaboration of the language of psychoanalysis at this point articulates with the institutional approach which has been pursued. It is possible to identify three types of psychological control which relate the person to the institutions of social control; *external*, *superego*, and *ego*

13. Dennis Wrong, "The Oversocialized Conception of Man in Modern Sociology," *American Sociological Review* 26 (April 1961): 182–93.

(or personal control.) These relations reflect the accumulated outcome of socialization, local and societal.

External control or the submission to external authority reflects a minimum of internalization and the minimum of development of personal autonomy. It must therefore be based on the immediate physical or symbolic presence of external authority, and extensive reliance on coercive authority. It reflects the subjective dimension of authority based on domination, and requires a pervasive component of physical coercion or a coercive psychological climate; submission to external authority is in effect the opposite to personal control. In contrast, *superego control*, or conscience control, reflects a concern with moral principle—that is, with collective responsibility and with the means for achieving group goals. Superego control implies that the person recognizes that a narrow, blind pursuit of self-interest is not an effective basis for a moral order. (Group goals can be formulated and expressed in terms of the importance of enlightened self-interest.) But the essential psychological aspect of superego control is that it relies on the availability of particular external agents—parents, teachers, religious leaders, political officials—to reassert and reinforce the relevance of the "higher moral" principles.

If superego control depends on continuous and continued external reinforcement, *ego control*—that is, personal control—has a critical element of self-generation and self-regulation. The antisocial and irrational tendencies of the person are moved to some extent into the sphere of consciousness and therefore become accessible to rational intervention. But there is no need to assert a sharp distinction or inherent opposition between emotional predisposition and ego control; rather, their complex interpenetration must be recognized. Again a wide range of psychological theories converge; personal control and rational behavior are not self-sustained but require emotive interaction and group attachments.

These forms of psychological control relate directly to the changed character of institutional authority and to the long-term shift from authority based on domination to authority incorporating manipulation—or authority based on consent, if one cannot use "manipulation" in a nonpejorative sense. Thus it is obvious that the trends in the social organization of the United States require stronger, more extensive reliance on personal control if effective social control is to be achieved.

It is equally obvious that the strengthening of personal controls has not proceeded at a sufficiently rapid pace to achieve this goal.

Since the social-control perspective rejects the "rational man" conception, it recognizes that even under the optimum social conditions, acceptance of external control would operate in wide areas of social behavior. In the process of socialization, the limits of personal control that is, ego control, are manifested in particular in the person's direct attachment to the nation-state and his sense of nationality. Acceptance of external authority in varying degree is dictated by the reality of the boundaries, both functional and symbolic, of the nation-state.[14] The limited growth of supranational institutions hardly alters the fundamental fact that the nation-state remains the organizing unit of the world community.

The strength of national attachments does not mean that local attachments become extinct; we have emphasized that local attachments become more specialized. Likewise, it is hoped that the growth of a world community perspective does not necessarily require the atrophying of national sentiments but rather a modification of their content and scope. There is no reason to assume that we are dealing with a zero sum game. In fact, it would be more appropriate to assert that the maturation of personal and social control increases a person's capacity to relate himself to more and more encompassing systems of authority.

Ethnicity, religion, regionalism, and the like are the intervening dimensions in a sense of nationality. Harold D. Lasswell's phrase, "world politics and personal insecurity" highlights the immediate interaction of social personality and national identifications. A sense of nationality reflects inner feelings which through socialization become externalized attitudes. In this process, the person, for better or for worse, manifests an acceptance of external authority and even of submission to external authority.

We do not have a body of trend data on the increase or decrease in the strength of national sentiments in the United States for the period since World War I. Social scientists have failed to include questions on this central topic in their sample surveys. It could be that social scientists' highly critical attitudes and indifference to national symbols account for this lack. But it would be in error to infer that the limited

14. Leonard W. Doob, *Patriotism and Nationalism: Their Psychological Foundations* (New Haven: Yale University Press, 1964).

number of trend data reflect an atrophying of national sentiment and patriotism in the United States.

There *has* been a growth of indifference, even of hostility, toward the symbols of nationalism among a very limited part of the population. This includes persons with extensive higher education and with strong oppositional attitudes. The events of Vietnam supplied the justification for the expression of such sentiments. Representatives of this segment are very visible and include persons in the mass media.

On the other hand, there has been a long-term countertrend in the growth of nationalism since 1920. One might even speak of the shift from "old-fashioned" patriotism into a more elaborate sense of national "spirit." The decline of ethnic nationalist sentiments and the incorporation of submerged groups into the social and political structure of the society mean that a larger proportion of the population feel that they are "Americans." For a small portion whose size is difficult to estimate, nationalist attitudes are defensive and stereotypic, a form of reactive nationalism. The nationalist feelings do not articulate with the realities of the position of the United States in the world community. However, for most of the population, World War II transformed or extended the meaning of nationalism. In contrast to the period after World War I, the new nationalism was compatible with extensive international perspectives and interests. The frustrations of the Vietnam War and the impact of domestic and economic tensions began to constrict the "enlightened" nationalism. Likewise, the persistent criticism of the United States in the mass media by oppositionist spokesmen and journalists contributed to the mobilization of defensive and stereotypic nationalism and old-fashioned "patriotism."

On balance, as of 1976, nationalist identifications in the United States remain pervasive and are central in the organization of citizen attitudes. However, we are dealing with a complex and unstable admixture of "enlightened nationalism" and strong components of "reactive patriotism." It is within this nationalistic context that societal socialization takes place and in which the following hypotheses about the consequences of the instrumentalities of the media and legitimate coercion are offered.

It is our general assumption that the mass media over a half-century have become more important in the process of societal socialization and accordingly in influencing specific political and electoral behavior of the citizenry. Again, this is not a predetermined, inevitable, or linear trend. There are built-in limitations and the possibility of a reversal. The increased importance of the mass media reflects fundamental changes in the social organization of an advanced industrial society. In our analysis, in particular, the increased disarticulation between the hierarchical bureaucracies of work and occupation and the structure of residential communities are the preconditions.

We are dealing not only with the traditional arguments about the increased complexity of the division of labor and enlarged magnitude of scale, but also with the result of the growth of the welfare state, which complicates a person's enlightened pursuit of his self-interest in the political arena. The interest groups, voluntary associations, and political institutions reflect the disarticulation between work and communal attachment. As a result, advanced industrial society requires higher levels of personal controls both to link the person to the nation-state and to contribute to the quality of citizen participation.

In this context, our central hypothesis is that the positive contribution of the mass media to institutional integration and effective social control has declined; in fact, there are significant disruptive consequences in the role of the mass media as agencies of societal socialization. Our analysis rests on the following: first, the popular culture content of the mass media, particularly the emphasis on violence, has a long-term effect of social personality which does not strengthen personal controls–and most probably weakens them. Second, while there is no basis for claiming that the mass media significantly depoliticalize the electorate, the public affairs content of the mass media contribute to the weakening of political identification and increased voter volatility. Third, while the mass media are essential for generating political consent for particular parts of the citizenry, they encourage distrust and suspicion rather than a critical sense of realistic political alternatives. Moreover, the socialization which results from exposure to the mass media must be linked to the consequences of the legal and legitimate sanctions, particularly those wrought by the criminal justice system. When these issues are explored subsequently in the next chapter, we will be more concerned with the impact of the coercive sanctions on the "law abiding" citizenry than on the social segments which are designated as criminal.

MASS MEDIA AND PERSUASION

The intellectual history of the study of the mass media needs to be taken into account in assessing their actual consequences on personal and social control. There have been two perspectives in this intellectual history.[15]

The first, which has been associated with the work of Paul F. Lazarsfeld, asserts that social research has refuted popular views, as well as those of journalists and public relations personnel, that the mass media are powerful and pervasive in industrial society. Instead, the mass media have limited, very specific influences which can best be identified by quantitative social research which focuses on the individual person and his response. This perspective led Lazarsfeld and his collaborators to formulate the concept of the "two-step flow" of communications, that is, mass communications have influence only when the contents are accepted by opinion leaders who in turn influence the mass of the public.[16] The research developed to document this perspective was launched in the 1940s and 1950s mainly by means of sample survey techniques. The stream of research convinced only social-science researchers, so that in 1959 Bernard Berelson, a disciple of Paul F. Lazarsfeld, published a statement anticipating the end of communications research because of the limited influence of the mass media.[17] Within a decade there had arisen within this "school" of research a second "look" which sought to correct the downgrading of the consequences of the mass media.

The alternative perspective developed after World War I and is associated with Harold D. Lasswell; it attributed ongoing and more pervasive roles to the mass media. Lasswell emphasized that modern society was dependent on mass communications and that the elite management of the systems of communication had a delimited but decisive consequence on social and political behavior. Harold D. Lasswell analyzed and highlighted the importance of mass communications during a

15. Morris Janowitz, "The Study of Mass Communication," *International Encyclopedia of the Social Sciences* 3 (New York: Macmillan and the Free Press, 1968), 41–53.

16. Elihu Katz and Paul Lazarsfeld, *Personal Influence: The Part Played by the People in the Flow of Mass Communication* (Glencoe, Ill.: Free Press, 1955); Joseph T. Klapper, *The Effects of Mass Communication* (New York, Free Press of Glencoe, 1960).

17. Bernard Berelson, "The State of Communication Research," *Public Opinion Quarterly* 23 (1959): 1–7.

crisis.[18] Lasswell was aware of the powerful resistances to communication appeals and the individual's capacity to select the contents of the mass media on the basis of one's predispositions. However, his outlook concentrated on the systemic consequence of the mass media and their long-term influence rather than on specific responses of individual persons. He implied that the mass media had influence both through opinion leaders—the two-step flow—and directly on mass audiences.

Lasswell's seminal writings have been applied continuously since and have been accompanied by increasingly sophisticated research clarifying the strategic role of mass communications. For example, in the 1930s, a comprehensive series of studies on the importance of the movies in molding youth behavior were completed.[19] During World War II, massive research observed the narrower limits of international political propaganda when directed against totalitarian states, as compared with the settings of World War I.[20] After 1945, extensive research was conducted on the effect of television. That research which emphasized the marginal influence of television has been displaced by a growing body of findings which clarified the strategic role of this medium. In short, the perspective originally formulated by Harold D. Lasswell has come to be accepted and to have central importance for our objective of exploring the mass media as instrumentalities of societal socialization.

As a result, the study of the mass media has been freed from methodological constraints. Much of the Lazarsfeld approach is a reflection of his empirical strategy, namely, the exclusive use of sample surveys. Carl I. Hovland has demonstrated that investigators who use experiments—laboratory or real life—are more likely to be impressed with the influence of the mass media; some of the most trenchant experimental work has been done on the effect of television on children.[21] On the other hand, many survey specialists have collected data which tend to emphasize the limited effectiveness of the mass media for pro-

18. Harold D. Lasswell, *Propaganda Technique in the World War* (New York: Knopf, 1927).

19. For overall presentation of findings, see W. W. Charters, *Motion Pictures and Youth* (New York: Macmillan, 1933); see especially, for detailed case-study analysis, Herbert Blumer and Phillip M. Hauser, *Movies, Delinquency and Crime* (New York: Macmillan, 1933).

20. William E. Daugherty, *A Psychological Warfare Casebook* (Baltimore: The Johns Hopkins University Press, 1958).

21. Carl I. Hovland, "Results from Studies of Attitude Change," *The American Psychologist* 14 (January 1959): 8–17.

ducing specific changes in attitudes and behavior. The survey approach deals with a person's response to specific messages or campaigns rather than the cumulative effect and fails to deal with the role of the mass media in "defining the situation" and posing alternatives.[22] In contrast, the results of content-analysis studies, especially those which cover long periods, tend to generate inferences which highlight the strategic influence of the mass media. These methodological issues can be handled by the utilization of multiple techniques and by careful comparison of the results of different methodologies. Moreover, the sophistication of survey research has increased, especially by the use of more refined statistical procedures than were applied by the Lazarsfeld group, so that survey research since 1965 has produced results which support the Lasswell perspective.

Moreover, the systemic investigation of the influence of the mass media is a very complex task because of the inescapable reality that the contents of the mass media both influence the processes of sociopolitical change in society and at the same time reflect the organization and values of society.[23] In the language of social research, the mass media are both independent and dependent variables. Contradictory conclusions—analytic and empirical—about the influence of the mass media in part reflect relative emphasis on either assumption.

The Gemeinschaft-Gesellschaft perspective has been extensively used as a major theoretical explanation of the effect of the mass media. In this view, the Gemeinschaft setting does not depend on mass communications and is relatively immune to them. But with the development of a more complex division of labor, the person finds himself more and more "individuated" and deprived of traditional guideposts. He is more exposed to and dependent on the contents of the mass media. The conditions of Gesellschaft create a fragmented social reality in which the communications processes and especially the mass media have increasing influence. This perspective has been applied vigorously to the analysis of the media and society, but not with compelling results.[24] The standard critiques of the Gemeinschaft-Gesellschaft model

22. M. McCombs and D. Shaw, "The Agenda-Setting Function of Mass Media," *Public Opinion Quarterly* 36 (1972): 176–87.

23. W. I. Thomas and Florian Znaniecki, "The Wider Community and the Role of the Press," in *The Polish Peasant in Europe and America*, 4 (Boston: Badger Press, 1920), pp. 241–71.

24. M. Defleur and S. Ball-Rokeach, *Theories of Mass Communication*, 3d ed. (New York: David McKay, 1975).

as presented in chapter 2 have undermined its relevance. Moreover, empirical research which seeks to link interpersonal communications to mass communication is hardly accommodated by this frame of reference. The strength of Gemeinschaft-Gesellschaft orientation is that it expresses a concern with a societal level analysis and thereby avoids the mechanical strategy of statistically aggregating personal responses as a means of assessing the influence of the media.

Instead, we shall apply our systemic analysis of the institutional structures to the mass media. An urban and industrial society—and in turn an advanced industrial society—supplies the institutional basis of the mass media, technological, economic, and organizational. By means of press, radio, TV, films, books, magazines, etc., small specialized groups are able to create and disseminate symbolic content to a large, heterogeneous, and widely dispersed audience. But at the same time the institutions of the mass media are indispensable mechanisms for overcoming the disarticulation of an advanced industrial society.[25] Without the mass media, an industrial society is "unthinkable." In this view, the mass media function as devices for (*a*) the surveillance of the environment, (*b*) the posing of personal, social and political alternatives—that is, defining the situation, and (*c*) the inculcation of standards of behavior—that is elements of morality and relations to authority—and the creation of a basis for citizen participation essential for democratic decision making.[26]

25. There have been vast historical studies, reports, biographies, autobiographies, and general accounts of journalism and the mass media. These materials are carefully annotated in three bibliographies: Harold D. Lasswell, Ralph D. Casey, and Bruce Lannes Smith, *Propaganda and Promotional Activities: An Annotated Bibliography* (Minneapolis: University of Minnesota Press, 1935); Bruce Lannes Smith, Harold D. Lasswell, and Ralph D. Casey, *Propaganda, Communication and Public Opinion: A Comprehensive Reference Guide* (Princeton: Princeton University Press, 1946); Bruce Lannes Smith and Chitra Smith, *International Communications and Political Opinion: A Guide to the Literature* (Princeton: Princeton University Press, 1956). More recent literature is covered in Donald A. Hansen and J. Herschel Parsons, *Mass Communications: A Research Bibliography* (Santa Barbara: Glendessary Press, 1968).

26. Charles R. Wright, *Mass Communications: A Sociological Perspective* (New York: Random, 1959); Harold D. Lasswell, "The Structure and Function of Communications in Society," in *The Communication of Ideas*, ed. Lyman Bryson (New York: Harper, 1948), pp. 37–52; Caren Siune and F. Gerald Kline, "Communications, Mass Political Behavior, and Mass Society," in *Political Communication Issues and Strategies for Research*, ed. Steven H. Chaffee (Beverly Hills: Sage Publications, 1975), pp. 65–84; Paul M. Hirsch, "Occupational, Organizational and Institutional Models of Mass Media Research: Towards an Integrated Framework," in *Strategies for Mass Communication Research*, ed. Paul M. Hirsch, P. Miller and F. Gerald Kline (Beverly Hills: Sage Publication, 1977), pp. 3–36.

The management of the mass media rests in the hands of various elite groups, and is subject to the pressures and conflicts between elite groups. By their nature, the mass media enable select elite and counterelite groups to appeal to large and "massive audiences." The political goals of these elite groups—and the professionals who actually operate the mass media—and the standards of performance they use are "real" independent variables in analyzing the influence of the mass media. The content which is excluded is as important as that which is emphasized.

There is a direct analogy between the analysis of the mass media and the classic essay by John Dewey criticizing the stimulus-response arc.[27] The mass media produce a continuous flow of communications, and the audience can be thought of as responding to this continuous flow. But a broader perspective is essential. The elites and the professional mass media experts are in effect being influenced by their audiences and audiences' responses. Rather than a stimulus-response arc, it is truly an interacting situation in which the stimulus itself is molded by the antecedent audience response and the larger societal context. (Moreover, the managers of the mass media are not apart from the process but are in fact influenced by their own communication; the person is both the subject and object of communication.)[28] There is a profound imbalance in influence and power—the initiative and power of the elites and the professional specialists overwhelmingly outweigh the contributions of the audience. However, in theory, under a parliamentary system, there are powerful self-correcting mechanisms because of the competition and diversity of content in the mass media. Competition in the mass media, within particular media, and among media, plus the notion that the mass media serve as a "common carrier" of diverse content and viewpoints, have persisted and been enhanced. Despite the growth of interlocking corporate controls, the number of distinct outlets still remains substantial. Thus, the basic question is to describe the balance between uniformity and diversity in the contents of the mass media.

27. John Dewey, "The Reflex Arc Concept in Psychology," *Psychological Review* 3 (July 1896): 357–70; see also Neil Coughlan, *Young John Dewey: An Essay in American Intellectual History* (Chicago: University of Chicago Press, 1975), chap. 8, for a discussion of the intellectual history and context of this formulation.

28. Harold D. Lasswell, "The Person: Subject and Object of Propaganda," *Annals* 179 (May 1935): 187–93.

As a result, content analysis in addition to surveys of audience enrich the analysis of the role of the media in social control.[29] Both short-term and long-term trends in the contents of the mass media supply indicators of trends in the normative content of the society. Over the long run, there is a interactive adjustment in the contents of the mass media to persistent and emergent tastes and predispositions. At the same time, sensitive analysis of the contents of the mass media highlights the activities of interest groups and thereby offers crude but revealing indications of the demands of sociopolitical groupings.[30]

Content analysis as a research tool and procedure has not achieved the same institutionalization and support that has been accorded to survey research. However, an accumulation of a body of separate studies permits a synthesis of some of the main trends in the contents of the mass media. The relevance of content analysis studies has grown in the light of the increased recognition of the limitations and difficulties associated with sample survey research. After 1965 efforts were made to place content on a time series basis for the first time.[31] The results are

29. The reassessment of the role of survey research involves a range of issues from technical considerations to broad moral and intellectual arguments. (1) Technical difficulties center on the increased costs and problems in the field procedures, including sharply increased field costs, local ordinances against survey operations, denial of permission to enter large apartment buildings, increased suspicion of householders, use of surveys for merchandising purposes, noncompliance with field instructions by interviewers, and interviewers' fear of completing particular assignments that they believe are risky and dangerous. All serve to complicate the execution of survey. (2) The issue of the rights of respondents is closely linked to the problems of field procedures. While survey research has an adequate record, certainly when compared to the major invaders of privacy such as business credit card companies and certain government investigating agencies, there have been enough abuses in survey practices to offend public sensibilities. (3) A growing intellectual criticism of the survey research strategy is that it does not adequately chart the dynamics of the public opinion process and the structure of the political and social movements that fashion industrial society. This is an old criticism that was emphasized by sociologists in the 1920s and 1930s, for example by Herbert Blumer in the concept "collective behavior." It has been argued that the extensive, and at times mechanical, reliance on surveys failed to chart and understand the explosive social and political movements of the 1960s. The survey approach, in this view, reflects the "state of mind" at a given moment rather than operating as a mode of analyzing popular expectations, demands for change, and the conditions under which new institutions are built.

30. Morris Janowitz, "Content Analysis and the Study of Sociopolitical Change," *Journal of Communication* 26 (1976): 10–21.

31. The violence content of television has been charted by continuing content analysis since 1967; George Gerbner and Larry Gross, "Violence Profile No. 6: Trends in Network Television Drama and Viewer Conceptions of Social Reality, 1967–1973," Annenberg School of Communications, December 1974; George Gerb-

already useful but the full significance of these enterprises will be apparent only after one or two decades.

The balance between uniformity and diversity of content is grounded in the technological base of the mass media. The end product is that of a massive national audience which attends to highly standardized content; at the same time the ordered social segments of an advanced industrial society have access to an almost bewildering range of specialized and diverse media content.[32] The uniformity of content is a result of the mechanics of television which enables three national networks to fashion the massive exposure of the U.S. audience to night television.[33] On the other hand, the diversity (and dissenting content) is the

ner and Larry Gross, "Violence Profile No. 7: A Technical Report," Annenberg School of Communication, 1976; George Gerbner and Larry Gross, "Living With Television: The Violence Profile," *Journal of Communications* 26 (1976): 172–99; John Naisbitt, *The Trend Report: A Quarterly Forecast and Evaluation of Developments in the United States* (Washington: Center for Policy Process, 1976).

32. Paul M. Hirsch, "Television as a National Medium: Its Cultural and Political Role in American Society," in *Handbook of Urban Life*, ed. David Street (San Francisco: Jossey Bass, 1978).

33. Students of societal change are especially concerned with tracing the effect of successive developments of technology. A good case can be made that with the shift from industrial to advanced industrial society, the size and complexity of the technological base have rapidly increased, and as a result the influence of particular technological developments has become both more rapid and more extensive. Military technology is a pointed example; with the introduction of nuclear weapons it can be argued that military strategy and societal change have been vastly increased in tempo, scope, and consequences. The introduction of television, it appears, since it is the most "powerful" of the mass media, has been the most extensive in its consequences. Of particular importance is the effect of television on the political process. But there is also good reason to resist such "linear thinking," especially about the mass media. However, a broader frame of reference calls into question an evolutionary conclusion. It may well be that successive developments have only a marginal influence; or at least there is no reason to accept the conclusion of increasing consequence. The introduction of movable type to supplant manuscript writing can be viewed as the important single development in the technological development of the mass media. This invention fundamentally altered the ability of man to disseminate information. It made possible broadening a sense of history in the population and supplied the communication basis for the modern nationalism which fundamentally transformed Western Europe and, in turn, the world community.

Second, the introduction of the rotary press, the next crucial threshold, is an important development but one of less importance. Third, radio, and fourth, television, plus fifth, the technological improvement of television via satellite, served to intensify trends, although television had a more powerful effect than the rotary press or radio or satellite transmission. Cable television will have important sociopolitical consequences but it will hardly rival those of movable type. There appears little reason for accepting the "culture shock" notion that technology must, of necessity, intensify and make more rapid—and more disruptive—the process of societal change.

result of extensive specialization of the other channels of the mass media, namely, those which operate in radio and print.

The simple facts of mass media consumption are obvious but remain astounding. It has been estimated, as of 1976, that 40% of the leisure time of the U.S. adult population is spent in exposure to the mass media, both broadcast and print. Television is the centerpiece, and adults on the average view television between two and three hours per day; 95% of U.S. homes have television. Much television exposure is accompanied by other activities. However, expenditure for television sets is taken for granted even by families supported by general assistance welfare payments. For old-age pensioners, television is defined as essential. There is no excluded social segment for television. Specifically, in total, the three major networks cover approximately 95% of the "prime time" television consumption.

In varying degrees the other mass media supply diversified and specialized content. Radio is predominately local and diversified as to audience and content. The press is midway, with considerable variation. Local newspapers reflect territorial diversification. Magazines and books contribute extensively to the variation in media content. Magazines, in particular, are specialized by occupation and interest grouping.

In terms of time, television is the dominant medium. It is compelling in its attractiveness and instant reality. Long-term trend data underscore the expansion of the television audience, and the capacity of the citizenry to consume mass media at the expense of other pastimes. National surveys covering the period from 1960 to 1974 report the person's favorite pastime. From zero in 1938 the television figure rose to 46% of the population in 1974. Television expanded its audience at the expense of reading, which dropped from 21% to 14%, of movies, from 19% to 9%; and of radio, from 9% to 5%. Even dancing suffered; from 9% to 5%. Only playing cards held its own. There were limited increases in staying home with family and visiting with friends, pastimes which can be combined with television viewing. The ability of television to claim leisure time, and in fact to increase its hold on mass audiences, has been precisely documented by the trend survey conducted since 1961 by the Roper Organization.[34] The question posed was simple and direct: "On an average day, about how many hours do you personally spend watching TV? The results indicate that the

34. Annual Reports by the Roper Organization.

trend in media exposure has been from two hours and seventeen minutes in 1961 to three hours and two minutes by 1974. While better educated persons spend less time than less educated, the college educated and upper economic levels have demonstrated a parallel upward trend in exposure as follows: One hour and forty-eight minutes in 1961 to two hours and twenty-three minutes in 1974.

Trends in Media Content

A considerably larger portion of the contents of the mass media is designed to entertain than to inform. More content distracts and diverts attention and less stimulates consideration of the social, economic, and political problems of the period. In other words, there is an extensive difference between the contents of the mass media and the contents of human existence—daily existence and "historical" existence. But the distinction between entertainment and information content is neither definitive nor necessarily appropriate. The entertainment content presents a flow of materials which fashion normative standards and which implant a picture of social reality. Instead our propositions about the content of the mass media deal with "popular culture," on the one hand, or with "public affairs," on the other. As a first step, if one leaves aside the limited but significant core of high culture, it is possible to characterize the long-term trends in popular culture content. For 1920 to 1976, obviously we are encompassing the changing technological spectrum from the dominance of print—in the case of popular culture, mass magazines to radio and movies and in turn to television.

Two observations about trends in popular culture emerge. First, Leo Lowenthal's observation of the shift in popular culture from "idols" of production to "idols" of consumption can be extended.[35] The idols in the mass media up until 1924 were men and women of economic, industrial, and technological achievement. They created goods and machinery. The change in emphasis came rapidly and decisively by the end of the 1920s. The development of an advanced industrialism, in the context of a consumer-oriented society, meant that the idols of consumption became more dominant and more central. There is, of course, no reason to assume that this was an inevitable process or "universal" outcome of industrialism. It is doubtful whether this shift in

35. Leo Lowenthal, "Biographies in Popular Magazines," in *Radio Research, 1942–1943*, ed. Paul F. Lazarsfeld and Frank Stanton (New York: Duell, Sloan and Pearce, 1944).

mass media content and underlying values has, for example, been as extensive in Japan as in the United States.

However, the Lowenthal observation can be extended for the period since the middle of the 1960s. In essence, the shift from mass media themes of production to consumption has been augmented by a third phase, namely, an emphasis on the details involved in the management of interpersonal relations. The economic tensions associated with stagflagtion have not led popular culture to reemphasize production. Themes of consumption still exceeded those of production; the concern is to include excluded groups in the culture of consumption. The new element deals with the strategies human beings use to handle the personal and emotional problems which are rooted in religion, ethnicity, geography, and family status. Occupation is at most a background dimension of tangential significance.

The popular culture content has come to focus on the moral problems of how one behaves in face-to-face situations as the result of the "big" and "little" issues of contemporary society, the appropriate interactions with close acquaintenances or with strangers. If the themes of production concentrated on heroes and men and women of importance and prominence, the shift to consumption broadened the range of idols to include "ordinary" people. The concern with the management of interpersonal behavior means also that ordinary people become the idols and become more important. Progressively, the range of "encounters" has been broadened to include race relations, mental health, and familial arrangements. The presentation of interpersonal management involves moral assumptions and moral implications. Superficially, the morality is relative; no overriding norms guide a person with certainty. The presentations offer a morality which borders on existential morality—the moral need to confront and master the immediate reality. The content trends, as documented by various empirical studies, have shifted the locus of responsibility of behavior and especially of defects in behavior from the individual person to the "social environment."[36]

The ethical guidelines are those which permit the "ordinary" person to demonstrate heroic qualities. Each person is a potential hero to the extent that he presses forward to determine and to display publicly his

36. Arnold S. Linsky, "Theories of Behavior and the Image of the Alcoholic in Popular Magazines," *Public Opinion Quarterly* 34 (1970–1971): 573–81; Charles Y. Glock, "Images of Man and Public Opinion," *Public Opinion Quarterly* 28 (1964): 539–46.

emotions and his enduring personal qualities. The externalization of emotions must be achieved and the benefits will justify the costs to the person, his group, and the larger society. This is a most abbreviated version of psychoanalytical thinking. Psychoanalytic thinking asserts that externalization is only a preliminary, partial, and tentative step in the development of personal control; maturity depends on the person's coming to terms with his strength and weakness.

The trends in the "idols" of popular culture are also linked to the relative emphasis on optimism and pessimism in the mass media. At this point we are dealing with both popular culture and public affairs content. One very interesting study on the contents of religious sermons has emphasized the growth of a pessimistic outlook—hardly a startling finding.[37] When incorporated with the content themes in public affairs, the inclination toward pessimism is pronounced. The public affairs contents, especially since 1945, have given strong emphasis to the possibility of nuclear war—and subsequently to nuclear "proliferation" and to the inability to control nuclear terrorism. Likewise, human population and world food themes contributed to the pessimistic outlook.

The themes of the management of interpersonal relations are part of this trend; in fact, one can argue that they constitute a denial or escapism from the unrelenting pressure of pessimistic realism. As Lester Asheim has noted, when serious novels are rewritten for mass audiences the unhappy ending gives way to an indeterminate ending.[38] This is the thematic strategy of the "new soap" operas which have moved from the morning for the housewife audience to the evening prime time for the adult audience. In the popular presentation of the ironies of interracial marriage, divorced status, or unconventional sexual arrangements, there are no outcomes but a series of ongoing dilemmas. The humanistic "coda" in the dramatization of interpersonal relations is a startling admixture of humor and tragedy—indicating the extent to which popular culture contributes to the trivialization of the prophetic aspect of human existence. No doubt the mass media phase of extensive stress on interpersonal "problems" will give way to new themes or rather become modulated. The new directions may have already made themselves apparent, but they unfortunately escape me.

37. Thomas Hamilton, "Social Optimism and Pessimism in American Protestantism," *Public Opinion Quarterly* 6 (1942): 280–83.

38. Lester Asheim, "From Book to Film," in *Public Opinion and Communication*, ed. Bernard Berelson and Morris Janowitz (Glencoe, Ill.: Free Press, 1950), 299–306.

The second trend in popular culture content is the rise and persistence of violent themes. The expansion of the mass media—movies and television in particular, as well as the comic books—increased vastly the availability of violent content. The amount of "symbolic" violence before 1920 was of a more limited order of magnitude and it appears less realistic and less immediate in content. Description of violence in books and newspapers, and even fairy tales was, on a cumulative basis, at best a fraction of the actual exposure of youngsters in 1976.

Moreover, the striking aspect, from the point of view of social control, is that parental, civic, and educational groups have extensively agitated to reduce the violence in the mass media. The institutional arrangements which preclude censorship and the powerful weight given to presumed consumer preferences have prevented this agitation from having much effect. The exception has been that pressure-group activity on comic books has reduced their violent content.

The trends in the mass media in thematic content dealing with violence cannot be accounted for in terms of the realities of modern society. Violent themes in the mass media are to be found primarily in the extensive popular culture content and not in the public affairs content. While one expects the public affairs content to reflect sociopolitical reality and thereby present reportage about actual violence, the emphasis on violence in the popular culture is a "market" decision by media specialists and media elites. The pervasive violence in the mass media is not the result of coverage of public affairs. During the Vietnam War, television coverage of the battlefield was extensive and greatly increased the violence content on the public affairs portion of the mass media. But since 1972 this topic has disappeared. Coverage of crime including the seizing of hostages and local natural disaster serves an equivalent "war" news, but the bulk of the violence is not in the public affairs coverage but in the popular culture and entertainment content.

Television epitomizes the extensive focus on violence in the mass media, although movies are by no means far behind. If the "average" adult attends to two to three hours of television daily, it is my estimate that as much as one-half of the context is violence-oriented. For youngsters the exposure to television and to violence is correspondingly greater. Starting in 1967, George Gerbner and his associates have prepared a detailed and continuous audit of violence in television.[39] Cov-

39. George Gerbner and Larry Gross, "Living With Television: The Violence Profile," *Journal of Communication* 26 (1976): 173–99; "Television World of

ering the period 1967 to 1973, they concluded that the "thematic structure of the world of television drama has not changed much." This was a period of concentrated agitation against the saturation of television with violence. These content analysts speak of "action programs which are crime, western, and miscellaneous action-adventure drama. They are almost synonymous with violent programming." These data indicated that nearly half of general and two-thirds of cartoon programming consists of "action programs." While the latter proportion declined for the period under investigation, the share of crime shows "nearly tripled," even in cartoons. Moreover, the "world" of television drama had become more "domestic, present-time and urban oriented." It appears that the limited effort to decrease the amount of violence content by the major networks has the result of shifting the setting from "exotic, historical and distant" to the more immediate.

It is no simple matter to characterize the normative context of violence in the mass media. The volume and extensive diversity dominate and obscure the details of the moral message presented. Commentators and critics have emphasized the pronounced tendency to present violent themes without reference to any moral code. Specifically, in the area of crime and law enforcement, the difference between the criminals and the police in motivation and tactics has been eroded in the name of realism. Even in the absence of careful and reliable content analysis studies, it does appear that the broadcast media have increasingly presented violent behavior, especially criminal violence, with less and less concern with normative evaluations and implications.

However, it may well be that another trend in the presentation of violence may be of more importance in terms of personal and social control. The thrust, has been to present and characterize violence and violent behavior as diffuse, pervasive, and undifferentiated from other types of social behavior. (There is an analogy with the presentation of the management of interpersonal relations, where there is a crude admixture of humor and tragedy almost at random and in an unpredictable fashion.) In part, we are dealing with the changed character of violence. For example, it has been pointed out that the character of warfare after 1945 has undergone an important change.[40] Classic na-

Violence," in *Mass Media and Violence*, ed. D. L. Lange, Robert K. Baker, and Sandra J. Ball (Washington: GPO, 1967), pp. 341–62.

40. Klaus Knorr, *The Power and Wealth: The Political Economy of International Power* (New York: Basic Books, 1973).

tional wars had an episodic nature; periods of violence were followed by periods of peace. There were boundaries to the scope and participants in the military operations. Progressively, the boundaries have become diffuse, and warfare or the threat of warfare has become an ongoing process in which violence and diplomatic persuasion are closely and simultaneously intertwined. It would be unreal if the mass media did not devote considerable attention to the actual patterns of violence in the real world. However, the diffuse, unpredictable, and unbounded character of violence, and its lack of differentiation from other forms of behavior, have become the essential nature of violence in the popular culture of the mass media.

The third trend in content analysis deals with the public affairs presentation in the mass media. The treatment of public affairs is a revealing indicator of modern society. This view was neatly formulated by Walter Lippmann, "on the whole, the quality of the news about modern society is an index of its social organization."[41] The almost endless array of topics and treatments of public affairs presented in mass media can be handled for our purposes by the overarching hypothesis that during the period under study there has been a shift in emphasis in the format for presenting public affairs from the "gatekeeper" style to that of the advocate journalist.[42] The gatekeeper format emphasizes the search for objectivity and the sharp separation of reporting fact from disseminating opinion, commentary, and editorials. Coverage of the real world required the journalist to select the important from the mass of detailed information. Therefore the notion of the journalist as gatekeeper rested on his ability to detect, emphasize, and disseminate that which was important as news, opinion, and human interest.

In contrast, the advocate journalist seeks to replace the search for objectivity with a conception of the journalist as critic and interpreter. In this view, the task of the journalist is to present the viewpoints and interest of competing groups, especially those of excluded and underprivileged groups. The role of the journalist is to ensure that all perspectives are adequately represented in the media, for the resolution of

41. Walter Lippmann, *Public Opinion* (New York: Macmillan, 1922), p. 274.

42. Morris Janowitz, "The Journalistic Profession and the Mass Media," in *Culture and Its Creators: Essays in Honor of Edward Shils*, ed. Joseph Ben-David and Terry N. Clark (Chicago: University of Chicago Press, 1977), pp. 72–96. See also Barbara Philips, "The Artists of Everyday Life," Ph.D. dissertation, University of Syracuse, 1975.

social conflict depends on effective representation of alternative definitions of reality. The journalist must "participate" in the advocacy process.

The gatekeeper model was based on a particular conception of professionalism. From the turn of the century, and especially after 1920, efforts were directed to fashioning journalism into a field similar to medicine, where the journalist would develop his technical expertise and also create a sense of professional responsibility. The journalist sought to apply the canons of the scientific method in order to increase his objectivity and enhance his effective performance. Through the application of intellectually based techniques, objective and valid results could be obtained. Those who pressed for the gatekeeper model were aware of the difficulties and inherent limitations, but the ideals supplied guidelines in their view.

In the middle of the 1960s, this gatekeeper model of journalist was called into question. Sociopolitical tensions led to a desire among some journalists for a more activist role. They came to believe that meaningful objectivity was impossible. One sociological investigator sympathetic to this viewpoint drew the conclusion from her field research into the practice of journalists that objectivity was a "strategic ritual" by news personnel to defend themselves from the "risks of their trade" and from "critical onslaught."[43] The model of the advocate journalist was the lawyer, in particular, the adversary lawyer.

The crusading journalist has, of course, a long history in U.S. journalism, but the main trend until the emergence of advocacy journalism was toward professional gatekeeper–and the result was the decline of "yellow journalism."[44] The intellectual and conceptual preparation for advocacy journalism was embodied in the work of the Commission on the Freedom of the Press, the so-called Hutchins report (after Robert M. Hutchins, one-time university president and occasional newspaper columnist.)[45] In its general report, dated 10 December 1946, it deemphasized the "factual" and the intelligence aspects of public affairs reporting and stressed the interpretative role of the press. Whether it

43. Gay Tuchman, "Objectivity as a Strategic Ritual: An Examination of Newsmen's Notions of Objectivity," *American Journal of Sociology* 77 (January 1972): 660–79.

44. Alfred McClung Lee, *The Daily Newspaper in America: The Evolution of a Social Instrument* (New York: Macmillan, 1947).

45. Commission on Freedom of the Press, *A Free and Responsible Press* (Chicago: University of Chicago Press, 1947).

intended to or not, it moved in the direction strengthening and justifying an expansion of the advocate role.

If the Commission of the Freedom of the Press gave unanticipated legitimacy to the advocate position, the findings and recommendations of the Kerner Commission, established to investigate the causes of the race riots of the 1960s, gave explicit support to the trend.[46] The Kerner Commission criticized the media for failing to cover adequately the plight of minorities and for their ineffective editorial support for necessary social and political change. The recommendations of the Kerner Commission included the employment of additional minority-group members in the mass media, in order to guarantee that the minority point of view would be adequately represented. These recommendations epitomized the advocate orientation. The critics of this aspect of advocacy journalism feel that reporting on the state of minority groups can be done through an effective gatekeeper outlook concerned with objectivity; to hold that only minority-group members can perform that function is to distort reality and to politicize excessively recruitment and performance in the profession. The recruitment of new journalists who were educated on the agitated campuses of the 1960s reinforced the trend in journalism toward advocacy reporting. Journalists had traditionally been more left of center than the citizenry at large; and this trend was strengthened in 1965 to 1975. The trend was much more pronounced in television, where the traditions and standards of gatekeeper journalism were the least developed and where the personalized style of broadcasting contributed to an advocate outlook.

John Johnstone's sample survey of over 1,300 journalists interviewed in 1971 has presented an overview of the concentration of gatekeeper versus advocate self-conceptions among journalists.[47] He used the more loaded terms "neutral versus participant" as the equivalent of the "gatekeeper versus the advocate." Of his sample, 8.5% were predominately participants in outlook, and 21.4% moderately participant. In addition, 35.4% held balanced views, 25.1% were moderately neutral, and 9.7% were predominately neutral. While these findings indicate that only a limited minority were polarized at each end of the continuum, more than 60% accept some aspect of the advocacy journalism. The result

46. U.S. National Advisory Commission on Civil Disorders, *Report* (Washington: GPO, 1968).

47. John Johnstone et al., *The News People: A Sociological Portrait of American Journalists and Their Work* (Urbana: University of Illinois Press, 1976), chap. 7.

has been an extensive shift in the standards and style of public affairs presentation, especially in the important and pervasive television news broadcast, where the distinction between news and comment has been in effect eliminated.

The advocate journalist has come to see himself in a variety of active roles. He sees himself justified in publishing confidential governmental communications or as the arranger of news events to dramatize an injustice.

The emergence of the advocate model in part represents a response to specific practices of political leaders. Political leaders have been more active in seeking to fashion "the news" through either subtle or more outright managements of information. In particular, those responsible for decision making in the Vietnam conflict at times engaged in such practices. In turn, mass media staff members came to believe that it was their obligation to "expose" relentlessly such practices and to inform the electorate of alternative information and opposing points of view.

Advocate or adversary journalism expanded extensively during the 1960s. It was built on the tradition of muckraking and investigative journalism, but represented a much stronger emphasis on commentary and an explicit policy position. Like many innovations initially it spread rapidly and was followed by a leveling off; there was even some retrenchment after a number of years. But the transformation it has wrought is more than marginal; it has presented a deep shift in style and format in the mass media. There is no need to exaggerate the accomplishments of the gatekeeper model; we are not dealing with the passing of the "golden age" of journalism. However, the gatekeeper format did after World War I contribute substantially to the decline of yellow journalism.

The fusion of reporting and comment of the advocate journalist has been called the "Europeanization" of the U.S. press, and the contents of the mass media have as a result become more argumentative, contentious, but not necessarily more penetrating or more revealing. With the background of these three trends in the contents of the mass media, it becomes more feasible to assess the influence of the mass media on social personality and social control. While a variety of research data are available, systemic inferences and some reasoned speculation are involved.

Audience Exposure and Popular Distrust

In analytic terms, the capacity of the mass media to mold attitudes and behavior is the result of both immediate or short-term effects and of long-term consequences. We are dealing with the accumulation of specific consequences which are manifestly discernible and long-term consequences which at any given moment are barely perceptible. The mass media have both an indirect effect through opinion leaders—national, metropolitan, and local—and a more direct effect on the person.

On the first issue, the research of Hadley Cantril on the Columbia Broadcasting Corporation's dramatic presentation on radio in 1939 of Orson Wells's "Invasion from Mars" documented the extreme behavior which specific mass media messages can produce under conditions of short-term panic.[48] Persons unable to check the authenticity of the Orson Wells program fled from their homes in the New York City area to the outlying areas of northern New Jersey in considerable numbers. By contrast, only from fifty individual studies, to be described below, could the gradual impact of televised violence on children and youngsters be discerned, and in this case mainly by inference. From the point of view of social control, it is these long-term consequences which are central.

Our underlying hypothesis is that the major trends in the mass media have not contributed to the growth of those personal controls required for more effective social control in advanced industrial society. More specifically, rather than strengthening those ego controls which contribute to realistic self-interest and stable group attachments required for effective political participation, the long-term effect has been to heighten projective (and accordingly suspicious) personality predispositions and defensive group affiliations. The most adequate research data center on the second content trend, of sustained concern with violent themes, rather than on the first theme, of mass consumption and interpersonal management, or the third one, the rise of advocacy in the presentation of public affairs. But it is the confluence of the three elements that is the essential component in accounting for the mass media contribution to the attenuation of social control.

First, popular culture content, the content dealing with both interpersonal relations and with mass consumption, is augmented by exten-

48. Hadley Cantril, *Invasion from Mars: A Study in the Psychology of Panic* (Princeton: Princeton University Press, 1940).

sive time and space devoted to mass advertising. By and large the audience views the mass advertisements as blending in with the popular culture portion. Raymond A. Bauer and Stephen S. Greyser have summarized the available survey research on attitudes toward advertisements.[49] The audience take advertisements for granted—indeed, they are a positive attraction. The overwhelming, uniform finding is the favorable attitude toward mass advertisements dating from the 1920s when such studies were first executed. Over time there has been no discernible trend. In 1964–1965 considerable debate began about truth in advertising, which led to various legislative and administrative steps. But there is no evidence of any basic change in attitudes toward institutionalized advertising. In fact, the interest of better educated persons in "artistic" advertisements in the "better" magazine has increased and reflects the strong appetite for the symbolic content of consumerism.

As indicated above, the notion of "consumerism" involves the increased use and reliance on material goods without a corresponding increase in sense of satisfaction; consumerism implies a growth of dissatisfaction. In the absence of effective personal and social control, increased material consumption creates only demands for more indulgence. Consumerism implies that the pursuit of material goods in the absence of appropriate moral standards is a destructive act, one with implicit and elicit aggressive overtones. This characteristic is manifested by the compulsive rather than satisfying overtones in the acquiring and utilizing and consumption of material objects.

In chapter 5, trend data on self-conceptions of one's economic well-being were presented. These data demonstrated that the rise in standard of living has not produced a corresponding increase in personal satisfaction, and therefore can be taken as evidence of the persistence and, in fact, growth of consumerism. Such an interpretation rests in part on the argument of relative deprivation, that is, one's feeling of being deprived as a result of comparison of oneself with the position of other persons.[50] The social definition of appropriate consumption and response to mass consumption reflect standards developed by mass advertising, as well as by the "idol" of consumption in popular culture.

49. Raymond A. Bauer and Stephen S. Greyser, *Advertising in America: The Consumer View* (Cambridge: Harvard University Press, 1968), passim; see also Leo Bogart, *Strategy in Advertising* (New York: Harcourt, Brace and World, 1967).

50. R. G. Runciman, *Relative Deprivation and Social Justice* (Berkeley: University of California Press, 1966).

At this point it is necessary to distinguish between the economics of advertising and the socialization that results from exposure to advertising and the mass media.[51] Economic analysis of advertising expenditures are hardly clear-cut and often indicate a low return. However, no single enterprise can afford unilaterally to reduce advertising expenditures. Moreover, the prospect that a particular campaign may produce "striking" results—as particular ones continually do—means that the gambling element is very powerful in advertising decisions. Thus there is an advertising culture which has its own internal dynamics and results in an expansion of advertising budgets and efforts.

In terms of social control, the response to mass advertisements—as well as the consumption content of popular culture—is not to be judged by the sales effectiveness of particular advertisements or campaigns but by the long-term consequences on attitudes and social personality. The most suggestive evidence is contained in the endless series of commercially sponsored research called "motivation research." Social scientists cannot dismiss these findings, although very few of them enter the published literature and most fail to meet minimum research standards. In addition, some of the intensive probing in this type of research may border on violation of privacy.

Such advertising research underlines that an important component of consumer decisions is based on the gratification of primitive impulses—on irrational motivation, if you will—rather than on rational economic choice.[52] Moreover, such research supplies guidelines for mass advertising designed to appeal to the nonrational aspects of social personality, and to give these aspects greater prominence. Of course, the results do not permit quantitative measures of the relative importance of these variables. But the advertising strategy which has been developed can well be described in terms of dynamic personality psychology. The "operational code" of the mass advertiser is, in the simplest language, to reduce conscience (superego) resistance, to appeal directly to primitive pleasure impulses (id), and either to avoid rational objections (ego) or at least to fuse the rational and the pleasure appeals.[53] The evidence of the success of appropriate advertising in

51. Lester G. Telser, "Advertising and Competition," *Journal of Political Economy* 72 (December 1964): 537–62.

52. Ernest Dichter, *Handbook of Consumer Motivation: The Psychology of the World of Objects* (New York: McGraw-Hill, 1964).

53. For the analytic background of this type of analysis, see Harold D. Lasswell, "The Triple-Appeal Principle," *American Journal of Sociology* (May 1932): 523–38.

specifics is interesting but not very persuasive. Competitive use of motivation appeals can well reduce the advantage one advertiser has but not the cumulative impact mass advertising has on social personality. One can make the analogy with the effect of the cumulative exposure to televised violence to be described. The long-term results have been to increase impulse buying, as it is called by the experts, which reduces rational considerations and contains personal controls.[54] The availability of credit cards reinforces such consumer behavior.

Mass advertising must, of course, balance primitive gratifications with appeals to economic self-interest, and this presents a delicate issue in "craftsmanship." Consumer guides which first appeared in the 1930s sought to protect the buyer from impulse buying and from consumerism. Material objectives were necessities—artifacts that one had to have; there was even an implicit hostility against material objects. The guide was designed to protect the person from the excessive intrusion of the material culture. Since the 1930s consumer guides as they have become popularized are devices to speed up the search for consumer gratification. The economic arguments and assessments are designed to strengthen the primitive gratification appeals. Whereas the pioneering guides were presented by consumer cooperatives and consumer groups, later guides are produced by commercial groups, integral to the mass advertising enterprise. There is a strong element of ritualistic behavior in their utilization; it is a technique for short-term reduction of anxiety about alternative and marginal choices. In short, consumer guides, once designed to contain "consumerism," have become part of "consumerism."

What can be said about the social implications of the popular culture content of the new style "sophisticated" "soap opera"—the serials concerned with "modern" interpersonal relations and tensions? The soap

54. A typical case is the change in advertising ice cream. Before motivation research, old-fashioned advertisement for ice cream cones was simple and realistic about size; the information content was that it was made of good ingredients (ego appeals), good for you (superego), and tasted good (id). The new format avoids any discussion that it is good for you, since to raise the conscience question might well raise psychic resistances; even ego appeals have been reduced. Instead, the approach is toward emphasis on primitive gratification. The cone is twice life size; the cone is packed to overflowing. Often it is presented as dripping slightly down one side, since the "mess" is thought to present a primitive appeal. Children are added in media with adult audiences, since the symbol of the child is a positive appeal of childlike gratification. The major social psychological issue the advertisers face is not to overemphasize the primitive appeals, but their scope has been greatly enlarged.

operas of the 1940s had explicit, simple moral messages. The analysis of housewife reaction to the "traditional" and moralistic "radio daytime serial" prepared by W. Lloyd Warner and William E. Henry showed the symbolic influence of this type of popular culture.[55] They describe these radio—and later television—presentations as "contemporary morality" plays which allowed the housewife vicarious indulgence in other people's adventures and wayward behaviors, but "in the end" her own day-to-day morality was validated. Drawing on the content analysis presented above, we cannot describe the new sophisticated soap opera as functioning in such a fashion. The comic interludes, even comic definitions of interpersonal strain and trauma, offer considerable catharsis and tension reduction, which no doubt account for the audiences. But the emphasis on the hostile and destructive impulses of the "outsider" and the reliance on humor to deal with hostility is likely to generate suspicious responses. There is little reason to assume that the viewer gains insight into his own motivations or is supplied with enriched understanding of social and psychological reality so as to reinforce or modify moral judgments and enhance self- and personal controls.

The growth in mass audience for popular culture raises the question of the discontinuity between popular culture and high culture.[56] Unfortunately, very little can be said on this topic which is not polemic and self-serving. The well-known argument is that the growth of popular culture has weakened the creation and in turn the influence of high culture. There are writers and artists who may have made a contribution to high culture who began producing popular culture for career and economic reasons. However, there is no evidence that there has been a decline in interest and exposure to high culture under advanced industrialism; if anything, the audiences for it appear to have increased.[57] This is not to pass judgment on the lasting quality of the newly produced high culture under advanced industrialism—either on its intrinsic and lasting humanistic quality or on its effect on society, and especially on elite groups.

55. W. Lloyd Warner and William E. Henry, "The Radio Day-Time Serial: A Symbolic Analysis," *Genetic Psychology Monographs* 37 (1948): 3–73.

56. Edward Shils, "Mass Society and Its Culture," in *Culture for the Millions: Mass Media in Modern Society*, ed. Normal Jacobs (New York: Van Nostrand, 1959), pp. 1–27; see also Herbert Gans, *Popular Culture and High Culture* (New York: Basic Books, 1975).

57. Edward Shils, "Daydreams and Nightmares: Reflections of the Criticism of Mass Culture," *Sewanee Review* 65 (1957): 586–608.

The long-term consequence of the strong concentration of violence content on personal and social controls has its crucial test in the impact of television on children and youngsters. Television is the major carrier of violent content. The new generation grow up in a setting of increased access to violent content and they continue to be exposed to varying degrees for a lifetime.

It was not academic interest which produced a comprehensive synthesis of the available analytic thinking and empirical research on televised violence. Rather, Congressional concern with public morality, crime, and aggressive behavior stimulated a cooperative and interdisciplinary review. As a result of the initiative of Senator John O. Pastore of Rhode Island, a government-sponsored panel of social scientists was created. The definition of the problem as a public health issue supplied a basis for the professional detachment of the effort. The Surgeon General's Scientific Advisory Committee on Television and Social Behavior, after two years in 1972 issued a report,[58] by a group of experts who had temporarily abandoned their specialized perspectives and risen above their institutional affiliation and interests.[59]

Aggressive behavior was the focus—the dependent variable. The results of over fifty separate studies, experimental endeavors and sample surveys, indicated that exposure to televised violence increased aggressive behavior as a result of imitation or instigation. The more clear-cut experimental findings were confirmed by sample surveys, although in general surveys produce, for the reason set forth above, less definitive results. The observed relations were low but repeatedly encountered. Given the multiple basis of aggressive behavior, if the encountered influence of televised violence on children and youngsters had been more

58. U.S. Public Health Service, The Surgeon-General's Scientific Advisory Committee on Television and Social Behavior, *Television and Growing Up: The Impact of Televised Violence* (Washington: GPO, 1972); G. Comstock Rubinstein and J. Murray, *Television and Social Behavior* (Rockville, Md.: National Institute of Mental Health, 1972); for British perspectives, see Hilde T. Himmelweit, A. N. Oppenheim, and Pamela Vince, *Television and the Child: An Empirical Study of the Effects of Television on the Young* (New York: Oxford University Press, 1958); J. D. Halloran, R. L. Brown, and D. C. Chaney, *Television and Delinquency* (Leicester: Leicester University Press), pp. 1–70.

59. The report has been criticized, among others by those who participated and who had second thoughts. The report also contained the expected rhetoric first about the limits of available knowledge. The result of 50 independent studies "constitutes some preliminary indication of a causal relationship, but a good deal of research remains to be done before one can have confidence in these conclusions"; in addition, there is strong but self-directed emphasis on the necessity of posing the correct rather than the incorrect question.

extensive, the results would have had to be judged as truly devastating. Moreover, if one makes the effort to read the descriptive details of the experimental studies one is struck by the scope and impact of instigated aggressiveness.

Of course, individual studies are only indicators; the essential inferences must be drawn from these findings. If the research methods which sampled social reality at particular moments in time had produced discernible results of increased aggressive behavior, then the long-term cumulative effects on the audience would most likely be stronger and clearer. Moreover, the correct question about televised violence involves a much sharper focus on societal socialization. In the frame of reference of social control, the increased complexity of the occupational sector and the disarticulation of work and communal residence require a higher level of personal controls. Thus, the task of the mass media is to develop a more adequate relation to authority—that is, greater capacity to store and manage aggression. In short, the findings of these researches indicate a tendency toward weaker personal controls, that is, just the opposite. In fact if the mass media exposure to violence had had no effect, the consequences could still be viewed as disruptive, since the societal requirements are for more effective personal control in order for there to be more adequate societal control. In part, this question was argued in 1937 by Mortimer Alder, when he was evaluating the effect of movies on the criminal behavior of youth.[60] As discussed previously, the content of the media sets the limits for their contribution to socialization. Adler's humanistic analysis and the findings of social research converge; if the proportion which has been allocated to violence had been used for civic education, the social personality of the U.S. citizenry would have been discernibly less accepting of illegitimate violence.

In assessing the consequences of the third indicator of mass media content, namely, the shift toward a stronger emphasis on advocacy, our focus must be less on specific subject themes, and more on style and format. Nevertheless, it must be remembered that less than 5% of all of the contents of the mass media, it is estimated, deals with public affairs. This limited amount is given prominent exposure and, because of its political importance and drama, it commands widespread attention. Media competition in the presentation of public affairs makes pos-

60. Mortimer Adler, *Art and Prudence* (New York: Longmans, Green, 1937).

sible a competitive electoral system with all its inherent and accumulated defects.

Media competition has the objective of ensuring relative accuracy in reporting the events of the day and in producing a measure of balance in opinion and commentary. There is competition among channels of the same medium, among different media, and especially among the generalized and specialized media. However, media competition does not guarantee that the relevant content will be disseminated; nor does it guarantee that in a particular medium an overall prepresentation—a holistic picture—of public affairs will be offered.

The strongest limitations on the competition of the mass media are the constraints which ensue from their profit-oriented management, producing widespread interlocks and a "community" of interests among the owners. However, there is no simple relation between type and patterns of ownership, including degree of concentration, and content. My reading of the scattered research on this issue is that the outlook of particular owners and managers, and the level of professionalism of the staff, are more decisive in determining journalistic performance.

Nor is it simple to assess the consequences of government-imposed regulation—legislative, judical, and executive. Such regulations are designed to enforce competition and maximize standards of performance. There is reason to believe that the degree of competition, although not necessarily the level of performance, has been enhanced by governmental intervention on behalf of competition. Government standards of performance—for example, amount of public service programming—strengthen minimum performance but do not ensure adequate achievement. The sheer administrative burden of the existing government regulations indicates that the point of diminishing returns has been reached. But on balance, it is reasonable to conclude that, without these regulations, as in the case of economic enterprise, the amount of media competition would probably be lower. However, the important conclusion to be drawn for the analysis of the structure of the mass media in the United States is that, under advanced industrialism, private ownership has not been a barrier to the growth in the movement toward advocacy journalism. In fact, the owners and managers appear to have stimulated and supported this trend, while the main incentive comes from the operating journalistic personnel themselves.

It is now necessary to spell out the requirements laid down for the mass media by democratic political theory. Political theorists and sociologists have elaborated these requirements in different language, but there is considerable agreement about the essentials. The mass media must (*a*) contribute to a high level of participation by all ordered segments of society; (*b*) stimulate effective political deliberation on the issues and candidates and contribute a meaningful basis on which citizens make their voting decisions; and (*c*) operate to preclude either side from monopolizing or even exercising pervasive influence by means of them. The mass media must also contribute to a sense of political self-confidence and enlightened self-interest on the part of each citizen. To the extent that these criteria are not met, the election process is not one of consent but degenerates into an exercise in mass pressure. In specific terms, the danger of an advanced industrial society with an elaborate system of mass communication is that the presentation of public affairs will contribute to suspicion and projective distrust and weaken the relevance and legitimacy of the electoral process. How far has this actually taken place in the United States? Does the extensive body of research on political participation make possible an estimate of the magnitude of influence of the mass media on voting behavior and the quality and character of this influence?

It has been argued by some critics that the mass media inherently contribute to suspicion and projective distrust. In this view, political democracy rests on face-to-face communications and in the real world there is an inherent element of remoteness between the mass communicator and his audience. In addition, there is an imbalance of influence and in "feedback" which undermines the process of building consent. Such a line of reason is extreme and self-defeating. The interpersonal basis of political democracy is essential, but one can still reject the assertion that the mass media inherently or uniformly undermine the process of political persuasion. In realistic and pragmatic terms, it is sufficient to offer the criterion that democratic debate and elections depend on the extent to which interpersonal influences operate substantially independent of the influence of the mass media. Thus the question is the strategy and tactics in the handling of public affairs content by the mass media. What is the character of the political struggle between the political elites? Is the approach one in which the emphasis is on building realism and insight (appeals to ego), or is it highly personalistic in format, combatative with irrational overtones and appeals to defensive group solidarities (distorted superego appeals)?

Human personality has a great capacity to simplify social reality and to select congenial elements from the mass media. In fact, the immense extent of self-selection is one of the most persistent findings of social psychological research on exposure to the mass media. But the political process of necessity involves simplification of complex issues. The human capacity to simplify the external world makes possible social relations and political decisions. From the point of view of social personality and social control, the basic question is whether these simplifications—stereotypes, in the sense used by Walter Lippmann—are being influenced by a component of personal control and by an appeal to insight, realism, and enlightened self-interest, or by the reverse, including accumulative distrust.

Our hypothesis is that the growing dominance of television, with its stress on a personalistic presentation of public affairs, and the increased emphasis on advocacy journalism make a discernible contribution to the distrustful and projective audience response to public affairs. In essence, the effects of the mass media on public affairs, particularly during election campaigns, conform more to the Lasswell model of systemic significance than to the Lazarsfeld tangential model.

When we offer the hypothesis of the increased influence of the mass media on political behavior after the 1952 election, of course, we are not certain that was the actual reality or whether we are relying on an improved mode of research and analysis. However, we do have more adequate bodies of data for 1952 to 1976, and we are dealing with the shift from radio to television. No one could overlook the significance of radio in the political strategy of Franklin D. Roosevelt. However, the weak political regimes have emerged and political party affiliation has declined during the growth of television, which has highlighted the salience of personality in the political campaigns. The electorate's assessment of the candidate's personality is an essential aspect of public affairs and political campaigns. But what are the consequences of an overwhelming reliance on television as the principal medium of news and commentary during a period of increased complexity of political decisions? The available evidence, I argue, is at least compatible with the observation that while, in 1952–1976, the electoral process operated as a system of generating consent, in varying and fluctuating degree, the mass media have contributed a discernible component of mass distrust and thereby to a weakening of personal and social controls.

The basis for the "disruptive" contribution of the mass media to the electoral process is a the convergence of the dominance of television as the major public affairs medium with its very personalized style plus the growth of the advocacy format. National samples demonstrate the long-term increased reliance on television as the source for "most of your news." The relative standing can be seen in Table 9.1, where citizen answers are presented. In 1959, 51% reported television, 57

TABLE 9.1 Trends in Mass Media Sources for News, 1959–1974 (Based on National Sample Surveys)

"First, I'd like to ask you where you usually get most of your news about what's going on in the world today—from the newspapers or radio or television or magazines or talking to people or where?"
most news:

Source of most news:	1959	1961	1963	1964	1967	1968	1971	1972	1974
Television	51%	52%	55%	58%	64%	59%	60%	64%	65%
Newspapers	57	57	53	56	55	49	48	50	47
Radio	34	34	29	26	28	25	23	21	21
Magazines	8	9	6	8	7	7	5	6	4
People	4	5	4	5	4	5	4	4	4
Don't know/ no answer (DK/NA)	1	3	3	3	2	3	1	1	*

SOURCE: Adapted for The Roper Organization, "Trends in Public Attitudes toward Television and Other Mass Media, 1959–1974," (New York: Television Information Office, 1975), p. 3.

newspapers, and 34 radio; by 1974 television had reached 65%, newspapers had dropped slightly to 47%, and radio had declined to 21%. Perhaps a clearer picture of the dominance of the television is obtained when responses are grouped. By 1974, the largest single group comprised those who relied only on television, 36%; the second, those who relied on television and newspaper, 23%; and the third, those who relied on newspapers only, 19%. By 1972 the reliance on television among the college educated almost equaled that of the less than college educated group. Moreover, television had emerged as the dominant source of news for national, state, and local elections.[61]

But the most striking aspect is the mass audience's trust and approval of television. The text of the specific question is relevant: "If you get conflicting or different reports of the same news story from radio, television, the magazines and the newspapers, which of the four ver-

61. A lower level of reliance on television for news is reported in a survey sponsored by the Newsprint Committee. See H. Bagdikian, *The Information Machines: Their Impact on Men and the Media* (New York: Harper and Row, 1971).

sions would you be most inclined to believe—the one on radio or television or magazines or newspapers?" (See Table 9.2.) From 1959 onward television credibility has grown from 29% to 51%, while newspapers have declined from 32% to 20%.

TABLE 9.2 Trends in Credibility of Mass Media: 1959–1974
(Based on National Sample Surveys)

"If you got conflicting or different reports of the same news story from radio, television, the magazines and the newspapers, which of the four versions would you be most inclined to believe—the one on radio or television or magazines or newspapers?"

Most believable:	1959	1961	1963	1964	1967	1968	1970	1972	1974
Television	29%	39%	36%	41%	41%	44%	49%	48%	51%
Newspapers	32	24	24	23	24	21	20	21	20
Radio	12	12	12	8	7	8	10	8	8
Magazines	10	10	10	10	8	11	9	10	8
DK/NA	17	17	18	18	20	16	12	13	13

SOURCE: Adapted from The Roper Organization, "Trends in Public Attitudes toward Television and Other Mass Media, 1959–1974," (New York: Television Information Office, 1975), p. 4.

These surveys also probed the performance of local television stations and compared "the job" they were doing with other local institutions. Again, on the basis of national samples, television stations were rated very high; and there has been a long-term increase in the view that they are "doing an excellent or good" job, from 59% in 1959 to 71% in 1974. The newspapers were rated somewhat lower and experienced a slight decline from 64% in the excellent and good category to 58% in 1974. The performance of television stations and newspapers was rated higher than that of schools and especially local government.

These findings are noteworthy, in the context of the marked decline in expressed trust in other institutions of U.S. society. The increase in trust in television has been gradual and therefore not linked to particular events. But coverage of the war in Vietnam and of the proceedings of the Watergate investigation has contributed to popular trust in television as a public affairs medium. However, I argue that television and its news commentators are trusted in part because of their consistently suspicious view of public affairs. The commentators help define public affairs as suspect; in effect, they direct suspicion away from themselves to other persons and institutions. They have assisted the audience to project their mistrust and to select targets for their mistrust, almost as if television were a counter "phobic device." The individual must have a focus for his trust, and to trust mainly the devices of the mass media with their exposé orientation is a weak basis for rational appeals and for strengthening ego control. The result is more and more a form of mass media dependency.

The style of the television commentator is to mix news and commentary, to emphasize advocacy posture—often less content and more style.[62] One can point to particular commentators who adhere to a "neutral" style, but the interpretative advocate posture is pronounced. The limitations of time requires more oversimplification than in printed media. If there is to be coverage in depth, one issue is selected—such as the war in Vietnam or Watergate—to the exclusion of others. Television, with its advocacy overtones, is concerned mainly with crises, tensions, and problem formation, not with performance and achievement.[63] Finally, the dissemination of public affairs by personalistic commentators heightens the definition of politics as a struggle between persons, and deemphasizes concern with and debate about underlying issues.[64]

The consequences of public affairs content for the mass media are most directly discernible in the outcome of elections. Such consequences are a function of the relative increase in change in voting intention in the course of the political campaign. The 1944, 1952, and 1976 campaigns supply periods for a trend analysis. In such analysis, it is necessary, to the extent possible, to separate the influence of the mass media from that of interpersonal and organizational pressure.

The People's Choice, by Paul F. Lazarsfeld and his associates, was based on a community study of Sandusky, Ohio, during the 1944 na-

62. Reuven Frank, "An Anatomy of Television News," *Television Quarterly* 9 (1970): 1–23.

63. M. Robinson, "American Political Legitimacy in an Era of Electronic Journalism: Reflections on the Evening News," in *Television as a Social Force: New Approaches to T.V. Criticism*, ed. D. Cates and R. Adler (New York: Praeger, 1975), pp. 97–140. This argument was in the past made about "sensational" newspapers. See H. L. Mencken, "Newspaper Morals," *Atlantic Monthly* 113 (March 1914): 289–97.

64. This analysis of the role of the mass media in creating projective distrust versus insight was stimulated by an essay entitled "Trends in Twentieth Century Propaganda," by Ernest Kris and Nathan Leites, first published in *Psychoanalysis and the Social Sciences* 1 (1947): 393–409. The authors of this essay emphasize the range of potentialities of the mass media in an advanced industrial society. They point out that democratic leaders such as Winston Churchill did make effective use of the mass media by skillful ego-oriented appeals; the contributions of the mass media—in particular television—are not inherent or predetermined.

tional election. It was "an old-fashioned" election in which the amount of shifting at the national level, and especially in the stable community which they investigated, was limited. Their frame of reference emphasized social stratification; position in the social structure fashioned voting intentions. Those at the bottom were more Democratic and those at the top more Republican. The complexities of the welfare state and stagflation were not operative. Because of the political setting and their use of a sample survey with limited statistical analysis, they encountered very limited influence from the mass media. The observed influence was largely of the two-step flow variety—that is, combined exposure to the mass media and to interpersonal persuasion.

The 1952 election, the intense competition between Dwight D. Eisenhower and Adlai Stevenson, was marked by a more extensive shift in voting patterns than the previous presidential election. The increased amount of voting shifts reflected changes in the social structure and in the strength of the personalities involved. It was also the first election which was studied extensively by national sample surveys.

Of the potential voting population in 1952, 46.5% were regular party voters, that, is they voted for the presidential candidate of the same party—Republican or Democratic—in 1948 and 1952; 16.1% were nonvoters, while all categories of changes amounted to 39.6%. Survey research soon after the 1952 election offered the conclusion that the effect of television on the election campaign was minimal and without real consequences.[65] However, subsequent reanalysis and a more systemic outlook pointed out the role of the mass media in that election, a role which contributed to the emergence of weak political regimes.[66] Three inferences can be drawn from the available analysis of the influence of the media in this campaign. Extensive exposure to the mass media reinforced and mobilized interest in the campaign, increasing final turnout. Increased exposure does not necessarily stimulate participation, although it generally does. (For example, Blumler found, in the British election of 1964, based on a very sophisticated analysis of

65. Angus Campbell, Gerald Gurin, and Warren E. Miller, "Television and the Election," *Scientific American* 188 (May 1953): 46–48.

66. Morris Janowitz and Dwaine Marvick, *Competitive Pressure and Democratic Consent* (Chicago: Quadrangle, 1964), pp. 57–71; Kurt Lang and Gladys Lang, *Politics and Television* (Chicago: Quadrangle, 1968); Michael J. Robinson, "Public Affairs Television and the Growth of Political Malaise," *American Political Science Review* 70 (June 1976): 409–32; Michael J. Robinson and Clifford Zukin, "Television and the Wallace Vote," *Journal of Communication* 26 (1976): 79–83.

sample survey data, that for young people with no or limited experience in national elections extensive exposure to the campaign on television depressed voting turnout, a sharp commentary of the quality of the election campaign.)[67] Second, in 1952, television assisted the Republican party to mobilize their "stalwarts" to a greater extent than it helped the Democratic "stalwarts." Finally, Eisenhower's appeal, especially on television, had a discernible effect on persons who might be called "indifferent" citizens, those who did not see the election as involving their essential self-interest. In other words, the mass media influenced those persons weakly linked to politics and most disposed to shift from one party to another. The quality of consent generalized by the 1952 election was also weakened by the low level of participation of blacks: 67.3% of the surveyed blacks did not vote.

Moreover, each person in the 1952 sample could be characterized by whether he or she were under concerned primary-group pressure—from relatives, friends, and work associates—to support one candidate or the other, or whether primary-group contacts were mixed between Democrats and Republicans. The minority of the total electorate (21.2%) which found itself under concerted primary-group pressure was an important target for the mass media.[68] These were the persons most likely to be influenced by the two-step flow of communications. Nevertheless, there were additional voters, especially those weakly involved in politics, who appeared to be more directly influenced by the mass media. Finally, the face-to-face political canvass conducted by both parties served as a counterweight to the assistance which the mass media gave to the Republican presidential candidate. Thus, if one seeks an overall assessment of the mass media influence on the quality of this election, the outcome could be judged as representing on balance a process of consent but not without discernible components of media "pressure."

In the 1976 election, available data indicate that the mass media also served to maintain relatively high interest and to stimulate turnout, although the citizenry had reservations about both candidates. The election produced a considerable shift in presidential preference from the previous campaign and changes in preferences in the course of the

67. Jay G. Blumler and Dennis McQuail, *Television in Politics* (Chicago: University of Chicago Press, 1969); see especially chap. 13 for discussion of long-term effects.

68. Janowitz and Marvick, *Competitive Pressure.*

campaign. Mass media appeals were especially important for those persons with strong political interests, in contrast to the 1952 election. As noted in chapter 4, the "independents" have changed their character and include a high concentration of persons with strong political involvements. However, given the complexity of the issues involved and the difficulties of aggegrating one's self-interest, the personality of the candidates was critical, and influenced not only persons with weak political interest but also some of those with strong political interest. This aspect of the campaign symbolism cannot be said to have strengthened rational responses and personal controls. In comparing the outcomes of the 1952 and the 1976 election, there is no basis to conclude that the 1976 election was characterized by more extensive one-sided persuasion or by more extensive media "pressure" in general, although these limitations were already operating. In any case, the 1976 election, like each election since 1952, did not produce a fundamental realignment or strengthen public trust in the process. Clearly, the increase in voting among minority groups, especially among blacks, meant that the final outcome was more of an expression of consent.

We are dealing not only with the outcome of specific electoral contests but also with a longer-term trend in media exposure and political response. Our analysis converges with the results of the reanalysis of survey data by Michael J. Robinson for 1960–1968 which emphasized the "counter phobic" or politically suspicious element in the response to television content.[69] He employs the term "political malaise" to describe the loss of political confidence which extensive exposure produces. Of course, an interactive effect is at work. Great reliance on television rather than on the other media for news is found among persons with a low sense of political efficacy. Some self-selection is at work, but this relationship holds for persons with low and high educational backgrounds. Self-selection then is not an adequate explanation of these and other correlates of high exposure to television news. For example, persons who rely more on television news believed more often that Congressmen quickly lose touch with people; and this relationship cuts across education and income groups as well.[70] These results under-

69. Robinson, "Public Affairs." See also Jarol B. Mannheim, "Can Democracy Survive Television?" *Journal of Communication* 26 (1976): 84–90.

70. As in the election of 1952, the 1968 election, which Robinson analyzes in some detail, television assisted Nixon, the Republican candidate, and Wallace as well, if both income and educational differences are considered.

line the projective influence of television content as it is actually organized and disseminated. Paralleling the consequence of violent content, the effect of television news is cumulative, so that its long-term contribution to political suspicion, which weakens political legitimacy, cannot be denied or overlooked.

In summary, the trends in mass media content and popular response highlight the vulnerabilities of the citizenry to appeals and content which weakened personal control. An advanced industrial society is dependent on the mass media to generate consensus and coordination, but the essential conclusion is that the vast apparatus of the mass media fails to contribute adequately to the articulation of the institutional sectors of society and to contribute to the socialization required for effective social controls. However, it is our assumption that the consent—cultural and political—which is generated by the mass media is conditioned by the extent of popular legitimacy according to the mechanisms and agencies of legal coercion and by the effect of coercive sanction of societal socialization. In this regard, the hypothesis examined in the next chapter, that there has been an effective weakening since 1920 of the popular legitimacy of the coercive sanctions, is perhaps more important than the influence of the mass media.

Ten

Societal Socialization: Legitimate Coercion

Law and Legitimate Coercion

Systemic analysis of the role of legitimate coercion in social control involves more than the consequences of legal institutions on those accused of criminal behavior. To focus on the effect of legitimate coercion on the "law-abiding citizen" is to draw on a long tradition in sociology.[1] The "criminal" is required so society can fashion and elaborate the rules by which it can function and endure. The law and the legal system operate in industrial and advanced industrial society by means of formalized, explicit rules and regulations—regardless of the limits of their effectiveness. The idea of social control is therefore compatible with the classic formulation of H. L. Hart, the legal philosopher: "A society develops special rules for curing the defects of a social order based on unofficial norms."[2] The critical term in this formulation is *special.*

If the special aspects of law are to be kept in mind and if it is not to be seen as "another set" of norms, it must be recognized that the law is supported by the coercive power of the state. But more than that, it must be seen as the legitimate coercion of the state. There have been unending efforts to "clarify" the classic formulation offered by Max Weber about the distinctive aspects of the legal system. But the irreducible element of legitimate coercion cannot be eliminated or denied. In the translation by Max Rheinstein, "there exists a coercive apparatus, i.e., that there are one or more persons whose special task it is to hold themselves ready to apply specially provided means of coercion (legal

1. Emile Durkheim, *Les règles de la méthode sociologique*, 8th ed. (Paris: Alcan, 1927).
2. Hornell Hart, *The Concept of Law* (Oxford: Clarendon, 1961), p. 91.

coercion) for the purpose of norm enforcement."[3] The threat of coercion does not necessarily constitute legal action. But to emphasize the socialization component of law—which is essential—does not obscure the fundamental basis of the legal system.

Such an orientation makes possible the juxtaposition of the instruments of mass persuasion with those of the legal system. In both cases we are interested in the ongoing process of socialization by which the person and his household are linked to the national society. As an indicator of social change and social control, our focus is on the criminal justice system, as it has come to be known, in fact on selected aspects of this. In some respects, the phrase "criminal justice" limits rather than clarifies the analysis of social change and social control. Criminal justice focuses our attention on offenders charged with crimes against property and against the person. But in terms of the basic issues of socialization in the national society, we are dealing as well with politically motivated and politically defined crimes.

A central theme of this study is that the decline in political legitimacy, the so-called crisis in the effectiveness of the electoral system, is a reflection of enlarged institutional disarticulation. Institutions are thought to be disarticulated when their interrelations contribute to the weakening of self-regulation and social control. Now we must add that disarticulation encompasses the institutional patterns for societal socialization. If the mass media have strained or weakened the linkage between the person (and his household) and the larger society, the parallel trend can be observed for the legal system, and especially for the procedures of criminal justice. Our task is to examine the scope and content of these strains so as to recognize their origin and reality and avoid exaggeration of their political implications.

Our basic hypothesis about the influence of legal institutions on social control is that there has been a long-term weakening, or more accurately attenuation, of the popular legitimacy of legal norms, especially those dealing with coercive sanctions. From the 1950s on, and probably earlier, the attenuation of the legitimacy of legal norms reflects the growing divergence between judicial reasoning and popular moral beliefs. Judicial reasoning and judicial decisions have had specific positive influence on popular attitudes appropriate for strengthening

3. Max Rheinstein, *Max Weber on Law in Economy and Society* (Cambridge: Harvard University Press, 1954), p. 13.

social control. However, on balance, the overall inability of judicial reasoning to have a decisive, guiding effect on popular attitudes can be understood in part as the result of two substantive trends.

First, the courts have worked to limit the scope of coercive sanctions in the area of criminal justice by extending citizen rights to the accused and the convicted. (They have sought to adapt the criminal code to the shift in authority in industrial and administrative sectors away from authority based on domination.) However, the rise in actual and effective crime rates has during the same period increased popular support for tougher law enforcement. Second, the courts have sought to extend social and economic citizen rights to minority groups, including women, and justified the use of coercive sanction to achieve particular citizen rights. While popular support for these rights has grown in the United States, the opposition to coercive sanctions—or sanctions defined as coercive by the citizenry—has persisted and even grown. The most profound indicator of the transformation of attitudes toward the legal system is the startling decline in trust and confidence in the U.S. Supreme Court, which has emerged as the symbol of the changes in the criminal justice system and the use of law to direct sociopolitical change.

Our analysis reverses conventional wisdom, which asserts that law embodies and organizes the operative norms. Instead, our strategy at the moment is to raise the question of to what extent does law, in particular the criminal justice system, operate as an instrument for directing social change. We will include the symbolic content of legal reasoning by which the coercive sanctions of the law are presented and rationalized to the larger society. The aspiration of legal reasoning and legal procedures is to create effective authority and to deemphasize coercive sanctions.

The previous categories of the person's relations to the authority and authority centers are directly applicable. In a parliamentary system, obedience to law is not submissive compliance. In social-psychological terms, the effectiveness of the legal system embodies more than acceptance of external authority and conscience controls. There must be a component of rational ego control. The law must make "sense" and be consistent. In the first instance, rational and personal control implies the citizen's popular acceptance of legal procedures and sanctions. But the criminal has the potentiality of rationally learning from his experiences with the criminal justice system; the striking conclusion to be drawn from the mass of criminological research is that, with the passage of time, an important number of convicted persons, regardless of their specific experiences with the system of criminal justice, become less and less involved in deviant behavior.

In institutional terms, legal authority generates a set of rules and procedures which enhance legitimacy to the extent that they are based on restraint.[4] These rules involve the adversary system, appeal procedures, and public scrutiny as well as a critical stance by the professional groups involved in the legal process. The important institutional mechanism is the existence and elaboration of a relatively autonomous judiciary which is continuously reformulating the law and supervising the agents of criminal justice.

Specialists in legal reasoning are aware of their symbolic role as advocates of individual persons from diverse social backgrounds. These specialists–in the legislative, administrative, and judicial system are engaged in unending efforts to formulate convincing arguments–arguments that will convince other legal specialists as well as elected and administrative officials and, in turn, the citizenry. Under advanced industrialism, the legal system is constantly modifying and altering both substantive and procedural law. There are profound differences between "conservative" and "liberal" specialists in the advocated scope and magnitude of change. But the striking element in legal institutions is the commitment grounded in the survival and extension of the common law tradition, that the legal system serves to adapt the society to technological, economic, and social change. This implies a central role for the courts in innovating law and in identifying those legal elements which are of more enduring relevance for a competitive political system.

Likewise, there is considerable agreement among legal experts, and among social scientists, about the consequences of judicial tradition and practice for coercive sanctions. The system of judicial reasoning grounded in common law tradition is most effective as a mechanism of social control when the courts are engaged in the continuous but limited and small-scale adaptions of legislative decisions. Judicial intervention is less effective when the courts seek to develop or to reject strategic, comprehensive solutions to old or new problems. Judicial

4. Philip Selznick, "The Sociology of Law," *International Encyclopedia of the Social Sciences* 9 (New York: Macmillan and The Free Press, 1968): 50–59.

procedures, in other words, are more effective when basic policy is settled and refinement of categories and procedures is needed.

However, since 1930, especially since 1960, there has been increased judicial activism; and therefore, our basic hypothesis about the decline of the legitimacy of coercive sanctions cannot be separated from this increased activism in traditional common law function and in the strategic redefinition of law.

First, the increased complexity in occupation and the growth of the welfare state have meant an enormous increase in the volume of legislative enactments and a parallel increase in administrative regulations, all of which are subject, in some measure, to judicial review. The sheer increase in legislative and administrative regulations, plus their inherent vagueness and inconsistency, implies a vast increase in the routine work of the courts. As of 1976, there were 77 regulatory bodies at the federal level, 50 of which were created after 1960. The mass of detailed regulation is striking. For example, the Occupational Safety and Health Administration has issued 21 pages of rules dealing with ladders. The Environmental Protection Agency had by 1975 issued 45,000 separate plant permits. One sympathetic government official analyzed the work of this agency: "It is forced to make thousands of decisions on detailed considerations it cannot possibly know and, even less, keep up with over time. These decisions are subject to multiple legal challenges."[5] The consequences have been longer delays in the court, a proliferation of cases in the long appeal process to the Supreme Court, and greater complexity of judicial decisions, including a significant enlargement of reversal decisions in contrast to more limited modification of law.[6] All these served in part to strain the legitimacy of routine judicial decisions.

Second, in addition to intensified "refinement" of law, the courts, and especially the U.S. Supreme Court, have during the period under investigation increased their strategic interventions to impose or to reject comprehensive solutions to old and new societal issues. A linear trend would not best describe the pattern of judicial activism; more appropriate is the characterization of periods of "outbursts" of new initiatives which have been increasing since the New Deal. Among the high points in the ensuing periods of increased intervention have been, in 1954, the school desegregation decision, in 1966, the Miranda case

5. *New York Times*, December 2, 1976, p. 45.

6. Hans Zeisel, Harry Kalven, Jr., and Bernard Buchholz, *Delay in the Court* (Boston: Little, Brown, 1959).

heralding a fundamental reorientation of the rights of the accused, and, in 1971, the Duke power case establishing new criteria of discrimination in employment.[7] This post–World War II activism of the courts has extended new social and economic rights to citizens and established new areas in which the authority of the federal government can be employed. The courts have sought to solve basic societal issues which they have judged were relatively insoluble or neglected by legislative action. While court actions have modified the practices in a wide range of institutions, they have also produced a marked decline in confidence in the legal system and in the legitimacy of the coercive sanction of the state.

The weakening of legitimacy of government authority, and the strain on institutions of societal socialization, raise the immediate probability of increased "private" violence, especially parapolitical and political violence. In the 1960s advanced industrialization was accompanied by intensified racial tension which produced extensive violence; likewise, the political debate about U.S. intervention in Southeast Asia resulted in repeated violent outbursts, especially in opposition to the Selective Service System. An essential aspect of the analysis of societal and social control is obviously an assessment of the consequences of these patterns of violence, despite the inherent difficulties of such a task.

The short-range effects of the confrontation over U.S. military participation in Vietnam are particularly difficult to disentangle. A case will be offered that group race violence, partly because it did not persist, produced adaptative societal change. But the essential argument that will be pursued is that, as in the historical past in the United States, the outbursts of political violence in the 1960s were not cumulative and were not institutionalized into a system for intervention in political decision making. No threshold was past. It is also doubtful whether these events had a decisive influence on popular attitudes, although they reinforced the strain on legitimacy. The basic and underlying disarticulation of institutional arrangements rather than the content of the violent outburst was more effective to this end.

Crime and Criminal Justice

The entrance to the social-control implications of the criminal justice system is the long-term trend in recorded and estimated rates of criminal behavior under advanced industrialism. A vast effort has been

7. *Miranda v. Arizona*, 384 U.S. 486 (1966); Griggs v. Duke Power Co. 401 U.S. 424, 91 S Ct. 849, 28 L. Ed. 2d 158 (1971).

invested in collecting, assessing, and criticizing trends in criminal behavior. Were criminal rates higher in the nineteenth century than in the twentieth century in the United States? What is the direction of the trend from 1920 to 1976? Emile Durkheim made use of suicide rates as measures of social integration; crime has come to be seen as a more adequate equivalent for advanced industrial societies.[8] The level of criminal behavior has come to be seen as a crucial indicator in the social order of a society and as an indirect measure of the effect of law on social personality, both of the accused and of the citizenry at large. Criminality for the sociologist is a direct measure of the moral climate of a society—forms and mechanisms of control are all involved.

It is possible to offer two observations which seek to come to terms with the complexity and the limitations on the available documentation. The results of historical investigations, for example, by Theodore N. Ferdinand, Roger Lane, and Mark H. Haller, are clear-cut.[9] Despite the difficulties presented by changing definitions and procedures of reporting crime, if one compares the period 1920 to 1976 with trends in the nineteenth century, it is possible to find urban settings in particular historical periods in which the rate of criminal behavior in the last century was higher than in the present century. Rapid growth of urban centers plus the weak organization of local police departments account for this. These findings make it difficult to adhere to a simple-minded model of evolutionary growth and expansion of criminal behavior under industrialization. But such a broad and sweeping comparison hardly clarifies the content and magnitude, as well as significance, of trends since the end of World War II.

For 1920 to 1976, homicide supplies a pointed indicator. It is one of the most visible forms of criminal behavior and the definition is relatively stable. It is one that has been most adequately observed and recorded by police officials. Since World War I, it is not possible to

8. Emile Durkheim, *Le Suicide: Etude de sociologie* (Paris: Alcan, 1897).

9. Theodore N. Ferdinand, "The Criminal Patterns of Boston since 1849," *American Journal of Sociology* 73 (July 1967): 84–99; Theodore N. Ferdinand, "Politics, The Police and Arresting Policies in Salem, Massachusetts since the Civil War," *Social Problems* 19 (1972): 572–88; Roger Lane, "Crime and Criminal Statistics in Nineteenth Century Massachusetts," *Journal of Social History* 2 (1968): 156–63; Mark H. Haller, "Historical Roots of Police Behavior: Chicago, 1890–1925," *Law and Society Review* 10 (1976): 304–23. See also D. J. Mulvihill, M. M. Tumin, and L. A. Curtis, *Crimes of Violence*, 2, Staff Report to National Commission on the Causes and Prevention of Violence (Washington: GPO, 1969).

account for trends on the basis of changes in definition or changes in recording or enumeration procedures. The homicide rate—or murder rate, as I prefer to call it—began to decline after 1935 as the nation emerged from the Great Depression; in increasing prosperity, it declined steadily through and after World War II; in 1965, with the onset of stagflation, the murder rate reversed itself and has continued to rise through 1976. (See Table 10.1.) The homicide rate per 100,000

TABLE 10.1 Trends in Number of Homicide Victims, 1920–1970

	Homicides	
Year	Number	Rate*
1920	5,815	—
1925	8,440	—
1930	10,331	12.4
1935	10,587	11.2
1940	8,329	8.4
1945	7,547	7.7
1950	7,942	7.2
1955	7,418	6.4
1960	8,464	6.9
1965	10,712	8.0
1970	16,848	11.6
1971	18,787	12.6
1972	19,638	13.0
1973	20,465	13.0

*Rate per 100,000 resident population fifteen years and over.
SOURCE: Adapted from U.S. National Center for Health Statistics, *Vital Statistics of the United States*, annual.

was 12.4 in 1930; in 1940 it had dropped to 8.4. It continued to decline, so that by 1955 it stood at 6.4 and by 1960 at 6.9; the rate started to rise to 8.0 in 1965, and by 1973 it had reached 13.3. In terms of actual numbers, by 1970 in the United States there were 16,848 homicides; the number had reached 20,465 by 1973.

Another visible and fairly stably defined type of criminal behavior is bank robbery. Bank robberies reported to the Federal Bureau of Investigation from 1946 to 1970 indicated a fivefold increase, hardly to be accounted for by the changing methodology of criminologists and police. To include more covert and more complex types of criminal behavior, the period 1965 to 1970 is appropriate for describing arrests in the United States for drug violations. In 1970, 3,381 police agencies, with a population of 122,233,000, reported 293,971 arrests for narcotic-drug violations compared with 43,550 arrests in the same jurisdictions in 1965. This amounts to a fivefold increase; again, changing definition and enumeration procedures could not account for this increase.[10]

Daniel Glaser, a sophisticated critic of criminal statistics, assesses these issues by describing the FBI index of crime, the index most vulnerable to distortion, in the following terms: "A large part of the annual crime increase announced by the FBI throughout the 1960's and early 1970's was only an increase in the percentage of crimes reported to the police and in the completeness of their recording crime reports."[11] In essence, he is prepared to state that a large part of the increase is due to data-collection procedures; but he does not deny the actual increase. The doubtful composite index prepared by the FBI rose from 2,423 in 1965 to 4,775 during the first six months of 1974. But the weakness of this FBI measure does not refute the specific trend data on homicides or other observations about the increase in actual crime especially since the mid-1960s.

It has become popular among university specialists concerned with advocating public policy to assert that social-science literature does not supply a guide to the causes of criminality—that is, to the understanding of the causes of criminality. No doubt some of the criminological literature is vague, and even contradictory; and the multicausal perspectives which have become dominant imply policy alternatives. But a careful and critical reading of the research literature offers a set of conclusions which are relevant for understanding the immediate factors which contribute to the trends encountered, especially since 1930.

Three underlying structural factors are relevant for our particular analysis; economic, demographic, and the deterrent consequences of the police and the criminal justice system. The economic and demographic elements are very closely linked. One does not have to press without limitation an "economic determinism" to recognize that crime rates are very closely linked to the level and pattern of distribution of economic behavior. The emergence of economic analysis of crime by

10. For an analysis of the social processes involved in drug addiction, see Alfred R. Lindesmith, *The Addict and the Law* (Bloomington, Ind.: Indiana University Press, 1965); Edwin M. Schur, *Crimes Without Victims* (Engelwood Cliffs, N.J.: Prentice-Hall, 1965); Leon Gibson Hunt and Carl D. Chambers, *The Heroin Epidemics: A Study of Heroin Use in the United States, 1965–1975* (New York: Spectrum, 1976).

11. Daniel Glaser, "The Classification of Offenses and Offenders," in Daniel Glaser, ed., *Handbook of Criminology* (Chicago: Rand McNally, 1974), pp. 45–83.

Gary Becker, for example, supplies not a substitute but rather a continuity with traditional sociological observations.[12] In the most general and crude terms, "economic prosperity" reduces crime, while "economic hardship" increases crime. Of course, such an assertion requires careful elaboration, but it is central. There is a body of data which conclude that crime is linked to unemployment, the incidence of the population below the poverty line, and even to unequal income distribution.[13] Thus, an economic interpretation helps identify the proximate factors in the decrease in crime rates in the years after the Great Depression and in the subsequent increase which started in the early 1960s and continued with the onset of stagflation. Despite the high level of economic prosperity which was reached by 1965, youth unemployment rates were increasing because of the growing number of young people and changes in work technology and organizations. Persistent stagflation has increased the level of youth unemployment.[14] Other economic-based factors operated in the same direction; for example, the failure of educational institutions to supply alternative modes of entrance into the labor market, racial prejudice, the location of employment opportunities, and increasing minimum wages for young workers.

The demographic increase of young cohorts in the 1960s contributed to the growth of criminal behavior. There were an excess of applicants for the number of youth employment opportunities. In addition, the size of the age groups between 14 and 24, the years of greatest crime-proneness, increased. Thus, the higher criminal rates since the early 1960s are connected to an increase in the size and proportion of the population in the crime vulnerable age groups. With the passage of time, whatever the criminal justice policy, the incidence of crime will decrease as the members of these age groups grow older, and the size of new youth groups decline.

12. Gary Becker, "Crime and Punishment: An Economic Approach," *Journal of Political Economy* 76 (March–April 1968): 169–217; George J. Stigler, "The Optimum Enforcement of Laws," *Journal of Political Economy* 78 (May–June 1970): 526–36.

13. Daniel Glaser and Kent Rice, "Crime, Age and Employment," *American Sociological Review* 24 (October 1959): 679–86; Belton M. Fleisher, *The Economics of Delinquency* (Chicago: Quadrangle, 1966); Harold L. Votey, Jr. and Llad Phillips, "The Control of Criminal Activity: An Economic Analysis," in *Handbook of Criminology*, ed. D. Glaser (Chicago: Rand McNally, 1974), pp. 1055–93.

14. For an alternative point of view, see James Q. Wilson, *Thinking about Crime* (New York: Basic Books, 1975).

Trends in criminal behavior need to be seen in terms of the interplay of population trends and the availability of prison facilities.[15] If crime decreases with age, especially as young men and women pass beyond 24 years, then the increase in "crime in the streets" is clearly linked to the failure of prison facilities to expand as rapidly as the age population. Data presented in the *Statistical Abstract* indicate that the prisoners in state and federal prisons per 100,000 population declined from 110.3 in 1950 to 103.6 in 1974.[16] This decline occurred while serious crimes known to the police more than doubled.[17] Likewise, during these years the cohorts between 12 to 24 grew both in absolute number and relative to the population at large. Thus the years per youth served in prison must have gone down during this period.

As a result repeated offenses were required for incarceration; youthful offenders remained at large and repeated their criminal actions. These figures merely confirm the general impression that youth with criminal backgrounds continued more frequently to remain on the streets rather than being placed in correctional institutions because of the lack of facilities. One can infer that the construction of prison lagged behind, and it can be assumed that in the 1980s the crime rate will decline because of the relative and absolute decrease in youthful population and the greater availability of correctional institutions. (The alternative to the expansion of correctional institutions would have been the organization of new educational and work institutions for youth in the vulnerable age groups—such as a national youth corps or a voluntary national service, which would serve youth from all the social segments of society.)[18]

Third, it is very difficult to assess the effectiveness of police forces, but there is no reason to believe it is as important as demographic struc-

15. Arthur Stinchcombe, pers. comm.
16. *U. S. Statistical Abstract* (Washington: GPO, 1976), p. 171.
17. Ibid., p. 153.
18. An important trend in the administration of criminal justice has been the movement to eliminate discretion in juvenile court, to eliminate flexible sentencing, and even to restrict parole procedures. Originally, these procedures were introduced to make the administration of criminal justice more humane and sensitive to individual needs. The reaction against them was not motivated by a "hard line." On the contrary, these changes were advocated and implemented in the name of greater universalism and fairness. The advocates were motivated by a distrust of the criminal justice system—that it was arbitrary and that these flexible procedures were administered without effective justification. When these flexible procedures have been eliminated or restricted, the result has been to complicate further the administration of criminal justice.

ture and socioeconomic opportunities. In accounting for past trends, especially since 1930, the effectiveness of police forces is probably of limited significance. This is not to deny the obvious assertion that the very existence of the police is essential for the viability of the criminal justice system and the resulting patterns of social order.[19]

However, as students of police behavior have demonstrated, most of the police efforts are directed to "keeping the peace," and the apprehension of criminals is a task which engages only a limited amount of their resources.[20] Moreover, the influence of the correction system cannot be judged by means of limited before and after studies of batches of inmates.[21] For 1965 to 1975, as mentioned above, the failure of the prison facilities to expand as rapidly as the youth population did strained the criminal justice system.

This type of systemic analysis which highlights social organization factors is fully compatible with the findings of a series of studies which seek statistically to identify the deterrent effect of punishment.[22] Analysis of the deterrent effect of criminal punishment, while hardly definitive, presents a body of evidence in support of the conclusion that speedy, consistent, and graded punishment does have such an effect. But the literature on deterrence does not negate the research on the sociological and economic "correlates" of criminal behavior.[23] In es-

19. John P. Clark and Richard E. Sykes, "Some Determinants of Police Organization and Practice in a Modern Industrial Democracy," in *Handbook of Criminology*, ed. Daniel Glaser (Chicago: Rand McNally, 1974), pp. 455–90.

20. Michael Banton, *The Policeman in the Community* (New York: Basic Books, 1965); Jerome H. Skolnick, *Justice Without Trial* (New York: Wiley, 1966); Egon Bittner, "The Police on Skid Row: A Study of Peace-Keeping," *American Sociological Review* 32 (October 1967): 699–715; William Westley, *Violence and the Police: A Sociological Study of Law, Custom and Morality* (Cambridge: MIT Press, 1970); David Bordua, ed., *The Police: Six Sociological Essays* (New York: Wiley, 1967); Albert J. Reiss, Jr., *The Police and the Public* (New Haven: Yale University Press, 1971).

21. Stuart Adams, "Measurement of Effectiveness and Efficiency in Corrections," in *Handbook of Criminology*, ed. Daniel Glaser (Chicago: Rand McNally, 1974), pp. 1021–49.

22. William Chambliss, "The Deterrent Influence of Punishment," *Crime and Delinquency* 12 (January 1966): 70–75; Charles R. Tittle and Charles H. Logan, "Sanctions and Deviance: Evidence and Remaining Questions," *Law and Society Review* 3 (1973); Isaac Ehrlich, "Participation in Illegitimate Activities: A Theoretical Investigation," *Journal of Political Economy* (May–June 1973): 521–65; for a summary of this type of research, see Frank E. Zimring and Gordon J. Hawkins, *Deterrence* (Chicago: University of Chicago Press, 1973); Charles R. Tittle and Alan R. Rowe, "Certainty of Arrest and Crime Roles, A Further Test of the Deterrence Hypothesis," *Social Forces* 52 (June 1974): 455–62.

23. Albert J. Reiss, Jr., "Discretionary Justice," in *Handbook of Criminology*, ed. D. Glaser (Chicago: Rand McNally, 1974), pp. 679–99.

sence, I infer that punishment is a meaningful deterrent (and hypothetically there could be no social order without a system of punishment) but differences in punishment systems are not as important as differences in social positions in accounting for the sources of criminal behavior.

The growth in the incidence of crime sets the context of the divergence of legal reasoning about criminal justice and popular beliefs and concerns. The trend in legal reasoning and judicial policy especially since the 1950s has been to extend citizen rights to the accused, to seek to improve criminal procedures, to limit police surveillance, to improve the conditions of imprisonment, and to remove the particular disabilities of low income and minority groups in the criminal justice process. Emphasis on controlling police brutality was also a pronounced theme and involved legislative regulation. Moreover, the courts have made a special effort to redefine the person's responsibility for his criminal behavior. In particular, the Durham decision of 1954—the same year as the school desegregation case—limited the responsibility of the "insane" criminal.[24] In the Court of Appeals for the District of Columbia Judge David L. Bazelon held that "an accused is not criminally responsible if his unlawful act was the product of mental disease or defect." Although this particular decision was reversed, the judicial trend has been in this direction.[25]

The body of new judicial decisions has been elaborate and continuous in 1955–1975, with the result that the practice of criminal justice procedures has changed. From the above reasoning, there is no basis for concluding that these judicial decisions are prime proximate factors in influencing the crime rate. No doubt these decisions contributed marginally to low morale among police officers, but the delay in courts and the limited correctional facilities are more important in complicating police procedures.

Nevertheless, the content of the changing body of law has been extensively covered in the mass media. In one sense, this trend reached a zenith in terms of public attention with the U.S. Supreme Court rulings on capital punishment. While these rulings have not been clear-cut, they constricted the application of the extreme coercive sanction. The overall judicial movement reflects internal developments in legal reasoning, the influence of humanitarian values, and selective support from

24. Durham v. U.S., 214 F 2 d862, 874 (D.C. Civ., 1954).
25. See U.S. v. Brawner, 471 F.2d 969 (1972).

social-science thinking and research. In the definition of the mass public, the courts have developed a more lenient attitude toward criminals; and this was taking place during a period of rising crime rates and increased fear of "crime in the streets."

One of the most revealing indicators of attitudes was the increasing popular preference for strong court action against convicted criminals. In 1965, 55% of the nationally sampled population thought that the courts were not harsh enough with criminals.[26] By 1974 the figure had grown to 85%. As can be seen from Table 10.2, the increasing

TABLE 10.2 Trends in Attitudes toward Treatment of Criminals by Courts, 1965–1974. (Based on National Sample Surveys)*

"The courts deal too harshly or not harshly enough with criminals?" "Not Harshly Enough"		Percent
	1965	57.5
	1968	75.0
	1972	74.2
	1973	80.5
	1974	84.2

*American Institute of Public Opinion 1965, 1968;
National Opinion Research Center 1972, 1973

SOURCE: Rebecca G. Adams, "Criminal Justice: Social Change Trend Report No. 42" (Chicago: National Opinion Research Center, 1975).

trend was not continuous. From 1965 to 1968 there was an increase in the demand for harsh treatment, from 1968 to 1972 the percentage remained relatively constant; it rose again after 1972. It could well be that the plateau reflected in the aftermath of the violence of the late 1960s and the short-term acceptance of the goals of social change, especially increased job opportunities for minority-group members as a strategy for dealing with increased crime rates.

The theme that the courts were not harsh enough was widely diffused throughout the social segments of society. However, the pattern of diffusion is most revealing of the influence of the criminal justice trends on popular attitudes. In 1965, males rather than females, the less educated rather than the better educated, believed more often that the courts were not harsh enough. By 1974 sex differences were eliminated and the better educated had come to emphasize that the courts were not harsh enough. Moreover, younger groups were strongest in their belief that the courts were not harsh enough.

26. Rebecca G. Adams, "Criminal Justice: Social Change Trend Report No. 2" (Chicago: National Opinion Research Center, 1975).

A similar hardening of attitude toward capital punishment has accompanied the increase in crime rates and the growth of apprehension about crime. Trend data are available for 1936 to 1974. In 1936 one-third of the population were opposed to capital punishment.[27] In 1953 those in opposition had fallen to 25%, but this appears to represent a short fluctuation in response to the espionage case of Ethel and Julius Rosenberg and to a dramatic kidnap-murder of a young child. Opposition to capital punishment increased until 1966 when 47% expressed such attitudes. Thereafter, the trend has been down, so that by 1974, 32% were opposed. These shifts follow closely the pattern of the decline and rise in the homicide and associated crime rates. Our argument is that the changes in the judicial posture are not prime factors in accounting for the actual trends in crime rates. However, popular opinion is based on the reverse estimate, namely, that the new judicial posture makes a decisive difference in the crime rate. Popular attitudes have been negatively influenced both by the presentations of these decisions in the mass media and by the direct impact of rising crime rates. The underlying age structure and "economic hardship" are not thought to be prime factors. As a result, the essential effect of the judicial decisions has been a weakening of popular legitimacy of the criminal justice system, and an increased distrust of a central institution of society.

The reactions of the "ordinary citizen" who comes into direct contact with the police and related enforcement agencies are also involved. The negative image of the lack of legitimacy and effectiveness of these officials is so widespread that most contact with them frequently produces a negative reaction. For example, it is possible to trace the reactions of a group of 210 encounters of persons who had minor "problems" or "difficulties" with government officials.[28] The data were collected by national sample survey interviews and unfortunately did not specify a time period, but sought information about such incidents at any time in the person's life. The results were as follows: problems

27. Tom W. Smith, "A Trend Analysis of Attitudes toward Capital Punishment, 1936–1974," in *Studies of Social Change Since 1948*, ed. J. A. Faris (Chicago: National Opinion Research Center, 1976), pp. 257–318.

28. Daniel Katz et al., *Bureaucratic Encounters: A Pilot Study in the Evaluation of Government Services* (Ann Arbor, Mich.: Institute for Social Research, 1975), pp. 63–116.

concerning driver's license, 4%; traffic violations, 3%; income tax, 6%; and police interference, 4%.[29]

A summary measure of the citizen's evaluation of his experience was constructed with a rating from favorable to neutral to unfavorable. These persons, in general, had a difficulty and in some cases a possible infraction. Therefore, one would not have expected widespread favorable reactions; a neutral response would have been a measure of acceptance, if not belief in the legitimacy of the procedures. However, as can be seen from Table 10.3, only 10% of the encounters produced neutral evaluations. Most, 58.5%, were unfavorable, while 30.5% were not ascertainable or probably also on the negative side. There was not a single neutral response to police encounters. Negative attitudes resulted despite the fact that one-half of the persons were aware that appeal procedures were available and almost one-quarter of the persons involved made use of these appeal procedures. The extension of police and administrative regulation to larger sectors of the population means that citizens have increased contacts with the coercive agents of government. Many persons, especially from middle social strata, including those who have their first contact with such agents, resent that they are being "challenged," even though they nominally accept the principle of equal treatment before the law.

Consequences of Judicial Activism

The second element in the strain in the popular legitimacy of legal institutions and the judicial process hinges on the activist role of the courts and especially the Supreme Court in directing societal change by extending the content of citizenship. The goals of the active court have rested on extensive popular support when the issues have centered on equality of opportunity and the elimination of arbitrary discrimination. In fact over time these goals have generated increasing support. Yet it is understandable that there has been increased citizen criticism of the means prescribed by the courts, especially when these means require extensive coercive sanctions. Likewise, there has been less popular support and more determined criticism when the social goals

29. For a discussion of criminality, see Edwin H. Sutherland, "White Collar Criminality," *American Sociological Review* 5 (February 1940), 1–12; Edwin H. Sutherland, *White Collar Crime* (New York: Holt, Rinehart and Winston, 1949).

impinge on personal morality, as in abortion and the distribution of pornography.

Moreover, in accounting for the declining popular legitimacy of the courts, as mentioned above, given the common law traditions of the United States, fundamental social and economic changes are facilitated by legislative enactment, while the underlying effectiveness of the courts rests on their ability to refine and clarify "the law." One of the most far-reaching societal changes in the United States during the 1960s

TABLE 10.3 Public Encounters with Regulatory Government Agencies: Overall Evaluation Favorable versus Unfavorable (Based on 210 "Encounters")

	Type of Problem					
Rating	Driver's license	Traffic violations	Tax	Police	Other	Total
Favorable	0	3.8%	0	0	0	1.0%
Neutral	12.2%	7.7	15.5%	0	8.1%	10.0
Unfavorable	73.2	42.3	57.7	65.7%	51.3	58.5
N.A.	14.6	46.2	26.8	34.3	41.0	30.5
Total	100	100	100	100	100	100
N	41	26	71	35	37	210

SOURCE: Daniel Katz, *Bureaucratic Encounters* (Ann Arbor, Mich.: Institute for Social Research, 1975), p. 103.

was the extension of the franchise to increase minority-group participation, especially blacks in the South, and subsequently the regulation of campaign expenditures which came into being in the 1970s. The increased participation of blacks as registered voters reflects the intense efforts of voluntary groups; voluntary efforts also stimulated reform of campaign finances. However, both of these basic changes which strengthened the legitimacy of electoral institutions have been the result of federal legislation. These legislative interventions improved the legitimacy of electoral outcomes and the resulting political balance because it was based on a broader citizen participation and because financial advantages were contained. In short, broader minority political participation, that is, the participation mainly of blacks, was more readily accomplished than school desegregation not only because of the weakened institutional barriers but also in part because of the greater legitimacy of the legislative authority in such matters.

In fact, the increased incorporation of blacks and other minorities into the electoral process occurred without significant strain on the processes of social control. The consequences of the regulation of financial contributions were marked, as will discussed in chapter 13, in that it reduced the advantage of those candidates who had been able to raise large amounts of campaign funds; again, these reforms have been accepted without significant resistance. Both these changes in the political process strengthened the effective electoral support for the welfare state.

In contrast, the redefinition of citizen rights resulting from judicial intervention in support of particular social and economic rights contributed to the extensive strain on institutional legitimacy. The most important—i. e., the most visible and publicized intervention—has been the outlawing of school segregation by the U.S. Supreme Court in 1954. At work has been not only the original decision by the U.S. Supreme Court but also the ensuing series of decisions by federal courts at all levels seeking to implement school desegregation by means of busing. In the school desegregation cases, the coercive power of the state rapidly emerged as crucial for implementing the revised legal reasoning. Equally important are mechanisms of societal change, but less dramatic have been the wide range of affirmative action steps in public and private employment and in institutions of higher education. While there are legislative components in these programs, the scope, definition, and strategy of "affirmative action" have been to a considerable extent the result of the activism of the courts and officials of the Department of Health, Education and Welfare.

Since the U.S. Supreme Court decision on school desegregation, mass attitudes as expressed in opinion surveys in support of school integration have continually increased. Public support for the goal of school integration has been measured for 1950 to 1972 by the question, "Do you think white students and Negro students should go to the same schools or to separate schools?" The white population's acceptance of racial school integration grew from 53% in 1950 to 78% in 1972.[30] The increase has been gradual and continuous without significant or persistent reversal. In effect, the trends represent an increase of slightly more than 1% per year. Regional differences in opposition to school integration have declined, so that differences between the South and the rest of the nation became smaller. The structure of attitudes —reflecting underlying social personality—is that younger and better

30. For an analysis of these trend data, see A. Wade Smith, "Racial Tolerance as a Function of Group Position," Ph.D. dissertation, University of Chicago, August 1977.

educated persons are more willing to express their acceptance of school integration than older and less educated persons. The mass media have contributed in refashioning societal norms in support of the objective of school integration, but the result has not been effectively internalized and therefore not necessarily binding on local communities faced with the realities of school integration.

The capacity of the federal government to accomplish school integration in particular locales has been striking, particularly in certain Southern cities. However, individual family and organized group resistance has been extensive. Families have sought alternatives to public education or have moved. There has been conspicuous and persistent group resistance, for example, in South Boston, which has strained not only the immediate community but also the environs. Moreover, organized political opposition to school desegregation erupts in a wide variety of legislative efforts to constrain and limit educational integration. These legislative initiatives serve as an index to the continuing opposition to the court decisions.

"Affirmative action" in employment and in higher education has operated on popular attitudes in a fashion similar to that of school desegregation; generalized acceptance of goals and controversy about scope and means. Although aspects of these programs are grounded in legislative enactment, it is judicial decrees which are visible and seen as the instruments of affirmative action. Trend data on popular legitimacy and acceptance of affirmative action are not extensive. However, there are greater opposition and criticism to affirmative action in access to higher education than in employment opportunities. This is not to overlook the tensions generated where equal opportunity for employment and promotion results in women's becoming supervisors of male personnel.

In effect, the courts' legal reasoning in affirmative action in higher education has permitted the imposition of numerical quotas in admissions and in academic employment. The response has been intense public debate and widespread opposition; such opposition has been concentrated among better educated and higher-income groups that have traditionally supported the elimination of segregation and discrimination.

Finally, it must be emphasized that popular criticism of legal reasoning is most intense on issues which have been defined as personal morality; in particular, the right to abortion and the distribution of pornography. Both these issues mobilize a minority of persons intensely and passionately opposed to judicial trends toward more "liberal" practices. But criticism of judicial decisions is not limited to this minority; the middle-of-the-road majority had by the early 1970s developed a compromise position on both these issues which was influencing legislative enactment and creating persistent controversy between legislative assemblies and the courts.

In partial summary, the consequences of a rising crime rate and dissatisfaction with the system of criminal justice plus the tensions generated by the activist role of the judicial system are highlighted by the long-term trend in attitudes toward the U.S. Supreme Court. It is understandable that the Supreme Court would be the focus of hostility and changed attitudes and an indicator of underlying reaction to authority. The Supreme Court and the images of the justices themselves as human beings have penetrated deeply into popular consciousness. But in the post–World War II period the downward trend in approval has been striking. On the basis of national samples assembled by the National Opinion Research Center, in 1949, 83.4% of the population expressed approval and trust in the Supreme Court, but by 1973, the figure had decreased to 32.6%.[31] The Harris Survey for 1975 showed even lower "confidence"; namely, 28%. Given the high prestige of the Supreme Court and its position as the most trusted institution in the society, this drop was more extensive than for any other institution in the United States. It amounted to approximately 2% per year and was in effect almost a "straight-line" decline. Those persons with higher education tended to be more favorable to the Supreme Court, but by 1972 this educational difference had attenuated. Likewise, other social differences —women and younger persons more favorable—declined during these years. Such changes in normative judgments are of deep systemic import; they imply significant weakening of the mechanisms of social control and the socialization process related to the acceptance and internalization of societal-wide norms.

The Meaning of Political Violence

Our systemic analysis of the consequences of legitimate coercion needs to be extended and amplified at this point. We have charted the divergence between judicial reasoning and popular norms concerning the

31. Karen Neuman, "Confidence in the Supreme Court" (National Opinion Research Center, 1976).

legitimacy of coercive sanctions, a divergence which is reflected in the long-term strains on both personal and social controls.

However, an alternative, but directly related issue requires examination. To what extent have the patterns and trends in political violence, the crescendo of militant action of the 1960s in opposition to the Vietnam War, and the racial confrontations left a mark on societal socialization? From the point of view of the direct participants, their use of coercion was legitimate, and at the time a minority—ranging from 10% to 25% in the population—gave varying verbal assent to the legitimacy of these outbursts.

Political violence, including parapolitical violence, comprises not merely outbursts of collective behavior but also deliberate decisions and collective efforts to produce societal change by force and coercion. There is a strong component of voluntarism in the application of political violence, and this was pointedly so in the 1960s. In the view of the participants, the actual tactics of violence had political relevance to the extent that they were able to make use of the mass media. The mass media portrayal of political violence emerged as being as important as the destructive consequences of the violence itself; coercion and persuasion became fused.

The history of political violence in general, and specifically in the United States, as it emerged in advanced industrial society, cannot be written without explicit reference to the justifications, or rationalization, if you will, offered for the use of violence and the objectives to be achieved by coercive sanctions. In the United States from the 1890s to World War I, the symbolism of the anarchists, epitomized by the agitations of the International Workers of the World, was dominant. The permanent destruction of the organized state was the goal. Immediately after World War I, the language of Marxism supplied the symbolic rationalization.[32] Violence of Communists and Trotskyists was justified as the instrument of the "dictatorship of the proletariat" to create a classless society. In the 1930s during the Great Depression, for the first time a native fascist movement arose with an explicit ideology of coercive violence.[33] The rise of fascist movements in Europe was influential. The U.S. native fascist movement was different than

32. Gabriel Almond, *The Appeals of Communism* (Princeton: Princeton University Press, 1954).

33. Morris Janowitz, "American Black Legions," in *America in Crisis: Fourteen Crucial Episodes in American History*, ed. Daniel Aron (New York: Knopf, 1952), pp. 305–25.

the nativist movements of the nineteenth century which agitated against recent immigrants. The term "fascist" is appropriate for the new movements of the 1930s which had broader concerns than these antiethnic agitations; they were explicitly seeking to alter the social structure fundamentally by force and violence. As a result, much of the political violence of the 1930s was between the extremists of the left and of the right. But with the outbreak of World War II in Europe, Communist groups modulated their appeal for political violence as they shifted their emphasis to a popular front in support of the USSR.

However, the impact of the Soviet-German Non-Aggression Pact and internal factionalism in the U.S. Communist party meant that the old left was not reassembled during the 1950s. Even in the early 1960s neither the "old left" nor the tiny residues of native fascist groups commanded attention as spokesmen of political violence. The civil rights movement and a segment of the antiwar movement of that period were strongly conditioned by nonviolent passive resistance and religious sentiments. But rapidly a "new left" emerged which was deeply divided about its commitment to political violence. One wing, seeking to reconstruct a "socialist tradition," eschewed political violence for an internal debate about the nature of "participatory democracy." However, the new left became rapidly "radicalized," in its acceptance of an ideology and practice of political violence as a mode of opposition to participation in the war in Vietnam. The dominant tone was supplied by the radical factions derived from "militant" Marxist and Maoist ideologies.

The symbolism and the imagery of "national liberation," as transmitted by the events in the "Third World" and by a number of intellectuals in the United States, rapidly supplied a new set of justifications. Societal change in the United States could be accomplished only by violence—and this maxim was applicable to the history of the United States. Violence is a form of mass education, to socialize the population at large, to create the preconditions of political action and political change. This was the case internally, to end the exploitation of racial minorities, students, women, and the like, and externally, to end the war in Vietnam.

The diffusion of this ideology was extensive because of the mass media, particularly as a result of the interviews on television with student and race "revolutionaries." The coverage of student and race confrontations offered the opportunity for their leaders to present their ideology. In the previous periods, militant movements were limited to their own press and face-to-face communications; but in the 1960s the "revolutionaries" had access to the television as an instrument of organizational communication. The effective audience was less the "masses" and more other student and educated groups.

It will remain for future historians to assess fully both the short-term and long-range consequences of the political violence against the war in Vietnam and in the racial arena. From the point of view of social control, our concern is particularly with the long-term effects on societal socialization and national norms. The outbursts of political violence of the 1960s did not become institutionalized. In fact, contrary to the expectation of various social scientists, the outbursts disappeared rapidly, following the historical tradition of previous periods of intensified political violence.[34]

The immediate, short-term political impact of the violent agitations against the war in Vietnam is more difficult to estimate than that of racial violence. It can be argued that the militant opposition had an effect, but probably a small one, in accelerating the withdrawal of U.S. forces and in encouraging greater flexibility on the part of the United States in negotiations with the North Vietnam regime. The violence may have contributed to speeding up the end of conscription. Vietnam was fought with a strong reliance on draftees. The end of the draft saw the atrophy of the student agitation; in contrast to Western Europe an enlarged and persistent radical student movement did not develop.

The political effect of racial violence seems clearer, if one imposes a short-term perspective. It needs to be emphasized that the race riots of 1964–1968, as various observers have documented, differed from the urban race riots in the period immediately after World War I.[35] The earlier outbursts were communal riots—they represented white resistance to the population expansion of the ghetto. They erupted at the boundaries of the black and white communities and involved attacks by whites on the black population, often with the assistance of local law enforcement officials. The riots of the 1960s were more parapo-

34. Sheldon G. Levy, "A 150 Year Study of Political Violence in the United States," in *Violence in America*, ed. Hugh D. Graham and Ted R. Gurr (New York: Bantam Books, 1969), pp. 94–100.

35. Morris Janowitz, "Patterns of Collective Racial Violence," in ibid., pp. 393–422.

litical; they represented black attacks against the symbols of white authority and power—against white law officers and against economic establishments. The violence took place almost entirely within the black community. It involved black rioters against white law enforcement officers and fire fighters, and included extensive looting of stores and widespread burning of buildings and apartment houses in which the blacks resided. In contrast to the early urban riots, whites from outside the black community did not participate or were blocked by the police from participating. The riots have been called "commodity riots" because of their parapolitical overtones and because they represented not only violence but also aspirations of the black community to participate in the institutions and material values of the larger society.

These riots produced "crash" political and economic programs of change by white leadership groups. There is every reason to believe that there was some immediate symbolic effect. However, it should not be overlooked that the destruction caused by the riots was felt heavily by blacks, thereby creating an increasing resistance to rioting. As a result there was the rise of counterrioters, both formal and informal leaders who worked to "cool it" and prevent new rioting. Moreover, police procedures for dealing with potential riots improved; by the use of "manpower not firepower," and the use of black policemen, the law enforcement officers contributed to a decline in the spread of disturbances.

It can be argued that the initial violence contributed to a positive response by the larger society; likewise, the rapid decline in violence further strengthened the "politics" of adaptation and conciliation. In short, one cannot rule out the hypothesis that prolongation of group racial violence could well have been counterproductive to institutional change. The racial tensions and rioting of this decade had a profound influence on the civil rights leaders, causing them to shift their priorities and leading to a closer collaboration with existing black leaders.[36] The civil rights movement stressed equal access to public facilities as a direct goal to dramatize the desire for equality of blacks in the larger society. The civil rights movement also was concerned with voting registration and desegregation of schools. These demands had a strong middle-class "orientation" and a longer time perspective. The race riots

36. William J. Wilson, *The Declining Significance of Race: Blacks and Changing American Institions* (Chicago: University of Chicago Press, 1978).

shifted priorities of goals to a concern with immediate job opportunities for unskilled and semiskilled blacks. Nevertheless, the most extensive effect of the violent agitations of the period was, in retrospect, the increased attendance of blacks at college and universities and their subsequent entrance into white-collar and professional employment in markedly increased numbers. As William J. Wilson has demonstrated, one decade later, by 1975, the socioeconomic position of middle-strata blacks had improved much more dramatically than the black "under class."[37]

But one cannot escape direct examination of the longer-term influence the political violence of the 1960s had on underlying patterns of personal and social controls and on mechanisms of societal socialization, or the claim of conventional wisdom that the resort to violence in order to end the war in Vietnam and to achieve racial equality contributed to a weakening of personal control and in turn to ineffective social control. We have very little pertinent systematic research; in fact, the complexity of the problem almost defies explication.

This is a research topic which is not effectively handled by the methodology of the standardized national sample survey. Thus in conducting a massive but conventional survey on attitudes "justifying violence" during 1969, Monica D. Blumenthal and her associates were aware of the ambiguity of their efforts.[38] The authors themselves question their central findings. Of what relevance is the central finding that 9% of the sample of adult males believed that "protest in which some people are killed" would be necessary to bring about change, while 19% to 23% felt that protest involving "some personal injury would be needed"?[39] They concluded their analysis with the assertion that "there are at least two ways of looking at these figures." One way is that "we can congratulate ourselves that the great majority of men are so commited to the idea that change can be produced without violence." The other way, "We can ask ourselves whether it is really desirable or safe to have one quarter of our male population believing that some degree of violence is required to produce change in our society." In the absence of a historical perspective and explicit standards of judgment, it is indeed difficult to use such data. Not only is the gap be-

37. Ibid.

38. Monica D. Blumenthal et al., *Justifying Violence: Attitudes of American Men* (Ann Arbor, Mich.: Institute for Social Research, 1972).

39. Ibid., p. 37.

tween attitudes and behavior great, but also the linkages are complicated and inconsistent. The expression of verbal hostility may well be an effective substitute in part of the population for agressive action in the political arena. The real danger rests in those citizens who are unaware of and unable to recognize their own hostile, violent, and aggressive proclivities.

In contrast to the variety of conventional attitude surveys conducted during these turbulent years, Barry Skura tried to trace out the aftermath of the race rioting of 1964–1968 on political behavior in the local communities of 94 large U.S. cities.[40] This enterprise is significant because of the range of data collected. He assembled measures of the severity of rioting; he reanalyzed large-scale surveys which measured community attitudes; he drew on systematic reports by community leaders and analyzed actual voting behavior.

The results are more revealing for black communities than for white ones. Skura's basic hypothesis is that in the aftermath of severe rioting in a city, there was an increase in the political and organizational activity in poor black communities. The data offer clear support of this hypothesis. However, it is important to underscore that the increase in political activity was not among the rank-and-file citizens who largely reacted with a heightened sense of black consciousness and solidarity. The increased political activity was among the leaders and reflected mainly interorganization activities and coalition building.

But one must ask the question whether this was a direct result of the riots; and no doubt to some extent it was. However, it was also the result of new resources and new programs generated in the white community to which the black leaders were responding. In other words, the political effect of the riots which Skura could discern resulted in part from the response of white leaders.

But what of the basic longer-term configuration of values and ideologies which emerged in the aftermath of the political violence of the 1960s? What was the normative influence of actual involvement in militant agitations as well as the imagery of riots and political violence in the mass media over a number of years? Conventional wisdom stresses the negative effect on existing citizen norms and a weakening of institutional legitimacy. These experiences had effects on the recruitment of new generations of political leaders, an effect which will grad-

40. Barry Skura, "The Impact of Collective Racial Violence on Neighborhood Mobilization, 1964–1968," Ph.D. dissertation, University of Chicago, 1976.

ually be revealed with the passage of time. However, the events of the 1960s left no permanent, visible cadre of radical leaders. Among the blacks, the experiences of the riot period had the effect of developing a more pragmatic and bargaining outlook which has characterized elected black leadership in the national elections of 1972 and 1976 and in countless local elections.

But the political violence reached two generations of college and university students and by means of the mass media touched wide audiences. Nevertheless, the hypothesis must be offered, and it can be no more than offered, that, one decade afterward, the political and racial violence was limited, indeed very limited, in influencing political perspectives or actual political behavior in the citizenry at large. If there was a discernible result, it was an additional contribution to the distrust of institutional effectiveness and strain on political legitimacy. Instead, the long-term increase in institutional disarticulation, I argue, has had more effect on the distrust of institutional authority and especially on the authority of governmental agencies.

More specifically, it appears that the discernible effect was on segments of students in college and universities who were "radicalized," not into new militant movements, but into deep and continuing suspicion and opposition to authority and distrust of the political process and to an increased acceptance of public disorder.

There is an indicator which is thought to relate to political violence or at least to violent ideologies namely, gun ownership. To what extent can the ownership of guns, especially of handguns, and the attitudes of their owners be used as measures of commitment to political violence? By and large, the private ownership of handguns especially is assumed to be an expression of "rightist" orientations. Of course, the gun culture in the United States has deep historical roots, especially in rural areas and in the South. But, of particular significance, is the post–World War II possession of weapons in urban areas. To what extent can this development be taken as another indicator of ineffective social control and declining legitimacy of official police and legal institutions? The approximately 13,000 annual homicides resulting from firearms and the estimated 23,000 accidental shootings are a profound national problem to the criminal justice system. Moreover, some observers argue the ownership and possession of these weapons have come to imply "parapolitical" overtones—especially rightist ideological ones. The claim that "in the wilderness of the cities, just as in the wilderness of the frontier, the gun becomes an effective equalizer" is a picturesque sociological aphorism.[41] Moreover, the political implications of gun ownership have been overstated, especially as an indicator of commitment to political violence.

First, personal and household ownership of guns has not increased in the United States in the period for which there are survey data (Table 10.4).[42] On the basis of national samples in 1959, 49% of the

TABLE 10.4 Trends in Ownership of Weapons, 1959–1973 (Based on Self Reports in National Sample Surveys)

	1959[a]	1973[b]	Change
Percent owning any weapon	49	47	− 2
Percent owning a rifle[c]	55	62	+ 7
Percent owning a shotgun[c]	65	58	− 7
Percent owning a handgun[c]	32	42	+10

a. *Source*: Gallup poll, September 4, 1959, as reported in Erskine (1972:456).
b. *Source*: 1973 NORC General Social Survey.
c. Figures for ownership by type are expressed as a percentage of those who owned a weapon, not of the total sample.
SOURCE: James D. Wright and Linda L. Marston, "The Ownership of the Means of Destruction: Weapons in the United States," *Social Problems* 23 (October 1975): 94.

adult population reported there were guns in their homes or garage; and the figure stood at 47% in 1973. While surveys of gun ownership have distortions, these types of data are relatively valid. The defects in these data are for young persons from very low-income areas where the underreporting of possessing weapons is extensive. Second, the bulk of gun ownership is that of rifles and shotguns designed for and owned as part of outdoor and hunting culture. Of those who reported owning a gun in 1973, 62% indicated that they had a rifle, 58% owned a shotgun, and 42% a handgun, which did represent an increase of 10 percentage points from 1959. The rifle and shotgun owners—the sports-oriented owners—tended to be concentrated in rural areas, small towns, and the South, and among higher-income groups. But the owners of handguns who define their weapons as for protection are more evenly distributed throughout the social structure. There is less difference in ownership between upper- and lower-income and education groups,

41. Lewis A. Coser, "Some Social Functions of Violence," *The Annals* 364 (March 1966): 10.

42. James D. Wright and Linda L. Marston, "The Ownership of the Means of Destruction: Weapons in the United States," *Social Problems* 23 (October 1975): 93–107.

and the ownership of handguns has penetrated into urban centers, particularly into suburban areas.

Because most gun owners are hunters, it was not unanticipated that the study of the attitudes of gun owners by James D. Wright and Linda L. Marston concluded that "most of the gunowners studied . . . are probably responsible persons who use their weapons for legitimate activities."[43] Even the majority of handgun owners are "lawabiding citizens"; and in general they consider that their ownership of handguns is compatible with existing law—which in general it is. They believe that they are acting in support of the duly constituted law enforcement officers of their community, since they are seeking to offset the "weakness" of the existing criminal justice system.

However, a comparison of handgun owners with owners of any type of gun revealed the expected differences and illuminated the associated political outlooks and ideologies. As anticipated, the handgun owners more often believe that the courts are not harsh enough (41.4% versus 20.2%). However, they were not more antiwelfare (too much is being spent on welfare, 21.0% versus 42.7%); this in part reflects the strong component of lower-income groups among handgun owners. Moreover, it is striking that fear of future encounters with criminal offenders rather than actual experiences with criminals or crime is associated with handgun ownership.

But these data do not adequately identify the limited minority of gun owners, especially handgun owners, who are motivated by deep fears with strong ideological overtones. They have come to assume that they must arm themselves because of an exisiting or impending breakdown in the system of criminal justice and in the political order. They hold distorted ideologies replete with authoritarian symbolism, particularly rightist language. There are no reliable measures of the size of these group, but their number are not limited to isolated individuals. We are dealing with 2% or 5% of the population, by my estimate. In chapter 4, the segment of the population who held antidemocratic ideologies was identified at about 10% of the adult population, and this figure had not increased since the 1930s. Among them are these persons whose fearful and hostile attitudes have led them to possess handguns. Their number measures the most hostile and most distrustful human beings in contemporary society. An examination of the rec-

43. Ibid., p. 104.

ord and achievement of such persons in native fascist groups and my interviews with such social personalities at least offer the assurance that they are so hostile, suspicious, and individualistic that they are not likely to be mobilized into "radical right" social-political movements. If such movements are to succeed, more realistic and more instrumentally effective persons capable of a higher degree of sustained organizational cooperation must be involved. Although these persons are very hostile, in a real sense, their social personality is highly privatized and it is difficult to speak of their "societal socialization."

In overviewing the role of the mass media and the coercive aspects of the legal system in socialization, it is necessary to remember that to examine a parliamentary regime without direct comparisons with authoritarian and totalitarian systems is to introduce strong distortion. From the perspective of social control, comparison of parliamentary with authoritarian and especially with totalitarian systems is not a matter of degree when one examines the balance between persuasion and coercion and the resulting patterns of societal socialization. There is a fundamental threshold difference in such comparisons.

The difference between a totalitarian and authoritarian nation-state hinges on the intensity and scope of internal coercion. In a totalitarian system, the level of internal coercion is markedly greater than in an authoritarian system. The concentration camp is the hallmark of the totalitarian society, and the totalitarian nation is one that must rule by use of the concentration camp. In an authoritarian state, the threat of coercion is decisive as a means of constraint.

In a democratic system, persuasion is the process by which political parties come into power and by which they seek to rule, while coercion is circumscribed and limited by the legitimating norms. Paradoxically, authoritarian and totalitarian movements make greater use of and rely more heavily on propaganda and persuasion in the struggle to achieve power than after their seizure of power, when they rule essentially by coercive sanctions and administrative decree. The "natural" histories of both Nazi Germany and Soviet Russia demonstrate that, after the seizure of power, the importance of the mass media for the single-party system declines, since the destruction of organized political opposition means that the elites no longer believe in the desirability, effectiveness, and relevance of mass persuasion. Of course, after the seizure of power these regimes must have an element of legitimacy, since there is a limit to the amount of coercion they have at their disposal. The strands of legitimacy rest on the personal appeals of the top leader or leaders as well as on the performance of administrative agencies.

Our analysis of the consequences of mass persuasion and legitimate coercion in a parliamentary setting has involved attitudes toward authority and societal socialization—that is, the resulting patterns of social personality. These are the intervening variables between the ordered social segments and the institutional sectors, on the one hand, and the resulting patterns of political participation and social control, on the other. There is and must be a "goodness of fit" among attitudes and social personality and the political institutions on which a parliamentary system rests. The socialization process, in short, must articulate with the institutional requirements for effective social control. We are not dealing with highly transitory relations, but with a process of gradual accumulation and transformation.

The intellectual process of systemic analysis, because it is concerned with values and value judgments, must make summary judgments about the consequences of the societal socialization, that is, about its adequacy and appropriateness for the maintenance of a democratic polity. Equivalent processes operate in authoritarian and totalitarian societies; these regimes demonstrate patterns of socialization which are compatible with their political formats. Our analysis of the socialization at the societal level in the United States points to the high strain between institutions and value patterns required for effective social control; but there is hardly any basis to concluding that there are broad trends which will anticipate or contribute to basic systemic transformation.

Thus we return to our original framework; under systemic analysis some measure of "explanatory" independence is given to attitude patterns and to underlying social personality. This is true for the citizenry and more so for the leader and elite groups. The great master trends of industrialization and military conflict do not account for the difference one finds in the social organization of parliamentary versus totalitarian nation-states. The accumulation of attitude patterns—the results of the process of societal socialization—operate at least as secondary variables. But even if these processes are seen as the source of secondary variables, they have an element of autonomy. In terms of the mechanisms of social control, they have a self-generating dimension. The idea of the accumulation and utilization of economic and technological resources is matched by the analog of the generation and accumulation and utilization of norms and values by means of socialization.

The influence of the mass media and the strains on legitimate coercion indicate that in the second half of the period under investigation moral resources were being overconsumed and overutilized without being adequately replenished. The growth of distrust and projective suspicion is a clear-cut manifestation. In terms of mass persuasion and legitimate coercion, the socialization that occurs in the community must articulate with that which takes place at the societal level. In political terms, the issue is that of "institution building" so that the electoral system can be more effective, that is, create more workable regimes and legitimate and meaningful majorities. Thus, the final section of this analysis deals with management of interpersonal relations and institution building.

The analysis of the social process over half a century has been pursued in terms of the impact of the threat of the garrison state and the consequences of the welfare state. The framework has been that of the contemplative perspective—the analysis of the unfolding of institutional history. The next step in the analysis takes the perspective of the manipulative standpoint. It examines the conscious efforts, including those of the social scientist, to alter the main lines of societal change, to deal with instabilities and disarticulations. The complexities of an advanced industrial society are matched only by the complexities of the conscious efforts to alter its putative character. The awkward but pointed terminology of Karl Mannheim in *Man and Society in an Age of Reconstruction* remains attractive to me.

IV

Rationality, Institution Building, and Social Control

Eleven

The Management of Interpersonal Relations

INSTITUTION BUILDING

The final portion of this study focuses on institution building for social control, and therefore the emphasis of analysis shifts.[1] Our strategy has stressed a "contemplative perspective" that is a reflective examination of trends in societal change.[2] The contemplative standpoint makes primary use of variables derived from technological, ecological, and economic processes to chart and account for these societal developments. But our systemic analysis has also been based on a clear recognition that at any given moment or period, leaders struggle to influence the structure of social organization and the direction and content of societal change. In this final portion it becomes more appropriate and necessary to focus on competing leadership groups—that is, to adopt a "manipulative" standpoint, to examine social processes as seen by leaders, both political and professional. This strategy implies a stronger and more explicit emphasis on the normative and voluntaristic dimensions in leaders and subleaders and their operating procedures and networks. In short, the underlying question is to assess the prospects for reasoned direction of societal change. As one seeks to explain the emergence of weak political regimes in the parliamentary nation-states, the elite dimensions become indispensable. The manipulative standpoint (again, used nonpejoratively) is an essential aspect of professional groups. The result of using it analytically need not be a diffuse eclecticism; it can be a reasoned and patterned "multivariate" analysis. The intellectual objective is to search for an imputed causal configuration

1. For a discussion of the sociological background of the term "institution building," see S. N. Eisenstadt, *Max Weber: On Charisma and Institution Building* (Chicago: University of Chicago Press, 1968), pp. ix–lvi.

2. Harold D. Lasswell, *World Politics and Personal Insecurity* (New York: McGraw-Hill, 1935), pp. 3–26.

which avoids the excessive abstractions of "materialist" or "idealist" interpretations of societal organization which have been stimulated by the Hegelian influence on social research.[3]

When I speak of institution building, I mean those conscious efforts to direct societal change and to search for more effective social control which are grounded in rationality and in turn are supported by social-science efforts. Two assumptions are immediately involved. First, conscious institution building does not assume a rationalistic view of man and society. The application of the scientific method to research and to public policy, as collective problem solving has come to be termed, moves in the opposite direction. It confirms the limits of rational economic and psychological man and denies the possibility and indeed the desirability of relying exclusively or mechanically on such models as the basis for institution building. The difficult and unending task is to identify the particular relevance of rationalistic models, for the limits of their applicability involve matters of judgment if not intuition.

Second, the notion of institution building means that, with the growth of the division of labor and the separation of work from the community of residence and family, the elites and subelites recognize the need and desirability of enlarging citizen participation in decision making. My underlying conclusion has been anticipated by members of the political elites. It is not possible to rely on periodic elections to maintain the legitimacy of parliamentary government; nor do periodic elections supply adequate mechanisms for decision making. To be concerned with institution building is therefore to distinguish the viable and effective forms of citizen participation from those which are ineffective, self-destructive, or merely ideological, a topic to be discussed in chapter 12.

Thus to consider institution building is to examine the actual and potential influence of scientific thought—especially social-scientific—on ongoing institutions. Conscious efforts at institution building include the fusion or, if you will, the balancing of scientific thought with the full range of disciplined creativity which draws on traditional and in-

3. See Sidney Hook, *From Hegel to Marx: Studies in the Intellectual Development of Karl Marx* (New York: Reynal and Hitchcock, 1936). The intellectual history of one important effort to avoid these formulations is presented in Neil Coughlan, *Young John Dewey: An Essay in American Intellectual History* (Chicago: University of Chicago Press, 1975).

novative humanistic enterprise.[4] Social scientists continue to have difficulty relating themselves to humanistic endeavor in a postindustrial society because they think of the humanities as mainly critical evaluations rather than creative and productive endeavors.[5] This is in part because the humanities have come to be practiced mainly in university settings. Effective social science, it must be repeated, highlights the limitations of rationalistic explanations of human behavior and achievement. And—no less important—the humanities leave an indelible record of the inherent influence of emotive impulse on societal change and the effective pursuit of intellectual goals (including the social sciences).

With the vast growth of the public and private institutions of social research, counterpuntally, it has become fashionable to attack the rationalism of social science as self-defeating and to decry the "eclipse of reason" which social investigation is accused of generating.[6] My approach and the approach of systemic analysis reject such a global perspective. This is not to deny the extensive distortions and exaggerations of purpose and achievement resulting from mechanical scientism in the social sciences. But it does reject the argument that organized social investigation of the real world undermines reason, and thereby necessarily and automatically contributes to the attenuation of the social order and to the weakening of social control.

On the contrary, the reverse assumption is more accurate. I wish to assert that, on balance, advanced industrial society is more tolerable, and the possibility of effective social control is greater, because there exists a cadre of social scientists who are devoted to the pragmatic—as opposed to the mechanical or ideological—application of the scientific method to social and political reality.

There is little point in arguing on behalf of the accumulated benefits of social research on formal and logical grounds. Such arguments are unconvincing and often self-serving. For me the question is an empirical one. I speak of modern times, the nineteenth and twentieth centuries, as the age of the emergence of institutionalized social science. The capacity of elites to fashion the most repressive societies have not been hindered by their failure to support or develop the social sciences.

4. John Dewey, *The Public and Its Problems: An Essay in Political Inquiry* (Chicago: Gateway, 1946).
5. Edward Shils, "Mass Society and Its Culture," *Daedalus* 89 (1960): 288–314.
6. Max Horkheimer, *Eclipse of Reason* (New York: Seabury, 1974).

(It is reported that Goebbels acknowledged two "important" social-science books in his library: Hans Thimme, *Weltkrieg ohne Waffen* and Albert T. Poffenberger, *Psychology in Advertising*.[7] Both are works of limited intellectual power, especially the Poffenberger. Moreover, it is impossible to demonstrate even the slightest connection between these volumes and Goebbels's mastery of mass propaganda. These volumes were in fact objects of his hostility and his anti-intellectualism.)

Rather, the initial steps of repressive totalitarian regimes center on the destruction of social science, on the elimination of those who are conspicuous in opposition. Moreover, the experiments of totalitarian nations with social science have only generated points of resistance to political repression.[8] These observations do not mean that social science will be decisive in the maintenance of democratic multiparty politics. Nor can one overlook the real possibility that the expansion and formalization of social science may lower the standards of performance and trivialize intellectual creativity so that the analytical dimensions of social science will sink into oblivion while its descriptive findings continue to have administrative relevance. Equally troublesome has been the extensive social and political criticism in the language of social science—as if such criticism were detached social analysis.

To argue on behalf of the positive influence of social science does not overlook the analysis of Joseph Schumpeter and those who have sought to develop his viewpoint, which highlights the negative contributions of the "intellectual" to the process of societal change.[9] I am trying to put his analysis into a historical perspective. In the simplest terms, it is necessary to take into account the fact that social scientists have demonstrated an ability to learn from their experiences and from their conscious self-appraisal and self-evaluation. They are also capable of responding to criticisms of their contributions to institution building which have been made by elected officials, policy makers, humanists, and associated professionals.

In fact, the idea of institution building encompasses the efforts to improve the organization and effectiveness of social research itself. There

7. Hans Thimme, *Weltkrieg ohne Waffen, die Propaganda der Westmächte gegen Deutschland, ihre Wirkung und ihr Auffrau* (Stuttgart: Colta, 1932); Albert T. Poffenberger, *Psychology in Advertising* (Chicago: A. W. Shaw, 1925).

8. Laura Fermi, *Illustrious Immigrants: the Intellectual Migration From Europe, 1930–1941*. (Chicago: University of Chicago Press, 1968). See also Walter Laqueur, ed., *Fascism: A Reader's Guide, Analyses, Interpretations, Bibliography* (Berkeley: University of California Press, 1976).

9. Joseph Schumpeter, *Capitalism, Socialism and Democracy* (New York: Harper, 1942).

has been a marked increase in self-awareness among social scientists, including sociologists. From 1920 through the early 1960s, the dominant posture of social scientists was optimistic, expansive, and in a sense unrealistic. However, there were self-critical and pragmatic sociologists who, from the very origin of academic sociology, were concerned with the institutional and moral issues of relating sociology to collective "problem solving." As early as 1894, Ira W. Howerth wrote about the "Present Condition of Sociology in the United States."[10] Edward A. Tiryakian offers an extensive bibliography which indicates that in the 1920s and 1930s there was already interest in what could be called the "sociology of knowledge" approach to sociology.[11] In particular, Robert E. Park was intellectually critical of the naïve and optimistic belief in the potentials of social research as a basis of "curing" societal problems.[12] Academic sociology never fully accepted the idea that sociologists would be philosopher-kings.

The tensions and disruptions of the 1960s did produce a reaction in social science and in sociology, no doubt an overreaction, as well as considerable confusion and even uncertainty about the worth of social science for decision making and professional practice.[13] Social scientists never paused to recognize that the expansion of their disciplines would at some point be interrupted. The end of a century of university growth contributed to the confusion and strain about the social and political role of social science.

In the middle of the 1970s, there has emerged increased realism about the complexities, limitations, and subtleties involved in the application of social research to institution building. The self-image of the sociologist as philosopher-king continued to be held by only a minority of social researchers. They believed that the imperfections of existing knowledge would be overcome by continued effort and that therefore in the future the influence of sociology and the social sciences would be more effective. Most sociologists, however, believe that, besides the intellectual limits and defects of their discipline, there were "tough"

10. Ira W. Howerth, "Present Condition of Sociology in the United States," *Annals of the American Academy of Political and Social Sciences* 5 (September 1894): 260–69.

11. Edward A. Tiryakian, *The Phenomenon of Sociology* (New York: Appleton-Century-Crofts, 1971).

12. Robert E. L. Faris, *Chicago Sociology, 1920–1932* (San Francisco: Chandler, 1967).

13. Alvin Gouldner, *The Coming Crisis of Western Sociology* (New York: Basic Books, 1970).

and at points almost intractable institutional, professional, and political barriers that had to be dealt with.

In addition to the societal strains of the 1960s, there are two other reasons for the increased realism among sociologists about the effectiveness of their work and about their social and political responsibility. During the "War on Poverty," some sociologists for the first time in their professional careers found themselves involved in administrative and community efforts oriented toward institution building and directed social change. Such experiences served as equivalent experiences of field work in graduate study. Many of them developed a sharper understanding of the limits of their knowledge and of the political processes which they had to confront in their efforts to make use of their all too fragile findings. Likewise, sociologists found that they and their colleagues had perspectives and recommendations on basic policy issues which changed over time.

Second, the continued debate in academic settings about the potentials of the social sciences for public policy did not produce consensus but did lead to the emergence of relatively clear-cut alternative strategies and to sharper and more realistic definitions of the issues involved. There were some sociologists who saw their discipline as producing knowledge which could be characterized as approximating an engineering model. In this view, the theories and empirical procedures of sociologists are able quantitatively to assess the consequences of alternative policies and practice; thus they have a rigorous applied sociology which offers binding prescriptions. The writings of Paul F. Lazarsfeld and James Coleman, author of the Coleman report, assessing the consequences of the social composition of mass public education, epitomize this model.[14] On the other hand, there are sociologists who see their efforts as conforming to an enlightenment model. For them, sociology produces knowledge which increased one's understanding of the social process, but it does not necessarily supply specific answers to "social problems." It assists elected officials, policy makers, administrators, and the citizenry to make more effective decisions, to think more effectively, both by sharpening their conceptual outlook and by supplying basic information.

Of course, it needs to be emphasized that, in day-to-day reality, the application of social research to efforts at institution building does not

14. James Coleman, "Policy Research in the Social Sciences" (Morristown, N.J.: General Learning Press, 1972); Philip M. Hauser, *Social Statistics in Use* (New York: Russell Sage Foundation, 1975).

necessarily correspond to these "idealized" alternative formulae. An advanced industrial society requires a massive amount of descriptive observational and statistical data—or social intelligence, as I prefer to call it.[15] Much social research, including that of sociologists, supplies such indispensable social intelligence, which is employed in the management of institutions with only limited regard to the theoretical and analytical concerns of sociologists. The collection and processing of these basic data have continued to expand under the direction of cadres of specialists whose professional commitments are mainly to the accuracy and validity of these data. The reaction against the excessive claims of social research has not retarded this expansion. The societal influence of these data is pervasive, although impossible to explicate precisely.

Likewise, the consequences of analytic social science and sociological writings should not be judged only in terms of particular studies or discrete findings, since we are dealing with a cumulative process. The literature on the "sociology of sociology" is replete with illustrative case studies of the imputed success or failure of selected research efforts; no doubt these studies supply pertinent findings, but they are partial in their scope and particularistic in their context. All too often they are written by persons actually involved in the research.

In assessing the role of social research in the management of institutions, as in the assessment of the mass media, we are not able to confine ourselves to particular messages or case studies. Instead, we are dealing with a stream of communications which comes to operate as a partial ideology addressed to multiple audiences. Social-science communications are attended to not only by decision makers but also by various professional groups and widely by the citizenry.

Social science is a language which has deeply penetrated the *Zeitgeist* of the United States.[16] There is no body of careful research which points up the consequences of this flow of communications and its effect on societal change. But our basic assumption is that in good measure the influence of social science on institution building involves these indirect and pervasive patterns of communications. In fact, it is

15. Morris Janowitz, "Professionalization of Sociology," *American Journal of Sociology* 71 (July 1972): 105–35; David Street and Eugene A. Weinstein, "Problems and Prospects of Applied Sociology," *American Sociologist* 10 (May 1975): 65–72.

16. Marvin Bressler, "Sociology and Collegiate General Education," in *The Uses of Sociology*, ed. Paul F. Lazarsfeld et al. (New York: Basic Books, 1967), pp. 45–77.

difficult to imagine the operation of a democratic polity without extensive institutions of social research and the widespread dissemination of the accumulated findings which buttresses the claims of competing interest groups. But having offered such an assumption, I must still explore as precisely as possible the effect of different streams of social-science thought on elite groups and on professional experts who make specific use of conceptually guided research findings.

To this end, the sharp distinctions in the disciplines of the social sciences become attenuated. We are interested in the "definition of the situation" as seen by persons with varying amounts of influence. How do social-science communications influence their outlook and then their behavior? To examine these sequences from the standpoint of the elites and the subelites does not mean that the social scientist abandons this methodology and accepts a cynical outlook; it does require a comprehensive and intensive standpoint, which in part cuts across existing institutional sectors and deals with the realities of social control. I propose to focus on three nodal points which highlight trends in stability and change: (1) the management of interpersonal interrelations and associated tensions, that is, the personal behavior syndrome; (2) the focal point of community organization, that is, the citizen participation syndrome; and (3) the interrelations of elites, that is, the definition of the nation in the world community.

Hedonism and "The Therapeutic Syndrome"

The task of separating the actual effect of social-science analysis, thinking, and language on the management of interpersonal relations from the basic consequences of changes in the social organization of an advanced industrial society might well be considered unmanageable. But it must be pursued despite the manifest pretentiousness of the intellectual goal. I have observed that in academic quarters there is a strong tendency to overemphasize the influence of social-science thinking. It is therefore important not to underemphasize its influence in an attempt to compensate.

Our systemic analysis has focused on the division of labor and the increased separation of the industrial work sector from the community of family and residence. These factors have made the management of interpersonal relations more complex. To explore with some precision the determinative contribution of social-science analysis to understanding these processes, it is appropriate to focus on two basic societal trends. There is the emergence of societal standards which have been labeled "permissive," and which encompass child rearing and adult gratifications which emphasize personal hedonism. On the other hand, there are the norms and practices associated with the treatment of interpersonal relations and illness—which represent an admixture of medical and "psychiatric" practice and have come to be labeled the "therapeutic syndrome."

Social-science analysis has contributed to both trends; however, it has been more determinative and more crucial in the fashioning of therapeutic perspectives. The trend toward increased "permissiveness" and the emphasis on hedonism result in good measure from increased affluence. The historical record is replete with linkage between hedonism and increased material conditions; but it is under advanced industrialism that hedonism became "democratized" and embedded in the language of social science. The idea of the therapeutic is a more recent concept, developed in the early decades of the twentieth century with the active assistance of social science.[17] By 1920, the main intellectual outlines had been effectively formulated, but the large-scale institutionalization and the confrontation of the difficulties and inherent limitation in implementing them have operated only since 1945.

As a result, our basic hypothesis focuses on the consequences that social analysis has had on the helping professions concerned with the therapeutic process, very broadly defined. Basically, on balance, the contribution of the social sciences, particularly dynamic personality theory and aspects of sociology, to the "humane" management of interpersonal relations has been positive. In other words, the social-science ideas formed in advanced industrial society have strengthened effective social control.

The scope of this argument includes the helping professions, that is, medicine and the vast proliferation of supporting professions concerned with interpersonal relations.[18] It must include the associated social

17. Philip Rieff, *The Triumph of the Therapeutic: Uses of Faith after Freud.* (London: Chatto and Windus, 1966). For an analysis of earlier concepts of mental health and "mental institutions," see D. Rothman, *The Discovery of the Asylum: Social Order and Disorder in the New Republic* (New York: Harper and Row, 1971).

18. The delimitation of the helping professions must be arbitrary, and it is limited to those who are directly concerned with the "psychic" state of the client. The focus is on specialists who are directly concerned with the personal controls of the client. The legal profession makes a decisive contribution to the management of interpersonal relations, but its approach is indirect, through the complex

movement of self-help. The support for this proposition is relatively persuasive and plausible but not definitive. The evidence underlines that it is not specific treatment practice or even specific institutional arrangements which are crucial; these are relevant. The argument rests on the contribution which social-science thinking makes to the professional ideologies—that is, the partial ideologies—of the helping professions. These partial ideologies contribute to maintaining the moral behavior of the helping professions and to helping establish standards of professional behavior. This perspective does not imply that the standards of moral and professional behavior are adequate for the tasks of institution building; rather, it highlights specific observable increments without which the management of interpersonal relationships would be less tolerable, and less supportive of a pluralistic political process.

Psychopathology or "mental illness" is one revealing measure of the management of interpersonal relations. It would be most helpful if the accomplishments of social research made it possible to bare in relatively objective and statistical measures the long-term trends in psychopathology—minor and gross—as well as the trends in permissiveness and hedonism. Since my systemic analysis rejects formulations of the transition from Gemeinschaft to Gesellschaft, there is no reason to believe that there has been a continuous growth in psychopathology with the advent of advanced industrialization. The available trends analyses are far from definitive, but the most penetrating studies have failed to find such a pattern of growth since 1850.[19] (In fact, if one uses rate of hospitalization in mental institutions, the incidence of mental illness varies strongly with the business cycle; depressions produce a higher rate of admission than periods of prosperity.)[20] Likewise, careful studies of stable homogeneous farming populations such as the Hutterites reveal markedly high patterns of mental deviance, related to the operative cultural and normative values.[21] If one emphasizes the impact of stress,

set of legal institutions. Members of the legal profession do not define the psychic state of their client as their primary concern, although they may become deeply involved in the same issues as the helping professional. (The tasks of the schoolteacher border even closer on those of the helping professions. Their contributions to social control will be explored in chap. 12.)

19. Herbert Goldhammer and Andrew W. Marshall, *Psychosis and Civilization* (Glencoe, Ill: Free Press, 1949).

20. M. Harvey Brenner, *Mental Illness and the Economy* (Cambridge: Harvard University Press, 1973).

21. Joseph W. Eaton and Robert J. Weil, *Culture and Mental Disorders* (Glencoe, Ill.: Free Press, 1955).

it is impossible to argue that the population in 1976 is under more psychic stress than their parents were in 1920. One can make a good case that the nature of the stress has shifted, from direct stress—fatigue, poor food, bad working and housing conditions, and the aftermath of infectious diseases—to more "psychological" stress—interpersonal tension reflecting complex group aspirations. However, from the point of view of social control, the essential trend is the decline in the reluctance or inhibition in admitting "psychic" discomfort, increased willingness to externalize private attitudes, and greater emphasis on the search for treatment or a resolution of one's felt strain. At least this is the assumption—enlarged self-indulgence—on which we shall proceed.

By contrast to the secular trends in psychopathology, the trends in permissiveness and the growth of hedonism are relatively clear. Changes in the contents of popular manuals for child rearing have been used to document the heightened permissiveness in this area.[22] Medical observers also attest to profound behavior changes, although changes in overt behavior do not necessarily mean changes in underlying psychological interaction. Practices which appear to be permissive can still signal rigid and repressive attitudes or at least confused relations between parents and children. However, a reaction in popular attitude and expert "advice" had set in by the early 1970s. Nevertheless, personal and societal norms press for more "humane" treatment as manifested by the increased effectiveness of the social movement to grapple with the violence of child and wife abuse.

The most dramatic changes have been acceptable standards for sexual behavior among adults. Perhaps future historians will record as the high point in this trend the official declaration of the American Psychiatric Association in 1974 that homosexuality could no longer be described as a "disease." In 1977, an official delegation of homosexuals were received by President Carter in the White House. The language, if not the findings, of social science has been central for the transformation of these societal definitions; but, as in child rearing, a reaction could be anticipated and detected.

However, it can be argued that the syndrome of "permissiveness" and associated hedonism is a direct function of the increased affluence

22. Daniel Miller and Guy E. Swanson, *The Changing American Parent: A Study in the Detroit Area* (New York: Wiley, 1958), chap. 1; Robert Sunley, "Early Nineteenth-Century American Literature on Child Rearing," in *Childhood in Contemporary Cultures*, ed. Margaret Mead and Martha Wolfenstein (Chicago: University of Chicago Press, 1955), pp. 150–67.

of an advanced industrial society. In this view, there have been other periods in which such psychic trends have reflected affluence, and of course, the pattern at a given moment in history has been concentrated in the upper strata of society. In effect, we are witnessing the penetration of these patterns through society—their "democratization," if you will—as a result of the unprecedented level of material resources available for consumption.

At least three trends can be used to chart the impact of hedonistic consumerism on the management of personal relations. As has been discussed above, inherent in these forms of consumerism is a strong manifestation of compulsive behavior which reflects an unsatisfying response and which, in fact, borders on and spills over into self-destructive behavior. The three measures of such consumerism are the increased consumption of food and alcohol and the intensified pursuit of sexual practice; in each case, the hedonistic pursuit has rested on increased affluence.

The consumption of drugs—addictive, or hard, drugs—is a revealing indicator of self-indulgence which produces self-destructive behavior. (In chapter 10, trend data on the criminal justice control of addictive drugs were presented.) Despite the difficulties of measurement, the increase in the use of addictive drugs has been striking—even overwhelming, in the 1960s—while it does appear that the rate of increase has leveled off during the first half of the 1970s. But this increase is not an effective measure of the growth of psychological consumerism. In fact, for a significant group, the use of such drugs does not represent psychological consumerism, but, on the contrary, failure to share in the abundance of an advanced industrial society. For these persons, addiction to hard drugs is a response to socioeconomic exclusion and an expression of social deprivation; the "journey back" from addiction comes when the drug victim is able to share in "the normal" forms of material indulgence.

As of the middle of the 1970s, explicit normative patterns, especially those emphasized by the mass media, define consumption of hard drugs as excluded from the accepted "culture" of consumerism. In other words, there persists a profound difference between the acceptance of the indulgences in food, alcohol, and sexual practice and that of the use of hard drugs. Hard drugs are essentially defined as unacceptable. From the point of view of social control of interpersonal relations, the basic question is the extent to which the increased consumerism of food, alcohol, and sexual behavior is not gratifying and actually reflects components of self-destruction.

In food consumption, variation among social groups remains, but more in quality than in quantity. While the amount of actual malnutrition is widely debated, the central issue is improper dietary routines rather than lack of food. The food stamps and school lunch programs have contributed decisively to wider food distribution.

At this point, our concern is with the overconsumption of food. A distinction needs to be made between overconsumption as a distinct form of psychopathology which leads to pronounced obesity and bodily deformity and a more culturally sanctioned excessive overeating which is more compatible with hedonistic norms. The latter is of direct interest. While there are no precise data, "normal" overweight is extensive and there is every reason to believe that it has increased since 1920. The statistical data, interestingly enough, indicate that by 1940 the United States had moved to its contemporary high levels of per capita food intake (Table 11.1). No single measure will suffice. By 1940, the Department of Agriculture's overall index of food consumption per capita stood at 91; by 1974 it had risen to 104. In terms of calories from food, the 104 index in 1940 remained at the same figure

Table 11.1 Trends in Food Consumption, 1940–1974
(Index of Per Capita Consumption of Selected Nutrients)

Nutrient	1940	1945	1950	1955	1960	1965	1970	1971	1972	1973	1974
Protein	95	104	96	97	97	98	102	108	103	101	100
Fat	95	92	97	97	95	97	105	105	105	103	102
Carbohydrate	115	112	108	101	101	99	102	102	102	103	101

Source: U.S. Dept. of Agriculture, Agricultural Research Service. Published annually in *National Food Situation.*

Overall Indices of Per Capita Food Consumption.
(1967 = 100)

Item	1940	1945	1950	1955	1960	1965	1970	1971	1972	1973	1974
Food consumption	91	97	95	97	96	97	103	103	104	102	102
Food use	93	101	96	98	96	97	102	104	104	100	101
Food consumed, pounds	109	116	106	104	101	99	101	102	102	101	100
Calories per capita	104	103	102	99	98	98	103	103	103	103	102

Source: U.S. Dept. of Agriculture, Economic Research Service, *Food Consumption, Prices, and Expenditures*, July 1968. (Agricultural Economics report no. 138, supplemented annually.)

in 1974. If one examines type of nutrition, the protein index of 1940 was 95 and it rose to 103 in 1974; during the same period fat intake grew from 95 to 105, while carbohydrate intake dropped from 115 to 104. On balance, the increased food consumption in part represented an improved diet, with the decline of carbohydrates but not an increased consumption of fat. While a 14% increase in the overall index is noteworthy, the full extent of increased consumption is the increased use of alcohol, described below, with its very high caloric content.

Nevertheless, these data indicate that we are dealing not only with an increase in actual food consumption but also with increased concern with overeating. Preoccupation with eating has been engendered by the content of the mass media, both in advertising content and in the textual and photographic portrayal of the "good life." The amount of overeating from a medical point of view can be inferred from observations (to be discussed below) that the control of overeating would produce a reduction of one-quarter of the death rate; overeating is among the significant contributory factors to the mortality rate in the United States.

The desire to control overeating and overweight is among the most frequent "pastimes" in the United States. It is a reflection of the unsatisfactory consequences of dietary habits, the lack of real gratification from eating in the absence of personal and social controls of this form of hedonistic consumerism. Basically, rituals and social protocols dealing with eating are weak. One older form of social control was the ritualized "medieval" feast at which one was expected to overindulge on infrequent occasions. It thereby was an effective form of social control over routine daily habits. Instead, overeating itself has become routinized on an almost continuous basis.

The nearly compulsive pressure to overeat is paralleled by frantic and unsuccessful efforts to control the very same practice. The most frequent—but generally unsuccessful—effort at control is the self-directed diet reinforced by regimes presented in the mass media or passed on by word of mouth. Diets supervised by doctors are extensive and are judged to have limited effects. Dieting—self-directed or even medically supervised—becomes a psychologically unstable routine.

The extensive overeating and the deep concern with its consequences has led to social movements and voluntary associations such as "Weight Watchers," which offer the person a set of external group pressures to assist in the group regulation of diets. To the outside observer, the most striking characteristic of these groups is their ability to combine positive group support and verbally punitive sanctions. They proceed on the basis of the manipulation of self-esteem—both positively and negatively—and are truly mechanisms for the management of interpersonal relations. Evidence of the enduring effectiveness of such groups does not exist, but there is good reason to believe that while a person is a member, there are short-term positive results achieved at high psychic cost, and clearly in counteraction to the presumed indulgences generated by dietary consumerism.

One can make reference to the limited but growing efforts to develop rituals and codes for eating. In the "upper middle" mass magazines the ritualized consumption of food has become more conspicuous: cooking clubs have grown which spend enormous amounts of time in preparing of food; guides to restaurant stress the importance of the service and the surroundings; all of these mechanisms are, in the United States, still in their infancy but are clearly growing, although weak, countertrends to "obsessive" patterns of food consumerism.

The long-term increase in alcohol consumption because of increased affluence is more manifest, more dramatic, and more self-destructive. The data on the production and per capita consumption of alcohol highlight the greater amounts consumed by the population. There is no reason to conclude that with increased affluence tastes have become more refined so that persons are consuming a wider range of beers and wines and less "hard liquor."

Table 11.2 shows that annual per capita consumption of beer rose from 25.0 gallons in 1950 to 31.0 gallons in 1974, a 24% increase. The growth in wine consumption was even more marked, although the total volume was limited by comparison. In 1950, the annual per capita consumption in wine gallons was 1.33, and by 1974 it had reached 2.26; a 69% increase. At the same time, "distilled spirits–hard liquor" per capita consumption increased from 1.48 wine gallons in 1950 to 2.90 in 1974, or a growth of 97% in a quarter of a century. The doubling of liquor consumption can only be described as extensive; the economic impact of stagflation serves more and more as the effective constraint.

The patterns of alcohol consumerism are amplified in the long-term trends in self-reported drinking. We are dealing less with an increase in the proportion of the population who drink—although this has

TABLE 11.2 Trends in Alcoholic Beverage Consumption, 1950–1974

	Unit	1950	1960	1970	1974
Beer Annual per capita consumption	Gallons	25.0	24.0	28.6	31.0
Distilled spirits Annual per capita consumption	Wine Gals.	1.48	1.87	2.61	2.90
Still Wines Annual per capita consumption	Wine Gals.	1.33	1.36	1.70	2.26

SOURCE: U.S. Bureau of Alcohol, Tobacco, and Firearms, *Summary Statistics*, annual.

grown—and more with an increase in the disruptive consequences of alcohol consumption. On the basis of survey data collected from national samples in 1939, 58% of the population were "drinkers"—"having occasion to use alcohol beverages such as liquor, wine or beer. . . ." By 1974, the figure had reached 68%, and by 1976, it stood at 71%.[23] The concentration of users in the age group 18 to 20 was comparable to the adult population; in 1974 it was 68%. Fluctuation in the upward trends was linked to the business cycle; for example, the figure for drinkers dropped to 55% in 1958. But the connection between affluence and alcohol consumption is strong. Among those earning more than $20,000 in 1974, 88% were drinkers, while of those with incomes under $5,000 the figure was only 46%.

From the available data, it is not possible to separate the results of increased affluence from the pressures of personal tension and insecurity, and from the interaction of increased affluence and personal insecurity. In any case, the important observation is the long-trend increased use of alcohol and the greater reliance on alcohol as a device for the management of interpersonal relations. In 1974, survey data revealed that nearly one-fourth of the drinkers or one-fifth of the total sample reported that they "sometimes" drink to excess. Even more striking is that 12% revealed that alcohol has been the cause of trouble in their family in 1974; and by 1977, the figure had grown to 18%[24]

23. American Institute of Public Opinion, Release, February 13, 1977, p. 4.

24. Ibid., p. 5; for a survey of the extent of drinking among young people, see "A National Study of Adolescent Drinking Behavior, Attitudes and Correlates," mimeographed (Research Triangle Institute, North Carolina, April 1975), pp. 140–58.

The smoking of tobacco is closely linked to the consumption of alcohol. Approximately one-half (48%) of self-reported drinkers are smokers, while only one-fourth (25%) of nondrinkers used tobacco. In the past, smoking was related to affluence; for significant parts of the population, to "start to smoke" represented entrance into the mainstream of society—for example, for women or young men coming of age.

However, smoking is no longer closely linked to affluence. Its persistent usage reflects its addictive qualities; as the case of drugs, but to a lesser extent, usage is concentrated among persons who are not effectively integrated, personally or socially, into the larger society. Revealing evidence on this point derives from the studies of those who seek medical and group assistance in order to cease smoking.[25] These studies demonstrate that persons who are more integrated into the social structure are more easily able to benefit from such programs. Men have given up smoking more easily than women, employed women more easily than housewives, and younger women more easily than older women.

The intense campaigns to reduce smoking have redefined the social acceptance of this consumer practice. The growing number of nonsmoking zones and the increased segregation of smokers from nonsmokers, for example, on airlines, are conspicuous manifestations. In fact, consumption of tobacco has declined from 12.29 pounds per capita in 1950 to 9.37 pounds in 1974. Smoking, in short, is no longer a revealing indicator of consumerism based on affluence.

Our third indicator of consumerism is sexual behavior. There is strong evidence that there has been an increase in the frequency and variation of sexual behavior—and not merely in greater visibility and awareness of extent of sexual practice. The replication in 1972 of the original Kinsey study as reported by Morton Hunt showed such an increase in sexual behavior, especially among older adults.

Increased affluence makes possible increased leisure and a decline in work-induced fatigue; wider segments of society have time budgets for self-indulgence once reserved for the upper strata. Likewise, affluence makes available the necessary devices for birth control. As sociologists have emphasized, the mass production and distribution of

25. Douglas Brian Heller, "Stopping Cigarette Smoking: The Social and Psychological Correlates of Directed Behavior Change," Ph.D. dissertation, University of Chicago, 1975.

the automobile in the 1920s created the physical setting for the massive extension of extramarital sexual behavior. Continuously since the end of World War II, mass advertising of material merchandise has been linked to sexual symbolism;[26] since 1960, the standards for acceptable pornography have undergone a fundamental transformation. In turn, public opinion and even judicial decisions have indicated that the societal limits of this transformation have been reached, but the countertrends are hardly destined to reverse the new patterns.[27]

Unfortunately, there is no body of data which indicate that the new sexual freedom and its increased intensity have produced greater satisfaction or self-esteem. The data presented in chapter 5 on long-term trends in satisfaction focus on economic well-being and reveal little of increased human happiness. Without the massive growth of consumerism, the level of personal and family satisfaction could have declined, although the topic defies explication. My estimate, on the basis of available research on consumer satisfaction and on attitudes toward sexual behavior, is that the new sexual freedom has not had a decisive or positive influence on human happiness and contentment. The compulsive overtones—as in eating and alcohol consumption—are too powerful and too obvious. In any case, from the point of view of the management of interpersonal relations, there is every reason to conclude that it is mainly the increased affluence of an advanced industrial society—in the context of ineffective social control—which is the root. In essence, the role of social science has been, at most, one of facilitating change and therefore rather minor. This is not to rule out the possibility that social-science language has complicated and retarded the search for new and more gratifying moral standards.

Nevertheless, these observations supply the context of the exploration of our basic hypothesis that, on balance, contribution of the social sciences have been positive in strengthening the effective human management of interpersonal relations. In essence, this hypothesis implies that institutional and professional practices operate as countertrends to the discontents and self-destructive responses to increased material affluence and the associated strains of an advanced industrial society. The hypothesis rests on the positive consequences of the organized profes-

26. Ernest Dichter, *Handbook of Consumer Motivation: The Psychology of the World of Objects* (New York: McGraw-Hill, 1964).

27. Commission on Obscenity and Pornography, *Technical Reports*, vols. 1–7 (Washington: GPO, 1971).

sional, paraprofessional, and lay groups whose practices are guided, or at least rationalized, by social-science analysis.

MEDICINE AS A "HELPING PROFESSION"

It is hardly outrageous to propose that the core of the conscious and professionalized management of interpersonal relations and associated tensions is the medical profession and the associated array of allied professions and related specialities.

Despite the repeated claim that doctors are indifferent to the psychological needs of their patients, medical specialists must confront, and for better or worse, respond to these needs. By 1920, the basic features of the institutions of medical practice in the United States have been established.[28] A variegated array of public, private, and voluntary association-based hospitals plus attending physicians and a system of university-affiliated medical schools are the essential components. In a half-century, the resources available for medical services have vastly increased, the scale of organization of the hospitals has expanded, and there has been a growth of group practice. But perhaps the most significant organizational change has been the intervention of the federal government and third-party associations in the fiscal management of medical services.

From the point of view of the mechanisms of social control, the practice of medicine has undergone during this period a fundamental transformation from the "medicinal" treatment of specific diseases to a continuous and relentless increased intervention and management of the social and psychological dimensions of interpersonal relations.[29] The personnel and resources of professional medicine and allied skilled groups—directly or indirectly, explicitly or implicitly, or effectively or ineffectively—must face the pressures of a "therapeutic" posture.

On the basis of available documentation on medical practice at the end of World War I, and especially from medical biographies and

28. See especially Odin W. Anderson, *Health Care: Can There be Equality?* (New York: Wiley, 1972), chap. 4.

29. Office of Health Economics, "Medicine and Society: The Changing Demands for Medical Care" (London: Office of Health Economics, 1972); see also Michael Balint, *The Doctor, His Patient and the Illness* (New York: International Universities Press, 1957); P. Ley and M. S. Spelman, *Communicating With the Patient* (London: Staples Press, 1967); D. R. Lipsitt, "Fragmented Medical Care: A Retrospective Study of Chronic Outpatients," pts. I and II, Bureau of Health Services, U.S. Department of Health, Education and Welfare. (Washington: U.S. Department of Health, Education and Welfare.)

autobiographies, the family doctor, even though seemingly reluctant, served to handle interpersonal and "therapeutic" problems. The striking trend in medical practice has been the increased demand for such assistance, and despite "loud" and "negative" protestations, the medical professional persists as central in the management of these services.

A medical definition of interpersonal strains and stresses still serves as the most accepted strategy for professional intervention. In part, this is due to the fact that the distinction between the somatic-biological dimensions of minor and major psychopathological behavior and social personality is very difficult to draw in many cases. Likewise, the centrality of medical practice is dictated by the immense expansion of drug treatment, which offers essential somatic relief without contributing to personal controls, but with partial reduction of destructive behavior—self and other.

The progress in pharmacology and in medical technology supplied the basis by the end of the first half of the twentieth century for the control of a wide range of diseases.[30] Deaths from tuberculosis have declined, diptheria has been eliminated, and infant mortality has been reduced, although for economic and administrative reasons the U.S. lags behind other Western industrialized society in control of infant mortality rates. By 1975, mortality rarely occurs before the age of 45. In the 1930s medicine was concerned with infectious diseases which had a high toll among young people. After 1950 medicine dealt with the incidence of death from cancer, heart disease, cerebrovascular disease, and pneumonia and bronchitis.

The increased effectiveness of medicine has produced cures for important conditions such as pernicious anemia, many kinds of high blood pressure, juvenile diabetes, and rheumatic diseases. There has been an extension of the scope and effectiveness of surgery; in particular, the advances in surgical repairs after accidents are remarkable. Particularly striking has been the increased effort to deal with mental illness. While the full results of these programs for mental health are debatable, the immediate outcome has been a reduction in the concentration of patients in mental institutions, accomplished mainly with the use of drugs.

The increased effectiveness of medicine has paradoxically not reduced the demands for medical services, nor is there any discernible

30. Office of Health Economics, "Medicine," pp. 3–6.

evidence that a half-century of "medical progress" has resulted in an increased citizenry feeling of well-being and satisfaction about their physical conditions. The contrary is probably the case. The best indicator of the increased demand for medical treatment during a period when it is more effective is the simple measure of patient-physician contact. From 48% of the population's having at least one contact with a physician during the last 12 months in 1928–1931, the figure rose to 68% in 1970 (Table 11.3). The number of physicians per 100,000 population has not increased markedly in the United States: from 149 per 100,000 in 1950 to 161 in 1968. Thus increased service is a result of more intensified contacts.

As the probability of early death has been reduced and as many serious diseases have been brought under control, three new and unanticipated trends have emerged in doctor-patient relations which influence the management of interpersonal relations. First, persons have come to "regard more seriously their minor diseases and discomforts. They perceive and act on symptoms which previously they would

TABLE 11.3 Trends in Patient-Physician Contact, 1928–1970

Percent of Population Having at Least One Contact with a Physician during the Last 12 Months	
Year	Percent
1928–1931[a]	48
1953[b]	60
1958[c]	66
1963[d]	65
1970[e]	68

*Since 1958 there has been a greater increase in physician contact for those 55–64 and 65 and over. The mean number of physician visits per person has remained quite constant at 40–44.

SOURCE: a. J. S. Falk, Margaret Klein, and Nathan Sinai, *The Incidence of Illness and the Receipt and Costs of Medical Care among Representative Families*, Publications of the Committee on the Costs of Medical Care, no. 26, p. 101 (Chicago: University of Chicago Press, 1963).

b. Odin W. Anderson and Jacob J. Feldman, *Family Medical Costs and Voluntary Health Insurance: A National Survey* (New York: McGraw-Hill, 1956), p. 73.

c. Ronald Andersen and Odin W. Anderson, *A Decade of Health Services: Social Survey Trends in Use and Expenditures* (Chicago, University of Chicago Press, 1967), p. 27.

d. Ibid.

e. Ronald Andersen, Joanna Lion, and Odin W. Anderson, *Two Decades of Health Services: Social Survey Trends in Use and Expenditures* (Cambridge, Mass.: Ballinger, 1976), p. 44.

have ignored."[31] In effect, "discomforts which they have considered irrelevant in the days when premature death and crippling disability from serious disease were commonplace are now thought to justify medical treatment." Many of these symptoms are obviously related psychosomatic manifestations of interpersonal stress. Second, enormous resources and psychic energy are invested in the prolongation of life, mainly for older patients; but various premature and deformed infants are also kept alive, as are groups of infants suffering from incurable diseases.[32] Not only are profound moral issues involved, but also there are enduring psychological strains associated with these medical efforts on the part of patients, relatives, and medical staffs.[33] Third, patients have come more and more to judge the performance of their physicians as educational level increases and as the demand for more effective performance grows. The practice of medicine has become more complicated and includes risk. In addition, the size of the medical establishment has meant an increase in the amount of malpractice–accidental or the result of ineffective standards. The growth of malpractice suits represents not only important financial burdens on medical services but also another point of tension between doctors and patients. The changed nature of medical practice means that the management of interpersonal relations becomes more and more central.

As a result, Lord Beveridge's original anticipation that the spread of effective medical care would produce corresponding economic benefits has proven to be a "miscalculation of sublime proportions."[34] The

31. Ibid., p. 5.

32. The social and moral issues involved in the medical treatment of genetically based diseases are discussed by James R. Sorenson, *Social Aspects of Applied Genetics* (New York: Russell Sage Foundation, 1971).

33. No doubt, the improvement in medical care and the prolongation of life reduce the psychological fears associated with death and disability from disease. But the fear of death and the psychological strains associated with death are not eliminated but transformed, and it can be argued that they are actually heightened. The prolongation of life means long periods of chronic illness which is physically painful for the patient and psychologically painful for him and his kin. The "problem of dying" emerges as a widespread popular concern. One manifestation is the interest in "analysis" of the psychological aspects of dying, and of the purported fear or denial of death. One such study by Ernst Becker has become a best-seller among educated persons; *The Denial of Death* (New York: Free Press, 1973).

34. J. E. Powell, "Health and Wealth," *Proceedings of the Royal Society of Medicine* 55 (1962): 1. For an analysis of the difficulties inherent in controlling the demand for medical services, see Odin W. Anderson, "Are National Health Services Systems Converging? Predictions for the United States," unpublished, October 1976. For an anlysis of health issues in strictly economic terms of supply

cost of medical institutions has grown faster than the gross national product and results in a staggering fiscal allocation of the welfare state. For the United States, the cost of health services as a proportion of the GNP in 1950 was 4.5%; by 1975 it had reached 8.2%. Distrust and hostility toward the profession have grown, for all the above reasons but basically because the profession is unable to deal with new problems—namely, the social and psychological rather than "medical" character of the problems it must confront.[35] The doctor, regardless of his training interest and technology, is faced with massive tasks in the management of interpersonal relations—a significant portion of which, given the present knowledge about social institutions, are without effective solutions and may remain so for a long time to come. Moreover, if there is to be a further reduction in the mortality rate, it is very likely to come from changes in human diet in an advanced industrial society as much as additional advances in conventional medical practice. To the extent that the medical profession becomes involved in modifying diet in order to extend longevity it will become further involved in the management of interpersonal relations. In January 1977, a Senate committee estimated that one-third of a million deaths per year could be avoided by changes in diet.[36] For example, a 25% reduction in mortality from heart disease was thought as a realistic objective, 20% in cancer, and 50% in infant mortality. The strategies of medical practice would have to be drastically altered to approach such "public health" objectives.

The expansion of medical services was in effect based on the assumption that cost was the barrier to effective medical practice. With the removal of price barriers by insurance and governmental subsidies, it was assumed that the minority of the population who were ill could perceive their symptoms and appreciate their significance. However, this has not been the case. Many persons who are sick do not seek medical assistance, while many of those who are not "medically" ill seek treatment.

The demand for medical treatment is strongly influenced by social, psychological, and cultural factors. The difference between those who

and demand, see Victor R. Fuchs, *Who Shall Live: Health, Economics and Social Choice* (New York: Basic Books, 1974).

35. Judith T. Shuval, "The Sick Role in a Setting of Comprehensive Care," *Medical Care*, vol. 10 (1972).

36. U.S. Senate Select Committee on Nutrition and Human Needs, January 1977.

repeatedly seek medical treatment and those who do not cannot be accounted for in purely medical terms.[37] Organized medicine has been unable to respond to these new fundamental changes. It largely persists with a narrow "medical" technique for dealing with patients, although the broader problems press continually into medical practice.[38] Such a narrow strategy is not only very costly but also often unsatisfactory to the patient. Moreover, the organization of the medical profession has come progressively to emphasize specialization. As a result, there are few mechanisms for early and overall assessment of patient needs. The classical system of tirage developed to assess war wounded would be applicable to the contemporary problems of medical practice. But this would require that the most skilled physicians and the most expert diagnosticians serve at the initial point of contact—as the "front lines" of medicine—which would reverse existing procedures and prestige hierarchies.

The changed tasks of medical practice are apparent to doctors, medical administrators, and professors of medicine. There have been conscious efforts to adapt the profession to these new requirements which require that it deal with the management of interpersonal relations. There is recognition of the need for medicine to be more "supportive" of the patient—to assist him (and his family) to monitor himself and to involve a wide range of institutions and personnel in the health care process. The term "community medicine" is a sign of the efforts to

37. N. Kessel and M. Shepherd, "The Health and Attitudes of People Who Seldom Consult a Doctor," *Medical Care*, vol. 3 (1965).

38. This perspective is summarized by the following statement: "With regard to medicine in general, I believe the basic problem is that physicians are trained to view problems organically, with treatment then devoted to organic intervention, e.g., chemotherapy (drugs), surgery. However, the problems which are increasingly at issue involve long term individual environment relations, rather than acute organic interrelations. Such problems can be classified into two types: a chronic problem, which if monitored individually, will require minimal organic intervention, e.g., diabetes, recovered cardiac arrests, certain spinal cord injuries; a chronic abuse problem which is unchanged may require drastic organic intervention, e.g., smoking, obesity, stress. Medicine is not equipped to handle (nor so inclined, in terms of practitioner economic incentive) the long term training and continual support of people to monitor themselves and follow a prescribed dietary regimen (e.g. diabetes) or to change such entrenched habits as smoking, food indulgence, argumentation with colleagues, etc. . . . Nor are psychiatry or clinical psychology so equipped. They are concerned with abnormal populations as defined by the relevant units in their respective professional divisions. The medical problems are those of normal people." (Personal communication from D. Israel Goldiamond to the author, 7 February 1977).

strengthen the role of the doctor as teacher and therapeutic agent.[39] The training of medical students has been modified to a limited degree to incorporate broader concerns. The most decisive attempt at institution building is the effort to create a medical "specialist" out of the family practitioner—that is, to reverse the trend toward more specialization. This effort parallels those in the "helping professions," including teaching, to overcome the trends toward specialization by a conscious model of aggregation of tasks.[40] The progress has been limited and mainly centers on the use of the community hospital, including the emergency rooms, for general medicine. No doubt in the search to contain excessive specialization, social science theory is involved, although common sense would dictate the same conclusion.

But the modification of medical practice proceeds without fundamental change in the structure of health institutions. The hostility of the patient toward the doctor hardly eliminates his dependency. If the traditional veneration of the doctor has declined or been strained, it has been replaced by a complex ambivalence which the doctor finds more and more difficult to deny. The interpersonal aspects of medicine—routine, acute, or chronic—cannot be avoided. The major response of the medical specialist is to refer patients to psychiatric experts or to mobilize associated professional expertise. Despite the efforts of doctors, especially of the highly skilled specialists, to define their tasks narrowly, the entire health setting has been plunged into a concern with the "human side" of practice. Like industrial managers, medical practitioners have come to recognize that neither they nor their institutions can operate on the basis of clear-cut or traditional authoritative sanctions. Even though most members of the medical profession verbally deny their central role in the management of interpersonal relations, they must make adaptations, however limited and segmented and even at times counterproductive.[41]

In these efforts at adaptation, the formulations of psychoanalysis are guideposts. The competing frames of reference to dynamic personality theory must address the central issues posed by psychoanalysts as they

39. Paul Roman and Harrison Trice, eds., *Sociological Perspectives on Community Mental Health* (Philadelphia: F. A. Davis, 1974).

40. Morris Janowitz, *Institution Building in Urban Education* (Chicago: University of Chicago Press, 1969).

41. Eliott Freidson, *Profession of Medicine: A Study of the Sociology of Applied Knowledge* (New York: Dodd, Mead, 1970).

seek to modify or reformulate its claims and expectations. At this point, we are interested in the broad intellectual and professional influence of psychoanalytic theories and doctrines.

Psychoanalysts complain about the indifference of their medical colleagues to the psychological dimensions of medicine. Moreover, psychoanalysts have declined in organizational authority as specialists in pharmacological treatment have become more numerous and influential in departments of psychiatry. In fact, with the growth of drug therapy, psychoanalysts have lost their administrative dominance in the department of psychiatry at the prestigious schools of medicine. Nevertheless, the psychoanalytical perspective toward personality, psychopathology, and "mental health" is at the core of medical and psychiatric orientations. The widely based, persistent attacks on psychoanalytical theory and practice only confirm this observation. The influence of this theory is to be judged in terms of its consequences on medical doctors and in the milieu of medical and semimedical institutions. It is a perspective which is "supportive" of the patient, since it gives validity to the subjective feelings of the patient and it encompasses the social life space of the patient. The psychotherapist acts as an intruder; he can be called a form of "public presence," since he is an "outsider." He operates as an outsider with special access, since he is a medical person by training and certification. Psychoanalysts serve as carriers of standards of treatment which are broader than conventional medical standards.

We are dealing with the "Hawthorne effect"; the consequences of intensive concern. These are variables or inputs which tend to become formalized and which tend to lose their power in an institutional setting. However, there is a body of research literature on the contribution of psychoanalytical and related psychological theory to the development of benign, and, it is hoped, therapeutic institutions, where the notion of intervention is not limited to the specific work of specialists but which have an effect on the entire institutional setting. The history of the medical and mental health setting is that of the movement from custodial to therapeutic, although the goals and aspirations of the therapeutic are often elusive. The therapeutic milieu is not limited to the mental hospital but has application wherever, as noted in chapter 7, institutions have the goal of handling or managing interpersonal relations. Probably persons who are exposed to health institutions which strive to conform to a milieu format experience positive benefits. The patterns of social control which operate in such institutions are more compatible with "humane" social norms and must therefore be judged as positive achievements in and of themselves.

In reality and on a day-to-day basis, we are not dealing with the construction of idealized environments, but rather with the search for improved interpersonal relations. Despite the negativism or indifference of medical specialists to the helping professions, they are aware constantly of the indispensable role the latter perform and more secretly than publicly acknowledge their dependency on them. More often than not, the presence of these helping personnel, especially those who also hold medical degrees, has a positive influence on the medical specialist in approaching his patients and his institution.

The enduring contribution of psychoanalytical perspectives in strengthening the "supportive" role of the medical profession requires explanation. We are dealing both with a body of scientific thought and a powerful professional dogma. Psychoanalytical thought gives the strong emphasis to the enriching of personal control by means of the development and reinforcement of autonomous ego controls. This professional goal has, of course, brought psychoanalytical specialists into conflict with others in the helping professions who believe that such goals are unrealistic, too expensive, or at variance with the realities of a hierarchical and segmented social structure. Nevertheless, precisely this basic commitment and professional ideology make the psychoanalytical perspective relevant for institution building for effective social control. The so-called pessimism of Freudianism does not thwart the analyst's belief in the patient's capacity to increase his self-regulation. The social implication of psychoanalytical theory is hardly "sheer" permissiveness, which the analyst rejects or views as likely to increase anxiety and personal disorganization. The goal is rather that of self-regulation, compatible with the person's abilities and with the objectives of effective social control. One is struck by the receptivity of psychoanalytic theories to social-science concepts related to social organization and to culture.[42]

The literature on psychopathology portrays both the routine day-to-day support and the more heroic acts of the psychoanalytically oriented

42. See, for example, Harry Stack Sullivan, *The Fusion of Psychiatry and Social Science* (New York: Norton, 1964); Stewart E. Perry, *The Human Nature of Science: Researchers at Work in Psychiatry* (New York: Free Press, 1966); Sidney Hook, ed., *Psychoanalysis: Scientific Method and Philosophy* (New York: Grove, 1960).

practitioner on behalf of his patients. There is a moral thrust in these characterizations, an element of transcendence, combined with a concern for the individuality of the patient. A set standard of professional performance is being offered in a period in which the attenuation of social control has been taking place. As a result, psychoanalytical thought has fused elements of professional practice with an "orthodox" morality—one with overtones of utopianism. The end product is a strong professional ideology. Anselm Strauss and his associates have carefully documented, by elaborate participant observation, the extent to which, in a variety of medical settings, this type of orthodoxy serves the positive goal of "speaking on behalf of the patient," the underdog in the social organization of medicine.[43] These investigators summarize their experience with the observation, "during the course of our research we rediscovered the sociological axiom that ideological convictions generate their own morality."[44]

The lasting focus of psychoanalysis is noteworthy. It is precisely because it raises the same questions and issues that it has had an enduring influence over the last half-century. This derives from the pointedness of its intellectual formulation; regardless of its substantive validity, it is an elaborated frame of reference with its own internal logic. While its intellectual development is incomplete and inadequate, it has enriched its content and scope with the shift from an instinctual emphasis to an ego psychology format.[45]

Moreover, psychoanalytical dynamic personality theory has enlarged its format from the person-to-person treatment to a variety of group and institutional approaches, particularly in the development of the therapeutic setting, in the evolving writings of figures such as August Eichorn and Bruno Bettelheim.[46]

43. Anselm Strauss et al., *Psychiatric Ideologies and Institutions* (New York: Free Press, 1964).

44. Ibid., p. 365; see also William E. Henry, John H. Sims, and S. Lee Spray, *Public and Private Lives of Psychotherapists* (San Francisco: Jossey-Bass, 1973), "The psychotherapist is clearly a person of deep conviction and whole-hearted devotion to his patients and to psychodynamics explanations of behavior" (p. 23).

45. Anna Freud, *The Ego and the Mechanisms of Defense* (New York: International Universities Press, 1946).

46. August Eichorn, *Wayward Youth* (New York: Viking, 1935); Bruno Bettelheim, "Therapeutic Milieu," *American Journal of Orthopsychiatry* 18 (April 1948): 191–206, "Milieu Therapy—Indications and Illustrations," *Psychoanalytic Review* 36 (January 1949): 54–68, and *Love Is not Enough: The Treatment of Emotionally Disturbed Children* (Glencoe, Ill.: Free Press, 1950); Jules Henry, "The Formal Social Structure of a Psychiatric Hospital," *Psychiatry* 17 (May 1954): 139–51.

But the continuity of psychoanalysis rests on its training and indoctrination procedures.[47] The use of personal analysis and the long period of supervised apprenticeship—on a one-to-one basis—have great effect. The process has effectively withstood the shift in patterns of personnel recruitment. In the early development of the psychoanalytic profession in the United States, young men entered medical training with the explicit goal of becoming analysts. The later trend has been toward medical students who late in their medical school careers decide to specialize in psychoanalysis; that is, psychoanalysis has become more and more one speciality among a variety.

Nevertheless, the training format has been maintained and been reinforced, particularly by a reluctance or inability to expand the numbers of trainees. The control of the production of analysts is the core in the strategy of maintaining orthodoxy, and on the other hand, it contributes to the vast proliferation of alternative and competing psychological and psychiatric specialities. Likewise, the central importance of one-to-one therapy contributes to the orthodoxy of psychoanalysis and its influence on medical practice. In the clinic and institutional setting this professional perspective must be modified, but in the one-to-one setting the classical modalities of psychoanalysis and its moral standards are perpetuated. This format of practice, in effect, supplies the basis of "self-regeneration" and professional social control of operative norms.

Converging Psychological Strategies

The changing character of medical practice, the societal strains on effective social control and the limited number of classically trained psychoanalysts have forced the typical doctor to become more and more concerned with "social" medicine. These trends have meant that doctors have been extensively supplemented by a variety of helping professionals concerned with the management of interpersonal relations. The demand for "supportive" services, direct and indirect, far exceeds the resources of "medicine." The growth of the "psychological" professionals, as will be noted, has been much faster than that of other types of professional groups during the last half-century.

The range and variation of these specialists are most bewildering and reflect the institutional pluralism of U.S. society. In fact, they en-

47. Arnold A. Rogow, *The Psychiatrists* (New York: Putnam, 1970); Bertram D. Lewin and Helen Ross, *Psychoanalytic Education in the United States* (New York: Norton, 1960).

compass not only professionals with elaborate codes of practice, but paraprofessionals, self-help enterprises, and social movements with explicit political overtones. Moreover, these groups are outspoken, almost fanatical, in their efforts to distinguish themselves from other groups in the spectrum. However, it is important not to be influenced by their self-designation, but to examine their actual goals and practices. Fortunately the expansion of the "helping professions" has been accompanied by considerable efforts to examine their organization and programs which have been carried out with reasonable care and objectivity. A central question is the extent to which these developments have been influenced, if not dominated, by medical practitioners and institutions. For our purposes four categories or modalities of "therapeutic" strategy can be identified. This overview excludes the deep division in the psychiatric professions between the organic and the psychological perspective; but the elimination of this division and the focus on the "psychological" point up the convergence of the medical and nonmedical divisions.

First, there is the group of specialists which William E. Henry so aptly calls the "fifth profession."[48] He refers to the four specialists who carry the bulk of the "professional" effort in individual psychotherapy—namely, the psychoanalysts, the medical psychiatrists, the clinical psychologists, and the psychiatric social workers. Second, professionals and paraprofessionals are engaged in various forms of group processes and group dynamics from T-groups to sensitivity training to encounter groups. This latter modality spills over to the next category.

Third, there are variants of group experiments which are self-directed and reflect social and voluntary associational movements. These formats include activists who consider themselves "radicals."[49] It was to be expected that the growth of psychological services and consultation would produce a countermovement—a critique of the concepts of psychopathology and of the processes of therapy. Its central figures, such as Theodor Szasz and Erving Goffman, supply the rationale for an onslaught on conventional forms of managing psychotherapeutic inter-

48. William E. Henry, John H. Sims, and S. Lee Spray, *The Fifth Profession* (San Francisco: Jossey-Bass, 1971); see also Maurice H. Krout, *Psychology, Psychiatry, and the Public Interest* (Minneapolis: University of Minnesota Press, 1956).

49. Dennis T. Jaffe, ed., *In Search of a Therapy* (New York: Harper and Row, 1975).

vention.[50] Their criticism—partly implicit—of society is as important as the particular forms of group intervention that they have stimulated. But from the point of view of the search for social control, there is no evidence that the interest in and growth of "unconventional" therapies and group confrontation have slowed the increase of more "conventional" psychotherapists, or of the services of the experts in "traditional" group dynamics.

Fourth, a range of behavior-modification techniques have emerged so rapidly and dramatically in a technological society which produces a strong anti-introspective response. For this modality, the issues of the civil rights of clients are deeply involved, although issues are operative in the other three modalities as well. However, no simple conclusions can be drawn, since it is especially necessary to examine the actual practices, which vary considerably, under this label.

The increase in the number of persons in the fifth profession—psychiatrists, psychoanalysts, clinical psychologists, psychiatric social workers and "professionalized" full-time psychotherapists—is indeed impressive. For 1960 to 1974, the United States had approximately 290,-000 physicians. Within this group, estimates of the number of active practicing psychiatrists ranged from 19,643 in 1970 to approximately 23,000 in 1974, or roughly between 7% and 8% of all M.D.s The number of psychoanalysts at this time was approximately 2,300 in all.

The psychologists have increased most rapidly. A central indicator is the membership of the American Psychological Association, which went from an index base of 100 in 1920, to 1,850 in 1950.[51] This growth was far more rapid than that of any other professional association. The next most rapidly growing professional group was the Federation of Societies for Experimental Biology, which expanded from an index base of 100 in 1950 to 735 in 1949. Another indicator of the rapid increase of psychologists is the fact that one-half the Ph.D.s in psychology as of 1976 received their degrees in 1965 to 1975. About 40% of the 40,000 psychologists, or 16,000, see themselves as health professionals. This self-designation encompasses those who view themselves as clinical psychologists and those who are engaged in counseling and

50. Theodor Szasz, *The Myth of Mental Illness: Foundations of a Theory of Personal Conduct* (New York: Harper and Row, 1961).

51. Kenneth E. Clark, *America's Psychologists: A Survey of a Growing Profession* (Washington: American Psychological Association, 1957), p. 23.

testing related to mental health programs.[52] Only a very small number are engaged in private practice; the figure was estimated as 6% of the membership of the American Psychological Association, while the remainder are in institutional settings.

Herbert Dorken and J. Frank Whiting, specialists in psychological manpower, have been emphatic in reporting that "Schofield [in 1969] was the first to describe psychology as a health profession without the qualifying term mental. Like other health professions, psychology strives to assure overall health, which includes the emotional and mental was well as physical condition of the individual."[53] Thus the struggle for "parity" by clinical psychology is carried on mainly within the structure of the medical institutional setting.

In addition, it has been estimated that in 1973 there were approximately 20,000 psychiatric social workers, of whom only 1,600 were in private practice. The number of psychiatric social workers and the number of those in private practice have also grown rapidly. To complete the inventory, in 1973 there were 9,000 employed trained psychiatric nurses, while in toto 33,000 nurses were working in psychiatric settings.

The development of these personnel and the network of services they supply rest on the increase of affluence in the United States. It requires considerable funds to train a member of the fifth profession, whether the funds be derived from personal or family income or from governmental fellowships (which have increased since 1960). Moreover, great resources are required to pay for the ongoing services. Only a small portion of the costs is provided by direct personal payments; the bulk of the payments comes from institutional support (e.g., military service schemes, educational institutional health services), third-party insurance payments, or group health schemes, and, increasingly, from welfare state–related programs which are mainly under medical categories.

Each of the constituent groups in psychotherapy believes that it represents the results of a unique and specialized training experience, as the research of William E. Henry and his associates has highlighted.[54] But

52. Bernard Lubin and Eugene E. Levitt, *The Clinical Psychologist: Background, Roles and Functions* (Chicago: Aldine, 1967).

53. Herbert Dorken and J. Frank Whiting, "Psychologists as Health Service Providers," in *The Professional Psychologist Today*, ed. H. Dorken et al. (San Francisco: Jossey-Bass, 1976). p. 1.

54. Henry, Sims, and Spray, *Fifth Profession*, pp. 1–8.

the reality is the extensive convergence among these groups in their actual practice. As Henry points out there are differences in ideologies and in particular therapeutic activities, but they are minimal, and, far more important, they do not differ along the lines of the profession in which therapists are members.[55] The psychiatrists emphasize their medical school training while the psychoanalysts add their personal analysis. Clinical psychologists refer to their research training, the psychiatric social workers to their exposure to the study and realities of community organization. But, in effect, these training experiences recede in the daily professional practice. The psychiatrist does not engage in physical medicine, the clinical psychologist does not do research, and the psychiatric social worker is not centrally involved in community organization; however, concern with family and community setting does give the social worker added information and an understanding of the potentials and limits of community resources for hindering or assisting psychotherapeutic goals.

In reality, the fifth profession of psychotherapy has an important element of convergence in the common aims that each of the four groups have accepted, namely, to deal with the psychic states and capacities of their clients and patients. They all assume the validity of the subjective state of their clients; they assume that feelings need to be dealt with. There is a unity in their recognition of an unconscious or at least an underlying and submerged set of attitudes and thoughts over which the individual must effect some degree of personal control. Again the empirical findings of William E. Henry underscore the pervasive reliance of these specialists on a converging framework which is "composed of psychodynamic concepts particularly psychoanalytic concepts derived from Freudian and neo-Freudian schools of thought."[56]

Moreover, Henry's empirical research into over 3,700 members of the fifth profession emphasizes additional sources of convergence, and resulting professional homogeneity. A major source comprises the similarities found in professional socialization. As he concludes, "Each requires of all members a distinctive set of skills."[57] In the development of these skills, formal didactic training in courses and nonclinical inter-

55. Ibid., p. 182.
56. Henry, Sims, and Spray, *Public and Private Lives*, p. 216.
57. Henry, Sims, and Spray, *Fifth Profession*, p. 7.

action are assigned only minor importance. These skills are developed in a clinical setting and on the job. This form of training reveals greatest similiarity across professional groups. His research also demonstrates that "the differences among the four groups are insignificant in such issues as relations to parents and sibling, reported sexual histories and aspects of cognitive development . . . they appear to have had highly similar formative experiences in significant areas of personality development."[58] Finally, the members of the fifth profession display a homogeneity in personal development and social background which contributes to a "therapeutic constellation."

These mental health specialists are recruited in overrepresented numbers from urban settings, culturally marginal ones in particular; and they have tended to reject their family values for more liberal ones. Psychotherapists are heavily recruited from a Jewish background, but it is important in this regard that these persons largely tend to be religious apostates. The data document the motif of these psychotherapists of the fifth profession as "liberal." (Some in the encounter group movement seem linked to a more radical outlook; and the behavior-modification groups reflect an emerging conservative trend.)

The sociology of the psychotherapist gives fuller meaning to the mass of evidence evaluating the direct effect of treatment on patients. The results point in a consistent direction. If one makes the systemic argument that the indirect effect of the psychotherapists is important in making an ongoing contribution to the therapeutic—that is "humane"—milieu to the medical setting. Moreover, evaluation studies of psychotherapy are pertinent because they address the interrelations between psychological distress and somatic illness. For example, a classic study of psychiatric services by W. Follette and N. Cummings demonstrates that psychotherapy includes in its consequences a reduction in the usage of conventional medical services.[59] If it is the case, and there is good reason to believe that it is, that patients consciously and "unconsciously somatize" their emotional problems in order to be able to obtain a response from a doctor, then the treatment of the underlying psychic state should and does reduce medical dependency.

The mass of evaluation studies, although they have complex problems of measurement, tend to support this positive influence, as the

58. Henry, Sims, and Spray, *Public and Private Lives*, p. 182.

59. W. Follette and N. Cummings, "Psychiatric Services and Medical Utilization in a Prepared Health Plan Setting," *Medical Care* 5 (1967): 25–35.

comprehensive review of the literature by D. H. Malan concludes.[60] This review emphasized the positive effect of psychotherapy on somatic manifestations; in part changes in such manifestations are more discernible than "psychic" states. The research literature stands in opposition to the constant criticism of psychotherapy by various sociologists and lay critics concerned with the imputed consequences of psychotherapy on public morality. Moreover, these observations supply suggestive evidence that forms of treatment reduce the costs of mental hospitals, in contrast to custodial procedures.[61] But cost effectiveness is only one criterion of performance, especially since a number of persons who suffer either mild or pronounced distress are prepared to search relentlessly for relief. These findings help explain why psychotherapy has continued to expand; there are a client population and their families and associates who have either directly or indirectly experienced some benefits, even though these benefits may well be temporary.

These observations about "conventional" psychotherapy are applicable to the second modality of psychological intervention, namely, group dynamics and group processes. One can argue that T-groups, sensitivity training, and related formats are an expression of the dilemmas and limitations of social control of a bureaucratized and disarticulated society. In this view, they are a deliberate attempt to make social institutions operate more effectively by training the members to take into account the sensibilities of "others," in particular, of organizational colleagues and associates. From this point of view, the psychological component appears limited, and to stress the idea of psychological intervention could be an overstatement.

But such a line of reasoning is incorrect, for it overlooks the effective psychic content of the group dynamics strategy which is not to be dismissed. The pioneer of such group interaction was J. L. Moreno.[62] He was directly influenced by Sigmund Freud and was aware of psychoanalysis and depth psychology. But the rationale of the group dy-

60. D. H. Malan, "The Outcome Problem in Psychotherapy Research: An Historical Review," *Archives of General Psychiatry* 29 (1973): 719–29. For a study which emphasizes moral values, see David Rosenthal, "Changes in Some Moral Values Following Psychotherapy," *Journal of Consulting Psychology*, 19 (December 1955): 431–36.

61. K. M. McCaffree, "The Cost of Mental Health Care Under Changing Treatment Methods," *International Journal of Psychiatry* 4 (August 1967): 142–57.

62. J. L. Moreno, *"Who Shall Survive?" Foundations of Sociometry Group Psychotherapy and Sociodrama* (Beacon, N.Y.: Beacon House, 1953).

namics perspective in good measure derives from the intellectual contributions of Kurt Lewin, who also was thoroughly familiar with the works of Freud.[63] Lewin's efforts, as well as those of his colleagues and disciples, were dictated by a desire to develop techniques which would have "popular" application. He was seeking to increase the availability of psychological approaches—to "democratize" them, if you will.

During World War II, he was involved in group experiments in the use of group discussion procedures to modify food habits. He and his followers believed that unconscious and submerged factors did not have to be confronted directly in the process of developing responsible psychological support. The need to manage and come to terms with these pressures, rather than let them work themselves out, was always present. The reliance on responsible and supervised group leaders was an essential part of the intervention process. In short, this modality grew out of and was aware of depth psychology. In fact, these group dynamics processes are fully compatible with deeper psychoanalytical techniques. There are psychoanalytical practitioners who have deliberately involved themselves in group dynamics strategies in order to deal in a circumscribed fashion with family relations, delinquency, and a range of emotionally charged tensions. For example, Bruno Bettelheim, the specialist in milieu therapy for disturbed children, has engaged extensively in group discussion techniques with mothers to resolve issues of child raising.[64] Such a strategy is not considered a "watering down" of more powerful techniques, such as free association and dream analysis, but rather the mobilization of group resources to deal with particular problems more effectively than on a one-to-one basis.

The key strategy of the group dynamics modality rests on a group leader who is trained and has professional and peer supervision. It is based on controlled face-to-face interaction in which the participants reveal and share previous and ongoing experiences. Small group processes are stimulated by feedback mechanisms, that is, by transmission of the experiences of participants and by the introduction of ex-

63. Kurt Lewin, *Dynamic Theory of Personality* (New York: McGraw-Hill, 1935); Kurt Lewin, *Principles of Topological Psychology* (New York: McGraw-Hill, 1936); Kurt Lewin, *Field Theory in Social Science* (New York: Harper, 1951).

64. Bruno Bettelheim, *Dialogues with Mothers* (New York: Free Press of Glencoe, 1962); see also L. A. Gottschalk and E. M. Pattison, "Psychiatric Perspectives on T-Groups and the Laboratory Movement: An Overview," *American Journal of Psychiatry* 126 (1967): 823–39.

ternal events. The goal is to increase self-understanding and to equip the participants with increased interpersonal skills in order to assist them in the performance of specific work tasks.

The strategies of the group dynamics movement evolved pragmatically but reflect the intellectual orientation of its founders. In 1946, a group of social psychologists led by Kurt Lewin conducted a series of workshops for Connecticut to assist community leaders to implement the Fair Employment Act. In 1947, the National Training Laboratory was formed as the outgrowth of these experiences and the term "T-group" (for training group) was used for their group experiments. These efforts supplied the core of the rapid diffusion of what would in time be called the strategy of group dynamics. The term T-group emphasizes the goal of assisting persons in institutional, community, and related settings to achieve specific occupational and social goals. This has been extended and adapted to encompass personal development and personal expression with less clarity and purpose.[65]

As a result, the participants in these group experiments and group interventions are mainly members of large-scale organizations, although these techniques have been applied in a variety of settings. The operating procedures articulate with the increased emphasis on managerial decision making and on manipulative authority, as defined in this study. The introduction of these techniques is in itself a demonstration of the commitment of the leaders of an organization to a stronger reliance on persuasion. The interventions are part of the extensive trend in the United States for bureaucratic organizations to hold "retreats," a modern version of religious retreats. As in the case of psychotherapy, the indirect influence, the norms, and the values which group dynamics and group processes represent are as important as the direct and immediate consequences which are generated in the participants. The attraction to participants involves the desire for new experiences; but the imputed or desired association of these procedures with improved performance "on the job" accounts for a considerable measure of their diffusion and institutionalization.

It is feasible to address these direct and immediate effects on individuals. There are over 200 evaluation studies of small group experi-

65. J. P. Campbell and M. D. Dunnette, "Effectiveness of T-Group Experiences in Managerial Training and Development," *Psychological Bulletin* 70 (1968): 73–104. For an overview, see Leonard D. Borman and Morton A. Lieberman, eds., special issue, *Journal of Applied Behavioral Science* 12 (July 1976): 261–463.

ences which document and sustain the hypothesis that participation in these types of experiments has at least the short-term consequence of improving—or, more accurately, enlarging—a person's sensitivity.[66] No matter how difficult it is to record and measure these effects, the findings cannot be dismissed. Moreover, it is inferred that enlarged sensitivity involves heightened self-respect and increased ability to accord self-respect to others; but this is yet to be adequately demonstrated.

Within a decade of the diffusion of conventional group dynamics, the third modality, the encounter group—involving more "acting out" —became a startling and widespread alternative.[67] The formal "label" supplies only a partial guide; the main outlines were subsumed under terms such as "encounter groups," "transactional analysis," and the like, as formulated by Eric Berne, and the "eclectic" Esalen Institute, in the writings of William C. Schultz.[68] These group processes were accompanied by experiments in "radical" therapy of longer duration. The emergence of the encounter modality had strong overtones of a social movement; a strongly motivated leader, the preparation of a basic text, and the recruitment of lay followers to extend the enterprise.

The goal was not that of training in insight or personal skills for bureaucratic performance. On the contrary, the goal was the uninhibited expression of psychological tensions and aspirations, with the

66. Leland P. Bradford, Jack R. Gibb, and Kenneth D. Benne, *T-Group Theory and Laboratory Method; Innovation in Re-Education* (New York: Wiley, 1964); R. J. House, "T-Group Education and Leadership Effectiveness: A Review of the Empirical Literature and a Critical Evaluation," *Personnel Psychology* 20 (1967): 1–32; Jack R. Gibb, "Effects of Human Relations Training," in *Handbook of Psychotherapy and Behavior Change*, ed. A. E. Bergin and S. L. Garfield (New York: Wiley, 1971), pp. 829–62.

67. The following set of categories have been offered by one psychologist to encompass the alternative approach to "small group" experiences: sensitivity experience (self-actualization); authenticity experiences (openness, authenticity, congruence, transparency, and confrontation); creativity-release experiences (body movements, sensory awareness, finger painting, free verse, interpretative dancing, psychedelic drugs, meditation, the Minerva experience, nude marathons, fight training, Zen, contextual maps, induced aggression, and nonverbal encounters); programmed experience; embedded experience (tm training, religious experience); and motivation-shift experience. See Jack R. Gibb, "Meaning of the Small Group Experience," in *New Perspectives on Encounter Groups*, ed. L. N. Solomon and B. Berzon (San Francisco: Jossey-Bass, 1972), pp. 1–12.

68. Eric Berne, *Transactional Analysis in Psychotherapy* (New York: Grove, 1961). William C. Schutz, *Joy* (New York: Grove, 1967); William C. Schutz, *The Interpersonal Underworld* (Palo Alto, Calif.: Science and Behavior Books, 1966).

purpose of establishing one's "real identity." If the strategy called for direct confrontation and direct release, the encounter group underscored the importance, the necessity, and the possibility of rapid transformation of the self. If the conventional and professional psychotherapists were concerned with the "regressive" aspects of their strategy, the advocates underlined the advantages of such tactics. It was a social movement which did not emphasize professional guidance. But the encounter movement did rapidly develop its dogmas and its specialized personnel.

The encounter movement is a direct reflection of the sociopolitical tensions and movements of the 1960s. It was an expression of the "radical" language which emphasized the potential for drastic societal change. In 1969, Carl Rogers spoke of the possibility that "the encounter group may be the most important social invention of the century."[69] The psychological equivalent of the imputed societal revolution in the United States was asserted. William H. Blanchard reported the disappointment leaders of the encounter movement experienced when the spokesman for the radical student movement, Herbert Marcuse, rejected their "philosophy." When they suggested the "revolutionary implications in the whole movement toward group therapy," Marcuse replied, in part, "I read the catalog of the Esalen Institute. To me, this is sufficient to be horrified."[70]

One striking aspect of the encounter movements has been the social heterogenity of the participants, who were essentially self-recruited and came from various institutional settings. There was none of the emphasis on organizational affiliations to be found in the more conventional T-group programs. In fact, the encounter group, from the point of view of social composition, represented the informal and disarticulated group that it was designed to counteract. If the T-group and sensitivity training session had overtones of a secular retreat, the encounter group was a form of confessional, a modern acting out of the confessional without religious sanctions or controls.

From a standard psychotherapeutic perspective, the central question was whether and/or to what extent such forms of "regressive therapy" would produce discernible personal damage. The study of encounter

69. Carl R. Rogers, "The Group Comes of Age," *Psychology Today* 3 (1969): 3; see also *Carl Rogers on Encounter Groups* (New York: Harper and Row, 1970).

70. William H. Blanchard, "Encounter Group and Society," in Solomon and Berzon, *New Perspectives*, pp. 1–12.

groups by Morton A. Lieberman and associates focused directly on this question.[71] They collected an enormous number of data on a variety of encounter groups—direct observational, test, and attitude material—and they developed their analysis with sophisticated concern for the societal context. The importance of the findings rested on their effort to investigate beyond self-designated labels and to examine practices. The actual variance between different encounter groups resulted from varying skills of the group leaders.

The central findings were that the expression of emotion is not necessarily or automatically beneficial. "Letting it all hang out" hardly guaranteed a "therapeutic" result.[72] The research concluded that only one-third of the participants had a beneficial experience; and the research team was prepared to debate whether this is a high or low payoff. They employed a sympathetic notion of beneficial, and they had to rely on self-reports and follow-up self-reports. They were dealing with psychic states which encompassed clearer self-definitions, better understanding of self, and the like. They were prepared to assert that, according to their psychological criteria, about 8% of the participants suffered psychological damage. The conclusion pointed out that this was the result as much of the skill and responsibility of the group leader as it was of the assumptions of this psychological modality. The researchers are concerned with that level of damage; is it socially acceptable? The study has only partial control groups. It would be important to estimate or to speculate what proportion of a comparable group of persons who had not participated in the study had during the similar period suffered psychological damage in the course of their "ordinary" life experiences.

Again, as in the more conventional T-group strategies, there is no evidence that the participants developed new interpersonal contacts or networks as a result of their participation in encounter groups, although they may have well emerged with an enriched rhetoric for describing their own psychic states. In essence, there was, as the researchers document, a strong temporary sense of participation or even of psychological community.

The term "synthetic community" has been applied to the temporary sense of communion, or to the sense of communion without lasting

71. Morton A. Lieberman, Irvin D. Yalom, and Matthew B. Miles, *Encounter Groups: First Facts* (New York: Basic Books, 1973).

72. Ibid., p. 422; for a careful empirical study which supports this hypothesis in family relations, see Murray A. Straus, "Leveling, Civility and Violence in the Family," *Journal of Marriage and the Family* 36 (February 1974): 13–29.

commitment which is produced.[73] In both the T-group and the encounter group, human needs are being satisfied, not the least of which is tension control. Thus it makes sense to assert that these processes are less oriented toward "people changing and more toward people providing."[74] As defined above, we are dealing with a form of psychological consumerism, a form of indulgence which is incomplete or minimally effective in the satisfaction which it provides. However, in both cases–group dynamics and encounter groups–if there is little support for our basic hypothesis that dynamics psychology assists the search for effective social control, there is also no reason to believe that these enterprises work effectively against the hypothesis. In essence, there is weak demonstration of the convergence of these modalities with the other intensive psychological interventions.

Does the fourth modality–behavior modification–present a distinctly different case? The theory and practice of behavior modification almost defies adequate explication. The manifest contents of many forms of behavior modification deny the subjective dimensions of social organization and eliminate personal control. Therefore, they pursue orientations in opposition to the normative goals of social control. Moreover, in practice, some of the dramatic applications of behavior modification have been in settings which have produced protest because of the violations of human and civil rights of "human subjects." In addition to the direct impact on the persons exposed to behavior modification, it has been argued that the indirect implication, the normative context of behavior modification, is at variance with the societal goals seeking to enlarge consent and effective social control.

But one cannot assert that these issues have escaped the responsible practitioners of behavioral modification.[75] However, we are concerned with the normative dimensions and the actual effect of the behavioral

73. Kurt W. Back, *Beyond Words: The Story of Sensitivity Training and the Encounter Movement* (New York: Russell Sage Foundation, 1972); Rolbert A. Luke, Jr., "The Internal Structure of Sensitivity Training Groups," *Journal of Applied Behavioral Science* 8 (July–August 1972): 421–37.

74. Lieberman et al., *Encounter Groups*, p. 453; for a more negative view, see Herbert S. Strean, "Social Change and the Proliferation of Regressive Therapies," *Psychoanalytic Review* 58 (1971–72): 581–94; Steven L. Jaffe and Donald J. Scherl, "Acute Psychosis Precipitated by T-Group Experience," *Archives of General Psychiatry* 21 (October 1969): 443–48.

75. Israel Goldiamond, "Toward a Constructional Approach to Social Problems: Ethical and Constitutional Issues Raised by Applied Behavior Analyses," *Behaviorism* 2 (1974): 1–84; Israel Goldiamond, "Protection of Human Subjects and Patients: A Social Contingency Analysis of Distinctions Between Research and Practice, and Its Implications," *Behaviorism* 4 (1976): 1–4.

modification modalities. In the writings of Israel Goldiamond, one can find a direct confrontation of the professional and ethical issues involved in behavior modification. The strategy that he advocates is an application of the standard aspect of professional practice, namely, a concern with informed consent in terms of the realities of the clinical setting. Moreover, when informed consent is not feasible or adequate, peer review and peer control become more and more central; and by inference, lay involvement needs to be expanded. The crucial element in the ethical responsibility of behavior modification as formulated by Goldiamond focuses on the alternative interventions available to the persons involved. He argues that, if alternative strategies have failed or the task of maintaining the person involved leads to the need for physical restraint, the use of behavior modification procedures can be seen as a reduction in coercive pressure and thus justified.

The wide range of actual operating techniques subsumed under this modality makes overall assessment of the available research literature very difficult. In particular, much of the literature deals with specific experiments rather than with institutionalized programs; it therefore becomes difficult to separate the special effect of the experiment—the well-known "Hawthorne effect"—from the actual effect of the special procedures. Nevertheless, when behavior modification is actually applied in relatively humane and simplistic procedures, the results are as would be expected. Generically, these procedures are rote training and fairly immediate reward for compliance. The results are temporary increases in the ability of the person to perform. These procedures are most appropriate for persons who are mentally retarded or deeply damaged psychologically and therefore potentially the least able to respond to procedures and intervention which require some voluntaristic response and enlarged personal control.

Training in behavior modification, especially in the form of the "token economy," means that important numbers of the clients are exposed to these procedures in sheltered environments. Observers of these "asylums" have pointed out that, while learning takes place in these experimental situations because the immediate environment is highly structured, the learning experiences are not closely related to the real situations which the inmates must confront when they depart.[76]

76. John H. Gagnon and Gerald C. Carison, "Asylums, the Token Economy, and the Metrics of Mental Life," *Behavior Therapy* 7 (1976): 528–34.

Thus, in summary and on balance, while there are practices of behavior modification which require the fullest scrutiny, this modality appears to be, by and large, supportive of its clients if not effective, and represents another form of benign accommodation of a society in which the pressure for solutions to human problems remains powerful. From the perspective of social science, the intellectual and analytic contributions to this modality are limited as compared with those to other modalities. The major contribution has been to "justify" or "rationalize" rote learning, a procedure of long historical standing, and to enlarge its application. But behavior modification, like the other three modalities, has emerged as an intellectually based strategy with explicit linkages to the university-trained professionals.

All four strategies, in varying degrees and with their inherent defects and limitations, represent positive contributions to the search for social control and the reduction of interpersonal coercion. Each of these intellectually based strategies for the management of interpersonal relations can be compared to "lay movement." Two impressive and comprehensive social movements with a voluntary basis have developed which have served as "therapeutic" strategies, without explicit intellectual justification. Both have strong overtones of the therapeutic milieu or even the therapeutic community. They include the extensive networks of programs offered by the Salvation Army and the more specialized control of the A. A. movement.[77] The central aspect of these supportive orientations rests on a moral commitment to a strategy of lay group assistance. The vast outpouring of self-help psychological books has a related relevance. (The drug control programs of Synanon can also be mentioned, but this movement relies on extremely negative, almost coercive, sanctions, and its growth and effective institutionalization have been limited.) But the relevance of the Salvation Army and the A. A. movement rests in their implicit but clear recognition that the idea of "cure" or even "treatment" is irrelevant. The underlying issue is the management of interpersonal relations which have important unresolvable elements. This modality seeks to provide continuing and effective assistance by creating a specialized subculture or psychological community, which exists in the larger societal setting and which enables "clients" to perform and survive without resort to self-destruc-

77. Thomas B. Richards, "The A. A. Halfway House and Service Center," in *Alcoholism: The Total Treatment Approach*, ed. Ronald J. Catanzaro (Springfield: Thomas, 1969), pp. 373–82.

tive behavior.[78] If the summary of the findings concerning the purposive management of interpersonal relations is that the contributions of dynamics psychology (and these lay movements) have on the whole been positive for societal practices and norms, there is no reason to assert that the men and women who represent these practices and partial ideologies are sufficiently aware of the prophetic and unresolvable dimensions of social control in an advanced industrial society.

78. Ralph Turner, "The Real Self: From Institution to Impulse," *American Journal of Sociology* 81 (March 1976): 989–1016.

Twelve

Experiments in Community Participation

Social Learning and Community Organization

Sociological analysis has dealt with the widest range of "social problems," so there is hardly a sociopolitical dilemma to which sociological thinking has not been applied. But the "social problem" of the social construction and the reconstruction of the "urban community" has been one of the central and persistent focal points. If one seeks to assess the consequences of sociological analysis on institution building, then the accomplishments and limitations of community sociology and urban sociology are of paramount significance. The term "community organization" with its varied content is one link between academic sociology and the related issues of public policy.[1]

Much sociological analysis has been devoted to identifying the limits of psychological strategies of social work. This type of critical analysis has sought to substitute community-based notions of institution building for interpersonal and intrapersonal concerns, when in effect, the essential public policy question is the area of convergence and reinforcement.[2] Nevertheless, mass media personnel, informed citizens,

1. Pranab Chatterjee and Raymond A. Koleski, "The Concepts of Community and Community Organization: A Review," *Social Work* (July 1970): 82–91.

2. I have long been interested in the historical origin of the dialogue between sociology and social work. It is well known that Robert E. Park became outrightly hostile to social work. In contrast, W. I. Thomas had many contacts with social work and he remained sympathetic, although critical. His essential point of view emphasized the necessity of understanding the values and culture of the immigrant population and the need for strengthening the institutions of self-help and community organization as a bridge into the large society.

In the following passage from *The Polish Peasant* (1918), it is possible to find persistent issues in social work: "It is a mistake to suppose that a 'community center' established by American social agencies can in its present form even approximately fulfill the social function of a Polish parish. It is an institution imposed from the outside instead of being freely developed by the initiative and co-operation of the people themselves and this, in addition to its racially unfamil-

and political leaders are prepared to attend to sociologists' ideas about the management of communities. This is a substantive topic on which the special intellectual competence and technical expertise of the sociologist are seen as valid or at least worthy of sustained attention and evaluation. And the search for more effective social control at the nation-state level has produced, especially since 1960, an intensification of intervention by the federal government in the neighborhood and residential community.

On a day-to-day basis, civic leaders and professional specialists think of "community organization" as an extensive array of substantive tasks—from improving the quality of public education in the neighborhoods of the inner city to expanding the facilities for family counseling in suburban settlements. As early as 1920, Joseph K. Hart used the term "community organization" in his textbook for social work practice, and its diffuse meaning has persisted.[3] But the variety of substantive goals does not obscure the "essence" of community organization as a strategy for strengthening social control. The institutional and moral difficulties of an advanced industrial society have in this analysis been cast in part in terms of the disarticulation between work and residence. The elimination or at least the reduction of the resulting tensions and conflicts is a goal of social control. As has been argued in chapter 8, the separation of work and residence implies that a dual but interrelated set of voluntary associations, one linked to occupation and work and one to residential community, are required in an advanced industrial society such as the United States.

iar character, would be enough to prevent it from exercising any deep social influence. Its managers usually know little or nothing of the traditions, attitudes, and native language of the people with whom they have to deal and therefore could not become genuine social leaders under any conditions. Whatever real assistance the American social center gives to the immigrant community is the result of the 'case method,' which consists in dealing directly and separately with individuals and families. While this method may bring efficient temporary help to the individual, it does not contribute to the social progress of the community nor does it possess much preventive influence in struggling against social disorganization. Both of these purposes can be attained only by organizing and encouraging social self-help on the co-operative basis. Finally, in their relations with immigrants the American social workers usually assume, consciously or not, the attitude of a kindly and protective superiority, occasionally, though seldom, verging on despotism."

3. Joseph K. Hart, *Community Organization* (New York: Macmillan, 1920). See also Sidney Dillick, *Community Organization for Neighborhood Development: Past and Present* (New York: William Morrow, 1953); Fred M. Cox and Charles Garvin, "Community Organization Practice: 1865–1973," in *Strategies of Community Organization*, 2d ed., ed. Fred M. Cox et al. (Itasca: F. E. Peacock Publishers, 1974).

From this perspective, community organization is a group effort, by increased social interaction and by institutional change, to deal with strained social control.[4] Community organization implies institution building internal to a territorial settlement—often professionals speak of the horizontal dimension.[5] But the results also depend on the vertical connections which are created with the political and electoral institutions of the metropolis and the nation-state.

Alternative strategies for community organization which reflect sociological thinking range from global schemes with utopian overtones to specific and narrow instrumental programs. They include strategies which propose withdrawal from the urban metropolis and the establishment of modern rural communes and the obverse demand for local political autonomy—especially for community control for depressed inner-city settlements.

One stream of thought, reflecting the dominant traditions of the Gemeinschaft-Gesellschaft formulations, has advocated comprehensive schemes for community reconstruction. These schemes essentially seek to reverse imputed societal trends by creating modern types of communes as well as complete self-contained new towns. As described in chapter 2, the emergence of Gemeinschaft-Gesellschaft theory produced sociological criticism which rejected its logic, substance, and rigid overdeterminism. This critical approach avoided an assessment which emphasizes the "idyllic" state of earlier human settlements and the superiority of simpler community structures. Such systemic analysis was compatible with and helped stimulate partial and pragmatic solutions to specific issues of community construction and organization.

4. Buell Bradley et al., *Community Planning for Human Services* (New York: Columbia University Press, 1952); Monna Heath and Arthur Dunham, *Trends in Community Organization* (Chicago: School of Social Service Administration, University of Chicago, 1963); Murray Ross, *Community Organization: Theory, Principles and Practice* (New York: Harper and Row, 1967); Arthur Hillman, ed., *Making Democracy Work: A Study of Neighborhood Organization* (New York: National Federation of Settlements and Neighborhood Centers, 1968); Robert Perlman and Arnold Gurin, *Community Organization and Social Planning* (New York: Wiley, 1972); Peter Marris and Martin Rein, *Dilemmas of Social Reform: Poverty and Community Action in the United States*, 2d ed., (Chicago: Aldine, 1973); Jack Rothman, *Planning and Organizing for Social Change: Action Principles from Social Science Research* (New York: Columbia University Press, 1974); see also bibliographic review by Richard H. P. Mendes, *Bibliography on Community Organization for Citizen Participation in Voluntary Democratic Associations* (President's Committee on Juvenile Delinquency and Youth Crime, Washington: GPO, 1965).

5. Roland L. Warren, *The Community in America* (Chicago: Rand McNally, 1963), pp. 267–302.

Thus it becomes necessary to address two sets of questions. First, what have been the main intellectual tendencies in the strategies of community intervention, especially the strategies which have been influential since 1945? Second, what are the consequences of these strategies on community institutions of social control?

The basic hypothesis to be offered is that on balance, the application of sociological concepts of the management of community relations has been maladaptive from the point of view of institution building for social control, or at least limited in achieving goals. The rationale for this assessment is that the actual consequence of community organization has been to create an additional set of interest groups which press for advantage without adequate mechanisms of societal adjustment. This is not to deny that community organization and the stimulation it has received from sociological analysis have reduced particular important components of disarticulation; in fact, without the existing linkages between community organization and existing welfare institutions, contemporary industrial society would be almost unthinkable—or at least unbearable. But these accomplishments hardly imply a decisive and significant contribution of community organization to societal articulation.

We are dealing with more than the "realities" of a disarticulated metropolitan community. Some of the proposed strategies of change have been defective because they have been excessively totalistic and, in fact, strongly ideological. Their results have little positive consequence. Even many specific programmatic elements have been offered and rationalized in overly ambitious and unreal terms, for example, the public park movements or public housing efforts. On the other hand, excessive reliance on ad hoc and short-term "tactics" does not contribute to overcoming fragmentation of community social organization.

In other words, an essential element in the underlying rationale about the ineffectiveness of sociological analysis of community organization is the format and content of the strategies which have evolved. The task of transforming the sociological orientation into pertinent and effective partial ideologies and professional perspectives has been long in progress and remains to be elaborated.

This line of reasoning does not rule out the possibility and the reality of social learning. The rationale of community participation and ethnic separatism of the 1960s has been subject to persistent, even excessive, criticism. The exploration of realistic and meaningful patterns of citizen participation has become more and more a topic of sociological scholarship and research. From the point of view of social control, it is essential to determine the extent to which community organization creates a more inclusive basis for collective problem solving. The task of social control is to articulate the demands of localistic organizations into a societal-wide system of political decisions. Since there has been considerable intellectual clarification, we can speak of social learning.

Our analysis of the trends in community organization strategies, practices, and consequences is guided by two hypotheses. First, while strategies of comprehensive and total restructuring have persisted and are periodically reemphasized, there has been a gradual increasing trend of emphasizing pragmatic and partial strategies. Second, since the turn of the century, the emphasis in community organization has shifted gradually from social interaction and local self-improvement to coalition building and political participation. However, the connections between community organization and the electoral process have been neither effectively clarified nor developed. The central dimension for classifying alternative recommended strategies is precisely the emphasis on a comprehensive or ideological framework versus one which represents a set of principles which are less comprehensive but offer a general direction. The partial perspective must take into consideration emerging uncertainty and the need for continuous adaptation and adjustment.

However, each strategy of community organization should also examine the role allocated to the organs of the central government in facilitating and fashioning community institutions, particularly the financial support accorded to voluntary associations by the federal government. This was a crucial, explosive aspect of the debate about the legitimacy of the "War on Poverty." The principle that the federal government should not support voluntary associations in opposition to existing local public administrative and political agencies proved to be a pervasive, powerful argument in mobilizing opposition to federally supported community action programs. However, as will be demonstrated below, this principle has come to be modified in particular programs, for example, legal service efforts.

Comprehensive versus Partial Strategies

Comprehensive—in fact, global—strategies of community organization had their origins in the nineteenth century and sociological stimuli have continued to elaborate these strategies. One of the most dramatic and attention-getting has been the communitarian movement—the commitment to the creation of a totally new physical and social community, especially one which created a new relation among work and residence and family. These utopian communities were grounded in religious thought as well as in secular political theory.[6] Nothing short of a comprehensive reversal of the "pathway" of history—the movement from Gemeinschaft to Gesellschaft—was required. Only by creating a new community outside existing society could the essential reconstruction be accomplished.

These communitarian movements have influenced sociology as much as they have incorporated sociological thought. The historical sequence of utopian communities and their success and failure has been a source of continuous fascination for sociologists, who have pursued the topic as if there were direct lessons to be learned for future communitarian settlements and for society more generally. Benjamin Zablocki's analysis of *The Joyful Community* is an explicit effort of this kind, based on the case study of the Bruderhof movement.[7] Rosabeth Kanter's comparative analysis of a sample of utopian settlements likewise sought to ascertain the factors which account for the survival of particular communes, on the assumption that length of existence is a measure of success.[8] Likewise, the enduring religious communitarian enclaves, such as the Hutterites and Amish, stimulate the sociological imagination; the focus of research on them has been the internal dynamics which has assisted survival. Interestingly enough, these enclaves have not been studied from a perspective which would identify the components in the larger social structure which have facilitated their survival, since the Hutterites and Amish have not flourished in Western Europe where they originated.[9] In a parallel fashion, the rural communes which appeared in the 1960s attracted sociological interest.[10] These

6. Percival Goodman and Paul Goodman, *Communitas* (New York: Random House, 1960); Lewis Mumford, *The Story of Utopias* (New York: Viking, 1962); Robert Boguslaw, *The New Utopians: A Study of System Design and Social Change* (Englewood Cliffs, N.J.: Prentice-Hall, 1965); John Humphrey Noyes, *Strange Cults and Utopias of Nineteenth-Century America* (New York: Dover, 1966).

7. Benjamin Zablocki, *The Joyful Community* (Baltimore: Penguin, 1971).

8. Rosabeth Moss Kanter, *Commitment and Community* (Cambridge: Harvard University Press, 1972).

9. John A. Hostetler, *Hutterite Society* (Baltimore, Md.: Johns Hopkins University Press, 1974).

10. Sallie Teselle, *The Family, Communes and Utopian Societies* (New York: Harper Torchbooks, 1971); Ross V. Speck, *The New Families: Youth Communes,*

settlements disappeared rapidly, despite the efforts of sociologists to strengthen their legitimacy by research and the publicity that such research generated.

In contrast, the urban "communes" which were launched during this period with more limited goals have demonstrated much greater vitality and endurance.[11] They have not sought to construct a total life space. The numbers of members range from four or five to fifteen or twenty, and they participate in the urban economy. The commitment to locality is very strong—even if the geography is limited to a block or two in an accommodating neighborhood.

The vitality of these "constituted" families has been enhanced by the rapid growth of voluntary associations which support these diverse enterprises. They require no "lifetime" commitment but a short-term and immediate concern with relatively principled management of interpersonal and social forms. If one examines the range of these constructed social enclaves, it is clear that they are based on opposition or rejection of a positive role of the agencies of government, although most urban communes have had to come to terms with the local ordinances and have learned to make use selectively of local services and amenities. They are characterized by a high turnover of residents who are seeking new pathways into adulthood; as a result these urban communes have considerable organizational instability.

The assumption that it is necessary to create new communities to overcome the disarticulation of work and residence has not been limited to these morally based communitarian enclaves but has had a secularly based motive. To start afresh has included the belief that a completely physically planned new community was required. This point of view, which gives priority to the manipulation of the physical environment, is epitomized by the writings of Ebenezer Howard, *Garden Cities of Tomorrow* which appeared in 1891.[12] Such aspirations have had considerable influence, and in varying degree the new town movement has pressed for such a strategy. These efforts strongly favored a high degree of self-containedness—the garden city, like one's

and the Politics of Drugs (New York: Basic Books, 1972); Kathleen Kinkade, *A Walden Two Experiment: The First Five Years of Twin Oaks Community* (New York: Morrow, 1973).

11. Denham Grierson, *Young People in Communal Living* (Philadelphia: Westminster, 1971); David French and Elena French, *Working Communally: Patterns and Possibilities* (New York: Russell Sage Foundation, 1975).

12. Ebenezer Howard, *Tomorrow: A Peaceful Path to Real Reform* (London: Swan Sonnenschein, 1898); *Garden Cities of Tomorrow* (London: Swan Sonnenschein, 1902).

garden, was a retreat from the inevitable pressures of an industrialized urban environment. One cannot avoid noting the utopian dimension of the new town movement and its efforts to create new solidarities without reference to the larger urban environment. But the advocates of these planned communities did not believe that they were creating pilot projects—showpieces, so to speak—but rather that they were launching a movement which would transform the metropolis, although first priority was given to the fringe sectors.

The new town movement and the efforts at totally planned community had to confront the issue of whether the new "community" should include the factory system.[13] In Great Britain, new towns have sought to include factories, while in the United States they have been almost exclusively residential. In the period from 1945 to 1975, in Great Britain, with its older established tradition and more centralized programs, 31 new towns were established. These new towns have provided homes for 1,179,880 people and jobs for 570,803.[14] In the United States, by contrast, where the program has been developed since the 1960s and where there has been greater reliance on private enterprise involvement, some 123 new communities have been undertaken. These constitute a diverse group of open-site new towns, add-on towns, and satellite towns. Thus, of the 123 proposed developments, only 60 or so can be called new towns. By 1975, the movement stimulated by the 1970 New Community Development Act had faltered seriously.

But the powerful attraction of the new town idea persists and has been modified to include "the new town in town"—that is, the construction of housing settlements in the renewal areas of the central cities. At this level, the planners are forced to avoid the utopian aspirations of the new town movement.

One aspect of these models of physical utopias was the stimulus they gave to the construction of public housing projects. In the 1920s and especially in the 1930s, physical planners gave their support to the idea that to build new physical structures on a massive scale would, in effect, create the conditions for the social reconstruction of the slums.

13. Carol Corden, "New Towns in Great Britain and the United States," Ph. D. dissertation, University of Chicago, 1974, chap. 8, p. 1.

14. Royce Hanson, *New Towns: Laboratories for Democracy* (New York: Twentieth Century Fund, 1971); Carlos C. Campbell, *New Towns: Another Way to Live* (Reston, Va.: Reston Publishing Company, 1976); Raymond J. Burby III and Shirley F. Weiss, *New Communities U.S.A.* (Lexington, Mass.: Lexington Books, 1976).

When the first evidence of failure was brought forward, the assumptions of public housing were not reexamined; rather, bureaucratic rigidities led to expanded problems, so that the negative aspects were self-compounding.[15]

Other manifestations of global thinking about the physical dimensions of community were the repeated efforts to prepare city and regional master plans to guide the physical and ecological expansion of the metropolitan centers. Given the mechanisms of economic decision making in the United States, the gap between the plan and the community reality has been immense, but there have been exceptions. Of course, the ecological disarticulation of the metropolis may well have been greater without the outlines presented by master plans.

The alternative strategies to the global and ideological oriented approaches to community construction and reconstruction have been these partial and highly pragmatic ones. They have focused on the uncertainty about the future that had to be confronted and the need for continuous adjustment in the context of a pluralistic polity with its emphasis on individualist choice and style. Moreover, the partial strategies have rested on the assumption that information and knowledge, including social research, would be an important asset, and that the judgment of the "common man" could balance the inherent limitations and defects of the expert and the specialist.

In fact, the piecemeal approach to "community improvement" is rooted in the empirical tradition of the social survey, in effect in the philosophical elements of the Enlightenment—plus the impulses of men and women of good will. Varying forms of social surveys were carried out in Great Britain, Western Europe, and the United States during the first half of the nineteenth century. But it was in the undertakings of Henry Mayhew and Charles Booth that the social survey developed its logic and visibility.[16] Between the turn of the century and the outbreak of World War I, the social community surveys became institutionalized as fact-finding devices involving both specialists and local citizenry with the objective of improving the life conditions of submerged social groups. The rationale was that the exposure of the realities of social inequality and the conditions of residential existence

15. Lee Rainwater, *Behind Ghetto Walls: Black Family Life in a Federal Slum* (Chicago: Aldine, 1970).

16. Henry Mayhew, *London Labour and the London Poor* (London: Griffin, 1851); Charles Booth, *Life and Labour of the People in London*, 9 vols., 2d ed. (London: Macmillan, 1882–97).

would inspire social intervention. The social survey movement received extensive private support, including assistance from the Russell Sage Foundation, and related social work to academic sociology.

Over the years, the community survey perfected its empirical methodology and evolved broad coverage of the social structure, since community disarticulation involves the middle social groups as well. The practitioners of community and social surveys stressed citizen involvement in their procedures as a prerequisite for policy implementation.

The work of the community survey was augmented by the development of government and especially federal census data collection. By 1920, sociologists were already helping fashion the national efforts of the U.S. Census so that statistics about small units could be assembled to delimit trends in neighborhood and community for administrative and policy considerations. Community and urban sociology, with its strong emphasis on descriptive social intelligence, linked with the statistical innovations of William F. Ogburn in the analysis of social trends. These efforts reached one threshold with the publication of Herbert Hoover's monumental committee's report on *Recent Social Trends*.[17] In the 1960s, the renewed interest in poverty and local community produced the term "social indicators," which, in essence, was a continuation of the long-standing tradition of social statistics cast in a demographic and ecological framework.[18]

From 1890 to 1920, the years of the growth and institutionalization of sociological research, especially of urban sociology, the central focus of attention of the pragmatically oriented community specialists was on the incorporation of the foreign-born into the social organization of the metropolis.[19] Native-born white immigrants from rural areas attracted less attention among sociologists and presented less of a social problem. Sociologists and community welfare specialists were aware of and sensitive to the social deprivation in the black community, but in the Northern cities where social research was developing, the numbers of blacks were limited compared with the European immigrants. World War I produced a great increase in black settlement

17. President's Research Committee on Social Trends, *Recent Social Trends in the United States*, 2 vols. (New York: McGraw-Hill, 1933).

18. Eleanor Bernert Sheldon and Wilbert E. Moore, eds., *Indicators of Social Change: Concepts and Measurements* (New York: Russell Sage Foundation, 1968).

19. Robert E. L. Faris, *Chicago Sociology 1920–1932* (Chicago: University of Chicago Press, 1970).

in the North and a corresponding increase in tension and sociological interest. In the aftermath of the disastrous riot in 1919, Charles S. Johnson directed the work of the Chicago Commission on Race Relations which produced a study described as a "striking document for its time."[20]

During this period, there was an uneasy but productive relation between the leaders of the settlement house movement and university-based sociologists concerned with social documentation. The sociologists applied a framework which blended institutional and cultural analysis and which motivated them to recommend a strategy for reducing the disarticulation between the foreign-born and the larger society. This strategy was at variance with the dominant emphasis on "Americanization" and on the overriding pressure for mechanical "assimilation." Instead, the counterstrategy called for a recognition of the positive elements of ethnic identification and placed high priority on locally based leadership, organization, and arrangements for self- and mutual assistance.[21] The goal was not to use local initiative and cultural resources to create self-contained and provincial enclaves, but to improve the linkage between the local settlements and the center of the metropolis. The proposed formula appears to be remarkably "contemporary"; the direct line of development from the settlement house to strategies of community participation is clear.

For these sociologists, stimulated by the writings of W. I. Thomas and Robert E. Park, assimilation did not mean renouncing one's immediate cultural background. On the contrary, they explicitly asserted that assimilation did not require complete cultural uniformity with an imputed set of national norms and values. It meant recognition by the larger society of the worth and aspiration of ethnic sentiments and themes. As discussed in chapter 8, these sociologists neither anticipated a rapid extinction of ethnic attachment nor an unchanging survival of such sentiments. While they believed that ethnic attachments would most probably attenuate, they argued that primordial attachments based on ethnicity supplied one basis of local organization and self-help.

20. The Chicago Commission on Race Relations, *The Negro in Chicago: A Study of Race Relations and a Race Riot* (Chicago: University of Chicago Press, 1922).

21. W. I. Thomas, with Robert E. Park and Herbert A. Miller, *Old World Traits Transplanted* (New York: Harper, 1921).

They paid attention to voluntary associations and political participation, although they were skeptical of political solutions. They gave greater emphasis to the social and cultural relations provided by the church, the school, and the settlement house. Thomas traces in detail the complex of voluntary associations and their national coalescence.[22] With considerable speed, national associations emerged which represented ethnic groupings. In short, local solidarities were supported by national arrangements.

World War I deeply complicated the process of assimilation, in this sense, for the German-speaking minorities in the United States, but for a number of ethnic groups it was a decisive threshold in their societal integration. The federal government in particular was explicit in its appeal to ethnic minorities to support military and homefront efforts. As a result, ethnic involvement went on as local participation and national recognition, without explicit reference to partisan politics.

The end of the World War I and the reduction of European immigrants paradoxically brought a temporary reaction against ethnic pluralism. Radical "left-wing" political movements produced nativist agitations against foreigners. In addition, the movement of blacks into the Northern cities produced deep tensions. The press for "nationalistic" Americanization was intensified, while the counterstrategy of pluralistic community organization was pressed by pragmatic and reform-minded leaders and reflected the thinking of certain university social scientists.

Patterns of community organization and purposes of intervention varied according to the income and social status of the area. However, one focal point was the public school, which led to the emergence of the school community movement after 1920.[23] The school touched the lives of the widest social groups of the local population and it had inherent legitimacy because it was mandated to serve the needs of the next generation. Furthermore, the school had explicit territorial boundaries which made it a particularly suitable focal point for efforts at community organization.

In middle-class areas, there were few barriers to the development of the school as the "center" of local community organization, especially

22. W. I. Thomas and Florian Znaniecki, *The Polish Peasant in Europe and America*, 5 vols. (Boston: Richard G. Badger, 1918–1920).

23. Eleanor T. Glueck, *Community Use of Schools* (Baltimore, Md.: Williams and Wilkins, 1927).

in suburban areas. Its central activity was a contribution to the socialization of the young in the context of the increasing difference between work and residence. Suburban communities were prepared to tax themselves extensively for educational purposes, since the system was so organized that such revenues essentially remained in the immediate community. However, the formal and informal school-community linkages after 1945 were progressively found to be incomplete or unsatisfactory for the socialization of the next generation because of the disarticulation of the young generation from meaningful contact with the world of work and because of the emergence of a more self-contained youth culture.

Thus it is understandable that the school in low-income and socially deprived neighborhoods attracted sociologists as an arena in which the sociopolitical issues of community organization could be confronted. The shift from the settlement house to the school building represented both the declining number of new immigrants and the recognition that governmental resources were required. Private charity could not underwrite the financial costs. The objective was to increase the ability of the local citizens to find their way in the economic order—not only for the young people but also for the adult population, whose influence was decisive in molding the orientation and aspirations of their children. The use of the school as a community center had the support of educational trends inspired by John Dewey which emphasized the fusion of academic and "practical" education. The school was to extend its clientele, its program, and its effectiveness. But the settlement house and the school community movement never fused the interests of professional educator and the professional social worker. The fragmentation which characterizes community organization and the welfare state could already be identified by the end of the 1920s. The fragmentation was increased by private charity agencies with specialized programs and even by police agencies which developed their own athletic and youth programs. The limited coordination of these efforts was in the hands of church personnel, but the vitality of these religious organizations was limited, and declining for such purposes.

The advent of the New Deal did not produce an increased concern with community organization or with the educational system of the slum. The New Deal economic and welfare programs rested on a series of categorical federal programs which used income transfers, unemployment compensation, and social security, and which avoided the issues of community institution building. These programs could be rapidly developed by the federal government and they had strong countercyclical objectives.

The New Deal did not have a "sociological theory" of poverty. In particular, it avoided improvement of the existing educational and community organization for preparing the residents of the slum for employment opportunities. The magnitude of the unemployment—the inability to use the able-bodied and trained labor force—led to an outright lack of concern with the persistent problems of incorporating the "lower" social groups into the labor force. To deal with these community-based issues, federal aid to public education would have been required. Such political initiatives were doomed to fail because Southern Democrats were opposed to the use of federal funds for educating blacks and for assisting Catholic schools in the North.

Particular leaders in the New Deal were interested in creating community organizations and enlarging "citizen participation." When such initiatives were undertaken, it was generally outside the metropolitan centers. The federal government was aware that agricultural development in rural and farming areas required active local organization and initiatives.[24] The county agent network was strengthened and it worked to assist voluntary associations which could in turn deal with federal agencies. Local leaders were given authority in the administration of farm economic development programs. A variety of rural education and social development programs were managed with local participation. There was not the sharp ideological opposition which developed when the War on Poverty sought to apply these strategies in urban centers. But it was the Tennessee Valley Authority which gave the federal government its major experience in citizen involvement. It was outside a metropolitan center. It was a natural resource development linked to multipurpose goals of education, community development, and local services. Various forms of local citizen participation and group representation were encouraged. Although there were controversial overtones, the outcome was extensive popular support. The regional scope resulted in a variegated social basis which was utilized to create linkages with outside institutions. Elements of this format were incorporated, with varying degrees of success, in the Rural Elec-

24. Richard S. Kirkendall, *Social Scientists and Farm Politics in the Age of Roosevelt* (Columbia, Mo.: University of Missouri Press, 1966).

trification Authority, the Columbia Valley Authority, and the Appalachian Regional Development Act of 1965.

Likewise, New Deal administrators tried to reduce the economic and social misery of the Indian population on the reservations by giving them an enlarged measure of self-regulation and local voluntary association. These efforts were slowed during the early 1950s when the "termination of the reservation" policies were launched by the Eisenhower administration. However, this shift in policy was only temporary, since strong local community organizations emerged in the wake of the civil rights movement.

Under the New Deal, there were a series of programs to create small new communities, such as Roosevelt, New Jersey, and self-help agricultural settlements. These experiments involved positive efforts by the federal government to create local voluntary associations to help direct them. As early as 1933, a Subsistence Homestead Division was established in the Department of the Interior; it was reorganized into the Resettlement Administration in 1935 and finally emerged in 1937 as the Farm Security Administration, which included about 195 separate projects.[25]

Paradoxically, the civilian mobilization of World War II increased the scope and intensity of "constructed" community organizations supported by the federal government. The expansion of the war economy relieved pressure from further welfare benefits. However, the massive movements of population into urban areas, the disruption of family life, and the need for emergency social services required extensive community organization. These social problems were found not only in the socially deprived but throughout the entire social structure, especially as race tensions and even violence erupted.

A portion of these community organization efforts rested on the initiative of the private sector. But the federalization of community organization represented a decisive threshold. The massive efforts of the Red Cross and affiliated agencies were, in effect, federally sponsored, as were a variety of efforts at community organization in the areas of public health and civil defense.

25. Edward C. Banfield, *Government Project* (Glencoe, Ill.: Free Press, 1951), pp. 15–22. For a discussion of New Deal policies toward the Indians see Kenneth R. Philip, *John Collier's Crusade for Indian Reform, 1920–1954* (Tucson: University of Arizona Press, 1977); Graham D. Taylor, "The Tribal Alternative to Bureaucracy: The Indian's New Deal, 1933–1945," *Journal of the West* 13 (January 1974): 128–42.

But the most striking development was the emergence of local committees on race relations under the leadership of mayors and stimulated by the staff of the President of the United States during World War II. These committees sought to mobilize community leadership and resources to deal with race tension. They involved an admixture of citizen groups, plus civil service personnel who were charged with organizing and stimulating voluntary associations. In time these groups developed official statutory basis and budgetary support with extensive citizen participation and made observable contributions to social control.

These developments from 1920 to 1945 were accompanied by writings and debate within the academic community. They were influenced by university personnel who became active in community and governmental programs. In this period more explicit conceptual elaboration and community strategy were being formulated. The process of social learning was not to have its full effect until the War on Poverty was under way. Community and urban sociologists were aware of the fragmented systems of welfare and education and the weakeness of community organization. They stressed the inherent limitations of bureaucratized external agents who were not attuned to local cultural norms and who were unable to involve local residents.

The strategy of placing high priority on developing local leadership and local voluntary associations of self-help was epitomized in the launching of the Chicago Area Project, under the guidance of Ernest W. Burgess.[26] Its immediate focus was on delinquency control, and its governmental support was based on this objective. However, it proceeded by means of broad programs of community organization. The underlying strategy was that increased citizen participation, even in the poorest communities was possible, and in fact essential, to achieve democratic political goals and to improve local educational and welfare services.

26. Clifford R. Shaw, "The Chicago Area Project," in *Criminal Behavior*, ed. W. C. Reckless (New York: McGraw-Hill, 1940), pp. 508–16; Solomon Kobrin, "The Chicago Area Project: A Twenty-Five Year Assessment," *Annals of the American Academy of Political and Social Science* 322 (March 1959): 19–29; Harold Finestone, "The Chicago Area Project in Theory and Practice," in *Community Organization*, ed. I. A. Spergel (Beverly Hills, Calif.: Sage Publications, 1972); Daniel Glaser, "Marginal Workers: Some Antecedents and Implications of an Idea from Shaw and McKay," in *Delinquency, Crime and Society*, ed. James F. Short, Jr. (Chicago: University of Chicago Press, 1976); Anthony Sorrentino, *Organizing against Crime: Redeveloping the Neighborhood* (New York: Human Science Press, 1976).

This project and other such efforts in the 1930s and 1940s trained many leaders in criminology and community organization. They included Leonard S. Cottrell, Jr., and Saul Alinsky, men of differing political assumptions and organizational tactics. At the time of the New Deal, they were at the periphery of planned social change. But by 1960, these figures and their alternative sociopolitical experiments were at the center of the federal effort. The strategies of community intervention that were being developed influenced the War on Poverty and have persisted, since we are dealing with long-term and chronic issues.

The "Natural History" of Community Control

It is possible to speak of a "natural history" in the development of strategies of community intervention, since we are dealing with a sociopolitical movement. The natural history of a sociopolitical movement is a long-standing idea in sociological analysis but one which must not be applied mechanically or arbitrarily. In the first phases of a sociopolitical movement, demands for change are limited. But the initial period is followed by a marked intensification of demands, a "radicalization" of outlook, if you will, which in turn gives way to a self-imposed or an externally imposed limitation of desired goals and is followed by a period of consolidation—or Thermidor, as it has been characterized. The final outcome is hardly a return to the status quo ante.[27]

If one looks at the full scope of the historical sweep from the settlement house movement to the militant demands for community control in the 1960s and the collapse of such demands, the natural history concept has applicability. In particular, the term "natural history" can be applied pointedly to the dramatic developments of 1960 to 1976, the years of the transformation and even maturity of the strategies of community participation. In fact, it is possible to focus on the language and symbols of these initiatives to observe the change. The pathway of escalation and deescalation is obvious. In the first, and limited objective period, the symbol, "community relations," was used, which in time gave way to more strident appeals for community action. The second escalated phase was heralded by the term "community control" —which encompassed the militant language of local separatism. The

27. For an early application of this approach, see Lyford P. Edwards, *The Natural History of Revolution* (Chicago: University of Chicago Press, 1970).

restructuring to more limited goals designed to relate the locality to the metropolis can be seen by the emergence, in the third phase, of the more instrumental terminology of community participation.

The intensification of community organization efforts actually started before 1960 with the initiative of the Ford Foundation's Gray Areas Program, which sought to give national scope to the then discrete and locally based programs. But, 1960 to 1964 contained the first steps of limited but increased agitation and the initial broad outlines of direct federal intervention.[28] In 1961, under the direction of Attorney General Robert Kennedy, the President's Committee on Juvenile Delinquency and Youth was established; it was the advance party of the War on Poverty. With the passage of the Economic Opportunity Act of 1964, there followed rapidly growing demands for community control with strong ethnic and racial exclusiveness and "nationalist" content; in essence, the second and more militant period came into being.

The election of Richard Nixon in 1968 resulted in the rapid dismantling of the administrative apparatus of the War on Poverty and a reduction of fiscal support. The next six years were characterized by chronic instability and confusion, plus considerable criticism and defeatism about these community-based programs; in fact, this was a phase of overreaction without clear recognition of the accomplishments, as described below. These included increasing electoral involvement of inner-city minorities, a contribution to the resolution of violence, some improvement in education and welfare programs, and, especially, expanded opportunities for industrial employment.

One cannot separate the natural history of community organization movements from the absence of a critical or realigning election during 1952 to 1976. Indeed, the underlying societal trends as well as the limitations on political party organization contributed to the intensification of community-based agitation. In 1960, for the first time since the U.S. entrance into World War II, there was a "rediscovery" of poverty. Intellectually, the publication of Michael Harrington's *The Other America*, and politically, the campaigning of John F. Kennedy, were the stimuli.[29] (Paradoxically, popular concern with inner-city poverty

28. S. M. Miller and Martin Rein, "Participation, Poverty, and Administration," *Public Administration Review* 29 (January–February 1969), 15–24.

29. Michael Harrington, *The Other America: Poverty in the United States* (New York: Macmillan, 1962).

was the result of the effect of the primary campaign in the remote regions of West Virginia on President John F. Kennedy.) The election of 1964 produced, for the moment, a "minirealignment" in the coalition of the national executive supported by a clear Congressional majority which supplied the basis for both extensive civil rights legislation and for the implementation of the War on Poverty. However, this political coalition was short-lived because of the domestic tensions and conflicts created by the war in Vietnam. By 1968 a political stalemate was in effect and the idea of the weak political regime was directly relevant.

Both the advocates of community organization strategies and their critics are prone to emphasize the lack of agreement in the official mandates for the President's Committee on Juvenile Delinquency and Youth Crime and in the enabling legislation of the Office of Economic Opportunity. But such a perspective overstates the case. If one examines the conceptual assumption of the various strategies for community organization that were extant during the 1960s, one sees that there was a rough continuum of increasing "militancy," based on differing sets of political assumptions. Most intellectual and academic specialists—but not necessarily the most visible spokesmen—adhered to political assumptions of coalition formation and bargaining in a pluralist society. Such an approach was embodied in the legislative mandate. The administrators sought federal assistance to achieve fuller citizenship and they placed high priority on community participation as a form of political participation and bargaining. They were, in effect, following T. H. Marshall's analysis of the extension of citizenship, with political rights as a prerequisite to economic and social rights.

Their basic assumption was that the existing education-welfare services did not meet the needs of slum dwellers. They failed to achieve their goals because they did not effectively articulate these populations with the larger society. Local participation, local leadership, and the use of local personnel were required to improve services and to effect the necessary connections of the locality to the metropolis and to the national political system. Within this type of community organization strategy, there was debate about the emphasis to be placed on improving services in contrast to community organization efforts and agitation.

There were competing strategies of community organization which could be labeled "militant."

For example, there was the political rhetoric epitomized by Saul Alinsky, who made frequent reference to "radical" tactics and in reality was using modified procedures of the trade union movement.[30] But although the day-to-day agitiation techniques were attention-producing and stimulated "confrontation politics," many of the community organizing drives which began with this type of language rapidly shifted tactics and became explicitly involved in ongoing political bargaining.[31]

However, with the growth of sociopolitical tensions, particular advocates of confrontation politics made persistent demands for "community control." The political assumptions of community control were at the borderlines or beyond of coalition and bargaining politics; the demand was for elements of political separatism, based on ethnic and racial solidarities.

Without specificity, these spokesmen sought a political format which would transform the local community into an "all-powerful decision-making center." There is no evidence that the philosophy of "community control" was an essential or central ingredient of the federal efforts. A scattering of persons and some groups held such views, but in essence such thinking evolved in the natural history of the War on Poverty. Community control was not an extension or modification of traditional democratic theory but rather the infusion of a "Third World ideology"–an anticolonial and national liberation ideology. These liberation appeals reinforced the thinking of intellectuals and academics associated with community control.

The anticolonial model was remotely linked to the intellectual tradition of violence–from Georges Sorel to Frantz Fanon.[32] In this view, persistent violence was needed both for political objectives and as social therapy to overcome the "repressed" socialization which the lower strata had suffered. This intellectualization of violence worked its way down the social structure by means of campus-based discussion and by the prominence accorded to its spokesman in the mass

30. Saul Alinsky, *Reveille for Radicals* (Chicago: University of Chicago Press, 1946). See also Frances F. Piven and Richard A. Cloward, *Regulating the Poor: The Functions of Public Relief* (New York: Pantheon, 1971).

31. John H. Fish, *Black Power–White Control: The Struggle of the Woodlawn Organization in Chicago* (Princeton: Princeton University Press, 1973).

32. Georges Sorel, *Reflections on Violence* (New York: Huebsch, 1914); Frantz Fanon, *The Wretched of the Earth*, trans. Constance Farrington (New York: Grove, 1963).

media.[33] But both the demands for community control and the arguments of anticolonialism set the terms of political debate of community organization.

During 1964 to 1968, the phase of militant agitation, particular political confrontations took place which were clearly stimulated by the efforts of federally financed community action programs. But it is impossible to assert that the racial violence and the general configuration of community conflict were the result of enterprises stimulated by the Office of Economic Opportunity. The contrary argument is more persuasive. Federal funds which supported community-based programs reduced the level of racial tension and overt conflict. No doubt racial violence and confrontation politics particularly, as portrayed by the mass media coverage of urban affairs, contributed to the popular reaction against community consultative and participation programs. Particular programs were rendered ineffective by the tensions generated over "community control." Such outcomes were more than rare isolated occasions but hardly typical or even frequent. Throughout this period of agitation and confrontation, the main body of pragmatic community organization strategy remained intact or reemerged in refined form during the consolidation in the 1970s.

Consequences of the War on Poverty

The magnitude and complexity of the War on Poverty produced an extensive research effort, in the form of both case studies and more ambitious analysis based on comparative community studies. It is understandable that, given the civic values of sociologists, they were involved in such research. Interest in "evaluation research" supplied another stimulus for these investigations. Evaluation research received support from administrators and elected officials who were intrigued with the claim that the effect of these federal expenditures could be measured, and academic researchers saw such procedures as generating new bodies of data.

33. Robert Blauner, "Internal Colonialism and the Ghetto Revolt," *Social Problems* 16 (1968): 395–408; Harry Scoble, "Effects of Riots on Negro Leadership," in *Civil Violence in the Urban Community*, ed. L. Masotti and D. Bowen (Beverly Hills, Calif.: Sage Publications, 1968); F. Fogelson, *Violence as Protest* (Garden City, N.Y.: Doubleday, 1971); C. McPhail, "Civil Disorder Participation: A Critical Re-Examination of Recent Literature," *American Sociological Review* 36 (December 1971): 1058–72.

The case study materials are rich and revealing in detail, but it is difficult to draw generalizations from them. This is not because of their lack of representativeness but because they usually had a narrow time frame and therefore did not describe the longer-term processes of sociopolitical change. They tended to focus on specific programs rather than to present systemic analysis of the articulation and disarticulation of the local community and the metropolis. While comparative research efforts collected data on the federal efforts at community organization, the findings are based heavily on survey research and not sufficiently on organizational and operational sources or on effective participant observation. Nevertheless, there are particularly useful research efforts based on differing methodologies, such as J. David Greenstone and Paul Peterson's comparative study of New York, Philadelphia, Detroit, Chicago, and Los Angeles, and James J. Vanecko's massive survey of 50 cities of 50,000 population or more, which help give coherence to the available research.[34]

The "social order of the slum" as it has been allowed to evolve in the United States supplied the grim, resistant realities which had to be dealt with. This body of research and analysis upon initial review emphasizes the limitations, defects, and superficial effect of federally subsidized programs, especially during the period of maximum expen-

34. J. David Greenstone and Paul E. Peterson, *Race and Authority in Urban Politics: Community Participation and the War on Poverty* (New York: Russell Sage Foundation, 1973); James J. Vanecko, "Community Mobilization and Institutional Change: The Influence of the Community Action Program in Large Cities," *Social Science Quarterly* 50 (December 1969): 609–30. See also National Opinion Research Center, "Community Action Programs as Agents of Change in the Private Welfare Sector," Chicago, August 1969; "Community Mobilization and Institutional Change: The Influence of the CAP in Large Cities," Chicago, August 1969; "Community Organization Efforts: Political and Institutional Change, and the Diffusion of Change Produced by Community Action Programs," Chicago, April 1970; "National Evaluation of Urban Community Action Programs," Chicago, June 1969.

35. J. Clarence Davies, *Neighborhood Groups and Urban Renewal* (New York: Columbia University Press, 1966); Daniel Knapp and Kenneth Polk, *Scouting the War on Poverty* (Lexington, Mass.: Heath, Lexington Books); Willis D. Hawley and F. M. Wirt, eds., *The Search for Community Power* (Englewood Cliffs, N.J.: Prentice-Hall, 1968); William W. Ellis, *White Ethnics and Black Power: The Emergence of the West Side Organization* (Chicago: Aldine, 1969); Harold H. Weissman, *Community Councils and Community Control: The Workings of Democratic Mythology* (Pittsburgh: University of Pittsburgh Press, 1970); Russell D. Murphy, *Political Entrepreneurs and Urban Poverty* (Lexington, Mass.: Heath, Lexington Books, 1971); Harvey Molotch, *Managed Integration: Dilemmas of Doing Good in the City* (Berkeley: University of California Press, 1972); Eric A. Nordlinger, *Decentralizing the City: A Study of Boston's Little City*

diture.[35] Some of this research literature was rapidly used by the mass media to highlight negative accomplishments. But more systemic analysis of these experiments and the associated local leaders reveals a more differentiated outcome.[36]

Any striking, enduring improvement and effectiveness of services were indeed limited. Nevertheless, the War on Poverty institutionalized increased local community participation. Even more noteworthy, as described below, the short-term effect was to increase the participation of inner-city minority groups, especially blacks, in electoral politics. The increased electoral participation by minorities in turn led to continued pressure for additional civil rights legislation and to increased employment opportunities, especially in the governmental sector.[37] In particular private sectors, such as the construction industry, there was little change. Blacks increased to a limited extent in the industrial labor force, where a shift in emphasis from prior vocational training to on-the-job training emerged. This is not to assert that the gap between white and black income levels dramatically closed; the re-

Halls (Cambridge: MIT Press, 1972); Kenneth J. Pollinger and Annette C. Pollinger, *Community Action and the Poor: Influence vs. Social Control in a New York City Community* (New York: Praeger, 1972); Irving A. Spergel, ed., *Community Organization: Studies in Constraint* (Beverly Hills, Calif.: Sage Publications, 1972); Lawrence Bailis, *Bread or Justice: Grassroots Organizing in Welfare Rights Movement* (Lexington, Mass.: Lexington Books, 1974); Richard L. Cole, *Citizen Participation in the Urban Policy Process* (Lexington, Mass.: Lexington Books, 1974); Norman I. Fainstein and Susan S. Fainstein, *Urban Political Movements The Search for Power by Minority Groups in American Cities* (Englewood Cliffs, N.J.: Prentice-Hall, 1974); Howard W. Hallman, *Neighborhood Government in a Metropolitan Setting* (Beverly Hills, Calif.: Sage Publications, 1974); Robert M. Hollister, Bernard Kramer, and Seymour Bellin, *Neighborhood Health Centers, What Do Demonstration Projects Demonstrate?* (Lexington, Mass.: Lexington Books, 1974); Martin L. Needleman and C. Needleman, *Guerrillas in the Bureaucracy: The Community Planning Experiment in the United States* (New York: Wiley-InterScience, 1974); George J. Washnis, *Municipal Decentralization and Neighborhood Resources* (New York: Praeger, 1974); Curt Lamb, *Political Power in Poor Neighborhoods* (New York: Halsted Press, 1975); David J. O'Brien, *Neighborhood Organization and Interest Group Processes* (Princeton: Princeton University Press, 1975).

36. For case studies in depth of community and organizational adaptation resulting in relative success, see Julia Abrahamson, *A Neighborhood Finds Itself* (New York: Harper, 1959); Irving Spergel, *Community Problem Solving: The Delinquency Example* (Chicago: University of Chicago Press, 1969); Mayer N. Zald, *Organizational Change: The Political Economy of the YMCA* (Chicago: University of Chicago Press, 1970).

37. William Wilson, *The Declining Significance of Race: Blacks and Changing American Institutions* (Chicago: University of Chicago Press, 1978).

straints of a stagflation economy were at work. The benefits of increased opportunity had special potentials for blacks who gained access to higher education. Thus following historical precedent, the process of societal change was one of the extensions of political rights followed by economic and social improvements.

These observations are not incompatible with the reality that there were large-scale and conspicuous "projects" couched in the language of community control which failed immediately or caused only tension and disruption. These failures received elaborate publicity which undermined public support for the War on Poverty. In particular, the term "community control" became linked to "unrealistic" educational decentralization, especially in the highly publicized effort in Brownsville in New York. It was a project which not only failed to achieve its organization objectives but temporarily also created throughout the nation polarized ideological and political positions.

The barriers which faced community action programs sponsored by the War on Poverty were of course formidable—both calculated opposition and institutional inertia. But the most persistent and difficult barriers were the expectations that were created for rapid, comprehensive societal change which were essentially unrealizable in the given time. From the extensive literature on the consequences of the War on Poverty, full pattern of barriers can be identified as including opposition of existing political groups, competition and instabilities among participating administrative agencies, limitations on the skills of local residents required for effective participation, and resistance by professional groups to cooperating with local community organizations and to accepting new social technologies.

The opposition and resistance of established political groups at the metropolitan and local level were pronounced but not monolithic or pervasive, as particular case studies emphasize. Entrenched political party leaders were able to divert resources to existing "arrangements." Perhaps more accurately, "city hall" both in large and in small urban centers had long experience of accommodating and surviving by adapting to new federal initiatives and programs. Given the tensions of the period, the willingness of particular leaders to search for new coalitions, or to coopt actively, if you will, insurgent community organizations, was striking. Rather than opposing community action programs, many leaders, especially in the larger metropolitan centers, were searching for new patterns of accommodation, although these accommodations were partial and often self-serving.

To what extent would the metropolitan political leaders delegate decision-making authority to local boards and agencies? The extents varied greatly, but there were clear, if temporary changes, given the increased available resources and the pressures from the federal government. Of course, certain political leaders were devious and at times merely gave in to external pressure without feeling long-term conviction and support. They then sought to recapture their dominance when community action programs ran into difficulty.

But such observations do not and cannot deny the experimentation and efforts at broadening the process of decision making. The variation from metropolitan area to metropolitan area was marked. But it is striking indeed that Greenstone and Peterson concluded that it was not the strength of the political party, size of the minority population, or the political effectiveness of black organizations which accounts for the variation in mayoral support for meaningful community-level decision making.[38] The immediate personal style and outlook of the mayor were decisive. This conclusion is plausible, since we are dealing not with long-term institutionalization of new forms of political power but rather with the initial, immediate, and short-term response to outside federal initiatives, over a period of less than four years. Likewise, the "downtown" chief political executive and his colleagues and staff were more inclined to experiment and share power or at least search for new coalitions, especially during racial tensions and violence, than were the middle- and lower-level political functionaries.

There is reason to believe that the administrative and bureaucratic difficulties were stronger barriers than opposition from elected party officials, although the distinction is at times difficult if not impossible to make. In the first instance, administrative barriers rose from the lack of coordination between the Office of Economic Opportunity and the two central federal agencies, the Department of Labor and the Department of Health, Education and Welfare, which were responsible for coordinating existing and augmented federal programs which had effects on neighborhoods and communities. These massive agencies resisted the Office of Economic Opportunity, which in turn had to

38. Greenstone and Peterson, *Race.*

decide whether it would be a policy and coordinating agency or whether it would develop into an operating and funding agency. While pressing to achieve its basic objectives of developing and overseeing community action programs, the Office of Economic Opportunity received authorization to implement a variety of operating programs, which, in effect, further fragmented the connections between the federal government and the recipient city governments. The OEO developed jurisdiction over "new programs" which could be administered without extensive coordination with existing federal agencies and local agencies, such as preschool education and the Job Corps.[39] The core of the welfare payments system was left intact and unchanged.

If the administrative philosophy of the Office of Economic Opportunity was to strengthen local involvement, the structure of this agency and its internal decision-making process worked in the opposite direction. It became a federal agency which penetrated directly into each metropolitan area. It contributed to the further fragmentation of federal involvement in education and welfare programs by creating a new governmental structure. It also reserved for itself a high level of centralized decision making, justifying this pattern as required if the executive branch of government were to innovate. Greater delegation of decision making to the cities was thought to hinder innovation, but the actual result was heightened bureaucratic tension and confusion.

The organizational difficulties reflected the rapid time frame under which the Office of Economic Opportunity had to operate. The President and the Congress of the United States, confronted with widespread racial tension and discontent, obviously wanted "quick" results. The "aspirations" of the elected officials, plus the demands of various interest groups, especially the minority groups, meant that their objectives were given an unrealistic timetable. The coverage of the mass media defined "success" only in terms of immediate consequences.

The experts who had spent a lifetime thinking about strategies of community organization hardly ever believed that they would witness such a rapid expansion of resources for community programs as took place in 1964–1968. If any doubted that local programs could be launched and successfully operated with the required speed—and there must have been many who did doubt—they did not express their reser-

39. Sar A. Levitan and Benjamin H. Johnston, *The Job Corps: A Social Experiment that Works* (Baltimore, Md.: Johns Hopkins University Press, 1976).

vations and did not advocate a more measured pace. The speed and the rhetoric of a "war" resulted in ineffective recruitment of key personnel, misallocations of resources, and a chronic tendency "to start and stop" programs before they had sufficient time to demonstrate their potentials.

An enlargement of citizen participation required a parallel decentralization of decision making in the public and private agencies which worked in the immediate localities. Such decentralization was neither adequately conceptualized nor organizationally implemented. Institutional decentralization is a complex idea and one that has not been clarified in analytical terms. The available scholarship on the topic in general and on the specific agencies of education, employment, public safety, and welfare at the community level is murky and underdeveloped. The failure to formulate a clear notion of the basic difficulties involved in institutional decentralization, and the massive bureaucratic resistance to even the first steps of decentralization, undermined the War on Poverty.

Conceptually, both academic and public leaders who were critical of existing structures were frequently in error when they asserted that at the metropolitan level, public education and public welfare agencies were overcentralized. In actuality, they were fragmented agencies, agencies which operated on the basis of arbitrary rules and procedures because supervisory personnel had neither the required information nor effective control over the operating personnel. There was an absence of mechanisms to enforce professional standards. To press for decentralization in general terms was counterproductive, since it only contributed further to fragmentation.

The simple distinction between policy and operations was at work. In fact, a stronger measure of centralization of policy was the precondition of a more equitable allocation of resources, of establishing standards of performance, and of collecting essential operational data. Such procedures would in time facilitate decentralization of operations. Only careful planning, extensive training, and strong organization sanctions produce "real" decentralization.

The immense difficulties of municipal decentralization have been carefully documented in reports published in a special issue of the *Public Administration Review*.[40] As observed in these reports, some

40. See especially Henry J. Schmandt, "Municipal Decentralization: An Overview," *Public Administration Review* 32 (October 1972): 571–88; John H. Strange,

of the limited efforts at decentralization in the 1960s served only to further fragment and make the municipal agencies involved even less effective. The most ambitious and most dramatic instance comprised the steps taken to "break up" the New York City Board of Education into over a hundred local school boards, which over the short run produced very limited results. On balance, the War on Poverty set in motion demands and some limited progress toward institutional decentralization. Decentralization became an issue which "permanently" confronted local political and administrative leaders.

Difficulties resulted from the limited skill of local residents in participating in community organization. The leadership resources in slum communities were indeed scarce, as was widely recognized but not acted upon. Leaders were not absent, and they could be effective in particular tasks, and developed and improved. Moreover, it was anticipated that "outside" leaders would be required, but they were not readily obtained.

In addition, difficulties resulted from the procedures used for recruiting local leaders and allocating responsibilities. The major effort was to establish comprehensive and inclusive community action groups and to recruit and allocate leadership on the basis of formal elections; the results were disappointing and often produced tension. The more successful procedures recruited leaders to participate in specific programs such as day care centers, after-school study groups, or youth employment programs. These projects required community participation which could be facilitated by local advisory groups. As these persons accumulated experience and influence, they could recruit and identify additional local community leaders. The process was slow, frequently interrupted, but not without results. War on Poverty programs extended beyond the lowest-income groups into modest-income areas, and in the latter, community participation was more extensive. In these areas, quality of life and transportation were important.

There is no reason to assume that there is a fixed quantum of local leaders who express the goals of contending interest groups. There is a strong voluntaristic component in community leadership in that it can be recruited and trained so that its contribution to social control reflects the consequences of deliberate efforts which often arise outside the local boundaries. No doubt, with the resolution of conflict and

"Citizen Participation in Community Action and Model Cities Programs," *Public Administration Review* 32: 655–669.

controversy or with the passage of time, such leadership atrophies, given the fragile social organization of community associations. But one can prepare an inventory of community leaders before and after intervention to create workable community organizations. Donald Bradley has presented a detailed study of the effect of federally sponsored community organization in two areas in Chicago in the early 1960s.[41] The influence of even limited efforts at community organization was clear-cut, enlarging the pool of local leaders.

But the assessment of the War on Poverty points to the striking retrospective conclusion that the limitation was not the weakness of local community leaders—existing leaders or the newly recruited ones. It is, rather, the fourth barrier, the fierce resistance of existing professional groups to cooperation with local community organizations and to accepting new social technologies, which was so powerful. Such resistance was concentrated in but not limited to low-income communities; it extended in the 1960s throughout the social structure.

The opposition of professional groups to citizen participation at the community level was one of the main themes documented by the case studies of community action programs. Professional groups responsible for the administration of urban education and welfare programs had weak or nonexistent mechanisms for developing and enforcing professional standards of performance in this regard. The community action programs only intensified defensiveness; given both bureaucratic inertia and trade union opposition, the specialists were able to resist change over the short run. In fact, they came to view the intrusion of community groups as arbitrary, partisan, and politically motivated pressure; as a result, the professionals could rationalize their opposition to change. Opposition to citizen participation in the inner city included an element of personal prejudice against minority groups and low-status persons among professionals who aspired to employment in more affluent locales.

Nevertheless, the increased flow of funds into the central city produced experimental efforts which demonstrated the potentials of new social technologies. The underlying problem was the inability of institutions to incorporate these innovations into massive bureaucratic structures. The innovations reflect the enthusiasm of particular dedi-

41. Donald Bradley, "Community Leadership in Two Inner-City Areas," Ph.D. dissertation, University of Chicago, 1969.

cated leaders and personnel. No doubt, these experiments produced results in part because of the Hawthorne effect—the fact that selected populations knew that they were being treated specially. However, some innovations failed, and some large-scale extensions of existing procedures also failed. Evaluations, if they are worthy of consideration, concluded that more resources for established procedures—such as reduced welfare case loads or better teacher-pupil ratio—had marginal effects. More "integrative" programs which overcame excessive and rigid division of labor were required. Community action programs had a real and a symbolic role in such experimentation. For example, excessive residential mobility interfered with acquiring basic reading and writing skills in grade school.[42] The innovative school principal therefore sent out his community aide to ask, often successfully, parents not to move, since frequently moving involved no more than a few blocks. The rules for remaining in a given school were loosened so that change of residence did not automatically mean a transfer. The result was a measure of increase in academic performance. Likewise, one-to-one tutoring programs for specific periods each week that used volunteers, older youngsters, and paid assistants produced measurable academic results for low expenditures.[43] However, the rigidities of school administration inhibited institutionalization of such programs, and ultimately forced their near extinction. One principal resisted the official reading program with testing limited to once each six months and began a flexible "continuous" program whereby the youngsters received biweekly feedback on their progress, with increased short-term improvements.[44] But the experiment was terminated when the principal left the school system. A decade later the same

42. Thomas S. Smith, C. T. Husbands, and David Street, "Pupil Mobility and I.Q. Scores in the Urban Slum: A Policy Perspective," in *Innovation in Mass Education*, ed. David Street (New York: Wiley, 1969).

43. Gayle Janowitz, *Helping Hands: Volunteer Work in Education* (Chicago: University of Chicago Press, 1965); Timothy Leggatt, "After School Study Centers: An Analysis of a New Institution," Working Paper no. 51, Center for Social Organization Studies (University of Chicago, November 1965); Richard Cloward, "Studies in Tutoring," *Journal of Experimental Education* 36 (1967), 14–25; Gayle Janowitz, "After School Study Centers: Experimental Materials and Clinical Research," *Center for Social Organization Studies* (Chicago: University of Chicago Press, 1968).

44. Mary A. Queeley, "Nongrading in an Urban Slum School," in Street, *Innovation*. See also Benjamin S. Bloom, *Human Characteristics and School Learning* (New York: McGraw-Hill, 1976).

procedures were being advocated and introduced on a more extensive basis in the same school system by an outside university specialist.

The improvement of education and welfare services requires labor-intensive, not capital-intensive, efforts, including the utilization of local personnel and family and kinship networks as well as a persistent attempt to overcome the specialized division of labor in public and private agencies and instead to "aggregate" functions and tasks into a more unified support system.[45] Effective operational decentralization of service bureaucracies and far-reaching professional accountability are needed.

We return to our early hypothesis. While no lasting and profound improvements of community services were generated during 1964–1968, the years of the War on Poverty, there is scattered evidence that the community participation strategies did have pertinence and continuing vitality. The conspicuous barriers prevented deeper and more lasting consequences, but the community participation strategies which have been evolving gradually since the turn of the century, and which are far from perfected, demonstrated their continuing relevance. The findings do not permit the explication of general principles or fixed rules of intervention—there is no equivalent to the techniques of psychotherapy. But the documentation does underline the importance of increasing the community's ability to organize itself—even with outside support—and to develop articulate attitudes and realistic demands.

The goal of community organization has been that of making the deprived locality a more viable interest group, in addition to improving its capacity in self-help. Such an objective has legitimacy, from the point of view of social control, in meeting minimum educational and welfare and related requirements. Obviously, the political process cannot operate if community organization only intensifies interest-group demands. But it is too much to expect that the leaders and residents of the most deprived areas would be in the forefront of institution building to adjudicate controversy and to resolve conflict between competing interests. Nevertheless, the strategy of building community organization does assume that increased linkages—volun-

45. Frank Riessman and Arthur Pearl, *New Careers for the Poor* (New York: Free Press, 1965); see also Eugene Litwak and Henry J. Meyer, *School, Family and Neighborhood: The Theory and Practice of School Community Relations* (New York: Columbia University Press, 1974).

tary, association, and electoral—of the local community to the metropolis should broaden parochial horizons and contribute to broader problem solving at the metropolitan level.

Most of the research on community organization, specifically during the mass experimentation of 1964 to 1968, highlights the "progress" that resulted, derived less from the delivery of services than from the expansion of community and civic participation, especially electoral participation. The community action agencies that were established in urban centers with the funds from the War on Poverty could emphasize the delivery of services or augment this goal with an emphasis on community participation with overtones of "civic" or "political education." (Some strategists advocated that these aspects of community organization should be financed solely from private funds or that at least the scope of these activities should be limited and institutionalized on a nonpartisan basis.)

For the deprived community, political education was enmeshed in new forms of community organization, namely, local community service centers. These centers sought to increase both individual and group access to local agencies, a realistic form of political activity. The technique was to obtain available and new services and information. Local leaders and groups became involved, with varying effectiveness, in making representations before agency staffs, administrators, and local boards, and became members of existing and/or newly created agencies. Often these experiments atrophied rapidly; but they involved an expansion of local activity and new patterns of interaction and communication, in part sustained by the pressure of the Office of Economic Opportunity staffs and by the mass media. As described below, it was not surprising that this type of activity should expand and "mobilize" citizen participation in the regular elections of metropolitan, state, and national governments.

One can use the more trenchant research and writing on the War on Poverty to document and elaborate these processes. For example, James J. Vanecko's study of 50 urban centers sought to compare the effects of differing goals of community action programs on local institutions—education, social welfare, and the like.[46] His results are relatively clear-cut; during 1964 to 1968 community action agencies which limited themselves to improving the delivery of services were

46. Vanecko, "Community."

less able to produce institutional change in existing education and welfare agencies than those agencies with an active program of community organization. The findings are not the result of other variables such as the size of the community or the concentration of blacks. He concluded that the results were the outcome of a particular type and mold of community organization. Those local organizations which engaged in militant action and in confrontation politics produced limited results or were even counterproductive. "The effective Community Action Program is one which has neighborhood centers actively involved in community organizing, which has neighborhood centers uninvolved in militant activities, and which does not spend time pressing specific demands on other institutions. Their effectiveness is in extending or complementing the activity and involvement of the residents of poor neighborhoods."[47] He stresses that the assistance is a form of political assistance—the facilitation of participation in electoral politics in particular and in making representation to public and private agencies in the area.[48]

Community organization efforts had the direct effect of extending and increasing minority-group voting, especially among blacks. Increased black and minority participation in the Northern and Western population centers was strengthened by voter registration drives supported by reform national legislation and was assisted by voluntary associations in the South. By 1974 approximately 59% of the black population were registered voters, reflecting the marked convergence with the white electorate. A measure of the increased political integration of the blacks was the fact that in the 1964 election 280 blacks throughout the United States were elected to public office; by 1971 the figure stood at 1,860.

This was tangible and had discernible national consequences. The expanded voting participation did not produce an electoral realignment; weak political regimes continued to emerge from 1968 to 1976. But the group demands of the lowest stratum were more effectively presented; political support for a continuation of essential educational and welfare programs was assured, although equally essential organizational reform was hardly developed, nor was the expansion of local

47. Ibid., p. 629.

48. Lester Salamon and Stephen Van Evera, "Fear, Apathy and Discrimination: A Test of Three Explanations of Political Participation among the Poor," *American Political Science Review* 67 (December 1973): 1288–1306.

community organization able to create the political basis for a resolution of the chronic issues of "stagflation." One measure of the resulting sociopolitical balance was that by 1976, the Democratic party, despite the declining number of Republican partisans, could elect a president only with the support of black citizens.

We are dealing with symbolic representation as well as the mechanics of electoral participation. As stressed by Paul E. Peterson and J. David Greenstone, the experiments in community participation of the 1960s emphasized social representativeness.[49] The "guidelines" of the federal government and the informal norms for recruiting local leaders focused on ascriptive characteristics. The immediate result was to continue the coalition building among ethnic minorities which had characterized municipal administration and politics in the United States but which had not been energetically pressed in the case of the blacks. Blacks and other relatively excluded minorities were mandated into community action agencies and community enterprises, and their opportunities for employment in local government increased. Federal intervention assisted their incorporation, which had been a "normal" political process for other ethnic groups in the past. The sequence of greater visibility as a result of greater community activity serves as a crucial stimulus to the black community's participation in ensuing regular partisan elections. In other words, community organization and participation propelled new entrants into partisan politics both as candidates and as voters.[50]

Some of the black militants demanding community control and community autonomy became frustrated and lost interest; but the natural history of the 1960s rested on the incorporation of the blacks and other minorities into leadership positions, both in the community and in organized partisan politics. Demands for community control and autonomy, which produced few lasting and visible results, gave way to more conventional bargaining. The decline of community racial tension by the end of 1967 was in part the result of the counterproduction of violence on the black community; it was the local citizens who suffered. The reduction in tension was also the result of

49. Paul E. Peterson and J. David Greenstone, "Racial Change and Citizen Participation: The Mobilization of Low-Income Communities Through Community Action," in *A Decade of Federal Antipoverty Policy*, ed. Robert Haveman (New York: Academic Press), pp. 241–78.

50. For analysis of the scope and consequence of increased black legislators, see ibid., pp. 272–74.

limited increased material benefits. But the symbolic visibility of new minority leaders, especially at the local community level, was an essential ingredient.

The Restructuring of Community Participation

The decline in the level of federal funds for community action programs and the dismantling of the administrative apparatus of the War on Poverty hardly brought a termination to the intellectual exploration of the realities and limitations of community participation. The election of Richard Nixon in 1968 did not produce an end to federal support for community participation; nor was the process of social learning about community organization ended.

On the contrary, the pragmatism which supplied the long-term rationale for institution building for community organization stimulated more self-critical reflection.[51] The notoriety given to particular treatises attacking community participation does not substitute for balanced assessment of potentials and limitations.[52] Gradually, after a period of uncertainty and confusion, it became possible to speak of the third phase in the natural history of community organization—the phase of consolidation which began to be manifest after 1972. The emphasis was on more attainable goals for community participation, with a longer time perspective. Both the civic advocates and the university-based experts revealed a greater realism.

On the one hand, the objectives of effective community organization had to face the difficulties, for example, generated by the implementation of school desegregation, continuous redistricting of electoral districts, and the persistence of a multitude of highly specialized federal-state funds for educational, welfare, and community development programs. On the other hand, there were new stimuli for more effective community participation which resulted from the developments of the 1960s, especially, for example, the institutionalization of the norms of community participation by both political leaders and the mass media, the entrance of new generations of professionals in education, medicine, and law who were more likely to accept the legitimacy

51. Roland L. Warren, Stephen M. Rose, and Ann F. Bergunder, *The Structure of Urban Reform: Community Decision Organizations in Stability and Change* (Lexington, Mass.: Lexington Books, 1974).
52. Daniel P. Moynihan, *Maximum Feasible Misunderstanding* (New York: Free Press, 1970).

and validity of the citizen participation, and the emergence of "somewhat" more effective community organizations. In each of these aspects of community organization—positive and negative—social science and sociological thinking have played a role.

The most significant and certainly the most prominent has been the analysis of federally supported policies and programs of school desegregation, especially those implemented by large-scale bus transportation. While the programs of school integration are compatible and germane for more effective social control in the United States, the techniques of implementation have weakened local community organization and self-regulation; and these costs must be taken into consideration in weighing the advantages. School desegregation, and reliance on extensive pupil transportation, was offered to achieve educational quality and effectiveness. In time, the advocates of school integration in large measure rested their case on the assertion that the social characteristics of the student population rather than teacher performance determined the outcome of primary and secondary school experience.

The evidence offered in support of these arguments could not be immediately dismissed but it was hardly adequate to be overriding or convincing. Social research evidence was used in connection with the original U. S. Supreme Court decision in 1954; by 1959, academic criticism appeared about the logic and adequacy of this evidence.[53] However, the "Coleman Report," which presented an elaborated body of research data, was later used to argue in favor of school integration, including large-scale busing.[54]

Unfortunately, subsequent research, as would be expected in such a complex issue of social policy, complicated public discussion. The evaluations of the effects of busing, for example, have not presented clear-cut conclusions.[55] But more important, research has called into question the basic thesis that teacher and institutional characteristics had no effect on academic performance.[56] Moreover, specific research studies raised the questions of whether "busing" increased white flight

53. Harold Garfinkel, "Social Science Evidence and the School Segregation Cases," *Journal of Politics* 21 (February 1959): 37–59.

54. *Equality of Educational Opportunity* (Washington: GPO, 1966).

55. David J. Armor, "The Evidence on Busing," *The Public Interest* 28 (1972): 90–126; Thomas Pettigrew et al., "Busing: A Review of the Evidence," *The Public Interest* 30 (1973): 88–118; N. St. John, *School Desegregation Outcomes for Children* (New York: Wiley, 1975).

56. Charles E. Bidwell and John D. Kasarda, "School District Organization and Student Achievement," *American Sociological Review* 40 (February 1975): 55–70.

to the suburbs and thus defeated the long-term goals of school integration.[57] It has long been recognized that the flight to the suburbs has been in process since the turn of the century, but these studies sought to measure the specific effect of busing on residential stability. In addition, sociologists who advocated busing drastically altered their position and stressed the limitations and social costs—with resulting public dismay about the relevance of sociological analysis to social policy dealing with community affairs.

In retrospect, it is difficult to understand why the type of evidence collected by sociologists on the correlates of school performance figured so prominently in the public debate on race relations. These analyses were manifest validations of existing educational practices rather than assessments of new and innovative educational strategies. The important contribution of social research was not that subsequent analysis weakened the conclusions of the "Coleman Report," but that there is a body of theory and a limited body of experience about alternative strategies of urban education, as mentioned above, which needed to be institutionalized in order to improve academic skills.

Moreover, the initial argument in support of integration by means of busing has strange overtones—one with racist implications. Namely, it is a formulation that advocated that only if white pupils were introduced into a school could a school be "good." In short, an all-black school could not be as "good" as a school with white pupils or as a school which was all white.

Nevertheless, the argument for school desegregation was and remains compelling. In order to effect the essential incorporation of the next generation into the societal structure and to contribute to a sense of citizenship, meaningful interracial experience is necessary for the youth of a democratic polity. The objective of school integration was political and therefore moral as much if not more than it was educational in the short term. Integration involved symbolic meanings. The essential issue was the appropriate scope, locale, and strategies of integration; and the social costs and benefits, especially as related to other programs of community intervention, had to be taken into account. There was no reason to assume that the school had to be the sole institution of interracial contact.

57. Reynolds Farley, "Is Coleman Right?" *Social Policy* 6 (January–February 1976): 1–10. Reynolds Farley and Clarence Wurdock, "Can Governmental Policies Integrate Public Schools?" paper presented at American Sociological Association Convention, New York, September 1, 1976.

In the 1960s, a variety of innovative and flexible strategies of school desegregation were suggested to balance costs and benefits, but the political context, and the pressures for immediate results, meant that they were not utilized.[58] Instead massive and mechanical procedures were applied.

It was also advocated by some specialists that metropolitan-wide rather than central city integration was required. This strategy was seen as necessary in order to involve sufficient numbers of white students and to avoid placing the burden on low-income youngsters whose cultural resources for handling school desegregation were the most limited. The movement for metropolitan-wide integration was very slow, and it appears that federal judges, including those of the Supreme Court, resisted such an approach either because of a lack of understanding of metropolitan social demography or because of a wish to limit school integration in suburban areas.

Flexible strategies for school integration allocated priority to teacher integration and initial reliance on permissive transfers, measures which were viewed as "foot dragging" by militant groups. But the core of innovation in school desegregation rested on recognizing that integration could be an instrument for diversifying and enriching the educational opportunities for both white and black youngsters. The central element was that it is not necessary to formulate desegregation—and integration—as a diurnal or daily occurrence; it could be part of a periodic or weekly educational experience. It would not be necessary to abandon one's affiliation to a neighborhood grammar school or a community high school in order to participate in integrated education. This approach would emphasize making available particular courses of instruction including specialized parts of the curriculum as well as work-study programs in specific locales, not necessarily in existing schools, which would be located to maximize integration with the most limited transport burdens.

While expressed public attitudes have been increasingly in favor of the principle of integrated education, busing as a tool for achieving school integration has remained unpopular. In 1974, 82% of a national sample of white respondents and 35% of a sample of black respondents opposed busing, as reported by the National Opinion Research Center.

58. George R. La Noue and Bruce L. R. Smith, *The Politics of School Decentralization* (Lexington, Mass.: Health, 1973).

By 1975, opposition to busing had become politically articulate, although verbal acceptance of the goal of integration remained high. There could be no formal withdrawal from a national commitment to school desegregation, and the courts were still strongly involved. In the Congress, fiscal support for school desegregation became more difficult to obtain, and in the judicial process the concept was evolving that one bona fide effort at school integration and its implementation would demonstrate the good faith of the local authorities and would be acceptable. Given the expanding dimensions of the ghetto in terms of population and geography, such legal reasoning implied a constriction of massive school integration by busing.

The negative impact of school desegregation based on daily busing obviously centered on the hostile and, at times, violent sentiments which were mobilized. It is striking that there is no available research on the effect of busing on youth culture and personal interaction in black residential communities. But the available observational data emphasize the weakening of identification with local institutions and educational agencies among young people without their being replaced by wider identifications. Likewise, there has been an observable effect on informal patterns and networks; the hypothesis has been offered that these patterns are more self-contained and detached from institutional and adult linkages. Such patterns can only complicate the socialization of young people into the larger metropolitan community. Busing has not increased adult participation in school-related voluntary associations, especially where distances inhibit parent involvement in the receiving school.

The attenuation of local attachments is even more marked and more disruptive in the case of the redistricting, and especially repeated redistricting, of election units. This is an instance of extensive unintended consequences, although the negative implications were anticipated by some students of community organization. The argument for redistricting rested on clear-cut examples of gerrymandering and the occasional pronounced underrepresentation of lower-status groups when particular election districts were unduly enlarged. The pressure for redistricting increased in the early 1960s as a part of the civil rights movement, and the major impetus and instrument have been court decisions. The results have not decisively increased the number of innercity representatives, because of population trends; instead, elected representatives have shifted from rural and small town areas to metropolitan suburbs, a trend which has been of only marginal political advantage to inner-city residents—of low or high income.

Court directives, given the population mobility and shifting social demography of the inner city, have produced numerical formulae which required repeated changes in boundaries and which avoided those natural boundaries and landmarks for mechanical and even computer-based entities. These shifts are particularly disruptive for low-income citizens with limited conceptions of the political process and limited knowledge of political institutions. Redistricting can disregard citizen knowledge and attachments to local leaders and produce a feeling of disenfranchisement. Repeated changes in the boundaries of the locality weaken local organizations' ability to mobilize their constituents. Such changes have attenuated the relations between these organizations and local political agencies. "South Shore is not much of a community anymore since they broke up the old Sixth Ward" epitomizes one type of popular reaction to altered political boundaries, boundaries which bear even less relation to the local natural area or to the format of administrative areas. Moreover, by and large, court-based redistricting has not produced political solutions or strengthened local community participation.

Students of public administration have long stressed the excessive numbers of local political and administrative units, the fragmentation of local services, and the lack of public accountability which results.[59] An additional complicating element has been the segmented funding of federal programs of intervention into the local community. Federal policy has emphasized direct linkages between local institutions and the central government, arguing that the structure of intermediate government, especially state government, thwarted innovation and local participation. Specialized programs of funding were created, each designed to achieve a particular goal. Within particular functional areas, the result was a marked increase in highly specialized programs. In educational grants to the central city, there were more than a hundred programs. If one adds housing, welfare services, and community

59. R. C. Wood, *1400 Governments: The Political Economy of the New York Metropolitan Region* (Garden City, N.Y.: Doubleday, 1964); see especially W. S. Sayre and H. Kaufman, *Governing New York City* (New York: Russell Sage Foundation, 1960).

development—even without including medical programs—the number rapidly multiplied. Skilled administrative staffs were required to manage the applications and accounting procedures. Basically, the division of labor generated by these individualized programs had little real connection with the tasks to be performed in the local neighborhood and community.

This pattern of funding had elements which ran counter to the goal of community action programs and citizen involvement. The feasibility of local participation is enhanced when the federal government makes use of block grants for broad functional areas. This approach is economical, simpler to administer, and more effective, and the task of influencing the allocation of these funds gives real and meaningful goals for citizen participation. However, the stress on specialized funding appeared to indicate that the federal government doubted the effectiveness of its own goals of local involvement. Gradually, since 1972 there has been a trend to recognize this dilemma and there has been a measured increase in block grants which have greater potential for effective local community participation. But the apparatus for administering these funds has produced an elaborate and heavy bureaucratic "stratum."

Despite the instabilities, limitations, and frustrations of the War on Poverty, popular acceptance of citizen participation has persisted, and in fact, popular belief in the desirability of such participation has been strengthened. There is no adequate body of data on popular attitudes, but a discernible growth of public support of the legitimacy of citizen involvement has occurred. The traditions of the democratic ethos supply the background which has been reinforced by populist leaders of national prominence. These perspectives have been pressed by advocacy journalists who favor community participation. Many local leaders, especially those in the most depressed localities, were deeply frustrated by the sharp constriction of the War on Poverty. However, they have remained interested and involved, although they are more cautious in making commitments and often their interests are limited to their own immediate locality.

It is of particular importance that the new groups of university-trained professionals who are involved in community-based services have become more accepting of the goals and procedures of community involvement, or at least consultation, although there is as much form as substance in their commitments.[60] The resistance of professionals in the 1960s to citizen participation, especially among teachers supported by their trade unions, has weakened. In the case of public school teachers, the declining school enrollment–including inner-city schools–has been a strong factor. More central has been the continuing influence of the federal government, which in numerous programs requires the formalities of citizen participation. Citizen participation is particularly mandated in the areas of public health, public education, low-cost housing, community development programs, and manpower training efforts administrated by voluntary associations. Of course, the federal government's intervention is not without ambiguity and contradiction. For example, in education, federal programs of desegregation of teacher personnel and equal opportunity for promotion take priority over citizen involvement in the selection and assignment of teachers and principals.

The younger professionals were exposed to the turmoil of the 1960s and have had experience with consultative bodies in their own education. Their professional training has come to include increased instruction in the social sciences, often with an explicit indoctrination about the relevance of citizen involvement.

Their commitment to such procedures represents, in part, a concern with "equality" and a rationalization of their privileged financial position. They have also experienced the operating advantages of dealing with clients who are organized into representative bodies. They have come to perceive that citizen involvement serves as a limited and insufficient procedure for dealing with the problems of allocating budgetary resources. Citizen involvement makes possible a measure of relief from overextended personal and professional responsibility.

But the central institutional question during the third phase of consolidation is the extent to which community organizations have maintained or increased their operating effectiveness. In making such an assessment, we are applying the complex and diffuse criteria of a contribution to effective social control. If a community organization can demonstrate its ability to operate as a veto group and to serve as a successful pressure group on behalf of its locality, that is only partial

60. Career experiences with community action programs have had a discernible effort on professional perspectives and types of practice. See, for example, Howard S. Erlanger, "Social Reform Organizations and Subsequent Careers of Participants," *American Sociological Review* 42 (April 1977): 233–48.

evidence. The criteria of social control involve participation in the resolution of broader metropolitan and even societal conflict. To what extent do local community institutions establish social priorities and thereby articulate enlightened self-interest which have positive consequences for more effective social control? One can marshall evidence for the continuous and even increased vitality of individual and groups of local community organizations. But even for pressure groups, the record is limited. And if one applies more inclusive criteria to the ability of a particular organization or a network of organizations to articulate the locality to the metropolis, positive evidence is meager. Thus, as of 1976, the accomplishments of local community organization are not commensurate with asserted potentials. Nevertheless, the existing level of performance is indispensable for the political process of a democratic polity grappling with the tasks of articulating the community of residence into the larger societal structure.

There is greater sophistication among civic leaders about local organizations and about the strength and weakness of professional assistance. One can speak of a decline in utopian thinking and a greater understanding of pragmatic realities. There has been an increased sensitivity to achieving results rather than creating organization forms. As a result, there are at least two trends in local community organization which superficially might be viewed as contradictory, but which reflect mutually supporting strategies.

There is an increase in organizations with specific and even short-term single goals or objectives. These organizations are based on informal interpersonal networks and intensive personal commitments. Such single issue groups are often but not necessarily always veto groups, and are involved in defeating initiatives which they believe to be undesirable. The limited longevity of such groups is not a defect since different issues mobilize varying clienteles and create new organizations.

On the other hand, there are community organizations which seek to provide a group of related services or to reflect a wide range of community needs; they are concerned with increasing their organizational stability. Continuity is particularly important in the most deprived communities. But the low-income localities of the central city have some advantage over the increasing enclaves of poverty in the suburban areas. Community organizations respond to the initiatives of public agencies and of ward political organizations. Such initiatives are more diffuse and irregular in the suburbs than in the central city. In the older central cities of the East and Midwest, the traditions of interaction among administrative agencies, political organizations, and local citizen groups are more institutionalized than in suburban and the newer cities, particularly in the West and Southwest.[61]

Field observations repeatedly emphasize that community groups, particularly in disorganized areas and throughout the metropolitan community, "purchase" and reinforce their stability by narrowing their attention and involvement to their immediate area and environment and by avoiding external coalitions. This observation does not deny the increase in the stability and longevity of community organization, including that in the central city, in the 1970s. Moreover, it does not deny the observation in chapter 8 that there has been a discernible trend toward coalition building among community organizations. The pattern has been the creation of roof organizations which link together groups of local organizations to deal with the problems of a particular sector of a metropolitan area.

However, the preoccupation of community organizations with their immediate local environments and their strong emphasis on establishing geographical boundaries of "jurisdiction" are self-limiting. The systemic analysis of community organization highlights the common interests and group identifications which are generated by common locality and place of residence. However, the goals to be pursued are not readily circumscribed by the local geography. Community leaders who come to define their role defensively in terms of a particular geographical subdivision–central city or suburban–weaken their potential for collective problem solving.

In short, the territorial patterns of settlement are different, usually smaller than the area required to deal with community issues. For example, Peter Hunt identified the functional area for a youth service facility in the inner city as encompassing between 12,000 and 18,000 residents. "This was the territory in which the kids hung out, the area in which there was some sense of neighborhood and some substantial face to face interaction between adults and between adults and kids, and the distance which it is feasible to expect kids to travel to attend programs at the center."[62] In essence, the territory involved a radius of five to six blocks, varying with the density of the area.

61. Roland J. Liebert, *Disintegration and Political Action: The Changing Functions of City Governments in America* (New York: Academic Press, 1976).

62. Peter Hunt, "Preliminary Self-Study Report," Chicago Area Project, mimeographed report, June 2, 1977, p. 6.

But the organization and institutional support for such a neighborhood facility, and the strategy for dealing with the issues which impinge on youth delinquency, involve a larger community—a population ranging between 60,000 to 200,000. It is thus necessary to fashion a larger community organization or a coalition of community groups, and Hunt emphasized that such organizations were slowly evolving. Sociologists have therefore sought to break away from "simpleminded" configurations of geographically defined perimeters for community organizations, without abandoning the ecological dimension. The continuing research on and assessment of community social organization have led to the notion that multitiered, or at least three-level, configurations of community social organization would be required to articulate the citizen with the metropolitan community.[63] The first level is the "social bloc"—the small, informal patterns—based on propinquity, homogeneity, natural boundaries, and diffuse interaction. It is based on a measure of joint responsibility and control. The demands it generates tend to be narrow and unmindful of the counterclaims of other social blocs. The second level is that of "organizational community"—the ecologically based residential interests which require a measure of formalized voluntary associations. This is the level that is conventionally called the local community. The demands of one organizational community must be balanced against those of other organizational communities. Their effectiveness is thwarted because they do not connect directly to the geographical pattern of administration and the political process; crucial decisions are made by larger or more remote or more centralized bodies. Therefore there is the necessity for a third level of ecologically oriented decision making, namely, the "aggregated metropolitan community." This level implies the emergence of much larger community organizations or coalitions of community organizations, with sufficient staff and civic leadership to figure persistently and meaningfully in the metropolitan-wide process and to shape policies as well as to seek a share of available resources.

Broader and more functional entities for community participation emerge only if they are fashioned by conscious efforts. In the reformulation of the strategy of community organizations, such entities have the potentials of serving as more effective veto and pressure groups, and thereby as counterweights to the voluntary associations

63. Morris Janowitz and Gerald D. Suttles, "The Social Ecology of Citizenship," in *Management of Human Sciences*, ed. Rosemary Sarri and Yeheskel Hasenfeld (New York: Columbia University Press, 1978).

based on the industrial division of labor. In addition, these enlarged networks and arrangements are effective if they have the ability to clarify self-interest by adjudicating the demands and pressures of competing social groupings. Enlarged forms of participation are designed to generate broader perspectives.

Democratic theory, that is, democratic political philosophy, predicates the centrality of electoral competition between political elites organized into partisan factions. Such theory is also sensitive to the widening range of alternate forms of citizen participation. But few political theorists would assert that these alternate forms can supplant the electoral process.[64] At least the assumption of this analysis of social control took periodic national elections as the point of departure. Experiments in citizen participation in the local community are seen as devices for assisting the citizenry to clarify self-interest and to resolve conflicts outside of the election arena. But over the long run, these modes of political participation, if they are to have significant consequences, must increase the effectiveness of elections, both local and national.

However, relations between community participation and the electoral process are by no means simple and straightforward. Research indicates that intensified local informal social contacts of a primary-group nature as well as increased participation in local community organizations generate more electoral participation.[65] Again, increased levels of community participation are no measure of improved quality of the electoral decisions or indicators of more effective social control.

In fact, one limited body of research on the linkages between local community organization and electoral behavior indicates that the result of increased community participation is overwhelmingly to produce greater support for the dominant party in the particular community. Robert D. Putnam has classified counties by the percentage who voted Democratic in the 1952 election, and he discovered that citizens who had stronger identification and involvement with their immediate locale voted by a significant amount more for the Democrats as the

64. Carole Pateman, *Participation and Democratic Theory* (Cambridge: Cambridge University Press, 1970); Dennis F. Thompson, *The Democratic Citizen: Social Sciences and Democratic Theory in the Twentieth Century* (Cambridge: Cambridge University Press, 1970).

65. Sidney Verba and Norman H. Nie, *Participation in America: Political Democracy and Social Equality* (New York: Harper and Row, 1972).

concentration of Democratic voters increased.[66] Whether one is dealing with a low-income central city ward or a relatively homogeneous suburban municipality, the "mobilization" of a greater participation does not automatically imply real consensus but includes pressure toward political uniformity.

Moreover, increased community participation can result in deeper controversy and more pervasive unresolved conflict. The findings of Sidney Verba and Norman Nie, based on a study of 64 communities in 1967, point in this direction.[67] They compared communities with high consensus and those of low consensus; by their definition high consensus localities were those where the active participants had the same policy preferences as the nonparticipants. In the communities with high consensus, "all modes of participation" were associated with an increase in responsiveness of the political leaders. But where community agreement was low, increased participation "can result in a diminished level of responsiveness." Or, in short, increased community participation does not mechanically have positive results.

We are dealing with a "delicate" process of "differentiation." Effective community organization depends on a minimum ability to maintain a strong element of autonomy or independence from partisan organization. Such independence facilitates community organizations in reaching out to involve uninvolved citizens and contributes to the formulation of consent. Moreover, community organizations require the capacity to form coalitions with other similar groups in the metropolitan area and to strengthen their national organization networks. The growth of national linkages among local community groups is steady, but incomplete. To be excessively partisan would be counter to this trend. National coalitions of local groups increase direct access by local community interests to federal administrative agencies and the national legislature.

At the same time, realistically, community organizations are and must be related to partisan politics. The "civic" education which community participation engenders has its "payoff" in the quality and extent of participation in partisan elections. Community organizations and partisan political groups converge to the extent that local organi-

66. R. D. Putnam, "Political Attitudes and the Local Community," *American Political Science Review* 60 (September 1966): 640–54.

67. Verba and Nie, *Participation*, p. 333.

zations serve as recruiting and training mechanisms for civic leaders who in due course enter politics. Community participation has increasingly served to diversify recruitment of the elected political leaders and to reduce the concentration of lawyers and of persons who have long and loyally served as minor party functionaries.

Integrating community participation and a partisan political career requires personal skill and flexibility, but few successful political leaders operate without some such community-based experience. But more fundamentally, we are dealing with the changing political parties, which, despite the presence of a cadre of enduring "professionals" remain relatively diffuse entities strongly dependent on affiliated voluntary associations for their institutional stability. Thus we must examine the analysis of the political parties by social scientists, and especially by "political economists," and the contributions of these studies to institutional building for social control, a topic which supplies the final element in our analysis.

Thirteen

Political Elites and Social Control

POLITICAL ANALYSIS AND "POLITICAL ECONOMY"

Research findings about U.S. national, state, and local politics receive wide attention. In particular, mass media content concerning U.S. politics—from sophisticated to the most popular reporting—has come to depend heavily on public opinion polls. In turn, the conduct of election campaigns is extensively fashioned by the findings of sample surveys. In the end, estimated popular reaction to specific legislative initiatives comes continuously to the attention of elected officials before they make their decisions.

The drama of the "political arena" ensures that journalists seek out the findings of academic social scientists and diffuse them widely, but it is the profound consequences of electoral and bureaucratic politics that produce the attention accorded to the findings of such academic research.[1] Thus it was to be anticipated that newspapers would develop staff members who would concentrate in "covering" the research community and undertake their own studies of politics in depth, using academic concepts, terminology, and procedures.

Unfortunately, there are no adequate content analyses of the growth and extension of such mass media content. Until the 1930s the amount of such content in the mass media was limited and reflected the modest visibility of academic specialists. However, with the emergence of presidential opinion polls in the 1930s, the allotted space increased rapidly and has grown.[2] But it was the combination of the expansion of "political research" and the increased intensity of sociopolitical tension in the 1960s that institutionalized the mass media's use of such

1. For a discussion of the prominence of selected academics in the mass media see Charles Kadushin, *The American Intellectual Elite* (Boston: Little, Brown, 1974).

2. George Gallup, *The Gallup Poll 1935–1971* (New York: Random House, 1972).

research findings. The interest of journalists not only in the findings of specialists in "political research" but also in their general comments, was striking. In volume, the economists and the psychologists exceed "political research specialists"; but the findings of political researchers are given real prominence in news and editorial coverage.

The diffusion of the findings of research on U.S. politics is augmented by an extensive apparatus of college and university teaching and public affairs seminars and workshops. Moreover, the search for "policy guidance" has meant that political leaders and their staffs have direct and elaborate access to the university research community. This network has come to include the commercial market research companies which engage in political research.

Assessing the contribution of these research efforts to institution building for social control is much more difficult—if not impossible—than assessing the consequences of personality theory and of community and urban research. Political scientists and political sociologists are strongly policy- and strategy-oriented; yet the vast amount of research on U.S. political institutions and electoral behavior is cast in a contemplative rather than a manipulative mode. There is little research equivalent to the evaluation of different strategies of psychotherapy or community organization. It is rare to find a political scientist like Samuel Eldersveld, who pursued field experiments of alternative campaign procedures.[3] The "macrostructure" of politics makes it difficult to pursue such research perspectives, but in good measure we are dealing with intellectual styles. The difference in intellectual coherence in these three areas as they relate to public and social policy is of real consequence.

As mentioned in chapter 11, the field of personality and psychotherapy is dominated by the format of psychoanalysis makes it possible to integrate research findings, even those which are based on assumptions different than those of dynamic psychology. The analysis of community organization and local citizen participation has at least a strong component of historical continuity over almost a century. In contrast, the analysis of elites and electoral behavior represents a loosely organized and multidisciplinary topic. The complexity of the problems encourages the application of variegated frameworks. But there is a central trend which makes an assessment essential and

3. Samuel Eldersveld, "Experimental Propaganda Technique and Voting Behavior," *American Political Science Review* 50 (March 1965): 154–65.

feasible. In particular, the influence and linkage of political analysis with economic analysis supply a basis for assessing the contribution—positive or negative—of elite and election studies to institution building; the term "political economy" has meaning. Therefore the assessment of "political analysis" spills over into aspects of economic research.

The long-run transformation in "political analysis" has not been from philosophical critique to empirical hypothesis testing. Academic political analysis continues to include an extensive domain of literary and moral criticism which could have been intellectually incorporated into the humanities or philosophy. Nor should one overlook the fact that a considerable amount of academic political analysis, especially of comparative politics, consists of informed institutional studies.

Since the end of World War II there has been renewed growth of a mode of analysis based on varying degrees and forms of individual and group rationalism.[4] The national political arena is seen as an analog of the economic marketplace. The political process is a vast competition, struggle, or conflict of individuals, pressure groups, institutional entities, or massive social groupings for whom economic decisions are paramount. The actions of political elites are, in effect, a series of economic decisions; and essentially, the same holds true for the electorate.

The economic model of politics has become intellectually dominant. Concern with the group processes inherent in the political function, as formulated by writers such as Arthur Bentley, Mary Follett, John Dewey, and David Truman, persists as a minor theme.[5] The psycho-

4. Herbert A. Simon, "A Behavioral Model of Rational Choice," *Journal of Economics* 69 (February 1955): 99–118; Herbert A. Simon, *Models of Man: Social and Rational* (New York: Wiley, 1957); Anthony Downs, *An Economic Theory of Democracy* (New York: Harper, 1957); William H. Riker, *The Theory of Political Coalitions* (New Haven: Yale University Press, 1962); James Buchanan and Gordon Tullock, *The Calculus of Consent* (Ann Arbor, Mich.: University of Michigan Press, 1962); V. O. Key, Jr., *The Responsible Electorate* (Cambridge: Harvard University Press, 1966); William H. Riker and Peter C. Ordeshook, "A Theory of the Calculus of Voting," *American Political Science Review* 62 (March 1968): 25–42; Michael J. Shapiro, "Rational and Political Man: A Synthesis of Economic and Social-Psychological Perspectives," *American Political Science Review* 63 (December 1969): 1106–19; William H. Riker and Peter C. Ordeshook, *An Introduction to Positive Political Theory* (Englewood Cliffs, N.J.: Prentice-Hall, 1973).

5. Arthur Bentley, *The Process of Government* (Chicago: University of Chicago Press, 1908); John Dewey, *The Public and Its Problems: An Essay in Political Inquiry* (New York: Henry Holt, 1927); Mary P. Follett, *The New State: Group Organizations, the Solutions of Popular Government* (London: Longmans,

pathological dimensions of politics have all but disappeared in academic circles or have been relegated to psychohistory.[6] The main contrapuntal view derives from the institutional analysis of Max Weber and converges with classic writers such as Alexis de Tocqueville, Gaetano Mosca, Roberto Michels, and Joseph Schumpeter, who focus on the specialized, unique tasks of political groups and political elites. These institutional perspectives are in university circles and do not extensively penetrate the broader discussions of the political process; but I will use them, for they are crucial for explicating the political aspects of social control. The institutional structure of political leaders asserts that politics, as a "profession," if you will, and the self-interest and moral perspectives of the elected political officials are important. The inherent limitations of economic rationality mean that political elites are forced to create or make use of mythic structures which have varying relevance for social control and self-regulation, if they are to rule in a multiparty setting. At the heart of our institutional analysis is the argument that the organized political parties have declined in effectiveness, and the rise of personalistic and relatively individualistic elected officials results in a political elite less able to perform the basic tasks of political coordination.

The general "economic" orientation, in varying formats, is offered by writers whose personal ideology is right, liberal, or even left. The right accepts this formulation and emphasizes the need for more sharply clarified and defined economic self-interest and for a contraction of government intervention. The liberal center accepts this "economic" model and seeks to improve the quality and fairness of the competition; from this point of view, there is no alternative if political freedom is to be maintained. The left claims that economic motives are the true mainsprings of politics and that the economic dominants are the effective power wielders; its evaluation is that one does not have a competitive marketplace but a one-sided economic conflict.

Green, 1918); David Truman, *The Governmental Process* (New York: Knopf, 1951). See also Harold D. Lasswell, *Democracy through Public Opinion* (Menasha, Wisc.: George Banta, 1941).

6. Harold D. Lasswell, *Psychopathology and Politics* (Chicago: University of Chicago Press, 1930); Fred I. Greenstein and Michael Lerner, *A Source Book for the Study of Personality and Politics* (Chicago: Markham, 1971); see also Brent M. Rutherford, "Psychopathology, Decision Making and Political Involvement," *Journal of Conflict Resolution* 10 (1966): 387–407.

This model of political analysis, I will argue, has an effect on institution building. The imagery of men and women—and their political elites—pursuing economic group interest is particularly diffused by the mass media. What is the influence of the perspective which casts political behavior—popular participation and elite behavior—in terms of "rationalistic" pursuit of economic self-interest and material gain?[7] The hypothesis is offered that the intellectual effect has not been very clarifying or constructive for strengthening the political institutions required for effective social control. From this economic perspective, political elites and political parties are seen as one additional type of interest group rather than the unique mechanism for actual and potential coordination of socioeconomic processes and for resolving societal conflicts. In other words, the economic perspective of politics has weakened or at least complicated institution building for social control.

The limitation in the "rationalistic" model is in fact inherent in our definition of social control, which postulates that economic self-interest cannot account for the social and moral order. However, the argument rests on the actual consequence of the economic models of politics diffused by the new political analysis. The political reforms which have been implemented to strengthen political competition, it will be argued, have actually weakened the political parties. There is no need to deny the overriding reality of elite concern with economic allocations. But an economic calculus neither accounts adequately for decisions made by political elites in the United States nor clarifies the procedures by which political conflicts are resolved or at least contained. The economic model of politics denies the pervasive institutional disarticulation which creates economic inconsistencies. The inherent weakness is that the economic model avoids the central problem of the political elites of the United States as an advanced society, namely, the inability of these elites to create the political conditions under which clear-cut political decisions can be made.

The effect of the study of "political economy" on societal change can be stated in alternative terms. Relatively speaking, of all of the social sciences, economics has had to face deepest "reassessment" in its self-estimate of its capacity to contribute to public policy. Without any interruption, for more than a century economists have manifested

7. W. A. John and H. W. Singer, *The Role of the Economist as Official Advisor* (London: George Allen and Unwin, 1955).

an increasing self-confidence about the growth of the coherence and precision of their discipline. Of all of the social scientists, they have demonstrated the greatest ability to use mathematical analysis. As a result, economists have expressed the belief that economics had reached the level where it could be applied as a "policy science." In fact, economists started to use criteria of policy performance as much as scholarly quality in judging professional achievement.

However, since the first years of the 1970s, the economists were shaken. The self-assuredness was mixed with a deep sense of doubt—even pessimism—about whether they could analyze the issues to which they had addressed themselves. By 1975 a sense of professional gloom or at least self-doubt pervaded the national meetings of the economists in the United States, not about financial rewards of their profession but about their scientific and advisory powers.

What has served as an indicator of productive debate in economic circles has been between the fiscalist and the monetarist strategies. This debate has been exhausted rather than resolved or even reformulated. The formulations of John Maynard Keynes in 1935 to 1965 involved more than economic theory.[8] They also provided a political strategy for managing and regulating the growth of the welfare state with the minimum amount of strain and conflict. The fiscalist approach generated professional support among an important group of economists, especially in the absence of inflationary trends in the two decades after 1945. However, the actual state of the economic analysis can be judged by the fact that other economists assert that the Keynesian strategy was of little or no consequence economically during this period. They argue that there was favorable economic performance despite the Keynesian policies, because of more fundamental variables such as the world market of raw materials and international monetary arrangements. It must be stressed that Keynes himself was aware of and accepted the importance of monetarist policies.

In any case, "stagflation" has meant that the political elites have had to recognize the limitation of fiscalist policies.[9] In varying degrees, most economists have accepted the relevance of both theories. The Keynesians have increased their concern with monetarist theory as a

8. For an overview of the relevance and limitation of Keynesian economics for public policy, see Harry Johnson, *On Economics and Society* (Chicago: University of Chicago Press, 1975).

9. Audrey Jones, *The New Inflation: The Politics of Prices and Incomes* (London: Deutsch, 1973).

means of dealing with inflation; the monetarists focus more and more on fiscal policy as it contributes to the volume of money—the central concern of the monetarists. A third group claim that they are committed to a fusion of both strategies. This convergence implies more a decline of the debate than a scientific resolution of competing paradigms, since each of the three groups has a different calculus for manipulating the variables which are asserted to "cause" stagflation.

These difficulties in the policy application of economics should not obscure the specific areas in which there is extensive agreement about economic policy among economists of different persuasions. Such agreement encompasses direct and first-order consequences of economic policies, for example, the regressive character of social security taxes or the limitations of property taxes as a means for financing local government. In addition, the agreement has come to involve more complex economic issues, such as the assertion that increasing the federal minimum wage produces greater inflationary pressure and a corresponding contraction of job opportunities for youngsters entering the labor market.

Economic analysis not only deals with the grand strategies of fiscal versus monetary intervention, it also encompasses "tools" of analysis which are applied to the formulation and administration of public policy, such as cost effectiveness systems, program budgeting, and the variant which has been labeled zero based budgeting. In each of these procedures, an economizing calculus is considered to assist the elected official to make fiscal decisions. A series of budgeting and accounting procedures have emerged which are indispensable for legislators and elected executives. These techniques become part of the struggle over resources allocation; they do not substitute for these struggles.[10] They do not displace "political" judgments; in fact, because of their inherent limitations, these tools probably intensify the competition for the allocation of resources. They make it more difficult to produce authoritative and legitimate decisions, since there is increased basis for disagreement.

These tools of analysis and the budgetary processes are applied differentially to the private sector and the public sector. There are two systems of budgeting in the United States, although this is generally

10. Aaron Wildavsky, *The Politics of the Budgetary Process* (Boston: Little, Brown, 1964); Robert H. Haveman, "Policy Analysis and the Congress: An Economist's View," *Policy Analysis* 2 (1976): 235–50.

overlooked. One system is for the private sector, which facilitates capital accumulation, since expenditures for capital development are carried as assets. The other system is for the public sector, which inhibits the accumulation of capital. Under it, expenditures for human capital and for physical capital are carried as liabilities and debts. By the 1930s economists had recognized this fundamental defect in the system of national accounts, but there has been no sustained examination of the influence of budgetary procedures on the welfare state.

Those tools of cost benefit analysis assume that the range of public choice and social benefits can all be reduced or equated to economic and price indicators.[11] The controversy generated by cost benefit analysis has persistently challenged this assumption and resulted in considerable mistrust and hostility to political decisions based on such procedures. Then, too, performance budget and zero based budgeting which seek automatically to eliminate expenditures unless they can be adequately justified have their own limitations. These procedures tend to produce extensive documentation which is hardly revealing of underlying realities and which can obscure the essential issues which have to be confronted. In addition, all of these procedures are subject to time lags which reduce their relevance and application. In the case of regulatory decisions, the costs of making use of these tools can become immense, almost to the point of outweighing the imputed benefits. Finally, and most important, the quality of the data often leaves much to be desired. Government statistics are often incomplete and inaccurate. This is particularly telling in the underenumeration of inner-city minority residents. Since census types of data are essential for allocating welfare funds, the result is distortion and inequity in such allocation. There is reason to believe that the inaccuracy and inadequacy of economic statistics are marked in cost of living indices, probably resulting in increasing inflationary adjustments.

It would be an error to stress these limitations without observing that straightforward, comprehensive, and definitive measures and procedures, which are based less on economizing logic and more on accounting procedures, are helpful in assisting political elites to make important decisions. The most outstanding development has been the revised federal budgeting mechanism which the Congress enacted in 1974. These procedures standardize the flow of data and develop an

11. Ida R. Hoos, *Systems Analysis in Public Policy: A Critique* (Berkeley: University of California Press, 1972).

overall reporting system which enables political leaders to see the relationship between a specific budget proposal and the budgetary limits which Congress has set for itself.

However, neither social scientists nor the informed members of the elite—political and economic—think of "political economy" as limited to tools for administrative purposes. It is rather seen as a crucial element in their ideology—total or partial. From the point of view of effective social control, rationalist economic models of political economy do not describe the actual behavior of the political elites. Therefore we must identify the main outlines of the operative political economy which guide the political elites as they confront economic decisions. These perspectives are responses to immediate political pressures and realities, but they incorporate elite conceptions of how the system does and should work.

Elite perspectives about the U.S. national economy have to be adapted to the context of the world economy. Two types of decisions are required from political leaders which are of a very different order. The national political elites are first engaged in maintaining and refashioning the framework in which public and private economic allocations are made. These decisions are mainly procedural. Second, they are confronted with the necessity of making the substantive allocations which constitute the public budget. Each decision is reached by resort to some conception of "forecasting"—that is, an anticipation of outcome of a specific set of policies and decisions.[12] For our purposes, the endless stream of specific decisions can be summarized into four categories. Under the framework of public and private allocations, we are concerned with *(a)* domestic prices, wage, and income policy; and *(b)* international trade and investment policy. Under the public sector allocations, the focus is on *(c)* allocations for national defense, and *(d)* allocations for welfare. The decisions in each area obviously closely influence the other three, but the pattern of decision making is segmented.

First, in the arena of prices, wages, and income policy, "management" and "labor" remain strongly institutionalized as "adversaries."

12. Fred Charles Ikle, "Can Social Prediction Be Evaluated," *Daedalus* 96 (1967): 733–62; Michael Young, *Forecasting and the Social Sciences* (London: Heineman, 1968); Otis Dudley Duncan, *Toward Social Reporting: Next Steps* (New York: Russell Sage Foundation, 1969); Daniel Harrison, *Social Forecasting Methodology: Suggestions for Research* (New York: Russell Sage Foundation, 1976).

The framework which the political elite has developed maintains the symbolic structure of adversaries and avoids the construction of new mechanisms of mutual self-regulation. In chapter 7, the acceptance of this partial ideology by both management and labor was underscored in the industrial sectors; and this perspective pours over into service and human services institutions. To a considerable degree, the political elites respond by seeking to make more "effective" the competitive process among these adversaries.

These normative commitments of adversary labor-management bargaining and rejection of governmental planning are seen as indispensable for effective allocation of resources and to the maintenance of personal and political freedom.[13] Among the members of Congress, one finds differences of emphasis in the interpretation of these "principles"; but the number who openly and decisively reject either is very small. In the background, there is the deep-seated opposition to the totalitarian model—the one-party system of centralized governmental economic management which is seen as inefficient and fundamentally incompatible with personal and political freedom. In the foreground, the political elite perspective in the United States overwhelmingly rejects the differing social democratic "models" of Western Europe. They reject nationalization as practiced in Great Britain as being economically inefficient. They reject the model of labor-management codetermination or even a limited "social contract" as practiced in Scandinavia and West Germany as potentially undermining personal and political freedom. One must describe the political code of the U.S. political elites, compared with Western Europe, as special if not unique, particularly given the extensive welfare state structure it has created.

The result of these perspectives is hardly profound limitations on legislative and executive intervention in economic processes. If it were possible to sum the volume of governmental intervention and regulation, the United States is as regulated as any of the Western European societies. The interventions and regulations are fragmented and guided by the notion of strengthening adversary and competitive relations, with the result that the disarticulated institutional structure of the industrial sector is reinforced.

13. Milton Derber, *The American Idea of Industrial Democracy 1865–1965* (Urbana, Ill.: University of Illinois Press, 1970).

Thus the political elites have erected a loose framework for handling domestic price, wage, and profit policies. Federal intervention is limited to efforts to facilitate the collective bargaining process, that is, the federal government supplies outside negotiators and collects and disseminates statistics about labor market conditions and the results of the collective bargaining. The formulation of advisory guidelines by the government is deemphasized and any positive contribution to defining national economic goals is even more circumscribed. These constraints, paradoxically, are compatible with extensive federal intervention in a variety of economic activities where very specific standards of performance are promulgated; for example, pollution control, safety and health standards, and the like. Moreover, the federal government reserves the right of extensive piecemeal intervention in the management of a variety of economic development programs, such as aid to small business, housing, transportation, etc.

Of course, there is a long history of legislation concerning trade union organization which has established the framework of the collective bargaining process. The long-term role of the federal government has been to pass legislation assisting trade union organizations; the Wagner Act of 1935 was the vital step in aiding unions to achieve a more appropriate balance. Over time, the Congress elaborated the jurisdiction of the National Labor Relations Board as a mechanism for regulating particular managment and labor practices. The Taft-Hartley Act of 1947 and the Landrum-Griffin Act of 1959 sought to assist the balance by limiting specific trade union practices. The federal government also has supported the growth of public employment unions, without requiring binding arbitration schemes. The political rationale has been the goal of a balance between labor and management to assist the competitive process among adversaries, and to avoid direct governmental intervention of bargaining.

At particular periods, the federal government has introduced forms of price control. With the exception of the World War II experience, spokesmen of organized labor and managerial leadership reject this approach. Moreover, even efforts to establish general voluntary guidelines for wage and prices are persistently resisted by management and labor leaders and there is general Congressional indifference to such strategies. The mainly symbolic effort by President Ford to hold a national economic summit was opposed or undermined by ritualized participation. Parallel efforts by President Carter have been limited to a series of informal minor meetings. The open adversary model of collective bargaining remains the persistent goal.

The political elites have also emphasized support for antimonopoly action, administrative and judicial. If success is measured in terms of resulting corporate reorganization or in fines paid or in cease and desist orders, the effect has been noteworthy. But the effect on economic performance is more difficult to assess. Moreover, by and large, trade unions have been exempted from antimonopoly actions. Likewise, the political elites have developed the welfare state and endured the emergence of stagflation without linking collective bargaining to the national welfare budget. As a result, the welfare budget is not directly related to capital investments and the growth of economic and labor productivity. In contrast, in countries such as the Federal Republic of Germany, labor-management collective bargaining encompasses the size and allocation of welfare payments.

Instead, in the U.S. the banking and taxation systems are seen as crucial regulatory mechanisms of domestic economic policy. In particular, the regulation of the volume of money has become an object of political concern. The political formula has been to accord a measure of independence to the Federal Reserve System as the regulator of the volume of money. However, it is more and more recognized that the central banking system has only partial, and probably declining, control of the volume of the money in the United States.

While tax policy is debated during elections in terms of equity and appropriate welfare transfers, economists focus on the role of taxation as an instrument for managing economic growth. Unfortunately, there is little professional agreement about alternatives. Even direct investment tax rebates are believed by a segment of "free market" economists not to have important consequences. Corporations have wide discretion in their investment policies. The decline in the early 1970s in investment ratios in U.S. corporations was in part self-induced. Corporations informed their executives that they would be rewarded and promoted on the basis of profits realized. This produced a short-term outlook in which funds were not allocated for reinvestment but were distributed as dividends. Only by 1975 did corporations modify this emphasis and encourage greater investment allocation.

In addition to the reluctance—in fact, opposition—to government intervention in collective bargaining, there is persistent opposition and massive indifference to labor participation in the management of industrial corporations. Such participation has been proposed as a device of social control designed to increase worker responsibility in wage negotiations, and as mechanisms for increasing worker productivity and satisfaction. The research literature on the influence of worker participation on industrial management and productivity is not clear-cut.[14] Compared with Western Europe, worker participation in the United States has been limited, and the political elites have not pressed for it. Even grievance procedures are cast in the adversary mold, with a strong emphasis on legalistic arrangements rather than consultative and participative ones among the parties directly involved.

The formula of economic adversaries penetrates even the efforts of government to deal with the organizational problems of quality control of production, of humanizing work, and of improving industrial safety. Again, one approach would be to make these issues part of the collective bargaining process, and to create a measure of worker participation. Instead, efforts are implemented by expanding federal and state inspection bureaucracies.

After a decade of stagflation, one could have expected that the opposing candidates in the national elections of 1976 would offer the potential of a critical or realignment election in which alternative strategies for dealing with the framework of prices, wages, and profits would be presented. There were differences between the presidential candidates, but they were relative. The failure to structure the election in more clear-cut alternatives was not due mainly to limitations in the deliberate capacity of the electorate; that was certainly operative. It was in part the lack of certainty about the consequences of alternative economic policies by the political elites who were essentially committed to competition between economic adversaries. But the underlying element was that the election reflected the complexity of aggregating and structuring self-interest among members of the electorate about prices, wages, and profits.

14. For an overview which emphasizes the limitation of worker participation, see George Strauss and Eliezer Rosenstein, "Workers Participation: A Critical View," *Industrial Relations* 9 (February 1970): 197–214. The positive contributions are stressed by Paul Blumberg, *Industrial Democracy: The Sociology of Participation* (New York: Schocken, 1969); Michael Poole, *Workers' Participation in Industry* (London: Routledge and Kegan Paul, 1975); Bengt Abrahamsson, *Bureaucracy or Participation: The Logic of Organization* (Beverly Hills, Calif.: Sage Publications, 1977).

In the 1976 presidential election, candidates were more explicit than in the past about their economic goals: the level of unemployment they sought to achieve and the amount of inflation that they believed that the economy could tolerate. However, the goal that attracted the most attention was Carter's pledge that he would seek to eliminate government deficit spending by 1980. This emerged as the most visible measure of the performance of a president during a historical period of weak regimes and inability to establish budgetary priorities.

Second, political elites are forced to orient their economic decisions to the realities of the United States in a world economy. For the United States, there has been a long-term increase in the magnitude of world trade as a portion of the gross national product. In 1960, 5.4% of the gross national product came from foreign trade; by 1974, the figure had risen to 10.0% The income on U.S. investments abroad stood as 3.3 billion dollars in 1960 and grew to 25.9 billion by 1974.

From the point of view of social control, the political elites are faced with difficulties in integrating domestic economic policy with the objectives of increasing world trade. Increased world trade carries with it the reality and continued loss of domestic employment opportunities to more efficient and lower-cost labor overseas. The outcome thereby strains further the institutions of the welfare state in the United States. The growth and persistence of a negative balance of trade which reflects in part high rates of consumption are a crucial economic indicator which the political elites must deal with.

Elected political leaders must create a framework of dealing with post-World War II changes in the international trade position of the United States which became fully manifest in the oil embargo in 1973. There has been a dramatic increase in the cost of raw materials, including energy resources. The major element in partially offsetting exports has been the increase in the sale of high technology and technical services, including the politically controversial sale of military equipment. In addition, the long-term trade position of the United States has reflected the marked growth of sales of agricultural products. However, a key strain has been the export of United States capital, either through international investment channels or through the operations of United States multinational corporations. Additional contribution to the outflow of capital comes from U.S. government grants for military and civilian economic aid. The export of U.S. capital is designed to produce, over the long run, profits which are in part returned to the United States and which create taxes. However, these revenues have hardly eliminated the chronic imbalance in foreign trade. Moreover, the major economic consequence of the movement of U.S. capital abroad by means of multinational corporations is the export of "jobs," which increases unemployment in the United States. U.S. government estimates indicate that, for the post–World War II period, the number of jobs lost by such export of capital has reached 10 million. Again, the loss of such employment opportunities increases unemployment and expands the demands of welfare support. These are inherent trends in differential economic development and cannot be avoided by economic "protectionist" policies. International "trade" has come to include the importation—both legal and illegal—of unskilled workers into the United States. While these workers are prepared to perform many menial tasks, the social welfare requirements of this population are immense and contribute to the strain on the welfare state. The chronic deficit in the balance of payments and the costs of stationing military forces abroad have emerged as factors in the long-term devaluation of the U.S. currency, which has increased the costs of living and exacerbates the management of the welfare budget.

Much economic policy concerning foreign trade is a short-term response to immediate pressure-group demands. Nevertheless, it is striking that up to 1976 political leaders have not resorted to a strategy of economic protectionism in the face of weakening U.S. position in the world economy. Instead, the U.S. has pursued a long-term program of foreign economic aid. Thus, the basic political approach to the world economy is not limited to a narrow and immediate interest in economic return but is rather an effort to adjust to long-term problems with some sense of international responsibility.

Next, it is necessary to turn to the political economy of the two crucial aspects of the public budget. One is the allocation for defense; the other, that for welfare. When one examines the defense budget, there is little basis for asserting that economizing models are of overriding importance.[15] There is continual pressure to reduce military expenditure and there is an extensive effort to use cost effectiveness tools to determine the required level of expenditures and to select among alternative weapons systems. But these calculations are sub-

15. Nancy J. Bearg and Edwin A. Deagle, Jr., "Congress and the Defense Budget," in *American Defense Policy*, ed. John E. Endicott and Ray W. Stafford (Baltimore, Md.: Johns Hopkins University Press, 1977).

merged by fierce political debates about international relations and the world military balance. There is one sense in which the decision-making process for military budgets conforms to the "economizing model," but in a complex fashion with unanticipated consequences. Given the pressure to reduce the military budget, the trend in the United States has been to replace manpower (general purpose forces) with high technology, especially with strategic nuclear forces. In the crude terms of military destructive capacity, this trend is more economical and articulates with the popular desire to avoid military service. However, greater reliance on nuclear forces tends to be destabilizing in the international community and in the world military balance.

The military budget is a combination of the political response to threat perception, plus the accumulated expenses of past military engagements. The budget-making procedures of the federal government tend during hostilities to postpone recording the full costs of military operations. Military costs are defined as "high" less because of the cost of weapons—which are in reality very expensive—and more because of retirement pensions and because of the increased personnel costs under the all-volunteer force. While the personnel costs of the "peacetime" conscription force of the 1950s was nearly 40% of the total military budget, under the all-volunteer force, the figure has risen to nearly 60%. It is estimated that the 8 billion dollar expenditure for retirement costs in 1975 will rise to over 20 billion during the 1980s.[16]

However, long-term expenditures on the military budget from 1945 to 1975 represented a declining percentage of the gross national product. By 1975, the trend had started to reverse itself and military allocations were increased. Congressional efforts to reduce the costs of military personnel, especially retirement costs, have also become intensified, but there is no reason to assume that these efforts will produce noteworthy reductions in the military defense budget, or to believe that the allocation for weapons will sharply increase. During a period of deterrence and "no war, no peace," changes for military expenditures are gradual. One can think of the military budget and deterrence as a form of fixed overhead costs. As described in chapter 6, high levels of military expenditures are not required to maintain economic

16. The socioeconomic aspects of military retirement are discussed by Albert Biderman, "Sequels to a Military Career: The Retired Military Professional," in *The New Military: Changing Patterns of Organization*, ed. Morris Janowitz (New York: Russell Sage Foundation, 1964), pp. 287–336.

growth and productivity under advanced industrialism; in fact, military expenditures are ineffective to maintain full employment. If there were a sharp reduction in military expenditures—for example, 25%—the newly available fiscal resources would rapidly be absorbed by existing and emerging welfare demands, especially for health and direct youth employment programs.

As in the case of the military budget, federal government allocations for welfare are difficult to explain in terms of an economizing model. Not only is there no marketplace for welfare services, but also it is extremely difficult for the political elites to choose between competing welfare programs. Therefore they make partial and continuous fiscal contributions to competing demands and programs. The rapid rise in welfare expenditures in the United States since 1965 represented partial responses to specific needs. However, the marked increase in expenditures is deeply influenced by normative and symbolic definitions, especially those of citizen rights. As Kirsten Grønbjerg has demonstrated, "welfare rolls" in 1960 to 1970 have grown in those states with the strongest economic base and where political pressure in support of welfare was strongest.[17] It is not a distortion to assert that the total allocations for welfare are a form of moral and political response—without effective economizing principles of allocation.[18] In addition, as mentioned, U.S. political elites have shown little interest in seeking more adequate social control of welfare expenditures by relating them to the collective bargaining process. Under such arrangements, the allocations for welfare would be linked to projected and desired rates of growth of economic productivity and accumulation of investment capital.

Instead, the political issues of social welfare have been cast symbolically in terms of adversary relations, in this case between respectable society and the social "outcasts." Administrative procedures and their symbolic implications have their independent importance. The reforms recommended during the Nixon administration included the negative income tax and a family assistance plan. The goal was to remove disincentives to employment, to introduce new economic incentives for the "working poor," and to simplify the administrative

17. Kirsten A. Grønbjerg, *Mass Society and the Extension of Welfare, 1960–1970* (Chicago: University of Chicago Press, 1977).

18. Theodore R. Mormon and Martin Rein, "Reforming 'The Welfare Mess': The Fate of the Family Assistance Plan, 1969–1972," in *Policy and Politics in America: Six Case Studies*, ed. A. P. Sindler (Boston: Little, Brown, 1973).

procedures. But the moral definitions were present. A critical aspect of the plan was that it would have shifted important parts of its administration from the Department of Health, Education and Welfare to the Internal Revenue Service. The moral assumption was that welfare was an unavoidable burden of an advanced industrial society and tight fiscal arrangements were required to contain the inevitable cheating—and these could best be made by the Internal Revenue Service.

The proposals for reform which emerged under President Carter's administration had many similar elements but a different moral definition. In the outlook of President Carter, welfare was defined as undesirable since it weakened moral character and demoralized the recipient. Therefore it was necessary for the government to create work opportunities. The recommended program included the proposal that the government should serve as the employer of the last resort and create jobs for the employable welfare recipients. The tasks of the government as the employer of the last resort are formidable, to say the least.

To accomplish this moral objective, the reform would shift the administration of important aspects of welfare administration to the Department of Labor from the Department of Health, Education and Welfare. The proposed transfer of administration was designed to symbolize the increased emphasis on work opportunities and the inherent limitation of "welfare." But, in effect, the lack of consensus and the weak political regimes which have emerged since 1952 have been unable to impose any consistent articulated model, either economizing or administrative, to deal with the political economy of welfare expenditures and have been engaged in a set of inconsistent compromises.

Generally speaking, the political elites in the United States demonstrate their strong commitment to the maintenance of private property and a competitive economy. This outlook is reinforced by their belief that the political process should be based on vigorous competition. But to maintain and enforce a competitive economic system considerable government regulation and extensive intervention are required.[19] However, the political elites are not "merely" a generic part of this competitive process, that is, another competitive element. If the normative structure of the United States produces a relative effective

19. Andrew Schoenfield, *Modern Capitalism: The Changing Balance of Public and Private Power* (London: Oxford University Press, 1965).

competition between the institutions of the economic and industrial sectors, it is because the political elites have some realistic sense of their special tasks. They are not competing but members of an institutional arrangement which manages the competitive process. They must, in turn, recognize the limits of competition in coordinating the political economy.

In other words, the economizing model of politics neither adequately accounts for the behavior of the political elites nor provides a comprehensive basis for guiding their behavior. Instead, political leaders are effective and increase their effectiveness to the extent that they remove themselves from economic competition. The perspective inherent in the institutional analysis of the political process has accumulated considerable research on the increased differentiation of the political elites from the economic dominants. Thus, it is necessary to examine the key linkages between business elites and the political elites. We are dealing with two hypotheses about long-term trends in the structure of political power. First, in the last century, and especially in the last half-century, there has been increasing structural differentiation of the economic dominants and the political elites which is rooted in the more complex division of labor and task requirements. To speak of this structural separation is not to imply the absence of powerful connections and elements of agreement of interest. It does imply that important components are mediated by organized interest-group bureaucrats and specialists rather than through intimate patterns of social interaction and cultural cohesion. Second, although under advanced industrialism the importance of social origins declines in accounting for political orientations and behavior, the political elites have over time been characterized by a broadening of their social origins at a more rapid rate than in the case of the economic elites. This shift in social recruitment plus the absence of common educational and socialization experience have attenuated the relationships between economic dominants and political leaders. The argument will be pursued that the political elites are a relatively differentiated "professional group" with at least a minimal conception of themselves as engaged in coordinating and balancing the competing institutional sectors of society.[20] This self-conception, rather than an economizing

20. Raymond Aron, "Social Structure and the Ruling Class," *British Journal of Sociology* 1 (1950): 1–16, 126–43.

model, supplies the basis for clarifying the issues of building political institutions required for social control.

THE STRUCTURE OF POLITICAL LEADERSHIP

The political sociology of the political leadership in the United States has been explored by a series of studies. The "naturalistic" and empirical interests which were generated by the Chicago school of political science in the 1920s have led to important specific studies of political elites which make a broad overview possible.[21] There is a straight line of intellectual descent and accumulation from Harold Gosnell, *Machine Politics: Chicago Style* to James Q. Wilson, *Negro Politics: The Search for Leadership* to Donald Matthews, *U.S. Senators and Their World.*[22] Without either excessive cynicism or utopianism, scholars of this persuasion believe that the realistic and detailed empirical research of political elites was a positive intellectual contribution to social control. On the other hand, particular political philosophers labeled these research efforts undemocratic or corrosive of good morals. As argued in chapter 3, this stream of research asserted and reasserted that political institutions were more than reflections or manifestations of societal structure. Social structure bears the imprint of political arrangements and political leadership. It made sense to pursue Max Weber's formulation of politics as a profession, but not because political leaders who organized parties could be compared with other professionals–doctors, lawyers, or professors.[23] On the contrary, the components of professionalism in politics, and in particular, those of skill and self-conceptions, were unique. Political elites had to be studied by the standard categories of professional analysis of social recruitment, socialization, career lines on an organizational format.[24] But their self-conceptions and the consequence of their tasks on their self-conceptions were cru-

21. Barry D. Karl, *Charles E. Merriam and the Study of Politics* (Chicago: University of Chicago Press, 1974).

22. Harold Gosnell, *Machine Politics: Chicago Style* (Chicago: University of Chicago Press, 1937); James Q. Wilson, *Negro Politics: The Search for Leadership* (Glencoe, Ill.: Free Press, 1960); Donald Matthews, *United States Senators and Their World* (New York: Random House, 1960).

23. Max Weber, "Polilitk als Beruf," *Gesammelte Politische Schriften* (Munich: Duncker and Humblodt, 1921), pp. 396–450.

24. Harold D. Lasswell, "Introduction: The Study of Political Elites," in *World Revolutionary Elites: Studies in Coercive Revolutionary Movements*, ed. Harold D. Lasswell and Daniel Lerner (Cambridge: MIT Press, 1965), pp. 3–28; Morris Janowitz, "The Systematic Analysis of Political Biography," *World Politics* 6 (April 1954): 405–12.

cial. In the simplest terms, men of political power were persons who sought to manage the totality of the modern nation-state and were prepared to be directly associated with the process which we call "government." Democratic polities required elites who were committed to a formula of shared power and decisions based on persuasion. There were no social structures which would automatically produce and maintain a democratic polity.

The line between social research and social criticism is not readily drawn, especially in the evaluation of the standards of behavior of men and women of power. Thus it is understandable that C. W. Mills in *The Power Elite* presents both a moral criticism of the U.S. society and his version of political conflict based on a stratigraphic image of economic classes.[25] Mills was influenced by the writings of Thorstein Veblen and James Burnham. He conceived of the U.S. elite as constituted of a highly integrated "ruling group."[26] It was an elite worthy only of total moral condemnation because of its self-centeredness and lack of responsibility. The U.S. power elite was functionally integrated as well as socially cohesive. The nation-state was in effect dominated and ruled by a triumvirate of economic dominants, political leaders, and professional soldiers.

The Power Elite generated a political polemic that received great attention and exhausted itself only very gradually. The terms of reference supplied by C. W. Mills had the effect of oversimplifying the alternative formulations of the elite structure. The argument of the "power elite" versus the "pluralistic model" became a set of new stereotypes. But such is the consequence of the intrusion of the language of social science into ideological political debate.

The decline in interest of the "theory of the power elite" was in good part a result of the changing interest of activist intellectuals. The rise of the black power and the women's liberation movements found this symbolism of limited pertinence; their leaders had different notions about the power elite. The spokesmen for these movements were more interested in enlarging the power elite than in analyzing its members' moral behavior. Of course, over the long run, the detailed research on the social origins of recruitment, socialization, task spe-

25. C. Wright Mills, *The Power Elite* (New York: Oxford University Press, 1956).

26. Roberto Michels, *Political Parties* (New York: Hearst's International Library Co., 1915); James Burnham, *The Managerial Revolution* (New York: John Day, 1941).

cialization, and decision making of the political elites challenged the substantive content of C. W. Mills's book. The key issue was the linkage between economic dominants and political managers.

One would have thought that four decades of trends in national legislation since the introduction of the New Deal and two decades of expansion of the welfare state would have offered extensive evidence in opposition to the power elite thesis.[27] The pressure groups of the "business community" have failed to prevent the extension of the welfare state and the intrusion of the federal government into the management of financial-industrial enterprises, regardless of the political affiliations of the president or the composition of the Congress. The fanatical-like public opposition of business community spokesmen focused on increased federal spending and the pattern of built-in fiscal expansion. The political constraints on the business enterprise system is epitomized by their continual alarm about these projections. Thus in 1972, it was estimated that by 1975 the federal budget would run a deficit of 17 billion dollars even at full employment and without any important new spending. In actuality the deficit was of course much larger; it was 34 billion.[28]

It requires a devious line of reasoning to argue that the "economic interests" are satisfied by the compromise which they have been able to extract—a line of reasoning which is denied by their extensive efforts to influence legislation. Likewise, there is little plausibility in the argument that the "capitalist class" wished to have expanded welfare expenditures and regulation of economic enterprise, since these arrangements represent a new form of economic relations which enables them to maintain their economic dominance. This line of reasoning is presented in such a fashion that it is subject to no negative proof, in effect. However, the legislative history of the welfare state, plus the expansion of civil rights and affirmative action laws, indicate that the complex coalition of ordered social segments such as the aged, minorities, and women, plus the collection of voluntary associations, especially organized labor, has been influential. The power balance includes the authority and influence which the federal bureaucracy has been able to accumulate in these areas.

27. William A. Muraskin, "Review of Piven and Howard: Regulating the Poor," *Contemporary Sociology* 4 (November 1975): 607–13.

28. Charles L. Schultze, et al., *Setting National Priorities in the 1973 Budget* (Washington: Brookings Institution, 1972), pp. 417–19.

In addition sociologists have spent considerable effort investigating elite networks by studying their social origins. They have pursued these indicators because they are available for statistical analysis, although the biographical directories are far from accurate. Likewise, the "theory" persists that social origins are revealing indicators of group affiliation and of political interests. But as the division of labor becomes more and more complex, the relevance of social origins for macrosociological processes declines. C. W. Mills himself has stated, "We cannot infer the direction of policy from the social origins and career of the policy holders. The social and economic backgrounds of men of power do not tell us what we need to know in order to understand the distribution of social power."[29] In fact, he overstates the case; his own writings contain extensive presentations of such social background and career data. These data have relevance when they are joined with the study of the internal organization of various institutional sectors.[30] It is worthwhile to know which social groupings are recruited into the different bureaucratic hierarchies of the industrial, political, and military sectors. These data are no substitute for the direct examination of actual political participation and power balances, but they do help one to understand the self-conceptions and perspectives which elite members develop in the pursuit of their tasks and their goals.

The increased structural differentiation of the various elements of the elite, especially the increased institutional separation of economic dominants from professional political leaders, is a result of the bureaucratic growth of the industrial enterprise.[31] Being a successful industrial manager is more and more difficult to reconcile with developing a national political career. The pressures of task specialization, the very growth of the size of economic establishments, and the scope of their operations have produced a strong trend toward elite specialization. There is an attenuation and specialization of informal face-to-face relations between elite groups, although there is no evolutionary reason to assert that they are completely displaced. There is good reason to speak of strategic elites in order to call attention to the patterns of

29. Mills, *Power Elite*, p. 208.

30. Lewis J. Edinger and Donald D. Searling, "Social Background of Elite Analysis," *American Political Science Review* 61 (June 1967): 428–45.

31. Richard J. Barber, *The American Corporation: Its Power, Its Money, Its Politics* (New York: Dutton, 1970); Neil Jacoby, *Corporate Power and Social Responsibility* (New York: Macmillan, 1973).

skill and career development and voluntary association membership which reflect the specialization among the powerful.[32] To point to these trends is not to overlook those members of the elite who move from one sector to another.

Massive documentation has been accumulated on the long-term trends in this process of elite differentiation.[33] One research technique has been the community study which analyzes the personnel and networks of local elites. Robert and Helen Lynd in "Middletown" identified in broad strokes the political dominance of the X family in the 1930s.[34] Yet they pointed out the limitations on the family's influence and a dispersion of power with the growth of trade unionism, local voluntary associations, and increased activity of local political managers. Since this study, a series of studies have covered much longer historical periods, focusing on the growth in scale of financial-industrial organization and the accompanying direct withdrawal of economic dominants from local political influence. The basic measure has been the decline in the number of men of great wealth who served themselves in elected and appointed municipal and local civic posts. The study of Robert Schulze, although it deals with a small manufacturing center, Ypsilanti, Michigan, measured statistically the bifurcation of the economic dominants from the public leaders for a period of almost a century.[35] The requirements of large-scale and bureaucratic financial and industrial enterprise meant that the posts of local public leadership were less and less filled by the economic dominants and more by small businessmen and local professionals who had definitions of the public interest different from those of the men of wealth, especially those who were absentee owners.

For New Haven, Robert Dahl replicated the same historical trend by observing the shift of political power from the "patricians" to the "entrepreneurs" to the "explebs" to the "new men."[36] The transforma-

32. Suzanne Keller, *Beyond the Ruling Class: Strategic Elites in Modern Society* (New York: Random House, 1963).

33. For an overview of the literature, see Terry Nichols Clark, *Community Power and Policy Outputs: A Review of Urban Research* (Beverly Hills, Calif.: Sage Publications, 1973).

34. Robert S. Lynd and Helen M. Lynd, *Middletown in Transition* (New York: Harcourt, Brace, 1937).

35. Robert Schulze, "The Bifurcation of Power in a Satellite City," in *Community Political Systems*, ed. Morris Janowitz (New York: Free Press, 1961), pp. 19–80; Robert Schulze, "The Role of Economic Dominants in Community Power Structure," *American Sociological Review* 23 (February 1958): 3–9.

36. Robert A. Dahl, *Who Governs? Democracy and Power in an American City* (New Haven: Yale University Press, 1961).

tion meant that men of wealth—landed and subsequently market wealth—were displaced by politicians from lower-status and minority groups and then by professional political leaders. The degree, extent, speed, and content of this transformation vary from city to city and from region to region. In Atlanta, studied first by Floyd Hunter and later by M. Kent Jennings, the rise to political power of the black community produced bifurcation between wealth and political power.[37] In the suburban areas, the most powerful economic elites never were extensively involved in local civic affairs. The growth of the suburban population has meant increased participation by small businessmen, lawyers, and professional specialists in the management of political and civic affairs.

The management of municipal affairs has traditionally been affected by the weakness of the local civil service. The older patterns of domination of municipal politics by the direct participation of the wealthy supplied a component of civic coordination.[38] With the withdrawal of these economic dominants because of broader national interests, the political party organization, in particular the old-fashioned political machine, sought to operate as a substitute mechanism. The decline of the big city machines meant an increased dispersion of political power; after 1950, when social scientists began to study community power structures, they were able to identify varying patterns of dispersion of local decision making. In no sense can it be said that economic dominants have been displaced by the professional political leaders; but the professional political leaders were crucial in determining the type of political balance which emerged in the coalitions which were built.

Two decades later in 1970 in his review of the accumulated research of 57 case studies augmented by his own analysis of 423 communities, Michael Aiken could describe broadly the variation in the patterns of community power—that is, the degree of dispersion.[39] He concluded

37. Floyd Hunter, *Community Power Structure: A Study of Decision Makers* (Chapel Hill: University of North Carolina Press, 1953); M. Kent Jennings, *Community Influentials: The Elites of Atlanta* (New York: Free Press of Glencoe, 1964).

38. In addition to institutional constraints, attitude changes take place among economic dominants whose wealth is inherited. When inherited wealth contributes to the formation of a "socialite" social group, rich people develop tastes and a style of life in which they become relatively indifferent to politics. See especially Gabriel A. Almond, "Plutocracy and Politics in New York City," Ph.D. dissertation, University of Chicago, 1938.

39. Michael Aiken, "The Distribution of Community Power: Structural Bases and Social Consequences," in *The Structure of Community Power*, ed. Michael

that the older Northern cities had more "decentralized" power structures and that there was direct linkage between patterns of economic ownership and the local power structure; the greater the degree of absentee ownership, the greater the degree of power dispersion. Social structure was also operative, in that the more heterogeneous the social structure the more dispersed the power structure. Moreover, nonreform city governments produced more decentralized power arrangements. In short, the differentiation of economic and political elites at the community and metropolitan levels was a broad trend which has contributed to the increased dispersion of political influence.

At this point the empirical conclusion is that the degree of dispersion of community power has had at least a short-term consequence for the management of municipal affairs. C. W. Mills himself was one of the early investigators who tried to document and grapple with the complex relations between the forms of economic organization and the management of local community welfare and civic programs.[40] In his study, commissioned by the U.S. Senate during World War II, he sought to relate the differential effect of "small business" versus that of "big business" on local social welfare, but without examining the actual details of local political institutions. He claimed that "small business" cities had more adequate local social welfare systems than "big business" cities, and this study helped stimulate research on the consequences of local political power structures.[41] Perhaps one of the most important contributions of Mills's study was that he pointed to the growing interest of trade unions and other voluntary associations

Aiken and Paul E. Mott (New York: Random House, 1970), pp. 487–525; see also John Walton, "Substance and Artifact: The Current Status of Research on Community Power Structure," *American Journal of Sociology* 71 (January 1966): 430–38; John Walton, "Discipline Method and Community Power: A Note on the Sociology of Knowledge" *American Sociological Review* 31 (October 1966): 684–89.

40. C. Wright Mills and Melville J. Ulmer, *Small Business of Civic Welfare*, Report of the Small War Plants Corporation to the Special Committee to Study Problems of American Small Business. U.S. Senate, 79th Congress, 2d Session, document number 135, serial no. 11036 (Washington: 1946).

41. See, e.g., Irving A. Fowler, *Local Industrial Structures, Economic Power and Community Welfare* (Totowa, N.J.: Bedminster, 1964); Amos Hawley, "Community Power and Urban Renewal Success," *American Journal of Sociology* 68 (January 1964): 422–31; Michael Aiken and Robert R. Alford, "Community Structure and Innovation: The Case of Urban Renewal," *American Sociological Review* 35 (August 1970): 650–65; Richard A. Smith, "Community Power and Decision Making: A Replication and Extension of Hawley," *American Sociological Review* 41 (August 1976): 691–705.

in civic affairs, which he believed would increase their influence in the conduct of community civic affairs.

Michel Aiken, when he subsequently summarized the accumulated research, was able to focus more directly on this issue.[42] He concluded that cities with dispersed political power "configurations" have been more successful in mobilizing local resources in order to participate in several federal self-help programs—low-rent housing, urban renewal, the War on Poverty, and model cities. These findings take on fuller meaning in terms of the broad conclusion he offers, namely, that contemporary American communities are not "tight social systems" but are fairly "open social systems" in which some subsystems may be largely independent of others. Moreover, "only a multicausal model can capture the complexity of the modern American community." I would add that the methodology of the studies on which Aiken depended underemphasized the importance of the self-conceptions and partial ideologies of key professional political leaders who supply the energies with which workable political coalitions could be built. Dispersed political systems do not automatically produce meaningful decisions.

Local community power structures supply only a partial and possibly misleading basis for generalizing about the trends in the structure and social composition of national political elites. There was reason to anticipate that at the national level, the extent of structural differentiation of economic dominants and political leaders would be less than at the community level. First, the withdrawal from direct community political participation by economic dominants resulted from the growth of regional and national goals among financial and industrial leaders, and even from the expansion of their international economic aspirations. Thus, the self-interest of business leaders would dictate more extensive and more direct involvement in national political arrangements. Second, the absence of bureaucratically organized political parties should have contributed to the less structured differentiation among the national elites.[43] The loose organization of political parties could mean that business leaders and industrial managers would be able to move easily into candidacy for elected office. Third, there has

42. Aiken, "Distribution," pp. 514–16.

43. Lester G. Seligman, "Party Structure and Political Recruitment," *American Political Science Review* 55 (March 1961): 77–86; Lester G. Seligman, "Political Parties and Recruitment of Political Leaders," in *Political Leadership in Industrialized Societies*, ed. Lewis Edinger (New York: Wiley, 1967).

been a new wave of literature by academic specialists emphasizing an economic determinist analysis of the political processes at work in both domestic and international policy. The older literature, as epitomized by Ferdinand Lundberg's *America's Sixty Families*, has been discarded as dated, crude, and lacking in sound scholarship.[44] Even the content of Mills's *The Power Elite* is viewed by the new group of economic determinists as lacking specificity and theoretical clarity, although his main theme is considered sound. The new literature is offered as being more sound empirically, more detailed, and theoretically more elaborated. This literature analyzes the goals of monopoly capitalists, and does not indicate an all-encompassing exercise of political power; rather, the economic elites are seen as able to intervene and to achieve their crucial national and international objectives of maintaining the capitalist economic system.

However, on balance, the available evidence on the structural differentiation of economic and political elites follows patterns which are roughly the parallel to the community patterns.[45] Likewise, the trends in social composition and career socialization, including social and cultural cohesion, contribute to this differentiation. The organizational requirements of a financial and industrial career operate in an equivalent fashion at the community and national levels, and if anything, they produce more structural differentiation at the national level. Political influence by the national economic dominants is likewise exercised by means of bureaucratic specialists and voluntary associations and through the complexity of a mediating political process and political elites.[46]

44. Ferdinand Lundberg, *America's Sixty Families* (New York: Halcyon House, 1940).

45. For an assessment of this issue by professional economists, see especially Clark Kerr, Frederick Harbison, John Dunlop, and Charles A. Mayers, "Industrialism and Industrial Man," *International Labour Review* (September 1960); "Although professional management is destined to sweep aside its political or patrimonial predecessors, its seldom becomes a ruling elite in any society. In other words, the state does not become the property of the professional managers, as James Burnham envisioned in managerial resolution . . ." See also *Industrialism and Industrial Man* (Cambridge: Harvard University Press, 1960) pp. 145–46.

46. The economic determinist literature written after 1965, which has been sympathetically summarized by Milton Mankoff, contains, interestingly enough, very little empirical analysis which bears directly on the central issue of the structural differentiation of the political elites. (Milton Mankoff, "Power in Advanced Capitalist Society: A Review Essay on Recent Elitist and Marxist Criticism of Pluralist Theory," *Social Problems* 17 [1970]: 418–30.) The new emphasis, designed to overcome the defects of the earlier literature, is on the pattern of polit-

The sociology of the national political elites reflects the extensive but declining concentration of lawyers, which has been continually emphasized, and the high concentration of relatively modest social backgrounds as well as the long-term broadening of their social representativeness.[47] We are dealing with persons who rose to power by means of their political skills, especially negotiating and bargaining skills. In one form or another, they have had to traverse considerable social distance; I argue that both their training and practice as lawyers and their social mobility contribute to their particular and uneasy self-consciousness, especially vis-à-vis other elite groups.

The relatively modest social origins of the members of Congress extend back into the nineteenth century. But the sociology of the political elite requires examination not only of occupational background but also of place of birth and educational careers. Senators

ical decisions and outcomes rather than on the underlying political sociology of elites. In fact, there is very little concern with the social origins, education, and careers of the national legislators. One structural element that has received attention is the social profile of the Cabinet, in order to highlight the extent of linkages between the financial-industrial sector and the political process. (Peter J. Freitag, "The Cabinet and Big Business: A Study of Interlocks," *Social Problems* 23 [December 1975]: 137–52.)

This type of analysis of economic decision making is less oriented toward examining the realities of the political cleavages among economic groupings and more oriented toward a moral criticism of the United States elites—both economic and political. In fact, as Milton Mankoff notes (pp. 428–29), the main burden of the most energetic scholars of this persuasion shifts from an analysis of economic relations and the resulting political conflicts to a concern with the popular acceptance of the culture of "capitalism." The intellectual task is to understand the "legitimacy of capitalism."

Such an orientation is paradoxical during a period in which the central political institutions of the multiparty democracies have been subject to a loss of public confidence and trust. The writings of Norman Birnbaum have been taken as the typical of the transformation of economic class determinism into a cultural model (Norman Birnbaum, *The Crisis of Industrial Society* [New York: Oxford University Press, 1969]). The elements which require critical analysis are the mass media, the church, the ideology of nationalism, and the socializing role of mass education, and these authors acknowledge the tradition of civil liberties and political competition, augmented by "relative prosperity and minimal but welcome social reform."

47. There is extensive literature on the effect of legal training and lawyers on the legislative process. See, e.g., Harold D. Lasswell and Myres S. McDougal, "Legal Education and Public Policy: Professional Training in the Public Interest," *Yale Law Journal* 52 (March 1943): 203–95; William Miller, "American Lawyers in Business and Politics: Their Social Backgrounds and Early Training," *Yale Law Journal* 60 (January 1951): 66–76; James D. Barber, *The Lawmakers: Recruitment and Adaptation to Legislative Life* (New Haven: Yale University Press, 1965). See also Joseph A. Schlesinger, *Ambition and Politics: Political Careers in the United States* (Chicago: Rand McNally, 1966).

and Congressmen in the past and even in the post–World War II period have been heavily overrecruited from small town backgrounds, in contrast to the disproportionate emphasis on metropolitan recruitment of big business leaders. In part, this reflects the political advantage of recruitment from the hinterland and the geographical boundaries of electoral districts. It also reflects the greater esteem accorded to public service outside the metropolitan centers.

A tabulation of 513 men who between 1789 and 1953 were president, vice president, speaker of the House, Cabinet members, and Supreme Court Justices includes some appointive posts.[48] One-fifth of this group were classified by C. W. Mills as lower class, including small businessmen, farmers, and wage earners; most were from prosperous business families who were hardly upper class. The 180 men and women who served in the United States Senate between 1947 and 1957 roughly replicates the same findings; most are from similar business and professional families, including one-third from farm families. But it needs to be stressed that they were mainly of the middle class from small town settings and circumscribed culturally.

The decline in small town recruitment lagged behind the increased urbanization of the United States, but the increased social representativeness reflects inclusion of more minority groups who were metropolitan residents. The documentation supplied by Garrison Nelson on the long-term changes from 1789 to 1975 in the House of Representatives reflects the increased "democratization" of social recruitment, produced both by the increased number of minority-group members and by women.[49] There is one minor countertrend in the pattern of recruitment whose scope remains difficult to estimate. In the Senate, the number of hereditary millionaires has increased since World War II. It is estimated that by 1970 there were at least six such persons; interestingly enough, they were not active in business but had inherited wealth, and almost all are Democrats.

48. Mills, *Power Elite*, chap. 10. See also R. Wences, "Electoral Participation and the Occupational Composition of Cabinets and Parliaments," *American Journal of Sociology* 75 (September 1969): 181–97; Paul Burstein, "Political Elites and Labor Markets: Selection of American Cabinet Members, 1932–72," *Social Forces* 56 (September 1977): 189–201.

49. Jeanne J. Kirkpatrick, *Political Woman* (New York: Basic Books, 1974); James E. Conyers and Walter Wallace, *Black Elected Officials: A Study of Black Americans Holding Governmental Office* (New York: Russell Sage Foundation, 1976). Garrison Nelson, "Change and Continuity in the Recruitment of U.S. House Leaders, 1789–1975," in *Congress in Change: Evolution and Reform*, ed. N. J. Ornstein (New York: Praeger, 1975), pp. 155–79.

Donald Matthews's data on Senators for 1947–1957 on the interplay of family background, education, and occupational career served as indicators of the extent of structural differentiation.[50] Educational achievement almost always outweighed occupational inheritance. Of the two groups which he studied, 85% had graduated from college but they had not generally attended prestige schools, even if prestige schools include the "Big Ten." Seventy percent went to schools other than the Ivy League, the twenty outstanding Eastern undergraduate schools, or the "Big Ten" state universities. However, 53% went on to law school, and a majority went on to high-entrance-requirement law schools; their academic records and their ambitions were already orienting them to positions of importance despite their modest backgrounds.

The American labor force has less than 1% lawyers, but 50% of the Senators were in the legal profession; 28% were involved in business enterprise before becoming Senators, almost all from small and middle-size establishments; 10% were from other professions with a strong admixture of teachers, journalists, and related "verbalizing" professions. The concentration of Senators with business experience was greater, as would be expected, among Republicans than among Democrats.

In overall terms, it is possible to speak of four types of Senators according to Donald Matthews–types which highlight the process of recruitment and professionalization. There are the very small numbers of patrician politicians (7% of Matthews's sample); there are persons of high social status and considerable wealth who have had long careers in public service and elected office. Then there are the "professional politicians," who constitute more than 50%. These are the persons of modest social background who were trained as lawyers, entered politics early in their careers, and who rose slowly to elite political positions, often having served in the House of Representatives before being elected to the Senate. The amateur politicians are 34%. They are the Senators from average middle-class backgrounds who first followed relatively successful careers in business and law and who had limited careers in public service before seeking office. They started their political careers later in life, often by accepting an appointive office. Finally, there were a handful (4%) who could be labeled agitators. They came from relatively low social origins, and entered the

50. Matthews, *U.S. Senators*, pp. 11–46.

Senate without a record of success as a lawyer or elected official, or in business or a profession. They tended to come from small Western states and from areas with extremely weak party organization and rapidly changing social structure. Although they divert the energies of the national legislature, they are hardly persons of enduring importance, and the election of such men has become even less frequent.

Compared with the integrated British parliamentary elite, based on unified national culture and common educational experience, the U.S. national legislative is a much more disparate group.[51] But it would be an error to underestimate the degree of their internal cohesion. The U.S. national legislators, and especially U.S. Senators as an elite group, despite modest social backgrounds and limited cultural settings, reflect the strong influence of the socialization of the law school and on-the-job training which comes from holding elected office; 90% held some form of elected or appointed office before entering the Senate and 55% held elected office. The broadening of the base of their recruitment serves to make the political elite more heterogeneous. But one cannot escape the observation that the structural differentiation of elected political leaders has come to rest on the impact of their roles, which they perceive to be highly specialized and of strategic import. This is reinforced by their conception of themselves as distinct from other influential groups.

Political analysts have been reluctant to acknowledge the extent to which these self-conceptions are operative, but the implications for social control and the tasks of societal coordination are paramount. Harold D. Lasswell, however, has emphasized the strong and specialized motivation of political leaders, and the crucial importance of their feelings of self-esteem, even if a powerful element of reaction is at work to counter underlying feelings of inadequacy.[52] One cannot escape the fact that the political elites are people who are aware of their humble social origins and are prepared to think of themselves as men and women who are searching deliberately to make a mark on the historical record. Edward Shils, in his penetrating analysis of elected political officials, in *The Torment of Secrecy*, highlights the extent to which the low prestige and limited deference accorded to political leaders in the United States complicate and weaken the processes of

51. W. L. Guttsman, *The British Political Elite* (London: MacGibbon and Kee, 1963).

52. Harold D. Lasswell, *Power and Personality* (New York: Norton, 1948).

government and place the elected political leader in a defensive stance.[53]

The tasks of elected office are onerous and time-consuming; the successful leader requires skills and personal talent, concern for detail, and the ability to create acceptable compromise. The political sociology of the elected official encompasses those self-conceptions which drive men and women to seek to associate themselves with the "supremacy of politics" and who, in turn, are influenced in their self-construct of the tasks which they seek to perform.[54] Successful legislative elites take themselves seriously—rightly so, because the roles they perform are unique. The serious student of the national legislative process notes, along with the petty vanities that emerge, that there is an awesome sense of history which pervades their deliberations and actions. In their own language, they are deeply conscious of the institutional disarticulation of an advanced industrial society and of the barriers which they face in seeking to implement directed socioeconomic change.

Aggregation of Political Power

The outcome of the structural differentiation of the political elites and the heterogeneity of their recruitment was not predetermined. At least hypothetically, bureaucratically organized political parties might have come into being.[55] Of course, there is no guarantee that such political parties would have served as more effective coordinating agencies of the disarticulated institutional sectors of society. However, political research has highlighted the decline, or at least attenuation, of the political parties; such analysis generally points to the resulting

53. Edward Shils, *Torment of Secrecy: The Background and Consequences of American Security Policies* (Glencoe, Ill.: Free Press, 1956).

54. There is a small but growing body of empirical literature which explores and documents the specialized self-concepts of legislative elites, for example, Allan Kornberg and Norman Thomas, "Representative Democracy and Political Elites in Canada and the United States," *Parliamentary Affairs* 19 (1965–1966): 91–102; Joel Smith and Allan Kornberg, "Self-Concepts of American and Canadian Party Officials: Their Development and Consequences," *Social Forces* 49 (December 1970): 1–17; John W. Kingdon, *Congressmen's Voting Decisions* (New York: Harper and Row, 1973); T. V. Smith, *The Legislative Way of Life* (Chicago: University of Chicago Press, 1940); Robert Presthus, *Elites in the Policy Process* (Cambridge: Cambridge University Press, 1974).

55. Maurice Duverger, *Political Parties: Their Organization and Activity in the Modern State* (New York: Wiley, 1951).

difficulties in achieving effective political decisions.[56] This trend of party decline should not be overstated. It actually deals with the fate of the big city "machine," and does not necessarily encompass the history of wide segments of the electorate. However, despite the diffuse structure of large parts of local and state politics, there has been a trend to more elaborated and more bureaucratic political organizations at the national level.

Since the 1950s the big city political organizations have progressively lost their organizational effectiveness. It must be emphasized that these machines were devices of the older Eastern and Midwestern cities. But with the growth of suburbs and especially the expansion of Western and Southwestern urban centers, an extensive percentage of the population found themselves in areas which never experienced the relatively structured political machines.

Starting with the classic study of Harold Gosnell, the literature has shown considerable agreement in accounting for the rise of the political machine and for its decline.[57] In essence, the political machine rested on an admixture of patronage, service, political program, and "nationalistic" ideology. It served a population of limited education —wave after wave of immigrants and migrants and their immediate descendants. Political leaders built their organization on the patronage posts over which they had control. They rendered a series of services to their constituents, from helping to obtain employment to facilitating access to the agencies of government to providing limited, informal welfare. But the big city machine became the political device for aggregating the coalition on which the New Deal was built and the welfare state begun. The political machine also played the ideological theme of legitimizing ethnic identification and simultaneously developing the positive aspects of acculturation.

Since 1950, the decline in the machine has been explained by higher levels of education and political sophistication in the electorate, by the emergence of the welfare state which has weakened the dependency

56. E. E. Schattsneider, *The Semi-Sovereign People* (New York: Holt, Rinehart and Winston, 1960); Samuel J. Eldersveld, *Political Parties: A Behavioral Analysis* (Chicago: Rand McNally, 1964); Everett C. Ladd, Jr., with Charles D. Hadley, *Transformations of the American Party System; Political Coalitions from the New Deal to the 1970's* (New York: Norton, 1975); Gerald M. Pomper, "The Decline of the Party in American Elections," *Political Science Quarterly* 92 (1977): 21–42.

57. Gosnell, *Machine Politics.*

of the citizen on the "favors" rendered by the political organization, and by the extension of civil service reform which has undermined the patronage system.[58] But each of these explanations requires amplification. First, no doubt higher levels of literacy and political awareness have undermined attachments to the "regular" party organization. But even among low-status groups, there has been a growth, if not of opposition, more certainly of indifference. The machine finds it more and more difficult to generate the overwhelming pluralities required to offset the suburban vote. The decline in the population concentration of central city compared with the suburbs compounds the decline of the "regular" organization.[59]

Second, there is little evidence that local political leaders in the central city or in the suburbs render fewer services to their voters. On the contrary, the amount of time and effort they expend in assisting their constituents has increased. They have larger staffs. The demands of citizens for assistance in obtaining public services and benefits grow partly because their variety has increased and partly because voters are more articulate in making demands. The growth of the welfare state also means that citizens are more likely to approach their elected officials for assistance in obtaining these expanded services and benefits; and because of the inefficiency of the welfare bureaucracies, more and more assistance is required.

The real and profound change has been in the local residents' self-conceptions—in their ideas about the rights and privileges of a voter and a citizen. The services rendered by elected officials are no longer thought of as favors or special benefits, but the just rights of a resident. To receive them places the person and his household under no special obligation to the official. In a study of the scope and consequences of the services rendered by a typical Chicago ward organization, Thomas Guterbock found that the recipients felt no particular loyalty or obligation to the elected official and his staff because of the

58. James Q. Wilson, *The Amateur Democrat* (Chicago: University of Chicago Press, 1962).

59. The effect of reform politics, especially the introduction of nonpartisan elections, has been statistically examined. The results show a measure of decline in responsiveness of elected officials. See Raymond Wolfinger and John Osgood Field, "Political Ethos and the Structure of City Government," *American Political Science Review* 60 (June 1966): 306–26; Robert L. Lineberry and Edmund P. Fowler, "Reformism and Public Policies in American Cities," *American Political Science Review* 61 (September 1967): 701–16; Willis D. Hawley, *Nonpartisan Elections and the Case for Party Polities* (New York: Wiley, 1974).

specific services they obtained.[60] Moreover, these services have very little influence on their voting behavior. His data were not based on retrospective recollection but consisted of ongoing observation and analysis of appropriate records.

Third, there can be no doubt that the decline of patronage has had effects on party organization. It must be remembered that many of the jobs available under patronage managements have lost their attraction to energetic and better educated persons. More central, throughout the United States, civil service procedures have reduced and eroded the scope of patronage appointments. (At the policy level, a trend in the reverse direction can be noted.) A city such as Chicago and a county such as Cook, which still had over 20,000 patronage appointments in 1976 are unique. Under the patronage system, the ward boss and city or county leaders had control over each patronage job and who would fill it. Patronage appointments gave the political apparatus extensive control over city and county employees.

Along with the decline of patronage, there has been a growth in public service unionism of municipal and county workers.[61] In fact, this growth of public service unionism as much as civil service reform weakened the regular organization. The public services unions have come to encompass municipal and county agencies that formerly contained patronage workers, for example, sanitation workers, police, and firemen. In addition, public service unions have developed in agencies which were not dominated by patronage workers, for example, local school systems and welfare and health agencies.

These unions have become powerful pressure groups which are able to limit the influence and political power of the regular political parties.[62] In the past the regular organization controlled or at least strongly influenced the manpower system of municipal and county employment through the patronage system. The rise of the public service union has altered the political balance. Public service unions have emerged as independent power centers which are able to negotiate with elected

60. Thomas Guterbock, "Favors and Votes: The Service Activities of a Local Patronage Party Organization," Ph. D. dissertation, University of Chicago, 1976.

61. David H. Rosenbloom, *Federal Service and the Constitution: The Development of the Public Employment Relationship* (Ithaca, N.Y.: Cornell University Press, 1971).

62. Harmon L. Zeigler and Wayne G. Peak, *Interest Groups in American Society* (Englewood Cliffs, N.J.: Prentice-Hall, 1972).

officials and local political leaders. The political parties have had to respond more and more to the pressure of these public service unions. These unions influence the selection of candidates and work as relatively independent agents in turning out the vote for local candidates.

The guidelines for labor negotiations have been weak and diffuse, reflecting the limits in the power of the local elected officials. Moreover, public service officials increasingly have been able to deal directly with state and Congressional leaders, again weakening the position of local political leaders. In other words, whereas the old machines enforced a measure of coherence on the structure of local government, at the price of inefficiency and corruption, the public service unions have contributed to the disarticulation of local government and weakened the ability of local political leaders to govern. Only with the threat of financial disaster and the intervention of the federal government signaled by the fiscal crisis in New York City has a new political balance started to emerge based on a more integrated management and stronger control of competing demands from public service unions.

With the decline of the old-fashioned machine, there is some convergence between the party organization of the central cities and that of suburban areas. However, in the central city, political organization remains more structured. The logic of a more inclusive governmental unit with highly visible boundaries and political subdivisions contributes to a more explicit hierarchical organization than does the diverse, fragmented political unit of the suburban areas. Because of larger population concentrations, more articulate residents, and greater economic resources, the suburban areas are more extensively characterized by individual and personalistic political entrepreneurs, as described below.

The attenuation of municipal political organization and the persistence of diffuse and personalistic political activity in suburban areas have been accompanied by the countertrend of the growth of a more structured national party organization. The diffuse pattern of local and state organization almost requires a national framework. The national organization for both the Republican and the Democratic parties rests in the Washington locale and is not based on a structured, intervening, middle level of organization.

The national organization of the party is a response to the national media, and the need to present a national image and to select a presidential candidate. It developed because funds can be raised on a national basis. The need to supply political documentation leads to large national staffs. The national organizations are required to establish standards for judging the representativeness of the delegates to national conventions and to implement these standards. Even more important, the national party apparatus reflects the growth of formal and informal caucuses and policy-formation groups of Senators and Representatives. These groups involve less the initiative of a limited number of key figures and more the interactions and aspirations of a sizable number of younger and newly elected national legislators.

Although American political leaders are professionals, they are not part of a bureaucratic party with strong internal discipline, as is the case with particular political parties in Western Europe. During the period of the big city machines, which was accompanied by a limited number of strong state organizations, there were at least a cadre of conspicuous political leaders who supplied the party leaders. The results of national conventions underline that the dominance of these favorite sons has been constricted as power within the parties has become more and more dispersed.

It is possible to speak of the constituent leaders of both parties' organizations as cadres of relatively "independent" professionals. They are groups of men and women who enter and leave politics, who succeed or lose to an important extent on the basis of their personal efforts and the staffs which they are able to mobilize. Even the candidates for the presidential nomination are persons who selected themselves and conduct their own campaigns to achieve the nomination rather than loyal party officials who are selected by the inner figures of a stable and cohesive hierarchy.

This type of party organization in the United States reflects the social stratification of an advanced industrial society and the normative values which stress populism and egalitarianism. It is difficult to explain why the degree of differentiation of the political elites from the economic elites has not led to more stable and more bureaucratically organized parties. Thus, the party organization in the United States has evolved into a highly complex but diffuse organization, deeply penetrated by particular interest- and pressure-group organizations.

In addition, new organizational technology has contributed decisively to the maintenance of personalized party political candidates. The person who seeks political office at all levels is less dependent on a bureaucratically organized political party for the election tasks which have to be performed. Instead, the individual candidate can mobilize finances and employ personnel which give him important autonomy and latitude. To a considerable degree this is a reflection of the increased influence of the mass media, as described in chapter 9, on the outcome of political campaigns. The candidate can employ public relations agents to assist in managing his relations with the mass media.[63] He can make extensive use of public opinion research specialists to report on the attitudes of his constituents. This procedure makes him much less dependent on party organization and party workers as sources of information about citizen attitudes and aspirations. Second, the candidate can employ specialized organizations which will assemble voter lists and conduct voter registration and political canvasses. The introduction of computerized technology has displaced—for better or for worse—the precinct worker's notebook and hard card. Then, the candidate can rely on personnel supplied to him by pressure groups, and in particular, if he is in the Democratic party, local trade union officials and their staffs serve as election workers.[64] The candidate can also mobilize volunteers, people with special interests, with broad ideological perspectives, or those who are seeking to test their interest in a political career. These types of local political workers are more effective and more reliable than the "conventional" patronage worker. They are clearly better able to communicate with the more informed parts of the electorate, and in fact wide groups of the population are not accessible to the "typical" patronage precinct worker.

The struggle to influence voters is not limited to the marginal and relatively uninterested citizen. As indicated in chapter 4, the independent voters include well-educated and politically interested people who are distrustful of party organization and who are faced with the continuous process of making candidate choices. In the conduct of campaigns—from the national elections to local elections—political lead-

63. Stanley Kelly, Jr., *Professional Public Relations and Political Power* (Baltimore, Md.: Johns Hopkins University Press, 1956); Dan Nimmo, *The Political Persuaders: Techniques of Modern Election Campaigns* (Englewood Cliffs, N.J.: Prentice-Hall, 1970); Robert Agranoff, *The New Style in Election Campaigns* (Boston: Holbrook Press, 1976). See also Thomas E. Patterson and Robert D. McClure, *Political Advertising* (Princeton, N.J.: Citizens Research Foundation, 1973).

64. J. David Greenstone, *Labor in American Politics* (New York: Knopf, 1969).

ers rely extensively and continually on periodic sample surveys because past experience is not a sufficient guide. The polls are designed to anticipate the outcome of the election and to guide the candidate and his personal staff in selecting themes which they will emphasize to help him fashion his personal image.

Since the development of political surveys in the 1930s, the record of this methodology in predicting the outcome of elections is indeed striking, particularly since there has been increasing difficulty in obtaining representative samples, in estimating the size of the turnout, and in coding the responses of undecided citizens. However, it appears that the interview situation generated by the standardized sample surveys does produce a set of responses which are closely linked to the actual electoral behavior. The ability of the standardized survey to probe candidate imagery and issue salience is much less revealing and more problematic.

Political candidates who have to assemble a coalition to create a majority have come to rely extensively on sample surveys to guide their campaigns. The standard approach is for the candidate to enter into a contractual relation with a commercial polling agency; the agency not only collects the information but also makes recommendations for campaign strategy. Often the candidate has a member of his staff who follows the published public opinion surveys and seeks out academic advice about trends in public opinion. Legislators frequently conduct their own mail questionnaire surveys, both to acquire information and to make the symbolic gesture of consulting their constituents.

Reliance on public opinion surveys has immediate short-term as well as long-term consequences.[65] Opinion polls influence the morale of candidates and their staff. The findings of surveys condition the decision to enter or not to enter a campaign.[66] Surveys influence the level and intensity of campaign activity, in particular the ability of candidates to raise funds. Financial backers are reluctant to underwrite candidates who appear to be doomed to defeat, while the challenging candidate who is moving to narrow the gap between himself and the incumbent is favored with financial assistance. One of the dramatic

65. Mark Abrams, "Political Parties and the Polls," in *The Uses of Sociology*, ed. Paul F. Lazarsfeld, William H. Sewell, and Harold L. Wilensky (New York: Basic Books, 1967), pp. 427–34.

66. Abrams, ibid.

examples of the negative influence of political surveys on staff morale and to some extent on the candidate himself was seen in the early days of Senator Hubert Humphrey's campaign for the presidency in 1968.[67]

The more general observation is that sample surveys contribute to an increased emphasis on the imagery and rhetorical style of the political candidate rather than substantive content. Obviously, the basic transformation of the social and political process which makes it more difficult for both the candidate and the voters to aggregate self-interest is at work. But the findings of the survey methods reveal weaknessess in the imagery of the candidate which he comes to believe he should be able to overcome. In turn, he tends to emphasize the positive elements of his image. However, the findings about substantive issues are more problematic. It is difficult to conclude clearly from surveys which issues are likely to mobilize more voters and, in particular, which combination of issues can be appropriately fused. Nevertheless, a democratic polity rests on effective feedback mechanisms between voters and candidates. The ongoing flow of information generated by surveys has considerable relevance for candidates in that they overcome the distortions created by the intrusion of professional lobbyists. But surveys contribute to a dampening of innovative leadership and risk taking as well as undermine the candidates' own political connections.

Public opinion polls focus the interest of the candidate on the problems and issues of getting elected, rather than creating the conditions for effective exercise of political power after assuming office. There is little concern with long-term trends; there is little concern with the consequences on the election of the attitudes of the electorate, and the extent to which the election operates as a mechanism for conflict resolution and for the strengthening or weakening political consent and consensus. No doubt these are issues which can best be probed by academic studies in depth. But the academic specialist in electoral analysis who uses survey data seems to converge with political candidates in their interest; the question is who voted for whom and on the basis of what issues.

The accumulated mass of survey data tend to present a model of self-interested voters, responding to economic issues—which are of

67. Leo Bogart, *Silent Politics: Polls and the Awareness of Public Opinion* (New York: Wiley, 1972), pp. 33–45.

course paramount—but without adequate exploration and assessment of normative values and the basic aspirations of the electorate. The systemic character of the electoral process and the realities and potentials of conflict resolution are thereby obscured. The contribution of these research procedures to effective institution building of social control are limited or incomplete and even disruptive.

The vigor and toughness in the political process are in the personal energies of the active contending candidates. The underlying social structure and the diffuse party organization require most candidates to assemble a majority coalition which reflects the immediate sociopolitical circumstances. The blocs of traditional voters are present but no longer to be taken for granted. The candidate must influence or at least convince the independents of his legitimacy. It is a process which must be reaffirmed for each election. One of the results of the volatility of the electorate has been the effort of the commercial opinion specialists to search for new bases of coalitions. Perhaps the most ambitious effort was by Kevin Phillips in 1969, which reflected the strategy of the 1968 Republican campaign and had an important influence on the Republican strategy in the elections of 1972 and 1976.[68] It was a search for a new "conservative" majority. On the Democratic side, Patrick Cadell sought to modify the traditional New Deal coalition. His campaign analysis likewise sought to infuse a conservative component into the traditional Democratic coalition and contributed to the outcome of the 1976 election.[69]

While there is a strong element of realism in these writings, they fail to contribute to a more effective electoral process in their exclusive concern with marginal and short-term advantage; they deal more with "getting elected" than with governing when in power.

In addition to political persuasion, the aggregation of political power involves chronic elements of corruption, intimidation, and conspiratorial behavior. These tactics not only influence the outcome of the electoral process and produce ineffective administration, they also con-

68. Kevin Phillips, *The Emerging Republican Majority* (New Rochelle, N.Y.: Arlington, 1969).

69. Patrick Cadell in the 1976 presidential campaign was a key adviser to Carter. He prepared a memorandum, "Initial Working Paper on Political Strategy," which received extensive publicity after the election. It contains a collection of sociological references to the "massive demographic changes" which were at work in the electorate—which hardly indicated specific lines of political strategy. However, he did accurately underline the volatility of the electorate and the necessity of creating a specific majority for the specific election.

strict the recruitment of dedicated leaders and weaken the confidence of the citizen in the orderly process of government. The extent of outright fraud in the conduct of election is difficult to estimate. By "outright fraud" I mean falsification of the results or distortion of the procedures to obtain an electoral majority. Although such procedures undoubtedly continue, they have become of marginal consequence. The payoff from outright fraud is so limited that old-fashioned machines have come to spend more time and energy in mobilizing their followers than in perverting the electoral process. The line between fraud and intimidation is a vague one and involves reliance on threats to influence the outcome of an election. Intimidation has declined, although it continues in some inner-city areas and in remote enclaves in the South.

Corruption is much more widespread and is a serious threat to effective election and political campaigns.[70] Corruption means the use of money and material advantage for illegal purposes. It is usually used to influence the behavior of officials after they are elected. However, it involves the use of illegally and criminally obtained funds to influence the selection of candidates and to underwrite political campaigns. In metropolitan areas, syndicate money is important in election campaigns, thus influencing certain officials, to weakening and undermining the legitimate function of party organizations. There is no reason to assert that the amount of such corruption has declined; there is some effort on the part of those involved to be more circumspect in their tactics, but corruption in political life is persistent. The fact that these practices have been of long standing is hardly a basis for reassurance.

The long-standing practices of political corruption have been augmented by covert and conspiratorial behavior which has a disturbing consequence for democratic political practices. Political leaders have traditionally sought to collect information about their opponents in order to assist their campaigns. At times, these efforts have bordered on or were actually illegal or clearly unethical. But since the end of World War II, two trends have developed which greatly increased the scope and disruptive implications of such tactics. First, the investigative agencies of government have expanded and have been used to

70. As a baseline for comparing corrupt political practices over time see V. O. Key, Jr., "The Techniques of Political Graft in the United States," Ph.D. dissertation, University of Chicago, 1934.

collect a variety of personal and political intelligence which clearly violates citizens' privacy. At times such materials have been used by political leaders for personal advantage and as a basis for intimidation.[71] Second, the strategy of covert operations generated in the "Cold War" has come on rare occasion to be used by political parties, and these procedures culminated in Watergate. These procedures involve the use of undercover agents to disrupt opposing political groups, the preparation of "black" propaganda, the use of illegal funds, and threat of blackmail.[72] Most such covert operations are of little political impact, except, of course, to undermine ethical standards and create public confusion and distrust of the political process and the machinery of government when such procedures are exposed in the mass media.

Strategies of Political Reconstruction

The academic specialists concerned with electoral politics have contributed to the formulation and adoption of a wide range of legislative enactments and judicial decisions designed to improve political campaigns, election procedures, and the operation of the national legislature. These have dealt with *(a)* the redistricting of electoral units, *(b)* extensive federal support for voter registration, *(c)* increased regulation of campaign expenditures, *(d)* the development of ethical codes of legislative conduct, and *(e)* the politicalization of the civil service. These "reforms," with the exception of federal support for voter registration, have obviously not had dramatic or profound consequences, although a case can be made that the political process would have been more strained without *(a)*, *(c)*, and *(d)*.

It is very difficult to assess the effect of these measures, especially since it is much simpler to make recommendations about recasting electoral politics than to engage in detailed research on their outcomes. The basic goal of these recommendations has been to improve political competition, that is, to make political campaigns and the legislative process more competitive. The central idea has been to increase the amount of participation and to strive for more equal participation and representation throughout the social structure. On the basis of the

71. Alan F. Weston, *Information Technology in a Democracy* (Cambridge: Harvard University Press, 1970). The growth of the technology for collecting, storing, and retrieving information makes possible increased opportunities for assemblying data of relevance in political contests.

72. Gary T. Marx, "Thoughts on a Neglected Category of Social Movement Participants: The Agent Provocateur and the Informant," *American Journal of Sociology* 80 (September 1974): 402–42.

available research and inference guided by a systemic overview of elections, two observations are reasonable. The emphasis on increased and intensified electoral competitions has produced no evidence of improved quality and more effective consequences of elections. The major persistent trend on these innovations has been to disperse political power and to continue to weaken the political parties.

First, to achieve the formula of one person, one vote, the Supreme Court has facilitated and required drastic redistricting, and in fact this has led to repeated redistricting.[73] The essential objective was to eliminate gerrymandering and grossly unequal election districts. However, as indicated in chapter 12, because of constant population shifts, there have been repeated boundary changes, which disrupts party organization and attenuates citizen identification with party organization. On balance, these essential electoral reforms by means of court-ordered redistricting have added to the dilemmas of political party organization.

Second, the massive voter registration drives have increased the political participation essential for the legitimacy of elections. Great progress has been made under the civil rights legislation; the special relevance of these efforts are that they have increased voting by black and other minority groups, groups which had to be integrated more effectively into the political process in particular areas. This expansion of the electorate is based on weakened literacy requirements. There is a point at which uninformed voting becomes a contrived form of political participation. In addition, the United States is a nation of high residential mobility, and residence requirements can be artificial barriers to electoral participation. Thus there has been considerable agitation to reduce residence requirements in order to increase political participation. But there are minimum limits required for involvement in and understanding of local political issues. The same length of residence is required for participation in national, state, and local elections, when in effect a case could be made for differential requirements, especially for shorter ones for participation in presidential elections.

Third, efforts to regulate campaign expenditures have included public disclosure procedures, legal limits on expenditure, and, in time, allocation of federal tax funds for political campaigns. These proce-

73. Robert G. Dixon, Jr., *Democratic Representatives: Reapportionment in Law and Politics* (New York: Oxford University Press, 1968) presents a detailed legal history of judicially inspired reapportionment.

dures are complex and it is difficult to assess their immediate and long-term effects.[74] It has been argued that these procedures assist the incumbent and the Democratic party, because it has had more incumbents during the period of growth of federal regulation of campaign funds. This observation has an element of plausibility but little supporting evidence. However, there is more reason to conclude that the reforms in campaign funding have weakened the political parties.

Public disclosure of campaign funds has been of limited consequence, although it does supply important information to candidates, political activists, and journalists. Much of the presentation of these data in the mass media highlights corruption or devious practices without clarifying the real problems of controlling campaign finances. Limitations on campaign expenditures have served to contain the escalation of the costs of political campaigns, although there are a variety of devices for increasing expenditures beyond the legal limits. However, the essential consequence of the controls appears to have been to limit the capacity of political parties to raise funds, compared to the capacity of individual candidates. The spirit and ethos generated by the legislation have stimulated contributions to candidates at the expense of contributions to party organizations.

In addition, the federal legislation has been important in terms of the balance of contributions from business corporations and labor unions. Over the short run and especially in the 1976 election, labor unions have been much more active in contributing funds directly or in encouraging their members to contribute than have been corporations. The inherent advantage of the Republican party with its affiliation with big business and wealthy donors has been to a noticeable extent neutralized.

Finally, the federal contribution to the Presidential nomination and election campaigns of 1976 represents a basic transformation in electoral procedures. Again, it does appear to have limited the escalation of campaign expenditures and created a greater balance in available resources between the two major competing candidates. Of course, there has been considerable criticism from political analysts about the equity and whether one candidate versus another emerged with an advantage. However, the more basic question is whether the reformed system will contribute to an increased ability of the president to avoid

74. David W. Adamany, "Financing National Politics," in Agranoff, *New Style*, pp. 379–414; Herbert E. Alexander, "Campaign Finance Reform: What's Happening in the Individual States?" in ibid., pp. 415–23.

excessive reliance on pressure groups. This question remains essentially unanswered.

Fourth, one must also mention the efforts to strengthen legislation and create codes dealing with ethical behavior and conflict of interest for elected representatives. The trend has not been to encourage stronger self-policing by the political parties of their own candidates and elected officials, but rather to subject the individual legislator to elaborate external controls and restraints.

The pressure for more ethical behavior has increased the scope of review of income tax auditing by the Internal Revenue Service, passed more explicit legislation dealing with conflict of interest and extra earnings, and written codes of ethical behavior and forms of disclosure of personal income. While the resulting positive results appear limited, there is good reason to believe that these additional burdens of public office and the need to expose one's personal behavior have deterred many a "good" person from seeking public office.

Finally, electoral innovation has led to increased politicalization of the civil service both by increasing the number of political appointments to top federal executive posts and by eliminating restrictions on direct participation of rank-and-file civil servants in partisan elections. Since 1952, both parties have wanted to increase the number of political party appointments that could be made at the highest level of government.[75]

The case for an enlarged number of political appointments to the highest posts has been argued by academic experts in order to make it possible for the elected president to implement his goals. It is an effort to develop a stronger political regime. The filling of these posts is the result not of political party decisions but mainly of the intervention of the office of the president and of his key supporters. By 1972, it was estimated that a newly elected president had between two and three thousand policy posts to be filled. The transition process and the "transition team" from one administration to the next have not faced a rewarding task of appointing a number of dedicated and skilled personnel to assist the new president achieve his goals. Instead, the transition tasks have been frustrating and most difficult to implement. Powerful rivalries are at work and immense dissatisfactions re-

75. For a study of the top career civil servants in the U.S. government, see John J. Corson and R. Sahle Paul, *Men Near the Top: Filling Key Posts in the Federal Service* (Baltimore, Md.: Johns Hopkins University Press, 1966).

sult. It is very difficult to recruit proficient personnel; in particular, it is very cumbersome to relate the appointment process to state, metropolitan, and local party organization. There is little evidence that the procedure strengthens party organization.

The converse aspect to the top political appointments by the office of the president is the political activity of middle- and lower-level civil service personnel. The long-term trend since the introduction of civil service reform after 1920 has been to remove civil service appointments from political patronage and to recruit, retain, and promote on the basis of training, qualification, and demonstrated skill. The "depoliticalization" process was sought not only to increase agency efficiency but also to make the political parties more subject to citizen control.

It was inevitable that a reaction would develop to this trend. Wide groups of the civil service developed excessive rigidities and bureaucratic procedures without being responsive to public requirements. However, the countertrend has not resulted in steps to improve the administrative effectiveness of the civil service. Instead, particular academic critics have emphasized the need to ensure civil service employees the political rights of other citizens without regard to their special position. Their solution to the problems of a responsible civil service has been to increase the political participation of public employees. These academic specialists supported the trade unions claim that increased political participation is a generic right of civil servants and a device for increasing the effectiveness of the political process. Thus the Hatch Act, which was passed to weaken patronage and to depoliticalize the civil service, was itself weakened by legislation passed in 1976. Federal employees at all levels could be active in partisan politics. It can be anticipated that the consequence will not primarily be a return to the patronage system, although this will take place for unskilled posts. Instead, the legislation will make the civil service into an even more effective pressure group and further fragment the control of the governmental agencies by elected officials.

The consequences of this series of legislative and judicial steps cannot readily be separated from the long-term changes in the institutional structure of Congress and in the relation of Congress to the office of the President. Within Congress there has been a trend toward greater dispersion of power, paralleling the dispersion of power in the larger society and in the electoral process. This trend has not necessarily improved performance and effectiveness. Likewise, since 1960, it is necessary to take into account the increased political and legislative initiatives of Congress vis-à-vis the presidency.

The basic literature on the structure and internal dynamics of Congress deals mainly with the 1950s and early 1960s and does not sufficiently take into account the subsequent period of increased internal "democratization."[76] Nevertheless, one can point to a number of trends which reflect the greater rank-and-file participation resulting from individual political initiatives and from legislative reorganization.

There have been clear signs of a decline in the importance of rigid seniority in allocating committee assignments. Expertise, political competence, and the political strength of the legislator have been more and more taken into consideration.[77] The committee system continues to dominate the flow and passage of legislation, but the rules and procedures of committee work show some increased flexibility and adaptation. Then, there has been a growth of important floor fights which reflect the wider participation of rank-and-file legislators and the necessity for members of Congress to respond to the pressures of their electorate. Also, the increased importance of the personal political entrepreneur has been accompanied by a growth of importance of party caucuses in the Congress. These party caucuses indicate the limit of the influence of the formal leader in the national legislature and the increased necessity of consultation in the building of coalitions.

In addition, an outcome of the increased dispersion of political power has been the increased turnover of elected personnel in both the Senate and the House of Representatives.[78] Incumbents have a strong advantage in elections, although there is some evidence that reelection of incumbents does not take into account increased voluntary withdrawals. The reluctance of men and women to stand for reelection, even in safe districts, results from the day-to-day frustra-

76. Lewis Anthony Dexter, *The Sociology and Politics of Congress* (Chicago: Rand McNally, 1969). See also Robert L. Peabody and Nelson W. Polsby, *New Perspectives on the House of Representatives* (Chicago: Rand McNally, 1963); Lewis Froman, *The Congressional Process; Strategies, Rules and Procedures* (Boston: Little, Brown, 1967); Ralph Huitt and Robert L. Peabody, *Congress: Two Decades of Analysis* (New York: Harper and Row, 1969); Norman J. Ornstein, ed., *Congress in Change: Evolution and Reform* (New York: Praeger, 1975).

77. Nelson W. Polsby, "Goodbye to the Senate's Inner Club," in Ornstein, *Congress*, pp. 203–16.

78. Morris P. Fiorina, David W. Rohde, and Peter Wissel, "Historical Change in House Turnover," in Ornstein, *Congress, Change: Evolution and Reform*, pp. 24–50.

tions, the decline in trust and confidence, and the increased work load.[79] Loss of the "gentlemen's club" atmosphere and the relaxed style of life in the national legislature is obvious. The introduction of a generous pension system has also facilitated the turnover rate in the Congress. However, seniority counts for less in the new Congress and this contributes to higher turnover. Resignation and retirement have shown an upward trend; they reached a high in 1976 when fifty withdrew from the House of Representatives, twenty-six of those withdrawing left public life. In the Senate, eight withdrew and all left public life. Thus, from an overall point of view, the relative dispersion of power in both houses of Congress means that the passage of many pieces of legislation involves to a greater extent conscious and elaborate efforts at coalition building; the party leaders can take their fellow legislators less for granted.

In this complex process, one is struck by the increase of areas in which Congress has expanded its legislative leadership vis-à-vis the President. Observers have noted, especially after the withdrawal of U.S. military forces from Vietnam, that Congress has intervened more directly in the details of the military budget and increased its deliberations and actions in foreign policy, ranging from the enactment of revised presidential war power to fashioning specific foreign negotiations, as in the case of Greek-Turkish relations.

In the arena of domestic decisions, the Congress has continued to display wide and extensive initiative, much more than in foreign affairs. Moreover the trend is in the same direction of exercising greater power vis-à-vis the President. The President's power is in shaping the general direction of legislation and in making overall budget recommendations. Likewise, in the name of reducing expenditures, the President selectively asserts his dominance, as for example President Carter did with his successful decision to reduce the public works budget, an area which has been the traditional preserve of the Congress. However, both the Nixon and the Carter administrations have been confronted by the ability of the Congress to "block" or to alter fundamentally legislation which the President considers crucial; welfare reform for Nixon and energy legislation for Carter.

Congressional power has been immense and conspicuous in taxation policy and in economic affairs such as minimum wages. Also Congress

79. "Why So Many Congressmen Are Calling It Quits," *Nation's Business* 64 (June 1976): 21–26.

has been prone to press for and often to succeed in obtaining higher levels of expenditure for welfare, education, and medical care. The split between the President and Congress reflects the chronic dilemmas in the fiscal management of the welfare state under weak political regimes and limited legislative majorities. The dispersion of political influence involves the increased policy differences between the Senate and the House of Representatives and the strong and long struggles to resolve their outstanding difference, for example, the half-year debate in 1977 between the House and the Senate on the issue of the use of federal funds for abortion.[80]

Likewise, the national presidential conventions of both parties present striking examples of the dispersion and discontinuity of power, but with a simultaneous decline of function. The increase in representation of women and minority groups has meant an influx of new and relatively unknown local leaders. Then, overall turnover of delegates remains high and in some groups has increased as party leaders become less able to determine the composition of state delegations. In addition, the political power of favorite sons has decreased as they are less able to control their delegates, who have developed their own candidate preference or are strongly committed to particular positions. Fragmented state delegations have become more typical and are an indication of the more complex social structure and the penetration of personalized political leaders.

These political trends have meant that the importance of the national convention in selecting candidates has sharply declined since 1952. The march toward the presidential nomination and the office of president has in effect been removed from the convention. As Gerald M. Pomper has emphasized, "no convention since 1952 has taken more than a single ballot to nominate its presidential candidate."[81] In essence, with the exception of the 1976 Republican convention, the presidential nomination has been determined before the convention. Increase in political participation and the dispersion of power in decision making do not automatically produce anticipated or desired results or necessarily improve the level of performance of the elected officials.

80. The more activist record of the Congress is supported by a marked increase in staff and operating expenditures. The cost of administering the Congress for 1960 was $131.8 million as reported by the *Congressional Quarterly* 18 (June 24, 1960): 1085; by 1977 the figure stood at $747.0 million, *Congressional Quarterly* 33 (July 26, 1975): 1625.

81. Pomper, "Decline," p. 31.

Throughout our analysis the dispersion of political power has been seen as the outcome of the social structure of an advanced industrial society and its institutional disarticulation, especially the increasing separation of the industrial and service hierarchies from the residential communities. The organization and practice of the political parties have in turn contributed to power dispersion. In addition, from the point of view of institution building, the outlook and behavior of the professional political leaders and the informed citizenry are observably influenced by the dissemination of social-science research on the political process. I must conclude that the rapid expansion of research since 1945 has not had a significant positive consequence on the electoral process and the associated political institutions to enhance effective social control.

If one wishes to argue on a point-by-point basis that there have been "helpful" contributions from political research in areas such as redistricting, the control of campaign expenditures, and the fashioning of ethical codes, then these contributions need to be matched by the negative influence of intensified candidate rivalry based on personal imagery which is a by-product of the heavy reliance on survey research. However, in broad systemic terms, it is plausible and reasonable to conclude that the consequences of research into political institutions has been to support and encourage the trend toward the dispersion of political power. In part this is the result of the use of economic models of competition to analyze politics which highlight the importance of increased lack of political and electoral participation and which are not necessarily oriented toward enhancing the deliberative content and quality of partisan elections. But more fundamentally, individualist and nationalist perspectives divert attention from the norms and patterns of authority found in political institutions which contribute to the resolution of political conflict. The consequence is both an ideological and practical contribution to the dispersion of political influence, since political organs are seen as merely another competing vested interest rather than as an essential coordinating mechanisms.

But increased participation and intensified pursuit of economic self-interest must be translated into the aggregation of new coalitions and to more effective deliberative processes if conflicts are to be resolved. Political leaders are continually engaged—generally unsuccessfully—in seeking to overcome the dispersion of political power. Again, because the political process has come to be extensively described as an analog to the economic marketplace, the outcome obscures, in my judgment, realistic analysis of coalition building for conflict resolution and the reduction of institutional disarticulation.

In contrast, it is striking that the historic and classic observation that electoral systems are strengthened by citizen participation in localistic associations has provided one of the most productive and most realistic points of reference for contemporary research into the political process. The analysis of community organization (chapter 12) emphasizes that increased separation of work and residence does not destroy but transforms and specializes local voluntary associations which have a geographical base. It is true that localistic organizations have shifted from but not abandoned self-help goals for a stronger emphasis on group representation, especially for obtaining services from the local government and the welfare state. These organizations become sustained points of contact with the elected political leaders and administrators of public agencies and institutions. One cannot escape the further overriding conclusion that the elaborated complex and networks of voluntary associations supply a matrix by which the weakness of party organization is contained, if not corrected.

At this juncture I must return to the premises with which I began if the overall consequences of "economic" model of politics are to be highlighted. The political "problem" of an advanced industrial society in systemic terms is that the periodic elections neither supply an adequate basis for clarifying citizen self-interest nor produce decisive political majorities for authoritative and consistent legislative decisions required for more effective social control. But the political parties and the electoral system remain the proximate and immediate instruments to achieve these goals. This is the meaning of the phrase "the supremacy of politics." These goals cannot be achieved by the mechanisms of the marketplace alone, or by analogy to the marketplace, although a workable marketplace is a precondition.

The pursuit of more effective social control involves every aspect of "man and society" to which higher moral principles can be applied. The intellectual aspects of institution building, including the conclusions of social research, have emphasized the expansion and especially the improvement of citizen participation outside the electoral system. In short, there is a nexus where the institutional analysis of politics converges with the assessment of social personality and the investigation of community organization. The ordering of socioeconomic priorities in the microsettings of the residential community is a viable and essential contribution to conflict resolution among macroinstitutions of the industrial and service sectors. But the whole body of research on participation—community and organization—does not lead to the conclusion that there is a priority in institution building which leads to a strategy of "working from the bottom upward." The resolution of conflict and the elaboration of social control rest as much on the conscious and deliberate initiatives of the elite leaders and groups who have strong, clear self-conceptions of the special role of the political tasks of societal coordination.

It is profoundly disappointing that the specialists in political economy and political analysis have not had more influence in strengthening political institutions and social control. Thus far, this lack has been linked to the limitations in their "theories" and their explanations of political behavior. But their failure to make more of a contribution to the reduction of the disarticulation between the institutions is a function of their procedures. It cannot be argued that they are handicapped by a lack of interest among leaders or informed citizenry; interest does not imply adequate understanding, of course.

I claim that these specialists have become excessively, disproportionately involved as partisans in the political process which they are mandated to analyze and make more understandable. Such an assertion is certain to be misunderstood. Clearly, direct contact with the political process is required for meaningful research. Certainly, political analysts have a wide variety of citizen and professional roles to perform. The academic profession concerned with political institutions requires a division of labor. But these academic experts have come to accept as dominant, the responsibility seeking to assist particular political leaders to achieve victory and to prepare the groundwork for their own involvement in appointed and advisory posts. To select the "appropriate candidate"—one who has a political future—is as important as the correct analysis of the political setting. In the pursuit of these tasks and responsibilities, the academic specialist takes on the perspective of the candidate, especially his concern with the tactics of electoral victory, at the expense of understanding and evaluating the electoral process.

Social scientists who serve particular candidates and political leaders are deprived of the opportunity to serve the citizenry as commentators and evaluators of the strength and weakness of the political system.

Within the university system there has not emerged a large enough cadre of scholars who have achieved outstanding distinction and reputation for the relevance of their academic assessments. They have not developed sufficient legitimacy that their knowledge has its fullest influence. In other words, the research specialist concerned with political institutions has been professionalized in a particular format—or, rather, has been only partially professionalized. The comparison with those social scientists concerned with interpersonal relations and with community development and organization is noteworthy, but need not be pressed too far. Of course, psychologists and psychiatrists, as well as sociologists and social workers and related professional groups, are deeply involved in the support of the immediate interests and claims of their clients. But the interplay of theory and practice, the mixture of research and policy, lead toward a larger number of persons and a more explicit concern with broad systemic responsibilities. The political adviser, the "intellectual" on the political staff, tends to reflect the model of immediate self-interest as the basis of political effectiveness—and the consequences of such a perspective, I have argued, are self-limiting in the search for effective social control.

This study has focused on parliamentary regimes and on the United States in particular. However, comparison with totalitarian and authoritarian regimes prevents distortions and encourages realism and objectivity. Social scientists have been interested in identifying the social and economic upheavals which have pushed societies with competitive elections across the political threshold into authoritarian and totalitarian forms. It is striking that no industrialized or advanced industrialized society which has gradually evolved effective parliamentary institutions has been pushed across this threshold. Of course, the danger is always present because of institutional disarticulation and the new tension of stagflation. However, the prospect is that a decisive movement in this direction may result not from an outburst of a "revolutionary" sociopolitical movement and the seizure of national power but from a gradual distortion of the electoral process and electoral choice.

Fourteen

Epilogue

This study has made use of the classic, and old-fashioned, meaning of the term "social control"; social control focuses on the capacity of a social group or a society to achieve self-regulation in terms of a set of "higher moral principles." The idea of social control is directly applicable to the political institutions of a society which makes use of competitive elections. The basic problem is to account for the increased difficulty legislative institutions have in mediating among conflicting group interests and in resolving social and economic conflicts. The United States has come to confront a chronic political stalemate similar to that faced by the other Western political democracies. We are in essence dealing, not with the monopolization of political power by tiny elite groups, but with new forms of dispersion of political influence which lead to the inability to create meaningful majorities which can effectively govern. If voting behavior and election outcomes are taken as measures of social control, existing procedures for creating political decisions and consensus are far from adequate.

The efforts of sociologists at global futurology are relatively pointless; even the forecasting of specific statistical time series is a hazardous task. But one must anticipate that the political stalemate will persist (and there will not be a "breakdown" or "radical" transformation of sociopolitical institutions). The underlying sources of disarticulation of the United States as an advanced industrial society indicate continued societal strain and tension.

Three master trends make it possible to describe the configuration of societal change since the end of World War II and thereby clarify the strains on the mechanism of social control. The changes in political participation, social stratification, and military participation represent long-term trends in the shift from an industrial to an advanced industrial society. While it is appropriate to stress the continuity in these trends, their results accumulate into a threshold of societal transformation. Each of these master trends helps to explain the attenuation of social control, or at least the failure of institution building to effect the level of social control which an advanced industrial society with a democratic policy requires. In retrospect, the national election of 1952 can be taken as the time marker of the threshold of societal change.

First, there is no evidence that there has been a significant "depoliticalization" of the citizenry or even a decline in political interest. The electoral procedures have not produced a critical election or a meaningful realignment of political affiliation or a new stable national coalition. (One can have a long-term Democratic legislative majority without an operative political majority.) Instead, there has been an increase in political volatility based on erosion of citizen attachment to one or another of the major parties, increases in party switching from one national election to the next, and continuous growth of ticket splitting.

Second, the long-term trend in the social structure has been toward a more differentiated pattern of social stratification, reflecting the complex division of labor and the persistence and growth of cleavages based on age, sex, region, and primordial attachments. The differentiation of social organization has also been conditioned by the fact that a person's position in the social structure is not only a function of his position in the occupational structure but is also increasingly related to the claims and expectations generated by the welfare state. These changes in social stratification make it more and more difficult for the individual citizen to calculate his self-interest. They therefore contribute to unstable patterns of electoral participation and to the resulting weak political regimes.

The third master trend involves both the change in U. S. military strategy to a deterrence posture which requires an expanded "force in being" and the shift from military service based on conscription and the citizen-soldier concept to an all-volunteer military. The new politico-military stance means that the issues of national defense, including particularly arms control, become ongoing and "permanent" political issues of intense debate, which complicates the work of the national political institutions. The decline of conscription and the mass armed force likewise means that civil-military relations are strained and that military service operates less as a device for maintaining and strengthening democratic ideals of citizenship.

Because of these three master trends, the political economy of the United States has been altered. The older economic dilemmas of "underconsumption" give way to a new pattern of relative "overconsumption"—that is, the economics of stagflation, in which chronic inflation and unemployment reflect the "permanent" deficit spending by the federal government, low rates of increase in economic productivity, and low rates of reinvestment of capital.

From the social-control perspective, these master trends in social organization produce extensive disarticulation of social institutions. The focal points of disarticulation are twofold. One set rests within and between the bureaucratic hierarchies—industrial and service—in which labor violence has been replaced to a large extent by "manipulative" organizational authority and labor-management relations in the adversary model. The other nexus of disarticulation results from increased separation of place of work and community of residence; this serves to fragment social and political relations. The result is hardly the emergence of a population of "isolated" persons and households but, rather, a complex of ordered social groups with striking primary-group solidarities.

Moreover, in an advanced industrial society the connections between these ordered segments are conditioned by the institutions of societal socialization which fashion personal controls. In addition to the local institutions of family, school, and church, the measure of an advanced industrialized society is the centrality of the mass media and the systems of law and legitimate coercion. From the vast body of empirical and almost conflicting research results, a plausible codification of the consequences of these agencies of socialization can be drawn.

About the mass media, the underlying assumption is that, without their contribution, the disarticulation of the institutional sectors of an advanced industrial society would be unmanageable. However, the empirical evidence supports the hypothesis that the contribution of the mass media to effective social control has declined and that there are significant disruptive or self-defeating consequences of the mass media as agencies of societal socialization. In addition, the mass media, especially the television style of personalized reporting and increased emphasis on advocacy journalism, do not necessarily contribute to clarifying political self-interest, but are more likely to strengthen mistrust and suspicion.

In the instance of the legal system and its coercive sanctions, the empirical evidence indicates that there has been a decline or at least a limiting in the ability of the law to serve as an agency of societal socialization. First, the response of the courts to the increase in criminality has been to emphasize the legal rights of criminals, but the result has been to undermine popular acceptance of legal judicial procedures. Then, too, while popular support for equality of opportunity for excluded social groups is extensive, implementation of such goals by administrative and judicial decision fails to provide self-generating acceptance, since the decisions are viewed as arbitrary. Again, the result is a decline in confidence and trust in the legal system.

These master trends help fashion the mass attitudes of the "new public opinion" of an advanced industrial society; and it is a public mood, with its inconsistency and with its potential for redirection. To extrapolate existing trends into the future is indeed hazardous and self-deceptive. Three dimensions of mass opinion are of particular relevance to the normative issues of social control. Personal annoyance and frustration underlie the limited trust in the political process and agencies of government, but in the context of extensive relative affluence. The enlarged distrust of political and public administrative institutions has been thoroughly documented. But such popular attitudes are accompanied by a pervasive feeling that the government must be more active rather than less in the solution of societal "problems." In a range of opinion surveys, a clear majority express their general acceptance of "more" rather than "less" government; and attitudes on specific issues revealed even stronger support. In 1974, 85.9% of the population, in a National Opinion Research Center survey, believed that the "government in Washington ought to see to it that everybody who wants to work can find a job." At the same time, the inconsistency, or at least internal strain, in attitude pattern is shown by the fact that fear of "big government" is widespread; in January 1977, 39% of the population labeled "big government" the greatest threat to the nation, a higher percentage than for "big labor," 24% and "big business," 23%.

For most citizens these attitudes "fit together." They believe that dedicated political leaders have the potential for collective problem solving. Such an outlook remains at least compatible with the basic consensus required of a democratic polity. But for a minority of the electorate, there is a strong element of substantive irrationality in the joint attitude of mistrust of the agencies of the state—political and administrative—and the demand for expanded governmental intervention. This syndrome was encountered in the analysis of the 1952 election. Although the size of this segment of the citizenry is difficult to measure over time, I believe it has grown at least modestly and probably significantly. This group includes citizens with strong affinities for adherence to antidemocratic sociopolitical movements, for extremist politics, and for sustained indifference to the existing processes for resolving conflict.

Second, in the context of stagflation, inflation has emerged as the paramount popular economic concern. Since 1972 popular concern about inflation has come to exceed that about unemployment. However, these attitudes are built on a new social cleavage—a new basis of ordered segmentation—which cuts through the entire social structure. The electorate is organized in terms of whether its wages are indexed or not—whether wage automatically increases with inflation—that is, the consumer price index. There is no direct, simple connection between indexed wages and position in the social structure, although over the long run, indexed wages create new privileged groupings. Indexed wages are to be found among federal employees and some employees of state and local government, as well as important numbers of unionized workers. If one speaks of social strata, income indexing has in effect created a new stratum and a divide in the social structure which deeply complicate effective social control in the economic area.

Finally, the long-term trends toward more "permissive" attitudes toward interpersonal relations and deviant behavior had by 1976 reached observable limits, and there were discernible countertrends. These shifts in attitudes did not necessarily represent reasoned moral positions, but reflected emotionally charged issues which supplied a basis for mobilizing popular attitudes. The "reaction" was epitomized in the campaign against governmental financial assistance for abortion which resulted in the enactment of restrictive federal legislation in 1977. The countertrend was also clearly manifested in public attitudes toward the control of pornography. On the question of local standards for the control of pornography, by 1977 national survey data indicated that almost a majority (45%) favored tougher standards, while the advocates of less strict standards numbered only 6%; 35% were for no change. These attitude patterns about positive government, the importance of inflation, and the "permissive" moral standards caution the student of societal change against extrapolating from existing trends or resorting to summary oversimplified categories of "liberal" and "conservative" attitude configurations.

The social-control perspective is both a mode of analysis and a value orientation. Self-regulation is a moral aspiration and is multivalued in orientation. There is in fact a hierarchy of values, one that requires continual clarification. As a moral aspiration, social control assigns the highest importance to the reduction of coercion. But at the same time it assumes that the pursuit of effective social control both depends on and will enhance personal and political freedom.

As a strategy of directed societal change, social control emphasizes the centrality of rationality and rational inquiry. Since the intellectual history of social control is grounded in pragmatic philosophical assumptions rather than in either materialistic or idealistic modes of thinking, the limits of rationality require concrete and specific explication. The centrality of rationality has been inherent in the explication of social control from the earliest usage of the concept. I can point to W. I. Thomas's formulation, in which he emphasized, with industrialization, "the growing importance which a conscious and rational technique tends to assume in social life." "We are less and less ready to let any social processes go on without our active interference and we feel more and more dissatisfied with any active interference based upon a mere whim of an individual or a social body, or upon preconceived philosophical, religious, or moral generalization." But sociologists concerned with social control have been and remain aware of the limits of rationality; it was for that reason that they formulated their framework in terms of "higher moral principles" and with full recognition of the elements of primordial attachments in effective social control.

As a result, I see the assessment of the social-science contributions to institution building as a key in the analysis of the macrosociology of an advanced industrial society. The strategy of systemic analysis avoids global and undifferentiated assessments and instead seeks to specify accomplishments and failures. In my view, there is no reason to conclude that the social sciences have undermined respect for common sense or reason; nor have they narrowed effective authority. There is equally little reason to assert that social science has served "the elite" in maintaining "undeserved privilege." If we were forced to a global assessment, which we are not, it would be that the strategic consequence of social science has been to contribute to the dispersion of political power. But one would have to add the observation that it has simultaneously rendered more understandable the underlying process of institutional disarticulation. However, it is more pertinent to trace out the specific implications of different bodies of social-science thought on those different groups which use its findings.

Since there is little basis for distinguishing sharply between basic and applied research in the social sciences, the intellectual worth and scholarly validity of a social-science contribution are at the core of its pertinence for institution building for social control. But, of course, we are dealing as well with professional sentiments of academic scholars and the partial ideologies of the practitioners who have been exposed to social-science ideas and findings. In the management of interpersonal relations, the elaboration of personality theory and its variants has contributed to some measurable degree to a more humane treatment of "mental" problems. These ideas have also helped fashion interpersonal norms of mutual respect appropriate for bureaucratic hierarchies. But such accomplishments have not been decisive in the effort to redefine authority relations in an advanced industrial society. Likewise, efforts to write off as failures the experiments in community participation which have been grounded in social analysis of the metropolis are premature. There has been a long, tortured process of social learning. Utopian aspiration as well as distorted representations in the mass media have been barriers to community-based institution building. But the efforts to enlarge citizen participation in the civic management of community life have persisted, and social science has gradually contributed to more realistic arrangements.

Even if the vast "industry" of survey research–based analysis of the political process has heightened political competition without improving the quality of electoral deliberation, these specialists have at least worked within the tradition of democratic persuasion and confronted the realities and defects of citizen participation. Likewise, while I have emphasized that the limitation of an economic model of political behavior serves to intensify interest-group pressure and to "downgrade" the political tasks of an advanced industrial society, I am prepared to acknowledge that on the whole such efforts have been presented as intellectual arguments within the scope of reasonable debate.

The systemic analysis of social control and societal change emphasizes that the legislative arena is too overburdened to effect adequate conflict resolution. The social scientist has no alternative but to assist in improving the capacity of extraparliamentary agencies to resolve conflicts and thereby overcome institutional disarticulation. I have repeatedly stressed that increased opportunities and levels of citizen participation, although required for complex industrial society, do not guarantee meaningful deliberative and reasoned outcomes. The basic issue is to enhance the clarifying outcomes of civic interaction, that is, the quality of the decision. The search for "higher moral principles" and their implementation are no longer concentrated in specialized institutions and agencies but occur wherever collective decisions are made. Each and every institutional sector can potentially assist the citizen to formulate his or her political self-interest.

There will be those who will use the term "corporatism" to describe the trend toward strengthening extraparliamentary political rule in order to enhance effective social control. The term "corporatism" has a mixed political history. It has a negative connotation from its association with fascist practice. However, it has a positive heritage in the long-standing political arrangements of the smaller European democracies which have used voluntary associations to perform administrative functions on behalf of the central government.

No doubt the idea of corporatism has pertinence in linking this study to the traditions of "political theory" which deal with group representation. However, we are speaking of corporatism as a social-science term, and not as a political slogan. In any case, there is little likelihood that, in the United States, the term "corporatism" will serve as the basis of extensive popular political appeals. On the contrary, there will be a real self-deception if the idea of corporatism and enhanced citizen participation come to be formulated as infinitely expandable procedures. The resources for these procedures are in very short supply and must be allocated accordingly.

In effect, one must formulate a priority of goals if the voluntaristic components of social organization are to overcome political stalemate. The essential strategy is for each group of organized adversaries to confront and deal with broader sets of issues than normally encountered in its routine practice in order to enhance its collective responsibilities. One basic aspect of institutional building is the massive machinery of labor-management relations; the goal is to encompass a more direct responsibility for the fiscal and administrative management of the welfare state and for handling chronic stagflation. Another basic element is the community-based voluntary association whose fixed geographic boundaries require enlargement and flexibility to include more diverse social groups and to articulate more effectively with existing political and administrative agencies. What is necessary is the social construction of new institutions which link the organization of work and community organization.

The social-control perspective encompasses the United States in the world community. It is possible to speak of a world "community" of nation-states—from the superpowers to the smallest states pursuing mutual economic and national security goals. To describe the world arena as one of endless, limitless economic conflict is a distortion. One does not have to deny the profound economic misery and economic inequality to recognize the existence of extensive networks of bilateral and multilateral arrangements of mutual economic benefit. To speak of three separate worlds of economic development—United States, Soviet Union, and the Third World—in the world community is a gross oversimplification. Concretely, the student of the influence of the world economy on the United States has come to recognize that the terms of international trade for the United States are hardly all favorable—they are, rather, decidedly mixed. Moreover, the position of the United States in the world economy has resulted since 1945 in the "exporting" of millions and millons of jobs, thereby complicating the domestic management of the welfare state.

The nation-states in the world community confront the emergence of the weapons of mass destruction, which means that national security converges with world security. A world governed by a delicate balance of terror means that the search for effective social control cannot be limited to any single nation, even a superpower. The institutional arrangements for controlling the weapons of mass destruction appear unequal to the required minimum tasks. Clearly, domestic political stalemate in the political democracies hinders the search for the control of nuclear weapons at the world level. However, the institutions of world security operate very differently. Nuclear weapons have their own self-limiting logic, so that one can again speak of a world "community"—an area of mutual self-interest—which comes into play at crucial moments. The superpowers have mobilized themselves to enforce minimum sanity and avoid an uncontrollable nuclear threat. Internationally monitored and self-enforcing accords have been developed at critical junctures. The accomplishments are illustrated by the sequence of steps including: the initial accord to ban nuclear devices in Antarctica; the various prohibitions against nuclear weapons in outer space or in the seabed; and the Strategic Arms Limitation Treaty-I, which eliminated the deployment of the antiballistic missile. The emerging agenda remains staggering but clearly realizable. If the internal political stalemate of the advanced industrial democracies, including the United States, does not imply collapse or self-destruction, but chronic tension, the analog applies to international security problems.

The emphasis of the social-control perspective on rationality and the simultaneous concern with the limits of rationality create obvious ambiguities for the social scientist. In particular, the pragmatic social scientist is reluctant to confront the role of political rhetoric and the fact of myth; political myths are required if elites, including democratic elites, are to govern. The development of social research and a critical outlook toward political institutions does not eliminate the role of creative political rhetoric. It has come to pass that the posture of social science has rendered the venerable term "political myth" unusable; one must refer to "political symbolism." In the context of rationality, "political symbolism" means the visionary ideal and zeal of political leaders, that is, their unverifiable slogans which combine their search for power and their creative concepts of the public interest.

Political symbols which facilitate the transformation of political systems emerge and have influence without being fully understood by social scientists. One does not have to be a rigid phenomenologist to acknowledge both the existential and transcendental dimensions of myths and political symbols. Rational, critical inquiry does not create new myths, but it does assist in assessing their social and moral worth. The ongoing efforts to probe the language of political rule highlight that there are both restraining and facilitating myths, although we have spent more time and energy in exposing the restraining myths than in explicating the facilitating ones.

In any case, social scientists have not been content to engage in scholarship and research; they have also been active in the formulation of political symbols and to a greater extent in the dissemination of political rhetoric. But there is no guarantee that training and adherence to the principles of scientific inquiry result in a positive contribution by intellectuals and social scientists to the language of politics. In the most charitable estimate, the unanticipated consequences of social-science efforts to fashion political symbols have been extensive. More precisely, the commitment of social scientists to political platforms which are antidemocratic is more than rare or accidental.

In exploring the relations between intellectuality and facilitating political symbols, there is no reason to overlook the conclusion that concepts of limited explanatory power can and have served wide political and societal ends. The case of "social class" is a most striking example. Appeals to "social class" served as a political formula in Western Europe to extend the institutions of political democracy and citizenship regardless of the descriptive validity of the term. In the United States, although the language of social class was less explicit and less strident, the same process took place. Progressively, since 1952, this political strategy has been less effective as a basis of resolving political conflict.

The rise to prominence of social-science endeavors has meant repeated efforts to use the terminology of social science as the basis for new political formulae and for new political symbolism. But social scientists are hardly creative political leaders and the result has been only to further fragment the electorate. Much of the symbolic residue of social-science language which appeals to political mass consciousness serves only to sharpen pressure-group demands of particular social segments of the electorate. The terminology of Keynesian economics had declined in importance. The renewed appeals of the language of competitive economics may produce specific political and socioeconomic developments, but not supply the basis of a new political majority and a new critical realignment.

Social scientists have been effective to some extent in their formulation of negative images and negative symbols which have served to retard the emergence of undesired societal trends. One prime example is the term "garrison state," formulated with political and policy objectives in mind. It may well be that an advanced industrial society which respects personal freedom must operate with a deficit of integrative political symbols. But I prefer to believe that the contribution of social scientists to societal changes must be indirect and must emphasize clarification more than direct political leadership and action. I have stressed that the United States as an advanced industrial society is one characterized by a high degree of institutional differentiation which unfortunately has resulted in extensive disarticulation of the component institutional sectors. It is a society in which conflict and strain are likely to remain chronic without resulting in fundamental political transformation.

Thus the idea of social control in turn serves not only as a basis for guiding the analysis of societal change but as an appropriate symbolism for mediating the interaction between the social scientist and the political leader who bears the continuing burden of reducing the sources and consequences of institutional conflict and disarticulation. Social scientists and political leaders, despite their wide array of contacts and occasional exchange of personnel, remain distinct professional groups. But I believe that the idea of social control serves as a focal point of clarification of the difficulties of societal change without assuming the burdens of being easily misunderstood or being used as an active political symbol.

Author Index

Analytic and Subject Index